OXFORD MEDICAL PUBLICATIONS

Cognitive Behaviour Therapy for Psychiatric Problems
A Practical Guide

Cognitive Behaviour Therapy for Psychiatric Problems
A Practical Guide

KEITH HAWTON

Consultant Psychiatrist, Warneford Hospital, Oxford;
Clinical Lecturer, Department of Psychiatry,
University of Oxford

PAUL M. SALKOVSKIS

Research Clinical Psychologist, Department of Psychiatry, Warneford Hospital, Oxford

JOAN KIRK

Top Grade Clinical Psychologist, Warneford Hospital, Oxford

AND

DAVID M. CLARK

Lecturer in Psychology, Department of Psychiatry,
University of Oxford;
Fellow, University College,
Oxford

OXFORD
UNIVERSITY PRESS

OXFORD
UNIVERSITY PRESS

Great Clarendon Street, Oxford OX2 6DP

Oxford University Press is a department of the University of Oxford.
It furthers the University's objective of excellence in research, scholarship,
and education by publishing worldwide in

Oxford New York

Athens Auckland Bangkok Bogotá Buenos Aires Cape Town
Chennai Dar es Salaam Delhi Florence Hong Kong Istanbul Karachi
Kolkata Kuala Lumpur Madrid Melbourne Mexico City Mumbai Nairobi
Paris São Paulo Shanghai Singapore Taipei Tokyo Toronto Warsaw

with associated companies in Berlin Ibadan

Oxford is a registered trade mark of Oxford University Press
in the UK and in certain other countries

Published in the United States
by Oxford University Press Inc., New York

© Keith Hawton, Paul M. Salkovskis, Joan Kirk, and
David M. Clark, 1989

British Library Cataloguing in Publication Data

Cognitive behaviour therapy for psychiatric
problems: a practical guide.
1. Medicine. Cognitive behaviour therapy
I. Hawton, Keith, 1942–
616.89'142–
ISBN 0 19 261587 4 (pbk)

Library of Congress Cataloging in Publication Data

Cognitive behaviour therapy for psychiatric problems: a practical
guide / Keith Hawton. . .[et al.].
p.   cm.—(Oxford Medical publications)
Bibliography: Includes index.
1. Cognitive therapy.   I. Hawton, Keith, 1942- . II. Series
[DNLM: 1. Behaviour therapy—methods.   2. Cognition   WM425   C6761]
RC489.C63C635   1989
616.89'142—dc19   88–38344   CIP
ISBN 0 19 261587 4 (pbk)

Printed in Great Britain
on acid-free paper by
Biddles Ltd., Guildford and King's Lynn

Foreword

M. G. Gelder
Professor of Psychiatry, University of Oxford

Cognitive behaviour therapy is a recent development in psychological treatment but it has already aroused much interest among clinicians. There are three principal reasons for this interest. First, unlike some other forms of behaviour therapy, cognitive–behavioural methods are directly concerned with the thoughts and feelings that are so obviously important in all psychiatric disorders. Secondly, cognitive behaviour therapy fills a gap that many clinicians perceive between purely behavioural methods and the dynamic psychotherapies. Thirdly, unlike dynamic psychotherapy, these newer methods of treatment are scientifically based and more amenable to evaluation in clinical trials.

Cognitive approaches to treatment probably came to the attention of most clinicians in the management of depressive disorders. However, cognitive behaviour therapy has much wider applications, many of which relate to conditions which often cannot be treated easily and effectively in other ways. These conditions include anxiety and obsessional disorders, eating disorders, certain somatic problems, aspects of the disabilities of patients with chronic mental illness, as well as sexual and marital problems.

Much has been written, both in books and articles, about cognitive behaviour therapy. However, only a very small part of this literature is concerned with the practical aspects of treatment. For this reason, it is difficult for an interested clinician to find out how to assess patients' suitability for cognitive behaviour therapy and how to carry out the procedures. The editors of this book identified this deficiency in the literature on cognitive behaviour therapy and set out to remedy it. They have succeeded extremely well. They have assembled a group of authors who are not only knowledgeable about cognitive behaviour therapy but also skilled in its use and in training others to use it. The book contains chapters dealing with all the important applications of cognitive behaviour therapy, which have been arranged so that each chapter follows a standard format with sections on relevant basic issues, assessment, and treatment. These accounts are clearly written and enlivened by extracts from therapy sessions, and they include much practical advice about ways of overcoming problems that can arise in treatment. Of course, to learn any new treatment, supervised experience is necessary as well as reading.

However the account in this book will ensure that learners will begin treatment with clear ideas about the procedures that they will be using, and supervision sessions will be the more fruitful because relevant theoretical issues have been understood.

The chapters in this book contain the basic information needed by trainees in psychology and psychiatry, as well as the kind of detailed advice that will be of value to more senior clinicians. For this reason the book is appropriate for readers of many kinds and levels of training. Cognitive behaviour therapy is developing rapidly, but the reader who has been introduced by this book to the basic and practical aspects of cognitive–behavioural techniques should have no difficulty in adapting his or her practice to other conditions for which cognitive–behavioural treatment may be shown to be of value. In short, the book is undoubtedly a most important addition to the literature on cognitive behaviour therapy, and it is a pleasure to introduce it to the reader.

Preface

How to use this guide

This book has been compiled for therapists who already have some experience in the clinical management of patients with psychiatric disorders, and its aim is to help them to start using cognitive–behavioural treatments in their clinical work. While there are many academic reviews which establish the efficacy of this approach, there are few guides sufficiently detailed to allow practitioners to work in this way in their everyday practice.

The book is intended to provide an integrated guide to the practice of cognitive behaviour therapy and it has been written and edited as a unit. The first chapter describes the basic principles of psychology which are relevant to cognitive–behavioural treatments and outlines the development and principles of this type of therapy. The second chapter provides a detailed description of how to carry out a cognitive–behavioural assessment. Since this covers the theoretical and practical bases of much of what is described in subsequent chapters it is recommended that it is read before turning to the chapters dealing with specific disorders. Within each of the succeeding chapters the authors have adopted a standard format, outlining the nature of each disorder and the development of current treatment approaches, and then providing a detailed practical account of how to carry out treatment. Particular attention is paid to dealing with difficulties encountered during treatment and reasons for treatment failure. Research evidence supporting the use of particular treatments is provided where appropriate, but the authors have deliberately not provided extensive reviews of research as these are widely available elsewhere and are not central to the aims of this book. Each chapter concludes with a brief list of recommended articles and books complementary to the chapter.

The authors have adopted a problem-oriented framework as a useful way of structuring the material, while avoiding the use of any rigid diagnostic scheme. The basic principle in all the chapters is that a treatment plan follows from a thorough cognitive–behavioural assessment and a formulation based on a psychological model of the specific disorder. It is not intended that the treatments described in this book should be viewed as standardized packages for particular conditions. Instead, the aim of each chapter is to provide the reader with sufficient information to carry out an assessment and plan individualized treatment for patients presenting with the wide range of problems seen in clinical practice.

Formulation and treatment are intimately linked and are modified as necessary in the light of patients' responses to therapy. Clinical illustrations have been used extensively to assist readers to understand the specific ways in which treatment may be applied.

Oxford   K. H.
1988   P. M. S.
                                                                                                          J. K.
                                                                                                          D. M. C.

Acknowledgements

We wish to thank the contributors for their wholehearted support and for putting up with not one, but four editors. We would also like to thank the following for permission to reproduce copyright material: Pergamon Press for Fig. 3.1 from Clark (1986a) and for Table 3.4 from Clark and Beck (1988); and *British Journal of Psychiatry* for Table 9.2. Melanie Fennell retains copyright for Tables 6.1, 6.2, 6.3, 6.4; Figs. 6.1, 6.2, 6.3, 6.4, 6.5, 6.6, 6.7; and the Handouts for Patients in Chapter 6. Anne Crowe, Carolyn Fordham, and Jackie Hodges provided invaluable secretarial assistance for which we are extremely grateful.

Contents

List of contributors

Gillian Butler
Research Clinical Psychologist, Department of Psychiatry, University of Oxford, UK.

David M. Clark
Lecturer in Psychology, Department of Psychiatry, University of Oxford; and Fellow, University College, Oxford, UK.

Peter Cooper
Lecturer in Psychopathology, Departments of Psychiatry and Experimental Psychology, University of Cambridge, UK.

Christopher Fairburn
Wellcome Trust Senior Lecturer, Department of Psychiatry, University of Oxford, UK.

Melanie Fennell
Research Clinical Psychologist, Department of Psychiatry, University of Oxford, UK.

Alan E. Fruzzetti
Doctoral Student in Clinical Psychology; and Research Coordinator, Center for the Study of Relationships, University of Washington, USA.

John Hall
District Clinical Psychologist and Clinical Lecturer, Warneford Hospital and Department Psychiatry, University of Oxford, UK.

Keith Hawton
Consultant Psychiatrist and Clinical Lecturer, Warneford Hospital and Department of Psychiatry, University of Oxford, UK.

Neil S. Jacobson
Professor of Psychology and Director of Clinical Training, University of Washington, USA.

Joan Kirk
Top Grade Clinical Psychologist, Psychology Department, Warneford Hospital, Oxford, UK.

Paul M. Salkovskis
Research Clinical Psychologist, Department of Psychiatry, University of Oxford, UK.

Karen B. Schmaling
Assistant Professor of Psychiatry, University of Colorado School of Medicine; and Assistant Staff Member, National Jewish Center for Immunology and Respiratory Medicine, USA.

1

The development and principles of cognitive–behavioural treatments

The Editors

The empirical foundations of cognitive–behavioural approaches to psychological problems can be traced back to the early part of this century. The Darwinian view that there is continuity between man and the lower animals allowed 'animal models' of behaviour to be applied to the study of how psychopathology developed and was maintained, with the assumption that principles derived from animal learning research could be generalized to man.

Early work identified two principles of animal learning. The first principle was based on the work of Pavlov and other Russian physiologists. They conducted experiments with dogs where first a bell was rung, and then food was given. After this sequence of events had been repeated a number of times, the dogs began to salivate as soon as the bell was rung, before the food was given. This phenomenon became known as *classical conditioning*. As food automatically produces salivation before learning (conditioning) has occurred, it was termed an *unconditioned stimulus*; the response of salivation to the food was termed on *unconditioned response*. Before any learning had taken place the bell did not elicit salivation. However, after several pairings of the bell and food, the sound of the bell (the *conditioned stimulus*) came to elicit salivation (the *conditioned response*). This paradigm is represented in Fig. 1.1. Pavlov also investigated what happened to a conditioned response when the bell ceased to be followed by the unconditioned stimulus (the food). After a number of such trials, the conditioned response gradually *extinguished*.

The Russian investigators also found that emotional responses such as fear can be conditioned. For this reason the classical conditioning paradigm has considerable implications for the understanding of psychopathological phenomena. In an unconditioned state, for example, an animal will respond emotionally to an electric shock, with an unconditioned response including an increase in heart rate. It will not initially respond in this way to an unconditioned stimulus such as a red light. However, if the red light is systematically paired with electric shock, the animal will begin to respond to the red light with a conditioned fear response. Thus the red light will have become a conditioned fear stimulus for the animal.

Cognitive behaviour therapy

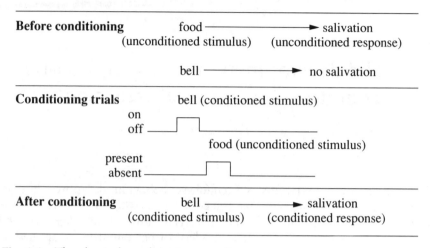

Before conditioning	food ————————→ salivation	
	(unconditioned stimulus)	(unconditioned response)
	bell ————————→ no salivation	
Conditioning trials	bell (conditioned stimulus)	
	on	
	off	
	food (unconditioned stimulus)	
	present	
	absent	
After conditioning	bell ————————→ salivation	
	(conditioned stimulus)	(conditioned response)

Fig. 1.1 The classical conditioning paradigm

The second principle, known as *operant conditioning*, derived from observations made in the USA by Thorndike, Tolman, and Guthrie. In a series of experiments they found that if a particular behaviour was consistently followed by a reward the behaviour was more likely to occur again. This phenomenon became known as the 'Law of Effect', which states that behaviour which is followed by satisfying consequences will tend to be repeated and behaviour which is followed by unpleasant consequences will occur less frequently. Skinner extended this principle by defining reinforcers in terms of the effect that they have on an individual's behaviour, not simply whether they appear to be either rewarding or unpleasant. Thus, in operant conditioning, if a behaviour is followed by a particular event and the behaviour increases in frequency, then the behaviour is said to be reinforced (see Fig. 1.2). *Positive reinforcement* describes the situation where a behaviour (e.g. being on time) occurs more frequently because it is followed by positive consequences (e.g. praise). *Negative reinforcement* describes the situation where the frequency of a behaviour increases because it is followed by the omission of an anticipated aversive event (e.g. anxiety, someone else complaining). Thus the term reinforcement always refers to situations in which behaviour increases in frequency or strength. Two further types of consequence are associated with decreases in the frequency of a behaviour. *Punishment* describes the situation where a behaviour decreases in frequency because it is followed by an aversive event (e.g. electric shock). *Frustrative non-reward* describes the situation where a behaviour decreases in frequency because it is followed by the omission of an expected reward (e.g. not

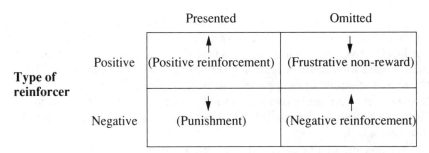

Fig. 1.2 The ways in which the frequency of a behaviour can be made to increase (↑) or decrease (↓) by manipulating its consequences

being praised). In using operant conditioning principles to help patients, treatments are planned using as reinforcers the events which have previously been shown to change behaviour in the desired direction; these are not necessarily those which intrinsically appear to be rewarding.

The development of these two conditioning paradigms and their subsequent integration by workers such as Hull and Mowrer were invaluable in the evolution of behaviour therapy. Of particular importance was the work of Mowrer (1947, 1960), who described a two-factor model (encompassing both classical and operant components) to account for fear and avoidance behaviour. He suggested that fear of specific stimuli is acquired through classical conditioning, and that as fear is aversive the animal learns to reduce it by avoiding the conditioned stimuli. Solomon and Wynne (1954) made the further important observation that if stimuli had become classically conditioned by previous association with strongly aversive stimuli, then avoidance responses to the conditioned stimuli were extremely resistant to extinction. That is, they demonstrated that avoidance responding to harmless stimuli could continue unabated long after the prior conditioning had ceased.

Early clinical applications of behavioural principles

Perhaps the most famous example of the application of behavioural principles to the problem of clinical anxiety was Watson and Rayner's (1920) description of conditioning procedures carried out with 'Little Albert', an 11-month-old infant. They found that they were able to produce a conditioned anxiety response to a white rat by pairing the appearance of the rat with a loud noise. This conditioning of anxiety extended (*generalized*) to similar stimuli such as the experimenter's white hair and cotton wool, but not to dissimilar stimuli. This work was adopted by Jones (1924), who applied Watson's recommendations for treatment; she discovered that only two treatment methods were consistently effective, one being to associate the feared object with an alternative pleasant response (eating), the other being to expose the child to the feared stimulus in the presence of other children who were not fearful. It is notable that these methods closely resemble those later adopted by Wolpe (systematic desensitization) and Bandura (participant modelling) (see below).

The next major development was the work of the Mowrers in the late 1930s on enuresis. They regarded enuresis as a failure of the patient to respond to bladder distension by waking up. They associated bladder distention (onset of urination) with wakening and consequent sphincter contraction, so that after several trials bladder distension should result in sphincter contraction on its own, thus preventing urination. Treatment utilizing an electrical 'bell and pad' device proved effective (Mowrer and Mowrer 1938). The work of the Mowrers was important not only because of this impressive outcome, but because the behavioural formulation and treatment of enuresis were novel. This work was significant in the later development of behavioural formulations and treatment.

Developments in the 1950s included several attempts to encompass concepts from outside the behavioural sphere. Particularly influential was the work of Dollard and Miller (1950), who conceptualized psychoanalytic theory in learning theory terms, and included factors such as cultural influences within a behavioural framework. This work demonstrated the broader explanatory power of behavioural theory, and laid the foundations for subsequent cognitive–behavioural formulations which incorporated findings from cognitive and social psychology research.

In South Africa during the early 1950s, Joseph Wolpe began to report work on 'experimental neuroses' in cats. This work was similar to previous research, for example by Masserman (1943), except that Wolpe emphasized new techniques for the elimination of experimentally induced fear and avoidance. He became particularly interested in the production of conditioned fear. Thus if an animal experienced a small shock when it approached food, subsequently the fear could be elicited by other situations which were similar to the situation in which the shock had previously been delivered. Wolpe proposed a neurophysiological explanation to account for this phenomenon. Since feeding was inhibited by conditions which elicited the 'symptoms' of the 'experimental neurosis', this suggested to him that conditioned fear and feeding were mutually antagonistic or *reciprocally inhibiting*. This led to the idea that feeding might be used to reduce the anxiety elicited by specific situations. Wolpe successfully demonstrated this in his experimental animals by feeding them in progressively closer approximations to the setting in which they had originally been shocked. He proposed that fear reduction could generally be accomplished by the simultaneous presentation of anxiety-provoking stimuli and stimuli evoking a response antagonistic to anxiety (the reciprocal inhibitor), provided that the antagonistic response was the stronger of the two. In order to ensure that the inhibitor was stronger, the anxiety-provoking stimuli were presented in a graded way, on a *hierarchy*, beginning with mildly anxiety-provoking stimuli.

In extending his work to humans, Wolpe considered three main responses which might act as reciprocal inhibitors: sexual responses, assertive responses, and progressive muscular relaxation. The most widely adopted of these was a modified and shortened version of Jacobson's (1938) relaxation procedure, which Wolpe believed to have similar neurophysiological correlates to the effects of eating. In Wolpe's method, the patient was taught relaxation, then encouraged to progress step-by-step through a *hierarchy* of feared situations while maintaining the relaxation in order to reciprocally inhibit the fear response. Initially, Wolpe used *in vivo* (real life) exposure, then changed to imaginal presentation because of the greater controllability and ease of presentation this offered. This procedure, which became known as *systematic desensitization*, was carefully elaborated in Wolpe's influential book *Psychotherapy by reciprocal inhibition* (1958), where it is made clear that patients were expected to carry out extensive *in vivo* homework between therapy sessions. Wolpe's contribution to the field was considerable, and has been a major influence on the practice of behaviour therapy. Its importance lay not only in his use of a theoretical formulation based on clear and testable hypotheses to devise a clearly specified treatment strategy, but also in his description of the extensive clinical application of this therapeutic technique. However, the theoretical basis of reciprocal inhibition is no longer influential. This is because it has been established that exposure in real-life situations is the most effective way to bring about reductions in conditioned anxiety, and that neither grading the exposure nor the use of reciprocal inhibitors such as relaxation are necessary. Nevertheless, systematic desensitization provided the practical foundation and the theoretical impetus for the research which has led to the development of current exposure-based therapies.

Wolpe was reporting his work at an important time, when the efficacy of psychoanalytic approaches was undergoing critical appraisal, following Eysenck's (1952) controversial review in which he argued that the improvement rates achieved by psychotherapy were no higher than the rates which would be expected if treatment were not given (spontaneous remission). At the Maudsley Hospital in London, Eysenck, Jones, Meyer, Yates, and Shapiro became interested in the application of conditioning theories to psychological problems, and held a series of seminars on this topic. From these discussions emerged a treatment approach exemplified in a series of detailed single-case investigations in which conditioning principles were successfully applied to clinical problems. The application of learning-based treatment at the Maudsley Hospital was extended with the involvement of Rachman, who had previously worked with Wolpe. Rachman was instrumental in the development of aversion therapy, behavioural medicine, and, especially, the behavioural treatment of obsessional disorders. Gelder, Marks, Mathews, and other colleagues at the Maudsley and Warneford Hospitals developed and elaborated *exposure treatments* for phobic disorders. At the same time American workers, such as Davison (1968), were also looking in detail at the process of desensitization and other fear reduction techniques, and demonstrated that *in vivo* exposure was the essential effective ingredient. The theoretical basis of the exposure approach is that feared objects are stimuli to which anxiety has become conditioned (*conditioned stimuli*), and that the conditioned fear has failed to extinguish because the patient has developed *avoidance and escape behaviours* which prevent the individual from being fully exposed to the feared stimuli. In order for fear to extinguish, the patient has to be exposed to the feared stimuli and not to escape (and thereby avoid exposure) once exposure has begun. Exposure should continue at least until anxiety begins to decline. Although this technique is similar to systematic desensitization, it proceeds much more quickly. One reason why behavioural approaches to fear reduction became influential was that their effectiveness was systematically investigated in controlled trials (e.g. Paul 1966; Marks 1975).

A parallel and conceptually related development to fear reduction was the attempt of early behaviour therapists to induce or increase the anxiety associated with unwanted stimuli or behaviours. This approach was called *aversion therapy*, and was used mainly to treat alcohol problems and deviant sexual behaviour. External stimuli, thoughts or behaviours associated with the undesired response were paired with an aversive stimulus, such as an unpleasant electric shock. After several such pairings, the original stimuli alone should elicit the same response produced by the aversive stimulus; that is, they should elicit conditioned anxiety. The initial enthusiasm for this approach declined both for ethical reasons and because it proved to be ineffective (Rachman and Teasdale 1969). *Covert sensitization*, a treatment method where thoughts of the unwanted behaviour are paired in imagination with unpleasant stimuli (e.g. arrest, humiliation), is a less emotive alternative approach (Cautela 1967), although its efficacy is uncertain.

The early 1960s saw a further expansion of behavioural treatments into a wide range of problems beyond fear reduction. This expansion was mainly based on studies which employed *single-case designs*, which have been an important element in the behavioural approach since Shapiro's (1961*a, b*) seminal papers on single-case methodology. Usually, single-case experiments involve obtaining a series of repeated measures of a clinically relevant variable at regular intervals (*a time series*); at a predetermined point in this series, an intervention is introduced, and the effect of this intervention is assessed according to changes in the variable. The effects of a variety of intervention strategies can be evaluated in this way. Later, complex designs which allowed single-case experiments to be applied to a wide range of clinical and research issues *as part of routine clinical practice* were developed (see Barlow, Hayes, and Nelson 1984). Although this methodology is theoretically not confined to cognitive–behavioural treatments, it has become intimately associated with the application of the cognitive–behavioural approach, and plays a continuing role in its development.

Applications of operant techniques: applied behaviour analysis

During the late 1950s, the potential applications of the operant approach (known as applied behaviour analysis) were described by Skinner and Lindsley, but no treatment work was carried out until the early 1960s. The first applications of operant techniques to clinical problems focused on measuring and changing the laboratory behaviour of mentally handicapped people and young children. In early applications to adult psychiatric problems, Ayllon worked on changing psychotic behaviour (such as violent acts, psychotic talk, and inappropriate eating behaviour) in institutionalized patients, using cigarettes and praise as reinforcers, and the withdrawal of attention from the patient as a means of extinction. He was able to demonstrate that disturbed behaviours would increase *or* decrease according to whether the behaviour was reinforced or reinforcement was withdrawn. This work illustrated the importance of Skinner's principle that reinforcement should be defined in terms of its effect on behaviour (see p. 2). Thus, for one patient it may be reinforcing to eat alone in a single room, while for another patient it may be reinforcing to eat with other patients in the dining room.

In 1961, Ayllon and Azrin designed a hospital ward environment in which reinforcers were applied to systematically change patients' behaviour. This system came to be known as a *token economy* because, as reinforcers, they used tokens which could be exchanged later for a range of privileges from which the patients could choose (Ayllon and Azrin 1968). This work was highly influential because it demonstrated that psychological intervention could be effective in patients (especially those with chronic schizophrenia) not previously regarded as amenable to such approaches. This study and later token economies all emphasized the importance of social reinforcement, particularly as an aid to both longer-term *generalization* (extension to other settings) and the *maintenance* of desired or acceptable behaviours. More recent work has cast doubts on the theoretical basis of the token system: for example, Hall and Baker (1986) indicated that the feedback and specific guidance about perform- ance at the time the tokens were given were the most important factors in such programmes. Nevertheless, the development of token economies was highly significant in terms of encouraging a general approach to treatment in rehabilitation settings. The use of structured social reinforcers (praise and attention by the therapist) was more widely adopted than the use of tokens, and the emphasis on altering and structuring social interactions remains an important influence in helping patients with schizophrenia (e.g. Falloon, Boyd, and McGill 1984).

Consolidation and elaboration of the behavioural approach

The 1970s saw the full emergence of behaviour therapy, with numerous new techniques being developed and experimentally validated. By the end of the decade there was general acceptance of these treatment approaches. Behaviour therapy became the treatment of choice for many disorders, such as the use of *in vivo* exposure with phobias, obsessions, and sexual dysfunctions, and operant and goal-setting techniques in rehabilitation. Sex therapy developed from Masters and Johnsons' pioneering work into the physiology of sexual responses rather than from behavioural research into sexual dysfunction. However, the emphasis on the empirical evalua- tion of treatments, and on operational definitions of treatment strategies, has gradually led to the inclusion of sex therapy in the mainstream of cognitive behaviour therapy. A further extension of behavioural ap- proaches was the development of *behavioural medicine*, a term coined by Birk (1973) to describe the application of biofeedback to medical disorders. In biofeedback, patients learn to control physiological respond- ing by receiving immediate information about changes occurring in the physiological system. Behavioural medicine later came to encompass a much wider field, including the application of physiological principles of treatment to disorders with a purely physical origin (e.g. painful burns), to those with a possible psychological aetiology (e.g. irritable bowel syndrome, psychogenic chest pain) and to the modification of risk factors (e.g. smoking). This period was also marked by the refinement of existing techniques (such as reducing the time required for effective exposure to bring about fear reduction and the development of abbreviated forms of relaxation) and the introduction of novel approaches (such as anxiety management training and social skills training).

Another major development was the adoption of a 'three systems' approach. Lang, Rachman, and others proposed that psychological prob- lems could usefully be conceptualized in terms of loosely linked response systems. The systems proposed were *behavioural, cognitive/affective*, and *physiological*. These systems, although linked, do not necessarily change at the same time, in the same way, or even in the same direction; thus they are said to be *desynchronous* (Rachman and Hodgson 1974). There is no *a priori* reason to specify three systems as opposed to four or even more, and indeed it is probably useful to differentiate between the cognitive and affective systems, resulting in a four-system classification. However, this alternative to a unitary view of psychological problems was important both because it helped account for the wide range of symptom patterns which patients report, and because it resulted in more systematic and appropriate evaluations of treatment outcome. It increased the extent to which treatment could be shown to have specific effects; for instance, relaxation treatments are initially likely to affect physiological aspects of a problem more than behavioural or cognitive aspects.

The late 1960s and early 1970s also saw the beginnings of discontent with the strict behavioural notions which dominated early developments. In particular, Lazarus (1971) rejected what he believed to be mechanistic notions underlying the practice of behaviour therapy. He argued that the majority of behavioural treatments could not be conceptualized simply in learning theory terms, and proposed the adoption of 'broad spectrum behaviour therapy', in which techniques of empirically established efficacy are employed regardless of their theoretical basis. In practice, this approach was increasingly adopted by clinicians, although the research literature did not systematically examine the limitations of behaviour therapy until rather later. One of the least satisfactory results of this 'technical eclecticism' was a tendency to apply treatment in a prescriptive way, so that particular techniques were mechanistically applied to particular problems with little or no regard to a full behavioural assessment and formulation. More usefully, discontent with the strict behavioural approaches resulted in attempts to add cognitive components to existing techniques, opening the way for the systematic development and application of cognitive approaches.

Towards the middle and end of the 1970s, there was general acceptance of the usefulness of behaviour therapy. No longer faced with the need to demonstrate the efficacy of behaviour therapy *per se*, some of those working within the field began to turn their attention to those patients who did not benefit from behaviour therapy even when it was competently delivered. This culminated in Foa and Emmelkamp's book on treatment failures (1983). It became increasingly clear, for example, that it was insufficient to regard patients' problems with compliance in terms of 'poor motivation', but attempts at more detailed behavioural analysis of poor compliance provided little in the way of further improvement. Another important development during this period was the attempt to develop behavioural theories and techniques which could be applied to other psychological problems, particularly depression. Lewinsohn (1974*a*), for example, proposed that depression is due to a reduced rate of response-contingent reinforcement. However, early attempts at therapy based on this notion (Hammen and Glass 1975) had limited success, probably because although patients engaged in a greater number of potentially reinforcing activities, they would often negatively evaluate the activities and their own successful performance. Thus it became increasingly evident that cognitive factors were involved in those patients who did not respond to simple behavioural treatment. These two developments contributed to the subsequent acceptance by many therapists of the importance of cognitive factors and the need to address them in therapy.

The integration of cognitive and behavioural approaches

Lang's notion of three relatively independent response systems had laid the foundations for the acceptance of cognitive notions within the behavioural approach. In the context of behavioural psychology (as distinct from behaviour therapy), the importance of cognitive variables had already become increasingly recognized. The slower acceptance of cognitive views within behaviour therapy probably related to the continuing influence of Watson's rejection of introspection, and the polemical position adopted by behaviour therapists towards other psychotherapies. Bandura's work on observational learning was particularly important in drawing attention to cognitive factors in behaviour therapy. In this approach an individual learns by watching someone else performing a behaviour; the behaviour is learned best if the observer subsequently performs the behaviour in question, but this is not a necessary condition. Bandura developed a model of self-regulation called *self-efficacy*, based on the idea that all voluntary behaviour change was mediated by subjects' perceptions of their ability to perform the behaviour in question. Another important influence was an increasing interest in the concept of *self-control*, based on a three-stage model of self-observation, self-evaluation (setting standards), and self-reinforcement. This model generated a great deal of research effort in which cognitive constructs, including attribution and self-instruction, were made explicit.

Probably the first wholly cognitive approach to generate interest among behavioural researchers was *self-instructional training* (Meichenbaum 1975). The popularity of this approach related to its simple theoretical basis, and its similarity to the concept of 'coverants' (mental operant behaviour) within operant theory. Meichenbaum suggested that behaviour change can be brought about by changing the instructions that patients give themselves, away from maladaptive and upsetting thoughts to more adaptive self-talk. The more sophisticated cognitive therapy described by Beck (1970, 1976), which is similar in many respects to Ellis'

(1962) Rational Emotive Therapy, was adopted much more slowly, but has now become the most important of the cognitive approaches. Initially, this approach was mainly applied to depression (Beck 1967). In contrast to the traditional psychiatric view of depression, Beck proposed that the negative thinking so prominent in the disorder is not just a symptom but has a central role in the maintenance of depression. This implies that depression can be treated by helping patients to identify and modify their negative thoughts.

Beck proposed that negative thinking in depression originates in attitudes (*assumptions*) which are laid down in childhood and later. In many situations these assumptions can be helpful, and guide behaviour. For example, an assumption such as 'To be worthwhile I must be successful' is likely to motivate considerable positive activity. However, the assumptions make the individual vulnerable to certain critical events. In the case of the above assumption, failing an examination might be such an event: this would be interpreted as a major loss and lead to the production of *negative automatic thoughts*, such as, 'I am worthless', 'I am a failure as a person'. Such thoughts will lower mood, which in turn increases the probability that further negative automatic thoughts will occur, producing a vicious circle which tends to maintain the depression. Once depressed, a set of *cognitive distortions* exert a general influence over the person's day-to-day functioning. These are manifest as the *cognitive triad*: negative view of self, current experience, and future. Other cognitive changes may maintain this view once it is elicited; for example, patients selectively attend to events which confirm their negative view of themselves. This model is elaborated more fully in Chapter 6. Beck (1976) extended the application of cognitive therapy to a wide range of emotional disorders.

The treatment described in this book represents an integration of cognitive and behavioural approaches. For this reason it is termed cognitive behaviour therapy. In this type of treatment the patient is helped to recognize patterns of distorted thinking and dysfunctional behaviour. Systematic discussion and carefully structured behavioural assignments are then used to help patients evaluate and modify both their distorted thoughts and their dysfunctional behaviours. Some aspects of treatment have greater behavioural emphasis and others a greater cognitive emphasis. As this book clearly demonstrates, cognitive–behavioural treatments have now been developed for most disorders encountered in psychiatric practice.

General principles of cognitive–behavioural treatment

In the cognitive–behavioural approach considerable emphasis is placed on expressing concepts in operational terms and on the empirical validation of treatment, using both group and single-case experimental designs in research settings and in everyday clinical practice. In order to ensure the replicability of findings, specification of treatment in operational terms, and the evaluation of treatment with a variety of reliable and objective measures are also emphasized. Much of the treatment is based on the here-and-now, and there is an assumption that the main goal of therapy is to help patients bring about desired changes in their lives. Thus treatment focuses on the opportunity for new adaptive learning, and on producing changes outside the clinical setting. Problem solving is an important integral part of treatment. All aspects of therapy are made explicit to the patient, and the therapist and patient endeavour to work in a collaborative relationship in which they plan together strategies to deal with clearly identified problems. Therapy is time-limited, and has explicitly agreed goals.

In this chapter we have summarized the earlier developments which have led to the acceptance of the applicability and usefulness of cognitive–behavioural treatment approaches for many psychiatric disorders. While the next few years will undoubtedly witness substantial changes and elaborations of these approaches, at the present time they offer both effective specific means of helping patients and also provide a valuable general approach to understanding psychiatric disorders and designing treatment programmes.

Recommended reading

Barlow, D. H., Hayes, S. C., and Nelson, R. O. (1984). *The scientist practitioner.* Pergamon, New York.

Davison, G. and Neale, J. (1984). *Abnormal psychology* (3rd edn). Wiley, New York.

Kazdin, A. E. (1978). *History of behavior modification: experimental foundations of contemporary research.* University Park Press, Baltimore.

2

Cognitive–behavioural assessment

Joan Kirk

Introduction

Cognitive–behavioural assessment is based on simple principles and has clearly defined aims. These can be readily understood by therapists new to this approach, although they may need two or more assessment sessions with their first patients in order to achieve the aims of the assessment. These are to have agreed a formulation of the target problems with the patient, and to have sufficiently detailed information about factors maintaining the problem to be able to design and present a treatment plan. In addition, the therapist should have begun to educate the patient about the psychological model.

The first, and perhaps central principle of cognitive–behavioural assessment is that the ways in which an individual behaves are determined by immediate situations, and the individual's interpretations of them. This therefore becomes the major focus of the assessment, with an emphasis on specific problems rather than global entities.

The characteristics of therapists which are believed to be important in other kinds of therapy are likely to be just as relevant in cognitive–behavioural treatment. The patient needs to feel safe to disclose important and often distressing information. This will be facilitated if there is a warm and trusting atmosphere, no risk of censure, and if the therapist is empathic and clearly committed to helping the patient overcome current difficulties.

Goals of cognitive–behavioural assessment

Cognitive–behavioural formulation of problems

Cognitive behaviour therapy has its basis in the experimental method, so the early sessions are used to devise an initial hypothesis (formulation) and treatment plan. The formulation is tested out in subsequent homework and treatment sessions, and modified if necessary.

Although most of the assessment takes place in the initial sessions, the assessment process continues throughout treatment. Therapists sometimes make the error of thinking that if they classify a problem (for example 'height phobia'), this will designate the treatment (for example graded exposure). Clinicians have become increasingly aware that diagnostic categories give broad indications about what treatment might be useful, but that this is only a preliminary step which must be supplemented by more detailed information. What is the person doing, overtly or covertly, which he or she would like to change? What are the precipitants (situational, mental, or internal), for the problem behaviour, and in what settings does the problem occur? What are the consequences of the problem behaviour? In particular, what seems to maintain the behaviour, either in the short-term or long-term? What changes might be made in any of these to produce changes in the problem behaviour?

Most of this chapter describes how to derive a formulation and treatment plan. However, before focusing on this, there are two other functions of the assessment which will be discussed first. These concern the use of the behavioural interview to inform the patient about the cognitive–behavioural model and approach to treatment; and also the therapeutic qualities of the assessment.

Educating the patient about the cognitive–behavioural approach

The patient should be informed during the assessment that the cognitive–behavioural approach is largely self-help, and that the therapist aims to help the patient develop skills to overcome not only the current problems, but also any similar ones in the future. The therapist should emphasize the role of homework assignments, pointing out that the major part of therapy takes place in everyday life, with the patient putting into practice what has been discussed in treatment sessions. The collaborative nature of the therapeutic relationship should be discussed; the patient is expected to participate actively by collecting information, giving feedback on the effectiveness of techniques, and making suggestions about new strategies.

Information about the structure of treatment should also be given at this stage; for example, how many treatment sessions there will be, how long each will last, and where treatment will take place.

A cognitive–behavioural assessment also has a general educational role and focuses the patient on internal and external variables which may not have been seen as relevant to the problem. The patient is asked about situations, physiological states, cognitions, interpersonal factors, as well as overt behaviour, and about how each of these groups of variables relates to the problem. This questioning will be discussed in detail later in the chapter. Drawing attention to such functional relationships is part of teaching the patient about the psychological model. During the early stage of treatment, this helps to increase the agreement between the therapist's and patient's expectations of treatment: if they remain too dissimilar, the patient may decide not to pursue treatment.

Initiating the therapeutic process

The assessment interview has an important role in beginning the process of therapy. Patients frequently present with an undifferentiated array of difficulties. As the therapist helps to clarify and differentiate between problems, so the difficulties are frequently reduced to manageable proportions, and the patient begins to believe that change is possible. For example, a patient who presented with a series of problems including weepiness and low mood, loss of enjoyment and interest, tiredness, sleep disturbance, self-dislike, hopelessness, was relieved to learn that these were all common symptoms of one problem (i.e. depression), for which there were well-established treatment approaches. In contrast, some patients erroneously assume that their difficulties reflect a single problem; for example, a patient believed that she had one major problem—a basic lack of control—but was relieved when it became apparent during the assessment that instead she had interrelated, separate problems, including binge-eating, alcohol abuse, debt, low mood, and poor interpersonal relationships, which could each be tackled separately.

The assessment emphasizes the possibility of change, by helping the patient to think of what may be achieved, rather than dwelling continually on problems. It also sets reasonable limits on what might be achieved through treatment; for example, it is unreasonable for an agoraphobic patient to aim never to experience unpleasant emotions, but it should be possible to go to a supermarket in comfort.

The assessment also allows the patient to see that variations in the intensity of distress are predictable in terms of internal and external events, and are not just arbitrarily imposed by fate. It is implicit that if the variations are predictable, they may also be controllable. Patients may not readily pick up functional relationships between symptoms and such events. For example a patient said, 'Yes, I've really had a dreadful week. I was premenstrual, then I had the awful row with my brother about the anniversary of my mother's death, then I had to start going to work without the car because it broke down, and to cap it all, I've been feeling awful and all my worries about the symptoms have started coming back. I don't know what's brought it all on again.' Questioning helped her to see that the increase in her symptoms was not unpredicted but could readily be explained by the associated events and her interpretation of what the 'relapse' signalled.

The therapist should offer non-judgemental sympathy and concern about the patient's problems and distress; this may provide enormous relief, especially if the patient has felt embarrassed, guilty, or hopeless, as is often the case.

Finally, an important function of the assessment is to establish whether there is anything which needs dealing with as an emergency. For example, if the patient is depressed, suicidal intent must be assessed; if someone is complaining of difficulties in managing children, the possibility of physical abuse must be explored.

In summary, the main goal of the cognitive–behavioural assessment is to agree a formulation and treatment plan with the patient. In addition, it

Table 2.1 Modes of assessment

Behavioural interview
Self-monitoring
Self-report (questionnaires, global rating scales)
Information from other people
   interviews with key individuals
   monitoring by key others
Direct observation of behaviour in clinical settings
   role-play
   behavioural tests
Behavioural by-products
Physiological measures

---

allows the therapist to educate the patient about the treatment approach, and to begin the process of change. It also allows emergency factors to be assessed.

Modes of assessment

Although the major part of the behavioural assessment takes the form of a behavioural interview, this is only one of the modes of assessment which may be relevant in any given case. When assessing problems, it is useful to differentiate between four different classes of response— behavioural, physiological, cognitive, and emotional. Different assessment procedures give information about different response systems, and so it may be useful to assess a problem in more than one way, to allow a more accurate picture of change following treatment. This is particularly true if there is likely to be a lack of synchrony between the different measures (Rachman and Hodgson 1974). For example, a patient may change behaviourally, but still feel distressed and experience physiological changes when in fearful situations. Thus, assessing only the patient's self-report of distress would mask progress and it would be usefully supplemented by a behavioural test (see p. 49) in which the patient is asked to carry out problem behaviours. Table 2.1 summarizes the major modes of assessment which may be considered when assessing problems.

The major part of the behavioural assessment takes the form of an interview, but this is supplemented by information collected and recorded ('self-monitored') by the patient after the interview. Much of a behaviou- ral interview will be directed at defining problems in the kind of detail necessary for subsequent self-monitoring. The principles of measurement which are relevant to self-monitoring also apply to the other aspects of assessment summarized in Table 2.1. Therefore, the principles of measurement relevant to self-monitoring and the other assessment modes will be presented here, before the behavioural interview and other modes of assessment are discussed.

Measurement in cognitive–behavioural assessment and treatment

The application of the experimental method to problems of individual patients, as advocated by Shapiro (1961*b*), is central to the cognitive–behavioural approach: a formulation is used to make predictions about the effects of particular interventions (treatment techniques, etc.), and these are then tested out in treatment. Thus, therapy with any one patient can be seen as a single-case experiment, and much of treatment revolves round measures taken both during treatment sessions, and between sessions. Such quantification can conveniently be restricted to self-monitoring and questionnaires in most patients, with direct observations or physiological recording seldom required. It may require ingenuity to find individualized measures which adequately reflect the patient's problem, although standard measures are readily available for many situations.

Advantages of measurement

1. Retrospective estimates by patients of the frequency of behaviours are notoriously unreliable (Barlow, Hayes, and Nelson 1984). Direct recording allows a more accurate description of the problem in terms of frequency, intensity, etc.

2. Measurements during treatment sessions, as well as between sessions, allow the patient and therapist to modify treatment if necessary. For example, 'thought satiation' (where the patient focuses on a distressing thought for a lengthy period) was being used with an obsessional patient who rated her distress every three minutes during treatment sessions, and also three times daily. Her rating sheet is shown in Figs. 2.1 and 2.2. Ratings of distress about the thoughts consistently decreased during treatment sessions, but daily ratings of tension indicated that this was increasing from day to day. Given the 'effectiveness' of the procedure during sessions, this deterioration would have been missed without the daily ratings.

3. Measurement can have therapeutic effects, providing the patient with consistent and accurate information about progress. For example, an agoraphobic patient reported, 'It's been dreadful, I've not been out at all, I couldn't do anything.' Examination of her daily homework diaries of trips from home (see Fig. 2.3) allowed her to see that although she had slipped back from the previous week, she was going out significantly more and feeling less anxious than a month previously. The session also

Please rate how distressed you feel at this moment, using the following scale:

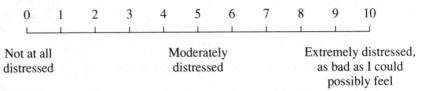

| 0 | 1 | 2 | 3 | 4 | 5 | 6 | 7 | 8 | 9 | 10 |

Not at all   Moderately   Extremely distressed,
distressed   distressed   as bad as I could
                                                            possibly feel

Fig. 2.1 Self-rating scale for distress during sessions of thought satiation with an obsessional patient

Please rate how distressed you felt during each part of the day, using the following scale:

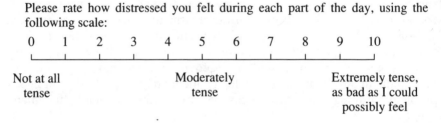

| 0 | 1 | 2 | 3 | 4 | 5 | 6 | 7 | 8 | 9 | 10 |

Not at all   Moderately   Extremely tense,
tense   tense   as bad as I could
                                                            possibly feel

Date	Morning	Afternoon	Evening
29 Nov	4	5	3
30 Nov	2	5	4
1 Dec	6	6	7
2 Dec	5	4	2
3 Dec	6	7	8

Fig. 2.2 Three-times-daily tension-rating scale for an obsessional patient

Date	Outing to	Anxiety expected 0–100	Time away	Shops ✓ ✗	Alone ✓ ✗	Actual anxiety 0–100
4 April	Cousin up road	75	30 min	✗	✓	40
5 April	Butcher and school	50	25 min	✓	✗	30
6 April	Abingdon on bus, shopping	75	2 hours	✓	✗	40
7 April	Butcher and school	60	25 min	✓	✗	35
	Pub in evening	80	1 hour	✗	✗	20

Fig. 2.3 Daily diary of trips from home by an agoraphobic woman

Date	Time spent alone		Anxiety initially 0–100	Anxiety 1 hour later	How you coped with being alone
	from	*to*			
3 March	10.20	10.45	85	15	I phoned my mother to ask her to come back
8 March	10.00	10.15	70	10	Phoned my neighbour and talked to her
12 March	10.00	10.30	60	5	Played my tape
21 March	2.10	2.40	60	10	Did some sewing to distract myself

Fig. 2.4 Diary of a patient anxious about staying alone

coincided with her menstrual period, and a review of other premenstrual weeks in the diaries indicated that she tended to be more anxious and less active at such times.

Patients low in confidence and self-esteem tend to give themselves little credit for progress. For example, a patient who had successfully overcome her fear of staying in the house by herself dismissed this by saying, 'Well, that was never a problem anyway; it's handling the children I really have difficulty with.' Reference to early record sheets revealed that at the beginning of treatment she had been very distressed if alone in the house, and avoided it as far as possible. This demonstrated how successful she had been in solving what had been a major problem (see Fig. 2.4).

Regular measurements also ensure that the therapist and patient remain focused on the agreed treatment goals.

4. Measurement allows the therapist to establish whether the treatment has been delivered as intended; for example, an exposure programme (see Chapter 4) may not work because the patient is not exposing appropriately. Many therapists check on homework informally; for example:

Therapist 'Are you going out regularly as we agreed?'
Patient 'Oh yes, I'm going out from time to time.'
Th. 'How often is "from time to time"?'
Pt 'Oh, whenever I need to.'
Th. 'And how often is that?'
Pt 'On most days.'

However, even this amount of questioning did not provide the precise information which a daily diary would provide. In this case the patient had actually been out three times in a week and this low frequency of exposure explained why little progress was being made.

In summary, measurement has a central role in cognitive–behavioural assessment and treatment, and may occur in different assessment modes. The behavioural interview is generally the starting point for assessment, and this will now be discussed in detail.

Behavioural interviewing

Initial stage

Most patients will have little idea what to expect of the assessment interview. It helps to put the patient at ease and to begin to establish rapport if it is clear that the therapist has read the relevant referral letters, and if the stage is set for the remainder of the session. After the therapist and patient have introduced themselves, the session might begin,

'Dr . . . wrote to me about the problems you would like help with. I gather that you are feeling tense and anxious most of the time, and that you are concerned about your drinking. Apart from that, I do not have a lot of detail. I would like you to tell me briefly how *you* see the problems just now. Then we will discuss for a quarter of an hour or so how the problem developed. And then we will go over how things are now in more detail. So can you begin by telling me briefly what you see as the main problems?'

It is useful simply to listen to what the patient has to say about the problems. He or she has probably spent a great deal of time thinking about them. On the other hand, it is easy for the patient to misinterpret what is required, and be ready to launch into an historical account of the problem, which is not useful at this stage. The therapist should listen carefully and communicate caring concern to the patient. Comments such as, 'This is obviously very difficult/upsetting for you' help to engage the patient, and to establish rapport. Summarizing and paraphrasing what the patient has said, and reflecting back feelings, allows the therapist to communicate that the problems are understood. For example, after listening to a lengthy description of a patient's problems, the therapist said, 'If I am right, you are saying that you try very hard to please other people, and to put their well-being before your own, but it sounds as though this makes you feel very worked up at times. Is that right?' The patient can be encouraged to expand in relevant areas if increased interest is shown, both non-verbally with nods and eye contact, as well as verbally through comments and questions. However, therapists should ensure that their initial preconceptions about patients' problems do not excessively influence either their questions, or their interpretations of the patients' replies.

Some patients find it difficult to describe their problems, or give only vague descriptions. It may then be helpful to ask questions such as, 'Can you describe to me what happened last time you were upset?', 'When was that?', 'What was the first thing you noticed?', 'In what way has your life changed since you developed these problems?', 'What does the problem prevent you doing?', 'What have you had to give up because of the problem?' The use of paraphrasing may then help the patient expand on relevant aspects.

At this stage, which lasts five or 10 minutes, only a general outline of the problems is required. The therapist picks up clues about possible antecedents and maintaining factors for use later in the interview, but only notes them at this stage. It is useful to provide the patient with a summary of the problems, and to obtain feedback on its accuracy. The therapist could say, for example, 'You seem to be saying that your major problem is palpitations, and your worry about them. But in addition to that, you are worrying about your daughter's current relationship, as well as your husband's attitude to it. Have I got that right? Are there any other problems we have missed out?'

When there is more than one presented problem, the therapist and patient should work out together which problem should be the initial focus of intervention (see p. 416).

The assessment then moves on to look at how each problem began and subsequently developed, before a more detailed analysis of the current situation is made. Each identified problem is analysed in turn, covering the steps summarized in Table 2.2.

Development of problem

This part of the assessment is considerably briefer than in other kinds of psychotherapeutic assessment, since historical information is only collected if it is of direct relevance to the development of the presenting problem, and the understanding of current maintaining factors.

Onset

There may have been a very clear onset for a problem; for example, a driving phobia may develop immediately after a car accident. However, even in such apparently straightforward cases, the therapist will require further information in order to understand the problem and how it is maintained. For example, the driving phobia may be maintained by thoughts about crashing, avoidance, and, perhaps, thoughts about disfigurement remaining from the initial crash.

For many patients, the problem will have developed gradually, with a succession of events contributing to the patient's recognition that there is a problem. These events may be directly related to what is eventually identified as the problem; for example, a patient may have left three jobs before recognizing that he has difficulty dealing with authority figures at work. The patient on the other hand, may realize that there is a problem which is getting worse, but be unclear about how it started, or why it is

Table 2.2   Stages in the Behavioural Interview

Brief description of problems
Development: precipitants
                        time course
                        predisposing factors
Description of problem behaviour: behavioural   ⎫   What?
                                                    cognitive   ⎬   When?
                                                    affective   ⎪   Where?
                                                    physiological ⎭   How often?
                                                                        With whom?
                                                                        How distressing?
                                                                        How disruptive?

Contexts and modulating variables: situational
                                                    behavioural
                                                    cognitive
                                                    affective
                                                    interpersonal
                                                    physiological
Maintaining factors: situational
                                    behavioural
                                    cognitive
                                    affective
                                    interpersonal
                                    physiological
Avoidance
Coping resources and other assets
Psychiatric and medical history
Previous treatment: response
                                  current medication
Beliefs about problem
Engagement
Mood/mental state
Psychosocial situation: family
                                      psychosexual relationships
                                      accommodation
                                      occupation
                                      social relationships
                                      hobbies/interests
Preliminary formulation

deteriorating. In such cases, there may be stressful life events or major changes associated with the onset of the problem and changes in its intensity. It may be useful to run through a list of some typical life events, for example, death or illness in family or friends, break-up in a relationship, moving house, job change, etc. There will be areas of particular relevance for any given problem; for example, loss would be especially relevant for a depressed patient, physical illness in a relative or friend for a patient with panic attacks.

Course

The way the problem has developed since its onset should be established. The problem may, for example, have persisted steadily, or it may have deteriorated or fluctuated. It is useful to establish why the patient presented for help at this particular time, as this may reflect other difficulties. For example, a woman with increasing social anxiety only presented for help when she changed jobs and could not face explaining to her colleagues that fears of contamination would prevent her using the staff canteen. If there have been fluctuations in the severity of the problem, and particularly if it is long-standing, then it is helpful to plot an event-time chart, with variations in problem severity down one side of a time-line, and life changes down the other side. An example is given in Fig. 2.5. As in other parts of the interview, the predictability of the problem is emphasized, to help the patient understand why variations in its severity have occurred. As well as life events, changes in mood should be enquired about, as should any 'treatment' interventions, either formal or informal (through, for example, self-help groups, voluntary bodies, churches, etc.).

Some patients will want to spend an excessive time describing the development of problems. This may be because of inaccurate expectations about the interview, or because they have spent hours pondering about their problems and wish to share their thoughts. It may be necessary to remind such patients that the major focus of treatment is on immediate circumstances. The therapist could say,

'We need to spend most of our time on what is happening now, because that is what we are going to try and change. Although we need an outline of how the problem developed, we need to spend most of our time on what we can change.'

It may also be worthwhile pointing out that a problem may have developed for reasons which have become irrelevant and that entirely different factors may now be maintaining it. For example, a man developed erectile failure at a time when he doubted his previous wife's affection for him; although he was now in a loving relationship, anxiety about his poor sexual performance maintained the erectile problem.

It is worth noting that the word '*why*' is avoided as far as possible, as it tends to produce the response, 'I don't know', or lengthy expositions

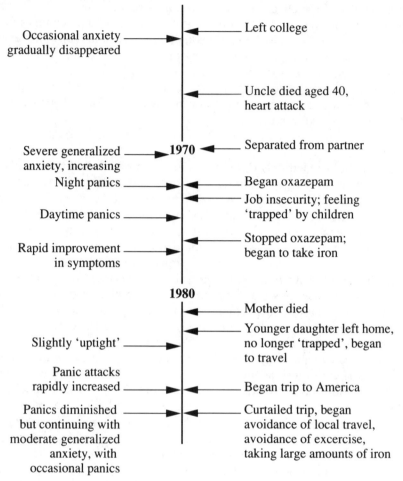

Fig. 2.5 Time-event chart for a patient with anxiety symptoms

about the origins of the problem in terms of lay psychology. Questions such as, 'What was difficult for you about that situation?' or, 'How did you stay calm in that situation?', on the other hand, produce more detailed information about factors currently maintaining the problem.

Predisposing factors

Information is sought about anything in the background which made it more likely that the patient would develop the target problem. More specific information about background factors relevant for specific disorders is available in the subsequent chapters. For example, if someone were depressed, then the patient would be questioned about family history of depression and childhood separation; an anxious patient would be questioned about emotional lability; a woman with orgasmic dysfunction would be questioned about sexual attitudes of her parents. However, depressed and anxious patients would not be asked about sexual attitudes, even though it could be argued that this might give a further understanding of the patient as a whole. Generally, the therapist only seeks information which makes it more likely that the target problem can be changed.

Behavioural analysis

This stage, during which problems are reviewed in detail, comprises the major part of the interview. The aim is to discover how the problem is currently maintained, in what way it is interfering with the patient's life, and whether the problem is serving any useful purpose for the patient. There are two commonly used approaches to this.

Each problem can be analysed in terms of what O'Leary and Wilson (1975) termed the A–B–Cs—the *Antecedents, Behaviours and beliefs*, and *Consequences*. Each of these factors may increase or decrease the probability that the behaviour will occur. For example, a common *antecedent* to smoking cigarettes is sitting with a cup of coffee at the end of a meal; if the antecedents are altered (immediately moving away from the table at the end of the meal, drinking tea instead of coffee), then the likelihood of smoking is reduced. On the other hand, changing *behaviour* by deliberately smoking cigarettes too rapidly can help bring smoking under control. Finally, if there are positive *consequences*, for example, money saved by not smoking put aside for a specific activity, smoking is less likely in the future. For any given problem, changes may be possible in any or all of the antecedents, behaviours, or consequences; the assessment aims to identify what might be maintaining the problem and what can be changed.

A similar but more straightforward way of carrying out a behavioural analysis is to describe the contexts in which the problems arise, to look at the factors which modulate the intensity of the problems, and to assess the consequences, including avoidance, of them. This scheme will be adopted here as it is less complex but allows an adequate analysis of most problems.

Detailed description of problem

As a first step, it is useful to ask the patient for a detailed description of a recent example of the problem. This gives more specific information than is obtained from a general description, and provides clues about maintaining factors. If patients have difficulty in describing a recent incident, it may be helpful for them to close their eyes and imagine the scene, as though it were being played on television. The description of the problem should include internal events such as thoughts, feelings, and physical symptoms, as well as overt behaviours.

A patient who presented with worries about bowel function was asked:

> 'Let's go over things in more detail. You say you worry about going to the lavatory. When was the last time you really worried about it?'

Patient   'This morning before breakfast.'

Therapist   'Could you talk me through it, letting me know what happened, how you felt, what you did, what thoughts were going through your head and so on. What was the first thing which happened?'

It may be helpful for the patient to talk freely for a few minutes, but this should be followed up with questions, until the therapist has a clear idea of what happened in the specific example and the sequence in which it occurred. The patient in the above example focused on how he felt, without describing what he did, and so the therapist questioned him about other aspects of the problem. The patient replied:

> 'I just felt terrible. I can't think about anything else at these times, and I get really uptight. My muscles were all tense, I got hot and sweaty, I got terrible butterflies, and my stomach felt all upset. But I knew that if I went to the loo I would tighten up and be unable to do anything.'

Therapist   'You say you felt all tense, hot and sweaty and so on. Were there any other physical sensations this morning?'

Patient   'I often feel lightheaded, but I know I won't faint.'

Th.   'And this morning, what did you do when you were feeling like this?'

Pt   'Oh, I paced around my room, but I daren't go outside, or into the kitchen in case I saw someone and they asked me what was wrong.'

Th.   'Would it be unpleasant if someone asked what was wrong?'

Pt   'Well, it would be so embarrassing. I could hardly *tell* them, could I?'

Th.   'I can see you'd find that difficult. How long did you stay in your room until you felt a bit easier, until you settled down?'

Pt   'About twenty minutes, then I could go out of the room.'

Th.   'And then what did you do?'

Attention then turns to a wider description of the problem, with the therapist continually trying to elicit specific detail rather than generalities. For each problem the therapist should have a picture of: what the problem is (when, where, how often, and with whom it occurs); how distressing it is; and how disruptive it is.

Contexts and modulating variables

As outlined in Chapter 1, an assumption of behavioural theory is that abnormal behaviour has been learned, and that such behaviours can be triggered by external or internal cues which have become associated with the problem behaviour. Thus, a woman with bulimia nervosa found that

Date	Mood *How strong* *0–100%*	Activity/thoughts before seeking a contact	Sexual feeling before contact How strong 0–100%	Contact made	Enjoyment from sexual contact 0–100%
6 June	Bored 70%	Watching TV by myself	20%	Yes	20%
8 June	Angry 60%	Unable to get booking for laboratory	10%	Yes	15%
9 June	Fed up 80%	Tidying flat, listening to music	25%	No	—
12 June	Bored 75%	Worked too late, can't be bothered to start anything	30%	Yes	10%

Fig. 2.6   Self-monitoring of casual homosexual contact

she had many more urges to binge when she was in areas of town where there were food shops; a woman with agoraphobia noted that she felt highly anxious in particular shops.

A detailed assessment of contextual triggers is required because treatment plans often include manipulation of the contexts in which problems occur; for example, the woman with bulimia could initially reduce her bingeing by planning routes which circumvented food shops. In addition, treatment frequently involves variations in the *modulating* variables associated with particular cues. The range of possible triggers is almost infinite: for example, an obsessional patient may constantly ritualize at home but never at work, an agoraphobic patient may be anxiety-free if in a town where she is unknown, a compulsive gambler may only gamble when angry.

The patient may not be aware of the contexts in which the problem occurs, nor of the modulating variables. It is generally necessary for further information to be collected, either through self-monitoring or a behavioural test. For example, a patient was distressed by his high frequency of casual homosexual contacts, but was unclear about what prompted him to seek them out. Daily monitoring helped him to see that the behaviour was related to boredom, irritability, and tension, and only occasionally to sexual frustration. A sample from his diary is shown in Fig. 2.6.

When considering contexts in which problems arise, six broad areas should be covered, as listed in Table 2.2; while it is not necessary to go through these in order, the interview should be sufficiently structured for each to be discussed: a major goal is to shift from a global, all-or-nothing view of the problem, to one in which the patient may begin to see it as predictable.

Situational cues Problems are often worse in some situations than others. For example, a patient with bowel problems gave the following account:

Therapist 'Right, that's a pretty clear picture of how things are when they are bad. Now let's look at the sorts of things which make the problem more likely to occur.'

Patient   'Actually, it's there all the time, I never stop thinking about it.'

Th.   'Yes, I'm sure it feels like that. But you've mentioned that at least some of the time you can put it to the back of your mind and get on with things. What is likely to set it off in the morning?'

Pt   'Well, if I wake up and can go to the lavatory straightaway then I'm OK. But if someone is around on the corridor, and I can't go, then I start to get uptight.'

Th.   'So, it's worse if people are around?'

Pt   'Oh yes, much worse.'

Th.   'And which people make it worse, anybody or are some people easier?'

Pt   'I'm not too bad at home with my family, because they know there's a problem and leave me alone. It's people on the corridor I particularly dread.'

Th.   'But what about total strangers in college, say?'

Pt   'Oh yes, they're difficult, nearly as bad as those in the flat.'

Th.   'Right, so having people around makes a difference. What else affects the situation? You are implying it is easier at home than at college. Is that just because of the people, or is it other things about the situation?'

Pt   'It's certainly worse if it's quiet.'

Th.   'What's so bad about quietness?'

Behavioural cues Symptoms may be precipitated by a wide range of behaviours. For example, an obsessional woman was not troubled by the presence of knives in her kitchen, but became very distressed whenever she used them; an obsessional man found going through doorways or over steps very difficult; a man concerned about his health found that any mildly strenuous activity resulted in anxious thoughts.

Cognitive factors Patients may believe that problems occur unpredictably because they pay little attention to what thoughts are going through their minds at the time and immediately beforehand. At the initial interview it may be difficult for the patient to identify the relevant thoughts, or to focus on thoughts at the appropriate level of specificity. This may be because the thoughts were not attended to; or it may be that, when the patient is not upset, the thoughts are discounted as ridiculous and exaggerated. The identification of dysfunctional thoughts, which is an important step in the treatment of many problems, is discussed in detail in Chapters 3 and 6. At the assessment stage, questioning about thoughts may introduce the patient to their role in precipitating problems. For example, one patient said:

> 'But sometimes I just start worrying about it for no reason at all. I can just be sitting in front of my typewriter, and suddenly feel awful.'

Therapist 'Can you think of a time like that?'

Patient 'Yes, it happened last week.'

Th. 'It's very unusual for symptoms to come out of the blue. Let's try and imagine the scene in as much detail as we can, and see if we can piece together what set it off.'

Pt 'I was sitting in my office, typing away, and suddenly I felt dreadful.'

Th. 'Do you often feel bad in your office?'

Pt 'No, as I said, I usually feel OK when I'm at work.'

Th. 'So, can you remeber what were you actually doing on this occasion?'

Pt 'I was typing an annual review.'

Th. 'So, you're sitting in your chair, typing the annual review, was anyone else around?'

Pt 'No, nobody was in, and I'd been left with a hugh pile of stuff to get through.'

Th. 'And can you think what actually went through your mind at that point?'

Pt 'I thought, I shall never get this lot done, I'll be tired out, and I shall be in a state for this evening.'

Other patients are fully aware that their thoughts play a major role in the presentation of symptoms, and may self-critically point out that they talk themselves into feeling bad. They sometimes feel hopeless and out of control about having got themselves into this mess, with all the responsibility for getting out of it thus resting fully on their shoulders. This offers an opportunity for pointing out an area of control.

Therapist 'You mean that if you start thinking "I'm going to feel bad", this brings on the symptoms?'

Patient 'Yes, it's ridiculous, I just bring it on myself. Anybody would think I enjoy feeling like this.'

Th. 'I am sure you don't. But you're in a very strong position, having realized that the way you *think* affects how you feel.'

Affective states A variety of mood states may affect the problem. Depression and anxiety are the most obvious areas, but other states like irritability, cheerfulness, excitement may be relevant. If, for example, a patient feels more anxious in phobic situations when she is irritable, she could look at what makes her irritable and whether this can be changed. It would also be useful to discuss whether she attributes her physical 'symptoms' to anxiety, when some could be attributed to irritability. A woman with a social phobia described this effect:

Therapist 'Do other sorts of mood make any difference? What about if you're excited?'
Patient   'I never feel excited, at least not for any length of time. If I feel excited about something, it reminds me that I shall probably be anxious when I get there, and that makes me nervous.'
Th.   'Do you mean that the feelings you get when you are excited are similar to the ones you get when you feel anxious?'

Interpersonal factors Social factors are relevant in the majority of problems presented. These include problems such as assertiveness or social anxiety in which interpersonal factors are central, through to a wide range of problems in which social variables are implicated but more peripherally. For example, a girl with an eating disorder was asked:

Therapist 'Does it make any difference if you're with someone?'
Patient   'Oh, I can't bear to eat if anyone is around.'
Th.   'What is it that you dislike?'
Pt   'Well, I can feel them watching me all the time to see if I'm eating normally, and I start thinking that they think I'm greedy as soon as I put the first mouthful in. Though I know that's ridiculous.'
Th.   'Is there anything else you dislike about it?'
Pt   'Well, if I'm honest, I guess it means that I can't go ahead and *really* binge, even if I want to.'

The behaviour of family members and other key individuals may have a marked effect on the problem; for example, criticism by another person frequently exacerbates obsessional rituals; the presence of a child may facilitate coping responses in a phobic patient. The beliefs of family members are also relevant, depending on whether they see the problem as physical, incurable, moral weakness, or whatever.

Physiological factors These can be relatively specific to the problem; for example, a palpitation may precipitate severe anxiety symptoms in a patient concerned about cardiac functioning. On the other hand, there are more general factors, like tiredness, phase of menstrual cycle, caffeine intake, which may affect either general arousal level, or may affect the problem directly. Furthermore, some behaviour may only occur in specific physiological states; for example, after alcohol consumption.

   As with many of the cues given in the above examples it is not sufficient simply to establish the antecedents for a behaviour; the patient's interpretation of the cues, whether these are situational, behavioural, physiological, or interpersonal, are central to the assessment.

Maintaining factors

Having built up a reasonable picture of the conditions under which the problem is most likely to occur, the next step is to look at what is maintaining the problem. The major focus is on the immediate consequences of the problem behaviour. In simple terms, as described in Chapter 1, behaviour which is followed by unpleasant circumstances is less likely to recur, behaviour followed by pleasant events is more likely to recur in the future. The most potent consequences of the problem are the patient's thoughts and other reactions to the problem, as these frequently set up a series of vicious circles which maintain the problem. Longer-terms events are usually less relevant, and indeed may appear to contradict the basic operant principle; for example, an obsessional patient may continue with time-consuming rituals even though in the long term this is jeopardizing both employment prospects and family harmony.

Immediate consequences As with the triggers, these reactions can be classified into six broad groupings, as shown in Table 2.2.

For example, a woman with increased frequency of micturition found that bladder sensations were triggered by a great many situations and behaviours, including arriving at work, beginning a journey by bus or car, eating a meal, bending over, carrying anything. She then thought, 'I must go to the loo', and if this were not possible, her *reactions* included behavioural responses like crossing her legs, sitting still; thoughts like, 'If I do not go immediately, there's going to be a terrible mess', and a whole series of thoughts about how uncomfortable she felt; affective changes, mostly in anxiety level; and a wide range of physiological symptoms including headache and stomach-ache, as well as more non-specific symptoms of anxiety. All of these reactions kept her focused on bladder sensations, which increased as a result; this then increased the reactions, and so on in a vicious circle. There were also interpersonal consequences; for example, her aunt might say, 'Are you not going to go to the loo now that you've eaten that sandwich?' As soon as she was able to empty her bladder, all of these reactions disappeared, thus reinforcing her belief that she had an abnormal bladder which she needed to empty frequently, and thus reinforcing her high frequency of micturition.

The patient will frequently give clues about maintaining factors during earlier parts of the assessment, but these need to be supplemented with detailed and specific questions. For example, a woman was feeling anxious much of the time because of a difficult family situation. She was increasingly worried about her ability to cope at work as a teacher.

Therapist 'You say that if you are anxious in the classroom then the children get out of control. What happens?'
Patient 'Well, they seem to sense that I'm feeling bad, and they play up. It can deteriorate into a riot within seconds.'

Th.   'Can you think of an example of when that happened, as quickly as that?'
Pt   'Well, it didn't happen within seconds, but one day last week it built up very quickly.'
Th.   'Can you tell me about that?'
Pt   'Well, I was feeling really bad, light-headed and tense, and they got more and more out of control.'
Th.   'What were you doing with them?'
Pt   'They were painting, and two or three started flicking paint, then it all built up. I should have noticed when it started really.'
Th.   'What were you doing instead?'
Pt   'I guess I was too busy thinking about how I was feeling.'
Th.   'Can you remember what thoughts were going through your head?'
Pt   'Oh yes, I spend all my time thinking—"I can't carry on like this, there'll be a riot if I don't pull myself together."'
Th.   'What happened that day? Did it build up to a riot?'
Pt   'No, it was playtime so I could go off to the staff room to cool down.'

The therapist then gave the patient a summary, so that she could begin to see which factors might be changed, and could provide feedback on the accuracy of the summary:

Therapist 'So what you seem to be saying is that if you are tense and worried in the classroom, this affects your concentration so that you're not so good at nipping trouble in the bud; if any trouble erupts, then you worry about it really getting out of control, get even more tense, and so it builds up.'
Patient   'That right. I can't do anything.'
Th.   'It sounds as though you just wait for relief, until you can get out of the classroom. And I suppose that is just strengthening your belief that you really cannot cope.'
Pt   'Well, it's true, I can't.'
Th.   'So we'll need to work out what you can do that would build up your self-confidence about coping at work.'

This summary has raised the possibility of altering a number of maintaining factors—nipping trouble in the bud, worrying thoughts about riots, increased tension—so that the situation can be improved without 'escaping', and so that the patient can again feel confident in the classroom.

The response of relatives and friends to the problem is obviously relevant, and it is usually necessary to ask in detail about particular situations. General descriptions of behaviour, like 'supportive', give little information; nor do phrases like, 'He never says anything'. A socially phobic woman gave much more useful information when specifically questioned:

Therapist 'How did your husband respond when you went red?'
Patient   'Oh, he never says anything really, he's not much help.'

Th.   'Can you remember what he actually said that day in the cafe?'
Pt   'He said he wasn't going to sit there if I was going to make a fool of
         myself.'

Avoidance   The avoidance of or relief from distressing emotion is frequently an immediate effect of a problem behaviour, and is often the most
potent maintaining factor (see Chapter 1). Many treatment plans will
include steps to overcome it, and the therapist therefore requires an
extensive description of what is avoided. The discussion of passive avoidance can be introduced with a general question like, 'What things have
you stopped doing, or what places have you stopped going to, because of
this?' Active avoidance can be addressed with a question like, 'Are there
things which you have started doing, or are doing differently, because of
the problem?' or 'What could you stop doing if the problem went away?'
This should be supplemented by questions about home life, relationship
with partner and children, work, social life, hobbies and interests, each of
which may be affected by avoidance. If the problem is chronic, the patient
may have become unaware of the extent of the avoidance, and questions
such as, 'How would your life be different if you did not have this
problem?', 'In an ideal world, if the problem disappeared, what would
you be doing that you can't do now?' are helpful. In addition, reports in
the literature can guide specific questioning; for example, patients with
worries about cardiac function may avoid any mildly strenuous activity
like going upstairs; patients with eating disorders may avoid a wide range
of fattening foods on 'health' grounds.
   Patients can be quite skilled at subtle avoidance even when they appear
to be exposing themselves to difficult situations. For example, a socially
phobic woman continued to go out socially but had developed an almost
total avoidance of eye-contact; this allowed her to avoid the disapproval
and boredom she feared she would see if she looked at people interacting
with her. Avoidance may be extensive even though the problem appears
to be circumscribed. For example, a woman with a phobia about vomiting had described how it affected her work as a nursery nurse where she
felt unable to deal with ill children. Specific questioning revealed a much
wider pattern of avoidance.

Therapist 'You say that if you see dirty people, or drunks, you get worried in
          case they are sick. Does this affect you socially? Are there places or
          people you avoid because of this?'
Patient   'I suppose there are. Hundreds of them. I won't go to pubs when they
          are busy . . . or go out late in the evening when people may have drunk
          a lot . . . I don't go to parties in case people get drunk.'
Th.   'Are there other social situations like that?'
Pt   'I'm not so bothered about dinner parties if I know the people, but I'm
          not keen on restaurants in case people eat or drink too much. I won't

	even fly because people might drink to settle their nerves before they fly and be sick in the departure lounge—I once saw that happen.'
Th.	'That was an unfortunate coincidence that you were there. It can't happen often. What about other public transport. Is that affected?'
Pt	'Well, I don't go on trips with the nursery in case the children are travel sick. And I wouldn't go on a long distance coach trip either— not because I'm travel sick but in case somebody else was sick.'
Th.	'Can you think of other situations like that?'
Pt	'It sounds ridiculous, but I stopped going to the squash club because somebody was sick once. They'd probably just got an upset tummy—if anybody says they feel ill, I do anything to get away.'
Th.	'Are there any other steps you take, in case anyone is sick?'
Pt	'Yes, I will never go out without wet tissues so that I could clean myself up if I was affected by it. And I carry barley sugar sweets to give to the children in case they feel sick. I'm very careful with my diet as well, particularly if I am going out.'

Further questioning about friends' illnesses and 'dirty' people was supplemented by a homework exercise, when she made a list of how life would be different if there was no problem. This was to give her more opportunity to identify avoided situations.

Long-term consequences   The pattern of avoidance described by a patient may raise the question of whether the presented problem is part of a wider difficulty. However, there is no supposition of underlying needs as in concepts such as 'secondary gain'. For example, it could be postulated that the vomit phobia described above allowed the woman to avoid social interactions. This could be pursued in the assessment interview, but the issue may not be fully resolved until further into treatment—successful resolution of a specific difficulty may reveal a wider problem, or failure to proceed may indicate associated difficulties. If there were an associated problem, it could be approached within the cognitive–behavioural framework described above without invoking underlying conflicts. Dealing with associated problems in this way side-steps the issue of whether the patient is really motivated to improve (p. 36), and evidence of a related problem can be taken at its face value with no implications of ambivalence about change.

After the detailed description of maintaining factors, it is worthwhile asking a broad question like, 'Are there any more general ways in which your life would change if you no longer had this problem?' This may simply point to a general increase in self-esteem for example; on the other hand, it may indicate longer-term changes, for example within a marriage, or in terms of independence, which may need building into the formulation.

Coping resources and other assets

People differ in their methods of coping with problems and distress, and in the extent to which they rely on themselves rather than on other people. This ranges from the individual's familiarity with specific strategies, like relaxing the shoulders when tense, through to more general assets, like being able to communicate distress to others.

Initially, questioning can be directed at coping with the target problem. For example, the therapist can ask, 'I would be interested to know what you do which helps you control the problem, even if it only has a small effect. Can you tell me what things you've found helpful?' It may be useful to give an example: 'You mentioned that you can sometimes prevent things building up if you go out of the room and count ten before coming back. Are there other things like that which you have found useful?' It is also helpful to discuss how the patient has dealt with other difficult situations, partly to highlight any demonstrable capacity for coping, and partly to determine which skills were used. For example, the therapist could ask, 'Let's think of another time in your life when you have had to deal with a difficult situation, something which was distressing. Can you think of an example?'

From this the interviewer can move to a wider discussion of the patient's assets, skills, and strengths. These include environmental features (for example, a supportive spouse, a satisfying job, having a car available for homework tasks); skills which may generally facilitate change (good record-keeping, highly skilled bee-keeping as a source of self-esteem); and strengths, such as a sense of humour, willingness to tolerate discomfort, persistence, interpersonal warmth, which make it more likely that treatment suggestions will be carried through.

Previous psychiatric and medical history and treatment

A description should be obtained of previous history, particularly of similar episodes. The patient's response to previous treatment is particularly important. This is partly because it may predict current response to treatment, and, in the case of poor outcome, might give information about pitfalls to avoid. In addition, the patient may have developed beliefs about the nature of the problem (e.g. 'It responded to tablets so it must be physical') or its possible outcome (e.g. 'It didn't even respond to tablets so it must be incurable') on the basis of previous response. Current medication should be noted, particularly psychotropic, but also other medication (e.g. hormone treatments) which may affect psychological functioning.

Beliefs about the problem and treatment

Patients are unlikely to engage in treatment if the approach the therapist offers is not congruent with their beliefs about the nature of the problem.

Although the therapist seeks to structure the interview so that information necessary for a treatment plan is obtained, and so that patients can be educated about the cognitive–behavioural approach, nevertheless opportunities should be given throughout the interview for them to educate the therapist about their perception of the problems. Patients should be asked, for example, whether they think their problems are likely to change and what they think would be likely to help them. It is helpful to ask whether anyone close to them has had similar problems, and what the outcome was.

The impact of the patient's beliefs on assessment and treatment need not be subtle. One woman with long-standing obsessional problems was unable to give a coherent description of her difficulties, or even to sit down during the interview. It would have been entirely useless to pursue a 'standardized' assessment interview, until it had been established that she believed that she was being reassessed for the lobotomy she had been offered 20 years previously. Other beliefs have indirect subtle effects; patients can provide detailed information about their problems, but reveal nothing about their general beliefs about them. For example, a woman had described a cancer phobia. It transpired that an aunt with hypochondriacal ideas had died after a long period of institutionalization in a psychiatric hospital; the patient believed that ultimately she would suffer the same fate, although vaguely hoping that treatment could stave off the evil day.

Patients with physical symptoms frequently believe that they have a physical condition which will only be helped by physical treatment, and this is also true for some depressed patients. While some beliefs require immediate intervention, others can be dealt with in subsequent sessions. Many change spontaneously during treatment; for example, a belief about the hopelessness of a condition may begin to change as soon as any improvement occurs. Ways of questioning and challenging beliefs are described in detail in Chapters 3 and 6.

It is preferable for the patient's beliefs to be elicited during the initial interviews, but occasionally the patient may be unwilling to disclose them at this stage, or even be unaware of them. As assessment continues throughout treatment, further discussion of beliefs may arise when there is a block in progress.

Engagement in treatment

Most cognitive–behavioural treatments demand a high level of commitment on the patient's part, and many treatments fail because the patient does not apply the agreed procedures. It would be useful to identify those people who are most likely to fulfil their side of the treatment bargain, but attempts to predict success in treatment by measuring a uni-dimensional or unitary 'desire for change' have been disappointing (Bellack and Schwartz, 1976). Instead it is helpful to discuss with the patient some of the components which make up a desire for change, correct any misconceptions, and together make an informed decision about whether it would be worthwhile continuing with treatment. First, the level of distress or inconvenience associated with the problem must be compared with the distress and inconvenience likely to result from the treatment. This balance is likely to change during treatment, and hence should be periodically reassessed. The patient's beliefs about the problem and treatment (as above) should be explored, and erroneous beliefs corrected. This could involve providing new information (for example, about probable outcome); or by getting the patient to question the validity of beliefs (for example, that the right tablet would take the problem away). Finally, it is useful to discuss whether changes on a broad front, in addition to those in the target problem, would, on balance, be positive. For example, a man is unlikely to energetically pursue treatment suggestions if he knows that his wife will leave home once she is sure he can cope.

Failure to progress
Even after an initial discussion of this kind, the patient may make some progress and then discontinue homework assignments. This kind of block can be associated with the homework itself, or with the patient's perceptions of the homework. Since similar principles apply whether engagement is an issue at the assessment or subsequent stages, the general principles will be reviewed here.

The homework task The patient and therapist should focus on what prevented completion of the homework. Was the homework merely suggested rather than explicitly planned? Was it too vague? Was it recalled accurately? Homework tasks should ideally be written down by therapist and patient. Had the therapist routinely reviewed homework on previous occasions? If homework is not reviewed, usually at the start of each session, patients come to perceive it as unimportant. Was the rationale for the homework understood? The patient should be asked to summarize the homework for the therapist, thus identifying gaps and misunderstandings. Were there practical difficulties which interfered with the homework? (e.g. diary forms were not accessible, patient had insufficient funds to complete the task).

Patient's beliefs about homework If the homework tasks were set up appropriately, then non-compliance indicates broadly that the patient does not except that the homework tasks will help achieve the goals for treatment—either that they are irrelevant, or that other factors (e.g. incompetence or hopelessness) will prevent progress. This may be because the task is irrelevant, perhaps revealing new facets of the problem; or because the patient fears the outcome of the homework; or because the patient has misperceived the relationship between the homework and the goal. For example, previous homework may have been aimed at the acquisition of a new skill, but the patient may have been dispirited that practice did not result in any discernible improvement in the problem, and hence be reluctant to spend further time on it. Further discussion of the role of skill acquisition in overcoming problems may make the homework more relevant.

On the other hand, non-compliance may tap into patients' more fundamental beliefs about either themselves or their problems. This can be followed up using the approach for eliciting cognitions described in Chapters 3 and 6. For example, the patient could be asked to imagine in detail what it would be like attempting a homework assignment, and to report any thoughts which went through his or her mind.

Psychosocial situation

Information is sought about the current situation as summarized in Table 2.2, without a detailed personal and family history. American texts emphasize the use of test batteries including inventories for demographic and background data covering family, religious, sexual, health, and educational histories (Cautela and Upper 1976). However, evidence for their usefulness is not strong, and there is less willingness in Britain to complete multiple questionnaires, and so there has been relatively little use of them.

Many patients expect to give lengthy descriptions of their past lives, and while they should be gently dissuaded from doing this, care must be taken not to communicate that they are not allowed to bring up difficult or embarrassing material.

Preliminary formulation

By this stage in the interview, the therapist should be in a position to give the patient a preliminary formulation of the problem. This would include a brief description of the current problem, an explanation of how the problem developed (including predisposing factors and strengths as well as immediate precipitants), and a summary of maintaining factors. As the treatment plan will be based on the formulation, it is important that the patient is asked for feedback on its accuracy.

For example, a 28-year-old woman presented with a five-year history of a bird phobia. Towards the end of the assessment interview, the therapist presented a preliminary formulation, in which liberal use was made of questions rather than statements in order to facilitate feedback. It is important that the patient is not overloaded with information, and is given ample opportunity to comment as the formulation is presented—a useful rule is for the therapist to talk in sentences, rather than presenting lengthy uninterrupted paragraphs.

The therapist began by giving a brief summary of the problem, emphasizing the symptoms experienced by the patient when she was confronted by a bird (or other feathery object) and her increasing avoidance of places where birds might be encountered. The discussion then moved on to the development of the problem.

Therapist: 'So, as I understand it, your first memories of unpleasant experiences with birds date back a long way, like the ones with the birds at the seaside when you were small, and you were terrified when you saw a gigantic bird in the pantomime "Sinbad the Sailor". There were no more frightening incidents until your teens when you saw the film of "The Birds". You also say you have always been a nervous, excitable sort of person, who reacts very strongly to things, and have been rather anxious at times of pressure, is that a reasonable summary?' . . .

'Let's go on to the time when your fear of birds really became extreme, and see if we can understand that. You say you had moved to your new house very recently, and although you'd been married for a couple of years, this was the first time you'd been away from your mother in the sense that you couldn't call on her for help, as you had previously. You had moved to the country, although you felt rather uncertain about the move and you had no friends in the village. So all of that had made you generally fairly tense, is that right?' . . .

'And then the problem became extreme when you came down into the living-room one morning and found a jackdaw flapping around; you became very frightened, rushed out and closed the door, and didn't go back until your husband came home and got rid of it for you. Now, I think if you had found the bird at any other time, it would have frightened you, or startled you, but you were generally tense anyway because of the other things we've mentioned. This extra fright pushed your anxiety up to a very unpleasant level, and you associated *all* of that anxiety with the bird. This would probably have settled down, but the next day when you went out, you saw a line of ducks walking past your gate. One of these ducks was flapping its wings, reminding you of the jackdaw. As the ducks approached you became very anxious and rushed back inside. This strengthened the association in your mind between birds and anxiety. Your body had learned to respond with fear each time you saw a bird, or even thought of going places where there might be birds. So what we will aim to do in treatment is to let you learn other ways of responding to birds, to weaken the association between birds and fear. Does that sound reasonable?' . . .

'If we think about what has kept the problem going, I think it may become clear what sort of steps we need to take to help you with this. I think there are two important factors. One is the way in which you have gradually *avoided* more and more bird situations—although it may be common sense to let the fear settle down, avoidance is one of the most important factors in strengthening fears of this kind. What happens is that each time you see a bird, or think about going anywhere where there might be birds, you get anxious; as you avoid the situation, your anxiety decreases, and you never get the chance to find out that nothing dreadful happens when you are near birds, or that you can cope with your anxiety feelings. This confirms your beliefs that being with birds is bound to make you anxious, and strengthens the association between birds and fear. Can you see any ways that we could begin to overcome that?' . . .

'The other important element is what happens when you are actually confronted by birds. You have given a very clear picture of your immediate response
when you see a bird—like your heart pounding, feeling cold; you get anxious
thoughts like, "What if it flies into me?" and an unpleasant image of a large black
bird flapping its wings right in your face; you begin to cry and cling to whoever is
with you; and you feel anxious. You describe this amount of fear as unpleasant
but just about tolerable, and it would probably die down quite quickly when
nothing dreadful happened; but because you know how unpleasant the anxiety
symptoms have been in the past, you react to these initial symptoms and the
whole thing builds up very rapidly. For example, you notice your heart pounding
and feeling light-headed, and you get the thought "I'm feeling all anxious, I shall
pass out", "The bird can sense I am anxious", "I must get out of here". These
thoughts rapidly increase your anxiety level, so your physical symptoms increase.'

'There are a whole set of vicious circles of this kind, which increase your fear
when you are in an actual "bird situation". This means that another thing we
need to do is to break into these vicious circles, and help you learn ways to
reduce your anxiety symptoms when they begin to build up, rather than to
increase them. For example, you said that when you become anxious in the house
when feathers come out of pillows, you distract yourself by thinking of what jobs
you have to do next. Are there other things that you do like that, which settle you
down when you are feeling slightly anxious?, for example, thinking about the
bird being trapped and scared itself, rather than thinking of it as a predator?'

The therapist then asked the patient to summarize the main points of
the formulation—that the problem developed at a time when the patient
was in a state of high arousal; that it was a learned response; that it was
maintained by avoidance, and a series of vicious circles. Further discussion of the treatment plan followed on from the summary.

The presentation of the formulation generally highlights the need for
further information, which can be obtained from either self-monitoring
or one of the other sources, described in the remainder of this chapter.
Alternatively, the preliminary formulation can be held over until self-
monitoring data is available; this allows the therapist to prepare the
formulation between sessions, and to incorporate the information from
self-monitoring. In either case the formulation is a working hypothesis,
which can be altered at any stage during treatment on the basis of new
information. While changes are more likely at the beginning of treatment,
treatment blocks may arise at any stage, and may alter the weighting of
various factors in the formulation. For example, the presenting problem
of a 30-year-old woman was her excessive fluid intake, amounting to
12–15 pints daily. The preliminary formulation emphasized her misinterpretation of a wide range of bodily signs (tiredness, tension, dry mouth,
having eaten, feeling hot, headache, as well as thirst) as cues for her
needing to drink. Initial intervention focused on her developing different
ways of responding to this range of cues, when it then became apparent
that another major factor was her misinterpretation of bladder signals.

The revised formulation was discussed with her, and new interventions planned.

Self-monitoring often provides the essential information around which the formulation can be tested, as well as allowing progress to be assessed. The latter is easier if there are agreed treatment goals. The advantages of setting goals, and the ways of doing this, will now be described.

Goal setting

Goal setting involves agreeing with the patient detailed, specific goals for each of the problem areas which are going to be worked on, as well as setting up intermediate sub-goals. Many of the principles involved in goal setting overlap with those for devising measurement, as the measures are usually related to goals.

Advantages of setting goals

There are many points in favour of setting goals at the assessment stage. First, it helps to make explicit what the patient can expect from treatment; for example, it is unreasonable to expect *never* to have an argument with your spouse. It can pin-point areas of miscommunication between therapist and patient, and may help the patient decide whether to continue with therapy. For example, a patient who was interested in learning about the historical antecedents for her panic attacks did not feel that a treatment aimed at reducing the frequency of her panics addressed the appropriate issue.

Setting goals also emphasizes the possibility of change, and begins to focus the patient on future possibilities rather than simply on symptoms and problems. It also reinforces the notion that the patient is an active member of the therapeutic relationship, and that full involvement is required: the patient will not be 'done' to.

Defined goals help to impose structure on treatment. This allows the presenting problems to be addressed, with less risk of diverting into a series of crisis interventions. It also prepares the patient for discharge, making explicit that therapy will be terminated when goals are achieved; or that therapy will be discontinued if there is little progress towards them. This is not to say that goals cannot be re-negotiated during treatment, but that this should be done explicitly, together with the patient, thus reducing the risk that patient and therapist are pursuing different agendas.

Finally, setting goals provides the opportunity for an evaluation of outcome related directly to the individual's presented problems.

How to set goals

1. Whenever possible, goals should be stated in *positive terms*, so that it is explicit what the patient is moving *towards* rather than away from. For example, a patient could aim to 'clean the kitchen calmly within one

hour' rather than 'have no handwashing rituals during housework'. Gam-brill (1977) refers to the 'dead man's solution' as that which could be achieved by a dead man; for example, a dead man would have no panic attacks, no urges to binge, no sleepless nights. She suggests that such solutions be avoided. As it is often difficult to turn the patient away from symptoms, and towards positive goals, it may be useful to say something like:

'It's as though you've been wearing glasses which are very good at focusing on symptoms and problems. I want you to start wearing glasses which pick up evidence that you're coping, evidence of success. So it's useful if we are clear what success would be like.'

Specific questioning may help to focus the patient on positive targets. For example, a patient said that she wanted to 'stop being irritable all the time', and she was asked, 'What would you do that was different if you were not irritable?' Barlow *et al* (1984) suggest asking the patient to make three wishes, or to describe a typical ideal day. It is also helpful to pick up positive goals as they are mentioned throughout the interview (for exam-ple, 'I wish I could just invite friends round for supper, like I used to'), and remind the patient of these if necessary.

2.   Goals should be *specific and detailed*. Patients are often aware in general terms of how they would like to be. For example, when the therapist asked what she would like to achieve through coming to the hospital, one patient replied:

            'I'd just like to be normal, like everybody else.'
Therapist 'Being normal means different things to different people. If you felt
            normal, how would you be different from how you are now?'
Patient   'I would be more like I used to be.'
Th.   'What would tell you that you were more like you used to be? What
            would you be doing that you're not doing now?'

The patient was eventually able to list the following goals for herself: to go out shopping alone in supermarkets; to stay overnight in the house alone; to initiate contacts with friends; to have friends round to her house. Questioning then helped to specify where/when/how often parti-cular behaviours would occur if each goal was met. If possible, goals should be phrased so that more than one person could agree if the goal was achieved, as this is likely to increase the reliability of measures related to goal achievement.

Self-monitoring

Self-monitoring is the most widely used adjunct to behavioural inter-viewing, and is almost invariably used both at the initial assessment stage and to monitor subsequent change. The introduction of self-monitoring at the beginning of treatment emphasizes the self-help, collaborative nature of treatment. It is flexible, can be applied to a wide range of overt and covert problems, and can give information about many aspects of problems. Barlow *et al.* (1984) point out that there are two stages in self-monitoring: first, the individual has to *note* that the behaviour, thought, emotion, event has happened; and secondly has to *record* that it has happened. These stages should be borne in mind when self-monitoring is initially devised and care taken to obtain accurate measurement.

Accuracy of self-monitoring

The accuracy of self-monitored information is increased if a few general rules concerning measurement are followed. Thus, only appropriate and meaningful information should be requested, without overburdening the patient. The importance of self-monitoring should be emphasized, it being made clear that subsequent treatment sessions will focus on the material. Explicit rather than tacit agreement to monitor should be obtained.

The accuracy of self-monitoring increases if the patient is aware that its accuracy will be assessed (Lipinski and Nelson 1974). This is often difficult clinically, but can be achieved most directly if the events can intermittently be monitored by someone else; for example, time spent handwashing by an obsessional patient could also be monitored by a spouse.

How to self-monitor

A measurement procedure should be relevant to the question asked, should measure what it is supposed to measure (valid), and should provide a reasonably consistent account of how things actually are (reliable). There are various ways of increasing relevance, validity, and reliability.

Specific, clearly defined targets

It is difficult to achieve reliable measurement of vague concepts like 'self-confidence'. The feature or event to be measured should be defined in detail, as far as possible in ways which would allow different observers to agree about its occurrence. For example, a patient who was lacking in self-confidence was asked,

'How would you know if your self-confidence improved? What would you be doing that you are not doing now?'

Patient   'I wouldn't be panicky like I am now, and I'd be doing all sorts of things I can't do now because I don't have the confidence.'

Therapist 'Can you give me some examples?'

Pt   'Well, I would invite some of my neighbours in for coffee—they must think I'm very funny because I never do. I would begin to show my pictures at local Exhibitions. I could drive myself and do the shopping on my own—I passed my test years ago.'

Further discussion elicited a list of indices of 'self-confidence' which were amenable to self-monitoring. The criterion that measurements should refer to events which are observable may be difficult for internal states but it may be possible to measure the external effects of an internal state. For example, it would be easy to disagree about 'Mr G was angry', but easy to agree about a more detailed 'Mr G shouted', 'Mr G kicked door/furniture'. This could be supplemented by Mr G counting the number of angry thoughts, and giving self-ratings of anger.

In general, the instructions about what to record should include requests for information about the frequency, intensity, and duration of the targeted problem where these are relevant.

Aids to recording

The therapist should provide the patient with a form or recording device which allows easy record keeping. Patients usually cannot draw up record forms for themselves until they have become skilled at recording. The patient should be clear about what and how to record information. This is best achieved by going through a worked example with the patient.

Meaningful and sensitive measures

The most meaningful measures are often different from the most sensitive ones. For example, a girl was being trained in assertiveness skills as a way of increasing her self-esteem. The most *meaningful* measures were self-ratings of behaviours associated in her mind with self-esteem (e.g. being able to initiate social contacts), and questionnaires related to self-esteem (Rosenberg 1965). However, these indices would be insensitive to small daily changes during therapy and could only be used, say, monthly. In order to look more immediately at whether changes were occurring, more *sensitive* measures (such as the number of times each day that she said 'sorry') were also used.

Simplicity of measures

It is usually helpful to use multiple measures for each problem since there is no single 'true' measure of a problem which will adequately reflect all aspects (see p. 8). However, patients should not be bombarded with demands for information. It takes time to acquire skill in record-keeping, and it is better to keep it simple, particularly at the beginning of treatment. Data should only be collected if the patient and the therapist are clear about what it will be used for. Patients are much less likely to keep records if they appear irrelevant.

Timing of measurement

Recordings should be made as soon as possible after an event (behaviour, thought, or feeling) has occurred. If the patient stores up examples and records them all at the end of the day, then some examples will be forgotten and others distorted. This will be particularly true if, for instance, the patient is depressed, low in self-esteem, or anxious, and is recording examples of achievement or coping. It is important, therefore, that the means of recording is easy to carry and use—a notebook, for example.

Types of self-monitored information

There are many different kinds of data which can be monitored. Specific examples are given in each of the subsequent chapters, but a broad description follows to allow the reader to design the most relevant self-monitoring for specific problems.

Frequency count

If there is a relevant and meaningful aspect of the problem which can be counted, then this will provide the most accurate information. This has wide applicability and it is worthwhile trying to find discrete aspects of a problem to count; for example, number of visits to family doctor per week, number of self-critical thoughts, number of hairs pulled out, number of panic attacks, number of arguments with spouse. The data can be recorded on diaries, or as frequency logs on cards; but for problems with high frequencies, it is easier to use a mechanical counter (for example, a golf counter or knitting counter).

Duration of problem

It may be appropriate to measure the duration of the target event or behaviour. Examples are: how long an agoraphobic patient spent away from home, time spent handwashing, time spent studying, and how long it took a patient to settle down after an episode of overbreathing. This information can be recorded in a diary, unless a stopwatch with an elapsed time indicator is available: this stores cumulatively how much time elapses whenever a switch is in the 'on' position.

Self-ratings

These are used when information is required about a patient's affective or subjective state, and are frequently obtained in addition to the frequency and duration measures described above. They are less reliable than more direct measures, and 'anchor points' may change as the patient improves unless great care is taken to specify what the points on the scale mean. For example, the meaning of 'mildly distressing' on a five-point scale from 'not at all' to 'extremely' distressing may change as the patient gradually has less frequent highly distressing experiences.

Ratings are more reliable if they are made at the time the problem occurs. If the problem or event occurs discretely and infrequently, the

Date

No eye-contact at all   × ————————————————   Normal eye-contact throughout the session

Fig. 2.7 Visual analogue scale for therapist ratings of amount of eye-contact shown by a patient

patient can be asked to rate each time it occurs; an example would be the intensity of 'urge to check' in an obsessional patient. If the problem occurs continuously or very frequently, then the patient may be asked to record for a fixed period of the day, either chosen because it has particular significance for the problem (for example, recording distress of 'fatness' thoughts in the hour following a meal), or because it is felt to be representative of the day. It may be necessary to arrange cues to remind the person to record; for example, there are portable timing devices which buzz when a recording is required, either at a fixed or varying time interval. Although less reliable, it may be more useful to ask the patient to make a rating of a subjective state averaged, for example, over a day, or hourly, or three times per day. Accuracy may be improved if the patient is also asked to rate the worst feeling during the day, to distinguish this from the remainder of the day.

Rating scales differ in their form, and range from visual analogue scales where a standard length line is provided and a mark can be made at any point along it (see Fig. 2.7 for an example), to numerical scales with a set of separate and distinct response categories, one of which must be marked (see Fig. 2.1 for an example).

Diaries

These are widely used, and often include frequency counts, duration measures, and self-ratings, but in addition include information about the circumstances in which the event occurred. It is important to specify closely what information is required; otherwise a vast amount may be recorded in a form which it may be impossible to assimilate, and with little check on whether the same material was attended to on different occasions (Figs. 2.3, 2.4, and 2.6 provide examples of diaries in addition to the numerous examples in individual chapters).

Reactivity of self-monitoring

When the patient begins to record the occurrence of an event, its frequency changes (Barlow *et al.* 1984). This phenomenon is called the reactivity of self-monitoring, and it occurs whether or not the monitoring is accurate. It may occur because the monitoring interrupts an automatic chain of behaviour, and allows the person to decide whether to continue; for example, the chain 'sight of stranger getting out a cigarette—urge to smoke—reaching in pocket—getting out cigarette' may be interrupted if the person has to rate 'urge to smoke' before getting out a cigarette. Clinically, it can be useful as the changes are almost always in the therapeutic direction. It is more problematic, however, when the data from self-monitoring are being used to establish, for example, a baseline.

In summary, self-monitoring has a central role in cognitive–behavioural assessment and treatment. If the patient does not self-monitor in spite of adequate care in setting it up, this can be treated as any other kind of non-compliance (see p. 37).

Self-report questionnaires

There is a somewhat arbitrary distinction between self-monitoring and self-report, but the latter refers to more retrospective and global information than self-monitoring. The most frequent source is questionnaires, which have the advantage that normative data are often available against which the patient can be compared. It is worth emphasizing again that self-report provides different but not necessarily inferior information to more direct measures. For example, there may not be a perfect correlation between physiological recordings of cardiac function, and a patient's self-report of palpitations. While the physiological data may be important, the patient's perception of cardiac function is equally relevant.

It is only worthwhile using questionnaires which have demonstrable psychometric soundness. Content validity is particularly important and refers to the extent to which the questionnaire adequately measures the relevant area. This should have been determined by the authors of the questionnaire on an empirical rather than logical basis, and validational data should be easily accessible.

Subsequent chapters give information about relevant questionnaires, but a wide range of examples is available in Cautela and Upper (1976) and Bellack and Hersen (1988).

Information from other people

Additional information may be obtained from other people, in each of the areas discussed so far. Thus, key people may be interviewed, may monitor information as it occurs *in vivo*, or may provide more global retrospective information. The relevant people include the therapist, relatives or other key individuals for the patient, or staff interacting with the patient.

Interviews with key individuals

The main aims of such interviews are identical with those when interviewing the patient. These are to derive and present a formulation of the problem; to educate the relatives or others about the nature of the problem and the psychological approach to treatment; and to engage them in treatment if this is relevant. More specifically, it is useful to establish during the interview what impact the problem has on the key individual; what that person's beliefs are concerning the problem; and how the person responds to, or copes with the problem. Information may also be available about avoidance which had not been mentioned by the patient. This part of the assessment may be longer than the interview with the actual patient if the problem behaviour is more distressing to others than to the patient. For example, the husband of a woman with panic attacks believed that his wife was suffering from madness, and that the major aim of treatment was to keep this distressing fact from her as long as possible. The husband's beliefs only became clear after a lengthy interview in which his pessimism about therapeutic outcome was discussed. Further examples of the central role of information from others are given in Chapter 9.

It is important to check whether the relative or other person wishes the therapist to keep any of the information confidentially (and to have made a similar check with the patient before interviewing the other person). If so, it is worthwhile discussing whether the request is based on unreasonable fears.

Monitoring by key others

This may be used to enhance the accuracy of self-monitoring, but it can also provide specific information about the impact of the patient's problem on others. This will be particularly relevant where other people are heavily involved in the problem; for example, a spouse reassuring a hypochondriacal patient, or relationship problems (including those with children). The general principles for obtaining accurately monitored data are exactly the same as for self-recorded data, and it should be set up with similar attention to detail.

Observations by staff in therapeutic environments are discussed in detail in Chapter 9.

Direct observation of behaviour

It is often useful to have direct observation of a problem behaviour; for example, a patient may broadly outline handwashing rituals, but be unable to give a detailed description. Sometimes it is difficult to arrange the observation in naturalistic settings. One example is where the patient describes gross inadequacies in social skills, and it is unclear whether these represent deficits or anxiety about social performance.

Observation of naturally occurring behaviours

If the relevant behaviours occur with the therapist, then measures can be taken at the time, provided that the situation can be standardized. Such measures can include frequency counts, duration measures, and ratings. For example, with a patient who complained of abdominal distension, the therapist counted the number of burps per session; with an electively mute patient, the therapist counted the number of words per session. In such examples, the length of the session should either be constant or the frequency count calculated on the basis of a constant session length. With a depressed patient, ratings of self-criticism and sad mood were made for the patient's response to the standard question, 'How have things been this week?' Another example of useful ratings were those made by a therapist of the amount of eye contact made by a socially withdrawn patient in each session, the visual analogue scale shown in Fig. 2.7 being used for this purpose.

If the target behaviours do not occur spontaneously in the clinical setting, it may be possible to contrive the situation so that the behaviour can be observed by the therapist. Two common examples are role-play and behavioural tests.

Role-play

If the problem involves interactions with other people, then role-play with a stooge allows direct observation of the problem behaviour, and can be repeated pre- and post-treatment to assess change. Where possible, the role-play should be videotaped, and then rated on relevant dimensions by independent observers who have practised using the rating scale; this method has been used to assess the efficacy of social skills training (Trower, Bryant, and Argyle 1978). In another study, couples with marital problems were asked to discuss problem topics, and their interactions were videotaped and subsequently coded (Bornstein, Bach, Heider, and Ernst 1981).

It cannot be assumed, however, that there is a high correlation between performance in role-played situations and that occurring in everyday settings. Role-played performance is sensitive to situational variables; for example, assertiveness may vary according to whether a good friend or acquaintance makes a request and whether or not a reason is given for the request. When ratings of role-play performance are used to assess treatment changes, treatment should not have focused specifically on the role-played tasks. It will otherwise be impossible to determine whether the improvement has generalized beyond those specific tasks.

Behavioural tests

These allow direct observation of a wide range of problem behaviours, and many examples are given in subsequent chapters; for example, avoidance tests for phobic patients (p. 106) and behavioural tests with obsessional patients (p. 143). The measures obtained from such tests can include specific, objective measures (for example, length of time spent confronting a phobic object), as well as ratings by both the patient and therapist. For example, an obese patient shop-lifted much of the food required for her binges; a behavioural test in a supermarket focused on the chain of behaviours which led up to stealing, with the aim of breaking into this chain at multiple points. The measures included the amount she stole (e.g. when carrying different bags, wearing different clothes), and self-ratings of urge to steal at various points in the shop. Another example was the behavioural test for a patient with writer's cramp, who was asked to write out a standard passage; the measures included the length of time taken and number of words completed, with ratings of discomfort by the patient, and therapist ratings of ease of pen-hold.

Behavioural by-products

These measures are indirect and do not focus on the problem behaviour itself. They have the advantage that they are objective and relatively free from observer bias. A common example is weight as a by-product of eating, used with patients with eating disorders. Other examples include the amount of money spent on food by patients who binge, the amount of soap used per week by obsessional patients, and the number of hairs pulled out by patients with trichotillomania.

Physiological measures

Physiological processes may be monitored indirectly; for example, a patient could self-monitor frequency of headaches, or a socially phobic patient could rate the amount perspired in social situations. Although there is an extensive literature on psychophysiological measurement, its use in routine clinical practice is limited by the cost and availability of equipment. However, psychophysiological changes may precede other changes, for example subjective and behavioural ones, and low-cost devices are increasingly available. Examples are given in subsequent chapters, particularly where the problems are largely somatic (p. 251).

Conclusions

The principal aim of a cognitive–behavioural assessment is to derive a formulation and treatment plan. Most of the information will be collected during interviews with the patient, and a preliminary formulation may be discussed following the initial interview. However, to complete the formulation it will almost always be necessary to obtain further information. Self-monitoring by the patient will generally be required and questionnaires may be relevant. In addition, information from relatives or others may be helpful. Direct observations of problem behaviour often highlight facets of the problem which it would otherwise be difficult to assess. Unless the behaviour occurs spontaneously in the clinical setting, it may be necessary to set up role-play tasks or behavioural tests. In some cases, physiological data may be collected, but these will often be indirect, for example ratings by the patient.

It may take two or even three sessions to complete this preliminary assessment and arrive at the formulation. Many studies have found that the majority of change occurs during the first few treatment sessions, and it would be unfortunate to minimize this by introducing inappropriate strategies before the therapist and patient had an adequate understanding of the problem. Having agreed together the nature of the problem and probable maintaining factors, the therapist and patient are in a position to make changes in the antecedents, consequences, or the behaviour itself, and to monitor the effects. The rest of the book focuses on the therapeutic approaches to specific problems.

Recommended reading

Barlow, D. H., Hayes, S. C., and Nelson, R. O. (1984). *The scientist practitioner*. Pergamon, Oxford.

Bellack, A. S. and Hersen, M. (1988). *Behavioural assessment: a practical handbook*, (3rd edn). Pergamon, New York.

3

Anxiety states
Panic and generalized anxiety
David M. Clark

The nature of the problem

The term 'anxiety state' refers to pervasive anxiety which is not restricted to specific external situations and is not associated with the consistent and extensive avoidance behaviour which characterizes phobias.

Because many anxiety state patients appear to be pervasively anxious in the absence of any obvious danger, anxiety states have sometimes been described as examples of 'free-floating' anxiety or 'anxiety the source of which is not recognized' (Lader and Marks 1971, p. 29). However, cognitive theorists (e.g. Beck 1976) have challenged this point of view, arguing that the notion of free-floating anxiety is based on the viewpoint of the observer, not that of the patient. When interviewed, anxiety-state patients frequently report thoughts and images which suggest that they perceive considerable danger in their current circumstances and their anxiety seems to be an understandable response to these misperceptions (Beck, Laude, and Bohnert 1974; Hibbert 1984). This observation has led to the development of cognitive behaviour therapies which attempt to treat anxiety states by helping patients to identify, evaluate, and modify their unrealistic appraisals of danger and the behaviours which may be maintaining these appraisals. The present chapter briefly discusses the main features of anxiety states and then provides a detailed description of the cognitive–behavioural treatment of these states.

Types of anxiety state

Recent research suggests that two different types of anxiety state can be usefully distinguished (Barlow, Blanchard, Vermilyea, Vermilyea, and Di Nardo 1986; Clark *et al.* 1988). In the first, the predominant problem is recurrent panic attacks which can occur unexpectedly and in almost any situation. A panic attack consists of an intense feeling of apprehension or impending doom which is of sudden onset and is associated with a wide range of distressing physical sensations. These sensations include breathlessness, palpitations, chest pain, choking, dizziness, tingling in the hands and feet, hot and cold flushes, sweating, faintness, trembling, and feelings of unreality. The unexpected and intense nature of these sensations often leads patients to think they are in danger of some physical or mental disaster such as fainting, a heart attack, losing control, or going mad. When not experiencing panic attacks some patients are perfectly calm. However, the majority remain somewhat anxious between attacks, often because they are anticipating another attack.

In the second form of anxiety state, the predominant problem is unrealistic or excessive anxiety and worry which is about various life circumstances and is not concerned with the anticipation of panic attacks. A wide range of physical symptoms may be associated with this anxiety. These include muscle tension, twitching and shaking, restlessness, easy fatiguability, breathlessness, palpitations, sweating, dry mouth, dizziness, nausea, diarrhoea, flushes or chills, frequent urination, difficulty swallowing, feeling on edge, difficulty concentrating, insomnia, and irritability. Thoughts associated with this form of anxiety are highly varied but revolve around the themes of not being able to cope, anticipating negative evaluation from others, performance fears, and diffuse somatic concerns.

These two types of anxiety state roughly correspond to the DSM-IIIR (APA 1987) categories of panic disorder and generalized anxiety disorder. However, it should be pointed out that a substantial proportion of patients experience both types of anxiety. As we will see later, there are some differences in the treatment procedures used for the two types of anxiety. Individuals with both types of anxiety often require both types of treatment.

Prevalence

Anxiety states are common in both psychiatric and general practice. Lader and Marks (1971) suggest that approximately 8 per cent of all psychiatric out-patients suffer from anxiety states, which is a higher figure than for phobic disorders (3 per cent) or for obsessive–compulsive disorders (1–2 per cent). Surveys of the general population (Weissman and Merikangas 1986) suggest that the one-year prevalence rate for panic disorder is in the range 0.5–3 per cent, while the one-year prevalence rate for generalized anxiety disorder is in the range 3–6 per cent. One recent study of health-care utilization found that patients with panic disorder are among the most frequent users of out-patient mental health services (Boyd 1986).

Mode of onset

Panic disorder usually starts suddenly with the most common age of onset being in the mid-to-late twenties (Rapee 1985). Some generalized anxiety states also have a sudden onset but many have a more gradual onset starting anywhere from the low teens onwards. For both disorders stressful life events are common around the time of onset. Most of these events involve threat of a future crisis (technically termed 'danger events') but in mixed anxiety and depressive states the events often also involve some element of loss (Finlay-Jones and Brown 1981).

Method of presentation

Some patients with anxiety states do not initially conceptualize their problems in terms of anxiety. When somatic symptoms (such as palpitations, difficulty swallowing) are particularly prominent, these may be the only symptoms discussed in an initial consultation with a general practitioner and the first specialist referral may be to a general physician, or to a neurology, cardiology, or respiratory clinic. When such patients finally reach the psychiatric services they frequently retain doubts about the psychological nature of their symptoms and these need to be addressed before the patient can be effectively engaged in therapy (see also Chapter 7).

Cognitive models of anxiety states

The central notion in cognitive models of emotional disorders is the idea that it is not events *per se* but rather people's expectations and interpretations of events which are responsible for the production of negative emotions such as anxiety, anger, or sadness. In depression the interpretations which are considered important relate to perceived loss of a relationship, status, or efficacy. In anxiety, the important interpretations, or cognitions, relate to perceived physical or psychosocial danger. In everyday life, there are many situations which are objectively dangerous. In these situations, individuals' perceptions are often realistic appraisals of threat. However, Beck (1976) argues that in anxiety states, individuals systematically overestimate the danger inherent in a given situation. Such overestimates automatically and reflexly activate the 'anxiety programme'. This is a set of responses which we have inherited from our evolutionary past and which were originally designed to protect us from harm in a primitive environment. They include:

(1) changes in autonomic arousal as preparation for flight, fight, fainting;

(2) inhibition of ongoing behaviour; and

(3) selectively scanning the environment for possible sources of danger.

In a primitive environment where many dangers were physical and life threatening (e.g. being attacked by a predator), the anxiety programme would serve the valuable function of helping people to protect themselves or get away from dangerous situations. In modern life, anxiety can similarly serve a useful function in many situations involving a real threat (such as getting out of the path of a speeding vehicle). However, when the threat arises from a misperception, the responses activated by the anxiety programme are inappropriate for the situation. Instead of serving a useful function, they are often interpreted as further sources of threat leading to a series of vicious circles which tend to maintain or exacerbate an anxiety reaction. For example, blushing may be taken as an indication that one has made a fool of oneself leading to further embarrassment and blushing; a shaking hand may be taken as an indication of impending loss of control leading to more anxiety and shaking; or a racing heart may be taken as evidence of an impending heart attack producing further anxiety and cardiac symptoms. Because of this reciprocal relationship between perceived danger and the symptoms of anxiety, a substantial part of cognitive behaviour therapy is devoted to dealing with fears about the somatic, behavioural and cognitive symptoms of anxiety.

Levels of cognition

Within cognitive models of emotional disorders, two different levels of disturbed thinking are distinguished. *Negative automatic thoughts* are those thoughts or images which are present in specific situations when an individual is anxious. For example, someone concerned about social evaluation might have the negative automatic thought, 'they think I'm boring' while talking to a group of acquaintances. *Dysfunctional assumptions and rules* are general beliefs which individuals hold about the world and themselves which are said to make them prone to interpret specific situations in an excessively negative and dysfunctional fashion. For example, a rule involving an extreme equation of self-worth with social approval ('unless I'm liked by everyone I'm worthless') might make an individual particularly likely to interpret silent spells in conversation as an indication that the others think he is boring. Dysfunctional assumptions and rules are believed to arise from early learning experiences and may lay dormant until activated by a specific event which meshes with them.

For example, a young woman whose father dies suddenly and unexpectedly at the age of 40 after a short history of unusual and misdiagnosed somatic complaints may develop the belief that any strong and unexpected physical symptom could lead to sudden death. However, this belief may have little influence on her emotions or behaviour until she experiences an unusual sensation such as blurred vision from overwork, or faintness and dizziness due to hormonal changes. These sensations could then activate the belief, leading her to become preoccupied with her health, repeatedly seeking medical reassurance and systematically misinterpreting innocuous bodily sensations in a catastrophic fashion.

Following the above general introduction to cognitive models of anxiety, the next section concentrates on the specific ways in which cognitions are said to contribute to the development and maintenance of generalized anxiety and panic attacks.

Cognitive model of generalized anxiety

Cognitive models of generalized anxiety (Beck, Emery, and Greenberg 1985) propose that individuals experience pervasive anxiety because their beliefs about themselves and the world make them prone to interpret a wide range of situations in a threatening fashion. The beliefs, or dysfunctional assumptions, which are involved in generalized anxiety are highly varied. However, most revolve around issues of acceptance, competence, responsibility, control, and the symptoms of anxiety themselves. Examples of assumptions related to acceptance would be: 'I am nothing unless I am loved', 'Criticism means personal rejection' and 'I always have to please others'. Assumptions related to competence include, 'There are only winners and losers in life', 'If I make a mistake, I will fail', 'I cannot cope', 'Others' successes take away from mine', 'I have to do everything perfectly', 'If something is not perfect, it is no good at all'. Assumptions related to responsibility include, 'I am mainly responsible for peoples' enjoyment when they are with me', 'I am mainly responsible for the way my children turn out'. Assumptions related to control include, 'I am the only one who can solve my problems', 'I have to be in control all the time', and 'If I let someone get too close, that person will control me'. Assumptions related to anxiety include, 'I must be calm at all times', 'It is dangerous to show signs of anxiety'.

Once an individual has developed generalized anxiety, attentional and behavioural changes further contribute to the maintenance of the problem. In situations which are perceived as threatening, patients selectively attend to aspects of the situation which to them appear to denote danger. For example, an individual who is anxious while talking to a group of people may be more likely to notice that someone in the group briefly looks out of the window and then interpret this as a sign that that person is bored. By definition, patients with generalized anxiety do not show consistent avoidance of specific external situations. However, they often engage in more subtle, or less consistent, forms of avoidance which maintain their negative beliefs (Butler, Gelder, Hibbert, Cullington, and Klimes 1987). For example, an academic who believed that everything he published must be outstandingly good, frequently put off writing because he was not sure that he was ready to write an outstanding article. This procrastination then became an additional source of anxiety as his failure to produce anything reinforced his doubts about his own ability and produced negative comments from colleagues. Similarly, a man who found social situations anxiety-provoking listened to others but avoided talking so as not to expose himself to the possibility of criticism or ridicule. This avoidance made it difficult for others to include him in the conversation, which reinforced his fear that he was not interesting.

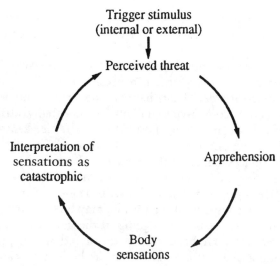

Fig. 3.1 The suggested sequence of events in a panic attack (reprinted with permission from Clark 1986*a*, p. 463)

The cognitive model of panic

The cognitive model of panic (Clark 1986*a*, 1988) states that individuals experience panic attacks because they have a relatively enduring tendency to interpret a range of bodily sensations in a catastrophic fashion. The sensations which are misinterpreted are mainly those which can be involved in normal anxiety responses (e.g. palpitations, breathlessness, dizziness) but also include some other sensations. The catastrophic misinterpretation involves perceiving these sensations as indicative of an *immediately* impending physical or mental disaster. For example, perceiving a slight feeling of breathlessness as evidence of impending cessation of breathing and consequent death; perceiving the feeling of faintness which accompanies anxiety as evidence of imminent collapse; perceiving palpitations as evidence of a heart attack; or perceiving unusual and racing thoughts as evidence of impending loss of control over thinking and consequent insanity. The specific sequence of events which it is suggested occurs in a panic attack is shown in Fig. 3.1. A wide range of stimuli can provoke attacks. These stimuli can be external (such as a situation in which an individual has previously experienced a panic attack) but more often are internal (thoughts, images, or bodily sensations). If these stimuli are perceived as a threat, a state of apprehension results. This state is associated with a wide range of bodily sensations. If these anxiety-induced sensations are interpreted in a catastrophic fashion, a further increase in apprehension occurs. This produces a further increase in bodily sensations, and so on round in a vicious circle which culminates in an attack.

Once an individual has developed a tendency to catastrophically interpret bodily sensations, two further processes contribute to the maintenance of a panic disorder. First, because they are frightened of certain sensations, patients become hypervigilant and repeatedly scan their body. This internal focus of attention allows them to notice sensations which many other people would not be aware of. Once noticed, these sensations are taken as further evidence of the presence of some serious physical or mental disorder. Secondly, certain forms of avoidance tend to maintain patients' negative interpretations (Salkovskis 1988*b*). For example, a patient who was preoccupied with the idea he may be suffering from cardiac disease avoided exercise (such as digging in the garden) or sex whenever he noticed palpitations. He believed that this avoidance helped to prevent him from having a heart attack. However, as he had no cardiac disease, the real effect of the avoidance was to prevent him from learning that the symptoms he was experiencing were innocuous. Instead his avoidance tended to reinforce his negative interpretation because he took the reduction in symptoms which followed avoidance as evidence that he really would have had a heart attack if he hadn't stopped what he was doing. As a further example, another anxious patient sat down or leaned against solid objects whenever she felt faint. She believed this behaviour prevented her from collapsing. Instead, it prevented her from learning that the feeling of faintness which she got when anxious would *not* lead to collapse.

Different types of panic
Some panic attacks are preceded by a period of heightened anxiety, others appear to come 'out of the blue' when an individual is not anxious. In both cases it is assumed that the crucial event is a misinterpretation of bodily sensations. In attacks preceded by heightened anxiety, these sensations are most commonly a consequence of the preceding anxiety, which in turn is either due to anticipation of an attack or to some anxiety-evoking event which is unrelated to panic, such as an argument with a spouse. In the case of panic attacks which are not preceded by a period of heightened anxiety, the bodily sensations which are misinterpreted are initially caused either by a different emotional state (excitement, anger) or by some innocuous event such as suddenly getting up from a sitting position (dizziness, palpitations), exercise (breathlessness, palpitations), or drinking coffee (palpitations). In such attacks patients often fail to distinguish between the triggering bodily sensations and a subsequent panic attack and so perceive the attack as having no cause and coming 'out of the blue'. As patients often take the

Table 3.1 Summary of topics to be covered in assessment

Brief description of presenting problem(s)
For *each* problem:
  (1) Detailed description of a recent occasion when problem occurred/was at
      its most marked
      (a) situation
      (b) bodily reaction
      (c) cognitions
      (d) behaviour
  (2) List of situations problem is most likely to occur/be most severe
  (3) Avoidance (situations and activities, active and passive)
  (4) Modulators (things making it better or worse)
  (5) Attitudes and behaviour of others
  (6) Beliefs about causes of problem
  (7) Behavioural experiments (where appropriate)
  (8) Onset and course
Medication (prescribed and non-prescribed)
Previous treatment (types, whether successful)
Personal strengths and assets
Social and financial circumstances

absence of any obvious triggers for these attacks as evidence that the attacks are due to some serious physical disorder, identifying the antecedents of a spontaneous attack can be a helpful way of challenging patients' catastrophic interpretations.

Assessment

Table 3.1 summarizes the main topics covered in the assessment interview. Normally the interview would start by asking the patient to provide a brief description of the main presenting problem(s). For example, feeling tired much of the time, being tense at work and at home, having difficulty coping with pressures at work and meeting people. For each problem identified, the interviewer obtains a *detailed description of a recent occasion* when the problem occurred or was at its most marked. This would include the situation ('Where were you?', 'What were you doing?'), bodily reactions ('What did you notice happening to your body?'. 'What sensations did you experience?'), cognitions ('At the moment you were feeling particularly anxious, what went through your mind?'—see also p. 66–70 below), behaviour ('What did you do?', 'Did you leave the situation?'), and the behaviour of others ('How did X react?', 'What did X say/do?'). Having obtained a detailed description of a recent occasion, the interviewer should check whether the occasion was typical. If not, further descriptions of other recent occasions should be elicited to provide a complete picture. Next a list of the *situations* in which the problem is most likely to occur or is most severe is elicited ('Are there any situations in which you are particularly likely to have a panic attack/feel tired/have difficulty coping?').

Avoidance behaviour is identified by asking questions such as: 'Are there any situations which you avoid because of anxiety?', 'Are there any things which you used to do before you developed the problem but don't do any longer?', 'When you notice the symptoms, are there any things that you won't do?', 'When you notice the symptoms, are there any things that you do in order to protect yourself (from fainting, going mad, losing control)?' *Modulators* are identified by asking questions such as: 'Are there any things which you notice make the symptoms stronger/more likely to occur?', 'Are there any things which you have noticed help you to control the symptoms/make them less likely to occur?'. As well as identifying the things which the patient does to control or exacerbate a problem, it is also important to identify the *attitudes and behaviour of significant others* such as the patient's spouse and close friends ('What does X think about the problem?', 'What does X do when you are particularly anxious?'). It is also important to assess patients' own *beliefs about the cause of the problem* as some beliefs may make it difficult for patients to engage in therapy. For example, someone who believes that their social anxiety is due to their personality, and that personality cannot be changed, is unlikely to show much interest in learning anxiety management strategies until this belief is at least partly modified. When somatic symptoms are prominent, and patients are sceptical about the idea that these may have a psychological cause, *behavioural experiments* can be a particularly convincing way of determining whether psychological factors are important. In a behavioural experiment, the interviewer manipulates a factor which he/she supposes may be responsible for producing the patient's symptoms and observes whether it does indeed reproduce the symptoms. Several examples of behavioural experiments are given on pages 83–85. Finally, a brief description of the *onset and subsequent course* of the problem is obtained. This description should particularly focus on factors which may have been responsible for the initial onset and for fluctuations in the course of the symptoms.

It is not always possible to obtain from the assessment interview all the information needed for a cognitive–behavioural formulation. Sometimes it is necessary to follow up the interview with homework assignments in which the patient is asked to collect more information which will clarify the formulation. For example, if it is unclear whether symptoms vary with time of day and the situation that patients are in, they may be asked to keep a diary recording what they are doing and how anxious (0–10-point scale) they feel each hour. Figure 3.2 shows an extract from a monitoring

Drink	Time	Activity	Anxiety (0–10)	Urge to Urinate (1–8)	Fluid produced (approx. in pints)
1 cup tea	8.30 a.m.	Getting up	1	6	1/2
	10.30 a.m.	About to go out	3	6	1/12
	12.15 p.m.	Back from shops	1	3	1/2
	1.15 p.m.	Pre formal lunch	4	5	1/6
2 glasses water	2.00 p.m.	Post lunch	2	3	1/6
	3.50 p.m.	Pre formal meeting	5	6	1/6
2/3 pint tea	5.00 p.m.	Reading	1	3	1/6
	6.10 p.m.	Reading	1	5	1/2
	7.15 p.m.	Pre formal dinner	3	5	1/4
2 glasses wine	8.15 p.m.	Post dinner	2	4	1/4
	9.00 p.m.	Reading	1	3	1/12
	9.55 p.m.	'Difficult conversation'	3	5	1/12
	10.45 p.m.	'Difficult conversation'	4	5	1/12
	12.30 p.m.	Before bed	2	3	1/10

Fig. 3.2 Extract from a self-monitoring sheet

sheet which was used to investigate the determinants of a patient's excessively high frequency of urination. Fluid intake, anxiety, activities, strength of urge to urinate just before urinating, and amount of urine produced were recorded. Inspection of this diary revealed that there was very little relationship between the strength of the urge to urinate and the amount of fluid produced. On some occasions when there was a strong urge a large amount of fluid was produced, on others very little was produced. On the latter occasions, the patient was usually in a situation where he thought it would be difficult to go to the lavatory and was anxious, suggesting that fear of not being able to urinate was intensifying the urge to urinate.

Monitoring progress

Once treatment has started, it is important to monitor progress continually in order to decide whether a particular treatment strategy is working or whether the case needs reformulating and/or new treatment procedures need to be implemented. Three of the most common monitoring procedures are:

1. *Standardized questionnaires.* Several standardized questionnaires can be used to monitor progress week by week. The Beck Anxiety Inventory (Beck, Epstein, Brown, and Steer in press) and the Beck Depression Inventory (Beck, Ward, Mendelson, Mock, and Erbaugh 1961) are useful measures of anxious and depressed mood respectively.

2. *Diaries* can be used to keep a daily symptom record. Figure 3.3 shows a diary which is specifically designed for panic patients. The left-hand side of the diary is used to record the situations in which a panic attack occurred and sensations experienced. The right-hand side of the diary is used to help patients to record their negative thoughts and answers to those thoughts once therapy has started. Ost (1988) suggests a useful form of the diary for generalized anxiety. Patients are asked to record every three hours whether they have experienced any anxiety in the preceding three-hour period. If anxiety has been experienced, it is rated for intensity on a 1–5 scale, if no anxiety is experienced, 0 is recorded. The measures which can be obtained from this diary are the mean number of periods of anxiety per week and mean intensity of anxiety during these periods.

When specific symptoms are the main concern, it is often useful to construct individualized diaries. An example of such a diary for a patient with an excessively high frequency of urination was given in Fig. 3.2 and was used to monitor progress throughout treatment. Two main measures of progress were obtained from it. First, daily urination frequency which gradually declined. Secondly, the weekly correlation between strength of urge to urinate and the amount of fluid produced. Before treatment, this correlation was low (0.3–0.4) indicating that the strength of the urge to urinate was not just determined by the amount of fluid in the bladder but also by a range of other psychological factors. By the end of treatment the correlation was substantially higher (0.7) indicating that now physiological factors were the main determinants of the strength of the urge.

3. *Belief ratings*. One of the main aims in cognitive behaviour therapy is to help patients to challenge their irrational beliefs and erroneous interpretations. In order to determine whether they have been successful in doing this, patients' beliefs in key identified thoughts are repeatedly monitored. How much a thought is believed can be assessed by asking a patient to rate it on a scale ranging from 0, 'I don't believe it at all', to 100, 'I am absolutely convinced'. Repeated belief ratings can then be used to monitor progress within sessions and between sessions, and also to help focus patients' attention on the important roles that specific beliefs play in the maintenance of their problems. Often belief ratings for anticipated catastrophes (e.g. 'I won't be able to cope', 'People will think I'm stupid if I speak up in class', 'When I am anxious and feel faint, I am likely to collapse') are higher when patients are in a fear-evoking situation or experiencing a frightening symptom than when they are calmly discussing these events in a therapy session. For this reason, it is important that therapists check that treatment has reduced beliefs in feared situations as well as in the clinic.

Suitability for treatment

Cognitive behaviour therapy is suitable for most anxiety state patients. However, some of the behavioural experiments described in this chapter may need modifying for patients with concurrent physical illness. For example, strenuous hyperventilation is medically contraindicated in patients who are pregnant or who suffer from cardiac disease, emphysema, epilepsy, or severe asthma. However, therapists could still demonstrate the role of hyperventilation in producing bodily symptoms by overbreathing themselves and then describing the effects of overbreathing to their patients. When an anxiety state appears to be secondary to some other major psychiatric disorder, such as an acute psychotic reaction or major depression, the primary disorder should be treated first. Similarly, some patients who are persistently intoxicated may benefit from a detoxification programme before the start of cognitive–behavioural treatment for anxiety.

Description of treatment

Cognitive behaviour therapy aims to reduce anxiety by teaching patients how to identify, evaluate, control, and modify their negative danger-related thoughts and associated behaviours. A variety of cognitive

Name ....
Week commencing...................

PANIC ATTACKS

DAY	DESCRIPTION OF SITUATION WHERE PANIC OCCURED	Breathlessness	Palpitations/heart racing	Choking	Chest tight/uncomfortable	Sweating	Dizziness/unsteady/faint	Unreal/distant feeling	Nausea	Hot or cold flushes	Trembling/shaking	Numbness or tingling	Fear of dying/going mad/loss of control	RATING OF SEVERITY (0–100)	PANIC FREQUENCY per day
Monday	At home, 11 a.m.	✓	✓		✓	✓				✓			✓	70	1
Tuesday	No attacks														0
Wednesday	In the bathroom	✓				✓	✓	✓		✓		✓			
	Shopping	✓	✓			✓	✓	✓					✓		2

Fig. 3.3 Example of a panic-attack diary

MAIN BODY SENSATIONS	NEGATIVE INTER-PRETATION (RATE BELIEF 0–100)	RATIONAL RESPONSE (RE-RATE BELIEF IN NEG. INTERPRETATION 0–100)
Palpitations breathlessness and chest tight	I am having a heart attack 80%	It's just anxiety and overbreathing. I've had this feeling many times before and not died. Furthermore it goes away when I distract myself and distraction wouldn't stop a heart attack. Maybe I had too much coffee 20%
Faintness, unreal, breathlessness Dizzy, breathless	I'm going to collapse 70% " " " " 80%	No I'm not going to collapse. My pulse is racing and my blood pressure is up. You need a blood pressure drop to faint. I feel faint because more blood is going to my muscles which is a normal response when people feel they are in danger, even if as now the thought is wrong. 5%

Fig. 3.3 *(Cont'd)*

and behavioural techniques are used to achieve this aim and many of these techniques are illustrated below. Some techniques are more relevant for panic than generalized anxiety and vice versa.

The general style of therapy is similar to that of cognitive therapy for depression (see Chapter 6). Patients are generally seen weekly for between 5 and 20 sessions. The style of therapy is 'collaborative empiricism' (Beck, Rush, Shaw, and Emery 1979). Although therapists may be convinced of the irrationality of their patients' thoughts, they should not 'lecture' their patients about the validity of a positive alternative to their thoughts. Instead therapy is closer to the work of a scientific team. The patient's negative thoughts are treated as hypotheses, and patient and therapist work together to collect evidence to determine whether the hypotheses are accurate or helpful. Instead of providing all the answers to patients' negative thoughts, therapists ask a series of questions and design a series of behavioural assignments which aim to help patients to evaluate and provide their own answers to their thoughts.

Therapy sessions are highly structured. They start by setting an agenda, which lists items to be dealt with during the session. Patient and therapist agree the contents of the agenda. It always includes a review of the previous week's homework and then covers one or two specific problems which will be the main focus of the present session. Within the session frequent feedback is used to guarantee mutual understanding and sessions always end with setting a homework assignment which follows up a topic discussed during the session. As a considerable number of topics and answers to negative thoughts may be discussed in a session, care needs to be taken to ensure that the important points which have been covered are remembered. Research on medical consultations suggests that people normally retain only a small proportion of the information given in a consultation (Ley 1979). Two techniques which can be used to overcome this memory problem are:

(1) writing down answers to thoughts as they are identified; and

(2) recording the session on audio-tape and giving the tape to the patient to listen to as homework.

Listening to therapy tapes as homework can considerably speed up the progress of therapy. In order to reduce the cost to the patient the same audio-tape can be used throughout therapy with each session being recorded over the last session.

The main techniques of cognitive–behavioural treatment are described below, starting with techniques for identifying negative thoughts.

Identifying negative thoughts

Some patients find it easy to identify their negative thoughts at the start of therapy. However, others require some training before they can confidently identify their key anxiety-related thoughts. There are several reasons why some anxious patients might find it difficult initially to identify thoughts. First, negative automatic thoughts may be so habitual and apparently plausible that they fail to attract the person's attention. Secondly, visual images play a prominent part in anxiety. These images can be extremely brief (less than one second) and hence are difficult to become aware of, or remember. In addition, the images associated with high anxiety can be bizarre (seeing oneself lying in a coffin; collapsed in a shop; screaming while others look on bemused; etc.). This sometimes makes patients reluctant to consider or discuss them, at least until they are warned that bizarre images are a normal accompaniment to high anxiety. Thirdly, because thoughts concerned with danger can produce anxiety, patients attempt to engage in various forms of covert and overt avoidance. Having experienced a brief image or thought related to an anticipated catastrophe, they may quickly attempt to suppress the image by distracting themselves or removing themselves from the situation which elicited the thought. This prevents detailed processing of the thought and so makes it difficult for patients to be aware of the exact nature of their anxiety-related cognitions. For example, Beck *et al.* (1985) describe a patient who attempted to cope with anxiety by whistling to himself as soon as he experienced an anxiety-provoking image. The whistling reduced anxiety but also interfered with recall of the thoughts which had triggered the anxiety. As Clark and Beck (1988) point out, the anxiety-inducing effects of thoughts related to anticipated danger means that some patients are reluctant to recall and discuss the exact details of thoughts which occurred during recent episodes of anxiety. Instead, they prefer to talk in general terms about topics which concern them or describe 'diluted' versions of their anxious thoughts. In such cases the therapist should gently persist in questioning until appropriate cognitions are elicited. A useful rule for therapists to apply to elicited cognitions is 'Would I be as anxious as my patient if I had this thought and believed it?' If the answer to this question is 'no', the elicited thought is probably inaccurate or requires further elaboration. Several techniques have been devised to help patients identify negative automatic thoughts. The most commonly used is detailed discussion of a recent emotional experience.

1. *Discussing a recent emotional experience*
Patients are asked to recall a recent event or situation which was associated with anxiety and for which they have a fairly clear memory. The event is described in some detail and the therapist elicits the thoughts associated with the onset and maintenance of the emotional reaction by asking questions such as: 'What went through your mind just then?', 'Did you have an image at that moment?', 'When you were most anxious, what was the worst thing you thought might happen?'. The extent to

Table 3.2 Examples of specific links between sensations and thoughts

Sensation	Thought (interpretion)
Palpitations/heart racing	I am having a heart attack; there is something seriously wrong with my heart
Breathlessness	I am going to stop breathing, suffocate and die
Faintness/dizziness	I will faint, fall over, pass out
Unusual thoughts, difficulty thinking	I am going mad

which patients believe anxiety-related thoughts often varies with their level of anxiety. When calm, patients can sometimes see that their thoughts are irrational and so attempt to discount and ignore them. For example, a panic patient who is concerned with the idea that there may be something wrong with her heart may reply to the question, 'What are you afraid of in a panic attack?' by saying, 'I used to think I would have a heart attack. However, my doctor has reassured me that my heart is OK and now I'm just worried about the anxiety.' However, if asked the question, 'Right in the middle of an attack, what is the worst that you think could happen?', she may reply, 'Despite what my doctor says, in the middle of an attack I really do believe that I'm about to have a heart attack.'

When listing the cognitions associated with panic attacks, therapists should try to help patients to see the links between specific sensations or groups of sensations and specific interpretations. This can be achieved by writing out a list of all the sensations which the patient experiences in a panic attack and also a list of the negative thoughts which occur in an attack. The therapist then asks which thoughts go with which sensations and suggests the possibility that the thoughts may be interpretations of the sensations. Examples of specific links between sensations and thoughts are given in Table 3.2.

2.   *Using imagery or role-play to relive an emotional experience*

When simple direct questioning fails to elicit automatic thoughts, it can be useful to ask patients to relive the recent emotional event by either replaying it in great detail using imagery or, if it is an interpersonal interaction, by role-play. Instructions for reliving an emotional experience using imagery might be as follows:

'It seems that it's difficult for you to remember exactly what was happening and what was going through your mind in the situation. When this problem occurs, we find that it is sometimes useful to get people to try to produce a clear image of themselves in the situation and then to run the image rather like you would run a movie film. To help you do this, first I would like to give you a little practice in producing clear images.' (The therapist then asks the patient to imagine a neutral object such as an apple or a rose, indicate when a clear image has been formed, and then check that the person really is visualizing the object by asking questions such as, 'Can you see the petals on the rose? What colour are they? Is there any dew on the petals? Are they curled?', etc.) 'Now you have had some practice in producing clear images, I'd like you to imagine yourself back in the situation we discussed, at the point just before you noticed yourself becoming anxious. Once you've got a clear image, can you briefly describe to me what you can see?' (Patient describes the scene.) 'Now, slowly run the image forward, noticing all the time what is happening, how you are feeling, and what's going through your mind. What do you see now? At the moment your anxiety suddenly increased, what was going through your mind?'

When the event that is being discussed is an interpersonal interaction (e.g. confrontation with someone at work), using role-play to reinact the interaction is often more effective than reliving it in imagery. After obtaining a detailed description of how the other person in the interaction behaved, the therapist plays the other person while patients play 'themselves'.

3. Shifts in mood during a session

Mood shifts during therapy sessions can be particularly useful sources of automatic thoughts. The therapist points out that a shift in mood has occurred and then asks the patient, 'What went through your mind just then?' This is illustrated in the following transcript from a session with an anxious patient who was preoccupied with the idea that her headaches indicated a serious brain abnormality (haemorrhage or tumour). Prior to the start of the transcript, the therapist had drawn a picture of a blood vessel and noticed the patient became very tense while looking at the picture.

Therapist 'What went through your mind when I drew that picture?'
Patient   'I was thinking about it.'
Th.   'What were you thinking?'
Pt   'About the blood coming out.'
Th.   'Did you have a mental picture?'
Pt   'Yes.'
Th.   'When you had that picture, how did you feel?'
Pt   'Horrible.'
Th.   'Did you feel tense?'
Pt   'Yes.'
Th.   'Where did you notice the tension?'
Pt   'In my head.'
Th.   'Did you have that tension before you had the image?'
Pt   'No.'

Th.   'What do you make of that? You had a mental picture and then
           noticed tension in your head.'
Pt   'If I think about it, it makes the pain come.'

4. Determining the meaning of an event

Sometimes, skillful attempts to elicit automatic thoughts are unsuccessful.
The therapist should then attempt to discern, through questioning, the
specific meaning of the event for the patient, e.g.

Therapist 'You are not quite sure what was going through your mind when you
felt anxious in [specify the situation]. Looking back at the situation now, what
did it mean to you?' (If this fails, the therapist may need to provide further cues
by giving patients an idea of the sort of thoughts that they might be looking for,
i.e. thoughts accompanying anxiety relate to perception of danger; thoughts
accompanying guilt relate to the belief that you have done something wrong;
thoughts accompanying anger relate to perceiving others as having broken one of
your idiosyncratic rules about what is right, etc.)

Modifying negative thoughts and associated behaviours

A wide range of procedures are used to help patients evaluate, control,
and modify their negative thoughts and associated behaviours. When
choosing specific procedures to use with a particular patient, the therapist
is largely guided by the assessment interview and, in particular, by the
hypotheses which he or she developed about the main cognitive and
behavioural processes maintaining the patient's anxiety state.

Rationale

Before therapist and patient can work together to test and modify negative thoughts, the therapist must first present the rationale for treatment
by demonstrating the relationship between thinking, feeling, and behaving. This can be done using an abstract example such as the one given by
Beck *et al.* (1979, pp. 147–8). In this example, patients are invited to
imagine they hear a crash in another room while they are at home alone
in the middle of the night. Questioning is then used to show that if they
had a thought such as, 'There's a burglar in the room', they would have
felt anxious and would have behaved in a way which might minimize the
danger (hiding or phoning the police). However, if they had had the
thought, 'The window is open and the wind has blown something over'
they would not have felt afraid and would have behaved differently
(calmly closed the window and gone back to sleep). In addition to this
abstract example, it can be helpful to use material which has been elicited
during the assessment interview to demonstrate the relationship between
thinking and feeling. Clark and Beck (1988) describe an example of a
generally anxious divorcee who was particularly anxious before and after
dinner parties. His negative thoughts related to the idea that people might

not enjoy themselves and then blame him. Questioning about whether his friends generally looked as though they were enjoying themselves during his dinner parties, whether he was totally responsible for their enjoyment, whether there were factors other than his behaviour which might determine their enjoyment, and whether he had any definite evidence that they had not enjoyed themselves, helped him to realize that his parties were in fact often successful, and furthermore, even if they were not, people would not necessarily blame him for this. He was also able to see that if on previous occasions he had been able to access some of these more realistic thoughts before dinner parties he would have experienced less anticipatory anxiety.

Giving information about anxiety

Early in treatment it can be useful to provide patients with a considerable amount of information about the nature of anxiety. This can include a description of the symptoms of anxiety, their possible evolutionary origins and function, the lack of relationship between anxiety and insanity, and the fact that the autonomic changes which occur in anxiety (such as a racing heart) are not dangerous. This information is tailored to the particular needs of each patient. It is used to effect problem-reduction (helping patients to see that a series of apparently unconnected difficulties—such as insomnia, difficulty making decisions, easy fatiguability, and occasional blurred vision—are all aspects of an anxiety state); to help patients to understand the cognitive–behavioural model of anxiety; and to correct any misconceptions about the nature of anxiety.

Distraction

A variety of distraction techniques are described on pages 187–8. These techniques can be used as immediate symptom management stategies. Early in therapy, training in distraction can be a very useful way of combating patients' beliefs that they have no control over their anxiety. Later in therapy, distraction can be a useful symptom-management technique in situations where it is not possible to challenge automatic thoughts—for example, while talking to someone. In this situation, the distraction exercise would involve becoming outwardly directed, perhaps moving closer to the person so that they fill the patient's field of view, and concentrating on the conversation itself rather than on thoughts concerned with evaluation of his or her own performance. Distraction can also be used to provide a potent demonstration of the cognitive model of anxiety. When patients are anxious during a session, they can be instructed to describe out loud the content of the room. This often reduces anxiety. Questioning can then be used to help them see that this is because they were momentarily distracted from their thoughts, suggesting that thoughts play an important role in the maintenance of their symptoms.

For example, a secretary suddenly became anxious in a treatment session. When asked what was going through her mind, she replied, 'Since we have been talking, I have started to get pins and needles on the surface of my head and down the left-hand side of my face. I am really frightened. I think it is a brain tumour or a haemorrhage.' The therapist then said, 'I understand. In that case, I'd like to do a brief experiment. Can you look around the room and describe to me in as much detail as you can all the objects you see?' Initially, the patient found it difficult to do this. However, with gentle encouragement from the therapist, she eventually became absorbed. After three or four minutes of distraction the therapist then asked, 'What's happened to the tingling on your head now?' To the patient's surprise, the tingling had now disappeared. On questioning, the patient agreed that it was unlikely that the symptoms of a tumour or haemorrhage could be made to disappear so simply, and it seemed more likely that the symptoms were produced by her fear that she had a tumour, especially as they had started when the interview turned to a discussion of this fear.

Activity schedules

In an activity schedule (see page 190 for an example), patients record their hour-by-hour activities, rating them (on 0–100 scales) for salient features such as anxiety, fatigue, pleasure, and mastery. Activity schedules can be used in a variety of different ways. In individuals who feel under intense time pressure they can be used to plan activities in such a way that they are likely to be able to engage in one task at a time (trying to do several tasks at once often increases perceived time pressure) and have brief breaks between tasks (running on from one task to another produces fatigue and increases perceived time pressure). Table 3.3 outlines the general principles of time management and may be helpful in planning activities with individuals who perceive themselves as being under considerable time pressure. Time pressure and other anxious concerns can lead some patients to stop engaging in leisure and social activities which they previously enjoyed. Often these activities contributed to their sense of worth and perceived control over their environment. Therefore, dropping activities often increases anxiety and perceived vulnerability. Once this problem is identified, the therapist and patient can use an activity schedule to reintroduce pleasurable activities. Inspection of activity schedules can also help to identify periods of anxious rumination, problems with perfectionism (suggested by highly polarized mastery and pleasure ratings—everything is either rated 10 or 0), and anxiety triggers.

For example, inspection of a housewife's activity schedule revealed that she usually woke at 5.30 a.m. but did not get up until 8 a.m. During this period her anxiety rating progressively increased. Discussion revealed that this was due to ruminating about all the things that could go wrong during the day and also that

Table 3.3 Principles of time management

1. Review your GOALS. Decide what you want to get out of the day at work, the weekend, etc.
2. Make a LIST of the things you think you have to do and things you would like to do, with time estimates.
3. If tasks and activities exceed the time available, decide on PRIORITIES. What *must* be done today, what can wait, and until when? What do I *want* done today? Can I *delegate* anything? If I can, to whom? What will happen if I don't do X? If nothing, consider omitting X.
4. Select an ORDER or SEQUENCE for tasks to be done. Find the sort of sequence that suits you best. For example, some people find that the day is more pleasurable if they start with a task they must do and then follow it with a task they enjoy. In that way, they have something to look forward to and the unpleasant task doesn't play on their mind all day.
5. Try to do ONE TASK AT A TIME and try to FINISH what you start. Don't jump from one task to another leaving behind a stack of partially completed activities. In general, each task takes longer this way as you waste time getting repeatedly started on the same task and uncompleted tasks remain on your mind, interfering with the present task.
6. Don't rush immediately from one task to another. Instead PAUSE. Plan brief BREAKS and times to relax; tea breaks, lunch breaks, times for yourself.
7. REVIEW priorities and progress midway through the day.
8. Look out for PROCRASTINATION. Are you putting it off because you're setting yourself too high a standard? Are you being unrealistic about what you could do? Could you do it now and get it out of the way?
9. At the end of the day, REMEMBER what you have achieved and GIVE YOURSELF CREDIT.

---

attempts to sleep after she had woken up were invariably unsuccessful. It was therefore agreed that instead of staying in bed and ruminating, she would get up and go for a jog. This was an activity she had previously enjoyed but had stopped since becoming anxious.

Verbal challenging of automatic thoughts
A series of questions are used to help patients to evaluate negative automatic thoughts and to substitute more realistic thoughts. Within sessions, patient and therapist work collaboratively to identify rational responses to automatic thoughts. Between sessions patients attempt to put into practice the questioning skills they have learned in the sessions by recording and challenging automatic thoughts as they arise. One particularly convenient way of doing this is to use the daily record of dysfunctional thoughts reproduced in Fig. 3.4 or (if panic attacks are the main problem) the panic diary reproduced in Fig. 3.3.

DATE	SITUATION Describe: 1. Actual event leading to unpleasant emotion, or 2. Stream of thoughts, daydream, or recollection, leading to unpleasant emotion.	EMOTION(S) 1. Specify sad/ anxious/ angry, etc. 2. Rate degree of emotion, 1–100.	AUTOMATIC THOUGHT(S) 1. Write automatic thought(s) that preceded emotion(s). 2. Rate belief in automatic thought(s), 0–100%.
21/6	2 a.m., still awake. Not able to sleep	anxious 70	I won't be able to do my work properly tomorrow because I need a full eight hours sleep. 80%
24/6	Joining colleagues having morning coffee in canteen. They didn't acknowledge me and carried on talking.	anxious 50	They don't like me. They think I'm boring. 40%
25/6	Asked to do some of my boss's work because he is going to the dentist for the afternoon.	angry 40	It's not fair. I shouldn't have to do his job, I've got enough of my own work to do. He's just off-loading on me. He should have got organized to go outside of works hours. 75%
		anxious 60	I'll make a mess of it. 65%

Fig. 3.4   Daily record of dysfunctional thoughts

RATIONAL RESPONSE	OUTCOME	FURTHER ACTION
1. Write rational response to automatic thought(s). 2. Rate belief in rational response, 0–100%.	1. Re-rate belief in automatic thought(s), 0–100%. 2. Specify and rate subsequent emotions, 0–100.	
This is not true. If I look back on other days when I've had a sleepless night I can see that I still got things done and my work was about the same quality as usual. I just felt terrible and that's something I can cope with on an occasional basis. 70%	1. 20% 2. 15	Felt too alert to sleep. Rather than just lie in bed thinking, read a light book. Fell asleep in half an hour.
They are enjoying their conversation and aren't really thinking about me one way or the other. They certainly don't look hostile. 75%	1. 10% 2. 30	Listen to what they are saying and find an opening to join the conversation. Ask a question. Stop mind-reading.
His secretary said he'd been in pain. It's not a routine check up and there probably weren't any out of hours appointments available at short notice. 90%	1. 0% 2. 0	
He wouldn't have asked me if he didn't think I could do it. There are many others he could have chosen. 85%	1. 15% 2. 20	Ask him a bit more about the job so I know exactly what to do.

Fig. 3.4   *(Cont'd)*

Some of the questions which are particularly useful for examining and testing the reality of negative automatic thoughts are:

1. *'What evidence do I have for this thought?'* *'Is there any alternative way of looking at the situation?'* *'Is there any alternative explanation?'* These questions, which are among the most commonly used, are illustrated in the transcript below, which also highlights the value of providing information about anxiety.

Patient	'In the middle of a panic attack, I usually think I am going to faint or collapse.'
Therapist	'How much do you believe that sitting here right now and how much would you believe it if you had the sensations you get in an attack?'
Pt	'50% now and 90% in an attack.'
Th.	'OK, let's look at the evidence you have for this thought. Have you ever fainted in an attack?'
Pt	'No.'
Th.	'What is it then that makes you think you might faint?'
Pt	'I feel faint and the feeling can be very strong.'
Th.	'So, to summarize, your evidence that you are going to faint is the fact that you feel faint?'
Pt	'Yes.'
Th.	'How can you then account for the fact that you have felt faint many hundreds of times and have not yet fainted?'
Pt	'So far, the attacks have always stopped just in time or I have managed to hold onto something to stop myself from collapsing.'
Th.	'Right, so one explanation of the fact that you have frequently felt faint, had the thought that you will faint, but have not actually fainted, is that you have always done something to save yourself just in time. However, an alternative explanation is that the feeling of faintness that you get in a panic attack will never lead to you collapsing, even if you don't control it.'
Pt	'Yes, I suppose so.'
Th.	'In order to decide which of these two possibilities is correct, we need to know what has to happen to your body for you to actually faint. Do you know?'
Pt	'No.'
Th.	'Your blood pressure needs to drop. Do you know what happens to your blood pressure during a panic attack?'
Pt	'Well, my pulse is racing. I guess my blood pressure must be up.'
Th.	'That's right. In anxiety, heart rate and blood pressure tend to go together. So, you are actually *less* likely to faint when you are anxious then when you are not.'
Pt	'That's very interesting and helpful to know. However, if it's true, why do I feel so faint?'
Th.	'Your feeling of faintness is a sign that your body is reacting in a normal way to the perception of danger. Most of the bodily reactions

you are experiencing when anxious were probably designed to deal with the threats experienced by primitive man, such as being approached by a hungry tiger. What would be the best thing to do in that situation?'

Pt   'Run away as fast as you can.'

Th.   'That's right. And in order to help you run, you need the maximum amount of energy in your muscles. This is achieved by sending more of your blood to your muscles and relatively less to the brain. This means that there is a small drop in oxygen to the brain and that is why you *feel* faint. However, this feeling is misleading in the sense that it doesn't mean you will actually faint because your overall blood pressure is up, not down.'

Pt   'That's very clear. So next time I feel faint, I can check out whether I am going to faint by taking my pulse. If it is normal, or quicker than normal, I know I won't faint.'

Th.   'That's right. Now, on the basis of what we've discussed so far, how much do you believe you might faint in a panic attack?'

Pt   'Less, say 10%.'

Th.   'And if you were experiencing the sensations?'

Pt   'Maybe 25%.'

In this example, the patient had never fainted. However, some panic patients have fainted in the past. Then the line of argument outlined above needs to be slightly modified to take this into account. First, the therapist should enquire whether the patients were anxious when they fainted. Usually, they were not and in fact the faint occurred very early on in the development of their panic attacks. It was probably produced by a variety of common physiological changes (such as hormonal shifts, a virus) but the patients were not aware of this and so subsequently whenever they were anxious and felt faint, they erroneously interpreted this feeling as evidence that they would faint. The misinterpretation then produced more anxiety and a more intense feeling of faintness. The only anxiety condition in which fainting actually occurs is blood injury phobia. Some patients suffer from blood injury phobia as well as experiencing panic attacks. For these, the therapist should explain that they are only likely to faint at the sight of blood and injury and also invite the patient to compare the feelings that precede an actual faint with those experienced in a panic attack. Invariably, they are not the same. Before actually collapsing, people often feel that they are fading away. In a panic, patients are all too painfully aware of their intense feelings of faintness.

2. *'How would someone else think about the situation?'* Patients' exaggerated perceptions of danger usually do not extend to other people (Butler and Mathews 1983). For this reason, asking how someone else would view the situation can be a particularly helpful way of restoring perspective.

3. *'Are your judgements based on how you felt rather than what you did?'* A common error in generalized anxiety is patients inferring that they cannot cope with a situation because they feel anxious in the situation. However, when asked how they actually behaved, they often realize that their behaviour was entirely appropriate and indicated that they coped well.

For example, a young nurse who had been told off for being late for work the previous day was about to leave for work when her pet cat knocked some poisonous cleaning fluid onto the floor and then rolled in it. The nurse immediately realized that if the cat licked its fur it would die. She felt a surge of anxiety, rushed to pick up the cat and held it under the tap while washing off the poison. The cat squirmed and scratched her, drawing blood. Once the cat was dry, she phoned the ward explaining that she would be late, dressed her wounds, and then rushed to work, arriving 30 minutes after the start of her shift. Throughout this time she felt anxious, worrying about her cat and what the ward sister might say when she was late. Noticing that she was anxious and seemed flustered while dealing with the cat, she inferred that this was yet another example of her not being able to cope. However, careful discussion of what she actually did revealed that her behaviour was an ideal set of coping responses for a very difficult situation.

4. *'Are you setting yourself an unrealistic or unobtainable standard?'* Some patients set themselves unobtainable standards and then feel anxious because they are inevitably frequently in danger of falling short of these arbitrary, self-imposed standards. An example of such a standard is 'I have to be at my best all the time'. By definition this is impossible. Two further examples are, 'I have to be perfectly calm at all times', and 'I have to be absolutely certain I am not developing cancer'. Both of these beliefs are unrealistic standards. Some anxiety is a necessary part of everyday life and, in some situations, can be an advantage. Similarly, medical tests can never establish with absolute certainty that an illness is not about to develop.

5. *'Are you forgetting relevant facts or over-focusing on irrelevant facts?'* For example, forgetting previous successful performances when faced with a difficult task or making the representativeness error, 'Because a friend of similar age has died of a heart attack, I will have a heart attack.'

6. *'Are you thinking in all-or-nothing terms?'* When anxious, individuals tend to evaluate themselves and on-going events in extreme, black-and-white terms. For example, 'If people don't show that they like you, then they dislike you', 'If I cannot do a job perfectly, it is not worth doing at all.' One particularly good way of breaking down all-or-nothing thinking is to try and construct a dimension. For example, someone who

believed that people either liked you or hated you might be asked to draw a 10 cm line with one end labelled, 'strongly hate', the middle labelled, 'neither like nor dislike', and the end labelled, 'strongly love'. They would then be invited to think about all the people they know and place each person on the scale. As this exercise progresses, it soon becomes evident that people do not just cluster at the ends of the scale but instead cover the whole range.

7. *'Am I over-estimating how responsible I am for the way things work out?'* *'Am I over-estimating how much control I have over how things work out?'* Anxious patients sometimes over-estimate the amount of control or responsibility they have for events. For example, a young mother constantly worried about whether she had made the right decision in sending her son to a particular school. Questioning revealed that she had made what she thought was the best decision on the basis of the information available, but this of course did not guarantee that her son would enjoy and benefit from the school. Her frequent ruminations were attempts to reduce this uncertainty but were doomed to failure because they were based on the erroneous assumption that it is always possible to know in advance whether a decision that you have taken in good faith will be the correct one. Excessive notions of personal control or responsibility can often be modified by using pie charts (see Fig. 3.5). When constructing a pie chart for this purpose, the therapist draws a circle which is meant to represent all the possible causes of a particular event (a marriage breaking up, unexpectedly feeling tired, guests not enjoying a dinner party) and asks the patient to list all the causes which are out of his/her control and then allocate a section of the circle to each cause. At the end of the exercise, there is often very little of the circle left for the patient's personal responsibility or control over the event.

8. *'What if it happens?'* *'What would be so bad about that?'* Perhaps because of cognitive avoidance, anxious patients have often not thought through in detail what would be so bad about the events they fear occurring or exactly how likely such events are. For this reason, pushing patients to consider the worst that could happen often helps them to discover either that the feared event will be less disastrous than anticipated or less likely than they had assumed.

For example, a student was concerned with the possibility of failing his forthcoming exams and initially thought that failing would be absolutely disastrous. However, discussion revealed that he would be able to retake his exams six months later, that if he continued to study in his normal way he would be very likely to pass the retakes and, that even if he did not pass the retakes, there were many jobs which he could consider doing which he might enjoy and which did not require these exams.

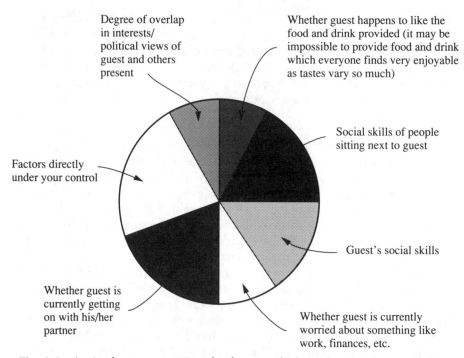

Degree of overlap
in interests/
political views of
guest and others
present

Whether guest happens to like the
food and drink provided (it may be
impossible to provide food and drink
which everyone finds very enjoyable
as tastes vary so much)

Social skills of people
sitting next to guest

Factors directly
under your control

Guest's social skills

Whether guest is
currently getting
on with his/her
partner

Whether guest is currently
worried about something like
work, finances, etc.

Fig. 3.5 A pie chart representing the factors which might contribute to guests enjoying themselves at one of your dinner parties

9. *'How will things be in X months'/years' time?'* This can be a useful way of putting anticipated losses, such as the breaking up of a relationship, in perspective. Often when thinking about the possibility of such a loss, patients exclusively dwell on the immediate impact of the loss. However, after the break-up of a relationship, for example, they may be distressed for several months but this will gradually decline in intensity; slowly they will start meeting new people and then possibly establish a further relationship. Forward time-projection can be useful not only when an anticipated loss is inevitable, but also when thoughts about a possible loss are producing behaviours which make the loss more likely. For example, someone who is excessively frightened about the prospect of a relationship breaking up may become excessively attentive and compliant, making the partner feel smothered and more likely to end the relationship. Forward time-projection can then be used to help reduce the patient's fear of a break-up, perhaps increasing the patient's confidence to such an extent that he or she ceases to engage in the behaviours which were interfering with the relationship.

10. '*Are you over-estimating how likely an event is?*' Anxious patients frequently over-estimate the probability of feared events (Butler and Mathews 1983) and their over-estimates vary with factors which are unrelated to objective probabilities. For instance, individuals who are anxious about flying may rate the probability that their plane will crash as 1 in 1000 a week before the journey, 1 in 200 on the morning of the journey, 1 in 100 at the check-in, 1 in 20 after seeing the plane, 1 in 5 during taxing, and 1 in 2 during take-off. Discussion of patients' inflated probability estimates and provision of data on objective probabilities can be a helpful way of reducing anxiety. However, some patients find that they remain anxious even when they are able to acknowledge that a feared outcome has a very low probability. This is usually because the perceived consequence of the event is very severe. In such cases, it is important to *decatastrophize* the event by looking at how the person could cope with it and what would be so bad about it, as well as dealing with inflated probability estimates.

11. '*Are you underestimating what you can do to deal with the problem/situation?*' Anxious patients often underestimate their own skills and resources for dealing with a problem. For this reason, it can be useful to review how they have dealt with similar problems in the past, how other people view their coping skills and rehearse ways in which they might cope with forthcoming difficulties.

So far the discussion has concentrated on the verbal thoughts. However, as noted earlier, sometimes the cognitions involved in anxiety are images rather than thoughts. Often images can be dealt with by challenging the meaning of the image with verbal questioning. On other occasions, it is necessary to work in imagery as well as using verbal questioning. This is particularly likely to be the case when patients experience vivid and repetitive images. For example, a young woman was disturbed by a recurrent image in which she visualized having been sexually assaulted when a child. Verbal discussion did little to reduce the distress provoked by this image. However, visualizing herself back in the situation, growing to her present size and dealing with the relative who assaulted her in an adult and assertive fashion was highly effective. Modifying images was similarly useful for a woman who feared fainting in public and often had images of doing so. Her images normally stopped at the point where she fainted. However, discussion helped her to see that in reality she would only briefly lose consciousness then slowly get up and return to normal. Visualizing herself doing this after fainting helped to reduce the distress normally produced by her image.

The examples given above have all concentrated on anxiety-related cognitions. However, anxiety state patients are often depressed as well as anxious and one of the great advantages of the cognitive approach to treatment is that similar techniques can be used for dealing with both depression-related thoughts and anxiety-related thoughts. Many of the questions given above are useful for challenging depression-related thoughts. Further depression-relevant questions are discussed in Chapter 6.

Behavioural experiments

As well as discussing evidence for and against patients' negative thoughts, therapists should also attempt to devise behavioural assignments which help patients to check out the validity of their negative thoughts. These assignments can be one of the most effective ways of changing beliefs. Some illustrations of behavioural experiments are given below.

Behavioural experiments used in generalized anxiety   The particular behavioural experiment chosen depends on the specific beliefs that it is designed to test. Three sets of beliefs and behavioural experiments are given below.

In the first experiment a young mother was preoccupied with the notion that she was a bad mother and was failing to cope with her role as a housewife and a part-time worker. When asked for her evidence for these beliefs, she gave as an example an event which had happened earlier that morning. Hoping to get to work a little earlier in order to catch up, she had taken her young son to the relative who looked after him three-quarters of an hour earlier than usual. He had then been very awkward during the day. She interpreted this as her fault (belief = 85 per cent) because she had spent very little time playing with him before going to work, and believed that she would just have to abandon her plans to get her work more under control. However, the therapist pointed out that an alternative explanation might be that her son was having an 'off day' and would have been difficult in any case. To test this alternative, she agreed she would persist with her early morning plans for a further week. To her surprise and delight, she found that her son adapted very well. Her belief that she was a bad mother reduced and, as a consequence of this experiment, she could then get her work under more control and consequently felt even better about herself.

A business man reported feeling extremely anxious when speaking in public. He believed that his colleagues would see that he was anxious (belief = 65 per cent) and, as a consequence, cease to respect him (belief = 40 per cent). When asked what evidence he had for the idea that others could see he was anxious, it transpired that he believed that because he *felt* anxious, others must be able to see that he was anxious. As a test for this prediction, the therapist asked him to give a short speech while being videotaped. During the taping he felt very anxious. However, to his surprise, he was unable to detect any external signs of anxiety when subsequently viewing the video. This then reduced his belief that others could see he was anxious (30 per cent).

A generally anxious laboratory technician with prominent somatic complaints provides a further illustration of a behavioural experiment. One of her most distressing symptoms was tingling in her fingers which was only elicted by touching solid objects. She believed that this must indicate some serious neurological abnormality (belief = 40 per cent). However, neurological investigations had proved negative. During an assessment interview, the therapist was able to ascertain that the tingling sensation started immediately after the patient had smoked hashish for the first time. As soon as she noticed the tingling she had had the thought, 'I have a brain tumour'. As an alternative to her negative interpretation, the therapist suggested the possibility that her tingling sensation might be due to her *thought* that she has a neurological abnormality and a change in tactile threshold produced by that thought. Consistent with the suggestion, she found that friends who were asked to gently stroke objects detected similar sensations to her own if asked to concentrate hard. During further discussion, patient and therapist agreed that if the sensation was due to her fears about its meaning, then it should decline if she repeatedly exposed herself to the sensation, as repeated exposure is often an effective way of reducing fear of specific objects (see Chapter 4). In order to test out this prediction, she agreed to attempt to bring on the sensation intentionally several times a day and, when it occurred naturally, to continue touching objects until it went away. To her surprise, she found that the sensation completely disappeared within a week and her belief that she had a serious neurological abnormality reduced (5 per cent).

Behavioural experiments used with panic   The main aim in the treatment of panic is to modify patients' catastrophic interpretations of the bodily sensations which they experience during panic attacks. Although discussion of the evidence for an alternative, non-catastrophic interpretation can be helpful, patients sometimes only believe that an alternative interpretation applies to them if its validity can be demonstrated by behavioural experiments in which their symptoms are reproduced and/or reduced. In a sense, panic patients are rather like Doubting Thomas, they are unlikely to believe the positive interpretation unless they can experience its effects. One particularly common alternative explanation is the idea that the sensations experienced in a panic attack are the result of hyperventilation rather than the more catastrophic things which patients usually fear (e.g. impending heart attack, insanity, loss of control). Behavioural experiments based on this hypothesis involve determining whether voluntary hyperventilation reproduces the bodily symptoms of panic and whether training in controlled breathing helps reduce the bodily symptoms. Voluntary hyperventilation is introduced as a diagnostic exercise which will help the therapist discover more about the problem. During the test, patients are asked to breathe through their nose and mouth quickly, fully emptying their lungs as they breathe out and filling them completely as they breathe in, for a period of up to two minutes, though they are at liberty to stop beforehand if necessary. Patients are *not* told exactly what sensations they are likely to experience, and they are not told that the effects of overbreathing may be similar to their panic attacks (to minimize the patients' prior expectations and to prevent difficulties arising if they fall into the approximately 30 per cent of patients who find that the sensations are unlike those experienced during a panic). Following voluntary hyperventilation, patients are invited to consider whether the sensations experienced during overbreathing are in any way similar to those experienced during a panic attack. In discussing this point, therapists should encourage patients to report differences as well as similarities between effects of hyperventilation and their naturally occurring attacks. Such differences can then be discussed. For example, the patients may say the physical sensations are very similar to their panic attacks, but they were less anxious. The therapist could then ask, 'If you experienced these sensations unexpectedly while you were away from the clinic, what would you have thought and how would you have felt?' Patients can then often see that they would have jumped to a catastrophic interpretation ('I'm having a heart attack') and felt panicky.

Once patient and therapist have established that it seems likely that hyperventilation plays a role in panic, this discussion can be followed up with training in controlled breathing. Such training has two aims. First, to provide further evidence for the hyperventilation reattribution by showing that controlled breathing can reduce the symptoms of panic. Secondly, to provide a useful symptom-management technique. Clark, Salkovskis, and Chalkley (1985) found that a convenient way of teaching patients controlled breathing is to use pacing tapes. On these tapes the pacing consists of a voice saying 'in' for two seconds (12 breaths/min) or three seconds (8 breaths/min), then 'out' for the same period; after a brief pause, 'in' again, and so on. Therapists choose the pacing rate which is most comfortable for the patient. By prolonging the articulation of 'in' and 'out', gentle and extended inspirations and expirations are achieved rather than the sharp gasps which are characteristic of hyperventilation. Training starts by asking patients to follow the pacing on the tape. Once they are comfortable in doing this, they are encouraged to turn the tape off and carry on breathing at the same pace for progressively longer periods of time on their own (e.g. 15 seconds, 30 seconds, 1 minute, and so on). When they are able to do this, they are then given practice in using controlled breathing to reduce the sensations which occur in panic. This is done in a graded fashion by asking them to overbreathe briefly during sessions and then to return to their slow controlled breathing in order to take away the induced sensations. Training in controlled breathing generally extends over a period of two to three sessions and associated homework.

Internal focus of attention sometimes accounts for the bodily sensations which panic patients are prone to misinterpret, and can be used in another behavioural experiment.

For example, a 42-year-old housewife erroneously believed she was suffering from cardiac disease (belief = 60 per cent). Negative medical tests and reassurance from her physician failed to modify this belief. When asked what evidence she had for the idea that she had cardiac disease, she said that she noticed her heart more frequently than did her husband or colleagues at work and she thought this must indicate that there was something seriously wrong with it. The therapist suggested an alternative interpretation that the problem was her *belief* that there was something wrong with her heart. This belief then led her to selectively attend to her body, which in turn increased her awareness of her heart. When asked what she thought of this alternative, she said, 'You psychologists are very good at thinking of clever explanations, and this would, no doubt, apply to some people, but I don't think that the effects of attention could be strong enough to account for my sensations.' Rather than argue with this assertion, the therapist said, 'You may be right. But perhaps to get more information it would be good if we did an experiment to see how strong the effects of attention are for you.' In this experiment the patient was asked to close her eyes and concentrate on her heart for five minutes. To her great surprise, she found that simply attending to her heart enabled her to detect the pulse in her forehead, neck, arms, chest, and legs without touching these parts of the body. Furthermore, when she was subsequently asked to describe out loud the contents of the room for five minutes, she ceased to be aware of her heart. This demonstration reduced her belief that she had cardiac disease (belief = 30 per cent), increased her belief in the alternative explanation, and encouraged her to use distraction as a coping technique when she subsequently felt panicky.

A further experiment which can be used involves directly demonstrating the role of thoughts in panic by trying to produce a panic attack using a purely cognitive manipulation. There are several ways in which this can be done. One useful way is to ask patients to dwell on, and read out loud, a series of word pairs printed on a large card (Clark and Salkovskis, in press). These pairs consist of various combinations of bodily sensations and catastrophes (e.g. breathlessness-suffocate; palpitations-dying). As patients read these cards, they tend to experience the sensations they are reading about. Imagery can also be used to invoke an attack. Patients are asked to imagine being in a situation which might provoke an attack, to start noticing bodily sensations, and then to dwell on and imagine their feared outcomes becoming realized. If this is successful in producing a panic-like state, the therapist can use this observation to show patients that cognitions have a role in their attacks.

Dealing with avoidance behaviour Although they do not show the consistent avoidance behaviour characteristic of phobic patients, many anxiety state patients avoid some situations or activities. Three types of avoidance can be distinguished. First, avoidance of specific situations: Butler *et al.* (1987*a*) found that approximately 40 per cent of generalized anxiety patients avoid social-evaluative situations (talking in public, eating in restaurants, eating with strangers), and approximately 20 per cent avoid agoraphobic-type situations (travelling on public transport, crowds, shopping). Secondly, avoidance of activities which might bring on feared sensations (e.g. exercise). Thirdly, avoidance strategies which are used once symptoms have started (e.g. holding onto solid objects when starting to feel faint). All three forms of avoidance tend to maintain patients' negative beliefs. For this reason, it is important that the therapist encourage patients to go into situations, or to engage in activities, which they have previously avoided in order to see whether the things they are afraid of actually occur. Patients are encouraged to expose themselves to feared situations or activities repeatedly and in a graded fashion (see Chapter 4). In addition, they are asked to predict in advance what they think will happen during an exposure exercise and then to see whether the outcome is less (or more) negative than predicted. When making predictions, patients specify not only their predicted fear level, but also (and more importantly) anticipated catastrophies ('I will have a heart attack', 'I will faint', 'I will make a complete fool of myself', 'I won't be able to cope', 'The anxiety will escalate uncontrollably'). Often patients accurately predict experienced fear but their predictions of anticipated catastrophes are rarely correct.

In addition to encouraging patients to expose themselves to situations or activities which they are avoiding, it is also important to modify behaviours which are used once symptoms have started and maintain a patient's belief that certain symptoms are highly dangerous (Salkovskis 1988*b*). Several examples of such behaviours were given on page 58. A further example is provided by a panic patient who believed that he was in danger of going mad during a panic attack. As he had already experienced many attacks, his therapist asked him, 'What has stopped you going mad so far?' The patient explained that he had always tried to control his thoughts during an attack and believed that these attempts at control always just saved him. In order to test this belief, he was encouraged to bring on his symptoms and then not to try and control his thoughts. As a consequence of this, he discovered that panic attacks do not lead to madness even when he made no attempt to control his thoughts during an attack. Indeed, he finally concluded that rather than stopping him going mad, his attempts to control his thoughts had been reinforcing his belief because each time he attempted to control his thoughts he inevitably noticed that several of his thoughts appeared to come into his mind unexpectedly. Attempts at control and checking behaviours played a similar role in maintaining the beliefs of a patient who was concerned that his hands might shake in public. Fearing this event, he repeatedly checked that his hands were alright by holding them out in front of him with his fingers stretched apart. Experimentation revealed that this posture was the ideal one for producing shaking even in individuals without such fears.

Learning new behaviours and skills

For some patients, part of the reason why they find social situations difficult is that they either lack, or have difficulty using, social and conversational skills. When this is the case, brief training in appropriate social skills can be helpful. Once a problematic situation has been isolated, role-plays and discussion of what the patient actually did in the situation are used to identify inappropriate behaviours. Once these behaviours have been identified, alternatives are suggested, modelled by the therapist and then practised by the patient, initially in the safety of a role-play in the therapy session and later in real-life situations (see Liberman, King, De Risi, and McCann 1975; or Rimm and Masters 1979, Chapter 4, for further details). Patients who have difficulty knowing what to say in certain situations and how to keep conversations going may benefit from reading sections of Alan Garner's (1980) excellent self-help book, *Conversationally speaking*. Where anxiety appears to be induced partly by difficulty in making decisions about real-life problems, brief training in problem-solving skills (see Chapter 12) can also be helpful.

Assumption techniques

This brief section specifically concentrates on some of the techniques which are used for dealing with dysfunctional assumptions. Several ways of identifying an individual's assumptions are given in Chapter 6. Two of the more common techniques are: looking for themes in the daily record of dysfunctional thoughts and using the downward arrow technique (see p. 204; also Burns 1980, p. 235). In the latter technique, instead of answering an automatic thought, patients aim to identify the belief behind the thought by repeatedly asking, 'If this thought was true, what would it mean to me?'

Table 3.4 (taken from Clark and Beck 1988) illustrates a generalized anxiety patient's dysfunctional assumption and the patient's rational responses to that assumption. The patient described himself as being anxious in a wide range of situations and for at least 80 per cent of every day. In discussing situations in which he became anxious, it quickly emerged that almost all the situations triggered performance worries. These worries appeared to arise from the assumption shown in the table. Several techniques were used to help challenge and modify the assumption. Following a *historical review* the patient was able to see that the assumption was probably a result of his early reinforcement history. This insight helped him to gain some distance from the belief. Discussion of the possible *advantages* and *disadvantages* of holding the belief enabled him to see that although valuing success increases motivation to achieve,

Table 3.4 Illustration of a dysfunctional assumption, rational responses to the assumption, and a plan for change (*from Clark, D. M. and Beck, A. T. (1988)*. Cognitive approaches. In *Handbook of anxiety disorders*, (ed. C. Last and M. Hersen), pp. 362–85. Pergamon, New York.

---

1. *The assumption*

   I hold the belief that, 'I am inadequate unless I succeed. All my past successes count for nothing unless I succeed again today. Nobody will love me unless I succeed.'

2. *Rational responses and plan for change*

   It is understandable why I hold this belief because in the past my parents have never given me unambiguous praise for my successes, but instead always suggested that there is another unseen important hurdle to attack.

   However, this belief is untrue because there are things about me from my past which are good and which nobody can take away from me. Also, I am the same person when I do poorly in school. No member of my family or friends treats me differently. They still love me.

   In addition, the belief is dysfunctional because it makes me constantly anxious.

   As I have held this belief for a long time I will have to work hard at changing it and it will take a while. Two things I can do to help change it are: (a) to make a list of my assets; (b) spend a little time each day doing something simply for the pleasure of doing it, not for what it will accomplish.

---

the extremeness of his belief led to constant anxiety and probably also underachievement. The assumption also revealed that the patient had considerable doubts about his self-worth. In order to counteract these doubts and build his *self-esteem*, he made a list of his assets and discussed with the therapist the evidence for and against his perceived deficits. Finally, he was encouraged to *act against the assumption*. In this way he found that he could enjoy life even when adopting a pattern of behaviour which was different from that implied by the assumption. Initially he found this difficult to do because whenever he tried to act against the assumption he experienced a series of automatic thoughts and became anxious. To help him continue to act against the assumption, he wrote the assumption and arguments against it on a flash-card (Table 3.4) which he carried around in his pocket and read when anxious.

A further illustration of dealing with assumptions is provided by the case of a generally anxious patient who frequently had the thought, 'I'll never get everything done.' Discussion revealed that this thought was based on the extreme perfectionist belief. 'I always have to do things perfectly.' Listing the *advantages and disadvantages* of holding the belief revealed that the belief's advantages (it could sometimes produce very good work) were vastly outweighed by its disadvantages (it produced considerable anxiety which prevented her from doing her best; it made her unwilling to take risks, unnecessarily restricting her range and preventing her from making the mistakes which are necessary for learning; it didn't allow her to let mistakes be noticed by others and therefore prevented her from obtaining valuable feedback). This information helped her to engage in a programme in which she was asked to act intentionally against the belief by doing all but the most important things less than perfectly. With practice she found that she then got more enjoyment out of everyday activities (because she was no longer judging her performance all the time) and became less anxious.

Relaxation techniques

Relaxation can be an effective way for patients to demonstrate to themselves that they have control over their symptoms. In addition, it may have broader cognitive effects. Peveler and Johnston (1986) found that relaxation increases the accessibility of positive information in memory and hence makes it easier to find alternatives to danger-related thoughts. One of the simplest ways of achieving some relaxation is through planning enjoyable and relaxing activities and planning breaks in busy routines. In addition, some patients benefit from more formal training in relaxation techniques. This may be particularly relevant for individuals who report finding it extremely difficult to relax or who report feeling continually tense. A range of relaxation techniques are available (Bernstein and Borkovec 1973; Goldfried and Davison 1976; Ost 1987). Whichever technique is chosen, it is important that relaxation should be presented as a skill to be learned through repeated practice with the aim being not just to relax in an armchair at home, but also to be able to use relaxation during everyday activities.

One of the most plausible types of relaxation training is the applied relaxation method devised by Ost (1987). The various stages in applied relaxation are outlined in the Appendix to this chapter.

It is advisable to demonstrate each of the stages in applied relaxation during a treatment session rather than just giving tapes of each set of relaxation exercises, as studies indicate that audio-tapes alone are rarely effective (Borkovec and Sides 1979b). Many anxiety state patients react favourably to relaxation training. However, some show a paradoxical reaction, becoming more anxious (Heide and Borkovec 1984). Relaxation-induced anxiety is particularly likely in patients with fears of loss of control who may find aversive the feeling of letting go which accompanies relaxation. In addition, the focusing on one's body which is involved in relaxation can lead panic patients to notice sensations which they are prone to misinterpret. These negative reactions can probably be reduced by warning patients that they may experience unusual sensations when at first practising relaxation. In addition, they can be exploited in therapy for reattribution purposes or by presenting relaxation as a way of reducing fear of certain sensations by providing graded exposure to those sensations.

Preventing relapse

Towards the end of therapy the emphasis shifts from symptom reduction to preventing relapse. In order to promote self-reliance, the interval between therapy sessions is gradually increased, attempts are made to anticipate any future setbacks, such as loss of a job or break up of relationship. Even if it is not certain that these events may occur, it is useful to discuss how they could be dealt with if they did occur. This usually will involve discussing how skills which have already been acquired in therapy could be applied to a new problem. To facilitate this, patients are asked to write out a list of things they have learned during therapy and to devise a plan for dealing with any future episodes of anxiety. As the cognitive model predicts that one of the major reasons for a relapse would be an incomplete grasp of arguments against negative thoughts, particular emphasis is placed on checking how strongly patients believe their own rational responses. *Point/counterpoint* can be a useful way of doing this. In a role-play the patient states his or her rational responses to a particular negative thought and then the therapist puts the counterpoint by trying to argue against the rational responses. This process helps the patient to pinpoint weaknesses in his or her rational responses. If weaknesses are identified, alternative, more convincing responses are then developed.

Alternative treatments

Benzodiazepines, beta blockers, and tricyclic antidepressants are the most frequently used alternatives to cognitive–behavioural treatment. While the short-term use of benzodiazepines may be helpful for managing an acute emotional crisis, these drugs appear to be of little value in more persistent anxiety. Catalan, Gath, Edmonds, and Ennis (1984) investigated the consequences of general practitioners not prescribing benzodiazepines to patients presenting with recent onset affective disorders, in most cases anxiety. Over the next six months, patients not given benzodiazepines were just as likely to improve as those given benzodiazepines. In addition to their restricted therapeutic effects, it is now evident that long-term use of benzodiazepines can produce dependence, further compounding patients' existing difficulties. Propranolol has been suggested as an effective anti-panic agent. However, controlled trials do not support this assertion (Noyes *et al.* 1984; Griez and van den Hout 1986). One case series (Garakani, Zitrin, and Klein 1984) suggests that imipramine may reduce the frequency of panic attacks in patients suffering from panic disorder. However, this result needs to be confirmed in a controlled trial.

Outcome

Cognitive–behavioural approaches to the treatment of anxiety states are a recent innovation. For this reason, relatively few outcome studies have been published. Treatment procedures similar to those described in this chapter have been used in eight case series (Hollon 1980; Waddell, Barlow, and O'Brien 1984; Clark *et al.* 1985; Clark 1986*b*; Gitlin *et al.* 1986; Salkovskis, Jones, and Clark 1986; Beck 1988; Clark *et al.* 1988), all of which obtained promising results. In two of the case series (Clark *et al.* 1985; Salkovskis *et al.* 1986*a*) a stable baseline was established before the start of treatment and significant improvements from that baseline were observed in a shorter period of time than the baseline itself. This suggests that the improvements were not simply due to spontaneous remission, a suggestion which is confirmed by recent controlled trials. Beck (1988) investigated the effectiveness of a form of cognitive therapy in panic disorder patients. Patients given this treatment, which is similar to the treatment used by Clark *et al.* (1985), improved significantly more than patients given a form of non-directive supportive psychotherapy. Recently, five further controlled trials have investigated the effectiveness of various combinations of cognitive and behavioural procedures. Barlow *et al.* (1984) found that panic disorder and generalized anxiety patients given cognitive treatment plus relaxation and EMG biofeedback improved significantly more than waiting list controls. Butler, Cullington, Hibbert, Klimes, and Gelder (1987*b*) found that generalized anxiety patients given Anxiety Management Training (exposure plus training in cognitive restructuring, distraction, and relaxation) improved significantly more than wait list controls, and these gains were maintained at six-month follow up. Durham and Turvey (1987) found that both behaviour therapy and cognitive behaviour therapy were associated with marked reductions in generalized anxiety, with cognitive behaviour therapy being marginally more effective. Finally, Ost (1988) found that panic and generalized anxiety patients given applied relaxation (see Appendix to this chapter) improved significantly more than patients given a more traditional form of relaxation (progressive muscle relaxation).

Recommended reading

Beck, A. T., Emery, G., and Greenberg, R. L. (1985). *Anxiety disorders and phobias*. Basic Books, New York.

Burns, D. D. (1980). *Feeling good*. New American Library, New York.

Clark, D. M. and Salkovskis, P. M. (in press). *Cognitive therapy for panic and hypochondriasis*. Pergamon, New York.

Garner, A. (1980). *Conversationally speaking*. McGraw-Hill, New York.

Liberman, R. P., King, L. W., De Risi, W. J., and McCann, M. (1975). *Personal effectiveness*. Research Press, Champaign Ill.

Rachman, S. and Maser, J. (1988). *Panic: psychological perspectives*. Lawrence Erlbaum, Hillsdale.

Shaffer, M. (1983). *Life after stress*. Contemporary Books, Chicago.

Young, J. E. (1981). Cognitive therapy and loneliness. In *New directions in cognitive therapy*, (ed. G. Emery, R. Bedrosian, and S. Hollon), pp. 139–59. Guilford Press, New York.

Young, J. E. (1982). Loneliness, depression and cognitive therapy: theory and application. In *Loneliness: a source book of current theory, research and therapy*, (ed. L. A. Peplau and D. Perlman), pp. 379–405. Wiley, New York.

APPENDIX
STAGES OF APPLIED RELAXATION TRAINING

The main stages of Ost's (1987) applied relaxation training are briefly outlined below, with the expected time it should take a patient to relax at each stage in the training programme given in parentheses. In most of the controlled trials investigating its effectiveness, the applied relaxation training programme has extended over 8–12 sessions and it is unlikely that the full training programme could be delivered in less than seven sessions. However, when clinical considerations mean that the number of sessions available for training is less that this, it may be possible to obtain worthwhile reductions in anxiety by teaching subsets of the training programme. Within a treatment session, training in applied relaxation can be easily combined with many of the other cognitive and behavioural procedures outlined in the present chapter.

Rationale

Before the start of treatment, it is important that patients understand the rationale for applied relaxation training. Presentation of the rationale should include the following information:

'When a person is anxious, there are three different components to his/her reaction: a physiological component (increased heart rate, sweating, muscle tension), a behavioural component (avoidance, trying to escape), and a cognitive component (negative thoughts such as "I am going to collapse", "I cannot cope"). The relative strength of these components varies from person to person but it is common for people to experience a physiological change, followed by a negative thought, which increases the physiological reaction producing a vicious circle. One effective way of breaking this vicious circle is to focus on the physiological reaction and learn how to control it. As anxiety can build up very quickly and can occur in a wide range of situations, an effective relaxation technique would be one which allows individuals to relax not just when sitting in a chair at home, but in any situation and to do so very quickly (20–30 seconds). This is the aim of applied relaxation training. As it is easiest to control an anxiety reaction if you start to relax before the anxiety reaches its peak, training starts with teaching you to recognize the early signs of anxiety. You will then be taken through a series of training exercises in which you are taught to relax in progressively less and less time. Throughout the period of training you are at liberty to use the relaxation skills you have been learning to manage naturally-occuring anxiety. However, you should not expect the skills to be fully effective until you have completed the training. In addition, during the early stages of training most relaxation practice will be conducted when you are not anxious as it is easiest to learn the skill in that state. Like other skills, such as riding a bicycle, applied relaxation requires a lot of practice. For this reason, daily homework practice is necessary throughout the training.'

Recognizing the early signs of anxiety

In order to increase patients' awareness of the early signs of an anxiety reaction, they are asked to keep a record of anxious episodes. The record includes information on the *situation* in which the anxiety occurred, its *intensity* (0–10), and the *earliest signs* which were noticed (most often bodily reactions such as increased heart rate or 'butterflies in the stomach'). Patients are encouraged to continue monitoring early signs throughout the different stages of relaxation training.

Progressive relaxation (15–20 min.)

The first stage of relaxation training involves the progressive relaxation technique in which the body is divided up into a series of large muscle groups and each group is tensed and then relaxed. By alternating tension and relaxation patients are taught to discriminate between these two states, and to become more aware of the parts of the body in which they are particularly tense. In order to facilitate transition to natural situations, patients do not lie on a couch during progressive relaxation training. Instead, they are asked to sit in a comfortable chair. First the therapist models how the different groups of muscles should be tensed and relaxed. The patient does the various tension-release exercises at the same time, with the therapist checking that these are done correctly. Then the patient closes his/her eyes and the therapist takes him/her through tensing and releasing the different muscle groups in the right order and at the right tempo. Tension is normally maintained for about five seconds, with the subsequent relaxation of a muscle group lasting 10–15 seconds. Normally each muscle group is tensed and relaxed only once. After going through all muscle groups in this way the patient is asked to rate the degree of relaxation obtained using a 0–100 scale. The same rating scale is later used to monitor progress during homework practice. Therapists should check whether patients are experiencing any problems in relaxing particular muscle groups and help deal with these. For the purposes of progressive relaxation, the body is divided into two parts. In the first session, relaxation of the hands, arms, face, neck, and shoulders is practised. In the second session, the rest of the body is also included. The main muscle groups involved in each session and instructions for tensing them are as follows:

Session 1 Clench the right fist, feeling tension in the fist and forearm . . . clench the left fist, feeling the tension in the fist and forearm . . . bend the elbow and tense the biceps, keeping the hands relaxed . . . straighten the arm and tense the triceps leaving the lower arms supported by the chair with the hands relaxed . . . wrinkle the forehead by raising the eyebrows . . . bring the eyebrows close together (as in a frown) . . . screw up the muscles around the eyes . . . tense the jaw by biting the teeth together . . . press the tongue hard and flat against the roof of the mouth with lips closed, notice tension in the throat . . . press the lips tightly together (as in a pout) . . . push the head back as far as it will go (against a chair) . . . press the chin down onto the chest . . . hunch the shoulders up towards the ears . . . hunch the shoulders towards the ears and circle the shoulders.

Session 2   First go through the exercises learnt in session 1. This should take about ten minutes. After completing the last shoulder exercise, go straight into the following set of exercises: breathe calmly and regularly with the stomach ... take a deep breath, completely filling the lungs, hold the breathe for a few seconds then passively exhale ... tense the stomach muscles ... pull in the stomach ... arch the lower back away from the chair ... tense the buttocks and calves by pressing the heels to the floor keeping the legs straight ... tense the calves by pressing the feet and toes downwards ... tense the shins by bending the feet and toes upwards ... continue breathing calmly and regularly with the stomach.

Following each session, the homework assignment is to practise progressive relaxation for approximately 15–20 minutes, twice a day. Patients should choose a place and time where they will be comfortable and unlikely to be interrupted. They should also keep a record of the time taken to relax, and the amount of relaxation achieved (0–100 scales) during each practice.

Release-only (5–7 min.)

The aim of this stage is to further reduce the time it takes to relax by omitting tension. A session starts with the patient being asked to breathe calmly and to relax as much as possible while doing so. The therapist then instructs him/her to relax each muscle group, starting at the top of the head and moving through the body to the tip of the toes. Instructions given to the patient (Ost 1987, p. 409) are as follows: 'Breathe with calm, regular breaths and feel yourself relaxing more and more with every breath ... just let go ... relax your forehead ... eyebrows ... eyelids ... jaws ... tongue and throat ... your entire face ... relax your neck ... shoulders ... arms ... and all the way down to your finger-tips ... continue to breathe calmly and regularly with your stomach ... let the feeling of relaxation spread to your stomach ... waist and back ... relax the lower part of your body, your bottom ... thighs ... knees ... calves ... feet ... and all the way down to the tip of your toes ... breathe calmly and regularly and feel how you relax more and more with each breath ... take a deep breath and hold it for a couple of seconds ... and let the air out slowly ... slowly ... notice how you relax more and more'. If a particular muscle group proves difficult to relax, patients are asked to briefly tense it and then release it again. Homework involves practising release-only relaxation twice a day keeping a record of the time taken to relax and the amount of relaxation achieved. After 1–2 weeks of practice most patients are ready to move onto the next stage, which is called cue-controlled relaxation.

Cue-controlled relaxation (2–3 min.)

In cue-controlled relaxation, the time it takes to relax is further reduced by focusing on breathing and establishing a form of conditioning between the self-instruction 'relax' and increases in feelings of relaxation. The session starts with the patient relaxing using release-only (without detailed instruction from therapist) and signalling when a satisfactory state of relaxation has been achieved. The therapist then gives the following instructions, cued to the patient's breathing pattern. Just before an inhalation, the therapist says '*inhale*' and just before an exhalation, the therapist says '*relax*'. This sequence is repeated five times and then the patient is instructed to continue the sequence silently. After a further minute, the therapist once again says '*inhale . . . relax*' several times, then the patient again continues on his/her own for several minutes. Normally cue-controlled relaxation is practised twice in a session. An interesting feature of this stage of the training is that patients invariably over-estimate how long it takes for them to become relaxed. For this reason, it can be useful for therapists to elicit estimates of the time taken to relax and to give patients feedback on their improving performance. As in the preceeding two stages, homework involves practising this type of relaxation twice a day, recording the time taken to relax and the amount of relaxation achieved on each occasion. Again, 1–2 weeks of practice is usually required before proceeding to the next stage.

Differential relaxation (60–90 seconds)

The main aim of this stage is to learn how to relax while engaged in everyday activities, not just sitting in an armchair. Many activities, such as standing, require tension in some muscle groups and the aim of differential relaxation is to teach patients how to avoid unnecessarily tensing those muscles that are not required for a particular activity. The first session starts with the patient using cue-controlled relaxation to relax while sitting in an armchair. Then he/she is instructed to move parts of the body while at the same time concentrating on keeping the rest of the body relaxed by frequently scanning for signs of unnecessary tension and relaxing as appropriate. The movements used are: opening the eyes and looking around the room without moving the head; looking around, moving eyes and head; lifting one arm while keeping the rest of the body relaxed; lifting one leg while keeping the rest of the body relaxed. During these exercises, the therapist continually encourages the patient to scan the body for signs of tension and relax all those parts of the body not engaged in the movement. When a problematic area is identified, ways of relaxing the relevant muscles are discussed. Once a patient has practised these movements while sitting in an armchair, the same movements are practised while sitting in an ordinary, upright chair, then while sitting at a desk (where practice in staying relaxed while writing on a piece of paper or talking on the telephone is also included). In the second session of differential relaxation, these exercises are extended to include practising relaxing while standing and while walking. During each exercise the patient is encouraged to repeatedly scan the body for signs of tension and relax as far as possible all the muscles which are not required. By the end of the second session of differential relaxation the time it takes patients to relax has usually reduced to 60–90 seconds. Homework involves practising differential relaxation twice a day with 1–2 weeks practice being necessary before progressing to the next stage.

Rapid relaxation (20–30 seconds)

In rapid relaxation, the aim is to further reduce the time it takes to relax and to give patients extensive practice in relaxing in natural, non-stressful situations.

Therapist and patient identify a series of cues which can be used to remind the patient to relax in the natural environment. For example, every time one looks at one's watch, is about to make a telephone call, opens a cupboard, goes into the bathroom, etc. To increase the distinctiveness of these cues it is often useful to put a small piece of coloured tape on the agreed cue (watch, telephone, etc.). The patient should aim to relax 15–20 times a day in natural, non-stressful situations. When relaxing he/she is instructed to:

(1)   take 1–3 deep breaths, slowly exhaling after each breath;
(2)   think 'relax' before each exhalation;
(3)   scan the body for tension and try to relax as much as possible in the situation.

Once patients have practised rapid relaxation for 1–2 weeks and are able to relax in 20–30 seconds the final stage of applied relaxation is introduced.

Application training

Application training involves practising applying the previously learnt relaxation skills in anxiety-provoking situations. Before starting this stage, it is important to remind patients that applied relaxation is a skill and, like any other skill, it takes practice to become completely successful. For this reason, patients should not expect to be able to fully control their anxiety at the start, but rather will gradually become more and more successful with practice. Practice usually involves frequent, but relatively brief (10–15 minutes) exposure to a wide range of anxiety-arousing situations. The aim of this exposure is to show the patient that he/she can cope with any anxiety experienced and eventually learn to control it. In order to promote control, the patient is reminded that it is important to start applying relaxation as soon as the first sign of anxiety is noticed and earlier anxiety diaries are reviewed to remind patients of their typical early signs. With phobic patients, it is fairly easy to identify a range of anxiety-eliciting situations which can be used for practice. In generalized anxiety and panic patients, it may be more difficult to identify specific situations which consistently provoke anxiety. However, techniques such as hyperventilation, physical exercise, and imaging anxiety arousing events can be used to produce anxiety both in treatment sessions and during homework practice.

Maintenance programme

In order to help maintain the improvements made during applied relaxation training, patients are encouraged to develop the habit of scanning their body for tension at least once a day and, if any tension is noticed, to use rapid relaxation to remove it. In addition, so they don't forget their relaxation skills, they are also encouraged to practise differential or rapid relaxation once or twice a week.

4

Phobic disorders

Gillian Butler

Introduction

A phobia is a persistent and excessive fear of an object or situation that is not in fact dangerous. Such fear results in a strong desire to avoid phobic situations, even though patients often recognize that this is not rational. They may be able to dismiss their fears when in a 'safe' place, but still believe they are in real danger when faced with the thing that they fear. Unlike other fears, phobias are disabling and not adaptive, as they interfere with ordinary activities.

Types of phobia

There are three main types of phobic disorder: simple phobia, social phobia, and agoraphobia. A *simple phobia* is confined to a single feared object or situation (e.g. spiders, heights, or the sight of blood). Simple phobics are usually free from their symptoms if they are neither in nor anticipating a phobic situation. *Social phobias* are more complex, as they centre around fear of unobservable events, such as negative evaluation, criticism, or rejection by other people. Social phobias may focus on particular aspects of social interactions, such as speaking, eating, or writing in public, in which case they resemble simple phobias. Usually they are more pervasive. Distressing thoughts, often related to the fear of scrutiny or of being evaluated negatively, are particularly important in social phobias. Successful avoidance may be less extensive than in other types of phobia, because it is not so easy to achieve.

In *agoraphobia*, anxiety is determined by distance from safety as well as by the proximity of the phobic stimulus. It effects a cluster of situations, of which the most commonly mentioned is fear of entering crowded places, and it may include fear of confined spaces (hairdressers, supermarkets, cinemas, etc.), of public transportation, and of being far from home. The symptoms include both fear and marked avoidance of situations from which it might be difficult to escape, or where it might be difficult to get help in the case of an emergency. Agoraphobics usually, but not always, feel safe at home, and more fearful the further they venture away from their safe place. They may also panic, or fear that they will lose control, faint or collapse if unable to escape. Some agoraphobics are less anxious if accompanied by someone they can trust, or when pushing a pram or carrying an umbrella, and may use these things as 'props'. Diagnostic systems such as DSM III (American Psychiatric Association 1980) distinguish two kinds of agoraphobics: those with and those without panic attacks, although it is not clear whether these are two separate disorders, which require different treatment, or more or less severe manifestations of the same thing. The techniques developed for the treatment of panic described in Chapter 3 can be combined with the treatments for phobias described below.

The frequency of phobias

It is difficult to calculate the frequency of phobias in the population as a whole because there is no hard and fast distinction between 'normal fears' and phobias, and because people tend to be secretive about phobias. Nevertheless, mild phobias are thought to be very common, affecting as many as one in nine adults (Agras, Sylvester, and Oliveau 1969; Robins *et al.* 1984). They are especially common in early childhood, although most of these fears disappear by the age of six. In adults phobias are slightly more common in women than in men; however, about 80 per cent of agoraphobics are women while the sexes are equally divided in social phobia. About 60 per cent of the phobic patients seen in outpatient clinics are agoraphobics, and social phobics form the next largest group.

Origins

It used to be thought that it is possible to be phobic about any object or situation. An alternative view, based on the observation that a limited set of phobias is observed in the clinic, is that the things feared may be, or have once been, potentially dangerous to the human race. This theory of 'preparedness' (Seligman 1971; McNally 1987) applies to phobias of small animals, illness or injury, thunderstorms, heights, strangers, and water, and to situations such as being far away from a safe place, and being rejected by other people. By extension it may also apply to the fear of flying, to sexual fears, and to things associated with illness such as vomiting or needles. However, there are rare but notable exceptions, such as the chocolate phobic mentioned by Rachman and Seligman (1976).

Although the exact cause of phobias is not known, they are generally considered to be learned fears, acquired through direct conditioning, vicarious conditioning (when the fear is learned by observing the fear of others), or the transmission of information and/or instructions (Rachman 1977; Ost and Hugdahl 1981). Conditioning is a form of learning during which a new association develops between a stimulus and responses to that stimulus. For example, a child playing with a pet dog (the stimulus) may unwittingly pull its tail and get bitten. The child responds with fear and distress, and learns to avoid dogs in the future (see also Chapter 1).

It is, however, unusual for a phobic patient to describe a single traumatic event, such as being bitten, to which he or she can date the onset of the disorder. Fear usually builds up gradually, as a result of repeated, more or less frightening experiences or through social learning. Sometimes this happens at a time of stress or high arousal, when fear responses are easily learned. Simple phobias may develop gradually out of childhood fears, and social phobias most commonly begin around late adolescence. Agoraphobia appears to start most frequently either in late adolescence, when women are expected to become more independent, or about the age of 30 (Marks and Gelder 1966). According to Marks (1969) the presence and nature of precipitating factors have no obvious relationship to the subsequent course of the disorder. It is certainly not necessary to know its exact cause in order to treat a phobia successfully.

Symptoms
The symptoms provoked by contact with something feared can usefully be categorized into three types: physiological, behavioural, and subjective (Lang 1968). The *physiological symptoms* include all the sensations that might be present if, for example, one had just missed being knocked down by a car: rapid heart rate, sweating, trembling, fast breathing, muscular tension and/or weakness, 'butterflies in the stomach', nausea, breathlessness, etc. Sometimes, more often in agoraphobia than in other types of phobia (Barlow and Craske 1988), these may be associated with panic attacks. A somewhat different pattern of symptoms is present in phobias of blood or injury, when there is a sudden fall in heart rate which can lead to fainting. Generally, the most obvious *behavioural symptoms* are 'fleeing' or 'freezing'; moving speedily out of the way or being momentarily rooted to the spot. *Subjective symptoms* obviously have to be inferred from patients' verbal reports and behaviour. They include thoughts: 'That might have killed me', 'People are dangerously careless'; and emotions such as shame, embarrassment, and anger, as well as fear. Physiological, behavioural, and subjective symptoms may or may not fluctuate together (Rachman and Hodgson 1974).

If one had narrowly missed being knocked down by a car, the symptoms of fear would quickly die away, and the experience might have beneficial, adaptive, consequences: making one more careful when crossing the road next time, or teaching one to avoid doing so while talking to a friend. The reactions of the jaywalker are sensible, and may even prolong life. Similar reactions become disruptive and maladaptive when they are provoked by something that is not really dangerous. By definition, phobic fear is disproportional to the source of danger, and reactions such as carefulness and avoidance in situations provoking such fear, are inappropriate.

Phobics react to fear in all three ways: physiologically, behaviourally, and subjectively, and these reactions prevent the symptoms from dying away. They maintain the problem because they prolong and increase distress, and also because they produce new symptoms such as anticipatory anxiety, apprehension, and dread. In many cases the most disruptive of all the reactions is avoidance. Subjective reactions are also important, and include thoughts such as 'Here I go again', 'I am going to lose control', 'I am shaking and everyone will notice', a strong desire to avoid, and a variety of distressing emotions such as frustration as well as fear and dread. Depression may aso become a problem in persistent phobias which interfere with daily activities (see below).

The interaction between symptoms and reactions

Figure 4.1 shows how the reactions to symptoms maintain the phobia by creating vicious circles that perpetuate fear. Avoidance maintains anxiety because it makes it difficult to learn that the feared object or situation is not in fact dangerous, or is not dangerous in the way, or to the extent that the patient thinks it is. Other important maintaining factors include thoughts, for example about the meaning of the symptoms of anxiety ('I'm going to faint', 'There's something really wrong with me'), or about the anticipated consequences of entering the phobic situation ('I'll get bitten', 'Nobody will speak to me'), and loss of confidence. External factors, such as the actions of people close to the patient, for example when they do things for them so that they do not have to face the things that they fear, also maintain phobias. In the absence of treatment, phobias are extremely persistent (Marks 1969), and precise identification of maintaining factors is necessary in order to plan effective treatment.

The rest of this chapter is concerned with the treatment of phobias. The theoretical background to treatment is presented first and more practical details follow, starting with assessment for therapy and continuing with a description of exposure and of the various cognitive and non-cognitive procedures that can be combined with it. The chapter ends with a brief account of the difficulties that may arise during treatment, of procedures for the maintenance of change, and of alternative treatments.

The theoretical background to treatment

Behavioural treatment for phobias developed directly out of the findings of experimental psychology, in particular the work of Wolpe (1958, 1961) on systematic desensitization. It was based on the hypothesis that most 'abnormal' behaviour, like 'normal' behaviour, is learned. It follows that what has been learned can be unlearned, and more adaptive reactions learned instead. This can be achieved by approaching instead of avoiding the thing that is feared; through 'graded exposure'. If the tendency to escape, withdraw, or merely avoid phobic situations is reversed, the

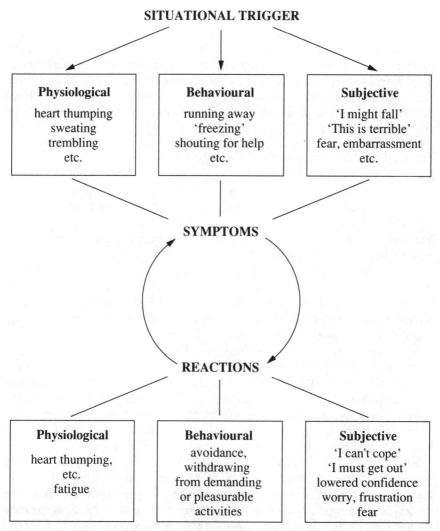

Fig. 4.1 A vicious circle model of phobic anxiety

phobic has the opportunity to learn that the situation is not in fact dangerous. The child who never goes near a dog again may remain fearful, while the one who approaches them is likely to regain confidence. Treatment therefore requires that patients repeatedly make contact with the things that they fear, and remain in contact with them until the fear starts to subside. Exposure breaks the vicious circles that maintain symptoms, and facilitates new learning. By facing the things that are feared, patients re-learn how to deal with them effectively.

Therefore, treatment is designed to extinguish (or reduce) anxiety and avoidance by exposing patients systematically to feared situations. It is immediately clear that the main problem for the therapist is to enable patients to enter situations which to them are unpleasant and frightening. Guidelines for overcoming this problem, and for ensuring the optimal effectiveness of exposure, have been derived from extensive research on the treatment of simple phobias, social phobia, and agoraphobia. These are outlined below.

The guiding rules of exposure

Exposure is defined as facing something that has been avoided because it provokes anxiety. Research suggests that for optimal effectiveness exposure should be graduated, repeated, and prolonged, and practice tasks should be clearly specified (e.g. Marks 1981; Emmelkamp 1982; Mathews, Gelder, and Johnston 1981.) In principle, this means that a patient must identify all the things that are avoided, and order them according to difficulty in a 'graded hierarchy' as described in detail below (p. 106). The first task selected for practice should be easy enough for the patient to be certain that he or she can attempt it, but sufficiently hard to provoke some anxiety. Tasks that do not provoke anxiety are not helpful (Borkovec and Sides 1979*a*), possibly because they do not provide an appropriate context for new learning. Tasks should be repeated frequently and regularly until they provoke little or no anxiety, and then the next task on the list should be attempted. Each practice task should be prolonged until anxiety starts to subside, and progress will be faster if the interval between practice times is short. For example, Mathews *et al.* (1981) suggest that patients should practise for one hour every day. In general, the more patients practise the quicker they improve.

So, for example, spider phobics would start by voluntarily making contact with something that provokes a definite but tolerable amount of fear, such as a small dead spider in a closed jar. They should look at the spider, examining it in detail, until the fear starts to subside. This exercise should be repeated until it provokes little or no anxiety. Then they should move on to a harder task, such as handling a dead spider, or watching a live one enclosed in a jar. This graded approach allows patients to become accustomed to contact with mildly fear-provoking situations before approaching harder ones, and in theory, effective treatment consists in the systematic repetition of this procedure.

The more complex the phobia the longer it will take to treat. Eight sessions should usually be adequate (fewer will be required in many cases), and by this time most patients have learned enough about the method for them to be able to continue to apply it with only minimal help. In all cases, patients should be encouraged to move quickly up their hierarchies, taking on new tasks as soon as the anxiety caused by easier ones has decreased. The earlier ones should be repeated occasionally later on, and incorporated into everyday life whenever possible.

Assessment

Assessment for the purpose of treating phobic disorders begins in the first session, and continues throughout treatment and follow-up. This is because measures of fear and records of practice provide the information upon which to base an effective and flexible treatment strategy. Assessment has three aims:

(1) to determine the precise nature of the phobia and suitability for treatment;

(2) to define the goals of treatment; and

(3) to identify appropriate measures of phobic anxiety.

Many phobic patients become anxious and distressed when talking about their phobia, and hence find this difficult to do. This may be because thinking about it in detail increases anxiety and is normally avoided, or because assessment forces the patient into a real phobic situation such as travelling to the clinic for an agoraphobic, or talking to a stranger for a social phobic. It is therefore important to build up rapport quickly, and to remember that patients may be reluctant to describe the phobia in detail because to them it sounds ridiculous or irrational.

The precise nature of the phobia and treatment suitability

General points

An assessment should be structured by asking systematically about physiological, behavioural, and subjective symptoms, and about reactions to them (see Fig. 4.1). The severity of the phobia can be estimated by finding out to what extent it interferes with daily life, including the ability to work, and to carry on normal relationships. It may help to ask the question both ways: e.g. 'What does the phobia prevent you doing?' and 'If you no longer had this problem, what differences would it make to your life?' Since exposure is likely to form a major part of treatment, detailed information is needed about avoidance. This includes finding out about the factors that make a particular situation easier or harder. A person with claustrophobia, for example, might be asked whether factors such as the size of a shower cubicle, or whether or not there is a window in it, make any difference. It will be necessary to determine the full range of avoidance in order to draw up a graduated list of exposure tasks, or graded hierarchy (see below, p. 106). Superficially, similar phobias may produce different patterns of avoidance, so that one spider phobic avoids cleaning out cupboards, while another is especially careful about cleaning under furniture. This is particularly clear in the case of social phobics, in whom the pattern of avoidance may be determined by the personal meaning of the situation to them, for example that they are being criticized or that they will never be able to form close relationships.

Maintaining factors

Assessment of background factors need not include a detailed history of the development of a phobia. It is more useful to identify maintaining factors, because they may interfere with progress. Avoidance is usually the main maintaining factor. Cognitive factors may also be important, for example thoughts about the dangerousness of the phobic stimulus and doubts about the value of treatment, or about having the ability to carry it through. The assessment should clarify whether other problems, such as generalized anxiety and depression, warrant specific attention (see below, p. 122), and whether there are reasons why it seems more comfortable to live with the phobia than to struggle against it. This could happen, for example, if a young person would be expected to move away from home once the phobia had improved, or if the greater independence achieved by an agoraphobic after treatment was perceived as threatening to her marriage. The therapist should try to find out whether such factors are important by, for instance, asking 'If you were successful in getting rid of the phobia, what problems would you be left with?', 'Would losing the phobia cause you, or anyone else, any other difficulties?'

Existing coping skills

The therapist should ask about which methods of coping the patient has tried in the past, because those which appear to be adaptive (such as keeping busy so as not to brood too much on the problem) might usefully be incorporated into the treatment programme. Others, such as sporadic attempts to face difficult situations, may have been unsuccessful. This could lead to reservations about the methods to be used in treatment unless possible reasons for failure (such as insufficient, ungraded, or irregular practice) are discussed. Alcohol and tranquillizers are frequently used, and may be difficult to give up because of their short-term effectiveness. However, they are both likely to lead to dependence if taken for long periods, and the patient may need other methods of control, of more long-term value, to take their place (see p. 118ff).

Resources

Patients' resources will influence factors such as their ability to tackle difficult situations, and their readiness to accept the active, self-help rationale of a cognitive–behavioural approach. Resources include hobbies and aspects of life that are relatively unaffected by the phobia, sources of pleasure and success, helpful relatives and friends, and personal characteristics such as persistence or a sense of humour. They can often be identified by asking how patients have dealt with difficulties in the past.

Suitability for treatment

Most phobias improve to some degree with treatment, and therefore there are strong reasons for making treatment available whenever possible. Patients who are severely depressed, or dependent on alcohol, may be unlikely to comply with suggestions until they have received other treatment. Those with long-standing personality disorders present other difficulties (e.g. fluctuating motivation, excessive dependence on or hostility towards the therapist), and take longer to treat.

Determining the goals of treatment

Although the general goal of treatment is usually self-evident in phobic disorders, it is important to discuss the patient's precise goals, as these may not correspond with those of the therapist. There are many sources of difference. Expecting the impossible is one. For example, a social phobic might wish never to feel anxious in company again. Since some degree of social anxiety is probably 'normal', this goal could not be achieved, and it might be more useful to set new goals by finding out to what extent others feel anxious in particular circumstances, for instance during a difficult interview, or if unexpectedly criticized.

Patient and therapist may also place differing degrees of emphasis on various goals. For an agoraphobic it may be more important, and indeed make a more practical difference to her life, to be able to go shopping with a friend, while to the therapist it may seem more important for her to build up the confidence to do things alone. Agreement about goals is necessary for full engagement in treatment.

It is difficult to know how wide ranging goals for phobic patients should be. There is some disagreement about whether it helps to confront the most frightening situations if these are unlikely to be experienced, for instance handling dangerous snakes or playing with tarantulas. Perhaps the most reasonable goal is one which would help maintain the gains made during treatment, such as planning regular spring-cleaning, country picnics, or visits to zoos for a spider phobic. Ost, Lindahl, Sterner, and Jerremalm (1984) suggest that blood/injury phobics should aim to become regular blood donors. Such goals are unlikely to be mentioned spontaneously, so may have to be suggested by the therapist.

Measuring the phobia

Measures are needed to provide information about progress, and to help plan treatment. They should be easy to use, sensitive to change, and capable of reflecting a patient's particular concerns.

Phobic severity
The most frequently used measures of phobic severity are the graded hierarchy and behavioural tests.

Graded hierarchies   A graded hierarchy is an ordered list of phobic situations used to guide exposure. It should reflect the full range of situations avoided by the patient, beginning with things that provoke only mild difficulty (e.g. hanging out the washing in the case of an agoraphobic), and ending with things that are well beyond the patient's present range (e.g. shopping in London before Christmas). The items in between these extremes should be carefully defined, should reflect aspects of the phobia that are of particular concern to the patient, and should, as far as possible, be evenly spaced in terms of the anxiety they provoke. Each item on the list is rated by the patient on a 0–10 (or 0–100) scale according to the amount of anxiety it would cause (and/or how much the patient would try to avoid it).

In practice, it may be easier for a patient to fill in items on a scale rather than think of a list of items and then scale them: i.e. 'We've got some relatively easy items which you have rated 5, and we've got this cluster of difficult items, all rated 90–100. Now, in order to plan treatment, we need items in the middle, so that you can gradually work up to the hard ones. Can you think of a situation on which you would score 50? . . . What would make that into a 60? . . . or a 40?' Considering modifying variables, such as the number of people present, or connecting themes, is also useful (see Table 4.1, and below, p. 111).

For a number of reasons, constructing a hierarchy is easier in theory than it is in practice. In the first place, fears are not always easy to grade into small-enough steps, and discontinuities may be inevitable (e.g. there can be no half measures when travelling by air). Secondly, a person may be fearful of diverse situations (e.g. crossing bridges and travelling in elevators). Finally, hierarchies may have to include internal sensations as well as external situations (e.g. fear of illness and fear of symptoms such as dizziness). An example of a relatively simple hierarchy is shown in Table 4.1, together with some notes to illustrate how the hierarchy can be expanded into a large variety of tasks (see also Wolpe 1982). Difficulties in devising practice tasks are described below (Treatment in practice, p. 112ff).

Behavioural tests   A behavioural tests consists of doing something that has been avoided, and rating the amount of anxiety experienced at the time (e.g. 0–100). It has the advantage that anticipatory anxiety, anxiety during exposure, and total duration of symptoms can be measured separately. It is particularly useful when avoidance is so extensive that the

Table 4.1   Hierarchy for fear of heights

	Rating scale 0–100
1. Look over banisters on upstairs landing	5
2. Look through closed 1st floor window	7
3. Lean out of 1st floor window	10
4. As above at friend's house, + 2nd floor windows	10–20
5. Look down from plate glass window in office, up to 6th floor	30–40
6. Look down from top of 'down' escalator	35
7. Use step ladder to change light bulb in centre of room	40
8. Walk across bridge over river, close to rail	50
9. Drive over suspension bridge	60
10. Church tower: walk up and out onto roof	70
11. Walk along cliff path	80
12. Drive along mountain roads, e.g. in North Wales	90
13. Eat a meal in Post Office Tower	100

Some ways of devising a variety of tasks relevant to this hierarchy:
Working on stairs and windows in increasingly unfamiliar places
Doing each task first with someone, and then alone
Watching films or looking at pictures of rock climbing, window cleaners, trapeze artists, aeroplane flights, ski-jumping, etc.
Practising looking down, allowing time for the eyes to become readjusted, e.g. by focusing on items at ever increasing distances

patient has to guess how bad a situation would be, as guesses are likely to be based on anticipatory anxiety. It is also useful when deciding where on the hierarchy to start working, or, at follow-up, to find out whether gains made during treatment have been maintained. One disadvantage of behavioural tests, from a measurement point of view, is that they may be therapeutic, because of the exposure involved, and therefore cannot both be frequently repeated and used as independent measures of change.

A behavioural test can be used as a source of information as well as a measure of anxiety, and in this way integrated into the assessment. Patients can, for instance, be asked to describe in detail what happens when they are in the testing situation, to find out exactly when anxiety is highest, or to pick up any thoughts that go through their minds at the time. Also the therapist could observe the patient and discover something not so far reported, such as a tendency to overbreathe, to avoid eye-contact or to hunch the shoulders. If the test is prolonged, it is likely that anxiety will peak and then fall, thus demonstrating the potential effectiveness of regular exposure. Patients often feel more willing to participate in this difficult test if its fact-finding function is emphasized when it is explained to them: 'In order to find out more about what it's like for you in real life, it would be very useful for you to go into one of the situations that you find difficult . . . '.

Self-monitoring

A daily record of exposure practice and of the level of anxiety experienced encourages patients to self-monitor and reminds them to complete homework assignments. It can also provide evidence to counter the tendency to remember failures rather than successes. Feeling panicky on a crowded bus may seem more important, and be more readily mentioned, than routine trips to the local shops. Written records are particularly valuable at the time of a set-back or relapse, when they provide a context within which present difficulties can be accurately assessed. They can help patients plan relevant practice independently, and keep track of progress. Anxiety, or 'subjective units of distress' (SUDs) can be rated on any scale that the patient finds easy to use (good/average/bad, 0–10, 0–100). Symptoms of particular concern (e.g. sweating or feeling faint) can be rated separately. An example of a completed practice record is provided in Table 4.2, and further information is given in Chapter 2 (p. 17).

Measures of cognitions

Accurate assessment of cognitions in phobias has only recently been attempted (see, for example, Last 1987), and there are as yet few relevant measures available. Notable exceptions include ratings of the Fear of Negative Evaluation (Watson and Friend 1969) and the Agoraphobic Cognitions Questionnaire (Chambless, Caputo, Bright, and Gallagher 1984). Their use is likely to increase because of their potential for alerting patients to the immediate effects of fearful thoughts, and to the benefits of exposure. For example, a patient might be asked to identify what he or she predicts will happen when entering a feared situation ('Anxiety will reach 7 on the 0–10 scale, and I will not be able to stay there for 1 minute'), and then to test the prediction in action. The prediction should be reassessed after exposure in order to find out whether the fearful expectations were confirmed, as predictions tend to be exaggerated or even catastrophic. Many patients make 'catastrophic' predictions when highly anxious or panicky, 'I will collapse', 'Everyone will laugh at me', 'I will go mad'. These predictions are especially likely to be inaccurate, and so the effects of identifying and disconfirming them can be quite dramatic (see also Chapter 3).

Standardized rating scales

These are useful for assessing the relative severity of phobias, for measuring the extent of generalization, or for identifying themes. Amongst the

Table 4.2 Practice record for an agoraphobic patient

Date.........

TARGET: Go to local shops daily. Travel to town once if possible.
NB Decide what to do before setting out, and fill in card before and after each trip.

Day Task		Expected Anxiety	Actual Anxiety	Shaky legs	Tablets
1.	Walk to post office in village	4	2	+	0
2.	Walk to 'far' shops: bus home	5	2	0	0
3.	Bus to 'far' shops, and back + chemist (Went very well)	3	1	0	0
4.	Bus to town, and back (can't get lift in!) (Terribly panicky)	4	5/7/2	++	0
5.	Felt awful and irritable. Stayed in a.m. Could not relax: took a tablet Local baker: 10 min	5	4	+	1
6.	Local shops, and supermarket (no bus) (Relaxed before going out. Met S, could go with her to town)	5	2	0	0
7.	Bus to town with S—2 hours (Not sure I could go alone)	6	2/4/1	0	0

best known are the Fear Questionnaire (Marks and Mathews 1979), the Fear Survey Schedule (Wolpe and Lang 1964), measures of social-evaluative anxiety developed by Watson and Friend (1969), and the Mobility Inventory for Agoraphobia (Chambless, Caputo, Jasin, Gracely, and Williams 1985).

Treatment in practice

Introducing treatment

In theory, phobias can be overcome by facing the things that are feared. When putting the theory into practice it is important to explain the model, using the patient's individual symptoms to illustrate how vicious circles maintain symptoms. For example, an agoraphobic patient described having felt hot and faint in a bus one day (a physiological symptom), and then walking to work the next week for fear of going on the bus again (an avoidance reaction that maintains the anxiety). Gradually she began to dread journeys (anticipatory anxiety, another reaction), and persuaded her husband or friends to drive her into town to shop (the behaviour of others maintained her avoidance). If this sequence is used to explain what has happened, the main message follows quite naturally: if the avoidance is reversed, gradually, in manageable steps, then the fear will subside. So at this point the patient may guess what the therapist is going to say next, and it is therefore worth asking: 'So the aim of treatment is to break the vicious circle. Can you see how to do this?' This not only encourages patients to think actively about what to do, but also helps the therapist find out more about their expectations.

The self-help rationale with which treatment is presented follows from this model, as the vicious circle cannot be broken without the active participation of the patient. The therapist should explain that treatment involves learning how to work on the problem effectively and independently. Treatment sessions should therefore be backed up by regular homework, and improvement will be the result of a collaborative effort. While the therapist contributes information about the model, and about treatment strategies, the patient contributes information necessary to fit the model and the strategies to his or her own case, and of course, the time given to practice. It is necessary to keep a record of practice, and to use this both to monitor progress, and to identify stumbling blocks. The function of practice is the same as when learning a physical skill, or in physiotherapy: that is, it is useful for its own sake and not for some wider purpose. The daily visit to the shop is not to get groceries, but to repeat exposure and to disconfirm expectations. The main job of the therapist is to advise the patient how to overcome the phobia. Only the patient can take the necessary steps, and therapists should remember that this can increase anxiety at first, and that practice demands persistence and courage. Encouragement should be given readily, especially when patients have to work at things that others find easy or enjoyable, such as going to parties or cinemas.

The rest of this chapter is concerned with the practicalities of treatment, and is divided into sections to cover the following topics: graded exposure, cognitive aspects of treatment, additional useful methods, complicating factors, maintenance of change, and alternative treatments.

Graded exposure

In practice, it is not always easy to stick precisely to the guidelines for exposure described above, and treatment demands much creativity from both patient and therapist. Exposure is described in detail here. Various other procedures can be combined with exposure, and these are described in the section on additional useful methods of treatment.

Devising practice tasks

It is frequently difficult to draw up a graduated list of tasks. A number of useful strategies are available when this happens. If the phobia is circumscribed, as in animal phobias or fears of specific illnesses, any means of communication can be used as a basis for practice. The patient may thus be able to extend the range of tasks by reading, writing, or talking about the phobic object; by watching relevant television programmes or films, or by listening to radio programmes, and so on.

Another strategy is to identify factors which moderate the level of anxiety experienced. For example, social situations may vary in difficulty according to the number of people present, their age, sex, and degree of authority in relation to the patient; or according to variables such as the formality of the situation, time of day, or ambient conditions. A hot room can provoke socially distressing symptoms such as sweating. It is always worth asking 'What would make this easier/harder for you?', and remembering that background factors such as feeling especially tired or having a bad cold may temporarily make practice somewhat harder.

Phobias are less similar than their definition would suggest, and social phobics probably vary most. Some social phobics are more comfortable when talking to strangers, and become more anxious the more intimate the relationship becomes. Others are more comfortable when talking to people they know well, and find it difficult to form new relationships. Agoraphobics also differ considerably from each other. Some find it easier to go out with their children, and others find this more difficult. In the first case the agoraphobic may be benefitting from the anxiety-reducing effect of caring for another person (Rachman 1978*b*), while in the second she may be thinking about what would happen to the children if the anxiety became unmanageably intense. Identifying such factors (which can include thoughts and beliefs) helps to determine which practice tasks will be appropriate.

Sometimes the situations that a patient avoids appear to be unconnected, for example speaking on the telephone, going to the hairdresser, and eating in the canteen at work. In this case one has to decide whether to build up separate hierarchies for approaching each situation or to use just one hierarchy. If the fears are connected by a single theme, such as thoughts of being trapped, it may be possible to order them on a single hierarchy. Common themes include rejection, hostility, worry about offending people, and loss of control (see also Wolpe 1982). An agoraphobic patient who had experienced a series of bereavements in quick succession, was unable to venture away from home for very long periods, as the longer she was away the more likely it seemed to her that a fatal accident might have occurred to a member of her family. In this case the important factor was 'time', and the theme 'fear of loss'.

The greater the variety of available practice tasks the better. Practice is hard work, and may be boring even though it provokes anxiety. Greater variety increases motivation, confidence, and the probability that improvement in one aspect of the phobia will generalize to other aspects (e.g. from waiting in the queue at the supermarket, to waiting in the dentist's waiting room, and waiting for someone who is late returning home). The strategies listed above can also be used to break tasks down into smaller steps when the next item on the hierarchy is too difficult. An agoraphobic patient who is unable to make the step from the small supermarket to the superstore may be able to do so if a friend waits in the car park, if she goes at a time when it is unlikely to be crowded, or if she visits it first just to look round. Encouraging patients to search for opportunities to approach instead of avoid helps them to adopt an 'ever-ready' attitude, and to overcome some subtle, but just as disruptive, types of avoidance. These include feeling reluctant to do something, postponing activities, prevarication, not thinking about the phobia, and giving excuses or rationalizations: 'It would be better to stay in today in case my mother/the electrician/the coalman calls', 'I can't carry all the shopping myself, so I'll wait until someone can come with me.' The therapist should make this point quite clear: e.g. 'Watch out for feeling that you want to get out of doing something. Try thinking instead about how you *could* do it.'

Conforming to the guidelines for exposure
The main guidelines suggest that exposure should be graduated, repeated, and prolonged, and tasks should be clearly specified in advance. In practice this is not always easy to achieve (Butler 1985), and three of the main difficulties are discussed here.

First, tasks cannot always be clearly specified in advance, repeated, or graduated, because phobic situations are variable and unpredictable (one never knows who will be at the party or when a big dog will come bounding down the road). One way over this problem is to stick less strictly to a hierarchy, and to practise a variety of tasks covering a range of difficulty in the same week. Another is to analyse the situation into its constituent parts. This gives patients the option of practising elements of situations over which they may have relative control, such as asking questions, listening attentively, and using non-verbal signs of communication. Asking questions is a particularly useful task for social phobics who feel uncomfortable if they think that attention is focused upon them, as this has the effect of shifting attention away from the speaker and on to the person who is expected to answer the question. Questions can also be prepared in advance.

Secondly, many situations, such as making a request, or signing a cheque, cannot be prolonged, so it is impossible for the patient to remain there until the fear subsides. Such tasks appear to be useful exposure tasks nevertheless, maybe because of their cognitive effect: they provide an opportunity to disconfirm expectations, for instance of being rejected or looking foolish.

The third problem is that of disengagement: a kind of 'absence of mind' which is especially likely when anxiety is high. Many phobic patients claim that they have already tried their own versions of exposure without success. One possible reason for this failure is that they were not fully involved in the things they were doing. Social phobics spontaneously report doing this, and, as we all know, it is relatively easy to go through the motions demanded by social situations without giving them our full attention: when listening to a boring story, or watching out for someone for instance. For phobic patients attention may be distracted by noticing internal sensations at these times (feeling hot and sticky, stomach churning, etc.). Unfortunately, symptom monitoring is more likely to maintain than to reduce symptoms, so disengagement prevents exposure being useful. Patients should be alerted to this, and told to make sure that they think about what they are doing when they practise: 'Dwell on the aspects of the situation that really bother you, so that you face up to them fully. If you ignore them, then the practice will not be nearly so useful. In fact it would be rather like trying to get used to heights by standing at the top of some steps with your eyes shut.'

Methods of applying exposure

Exposure as described above can be applied in many ways. As treatment has to be adapted to the patient's needs, phobics are frequently treated individually, and a 45-minute session is used to review progress and to plan exposure tasks to be completed outside the session. Home-based treatment, in which the partner or a relative of the patient is also taught about treatment and co-operates with the therapist to encourage, motivate, and advise the patient, has been found to be particularly successful with agoraphobics (Mathews *et al.* 1981). It is also extremely economical of therapist's time, good and lasting results having been obtained during research trials in five brief sessions.

Real-life exposure A major goal of treatment is to give patients the confidence to face the things they have been avoiding. This is why strong emphasis is placed on homework, and on the realistic setting of practice. Nevertheless, it can be useful to accompany a patient during exposure to begin with. This may reduce anxiety and/or make it easier to move faster up the hierarchy. It may also be a way of demonstrating particular skills, for instance in managing anxiety or social interactions. The danger is that patients will come to rely on their companion rather than on themselves, so it is advisable for patients to work independently if possible, and to phase out accompaniment well before treatment ends. Phasing out for an agoraphobic patient might progress, for example, from the companion riding on the bus with the patient to travelling in a different section of it, to meeting the patient at the bus stop, and, eventually, to meeting at the end of the journey.

Treatment in groups   Similarities between phobics also make them suitable for treatment in groups (e.g. Hafner and Milton 1977; Emmelkamp, Mersch, Vissia, and van der Helm 1985; Heimberg, Dodge, and Becker 1987). Members of a group are often able to share ideas about coping and give each other much support and encouragement.

Group exposure for agoraphobics is usually planned round a joint expedition to a town or shopping centre, from which base members of the group can work singly or in pairs according to their needs. Three group sessions in a week, each occupying about half a day, may produce sufficient improvement to motivate patients to continue working on their own with relatively little further support, some of which may be available from group members. Social phobics may also benefit from group treatment, and in both cases gains made during treatment sessions will be enhanced if they are backed up with individually designed homework assignments.

Imaginal exposure   In some cases, for example thunder phobia or fear of flying, it is not easy to arrange real-life exposure, and imaginal exposure has to be used instead. Imaginal exposure should be graduated in the same way as real-life exposure, and the two should be combined whenever possible. So the flying phobic may have to prepare for a journey in imagination, but will also benefit from reading or talking about flights, from visits to airports, and, of course, from regular travel by air (local clubs or flying schools are sometimes willing to help).

Imaginal exposure is difficult for the patient to do alone, and usually has to be directed by the therapist. The standard procedure involves asking the patient to imagine an item from the phobic hierarchy while he or she is as relaxed and comfortable as possible. Progressive muscular relaxation may be taught for this purpose if necessary (see p. 93). The patient starts by imagining the item vividly enough to induce anxiety, and goes on thinking about it in as much detail as possible until anxiety subsides. Items should be repeated until they provoke little anxiety, before moving on to the next item on the list. There is much variation in the ability to use imagery, so some patients may need a little prompting before they can get a clear image, and others need the therapist to describe the scene to them. For this reason, much of the exposure takes place during the treatment sessions. However, homework should still be an integral part of the treatment, and if the patient notes down the imaginal scenes used, and is shown how to keep a record of anxiety and how it changes during imaginal exposure, it should be possible to continue the exercise at home for half an hour each day.

Cognitive aspects of treatment

This section starts with a discussion of three general biases that influence the way phobic patients think about their difficulties, and may maintain symptoms if left unchallenged, and goes on to consider some more specific cognitive aspects of phobias and how to deal with them. Finally general cognitive factors that can accelerate or retard change are described. The cognitive methods described in Chapters 3 and 6 of this book are also useful in the treatment of phobic disorders, and further details of both theory and practice can be found in Beck, Emery, and Greenberg (1985).

Counteracting general biases

Biases affecting the past   In general, it is relatively easy to remember events which have particular significance (being criticized), or which were associated with strong emotions (stumbling at the top of a cliff). It is also relatively easy in any one mood to remember events that occurred when one was previously in that mood. This may account for why even simple phobias can dominate a person's life, and why, when distressed patients describe the events of the previous week they frequently report a series of more or less distressing events. In addition, successful exposure may be thought of as 'normal behaviour', or as what the patient ought to be able to do anyway, and therefore treated as a matter of course, and not registered, remembered, or reported. Once a patient is able to do something without thinking about it, such as fetching the children from school, cleaning the house, or using the telephone, the event may be overlooked. This bias maintains the 'problem-focused' perspective of the patient, and reduces the sense of achievement which brings hope, and forms the basis for further improvement. The therapist can help restore perspective by asking explicitly about successes, and focusing on the successful aspects of particular events. It may also help to ask patients to write down their successes. Those who can do this will feel encouraged, those who find it difficult may need to work against this bias.

Biases affecting the present

   1. *Hypervigilance*   Anxious people have a relatively low threshold for the perception of threats. This is like being tuned in to a particular wavelength. If well tuned in, as a spider phobic might be to the presence of spiders (or cobwebs), these things are noticed more readily. Flying phobics notice the small print in the newspapers referring to near misses, engine trouble, or the difficulties pilots experience in fog. This 'hypervigilance' is counterproductive, and maintains symptoms. Sometimes it is reduced by exposure, and sometimes relaxation or distraction may help (see below, p. 120). At other times the patient is only 'half-exposed' to the

phobic situation, and avoiding full exposure (e.g. by glancing at the newspaper but not reading it or thinking about it). In this case appropriate, engaged, exposure should be planned in the usual way.

2. *Misinterpretation* Anxious people tend to interpret events in a threatening way, especially if the events are ambiguous (Butler and Mathews 1983). Ambiguous events can be either external or internal. So when an agoraphobic notices her legs 'turn to jelly' she thinks she is about to collapse, and when a friend fails to return a telephone call a social phobic thinks he or she has been rejected. In both cases the interpretations should be identified, and then re-examined to find out whether there are alternative, and more plausible, explanations (methods for finding and examining alternatives are described in more detail in Chapters 3 and 6). Alternative explanations can then be tested during exposure. For instance, the agoraphobic may find that thinking she is about to collapse makes her legs feel wobbly, but that they feel stronger after starting a distracting conversation with her companion. She may therefore be able to accept that the feeling may be a symptom of anxiety rather than of imminent collapse, thus increasing the potential for her to control it. It is important to ask patients to find their own alternative explanations, so that they learn how to do this, although initially the therapist will often have to make suggestions.

An example may help to illustrate this point:

A claustrophobic felt breathless in a lift and became panicky when she thought she was going to suffocate:

Therapist So you felt breathless, and thought you might suffocate because there wasn't enough air?

Patient Yes.

Th. Might there be any other reason why you felt breathless just then?

Pt I can't think of one.

Th. Well, had you been hurrying to get the lift?

Pt No.

Th. Were you worried about getting into it?

Pt Yes—very!

Th. What other feelings did you have?

Pt Heart thumping, bit sweaty, had to hang on tight to my bag, breathing heavily.

Th. Did you know that anxious breathing and feeling tense can make you feel breathless?

Pt I think I had been told, but it didn't occur to me just then. Perhaps the feeling of breathlessness was another sign of anxiety.

Th. It certainly could be. How could you find out whether that was what was happening to you?

The next step would be to collect some relevant evidence, by for instance noticing what happens next time, or by overbreathing in the session (see also Chapter 3).

Biases affecting the future Anxiety also biases predictions about the future so that threatening events seem more likely, and it also seems more likely that the threat will be serious. 'Not only will the lift get stuck, but also there will be no one available to mend it.' This bias helps to explain the degree of anxiety experienced by phobic patients, and it may also affect their attitude to treatment. 'Not only will the treatment be painful, but also it may not help.' Once again the bias can only be dealt with if it has been identified, and phrased in the patient's own terms. Exposure is an effective way of testing specific predictions, and when the results of exposure are evaluated in relation to the initial predictions, behavioural and cognitive factors interact, and both kinds of change may occur. 'Not only did I pick up a spider, but also it did not run wild all over me (and I managed not to scream). In fact it seemed to want to get away from me.'

Specific cognitive aspects of phobias

Social phobia has obvious cognitive components: e.g. thoughts about being negatively evaluated, criticized, or rejected. The cognitive aspects of agoraphobia (Chambless and Goldstein 1982; Hardy 1982) are more likely to focus on thoughts about collapsing, or losing control. The thoughts of individual patients are often idiosyncratic, and can usually be identified by asking 'When you are feeling anxious, what is in your mind?' or 'What is the worst that could happen?' However, it does not follow that exposure to the worst fear would be helpful. In social phobia, for example, exposure to negative evaluation would be difficult to arrange, and probably distressing. Exposure to situations in which negative evaluation *could* occur, but which allows the worst fears to be disconfirmed, is more useful.

Superficially this may be the sort of exposure that takes place during the course of everyday life, and which appears not to be beneficial. In order to be made useful it should be set in the context of specific expectations, and then later re-evaluated. For example, social phobics may expect others to be unfriendly, or think that they do not wish to communicate. But if they smile at a stranger they may receive a smile in return, and if they ask a question or disclose something about themselves they may end up starting a conversation. These events disconfirm the original expectations (see also Chapters 3 and 6). In this way cognitive procedures help the patient assimilate the new information collected during exposure, and potentiate the change in thinking that is required for stable long-term change (Goldfried and Robins 1983; Kendall 1984).

Cognitive factors preventing engagement in treatment

Cognitive factors may also retard change, or even prevent the patient becoming engaged in treatment at all. Two examples should make this clear.

In the first case an agoraphobic girl, unable to travel alone at the time of referral, came for treatment shortly before she was due to start training as a systems analyst. She made rapid progress with graded exposure, and attended the first day at college. She then started to relapse, and was unable to make the journey again. The reason for the relapse did not become clear until she was asked what thoughts went through her mind as she left home. Her answers suggested she was ambivalent about going to college. Weighing up the pros and cons of going to college revealed a number of real difficulties, such as anxiety about leaving home, together with a strong desire to become independent, and worries about the suitability of her chosen career. These problems could not be solved in one short session, but the systematic examination of her thoughts brought her to the conclusion that the best way to find out what she needed to know in order to solve the problems was to attend her course lectures. This single session re-mobilized her and she went to college, and reported later that she had learned a useful strategy for the future: identify the problem carefully, pay attention to thoughts when feeling anxious, and then examine the problem systematically and coolly, perhaps with the help of another person.

In the second case, idiosyncratic thoughts prevented a socially phobic man from complying with homework assignments. The phobia was interfering severely with his life, and he had had previous brief courses of behavioural treatment, which had provided limited, temporary relief, and during which he had consistently failed to complete independent exposure assignments. When asked what he thought about these assignments he revealed a fear of changing based on the thought 'If I try out different roles, or change my behaviour, people won't like me.' This meant that people would think he was not genuine, which would make him less likeable and also make him feel guilty (for pretending to be something that he was not). Two lines of questioning proved fruitful: asking what alternative views there were, and asking whether it would matter to him if other people's behaviour varied over time. The discussion, in outline, made the following points: other people have many sides and many goals; behaviour changes as a function of goals, and variability could be interesting to others, making a person less boring. If others change their behaviour, this would not be important if you could still 'get on'; it might mean that you knew the person better, and could feel more confident in the relationship knowing that it could withstand variability. His conclusion was 'Therefore I can try to change', which he then did.

Additional useful methods of treatment

All the methods described in this section can be used in conjunction with the cognitive–behavioural methods already described. Two kinds of psychological techniques will be considered: techniques for controlling anxiety and behavioural techniques for preparing for, or enhancing exposure. Anxiolytic medication may also be helpful in some cases (but see p. 123).

Techniques for controlling anxiety

Generally, in order to be effective, exposure should provoke anxiety. These techniques do not undermine exposure by removing anxiety completely, but facilitate it by developing skills for controlling symptoms in phobic situations. Patients who can control their symptoms will move faster up the graded hierarchy, will be better able to deal with anticipatory anxiety, and will be able to apply these skills whenever they feel anxious in the future, thus increasing both self-confidence and generalization.

The three main techniques are *relaxation, distraction,* and *answering thoughts.* Many phobics have attempted to use these methods (and others as well) before coming for treatment. Indeed, they are very similar to the techniques recommended by 'common sense', but it is not easy to learn how to use them effectively. They need to be practised and applied systematically and regularly if they are to become useful, so it is always worth trying again during treatment to use a method that a patient has not previously found helpful. All the techniques are harder to use at high levels of anxiety, and should be applied first when anxiety is low.

Relaxation There are various ways of learning to relax, of which progressive muscular relaxation and applied relaxation are the best known (for further details see Chapter 3). The techniques can be practised at home using tape-recorded instructions, but patients should initially be taken through each new exercise during a treatment session. Relaxation will not be much help unless it can be applied quickly when needed. Therefore patients should learn to notice the early signs of anxiety, and use these as cues to relax. They should practise relaxing in successively shorter periods, and while sitting, standing, and carrying on with normal activities (pp. 89, 92–6). Patients often find it helpful to use a readily visible reminder, for example coloured paper dots to stick where they can easily be seen (on a wristwatch, mirrors, the telephone, etc.), and to make up a personal self-instruction or mnemonic ('keep calm', 'let go').

Ost has suggested, on the basis of his work on claustrophobia and social phobia, that patients whose predominant symptoms are physiological respond best to applied relaxation, which combines exposure with training in relaxation, and those whose predominant symptoms are behavioural respond best to purely behavioural treatments (Ost, Jerremalm, and Johansson 1981; Ost, Johansson, and Jerremalm 1982). However, the findings are not always clear cut (Michelson 1986) and it is likely that the combination of exposure and applied relaxation is helpful in most cases, with the exception of blood-injury phobia.

Applied tension In blood/injury phobia there is an atypical symptom pattern in which an initial increase in heart rate and blood pressure is followed by a sudden sharp drop, and often by fainting. In this case applied tension, in which the muscles of the arms, legs, and torso are tensed but not relaxed, will prevent the drop in blood pressure and fainting. The diphasic pattern of symptoms and reasons for feeling faint should be explained and the treatment presented as a coping skill that can be applied quickly and easily in almost any situation. First, patients learn, through modelling and practice, to tense gross body muscles for 10–15 seconds at a time, releasing them so as to return to 'normal' rather than to a relaxed state. Then they are exposed to a series of increasingly threatening blood/injury stimuli, so that they become skilled both at identifying the early signs of a drop in blood pressure and at reversing this by applying tension. This treatment is described in detail by Ost and Sterner (1987).

Distraction Paying attention to symptoms of anxiety perpetuates the vicious circle, and makes the symptoms worse. Distraction can reverse this process. This is a useful short–term strategy, but can be unhelpful in the long term if used as a way of avoiding symptoms, or of disengaging from exposure. There are many distraction techniques, most of which involve focusing on external factors, and many patients like to devise their own. Distraction is discussed in more detail in Chapters 3 and 6.

Identifying thoughts and finding alternatives The cognitive techniques for identifying and then examining the thoughts associated with anxiety can be used to control symptoms, for example of panic, as well as to challenge thoughts about the phobia. They are particularly useful for dealing with worries about future events or anticipatory anxiety, during which patients often underestimate their capacity for coping, and over-estimate the likelihood of disaster (see Chapters 3 and 6).

Additional behavioural techniques

Role-playing, rehearsal, and modelling are the most frequently used behavioural adjuncts to exposure. All of them can be seen as ways of preparing for exposure, and of increasing skills. Thus, they may be useful whatever the nature of the phobia. Training in assertiveness and in social skills are particularly useful in the case of social phobias, and applied tension, as mentioned above, in the case of blood/injury phobia.

Role-playing Role-playing and rehearsal are more often used in the treatment of social phobias than of other phobias, and a role-play may itself be a type of exposure. For example, a patient who finds it difficult to say no, or to be assertive, can practise being assertive during a role-play with the therapist. This has many advantages. It may reveal a lack of skill or knowledge, such as difficulty in moderating responses, or being unable to be assertive without being aggressive. The role-play can then be re-peated in various ways, until the patient discovers how he or she wishes to change. The technique can be quite simply introduced: e.g. 'I'll be your boss, and you show me how you would ask him to rearrange your time off.' Reversing the roles, so that the therapist plays the role of the patient, alerts the patient to the effects of unassertive behaviour on others, and to the advantages of being more assertive. It also clarifies exactly how to change. Role-plays are particularly useful in preparation for events such as interviews. Video (or audio) recordings, if available, allow patients to make the most of this type of practice. Watching the video provides accurate feedback as well as new information: for instance that they may feel much worse than they look.

Rehearsal This is a way of preparing for exposure. Many phobics find that their minds go blank when they are faced with phobic objects or situations, or when feeling panicky. Techniques for managing the symptoms of intense anxiety, especially panic attacks, should therefore be rehearsed. When this 'blankness' occurs in social situations it creates awkwardness, which rapidly increases anxiety. It is less likely to happen if appropriate strategies are rehearsed, and appropriate material prepared, such as lists of questions to ask, or topics to talk about. Social skills can be separately rehearsed and may improve with practice (Trower, Bryant, and Argyle 1978). Rehearsing difficult events, such as speaking in public, making a request, or introducing someone, both increases confidence and reduces anticipatory anxiety. Lastly, detailed rehearsal helps to reveal 'blocks' that might prevent exposure: 'What will you do if there is a queue in the post office?', 'How will you explain your trip to your mother-in-law?'

Modelling This is a less direct technique, in which the therapist demonstrates how to approach the phobic object, for example a snake or the edge of a high building, while being observed by the patient. Modelling is most effective when the model exhibits, and overcomes, anxiety, and it is suggested that observation of such a 'coping model' facilitates the patient's own coping skills. These might be poor either because patients do not know what to do, or because they are unable to think what to do at the time.

Anxiolytic medication

Patients usually wish to reduce their consumption of medication, and this should be encouraged (see below). In fact the beneficial effects of exposure may be attenuated if tranquillizers are used at the same time. This is because the patient attributes calmness in the face of the phobic object to the action of the drug, instead of to his or her own actions. Nevertheless, there are times when tranquillizers can be helpful. For example, they may make it possible to face a situation for which there has been no opportunity to prepare, or which is presently beyond the reach of the patient but cannot be postponed (this applies to those patients who have not previously taken tranquillizers also). Tranquillizers used to build confidence for practice without tranquillizers may be helpful, but their regular use should generally be discouraged.

Complicating factors in treatment

Affective disorders

Difficulties arise more frequently in the treatment of complex than of simple phobias. The most common complicating factor is the presence of another affective disorder, for example generalized anxiety, depression, or panic disorder. The latter is especially likely in the case of agoraphobia. Methods for dealing with affective disorders described in this book are consistent with treatment for phobic disorders, and can be carried out simultaneously in the case of generalized anxiety and panic. The combination of controlled breathing, cognitive restructuring, and exposure is very effective in the treatment of patients who suffer both from repeated panic attacks and from situational anxiety (see Chapter 3 and Clark, Salkovskis, and Chalkley 1985). Severe depression, associated with loss of energy, fatigue, and poor concentration can interfere with the ability to implement the treatment (e.g. carry out homework assignments). It may therefore need treating first. The decision as to which problem to tackle first can be made easier by considering whether the phobia is the primary problem, and is the main cause of the depression. If so, it is important to start working on the phobia as soon as possible. In both agoraphobia and social phobia, depression can exacerbate the phobia, by increasing the wish to withdraw. In these cases the easiest exposure tasks can be planned as part of a re-activation programme, and monitored using activity schedules in the way described in Chapter 6. Phobics who are depressed are easily discouraged. Special care should therefore be taken to plan exposure tasks that can be achieved, to rehearse these tasks so as to identify blocks in carrying them out, and to counteract biased interpretation of the results. These patients are particularly apt to think that residual signs of anxiety, for example, are a sign that they have failed, or that exposure will not work for them.

Personality disorders

Phobic disorders are not uncommon in patients with personality disorders. However, psychological treatments for phobias have a good chance of providing some relief, and the presence of a personality disorder is not a reason for withholding treatment. Progress may be relatively slow, and excessive hostility, dependency, or low self-esteem may, for example, interfere with the process of treatment. There is little point in working on a phobia in fits and starts, so if another problem prevents steady application of the treatment it would be better to treat the problems successively.

Dependence on drugs or alcohol

If the dependence is severe, which according to Amies, Gelder, and Shaw (1983) is likely to be the case in about 7 per cent of agoraphobics and about 20 per cent of social phobics, it should be dealt with before starting to work on the phobia. In some less severe cases, gradual withdrawal can be combined with techniques for controlling symptoms, so that the patient substitutes one form of control for another (more helpful) one. If consumption of alcohol or drugs is precipitated by phobic, or anticipatory, anxiety, it may be possible to reduce this need by extending the lower end of the graded hierarchy, and increasing the amount of practice time devoted to tasks that barely provoke anxiety. According to Bibb and Chambless (1986) about half of all agoraphobics have at some time used alcohol to control their symptoms.

It is generally agreed that anxiolytic medication should be stopped gradually. Withdrawal may be difficult, and is likely to be harder the longer the patient has been taking the drug. Short-acting drugs are the hardest to give up, and it is sometimes helpful to transfer the patient to a long-acting preparation prior to withdrawal. Patients should be warned that the symptoms that accompany withdrawal may be similar to those of anxiety. Cognitive–behavioural techniques may be used, e.g. to help patients attribute these symptoms to drug withdrawal rather than to an increase in 'normal' anxiety, or to additional illness, etc.

Problems with relationships

These are common in agoraphobia, and fears about the permanence or stability of a relationship may contribute to the maintenance of the phobia. It is quite hard to abandon someone who is clearly unable to cope on their own. Alternatively, a spouse may find it difficult to be sympathetic to the 'irrational' fears of the patient, might misunderstand the problem and how it can be dealt with, or might take over difficult tasks for the patient, and thereby prevent exposure. Nevertheless, a close relative or spouse can often be very helpful during treatment, and there is no clear evidence to suggest that having a difficult relationship is associated with failure to respond (Himadi, Cerny, Barlow, Cohen, and O'Brien 1986). Indeed, treatment may relieve some difficulties that arise when one partner has a problem. These include having fewer shared activities, more restrictions or additional pressures, and general dissatisfaction and irritability. It is therefore advisable to enlist the help of close family members as often as possible, and to explain treatment carefully to everyone involved.

General points

Difficulties such as failure to complete homework assignments or to comply with other requirements of treatment are best dealt with by using cognitive techniques. These can be used to explore the reasons for the failure, which range from practical difficulties in organizing time, to 'irrational' beliefs, for example that phobias are inherited or unchangeable. In order to start working collaboratively the patient must be able to accept the hypothesis that the treatment might work, and be willing to try it and see. So therapists should provide hope without guaranteeing success, which will depend, at least partly, on the patients' own efforts. They should encourage patients to work hard, while remembering that this takes much courage.

Sometimes patients do not carry out suggested tasks because the tasks seem to them to be unreasonable. Going up and down repeatedly in a department store lift, or climbing to the top of all the tall buildings in town, seems to be unrelated to everyday life, or unnecessary. Explaining that these are rather like the exercises that physiotherapists teach people after sports injuries is helpful. Artificial exercises can be stopped once they have served their purpose of re-establishing functional behaviours.

In general, when difficulties arise in treatment, the therapist should:

(1) establish that the rationale and treatment model have been adequately understood;

(2) determine whether symptoms can be attributed to anxiety, and, if so, explain that they are therefore potentially controllable;

(3) together with the patient, look for evidence that exposure has beneficial effects, noting that the biases described above may make it hard for the patient to find such evidence without help; and

(4) expect progress to be slower than otherwise.

Maintenance of change

If the lessons learned during treatment are made explicit, then the patient will also learn how to deal with the problem again should it recur. So preparation for dealing with future difficulties begins in the first session, and each success thereafter can be used to endorse the main point that phobias can be reduced by approaching rather than avoiding the phobic object or situation.

One advantage of the cognitive–behavioural approach is that it helps to structure discussion about reasons for improvement. The active, self-help rationale, and the emphasis on independent homework, strongly suggest that change results from the patient's work. So when improvement has started the therapist should make sure that the patient understands why the phobia is diminishing, for example by asking; 'Why was it easier to go into the supermarket this time than last time?', 'What made the difference?' Occasions of exposure vary so much that, even when the same task is repeated, many patients think that change is due to chance, or that it is an indirect effect of talking to the therapist. If the therapist suggests an explanation consistent with the rationale, for instance 'Is it possible that you felt more confident because you have got used to smaller shops now?', or 'because you got interested in adding up the cost of the things in your basket and forgot to think about how you were feeling?', then future exposure can be planned as a test of this explanation (more practice, or more distraction).

In addition, by asking 'What does that [the 'easy' trip to the supermarket] tell us?', the therapist can highlight important implications of the patient's new experience, and look for answers that fit with the treatment rationale. Examples would be: 'The more I practise the better I feel', 'I *can* go to the supermarket without having a panic attack', 'I can control these symptoms after all.' If patients both understand the rationale and practise exposure tasks, they have the opportunity to learn that they are responsible for improvement, and to disconfirm their worst fears. But they may not make best use of this opportunity, even when they have the evidence in front of them in the form of record sheets, unless the topic is discussed. Conclusions can be written down for future reference.

A number of other strategies also increase the probability that gains will be maintained.

Expectations for the future should always be discussed, as fluctuations in phobic anxiety are common, and minor set-backs are likely. This can be distressing if not expected, so warning patients to expect them is a good way of helping them remain hopeful and active when they occur. Most patients are aware that the amount of phobic anxiety experienced varies not only with the difficulty of the phobic situation, but also with indices of stress, such as fatigue, physical health, and the number of other problems in their lives. So relapses are more likely at a time of stress, and it may be unrealistic to expect a 'phobia-free future' in some cases. Nevertheless, a relapse, whether or not it is precipitated by stress, can be dealt with using the same methods, and further deterioration can be prevented if action is taken early. In general, relapse will be less likely if regular exposure is planned, even though this may have to be contrived, for instance by becoming a blood donor or by choosing to stand in the longest instead of the shortest queue at the supermarket.

Before treatment ends it helps to draw up a plan for the future, or 'blueprint', specifying how to handle future difficulties. This should be phrased in the patient's words, and should list all the strategies that were useful. As well as reminders about exposure and conclusions from the discussions about improvement mentioned above, it should include self-

Table 4.3 Example of blueprint

1. Don't shy away from doing things that are difficult. Do them quickly, before you have time to start worrying again.
2. Remember how many times you had to visit the post office before you felt OK. Now even the shops in town are OK.
3. Do the relaxation exercises properly once a month as a reminder.
   (NB Write this in diary so it doesn't get forgotten).
4. Don't get bogged down in the horror of it all: it's more encouraging to think about the progress I have made before, and what to do next.
   Write down the steps.
5. Look back at the old record sheets. They show which order I did things in before, and how much practice I had to do before it got easier.
6. Go into the supermarket alone sometimes. Don't always go with the family, even if it's more convenient to do so.
7. Plan to go to all the school concerts next term.
8. Breathe slowly when you feel bad.
9. Watch out for thinking the worst will happen. It hasn't happened yet.

If things get difficult again

   Remember set-backs happen to everyone. You can't get through life without having some bad times.

   Work out how to practise in steps. Write the steps down, and make sure you tackle them one by one. Write down how you felt each time.

   Practise every day. There's no need to try to run before you can walk.

   Don't bottle it up. Talk to the family about what's happening.

monitoring techniques such as keeping records and diaries, and additional techniques such as relaxation. An example is given in Table 4.3.

One of the aims of treatment is for the patient to develop the confidence to cope with the problem independently. Therapists can further this aim by gradually handing over responsibility for the work of the session, by becoming progressively less directive, and by leaving increasingly long intervals between sessions, so as to phase out help gradually. Follow-up sessions, scheduled a relatively long time after treatment has ended (e.g. three months later), keep the patient motivated after more frequent contact has ceased.

Alternative treatments

Alternative treatments that do not use exposure have not been found to be as effective as those that do. However, the matter is not so simple as it might seem. Once a phobic patient feels better he or she will be able to enter the phobic situation. Once he or she enters the phobic situation, exposure is taking place. Therefore any effective treatment will lead to exposure, although this may not follow the guidelines for optimal effectiveness.

There are two main alternatives; pharmacotherapy and another form of psychotherapy. Few comparative trials have been completed. Both anxiolytic and antidepressant medication, usually in small doses, have been found to be helpful in the short term. However, neither class of drugs appears to produce stable long-term gains, unless administration of the drug is combined with exposure (e.g. Telch, Agras, Taylor, Roth, and Gallen 1985). Beta blockers (e.g. propranolol) are widely used as a treatment for performance anxiety, for example by professional musicians, in order to control the symptoms that interfere with performance. But anxiolytics in general have the disadvantage that they may be difficult to give up, and may have long-term harmful consequences (Tyrer and Owen 1984). Using them regularly may also be a way of avoiding the symptoms of anxiety, or the difficulties of learning how to manage the phobia, and therefore serve indirectly to maintain symptoms.

Psychoanalysis and psychodynamic therapy are not effective in reducing avoidance behaviour (see accounts by, for example, Mavissakalian and Barlow 1981; DuPont 1982; Klerman 1986). Indeed, there is some general agreement that no treatment in which patients play a passive role is helpful, and that it is extremely important that patients return to the situations that they avoid if they are to improve. Graded exposure has the advantage that it is very economical of therapist time while other forms of psychotherapy take longer.

The effectiveness of exposure

Exposure-based treatments for phobias have been remarkably successful (see, for example, Rachman and Wilson 1980; Barlow and Wolfe 1981; Mathews 1985; Marks 1987). Indeed, the success in treating phobias contributed much to the widespread acceptance of behavioural approaches to psychological problems. There is good evidence that they also have more generalized benefits, such as improvements in relationships, and enhanced self-confidence.

The model upon which they are based is relatively simple and well grounded in learning theory, and more detailed guidelines about the best way to proceed have been derived from extensive clinical research. The main findings show that exposure works, and that the effects are not simply due to non-specific factors (Paul 1966; Gelder, Bancroft, Gath, Johnston, Mathews, and Shaw 1973; Mathews *et al.* 1981); that in some cases the effects can be potentiated by adding anxiety management or cognitive procedures (Butler, Cullington, Munby, Amies, and Gelder 1984; Butler 1989; Mattick and Peters 1988); and that improvement is maintained for many years (Munby and Johnston 1980). Other findings suggest that variations in the level of anxiety during exposure make little difference to outcome, and that, in general, prolonged exposure is more effective than brief exposure (see, for example, Stern and Marks 1973).

However, we still do not understand exactly how exposure works. When a patient improves, changes are observed in both behaviour and thinking. Exposure has cognitive as well as behavioural effects and, as has been described above, it frequently incorporates a variety of cognitive procedures. Distinctions between cognitive and behavioural procedures have only recently been clarified. Some of the aspects of exposure that used to be described as 'non-specific', such as arriving at a realistic interpretation of the week's events, or at accurate expectations for the future, or dealing with reservations about treatment, are now described in cognitive terms. Cognitive therapies are sufficiently well developed, and the theories upon which they are based are sufficiently well worked out, to provide a greatly improved structure for these aspects of treatment. Nevertheless, the simplicity of the theory should not tempt therapists into working mechanistically, or suggest to them that therapy will be easy. No two people are ever exactly the same, and working with phobic patients requires much creativity from the therapist. Because these treatments have a high chance of being successful, it is both rewarding and interesting.

Recommended reading

Beck, A. T., Emery G. and Greenberg, R. (1985). *Anxiety disorders and phobias: a cognitive perspective*. Basic Books, New York.

Butler, G. (1989). Issues in the application of cognitive and behavioural strategies to the treatment of social phobia. *Clinical Psychology Review*, in press.

Chambless, D. L. and Goldstein, A. J. (ed.) (1982). *Agoraphobia: multiple perspectives on theory and treatment*. John Wiley, New York.

Dupont, R. L. (ed.) (1982). *Phobia: a comprehensive summary of modern treatments*. Brunner/Mazel, New York.

Marks, I. M. (1978). *Living with fear; understanding and coping with anxiety*. McGraw Hill, New York.

Mathews, A. M., Gelder, M. G. and Johnston, D. W. (1981). *Agoraphobia: nature and treatment*. Guilford Press, New York.

Mavissakalian, M. and Barlow, D. H. (1981). *Phobia: psychological and pharmacological treatment*. Guilford Press, New York.

Michelson, L. and Ascher, M. (ed.) (1986). *Anxiety and stress disorders: cognitive–behavioral assessment and treatment*. Guilford Press, New York.

Rachman, S. (1978). *Fear and courage*. W. H. Freeman, San Francisco.

Weekes, C. (1972). *Peace from nervous suffering*. Hawthorn books, New York.

Wolpe, J. (1961). The systematic desensitization treatment of neurosis. *Journal of Nervous and Mental Diseases* **132**, 189–203.

5

Obsessional disorders

Paul M. Salkovskis and Joan Kirk

Obsessive–compulsive disorders are not a new phenomenon; the notable fictional example is Lady Macbeth. John Bunyan and Charles Darwin are amongst the many prominent people afflicted in the past by this disabling disorder. Many of the early descriptions emphasized the religious content of obsessions, which provides an important clue to the nature of the disorder. The content of obsessions reflects the principal concerns of the time, whether these are the work of the devil, contamination by germs and radiation, or the risk of acquired immune deficiency syndrome (AIDS).

During the nineteenth century, obsessions ceased to be regarded as the work of the devil and were seen as part of depression. After the turn of the century, obsessions began to be viewed as a syndrome in their own right. In his early writings, Freud proposed that obsessional symptoms represented regression to a pregenital anal–sadistic stage of development, with conflicts between aggressiveness and submissiveness, dirt and cleanliness, order and disorder. Subsequent psychodynamic formulations imply that obsessional patients have 'weak ego boundaries' and may therefore be 'pre-psychotic'. Such views may result in inappropriate treatment (such as the prescription of neuroleptics) and opposition to behavioural treatment on the grounds that this will undermine the patient's defences and precipitate psychosis.

Prior to the 1960s the prognosis for obsessional disorders was poor, with recommended treatments being support, long-term hospitalization, and psychosurgery. Against this unpromising background, Meyer (1966) reported the successful behavioural treatment of two cases of chronic obsessional neurosis, followed by a series of successful case reports. Meyer's work heralded the application of psychological models to obsessions and the development of effective behavioural treatments. He took as his starting point animal models of compulsive behaviour (see, for example, Metzner 1963), which proposed that ritualistic behaviours were a form of learned avoidance. Behaviour therapy for phobias, based on similar models, had proved successful in the treatment of phobic avoidance through desensitization, but attempts to generalize these methods to obsessional rituals had been unsuccessful. Meyer argued that it was necessary to tackle avoidance behaviour directly by ensuring that rituals did not take place within or between treatment sessions. His approach anticipated cognitive approaches in that he emphasized the role of the expectations of harm in obsessions and the importance of invalidating these expectations during treatment. Meyer included graded exposure to obsessional situations in his treatment, but this was regarded as peripheral to the major task of preventing ritualizing. However, at around the same period, Rachman, Hodgson, and Marks (1971) developed treatment methods in which exposure to feared situations was the central feature. These differing approaches were subsequently incorporated into a highly effective programme of behavioural treatment incorporating the principles of *exposure* with *response prevention*. More recently, cognitive methods have been incorporated, based on the view that obsessional thoughts are exaggerations of important aspects of normal cognitive functioning (Salkovskis 1988a).

The nature of the problem

Obsessions are unwanted and intrusive thoughts, images (mental pictures), and impulses (urges). They are usually regarded by the individual experiencing them as repugnant, senseless, unacceptable, and difficult to dismiss. A wide range of *triggering stimuli* can provoke obsessions. Once an obsessions occurs, it is accompanied by feelings of *discomfort* or anxiety, and the urge to *neutralize* (put right) the obsession (or its consequences). Neutralizing often takes the form of *compulsive behaviour* (such as washing or checking). Sometimes this behaviour is accompanied by a subjective sense of resistance to performing the compulsive behaviour. Compulsive or neutralizing behaviours are usually carried out in a stereotyped way or according to idiosyncratically defined 'rules', and are associated with temporary anxiety relief or the expectation that, had ritualizing not been carried out, anxiety would have increased. Neutralizing behaviours include changes in mental activity, such as deliberately thinking a different thought in response to an obsessional thought. Patients also develop *avoidance behaviours*, particularly avoiding situations which could trigger obsessional thoughts. An important feature of obsessional problems is that, on calm reflection, patients usually regard their obsessional thoughts and behaviour as senseless or excessive, at least in degree.

For example, a patient had the thought (obsession) that she might pass cancer on to her family and scrubbed her hands (compulsive behaviour) with disinfectant up to 40 times each day, for between 5 and 20 minutes each time. She knew that cancer is not transmitted by contact (although she could not be 100 per cent certain), and most of the time realized that washing was both futile and upsetting. However, when she experienced the obsessional thoughts, she became anxious and distressed and only by washing could she gain the certainty that she had not harmed her family. Her washing was stereotyped, involving the washing of each finger and part of the hand in a strict order (otherwise having to repeat the wash), employing stilted, stereotyped movements.

Clinically, obsessional–compulsive phenomena have generally been divided into obsessional thoughts without obvious compulsive behaviours (*Obsessional ruminations*) and obsessions with overt compulsions (*Obsessional ritualizing*) (Rachman and Hodgson 1980). This simple division of obsessive–compulsive phenomena into overt and covert mani-festations is superficially appealing, but may mask important functional qualities. The psychological model of obsessions (Rachman 1978*a*), emphasizes the functional significance of overt *and* covert compulsions (known as neutralizing behaviours). On this basis, obsessions are the intrusive thoughts, images, and impulses which are *involuntary* and are accompanied by increased anxiety, whereas neutralizing (overt and covert compulsive behaviour) is *voluntary* behaviour which the patient carries out with the intention of reducing anxiety (or the risk of harm). Patients' covert neutralizing behaviour can be identical in many respects to the obsessional thoughts. An example was a patient who had the obsessional thought that a stranger would be violent towards him; if this thought occurred, he would have to make himself have the thought again (i.e. an even number of times) in order to feel better. This could lead to long sequences of intrusion–neutralizing–intrusion–neutralizing–intrusion . . . and so on, giving a chain of thoughts which differed in function, but not in their content.

Content of obsessions

Obsessional thoughts, impulses, and images usually concern topics which are personally repugnant. The more personally unacceptable an intrusive thought, the more uncomfortable an individual will be on its occurrence. This explains the apparent paradox of the priest who thinks blasphem-ously, the pacifist with violent impulses, or the concerned mother who has thoughts of harming her child. The more common content areas for obsessions are shown in Table 5.1, together with examples of the types of thoughts and associated compulsive behaviours.

Types of compulsive behaviour

A theme common to many patients with obsessive–compulsive disorder concerns future harm and the urge to prevent it, usually accompanied by attempts to do so. However, compulsive cleaning patients have been found to differ from patients who mainly exhibit checking behaviour (Rachman and Hodgson 1980). *Cleaning* obsessions resemble phobias, and are characterized by a greater range of 'contaminated objects' and with more avoidance behaviours designed to prevent harm; when avoid-

Table 5.1 Principal content areas with examples of obsessions and associated compulsive behaviour

Example of obsession	Example of compulsive behaviour
Contamination (ideas of being harmed by contact with substances believed to be dangerous, e.g. dirt, germs, urine, faeces, blood, radiation, poison, etc.)	
The hairdresser's comb had AIDS virus on it	Ring doctor; check body for symptoms of AIDS; wash hands and hair; sterilize all things which others may touch
Physical violence to self or others, by self or others	
I will harm my baby	Won't be alone with the baby; seeks reassurance; hides knives, plastic bags
Death	
Images of loved ones dead	Imagines the same people alive
Accidental harm (not due to contamination or physical violence, e.g. accident, illness)	
I may have hit someone with my car	Telephones hospitals, police; retraces route driven; checks car for marks
Socially unacceptable behaviour (e.g. shouting, swearing, losing control of behaviour)	
I am going to shout an obscenity	Tries to 'keep control' of behaviour; avoids social situations; asks others whether behaviour was acceptable in particular situation
Sex (preoccupation with sexual organs, unacceptable sexual acts)	
I am going to commit rape	Avoids being alone with women; tries to keep mind off sexual thoughts
Religion (e.g. blasphemous thoughts, religious doubts)	
I am going to offer my food to the devil	Prays; seeks religious help/confession; offers other things to God
Orderliness (things being in the right place, actions done in the right way, according to a particular pattern or number)	
If I don't clean my teeth in the right way, I'll have to do it again until I get it right	Repeats action a 'good' number of times; repeats until it 'feels right'
Nonsense (meaningless phrases, images, tunes, words, strings of numbers)	
Hears (in head) tune of a TV sports programme while reading	Repeats action until manages to read the same passage without the tune occurring

ance fails, the patient 'puts things right' by washing or cleaning. Thus, a patient who was worried about bringing germs into the house avoided buying things from particular shops; when she bought groceries, she washed them seven times so that germs were not brought into the house to infect the family. In *checking* obsessions, the patient strives to be sure that he has not been responsible for harm coming to himself or others. For example, a patient was worried about people coming to harm because of his carelessness; he would frequently turn his car round and speak to pedestrians to ensure that he had not inadvertently knocked into them as he drove by. There is a considerable overlap between the presentation of cleaners and checkers, and the functional significance of the compulsive behaviours (checking and cleaning) is identical. A similar distinction can be made with respect to obsessions without overt compulsions; mental (covert) compulsions can be roughly classified as restitution (putting right, like cleaning) and verification (like checking).

The psychological model of obsessive–compulsive disorder

The core features of obsessional problems are:

(1)   avoidance of objects or situations which trigger obsessions;

(2)   obsessions; and

(3)   compulsive behaviours and thought rituals.

Patients attempt to avoid obsessions by keeping away from situations or objects which trigger them. For example, a patient with violent impulses locked away all the knives in her house and made sure she was never alone with the people involved in her violent thoughts. Many patients limit their activities and environment to minimize contact with their obsessional stimuli, such as the checker who moved to a house with only one door, and only left the house if someone else locked the door and kept the key for her.

When, despite avoidance, obsessions occur, rituals usually result. These are more recognizable as characteristic obsessional behaviours, particularly when they are repetitive and associated with temporary anxiety relief or the expectation that, without ritualizing, anxiety would have worsened. As the obsessions persist and rituals become extensive, patients can present with ritualistic behaviour apparently *independent* of the obsessions: when confronted with an obsessional 'trigger', the patient neutralizes before the obsession occurs, and thereby prevents its occurrence. For example, a patient checked her door 50 or 60 times whenever she used it so that the original obsessional thought of being burgled never occurred.

Table 5.2   The psychological model of obsessive–compulsive disorder

1. Obsessions are thoughts which have become associated with anxiety (conditioned). The anxiety would usually decline if the thoughts recurred without further conditioning; in obsessional thoughts it does not decline because of the occurrence of compulsions.

2. Compulsions are voluntary behaviour (overt or thoughts) which terminate exposure to these thoughts and may provide relief from the anxiety or discomfort produced. Compulsive behaviour becomes more likely as it is reinforced by anxiety relief. In this way, compulsions provide a short-term escape from distress.

3. In addition, patients learn that avoidance behaviours can prevent the obsessional thoughts (and anxiety), so that exposure to the thoughts occurs less often.

The psychological model is used as the basis for cognitive–behavioural assessment and treatment. The basic assumptions are shown in Table 5.2. In summary, avoidance prevents exposure to the feared thoughts, and compulsions (overt or covert) terminate exposure; both types of behaviour prevent the patient from confronting (being exposed to) his feared thoughts and situations. Compulsions and avoidance thus prevent reappraisal: if the patient stops these behaviours, he (or she) discovers that the things he is afraid of do not actually happen.

Treatment thus involves exposing patients to the feared stimuli, while encouraging them to block any behaviours which prevent or terminate this exposure. At the same time, reappraisal of the fears is encouraged so that patients discover that the things which they fear do not actually happen.

Assessment

Assessment consists of a detailed clinical interview, self-monitoring, homework assignments, and direct observation. The main purposes of assessment are:

(1)   to agree a problem list;

(2)   to reach a psychological formulation of each problem, including predisposing factors, precipitants and present maintaining factors;

(3)   to assess suitability for psychological treatment; and

(4)   to provide a means of assessing progress.

As usual in cognitive–behavioural treatment, assessment and treatment merge into each other, so that a crucial aspect of assessment is the response to exposure (without neutralizing) both within and between therapy and homework sessions. The assessment is covered in greater detail in this chapter than in others because, once the links between triggers, thoughts, neutralizing activities, and avoidance are clear, then the therapist and patient can rapidly implement a treatment plan. The treatment, based on the two principles of exposure and response prevention, is relatively straightforward once the detailed assessment is complete.

Factors determining suitability for treatment

Decisions about treatment suitability largely focus on whether the obsessional problem is primary, or secondary to another psychiatric or organic disorder, and willingness to engage in treatment. If there is evidence that the obsessional problem developed immediately after the onset or during an exacerbation of another disorder which is still present, then treatment of the primary disorder is indicated (particularly depression). However, it is not unusual to find that obsessions which have been defined as secondary persist despite resolution of the primary problem and require subsequent intervention. Although the incidence of schizophrenia in obsessionals is no greater than for the general population, schizophrenic patients often show obsessional features. These symptoms are clearly distinguishable from true obsessional disorder because they are linked to other, first-rank symptoms; the attribution is to external forces; and (often) the patients fail to regard them as senseless. In patients who have been previously diagnosed as schizophrenic it is important to verify this diagnosis, because sometimes severe obsessional patients are labelled 'psychotic' with no justification other than the severity of the disorder. Organic factors should be considered in the (rare) cases of primary obsessional slowness and when compulsions are mechanical, 'primitive', and appear to lack intellectual contact and intentionality.

Reluctance to agree to treatment is an important factor; treatment is based on a collaborative relationship and active participation in treatment. Non-compliance can be overcome using cognitive techniques; if, however, the patient is unwilling to participate actively in treatment despite efforts to deal with objections and worries (Salkovskis and Warwick 1988), then treatment is unlikely to have any impact and should not be attempted.

First steps in the initial interview

The initial interview follows the general format outlined in Chapter 2. Thus, it begins with open questions, such as, 'Could you tell me about the problems you've been having recently.' The interviewer then narrows the scope a little by asking for an account of the way the problem has affected the patient over the last week; once a general picture of current problems is obtained, the focus moves to recent examples of the problem. The therapist should look for clues about possible functional links, such as events which tend to trigger off particular thoughts or behaviours. If the obsessional problem is highly involved and the patient is giving an over-inclusive account, it may be useful to direct the interview with statements such as, 'I am especially interested in upsetting thoughts which go through your mind and anything you feel you have to do because of the thoughts.' Obsessions may also involve intrusive images ('mental pictures') and impulses ('feeling an urge to do something you don't really want to do'), and the patient should be questioned about these. A summary of assessment procedures is presented in Table 5.3, and elaborated below.

Detailed behavioural analysis

Once the general picture has been obtained, the interview progresses to a detailed analysis, using specific examples which typify the problem. This can be structured in terms of response systems (pp. 8–9), where the therapist enquires about cognitive, subjective/emotional, physiological, and behavioural aspects of the problem. Direct questions are used, such as, 'Now I want to go over the type of things which you *do* in relation to your problem.' Information is sought about the obsessional thoughts and their triggers, avoidance and ritualizing in each response system. At each step, the accuracy of the assessor's understanding is checked by the use of summaries.

For example, with the behaviour of an obsessional washer, 'Let's see if I have a full picture of what you *do* when bothered by the obsessions. There are a number of things which you do because of your problem; you try to avoid going to places where dirty people may have been. If you can't avoid these places, then you avoid touching anything you think dirty people may have touched. If you have to touch things, then you usually wash your hands a number of times, until they feel 'right'; this can take between half an hour and two hours. If you have touched anything in your house before you washed, you have to scrub it until you are

Table 5.3 Summary of assessment procedures

General description of nature of the problem
  Open questions
  Recent and specific example, described chronologically
  Description of situations in which obsessions are most likely or least likely, looking for functional links ('triggers' or maintaining factors)

Detailed specific description and behavioural analysis
  (1) *Cognitive and subjective*
     Form of obsessions: thoughts, images, or impulses (urges)

Table 5.3   *(Cont'd)*

Content of obsessions (see Table 5.1)
Cognitive factors triggering obsessions (e.g. other thoughts)
Cognitive neutralizing (mentally checking or 'putting right')
Cognitive avoidance
Perceived alienness and subjective resistance to obsessions
Senselessness
(2) *Emotional*
Nature of mood changes associated with obsessions (anxiety, depression, discomfort); nature of the association, i.e. whether mood changes precede or follow obsessions, or both
(3) *Behavioural*
Triggers for the obsessional thoughts
Overt avoidance of (not going into) situations in which obsessional thoughts might occur
Overt active avoidance; behaviours which are intended to control occurrence of the obsessions
Overt ritualizing
Asking for reassurance, asking others to carry out tasks which would otherwise be associated with the obsession
(4) *Physiological*
Triggers
Physiological changes consequent on obsessions

Background to the problem
History
Development of the problem and its components (obsessions, neutralizing, avoidance)
Degree of handicap in work, sexual, social, and domestic functioning
Significant relationships
Benefits and costs of change

Behavioural tests
In the clinic
In target situations

Direct observation
By relatives
During home visits

Questionnaires
Maudsley Obsessive-Compulsive Inventory
Compulsive Activity Checklist
Beck Depression Inventory
Beck Anxiety Inventory

Self-monitoring
Diaries of mood, thoughts, ritualizing, behavioural by-products

totally satisfied that it is clean. Sometimes you have to do the washing even although you have not touched anything, but feel unsure. Also, you repeatedly ask your wife whether she thinks you might have passed anything on to her or the children. Have I got that right? . . . Have I missed anything out?'

Cognitive and subjective aspects

The principal focus when evaluating the subjective experience of obsessions is on the *form* (whether thought, image, or impulse) and *content* of the intrusions. The content will be idiosyncratic and should be assessed in detail. The patient is asked questions such as, 'Do upsetting thoughts, urges, or mental pictures come uninvited into your mind?', 'What kind of thoughts are these?', 'Could you describe the last time you were troubled by these?' Many patients show signs of experiencing obsessional thoughts during the interview (becoming distracted or upset); it is particularly helpful to question the patient about what happened at these points. For example, the patient is asked, 'Did you have one of these thoughts just now?', 'What went through your mind just then?'; this is then followed through in detail.

Subjective *triggers* for the obsessional thoughts can be assessed at the same time as content of the thoughts. Triggers can include non-obsessional thoughts or images. Examples provided by the patient earlier in the interview can help illustrate what is being sought. For example, a patient was asked, 'You mentioned before that when you were bothered by the thoughts yesterday, the thoughts had been set off by reading an article in the paper about a mother who had mistreated her children. Are there other things which can set off the thoughts in this way?'

Covert neutralizing   Mental rituals should also be assessed. The patient should be carefully questioned about recent occasions on which the thought occurred, focusing on thoughts or images the patients tried to form in their minds, or any other mental activity which they deliberately tried to form or carry out, e.g. 'Did you try to get any other thoughts? Did you try to think things to put the thought right?' In more chronic cases, the content of the obsessions can be obscured by overt or covert neutralizing. This can be assessed by asking the patient to provoke the obsession, prevent neutralizing, and then describe the resulting phenomena.

For example, a woman complained that she repeated almost every action carried out during the day—getting dressed, walking across rooms, picking up objects, closing doors, etc. She could not say why she repeated things other than because of a feeling that she 'had to'. She readily agreed to perform one of her most troublesome tasks (filling the kettle with water to make tea) without neutralizing (i.e. without emptying the water and starting again). On filling the kettle, she reported the thought, 'If I do not do that again, it will be the last time I do it', followed by the thought, 'That would leave my children motherless.' She recognized the thought as one she had frequently experienced in the past, but was much less common now that she routinely repeated actions.

Avoidance   This may occur cognitively, with the patient either trying not to think things or frantically trying to think of other things. This can not only prevent exposure and reappraisal as described above, but also paradoxically increases preoccupation by focusing thoughts on things which the patients does not want to think about (p. 147).

Many of the salient characteristics of obsessions are subjective and can only be assessed verbally; there are no external criteria for a sense of alienness, for example. It is nonetheless crucial to establish whether or not patients believe the obsessional thoughts to be integral to their personality. It is also important to establish the extent to which patients have resisted both the obsessions and the associated rituals, as this will affect their acceptance of the rationale for response prevention. The absence of resistance does not imply that the patient is not a true obsessional; many patients, particularly those with cleaning rituals, show little or no resistance. It is also necessary to assess the extent to which obsessional thoughts and behaviour are viewed as senseless; if patients are convinced, even when not particularly anxious, that the thoughts are sensible, then they would not normally be regarded as obsessional. This is especially so when the patient feels the thoughts have an external origin (e.g. 'Radio waves coming through the wall make me wash'). However, judgements of senselessness change as a function of anxiety. For example, a man was able to recognize the irrationality of repeating prayers in a stereotyped way in response to obsessional images. Despite this general belief, he stated that, 'If I get these thoughts when I am praying, then I really am being sinful and must atone.' Most patients believe their behaviour to have a rational *basis*, even though it has become exaggerated in its present form. Treatment often depends on agreement that the highly improbable 'risks' associated with stopping the obsessional behaviour do not justify the costs incurred; e.g. hairwashing for eight hours each day is not justified by the reduction in the risk of contaminating others.

Emotional factors

Mood changes associated with the occurrence of the obsessions (particularly anxiety, discomfort, and depression) should be examined. There is a tendency to assume that the predominant emotion will be anxiety; however, many patients report the emotional impact of the obsession as being of discomfort, specific tension, anger, or repugnance. To clarify this, it helps to use analogies, e.g. 'Is the feeling like you get before an examination?', 'Is it like being very fed up?' It should be established whether mood changes precede or follow the obsessional thoughts and behaviours.

Behaviours

The assessment of behaviours is crucial. Any behaviours which may trigger the obsessional thoughts, prevent exposure to them (avoidance), terminate them, or prevent reappraisal are examined in detail.

Behaviours often serve as *triggers*, because the scope for having caused harm to oneself or others is considerable. A common example is driving a car; one patient had the thought that he had knocked someone over whenever he turned left, and would often turn round and drive back to make sure that no one was hurt. Turning left thus served as a trigger for the obsessional thought and the urge to check.

Active and passive avoidance are both investigated by asking, 'Are there any things you do to prevent the obsessions occurring?' and, 'Are there any things you don't do because they might set the obsession off?'

Overt rituals are readily elicited by asking 'When you have one of these thoughts do you do things to put things right or stop things going wrong?', 'Do you ever feel that you *should* do things of this type, even if you seldom actually do?' Covert rituals (neutralizing) sometimes take the place of overt ritualizing at times when the patient is prevented from using overt behaviours. Patients should be routinely asked about these. An additional neutralizing behaviour often prominent in obsessional patients is the seeking of reassurance. This serves two functions: first, a checking function ('Do my hands look clean to you?'); secondly, reassurance allows the patient to spread responsibility to trusted individuals—if there truly were a problem, the other person would take action or otherwise comment. Reassurance thus terminates exposure to the upsetting thought and affects the degree to which reappraisal can take place. Neutralizing behaviour (including reassurance) can be stored up and carried out some time after the occurrence of the initial obsessional thoughts.

For example, when a patient was unable to wash her hands for eight hours during a day trip, she 'stored up' the washing until the next day when she washed herself and anything she might have touched continuously for two hours. Patients may also develop subtle or delayed forms of neutralizing: one woman repeatedly sought reassurance from her family that she had not accidentally harmed someone; as the family became increasingly reluctant to respond she began to ask irrelevant questions (e.g. 'Is it going to rain?' asked on a clear day); she stored up 'no' responses and used them later when she was filled with obsessional doubt about another issue.

For each behaviour, detailed information is sought about the actual form it takes and its duration, frequency and consistency ('Do you always do this?'). Factors making behaviours more or less intense are evaluated; 'Is there anything which tends to make you do this more/less?.' These 'modulating factors' can be situational, affective, cognitive, or interpersonal. A preliminary assessment of the scope of the behaviours is gained at the interview, with more detailed information being derived in the subsequent stages of assessment and treatment.

Physiological factors

This part of the assessment resembles that in other anxiety disorders (see p. 59, p. 99), particularly when the bodily sensations are a source of distress in themselves. An account of the bodily sensations which occur with the obsessions is usually sufficient. Occasionally, more direct physiological recording is useful when verbal ratings during a procedure would interrupt the response. For example, a patient who had obsessional thoughts about losing her mind neutralized them by talking out loud. A behavioural test including overt rating of her thoughts was impossible, as the spoken ratings would have provided sufficient neutralization; to overcome this difficulty, her heart rate response to sitting quietly thinking about losing her mind was monitored. However, physiological measurement is seldom practicable in clinical practice, and results are difficult to interpret.

Bodily sensations may trigger obsessional thoughts and behaviours. For example, a patient had the thought that he was contaminated and needed to wash whenever he detected feelings of sweatiness. Bodily changes can result from obsessional behaviour, as for example, when skin is damaged by excessive washing, or when severe and persistent constipation arises from obsessions about the use of toilets. Some patients with health-related obsessions check bodily areas by feeling them repeatedly and thereby make them swell up (p. 243).

Other aspects of assessment

The more general assessment of history follows the lines discussed earlier in the book (Chapter 2). The circumstances surrounding the onset of the problem are important. Onset in early adolescence may have interfered with the patient's socialization and general ability to cope; difficulties in social interaction may have to be dealt with along with the obsessions if severe and long-standing impairment is evident. Involvement of other family members in the patient's compulsive behaviour needs to be assessed. Effects of the problem on work, sexual functioning, and home life should all be enquired about. A final important part of the behavioural interview is to assess any possible functional value of the symptoms, and to focus the attention of the patient on the relative costs and benefits of change. The patient might be asked, 'Supposing it were somehow possible for you to become completely clear of your problem from tomorrow;

what are the main ways in which your life would be different?' Although the benefits of getting rid of the problem may far outweigh the disadvantages, this is not invariably the case. In one instance, a patient who had only been married for a few years replied, 'My husband will leave me.' In such circumstances more detailed assessment of the marital situation is indicated, if the partner is willing (see p. 341).

By the end of the assessment interview (which normally takes 1–2 hours) the therapist should have reached a tentative formulation of the nature and scope of the problem. This formulation should be discussed with the patient, so that the rationale for treatment can be introduced. For example:

'From what you have described, it seems like you have a psychological problem called obsessive–compulsive disorder. What happens in this problem is that people notice upsetting thoughts more than usual and become very worried about these. In your instance, you had thoughts about germs and the possibility that you might pass germs on to your family. You knew that this was unlikely to happen, but couldn't take the risk if there seemed any way of preventing this, so you started to clean lots of things. You also stopped touching your children, started washing your hands for up to an hour at a time, and avoided anything which you thought might be connected with cancer. Unfortunately, all of these things only made you feel better in the short term, so that over a longer period the problem got worse and the thoughts and behaviours became more of a problem. This is what usually happens in this type of problem—the more you try to deal with the problem by avoiding, the more real it seems and the more the thoughts get stuck in the front of your mind. Does that seem to fit with your experience?'

Following any modifications suggested by the patient, the treatment rationale is described. Thus, in the example above:

'The best way to deal with the thoughts is to get used to them without doing the things like handwashing and avoidance. This helps in several ways; you can get used to the things which frighten you, you get back to a more usual lifestyle, and you discover that the things which your are most afraid of do not happen. The main part of treatment aims to find ways of helping you to do this, to come more and more into contact with the things which bother you until you get used to them. It is important that we work out ways of stopping behaviours like washing and avoiding so that you discover that the things you are worried about don't happen. As you do these things, then you will get anxious at first, but you will find that anxiety gets less, usually more quickly than you would expect. How does this type of treatment sound to you?'

The discussion should stress the importance of both self-control and collaboration in therapy. It is emphasized that, 'Our therapy sessions are 2–3 hours in a week, as opposed to the other 165 hours in the week; this means that our sessions can be useful for finding things which help the problem, but these have to be put into practice at home. The most important therapy work is done at home by you, especially in the situations where the problem is at its most difficult.' Patients are encouraged to express any fears or worries they may have with respect to treatment; for example, 'I don't think I can do this; I've tried before; I think it's too risky.'

In most instances the patient is offered a time-limited treatment (20 sessions, for example), depending on the severity and chronicity of the problem. This limit may be changed, depending on the way treatment has progressed.

Behavioural tests

In most obsessions a behavioural test will clarify the details of the problem. In order to report on their reactions, patients are asked to enter or provoke a situation they would normally avoid and not to make any attempts to reduce their anxiety. For example, a patient with worries about contamination by discarded objects was asked to handle the contents of a waste bin; he was then asked to describe his thoughts, the behaviours he felt compelled to carry out, and his subjective state. Ratings of anxiety/discomfort and urges to neutralize were also collected. Behavioural tests carried out without neutralizing are particularly informative in those more chronic patients who are unaware of their upsetting thoughts because stereotyped rituals prevent their occurrence.

In general, patients' descriptions of their problems are influenced by familiarity, so that they may omit details which seem trivial or normal to them but are crucial to therapy; for example, a patient did not mention that he picked things up in an unusual way (using tissues) because of fear of contamination. Behaviour tests are thus best carried out with the therapist observing. Sometimes this is not possible, especially with checkers when the presence of the therapist reduces anxiety. Detailed self-monitoring is then used; sometimes, video-recordings may be a helpful adjunct.

The behavioural test may be carried out in the clinic if the behaviour is easily elicited; for example, if contamination by dirt or germs is involved, asking the patient to touch the soles of shoes may suffice. More frequently the problems centre on home and family, making a home visit necessary. In patients who have difficulty describing their problems in detail, or where the scope is extensive, this is recommended in any case.

A man reported that he was washing his hands up to 70 times daily because of fears of contamination by weedkiller. When the therapist visited his house, he noted that there were newspapers covering all the floors, and that the furniture was arranged around the walls. His wife described a number of additional behaviours, including the patient's inability to throw away old clothes and shoes and his repeatedly buying new ones; the garage was full of carefully sealed boxes of clothes, which he would not throw away in case he harmed the men who collected the rubbish. He agreed to a behaviour test, which involved walking across and touching with his hand a nearby patch of grass he knew had been sprayed with weedkiller the previous year. His ratings of discomfort and his comments are shown in Fig. 5.1. At the end of the behavioural test, he reported a strong urge to wash. For a previously agreed period of 30 minutes he discussed with the therapist the thoughts he was experiencing and then demonstrated the way he washed his hands. This involved stripping to the waist and washing his hands in a stereotyped fashion; if he was not satisfied, then he would have to re-wash a further 12 times. The handwashing included his arms up to his elbows; he said that sometimes it would include virtually his entire body. A single wash at the time of the visit took 15 minutes, which was slightly quicker than normal. He volunteered that it usually took longer if he was in a hurry. The behavioural test thus quickly revealed a great deal of information which extended far beyond the test itself.

Interviewing relatives

When there is extensive involvement of the family in the patient's thoughts or rituals, it is important to involve them in treatment. Usually the relative is interviewed in the presence of the patient. Considerable sensitivity may be required because of the unusual nature of the behaviours involved. For example, the parents of a 17-year-old patient reported that he got his family to sit on the kitchen table with their legs up for 15 minutes at a time while he carried out cleaning and checking.

Questionnaire measures

Questionnaire measures of obsessional behaviour are principally used as a shorthand way of obtaining repeated measures during treatment. Most useful are the Maudsley Obsessive–Compulsive Inventory (Hodgson and Rachman 1977) and the Compulsive Activity Checklist (Freund, Steketee, and Foa 1987), both of which focus on rituals.

Self-monitoring

Self-monitoring begins as early as possible in assessment and treatment. This introduces regular homework, provides detailed information about the problem, and is a useful indicator of treatment progress. Patients can be asked to self-monitor a variety of variables, depending on their specific problems. Common measures include:

Diaries of obsessional thoughts   In its simplest form this is a frequency count. A golf counter (available from sports shops) is a useful adjunct: the patient presses a button each time the thought occurs, and records the totals at agreed intervals.

Diaries of compulsive behaviour (e.g. time spent on rituals)   These are often combined with thought recording; a stopwatch can be helpful if

NAME

DATE /2 - 2 - 88

For each situation listed, give your rating by circling the cross underneath the number which best describes how you *feel at that time*. Use spaces between numbers if you want, such as '55' if 50 is too low and 60 is too high. Do the rating *in the situation itself, NOT* later when you think back.

GENERAL DESCRIPTION: *Walking to the grass where weed killer had been without washing for 30 minutes*

I don't feel at all uncomfortable

I feel the most uncomfortable I have ever felt

TIME	SITUATION	0	10	20	30	40	50	60	70	80	90	100	mean
2 pm	Before leaving					40							100
2.05	Outside house						50						100
2.08	Just on grass										90		100
2.10	In middle of grass										90		100
2.15	Walking off grass									80			100
2.16	Across road						50						100
2.18	Outside house								70				100
2.19	In sitting room									80			100
2.24	In sitting room								70				100
2.34	In sitting room						50						100

I don't feel at all uncomfortable

I feel the most uncomfortable I have ever felt

		0	10	20	30	40	50	60	70	80	90	100	
2.50	/6 MINS LATER (before wash)					40						100	
	5 MINS LATER (after wash)	0										100	

Fig. 5.1 Record sheet from a behaviour test, including discomfort ratings

slowness is a problem. The patient is asked to record on a diary the time spent on each ritual. Such measures are especially useful when the rituals concern everyday activities, such as eating or using the toilet. Recording of frequency may be preferred, depending on the patient's specific pattern of problems.

Ratings of discomfort, urge to neutralize, depression, and anxiety   These are often relevant. During exposure treatment these provide important information about how subjective responses change both within any particular session and between sessions as treatment progresses (see Fig. 5.2 for an example of this type of self-monitoring).

Behavioural by-products   These are incidental correlates of the obsessional behaviour which indicate its extent and are easy to measure, especially in cleaners. Examples are the amount of soap, toilet paper, or cleaning material bought each week.

Difficulties in assessment
By definition, the content of obsessional thoughts is unacceptable and often repugnant. This often makes patients very reluctant to describe their thoughts. They may believe that the thoughts reveal that they are unpleasant people; that others (including their therapists) would reject them, or believe them to be insane. There are a range of specific fears, including the following:

Effects of discussion
Some patients have obsessional fears that talking about the obsessions may make them worse or more real, or even make them act out the thoughts.

Implications of the obsession
Patients may have specific fears, such as the obsession being a sign of schizophrenia (perhaps implying immediate hospitalization against their will). When the thoughts or impulses concern violence or other illegal or morally repugnant acts, patients often worry that the therapist will have them arrested.

Embarrassment
The thoughts may be socially embarrassing, for example when they concern contamination by faeces or semen. Patients with severe problems (especially when extensive compulsive behaviour is involved) can be ashamed by the extent to which their obsessions are out of control, especially since most patients regard obsessional thoughts as intrinsically senseless.

Chronicity

With chronic problems, compulsive behaviour and avoidance may have become so extensive that the patient is no longer aware of the previously associated pattern of thoughts.

These difficulties demand sensitivity and empathy on the part of the therapist. The therapist should be alert for clues about possible areas of difficulty, or for reasons which account for the patient's reluctance to talk about his or her thoughts.

For example, a young non-psychotic woman was referred for anxiety management. During the initial interview she was very shy and indicated that she was anxious mainly about thoughts, although she said that she was unable to say what the thoughts were.

Therapist 'Are they about something awful happening?'

Patient 'Well . . . kind of. I can't talk about them.'

Th. 'It sounds like these thoughts are very upsetting for you, and difficult to talk about. That often happens; it can be very difficult to discuss the kind of thoughts which are especially upsetting. Often, people come to see me about thoughts which they haven't even told their own family about, because the thoughts seem so awful to them. Have you ever been able to tell anyone about these thoughts?'

Pt 'No. It's . . . very difficult. Do other people really have thoughts they can't talk about?'

Th. 'Yes. Very often people find it easiest to tell me first why the thoughts are difficult to talk about. Of course, there are lots of things which may make talking difficult. For example, sometimes people worry that I'll think they are crazy, or that I will think they are bad people. Other times it's that the thoughts themselves are embarassing, or people think I'll be shocked. What is the worst thing about these thoughts for you?'

Pt 'I'm very worried . . . that you'll think I'm bad and have me locked up. Because the thoughts are so bad; I don't think anyone else has thoughts this bad; you might think I'm dangerous.'

Th. 'Would it be helpful to you if I went through some of the worrying kinds of thoughts that other people have?'

Pt 'Yes.'

The therapist goes through some of the examples of the types of thought experienced and reactions to them as in Table 5.1, stressing their alienness.

Therapist 'There is a very important thing to remember about these kind of thoughts: the people who get most upset about a particular thought are the people for whom it is most difficult; for instance, if you have strong religious beliefs you are more likely to get upset by blasphemous thoughts; if you are very gentle you will get upset about violent thoughts or impulses. Think about someone who deliberately gets into fights a lot; do you think violent thoughts upset them?'

Patient 'No, I see what you mean. But would you take someone's child away from them if they had thoughts about doing awful things to them?'

Th.	'One of the most important features of these kind of thoughts is how upset they make the person having them. It might seem odd, but very often the thoughts happen because you are trying hard *not* to have them. Could you try right now NOT to think about a giraffe.' (pause) 'What happened?'
Pt	'I had a picture of a giraffe!'
Th.	'Right, that's what happens with a thought which is *not* upsetting when you try not to have it. If the thought *is* upsetting, then it comes on even more than that. Would it be sensible to take someone's child away from them because they were trying *not* to think about harming them?'
Pt	'That's just what I do. I try really hard not to have these thoughts and they just keep on coming. Then I try to wipe them out. It's really difficult.'

Rather than making direct guesses it is usually better to deal with the patient's worries about the obsessional thoughts, using examples which appear to have some similarity to the patient's own difficulties. Sometimes the assessment will have to be spread over two or even three interviews in order to complete it thoroughly.

Treatment of obsessions with overt compulsive behaviour

Exposure and response prevention
The principles of treatment are derived from the psychological model outlined earlier. The procedures are:

(1) deliberate exposure to all previously avoided situations;

(2) direct exposure to feared stimuli (including thoughts);

(3) Prevention of compulsive rituals and neutralizing behaviours, including covert ones (i.e. response prevention).

Treatment as described in this chapter aims at the highest possible level of exposure with no neutralizing of any kind taking place. Otherwise, neutralizing has the effect of terminating exposure without full confrontation of the patient's fears. Therapy is collaborative with the target being for patients to take responsibility for planning and carrying out their own treatment as quickly as possible as treatment proceeds. The aims of therapy are achieved more quickly and generalize more effectively when extensive use is made of homework; later in treatment, the patient takes responsibility for implementation *and* planning of homework.

Presenting the rationale
At the beginning of treatment the preliminary formulation is expanded and revised to accommodate any new information derived from the

patient's responses to treatment. The rationale for exposure and response prevention outlined on p. 142 is discussed further, and the patient encouraged to raise any objections or worries. The usefulness of exposure going beyond everyday behaviour must be discussed: exposure to difficult situations makes it easier to cope with everyday situations. For example, a patient with fears about contamination by urine might be asked to pick a comb out of a lavatory. Explaining the importance of confronting the anxiety 'without switching it off with the rituals' is a useful way of conveying the reponse prevention component. To check the patient's understanding of the rationale, the therapist can ask, 'Just to make sure that I have been clear, could you describe what the treatment consists of?', followed by questions on points about which the patient is not totally clear.

One of the most frequently expressed worries is that the anxiety will be overwhelming when exposure is carried out, rather than decline as predicted by the therapist. Bland reassurance ('everything will be alright, don't worry') can be unhelpful, and it is counterproductive to argue with the patient. Instead, the therapist should agree that it *may* be true that anxiety will not decline. The patient could be questioned about the longest period for which the compulsive behaviour was resisted, and how certain it was that the anxiety would not have declined. Asking about possible ways of discovering whether the worries are true or not can be used to lead into a behavioural experiment. This is designed to investigate what happens (both in terms of anxiety experienced and worries about the feared consequences) if the patient is able to resist neutralizing for a preset period, usually two hours. This is then used as the basis for further sessions of exposure with response prevention.

Formulation of treatment plan with the patient

The treatment plan is negotiated with the patient by agreeing short-, medium-, and long-term targets. All exposure is discussed in advance, and it is emphasized to the patient that there will be no 'surprises'. For the man with obsessions about weedkiller (p. 143), the long-term target was to put weedkiller on his garden without washing his hands afterwards. The target set for 10 weeks was to be able to handle packets of weedkiller and then touch objects around the house without washing his hands or the objects. The short-term target for the first week was to remove the newspaper from the house floor without increasing avoidance and without handwashing for an hour afterwards. The short-term target was updated weekly.

The choice of early tasks and the order in which problems are dealt with depends considerably on the patient's confidence, the degree to which each aspect of the problem is handicapping, the extent to which a given aspect occurs in the patient's normal environment and, of course, the patient's readiness to carry out the task. As a general principle, exposure should begin with a task which readily lends itself to *in vivo* exposure; the rate at which discomfort will decline is unknown for any particular patient, and so the task chosen should be one which will provoke moderate discomfort; the target problem should be relevant to the patient's lifestyle, so that success will be self-reinforcing.

Obsessional patients are often severely distressed by their problems, which not infrequently leads to problems of compliance, particularly with homework. This may result in their not being fully truthful about homework, or stopping treatment altogether. The patient can be prepared for this kind of difficulty if, for example, the therapist explains that difficulties with homework are not uncommon, but, 'That's fine, because every time you find homework difficult we can learn more about the problem and the way it affects you. It's important that you try your hardest with all the homework we agree, but if you are not able to manage it, then it is helpful if you write detailed notes about what happened so that we can deal better with similar problems when they arise in future. Often the problems which come up are just different aspects of the obsession which we have not yet worked out.'

Introduction of exposure

Many therapists find this stage difficult because the patient may experience considerable distress as a result of exposure. However, obsessional patients are usually willing to tolerate high levels of distress if they believe that treatment will be effective. Firmness tempered with understanding of the patient's distress helps set the precedent for a trusting and task-oriented relationship. Failure to establish a confident and structured approach at this stage can be very difficult to correct later. The patient should be reminded of the exposure rationale:

'Usually, some anxiety occurs when you start this type of programme. This is actually an important part of treatment, because often people think that the anxiety will continue and become intolerable. One of the valuable things you learn through treatment is that the anxiety does not increase to intolerable levels and it often subsides more rapidly than you might expect. Sometimes, anxiety starts to reduce within 20 minutes; more usually, half an hour to an hour. Another important thing which you will notice is that after you have done exposure two or three times, the amount of discomfort you get at first becomes less and less. This is the best indication of how the treatment is working; as time goes on, you will find you will be able to do the exposure in this way and get no discomfort at all.'

Anxiety and its reduction is discussed in an empathic way, but there is no attempt to reassure the patient about the safety of the particular task; for example, there would be no reassurance about the safety of weedkiller. Exposure to feared, obsession-provoking stimuli is graded in difficulty so that therapy is not experienced as so unpleasant that the patient cannot continue. It is best introduced by a demonstration of the required behaviour to the patient (modelling).

Modelling This involves the therapist carrying out the required task before the patient does so; compliance is increased if the therapist is exposed to the feared stimuli *more* than the patient is asked to. While research evidence on its usefulness is equivocal, clinical experience indicates that modelling is helpful in two important respects. First, it is the clearest way of demonstrating which behaviours are required during exposure and response prevention, especially as these are often unusual (e.g. running hands over toilet seats, closing doors without looking at them). Secondly, modelling *early on in treatment* is accompanied by better compliance with exposure during treatment sessions and with homework. Modelling should be rapidly faded out once treatment has started because it can serve as a powerful form of reassurance.

In the case of a patient who feared contamination by bathroom products which could be carcinogenic, the therapist introduced exposure by asking the patient to smear shampoo on the back of her hand. First, the therapist smeared a large amount of the shampoo on his own hands and face and licked his hand. The patient then smeared a small amount and agreed not to wash for three hours and to give ratings of discomfort and urge to wash at periodic intervals. Throughout the session the patient was repeatedly praised and her attention drawn to the degree of anxiety reduction and the decay of the urge to wash which occurred without any neutralizing behaviour.

In patients who check, the general strategy is the same, but more emphasis is placed on the actions of the patient themselves. For example, the therapist may model putting an iron on for a while, then switching it off and leaving the room without checking. The patient is invited to do the same (without the therapist watching when the iron is switched off), then both leave the house for a pre-determined period.

Continuous high level exposure and response prevention
In the first two weeks of outpatient treatment it may be helpful if the patient is seen two or three times each week. Progression through tasks is often rapid during the early stages. *In vivo* exposure sessions typically take one to one and a half hours, but the therapist should allow up to three hours at this stage in order to be able to extend the session if necessary. Generally, it is undesirable to finish a session when the patient's anxiety is reaching a peak; the session should be prolonged until there is some reduction in discomfort. After two weeks, appointments are reduced to weekly or fortnightly.

Treatment progresses with the patient carrying out homework assignments, starting with tasks practised with the therapist. In all sessions and homework the patient rates discomfort and urges to neutralize; this improves compliance and helps identify difficulties which arise. Ratings from a man with checking rituals are shown in Fig. 5.2, illustrating typical decreases in discomfort. Changes in discomfort during the session are discussed, as well as the overall reductions from session to session.

Subsequently, self-directed response prevention for any avoidance or neutralizing is crucial. Such behaviours may not be immediately obvious to either therapist or patient. Useful questions for patients to ask themselves are: 'If I didn't have an obsessional problem, would I be doing this?' (identifies neutralizing and avoidance), 'What extra things *would* I be doing if I didn't have the problem?' (identifies avoidance). As treatment progresses, the intensity of self-directed exposure and response prevention is built up as rapidly as possible.

In many patients (especially checkers) anxiety about being responsible for harm to self or others is prominent. In order to reduce responsibility should anything go wrong, the patient may seek frequent reassurance from the therapist or carry out homework literally as directed. This is a form of avoidance and indicates the need for direct exposure to responsibility as part of the treatment programme, after a discussion about the role of worries about responsibility. This involves the patient being given homework in which the entire assignment is self-initiated and the *details* not discussed with the therapist. The therapist says: 'I would like you to plan this week's homework yourself; it should be the normal type of assignment, but I don't want you to tell me any details of what you do. I want you to record, as usual, how uncomfortable you get. It is important that you set things up so that you become uncomfortable but don't check, avoid, or neutralize. Try not to tell or even hint to anyone what you have done. Next session we will discuss how you *felt* but you and only you will be responsible for the assignment. So, without telling me any details of what you will leave unchecked, can you outline what the homework is for this week?'

Reassurance

Reassurance seeking is a prominent feature of obsessions. Obsessional thoughts almost always involve the fear of responsibility for harm, through things done or omitted (Salkovskis 1985). Examples are the thought that touching someone's hand without washing will pass on contamination; the thought that not picking up pieces of glass in the road may lead to someone being badly cut. Asking for reassurance is usually an attempt to ensure that harm has not been caused to self or others; it also has the effect of sharing or passing on responsibility. It is tempting for the therapist to reduce the patient's anxiety by providing such assurance, but the enterprise is doomed to failure: proving that harm has not and will not be caused is an impossibility. For example, a patient told her therapist that she had not checked her rubbish bin to see if there were any tablets in it, and asked whether the therapist thought that was alright? Telling the therapist provided sufficient reassurance regardless of whether an answer was given; the therapist had the opportunity to suggest corrective action and the patient could gauge the therapist's reaction. The repetitive, persistent, and stereotyped way in which reassurance is sought closely resembles other forms of ritualizing. In order to work out a treatment rationale for this problem, the therapist should question the patient about whether the relief obtained from reassurance is persistent or transient, and compare reassurance with other forms of neutralizing. Reassurance seeking within therapy is transformed from a frustrating experience which blocks other useful discussion into an ideal opportunity to deal directly with the obsessional problem.

Therapist	'You seem to be going over your worries about cancer again and again right now; are you wanting me to respond in a particular way?'
Patient	'Yes, I suppose so. I just need to know that I won't get cancer. I don't see what's wrong with finding that out.'
Th.	'In the last couple of sessions we discussed the way that washing hands can actually continue the problem when feeling contaminated, and that it was likely that asking had similar effects when it came to your doubts and fears. Am I right in thinking that asking for reassurance seems different to you?'
Pt	'Well, I feel you would know about it, so why not just tell me and make me feel better?'
Th.	'You are right, I obviously should if it will help the problem. OK, I can do it right now. How much would I have to reassure you to last the rest of this month?'
Pt	'The rest of this month?'
Th.	'Yes, I've got at least another two hours now. If it'll solve the problem for the rest of the month I should tell you. How much would you need for that?'
Pt	'It doesn't work like that. It'll only help for a few minutes.'

The therapist can go on to discuss how reassurance prevents the patient from confronting the anxiety about being responsible for harm, and hence that self-imposed response prevention is required (Salkovskis and West-brook 1987). Involvement of other family members is helpful in extending reassurance prevention and in reminding the patient about it, particularly when the patient is having difficulty. Sometimes it is useful for the therapist to suggest an alternative to reassurance for relatives. The relative can be given a response such as, 'Hospital instructions are that I don't answer such questions' (Marks 1981). If the patient and relative role-play a recent occasion when reassurance was sought, the relative can practise using the alternative response in a caring way. Sometimes it is helpful to role-play further difficulties and the response to them. For

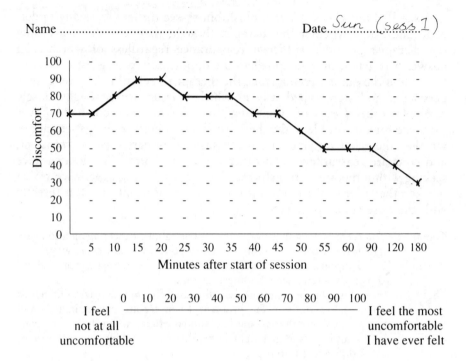

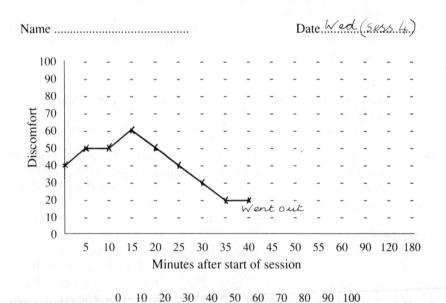

Fig. 5.2 Patient's records of discomfort over the period of four homework exercises

Name ....   Date........ Sat (sess 8)

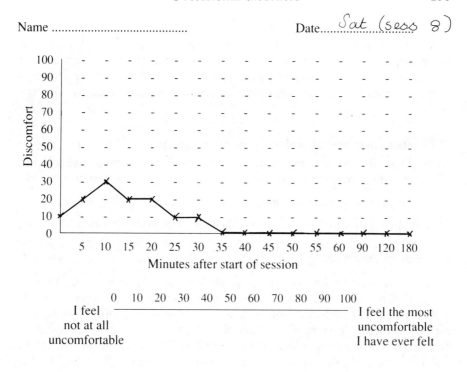

Name ....   Date.. Fri ..(sess.14)

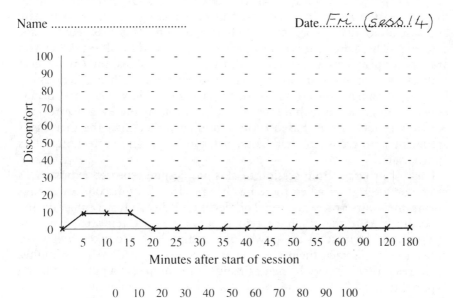

Fig. 5.2 (*Cont'd*)

example, if the patient is insistent, the relative can say, 'At the hospital I was told to walk away from you when your are doing this', and then walk away. However, the patient should be clear about the function of reassurance, and the relatives' responses only used as a back-up if necessary; this means that the onus for response prevention remains with the patient.

Difficulties encountered in the course of treatment

In the majority of cases, exposure and response prevention are successful. However, three major patterns of difficulty may arise during homework:

(1) habituation (anxiety reduction) may not occur during sessions;

(2) despite full compliance, little progress may occur between sessions; and

(3) non-compliance.

The first of these seldom occurs, and when it does the reasons are usually obvious. The most likely are sessions being too short; or severe concurrent depression which was not identified on assessment, and may demand direct treatment. Very rarely, failure to obtain within-session change may result from overvalued ideation (Foa 1979). This may be amenable to cognitive procedures (Salkovskis and Warwick 1985, 1988; Salkovskis 1989). In particular, questioning can be used to allow patients to identify inconsistencies in their beliefs, and to encourage them to formulate and test alternative hypotheses of their situation. This proceeds as, for example, 'There are two ways of considering your difficulties; either you are having problems with germs, and need to be obsessional to protect yourself, or you have an obsessional problem which is being kept going by type of things you do as we outlined earlier. How could we decide between these two possibilities?' The discussion of the evidence for the patient's beliefs (again, based on questioning rather than the therapist's arguments) proceeds on that basis, using other cognitive techniques as appropriate.

Lack of progress from session to session, despite repeated exposure, is more common, even when there has been a decline in discomfort ratings during the course of exposure. The decline in discomfort ratings during exposure can be the result of two processes: either repeated exposure leading to a decrease in the power of the stimuli to provoke anxiety, *or* patients can distract themselves from the anxiety-provoking stimulus, or decrease their anxiety by neutralizing. For example, if a patient is being exposed to being in the same room as a knife, distracting himself from the knife would reduce ratings but would not lead to any enduring reduction in anxiety between sessions. Any neutralizing which the patient carries out during the session (including reassurance seeking) can have this effect

Table 5.4 Failure to progress between sessions, and some suggested solutions

Reason	Remedy
Non-compliance with exposure	Assess and deal with thoughts about exposure homework (see below)
Non-compliance with response prevention	Check patient's understanding of rationale; carry out therapist-directed session to identify difficulties
Exposure sessions too brief	Discuss any worries about consequences of lengthening sessions; do a demonstration exposure session; set homework to be of a specified duration
Covert neutralizing replacing overt rituals	Discuss rationale of response prevention with respect to covert neutralizing and institute covert response prevention
Reassurance seeking	Discuss rationale of reassurance as a form of compulsive behaviour (see p. 153); involve as necessary those from whom reassurance is being sought (p. 153)
Transfer of responsibility	Increase exposure to responsibility (p. 152); involve those to whom responsibility is being transferred
Exposure and response prevention too circumscribed	Include generalization in the homework; homework assignments to involve increasing amounts of the patient's day
Avoidance of situations which trigger thoughts	Extend homework to include exposure to feared situations outside specific homework periods; set goals for exposure to feared situations (see Chapter 4, p. 106)
Reasons not clear	Further assessment, using self-monitoring and exposure sessions in the clinic or the patient's home, to gain more direct information

and must be eliminated. The most likely causes and some suggestions are listed in Table 5.4.

Non-compliance

It is crucial for compliance that the formulation and treatment rationale are acceptable to the patient. Furthermore, if homework assignments are not completed, then the therapist should initially check the general principles for improving compliance (p. 37). It is not uncommon for patients to make some progress and yet discontinue homework assignments after minor setbacks. As described above (p. 150), difficulties with homework should be anticipated by the therapist, and any problems which arise reinterpreted as an important source of information about the problem itself. For example, a patient was successful at eliminating washing rituals at all times of the day except mornings. As she began to tackle response prevention in the mornings, things became difficult; at the same time, her menstrual period began. Discussion and subsequent observation confirmed a strong tendency for symptoms to worsen at this time, although she had not previously been aware of this.

Careful planning of homework assignments can identify potential difficulties before they arise. Questions such as, 'If an obsessional thought occurs then, what will you do?', 'If you feel you must neutralize, what then?' can be helpful, as well as detailed planning of the what, where, when, and how long of the task itself. As noted above, the responsibility for such details are gradually assumed by the patient during the course of treatment. Therapist and patient should always make a note of the details of homework, and the patient should be asked to record the outcome of the assignment for review at the beginning of the following session.

Some patients are able to accept the treatment rationale while calm, but are unable to take 'risks' when anxious and troubled by obsessional thoughts. If this is the case, the therapist can provide the patient with strategies which can be used during anxious periods as reminders of the key points of the rationale; for instance, flashcards can be used, with the patient's fearful thoughts written on one side and the rational responses and evidence against on the other. Rehearsal is also helpful. This usually involves imagining an anxiety-provoking situation, then imagining a range of coping strategies, such as approaching the sink to wash, then turning away and going for a walk instead. While thinking about the scene, the patient is also encouraged to imagine the anxiety, urges, and bodily sensations, then imagine their gradual decline.

Style of therapy

For therapy to be successful the principles of treatment have to be adapted to the patient, and this often involves considerable inventiveness on the part of the therapist and the patient. A sense of humour can be particularly helpful, and may allow a patient to complete tasks which would not otherwise be possible. *This never involves laughing at the patient*, but only laughing with the patient at the problem and at yourself.

For example, a patient was unable to bring herself to touch a chair which she regarded as contaminated. The therapist and a nurse who was assisting modelled touching the chair, but the patient was unable to do so. The therapist asked whether the patient knew of a children's game, in which people put their hands, one after another, on top of the previous hand; the bottom hand is then pulled out and put on top, and so on. This game was played on the contaminated chair (with a great deal of laughter); the patient had touched the chair several times, and the programme was begun.

Treatment of obsessions without overt compulsive behaviour

Obsessions without overt compulsions can be considered as a difficult category of obsessive–compulsive disorder in which avoidance and compulsive activity are almost totally *covert* and are therefore especially difficult to gain access to and control. The term 'obsessional ruminations' is confusing because it has been used indiscriminately to describe both obsessions and mental neutralizing. For example, a patient reported that she had thoughts and images about her family dying; she would ruminate about these thoughts for periods of up to three hours at a time. Careful questioning elicited two functionally different types of thoughts; first she had intrusive thoughts such as, 'My son is dead.' If she had thoughts like this, she would neutralize it by making herself have the thought, 'My son is NOT dead' and by forming a clear image of her son carrying out normal activities.

The psychological formulation of obsessions will be outlined, followed by a description of two treatment approaches to obsessional thoughts.

Psychological model of obsessions without overt compulsions

The psychological formulation of obsessions on page 134 requires only slight extension, acknowledging the role of *mental* neutralizing and avoidance behaviours which are difficult to detect and control. The underlying principle is that anxiety can be reduced by repeated exposure to the feared thoughts, if there are no overt or covert responses which terminate or avoid exposure. A further specific consideration is that rapid and enduring anxiety reduction is best achieved by ensuring that stimuli to which the patient is exposed occur as *predictably* as possible. In obsessions without overt compulsions, exposure is to *thoughts*, and these are more difficult to make predictable than the stimuli used in exposure with obsessions with overt compulsions. That is, vividness, time of onset, speed of onset, intensity, duration, rate of occurrence, and the actual detailed content of the thoughts are all beyond the control of the patient and the therapist, and usually vary from presentation to presentation. Although habituation might *eventually* occur even with irregular presentation of thoughts, this is not evident to the patient, who may therefore continue to neutralize ('It's the only way I can feel any better') or even abandon treatment.

Assessment

The assessment follows the general principles outlined earlier in this chapter. Specifically, both obsessions and neutralizing thoughts are mixed together in the cognitive domain, and discriminating between them is crucial to treatment. *Intrusive, involuntary* thoughts which produce anxiety must be differentiated from thoughts which the patient *deliberately initiates by voluntary effort* and which are intended to reduce anxiety or risk. There may also be covert avoidance behaviours, such as attempts *not* to think particular thoughts (see also p. 139). Avoidance is not defined in terms of how successful it is in preventing anxiety, but rather in terms of what the behaviour is intended to do. Covert avoidance and neutralizing are assessed by asking the patient about any mental efforts that are made because of the problem (see p. 138).

For example, a patient felt compelled to think every 'bad' thought an even number of times. He spent much of his day trying not to have 'bad' thoughts (avoidance); these efforts were frequently followed by thoughts such as, 'I never liked my father' (obsession). He would then have to think, 'I never liked my father' again (neutralizing) and try to stop (avoidance); this cycle then repeated. The obsessional thought can become a neutralizing thought if there is voluntary effort; e.g. the patient who makes himself think particular thoughts before they occur on their own.

Treatment procedures

Two treatment approaches will be described: first, habituation training as an extension of exposure and response prevention to obsessional thoughts; secondly, a pragmatic approach—thought stopping.

Habituation training

This is based on the idea that the practical task early in habituation training is repeatedly and *predictably* to elicit thoughts over the period required for anxiety reduction, while at the same time preventing any covert avoidance and neutralizing behaviours. Once habituation to predictable stimuli has been achieved, treatment progresses to more unpredictable stimuli and habituation while the patient is anxious.

Treatment begins with a detailed discussion of the problem formulation, with emphasis on the unpredictability of thoughts and the role of covert neutralizing. The rationale for habituation training with response prevention is introduced by drawing attention to the way in which avoidance prevents the patient from confronting anxiety and getting used to it. Neutralizing thoughts are similarly discussed. Once these principles have been agreed, the patient is asked if this suggests ways of dealing with the problems, that is, 'getting used to the upsetting thoughts without doing anything about them'. In order to present the thoughts repeatedly in a predictable way, a number of strategies are possible:

(1) deliberate thought evocation ('form the thought, hold it until I say, then pause; repeat this several times');

(2) writing the thought down repeatedly; and

(3) listening to a 'loop tape' of the thought in the patient's own voice.

A combination of these strategies can be particularly powerful, beginning with the loop tape. The patient is asked to record an intrusive thought or a series of the same thought for 30 seconds. For example, a patient might record the thought, 'I may harm my son, I may stab him with the kitchen knife so that he bleeds to death.' It is very important that no neutralizing thoughts are included on the tape. The loop cassette (which can be bought from audio stores) will then continuously repeat the intrusive thoughts on a 30-second cycle. The patient is instructed to listen to the tape as closely as possible, without any neutralizing, for 10 presentations. After each presentation, discomfort and urge to neutralize are rated on 0–100 scales (see p. 146, p. 154, Fig. 5.2). After listening to the tape, any urges to avoid or neutralize are discussed in detail; if any actually took place during or after the tape, ways of preventing this are discussed and tried out with the tape for a further 10 presentations until a non-neutralized presentation is achieved. This may involve changing the content of the tape, adding another thought (perhaps on the other audio channel), closing the eyes, playing through headphones, producing an image to go with the thought, or whatever else might prevent neutralizing. The tape is then played continuously for about 15 minutes with ratings of discomfort and urges to neutralize made at intervals of, for instance, three minutes. Any difficulties with avoidance and neutralizing are again discussed.

The patient is asked to practise with the tape at least twice daily for periods of at least an hour, preferably until anxiety has reduced to 50 per cent of its highest level during the practice session. Response prevention of any neutralizing is again stressed. In addition, the patient is asked to eliminate any neutralizing which occurs throughout the day and to keep records of the occurrence of thoughts, discomfort, and urges to neutralize. In subsequent sessions, difficulties experienced with the homework tape or self-directed response prevention are discussed. All activity directed at avoiding or terminating the obsessional thoughts should be identified and prevented. Once the patient can listen to the tape without neutralizing and with only minimal anxiety occurring, then the thought on the tape is changed and the procedure repeated with the new thought. Once the patient has habituated to one or two thoughts, there is usually generalization to other thoughts, which become less distressing. This can be checked by reference to the patient's diaries. Specific techniques to enhance generalization can then be employed. These include:

(1)   having the patient listen to the tape in very difficult situations, possibly using a personal stereo (e.g. patients with thoughts about harming people in the street can listen to the tape when out walking);

(2)   getting the patient to listen to the tape while anxious, either from naturally occurring stress (e.g. going to the dentist, capitalizing on natural mood variations) or for contrived reasons (e.g. imagining a stressful situation or using mood-induction procedures; Clark, 1983); and

(3)   deliberate variation of the taped habituation (e.g. using a non-looped cassette tape, varying the thoughts' content, loudness, vividness, and so on); loud noises can be introduced into the tape to elicit startle responses.

Finally, the patient is asked to provoke thoughts deliberately, proceeding through a similar sequence of using single thoughts, multiple thoughts, in a range of situations, and so on, without neutralizing.

As with the general approach to obsessive–compulsive disorder, the problem of reassurance is emphasized, and the patient is increasingly made responsible for the details of treatment and homework.

Thought-stopping
The major alternative to habituation training is less closely tied to the psychological model outlined above, but is consistent with research findings about the differences between intrusive thoughts in normal and clinical populations (Rachman and De Silva 1978): clinical obsessions are more difficult to dismiss, last longer, and cause more distress. Thought-stopping aims to provide a strategy for dismissing thoughts and thereby reducing their duration. This may also have the effect of increasing the patient's sense of control and hence reduce discomfort. As the cognitive–behavioural model predicts that obsessional thoughts are maintained by neutralizing and avoidance, effective thought-stopping is accompanied by a programme to eliminate neutralizing (including reassurance) and avoidance.

The rationale begins with a discussion of the similarities between normal and abnormal intrusive thoughts. This leads to an agreement to try to reduce the duration of the obsessional thoughts *without neutralizing*, thus making them more 'normal' and increasing the patient's sense of control. It is emphasized that thought-stopping is a skill which cannot be learned in stressful situations. A useful analogy is with driving: 'First you need to practise a lot when you are calm and there's not much traffic. Second, you need to practise to build up your skill, when you are not faced with a problem. In the same way, you should not try thought-stopping with distressing obsessions in everyday life until you are really good at it.'

Following assessment, the therapist and patient draw up a list of up to four obsessional thoughts, and a longer list of triggering situations. In addition, a list of four alternative relaxing or interesting thoughts are listed; for example, remembering a pleasant walk, a sporting incident, or a specific scene from a film. It is crucial that no neutralizing thoughts are included in either list of thoughts. Each obsessional thought is rated for the discomfort it generally produces and the vividness with which it can be evoked.

In the first session, the method is demonstrated to illustrate that it is possible to rapidly dismiss obsessional thoughts.

The therapist says, 'I want you to sit back in a relaxed way with your eyes closed. I am going to describe a scene to you and then describe you getting an obsessional thought. I want you to raise your hand *as soon as you begin to think the obsessional thought*, even if I am only describing the scene. Do not try and get the thought in detail. It is important that you raise your hand as soon as you have even the beginning of the obsessional thought. Settle back and close your eyes.'

The therapist then describes a typical triggering scene and, if necessary, goes on to describe an obsessional thought. As soon as the patient raises a hand, the therapist shouts 'Stop!' very loudly and then asks the patient what happened to the obsessional thought. It will have disappeared. The therapist points out that, while 'stop' cannot be shouted in public, it will gradually be possible to associate the word 'stop' with cessation of the thought. The procedure is repeated with the therapist describing the precipitating scene and the subsequent obsessional thought. When the patient raises a hand the therapist says 'Stop' in a firm voice and instructs the patient to switch to an alternative scene. The patient is encouraged to think in detail of this scene and to raise a hand when there is a clear thought or picture of it in his or her mind. The discomfort and vividness which was associated with the obsessional thought are then rated by the patient. The therapist checks whether the obsessional thought went away and that it was possible to imagine the alternative scene in some detail. The patient should also be questioned about covert neutralizing with further emphasis on the importance of response prevention.

The session continues with 10 minutes of thought-stopping with a variety of triggering scenes and alternative thoughts. The patient is allowed to imagine the alternative scene for up to one minute, with 30 seconds' relaxation before ratings of distress and vividness. Next, the procedure is altered so that the therapist describes the triggering scene and obsessional thought, but the *patient* says 'Stop' and describes the alternative scene. This continues for five minutes, and then the procedure is again changed when the therapist says, 'I want to put you more in control of the whole procedure. This time, I will describe the scene; as soon as you have the thought, I want you to lift your hand and say 'stop' *mentally to yourself*; the same with the alternative scene, which I want you to describe to yourself in your head. When you have the alternative scene, lift your hand again. Let's just go over that; when I describe the scene, what happens next?' This third stage continues for another five minutes. Thought-stopping is practised with the patient during the next two or three treatment sessions, emphasizing the importance of not neutralizing.

Homework consists of approximately 20 minutes' practice each day at times when the patient is not distressed by the thoughts. A diary of practice is kept, with ratings from 0–100 made of the distress and vividness associated with each evocation of the obsessional thoughts. After at least one week's practice, the patient is encouraged to begin using the procedure to dismiss mildly or moderately distressing thoughts as they occur, gradually moving on to more difficult thoughts. At this stage, patients are asked to enter situations they previously avoided. It is stressed that there will be limited success at first, and that spontaneously occurring thoughts will be dismissed only temporarily with frequent recurrences. The procedure should then be repeated with the expectation that the delay before recurrence will gradually increase over days and weeks. As the patient's sense of control increases, the thoughts should become less distressing and vivid when they occur, until the patient is unconcerned about them.

Difficulties with thought-stopping   Difficulties may arise at two stages in treatment, either during practice sessions with the therapist or in subsequent homework sessions. In the first case, the patient may have difficult in imagining the triggering or alternative scene, in which case imagery should be practised as a preliminary step (see Chapter 3, p. 68). Alternatively, it may be difficult to remove the obsessional thought; should this arise, the therapist could either switch to a less distressing obsessional thought for initial practice or revert to the procedure of shouting 'stop' until the procedure is better established; this is very rarely necessary.

The patient may stop doing homework; if the general principles on compliance have been followed, the most frequent explanation is that the patient has tried to apply thought-stopping to difficult thoughts outside practice sessions but not found it helpful. This may be because thought-stopping has not been sufficiently practised. The patient may, on the other hand, simply have found homework sessions too difficult either because of practising with thoughts which were too distressing, or because the practice situation itself was inappropriate (for example, in the morning when mood was relatively low, or at tea-time when there were many competing demands).

If the patient has practised the procedure in the recommended way, but ratings of distress and vividness of the thoughts have not decreased, then it is most probable that there is continuing covert neutralizing, or reassurance-seeking. Questions such as, 'What are you having to say to yourself that you wouldn't have to say if you didn't have the thoughts?' will identify covert neutralizing, and can lead on to a further discussion of its role in the maintainance of the thoughts. If reassurance seeking is a persistent problem, then a joint session with relatives or others involved may be helpful.

Alternative treatments

Behavioural treatment is now the treatment of choice. Psychotherapy has been used at times, although Storr (1979) suggests that psychodynamic treatment is only appropriate for patients with obsessional traits, not for obsessive–compulsive disorder. This view is consistent with the outcome data (Cawley 1974). It has been suggested that obsessions are a manifestation of affective disorder because obsessions can be triggered and/or worsened by depressed mood (Gittleson 1966), and because proper treatment with antidepressant medication results in improvement in some depressed patients (Rachman *et al.* 1979; Marks *et al.* 1980). However, a recent meta-analysis of outcome studies has suggested that antidepressant medication may exert a direct effect on obsessions (Christensen, Hadzi-Pavlovic, Andrews, and Mattick 1987). Antidepressant medication is probably best employed in those patients in whom obsessions are associated with a considerable degree of concurrent depression, and possibly those whose obsessions developed or worsened after the onset of depression. It also seems likely that such patients will also respond to psychological treatment of depression (Chapter 6).

The extent to which psychosurgery has been proposed as a treatment for obsessions is more a testimony to the former intractibility of the condition than to the effectiveness of this intervention. Sternberg (1974) reviewed the evidence and concluded that the patients who appear to improve most with psychosurgery are those with previously good personality, over the age of 40, having stable home and work environments and recent onset of illness. Rachman (1979) points out that there is no convincing evidence for the efficacy of psychosurgical procedures with patients who could not be helped by less intrusive methods.

In-patient treatment may occasionally be considered. Most treatment outcome studies have been of behaviour therapy carried out in in-patient settings, because of the greater control over the patient's physical and social environment. There are occasions where this is desirable, although it is seldom necessary. The disadvantages of in-patient treatment are that it requires a major time commitment from staff who are fully trained in behavioural methods, and generalization from the ward setting can be very poor. The generalization issue arises because obsessional patients perceive hospitalization as removing responsibility for many of their actions; this means that many patients, particularly checkers, improve immediately upon admission and deteriorate rapidly on discharge. This phenomenon may lead to false conclusions about the basis of their problems. Hospitalization can be a helpful way of *starting* a treatment programme in patients whose problems primarily concern contamination and who find self-directed exposure particularly difficult to initiate. Admission should be planned (i.e. not in response to a crisis), and time-limited (usually for a week or less). During the admission, 24-hour exposure and response prevention is the best approach, with considerable skilled input from staff over the first day or two (Foa and Goldstein 1978). Generalization to the home setting should begin from the second day onwards, with a programme of initially supervised visits to home for the purpose of extending the programme.

Treatment outcome research

Treatment outcome research has been carried out by three main groups, led by Rachman, Hodgson, and Marks in London, Emmelkamp in Groeningen, and Foa in Philadelphia. The London group carried out an important sequence of studies, in which they showed that exposure combined with response prevention was an effective treatment (Rachman and Hodgson 1980, Chapter 22; Marks 1987, Chapter 14). They recommend a domiciliary basis as the most effective way of delivering treatment. More recently, two large-scale trials compared exposure with and without the antidepressant clomipramine (Rachman *et al.* 1979; Marks *et al.* 1980 and Marks 1987). The results showed that the efficacy of exposure was greater than relaxation, and that drug effects on rituals were mediated by the effects on mood. Marks (1987) also suggests that there were somewhat higher relapse rates on cessation of the drug treatment, and that there was a high incidence of troublesome side-effects.

Foa's results are consistent with the earlier conclusions drawn by Rachman and Marks' group. She investigated the relative contribution of the exposure and the response prevention components, and found that a combination was most effective. Foa also investigated the effectiveness of exposure with 24-hour response prevention, resulting in unusually high success rates of 85 per cent (Foa and Goldstein 1978). Emmelkamp's series of studies replicated the good outcome obtained by the London group, and investigated the impact of different ways of carrying out exposure. Emmelkamp's results suggest that therapist modelling does not substantially alter outcome, but that involving the family in treatment can be helpful (Emmelkamp 1982). Although an early study suggested that self-instructional training did not enhance exposure treatment (Emmel-kamp, van der Helm, Van Zanten, and Plochg 1980), more recent work demonstrated that a form of cognitive therapy was as effective as expo-sure (Emmelkamp, Visser, and Hoekstra 1988).

The literature on the outcome of the treatment of obsessive–compulsive disorder reveals median success rates of 75 per cent improvement in those who complete treatment. The outcome of treatments for obsessions *with-out* compulsions is considerably worse, with little data to show that specific treatments improve on non-specific effects (e.g. Emmelkamp and Giesselbach 1981). There are several reasons why this might be so; notably, the sample sizes employed in outcome trials have invariably been very small. Other reasons for the poor treatment outcome are discussed on p. 159. These factors suggest that there is a great deal of further scope for the application of behavioural treatment in obsessions without com-pulsions, and that outcome could be improved considerably. For example, Kirk (1983) showed better results in a study employing some of the modifications of treatment outlined here, and obtained better results in a clinical series of patients treated in routine clinical practice.

Despite the improvement in outcome brought about by the adoption of behavioural treatments, a range of serious problems remain to be dealt with. In particular, treatment refusal, drop-out, and failure mean that less than 50 per cent of patients suitable for and seeking treatment improve (Salkovskis 1989). During follow up, relapses certainly occur, although the rate has not been adequately investigated. The adoption of high levels of exposure with 24-hour response prevention suggests that there is little scope to improve further the outcome of treatments for obsessions with compulsions by increasing exposure levels. An obvious alternative would be the incorporation of cognitive techniques into existing behavioural treatments (e.g. Salkovskis and Westbrook 1987; Salkovskis and War-wick 1988).

Recommended reading

Emmelkamp, P. M. G. (1982). *Phobic and obsessive–compulsive disorders*. Ple-num, New York.

Foa, E. B. and Steketee, G. S. (1979). Obsessive–compulsives: conceptual issues and treatment interventions. In *Progress in behaviour modification*, (ed. R. M. Hersen), pp. 1–53. Academic Press, New York.

Marks, I. M. (1978). *Living with fear*. McGraw Hill, New York.

Marks, I. M. (1987). *Fears, phobias, and rituals*. Oxford University Press, New York.

Rachman, S. J. and Hodgson, R. (1980). *Obsessions and compulsions*. Prentice Hall, Englewood Cliffs, NJ.

Salkovskis, P. M. (1989). Obsessions and compulsions. In *Cognitive therapy: a clinical casebook*, (ed. J. Scott, J. M. G. Williams, and A. T. Beck), pp. 50–77. Routledge, London.

Salkovskis, P. M. and Warwick, H. M. C. (1988). Cognitive therapy of obsessive–compulsive disorder. In *The theory and practice of cognitive therapy*, (ed. C. Perris, I. M. Blackburn, and H. Perris) 376–95. Springer, Heidelberg.

Salkovskis, P. M. and Westbrook, D. (1989). Behaviour therapy and obsessional ruminations: can failure be turned into success? *Behavior Research and Therapy*, **27**, 149–60.

Turner, S. M. and Beidel, D. C. (1988). *Treating obsessive–compulsive disorder*. Pergamon, New York.

6

Depression

Melanie J. V. Fennell

Introduction

The nature of depression

Clinical depression is so widespread that it has been called the common cold of psychiatry (Seligman 1975). At any given point in time, 15–20 per cent of adults suffer significant levels of depressive symptomatology. At least 12 per cent experience depression severe enough to require treatment at some time in their lives, and depression has been estimated to account for 75 per cent of psychiatric hospitalizations. For reasons as yet unclear, the rate of depression among women in Western industrialized nations is approximately twice the rate among men (Brown and Harris 1978). It seems likely that no single factor can explain the occurrence of depression, but rather that it results from an interaction between many different factors. Its onset and course have been shown to relate to a variety of biological, historical, environmental, and psychosocial variables. These include disturbances in neurotransmitter functioning, a family history of depression or alcoholism, early parental loss or neglect, recent negative life events, a critical or hostile spouse, lack of a close confiding relationship, lack of adequate social support, and long-term lack of self-esteem. (For a recent review of epidemiology, see Boyd and Weissman 1982.)

Clinical depression as a diagnostic category has been subclassified in a number of ways. In particular, distinctions have been made between bipolar and unipolar disorders, and between endogenous and reactive (or neurotic) depressions. The term 'depression' in this chapter will generally be used to refer to non-bipolar, non-psychotic (i.e. not hallucinated or deluded) depressive disorder, since this is the type of mood disturbance for which cognitive behaviour therapy for depression was designed and with which it has been most extensively tested. Clinical depression in this sense is quite different from the transient low mood experienced by most people as a normal reaction to loss, and disturbs many aspects of functioning. When people become clinically depressed, they feel sad, and are often tearful. They are troubled by guilt, believing that they are letting people down. They may become more irritable than usual, more anxious and tense. When the depression is at its worst, they may lose the ability to react emotionally, and find that good and bad feelings alike are lost in numbness. It becomes difficult to enjoy or to be interested in normal activities. Energy is low, and everything seems an effort. So they tend to withdraw from the things they would normally do, and may spend long hours hunched in a chair, or lying in bed. Ordinary pleasures, like reading the paper or watching TV, become difficult and burdensome because it is hard to concentrate and to remember what has been read or said. They become preoccupied with how bad they feel and with the apparently insoluble difficulties that face them. Even basic bodily functions may be disturbed. Sleep is difficult, appetite declines, sexual desire disappears. Most dangerously, it may seem as time goes on that there will be no end to this state, that nothing can be done to change things for the better. So hopelessness grows, and can lead to a longing for death, and to thoughts of suicide. Among the severely depressed, 15 per cent eventually kill themselves (Coryell and Winokur 1982).

In most cases, depression is time-limited. Untreated episodes usually resolve within 3–6 months. However, relapse is frequent, and some 15–20 per cent of people follow a chronic course. For this reason, treatment must aim not only to speed recovery from the current episode but also to maintain improvements and, if possible, to reduce the likelihood of recurrence. This concern has encouraged the development of psychological treatments designed to teach patients active depression-management skills.

The development of psychological treatments for depression

The past ten years have seen the rapid development of a range of short-term psychological treatments for depression (Rush 1982). Until the mid-1970s, psychiatric conceptualizations of the disorder viewed behavioural and cognitive deficits present in depression as consequences of a primary disturbance in mood, and not as appropriate targets for treatment in their own right. Within clinical psychology, depression was a focus for growing theoretical speculation (e.g. Lazarus 1988; Costello 1972; Ferster 1973; Lewinsohn 1974b; Seligman 1975), but attempts to understand its phenomenology and process had not yet led to the development of sophisticated, coherent, practice-based therapy programmes.

The clinical effectiveness of a number of behavioural and cognitive–behavioural treatment packages has since been demonstrated. Cognitive behaviour therapy for depression, as developed by Beck and his colleagues in Philadelphia (Beck, Rush, Shaw, and Emery 1979), is now one of the most widely adopted, extensively evaluated, and influential of these. Cognitive behaviour therapy at its best comprises a complex interweaving of cognitive and behavioural techniques. These to some extent include interventions advocated by other workers, for example pleasant-event scheduling (e.g. Lewinsohn, Sullivan, and Grosscup 1982),

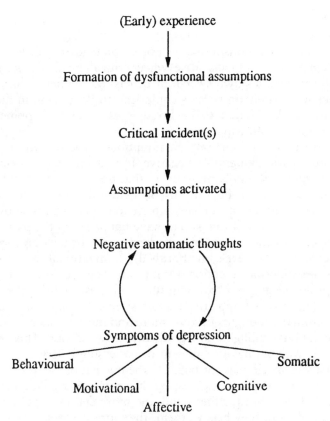

(Early) experience

Formation of dysfunctional assumptions

Critical incident(s)

Assumptions activated

Negative automatic thoughts

Symptoms of depression

Behavioural

Motivational

Affective

Cognitive

Somatic

Fig. 6.1 The cognitive model of depression

and re-evaluation of dysfunctional standards of behaviour (e.g. Rehm 1982) and of depressive attributions (e.g. Abramson, Seligman, and Teasdale 1978).

The cognitive model of depression

Beck's cognitive model of depression (Beck 1967, 1976) is illustrated schematically in Fig. 6.1. It suggests that experience leads people to form assumptions or schemata about themselves and the world, which are subsequently used to organize perception and to govern and evaluate behaviour. The ability to predict and to make sense of one's experiences is helpful, and indeed necessary, to normal functioning. Some assumptions, however, are rigid, extreme, resistant to change, and hence 'dysfunctional' or counterproductive. Such assumptions concern, for example, what people need in order to be happy (e.g. 'If someone thinks badly of me,

I cannot be happy'), and what they must do or be in order to consider themselves worthwhile (e.g. 'I must do well at everything I undertake'). Dysfunctional assumptions alone do not account for the development of clinical depression. Problems arise when critical incidents occur which mesh with the person's own system of beliefs. So the belief that personal worth depends entirely on success could lead to depression in the face of failure, and the belief that to be loved is essential to happiness could trigger depression following rejection.

Once activated, dysfunctional assumptions produce an upsurge of 'negative automatic thoughts'—'negative' in that they are associated with unpleasant emotions, and 'automatic' in that they pop into people's heads rather than being the product of any deliberate reasoning process. These may be interpretations of current experiences, predictions about future events, or recollections of things that have happened in the past. They, in turn, lead on to other symptoms of depression: behavioural symptoms (e.g. lowered activity levels, withdrawal); motivational symptoms (e.g. loss of interest, inertia); emotional symptoms (e.g. anxiety, guilt); cognitive symptoms (e.g. poor concentration, indecisiveness); and physical symptoms (e.g. loss of appetite, loss of sleep). As depression develops, negative automatic thoughts become more and more frequent and intense, and more rational thoughts are gradually crowded out. This process is helped on its way by the development of increasingly pervasive depressed mood. So a vicious circle is formed. On the one hand, the more depressed a person becomes, the more depressing thoughts they think, and the more they believe them. On the other hand, the more depressing thoughts they think, and the more they believe them, the more depressed they become.

The cognitive therapist breaks into the vicious circle by teaching patients to question negative automatic thoughts, and then to challenge the assumptions on which these are based. The rest of the chapter will describe how to do this. First, however, it is worth making two general points about the cognitive model:

1. The model was first developed, and has been most extensively studied, in relation to depression. However, it is not relevant only to depression, or indeed only to emotional disturbance of clinical intensity. To distort incoming information in line with pre-existing conceptual frameworks is not in itself abnormal (Nisbett and Ross 1980; Hollon and Kriss 1984). There is thus no *qualitative* difference between the thinking processes of most depressed patients and of those who attempt to treat them; rather, depression exaggerates and intensifies processes present in all of us. A recognition of this may be important to the formation of an equal, collaborative relationship between therapist and patient.

2. The fact that cognitions influence mood does not imply that negative thinking *causes* depression. Depression may be seen as a final

common pathway for a range of biological, developmental, social, and psychological predisposing and precipitating variables. Depressive thinking does not *cause* depression; it is part of it. Cognitions may, however, have some temporal priority in the development of mood disturbance, and they can act to trigger, enhance, and maintain other symptoms. For this reason, they form an ideal point for intervention.

Cognitive behaviour therapy for depression: general characteristics

Cognitive behaviour therapy is 'an active, directive, time-limited, structured approach... based on an underlying theoretical rationale that an individual's affect and behaviour are largely determined by the way in which he structures the world' (Beck *et al.* 1979, p. 3). It is:

- based on the coherent cognitive model of emotional disorder outlined above, rather than simply a rag-bag of techniques with no unifying rationale;
- based on a sound therapeutic collaboration, with the patient explicitly identified as an equal partner in a team approach to problem-solving;
- brief and time-limited, encouraging patients to develop independent self-help skills;
- structured and directive;
- problem-oriented and focused on factors maintaining difficulties rather than on their origins;
- reliant on a process of questioning and 'guided discovery' (Young and Beck 1982) rather than on persuasion, lecturing, or debate;
- based on inductive methods, so that patients learn to view thoughts and beliefs as hypotheses whose validity is open to test;
- educational, presenting cognitive–behavioural techniques as skills to be acquired by practice and carried into the patient's environment through homework assignments.

Cognitive behaviour therapy can be conceptualized as a type of problem-solving. Patients arrive with a number of problems, including the depression itself. Depressive thinking prevents them from solving these. Tackling negative automatic thoughts is thus a means to an end, not an end in itself: the goal of therapy is to find solutions to the patient's problems, using cognitive–behavioural strategies, not merely to help the patient to think more 'rationally'. The immediate target is symptom-relief. In the longer term, the same strategies are used to solve life-problems (such as situational or relationship difficulties) and to prevent, or at least attenuate, future episodes of depression.

In most research protocols, a maximum of 20 one-hour sessions is offered, twice a week for the first 3–4 weeks so as to provide momentum and combat hopelessness, and once a week thereafter. In practice, the number of sessions required varies considerably. Some people, particularly those who clearly coped well with their lives before becoming depressed, respond well to five or six highly structured, educational sessions. Others, whose difficulties are more longstanding, may require the full 20 sessions, and more (Fennell and Teasdale 1987a). Session frequency can also be varied according to need. Weekly sessions throughout suffice with less disabling depressions. In contrast, severely depressed inpatients with poor concentration and low activity levels may, at the beginning of treatment, benefit most from brief (e.g. 20-minute) daily sessions concentrating on specific behavioural tasks. Whatever the number and frequency of sessions, it should be made clear from the outset that the patient is expected to develop independent self-help skills, and that the therapist will be available only for a limited period.

Selection of patients for cognitive behaviour therapy

The following questions are intended as guidelines in deciding whether or not to attempt cognitive behaviour therapy with a particular patient:

Is the patient depressed?

Controlled outcome trials have demonstrated the effectiveness of cognitive behaviour therapy with non-psychotic (i.e. not hallucinated or deluded), non-bipolar outpatients meeting formal diagnostic criteria for Major Depressive Disorder. Research Diagnostic Criteria (Spitzer, Endicott, and Robins 1978), for example, require for a definite diagnosis: at least two weeks' persistent depressed mood or pervasive anhedonia; at least five out of eight other psychomotor, cognitive–affective, motivational, and somatic symptoms; and significant impairment in overall functioning. While such criteria provide useful guidelines for determining whether a person is depressed, patients should not be rejected simply because they do not present with the required number of symptoms.

What is the nature of the depression?

Beck *et al.* (1979) suggested that 'standard' treatments such as hospitalization and medication should be used with very severe, highly suicidal, and bipolar depressions. Rush and Shaw (1983) added that cognitive behaviour therapy is unlikely to succeed with endogenous or melancholic depressions. However, there is no clear evidence to date that an endogenous symptom pattern predicts poor response (Blackburn, Bishop, Glen, Whalley, and Christie 1981; Kovacs, Rush, Beck, and Hollon 1981). It is possible that cognitive–behavioural methods could be used (in combination with physical treatments and hospitalization) to manage the symptoms and consequences of more biological depressions, just as they have been used to manage physical pain and disability. In practice, physical treatment and cognitive behaviour therapy can be combined, though problems may arise if the patient fails to make use of psychological methods because improvement is attributed to the drug.

How severe is the depression?

Assessment of severity is important because it may reveal a need for alternative (or concurrent) physical treatment or hospitalization, and because severity influences what symptoms and techniques form the initial focus for treatment. The Beck Depression Inventory (BDI; Beck, Ward, Mendelsohn, Mock, and Erbaugh 1961), a 21-item self-rating scale, allows rapid assessment of overall symptomatology and can be routinely completed by patients before each session. Scores may be categorized as follows: less than 10 = not depressed; 10–19 = mildly depressed; 20–25 = moderately depressed; 26 or more = severely depressed. Alternatively, severity can be assessed using interview data such as intensity and pervasiveness of depressed mood, reactivity to external events, extent of behavioural deficits, and how far normal functioning is disrupted.

Does the patient report depressive cognitions?

Therapists should look for evidence of the 'negative cognitive triad' seen by Beck as central to depression (p. 192). Particular care should be taken to elicit hopelessness, suicidal intentions, and negative expectations of treatment, since dealing with these must be a priority.

How willing is the patient to accept the treatment rationale?

Patients who respond to the treatment rationale with recognition of its relevance to their own experience ('Yes, that's me') and who are willing to give cognitive–behavioural techniques a try, are likely to respond better to treatment than patients who reject the personal relevance of the model (e.g. 'I see what you're getting at, but I can't see how that applies to me') and deny that it could be of any use to them (Fennell and Teasdale 1987*a*).

How far is the patient able to form an equal, collaborative relationship?

It is difficult to apply cognitive behaviour therapy as a brief, focused, problem-solving treatment if the patient has significant difficulties in working as a member of a team. Problems include fear of revealing thoughts and feelings, insistence on managing alone, and believing that the therapist should do all the work. Such difficulties need not contraindicate cognitive behaviour therapy, but they will affect the way is which it is carried out and may require direct intervention. For example, the therapist may need in early sessions to concentrate more on building the relationship than on teaching the patient technical therapy skills. It may also be necessary to work explicitly on helping the patient to identify and re-evaluate thoughts and assumptions that prevent active collaboration, such as, 'If I tell her how I really feel, she will reject me', or 'It's his job to make me better without any effort on my part'.

How extensive is the patient's existing repertoire of coping skills?

Patients with a good repertoire of behavioural and cognitive coping skills are likely to respond more quickly and completely to cognitive behaviour therapy than patients without such a repertoire (Simons, Lustman, Wetzel, and Murphy 1985). This may be because they readily accept the treatment rationale (see also Fennell and Teasdale 1987a), or because treatment has merely to re-establish existing skills disrupted by depression, rather than to teach completely new adaptive behaviours. That said, attention is now increasingly being directed towards using cognitive behaviour therapy with more severe, chronic, and recalcitrant depressions (e.g. Shaw, cited in Beck *et al.* 1979, p. 392; Fennell and Teasdale 1982; De Jong, Triebe, and Henrich 1986).

The structure of treatment sessions

The initial interview

An overview of the first treatment interview will be found in Table 6.1. The interview, which normally takes 1–1½ hours, comes after diagnostic assessment and evaluation of suitability for treatment as outlined above. Its prime purpose, in the interests of encouraging hope, is to begin active therapy immediately and to provide the patient with experience of the structure and process of cognitive–behavioural treatment. The therapist's main tasks are:

1. *Assessment of current difficulties*

It is not necessary at this stage to know everything about the patient. In particular, the historical data routinely gathered in formal psychiatric assessments (details of family of origin, school history, etc.) are not included unless obviously relevant to current functioning. The goal is to obtain an overall picture of the present situation as the patient sees it. This involves pin-pointing major problems, and gathering enough information about their onset, development, and context (living circumstances, resources, social support, etc.), and about associated negative automatic thoughts, for the therapist to make a preliminary formulation of the case, guided by the cognitive model of depression. An example of a formulation will be found in Fig. 6.2. Such a formulation (which is shared with the patient) is essentially a hypothesis, to be validated during treatment as more information comes to light. Indeed, in many cases the data necessary for a complete formulation (especially information about

Table 6.1 The structure of the initial interview

1. *Assessment of current difficulties:*
   Symptoms
   Life problems
   Associated negative thoughts
   Onset/development/context of depression
   Hopelessness/suicidal thoughts

   → agreed problem list

2. *Goal definition*

3. *Presentation of treatment rationale:*
   Practical details
   Vicious circle of negative thoughts and depression
   Possibility of change

4. *Beginning treatment:*
   Specific: Select first treatment target
   Agree appropriate homework
   General: Give patient experience of style of cognitive–behavioural therapy

Overall aims:
Establish rapport
Elicit hope
Give patient preliminary understanding of model
Get working agreement to test it in practice

fundamental assumptions and the early experiences which led to their formation) do not become available until treatment is well under way.

Assessment of current difficulties is summarized in a 'problem-list', agreed with the patient. An example will be found in Table 6.2. The list will normally include two types of problem: symptoms of depression and 'life-problems'. The latter refers to problems other than the depression itself, which may be more-or-less closely associated with it, for example:

(1) practical problems (such as poor housing or unemployment);

(2) interpersonal problems (such as difficulties in forming close and confiding relationships); and

(3) intrapersonal problems (such as lack of self-confidence predating the onset of clinical depression).

Drawing up an agreed problem-list gives the patient immediate experience of cognitive behaviour therapy as a collaborative enterprise. It helps the therapist to understand the patient's perspective, and allows patients

Early experience

Unfavourable comparisons with twin sister
Father (and main supporter) dies

↓

Dysfunctional assumptions

I am inferior as a person
My worth depends on what other people think of me
Unless I do what other people want, they will reject me

↓

Critical incident

Marriage breaks down

↓

Negative automatic thoughts

It's all my fault—I've made a mess of everything
I can't handle my life
I'll be alone for ever—it's going to be dreadful

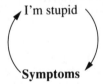

I'm stupid

Symptoms

Behavioural: Lowered activity levels, social withdrawal
Motivational: Loss of interest and pleasure, everything an effort, procrastination
Affective: Sadness, anxiety, guilt, shame
Cognitive: Poor concentration, indecisiveness, ruminations, self-criticism, suicidal thoughts
Somatic: Loss of sleep, loss of appetite

Fig. 6.2   The cognitive model of depression: Mrs R

Table 6.2   Problem-list: Mrs R

---

1. *Inability to express myself:*
   difficulty saying 'no'
   difficulty disagreeing
   difficulty saying what I want if others want something different

2. *Feeling inferior as a person*

3. *Difficulty adapting to the breakdown of my marriage:*
   I won't be able to cope alone with practical things (bills, finding somewhere
      to live, etc.)
   I will never find another satisfactory long-term relationship

4. *Depression:*
   overwhelmed by everyday demands
   avoiding people
   sitting around ruminating
   doing nothing
   not being able to concentrate
   not enjoying anything
   etc.

5. *Feeling depressed about being depressed:*
   It's my fault for making a mess of things; I deserve to feel this way

---

to feel that a genuine effort is being made to grasp their internal reality. The therapist makes brief, frequent summaries of what has been said and asks for feedback to ensure that these accurately reflect what the patient means to convey. For example, 'Let me just check that I'm following you. The first problem is that you've lost your job. There seem to be two sides to that. One is that you think it's your fault that you lost the job; you weren't good enough. The other is that you're having difficulty filling your time. Does that sound about right?'. As discussed in Chapter 12, the problem-list also imposes order on chaos. A mass of distressing experiences is reduced to a number of relatively specific difficulties. This process of 'problem-reduction' is crucial to the encouragement of hope, since it implies the possibility of control. The problem-list in Table 6.2, for example, lists a number of items under the heading 'symptoms of depression'. The patient, who presented each symptom as a separate problem, felt overwhelmed by the sheer number of her difficulties. Drawing up the problem-list reduced this seemingly endless catalogue to different aspects of a single problem. (See Chapter 12 for more details on the preparation of problem-lists.)

It is crucial when working with depressed patients to ensure that hopelessness and suicidal thoughts and intentions are elicited in the initial interview. Suicidal thoughts may not be readily admitted and, where hopelessness is present, should always be inquired after. For example:

Therapist 'It sounds as if you have been feeling very gloomy about the chances of things improving.'
Patient 'Yes, I have. Someone asked me the other day what I was going to do when the children left home. And I realized I just couldn't see that far ahead. I can't see a future for myself—not one worth having, anyway.'
Th. 'So it seems there's nothing to look forward to?'
Pt 'That's right.'
Th. 'Sometimes when people feel that way, they start to think there isn't much point in living. I wonder whether you have ever felt that way?'
Pt 'As a matter of fact, yes, I have, I know I shouldn't say it, but I have.'
Th. 'And have you gone so far as to think of ending your own life?'
Pt 'Yes, I have. I think about it quite often.'

Once suicidal intent has been admitted, seriousness should be assessed by gathering more details about whether or not plans have been made, what prevents the person from taking action, and so forth. Where extreme hopelessness and suicidal thoughts are present, they must form the first point for intervention. Therapists sometimes think that they should not mention suicide in case they put the idea into patients' heads. In fact, it is often a relief to talk freely about it. Suicide is usually a response to thinking that one's situation is intolerable, and that nothing can be done to change it. Self-destruction thus represents an attempt at problem solving. Discussion opens the way to consideration of alternative solutions, or at the very least to an agreement that the option will be shelved until therapy has had a chance to bite. (For a full discussion, see Beck *et al.* 1979, Chapter 10; Burns 1980, Chapter 15.)

2. *Goal definition*
Goals in relation to each problem area are defined in Session 1. Helpful questions include: 'How would you like things to be different in this area?', and 'Supposing the treatment works, how will things be different in relation to this problem?' Goals often change over the course of treatment. Some later seem irrelevant, some need modification, and new ones emerge. Nonetheless, defining goals at the outset helps the therapist to correct unrealistic expectations of therapy, provides a standard against which progress can be monitored, and focuses attention on the future.

3. *Presentation of the treatment rationale*
Patients are given information about practical matters such as number, duration, and frequency of sessions; use of homework assignments; arrangements for making contact in case of need; and the like. More importantly, the core principles of therapy must be simply and clearly conveyed. The first of these is the idea that depression can be understood

in terms of the vicious circle of negative thinking and low mood described above. The second is that change is possible, i.e. the patient can learn to 'catch' and test depressing thoughts, and to break out of the vicious circle by finding more realistic and helpful alternatives to them. Patients need not fully grasp the complexities of the cognitive model, nor accept without reservation that treatment will help. Rather, a working agreement is needed that the therapy's central ideas make sense of their own experience of depression, and that they are willing to try it out.

Such an agreement is reached by using information given by the patient when drawing up the problem list to demonstrate the personal relevance of the cognitive model, by asking for immediate reactions to the rationale, by facilitating free expression of doubts and reservations, and by encouraging willingness to test the therapy's effectiveness in action. Helpful questions include: 'What is your reaction to the idea that depressing thoughts can keep depression going?', 'How do you think these ideas might apply to you personally?', and 'How far do you think this might be helpful to you?' Eliciting doubts and reservations is particularly important where patients have failed to respond to previous treatment. Here it may be helpful openly to invite scepticism, for example, 'I know that you've made other attempts to sort these problems out, and they don't seem to have worked. So I suppose you may well feel doubtful about your chances here. If you do have doubts, I'd be really pleased if you would tell me about them, so that we can bring them into the open and take a look at them.' When reservations are openly expressed, they can be constructively tackled, if only by acknowledging that the patient's opinion is of value ('I'm very glad you brought that up') and by reaching an agreement that the best way to find out if cognitive behaviour therapy works is to try it.

4. *Beginning treatment*

Specifically, beginning treatment means identifying a target for immediate intervention and agreeing on homework assignments to be carried out before the next session. More generally, it involves demonstrating what therapy will entail in practice, i.e. the focus on specific problems, the requirement for active collaboration, and so forth. Useful assignments after the initial interview include:

(a) the patient listening to an audio-tape of the session to ensure that the information given does indeed reflect his or her current situation;

(b) reading *Coping with depression* (Beck and Greenberg 1974), a booklet produced by the Center for Cognitive Therapy in Philadelphia, which describes treatment in more detail;

(c) monitoring activities and mood; and

(d) monitoring negative automatic thoughts.

Table 6.3   The structure of subsequent therapy sessions

---

1. *Set the agenda*

2. *Weekly items:*
    review of events since last session
    feedback on previous session
    homework review:
        outcome?
        difficulties?
        what has been learned?

3. *The day's major topic(s):*
    specific strategies
    specific problems
    long-term problems

    List in order of priority

4. *Homework assignment(s):*
    task?
    rationale?
    predicted difficulties?

5. *Feedback:*
    understanding?
    reactions?

Subsequent therapy sessions

With rare exceptions, later sessions follow the pattern shown in Table 6.3.

1.   *Setting the agenda*

Agenda-setting is introduced at the beginning of Session 2; for example, 'Before we start, I would like to set our agenda for today's session. That means deciding what we want to work on today. We'll do this at the beginning of each session from now on. We only have a limited time each week, and the idea is to make sure that we cover what seems most important to each of us. How does that sound?' In addition to listing major topics for the day, the agenda automatically includes a review of events since the last session, feedback on the previous session, and a review of homework.

2.   *Weekly items*

Review of events   This should be brief but sufficient to show the therapist how things have gone since the previous session, and to allow issues and incidents relevant to therapy to be brought to light.

Feedback on the previous session   Questions such as 'Have you had any further thoughts on what we covered last time?', and 'When you had time to think about it, what were your reactions to our last session?' show patients that they are expected to reflect on and to learn from therapy.

Homework review   This emphasizes the importance of self-help, allows the therapist to identify difficulties and misunderstandings that might otherwise go undetected, and provides as opportunity to reinforce independent functioning. Useful questions include, 'What were the results of your homework assignments?', 'What difficulties did you encounter?' 'What could you do to overcome these in future?' 'What have you learned?' and 'How can you use what you learned to tackle other problems?'

3.   The day's major topic(s)

In the majority of sessions, most of the time is devoted to this item. Major topics, which are defined by therapist and patient in collaboration, vary from week to week. They include working on specific cognitive–behavioural strategies (such as learning to question negative automatic thoughts), working on particular difficulties that have arisen during the week (such as set-backs), and working on long-standing problems (such as marital difficulties) which form a continued focus over a number of sessions. When several topics seem important, therapist and patient decide priorities together. Similarly, when issues which were not originally identified as agenda items arise during sessions, the decision as to whether to change tack, or to continue working on what has already been agreed, is taken collaboratively. Generally speaking, it is better to deal thoroughly with one or two issues than to tackle several superficially and fail to reach closure on any. What has been learned in dealing properly with one difficulty can be generalized to deal with others.

4.   Homework assignment(s)

Self-help assignments to be carried out between sessions are most likely to be helpful if they:

(a)   *follow logically* from what has occurred during the session;

(b)   are *clearly and concretely defined*, so that success is easily recognizable (e.g. 'to spend five minutes knitting every day' not 'to become a better person by next week');

(c)   have an *explicit rationale* which is understood and accepted by both therapist and patient (e.g. 'in order to test the idea that I can't do anything' not 'to see what happens'); and

(d)   are set up as *'no lose situations'* from which something useful will be learned whether the desired outcome is achieved or not.

In order to reduce the chances of misunderstanding, it is useful for both therapist and patient to write down what the task is, and what it is designed to achieve (the rationale). Equally, a written record of what was done and what the outcome was should be kept by the patient (using, for example, the standard record sheets illustrated in Figs. 6.3 and 6.4).

Even when these guidelines are followed, low motivation, lack of interest, and hopelessness will inevitably influence whether (and how) self-help assignments are carried out. To maximize the chances of success, it is helpful to predict with the patient what difficulties are likely to arise and to work out in advance how to overcome them. This includes identifying and challenging blocking negative automatic thoughts such as 'It won't work', and 'There's no point' (see 'Cognitive–behavioural strategies', p. 192, for how to do this). Similarly, when patients fail to carry out agreed assignments, the cognitive therapist acts on the assumption that negative automatic thoughts such as these got in the way. 'Lack of compliance' thus becomes a problem to be solved, rather than a lack of moral fibre or defiance on the part of the patient.

5. Feedback

The therapist's final task is to obtain feedback on the patient's reactions to the session as a whole. First, this involves asking patients to summarize what they have learned; for example, 'If I tackle problems step by step, a bit at a time, I can deal with them', 'I discovered it's not that I *can't* do anything, it's that I *think* I can't do anything', 'After therapy has ended, I will still be able to cope on my own by using what I've learned'. Secondly, it means finding out how they feel about the session and, in particular, if anything has upset or offended them. It should be made clear to the patient that honest feedback is always welcome, no matter how negative, since it allows misunderstandings to be clarified and helps the therapist to act in accordance with the patient's needs.

Major cognitive behaviour therapy strategies

The main treatment strategies used in cognitive behaviour therapy are summarized in Table 6.4. Each will be described in full in the sections which follow. In most cases, progress through these occurs in roughly chronological order, the majority of sessions being spent on applying cognitive–behavioural skills (Step 3) to a range of different problems. As a general rule of thumb, it is as well to ensure that each strategy is well established before moving on to the next. That said, the boundaries between strategies are not as clear as the Table would imply. It is perfectly possible to use two or more strategies together. Equally, in some cases only a limited range will be put into practice (for example, distrac-

Table 6.4 Major cognitive behaviour therapy strategies

1. *Cognitive strategies*	Distraction techniques
	Counting thoughts
2. *Behavioural strategies*	Monitoring activities, pleasure, and mastery
	Scheduling activities
	Graded task assignment
3. *Cognitive–behavioural strategies*	Identifying negative automatic thoughts
	Questioning negative automatic thoughts
	Behavioural experiments
4. *Preventative strategies*	Identifying assumptions
	Challenging assumptions
	Use of set-backs
	Preparing for the future

tion techniques are unlikely to be used with a person who is able immediately and effectively to question and test negative automatic thoughts). Broadly, choice of strategy at any point is determined by an assessment of which deficits are the most appropriate targets for intervention at that moment. The following questions may be useful in deciding which strategy to use with which patient at what point in therapy:

How severe in the patient's depression?

What deficits are currently most prominent? The more severe the depression, for example, the more likely it is that patients will have difficulty in maintaining normal levels of activity. If so, monitoring and scheduling activities are a first priority, not least because periods of inactivity provide fertile ground for depressive ruminations.

At what point in therapy is the patient?

In general it is useful to build on existing knowledge and skills. A person must know how to recognize negative automatic thoughts, for example, before learning how to test and question them.

What problem is currently most distressing to the patient?

It is essential to work on problems which patients perceive as relevant to their immediate concerns. Where there is disagreement between therapist and patient as to what problem should be tackled next, open discussion of the pros and cons of options available (see p. 421) can provide a mutually satisfactory solution. One severely depressed patient, for example, wanted to work on his difficult and painful relationship with his parents immediately after entering treatment. The therapist, on the other hand, thought that he would be in a better position to deal with this problem constructively once he had some control over his depression. When they examined the pros and cons of the two options, it was clear that independent attempts to solve the problem were always undermined by intense depressed mood resulting in hours of futile rumination. A compromise was reached: in sessions, where it was 'safe', therapist and patient worked together to unravel the problem relationship; between sessions, the patient devoted his energies to developing depression management skills. If the difference of opinion had not been openly resolved, symptom-relief techniques which might otherwise have proved helpful would have been perceived as irrelevant by the patient.

What problem is currently most open to change?

To encourage hope and foster engagement in treatment, it is crucial that therapy sessions and homework assignments furnish success experiences (no matter how small) which patients can attribute to themselves, and which provide direct experiential evidence that depression can, through their own efforts, be controlled. This is especially important at the beginning of treatment.

Step 1. Cognitive strategies

These techniques are presented to the patient as a way of cutting down on time spent ruminating where this is clearly leading to increased distress rather than to constructive problem-solving. They are particularly useful early in treatment, before the patient has become skilled at finding alternatives to negative automatic thoughts. They do not produce fundamental cognitive change but, by reducing the frequency of depressing thoughts, lead to improvements in mood which can then be used to facilitate problem-solving. This should be clearly explained to the patient, for example:

Therapist 'So at the moment you are spending a lot of time going over and over the problems in your mind?'
Patient 'Yes, I am.'
Th. 'And how does that make you feel?'
Pt 'Terrible.'
Th. 'What happens if you manage to distract yourself, make yourself concentrate on something else?'
Pt 'Well, I find that very difficult, but if I can do it, it helps.'

Th.   'So how would you feel about learning to shut out the thoughts more effectively? What do you think might happen if you could?'

Pt   'I suppose I might feel better.'

Th.   'That sounds like a possibility, doesn't it? Of course, the problems won't go away, just because you're not thinking about them. The idea is to get some control over how you feel. That way you will find that in the longer run you can look at things more constructively and be in a better position to sort them out.'

Some patients use distraction as a way of avoiding painful issues ('cognitive avoidance'). They can be encouraged to assess the advantages (feeling better in the short term) and disadvantages (leaving problems unsolved in the longer term) of this policy. Thoughts that prevent patients from tackling painful issues (for example, 'It'll be too much for me', or 'If I forget it, it'll go away') can be identified and questioned in the same way as any other negative automatic thoughts (see Step 3 below).

Distraction techniques

Focus on an object

Patients are taught to focus attention on an object, describing it to themselves in as much detail as possible. Cue questions include: 'Where exactly is it?', 'How big is it?', 'What colour is it?', 'What is it made of?', 'Exactly how many of them are there?', 'What is it for?', etc.

Sensory awareness

Patients are taught to focus on their surroundings as a whole, using sight, hearing, taste, touch, and smell. Cue questions include: 'What exactly can you see if you look around you? And what else? And what else?', 'What can you hear? Inside your body? Inside the room? Outside the room? Outside the building?', 'What can you taste?', 'What are you touching? Can you feel your body in the chair? Can you feel your clothes on your body? Your hair? Your glasses? Your shoes?', 'What can you smell?', etc.

Mental exercises

This includes counting back from 1000 in 7s, thinking of animals beginning with each letter of the alphabet in turn, remembering a favourite walk in detail—indeed, any absorbing mental activity.

Pleasant memories and fantasies

Vivid, concrete memories of past pleasures (e.g. an enjoyable holiday) and fantasies (e.g. what patients would do if they won the Pools) can be used as distractors. The disadvantages of these are that access to pleasant memories may be difficult (cf. Clark and Teasdale 1982) and that positive cognitions are only too readily overwhelmed by negative ones.

Absorbing activities

It is important to select activities which occupy mind and body alike, e.g. crosswords and puzzles, or playing tennis. Those which do not require much thought can be made more absorbing by combining them with others, for example listening to the radio while doing the ironing.

To begin with, poor concentration often makes it difficult to use these techniques successfully for more than very brief periods. With practice, however, they will block out ruminations more and more effectively.

Counting thoughts

Counting thoughts (Burns 1980, pp. 64–6) is designed to promote distance from negative thinking. It involves learning to note the occurrence of negative automatic thoughts (for example by pressing a golf or knitting counter, or by making a mark on card), and to put them to one side rather than allowing them to influence mood. A disadvantage of this technique is that its immediate effect may be an actual or apparent increase in negative automatic thoughts, and thus in depressed mood, as the patient becomes increasingly aware of thoughts without having the skills to modify them.

Step 2.   Behavioural strategies

The goal of behavioural strategies such as monitoring and scheduling activities and graded task assignment is to maximize engagement in mood-elevating activites. This is not dissimilar from 'pleasant-event scheduling' (Lewinsohn, Munoz, Youngren, and Zeiss 1978, Chapter 7). However, the techniques are presented within the framework of a cognitive rationale, i.e. they are explicitly used to test thoughts which block engagement in such activities, or lead people to discount or devalue what they do, and thus help to maintain the depression. (See pp. 210–18 for a handout which may be given to patients to explain the use of behavioural strategies.)

Monitoring activities

An example of a completed record-sheet is shown in Fig. 6.3. Patients are asked to record what they do on an hour-by-hour basis, and to rate each activity out of 10 for pleasure (P) and for mastery (M). 'P' ratings show how much the person enjoyed the activity. 'M' ratings show how much of an achievement the activity was, given how the person felt at the time.

Self-monitoring provides hard data on overall levels of activity. This allows therapist and patient to test thoughts such as 'I'm not doing anything'. Such thoughts may or may not be correct. If they are incorrect, the record makes this clear. If, on the other hand, there is some truth in them, identifying where and how difficulties in engagement arise is a first step to finding a more satisfying pattern of activity. Self-monitoring also demonstrates the relationship between mood and activity. Rating specific activities for pleasure and mastery tests thoughts such as 'Nothing I do makes any difference to how I feel' (which may reflect a failure to perceive positive experiences) and 'Nothing I do is worthwhile' (which may reflect the depressive tendency to discount perceived positives because they fail to meet some notional standard or behaviour). A depressed person's sense of mastery is often undermined by thoughts like 'Well, so what? It's only what's expected of me', and 'Yes, but I used to do it much better than this'. These thoughts fail to acknowledge that, in depression, the simplest tasks represent a major expenditure of effort which should receive due credit. Thus, available reinforcement is reduced, discouragement and self-criticism increase, and activity levels fall still further. Introducing a more realistic concept of mastery (i.e. one that takes account of how the patient feels instead of demanding 'normal' performance) forms a crucial part of remobilization.

Scheduling activities

Once accurate information is available on what patients are doing and what satisfaction they obtain from their activities, the schedule is used to plan each day in advance on an hour-by-hour basis. The goal is to increase activity levels and to maximize mastery and pleasure. This strategy has a number of advantages. It reduces an apparently overwhelming mass of tasks to a manageable list, removes the need for repeated decision-making ('What shall I do now?'), makes it more likely that activities will be carried out, encourages an increase in the proportion of satisfying activities, and increases patients' sense of control over their lives. Information from the schedule can be used to challenge negative automatic thoughts like 'I'll never get everything done', 'I shouldn't take time to enjoy myself', and the like (see Step 3 below). In some cases, the schedule will aid a return to normal, non-depressed functioning only by successive approximations. A severely depressed person, for example, may initially only be able to plan and carry out half an hour's activity a day.

Graded task assignment

This refers to the practice of maximizing the chances of success by breaking tasks down into small, manageable steps, each of which is reinforced in its own right. Within cognitive behaviour therapy, each step is facilitated by identifying and challenging cognitive blocks to progress ('I won't be able to do it', 'It's too much for me', etc.). The technique can be used to overcome procrastination and to help patients to deal with inertia and to face anxiety-provoking situations. Depressed patients often report

Cognitive behaviour therapy

Name ....

	M	T	W
9–10	Asleep	Got up, had tea (P2, M5)	Got up, had tea (P2, M7)
10–11	Got up, had tea (P2, M4)	Washing-up Radio (P1, M4)	Back to bed (P0, M0)
11–12	Shopping (P3, M3)	Shopping (P1, M3)	Asleep
12–1	Looking for lost cat (P0, M10)	Washing (P0, M4)	Asleep
1–2	Sat in garden (P0, M0)	Listened to radio (P1, M0)	Got up Lunch (P2, M5)
2–3	Listened to radio in garden (P1,M0)		Listened to radio (P1, M0)
3–4			Spoke to friend (P5, M1)
4–5	Fed cats (P1, M0)	Asleep	Watched TV (P1, M0)
5–6	Listened to radio (P1, M0)	Took cat to vet (P0, M6)	
6–7	Watched TV (P1, M0)	Got supper (P1, M4)	Went to cinema and had dinner with friends (P6, M2)
7–8	Got supper (P1, M2)	Watched TV (P1, M0)	
8–12	Watched TV (P1, M0)		

Fig. 6.3 Weekly activity schedule: Mrs R

Week beginning ....

Th	F	S	S
Asleep	Asleep	Asleep	Asleep Got up (P0, M4)
Got up, had tea (P3, M4)	Got up, had tea (P2, M6) Fed cats (P1, M2)	Asleep	Listened to radio. Had tea (P3, M0)
Went to bank and shops (P3, M6)	Spoke to friend (P5, M2)	Got up, breakfast (P2, M4)	Read paper (P3, M3)
Listened to radio (P2, M0)	Drove to meet friend for lunch (P1, M6)	Listened to radio (P4, M0)	Phoned friend about job (P5, M5)
Drove to friend's house (P1, M5)	Lunch with friend (P5, M2)	Went shopping (P2, M2)	Read paper (P3, M0)
Visited friend with new baby (P5, M1)	Visited mother (P4, M1)		Ironing, radio (P3, M1)
		Read paper (P1, M3)	Talked to sister (P8, M0)
	Argument (P0, M6)	Read book (P2, M3)	Shopping with sister (P5, M4)
	Hair cut (P5, M4)	Cleaned silver (P1, M5)	Talked to sister (P5, M2)
Drove home (P2, M5)	Drove to flat Supper (P2, M3)	Got supper (P2, M3)	Got supper (P3, M4)
Got supper (P3, M3)	Drink with neighbours (P5, M1)	Watched TV (P3, M1)	Watched TV (P3, M0)
Watched TV (P3, M0)			

Fig. 6.3 (*cont'd*)

that they repeatedly fail to carry out tasks they have set themselves, and use this fact as evidence of personal inadequacy and decline. This may be because they have not adjusted their standards to take account of how they feel, and are still expecting as much of themselves as if they were not depressed. Apparent failures contribute to hopelessness about the possibility of change. Graded task assignment counters hopelessness by encouraging patients to reduce tasks to manageable proportions, to increase the frequency of self-reward, and to redefine success realistically, taking into account how they feel. (See the handout for patients on p. 214 for more detailed instructions on graded task assignment.)

Step 3.   Cognitive–behavioural strategies

Most treatment sessions and homework assignments are directed towards teaching the patient to identify, question, and test negative automatic thoughts. These skills form the heart of cognitive therapy, and are used to reduce depressive symptomatology and later to tackle 'life-problems'. (A handout for patients giving details of how to identify and question depressing thoughts will be found on pp. 218–34.)

The nature of negative automatic thoughts

The content of depressive thinking has been categorized (e.g. Beck 1967) in terms of a 'cognitive triad'. This comprises distorted, negative views of:

(1)   the self (e.g. 'I'm useless');
(2)   current experience (e.g. 'Nothing I do turns out right'); and
(3)   the future (e.g. 'I will never get better').

Depressive automatic thoughts have a number of characteristics which may influence how therapy is carried out and affect the relationship between therapist and patient. They are *habitual*, and so may be difficult to identify. They are *automatic and involuntary*, and so may be hard to control. They are *plausible*, especially when accompanying emotions are strong, and so may be difficult to challenge. Finally, they occur in response to an *extensive* range of stimuli, including therapy itself. So talk of ending treatment may be interpreted as rejection (e.g. 'She just wants to get rid of me'), and homework assignments may be abandoned because the patient predicts inevitable failure (e.g. 'I'll do it wrong'). Negative automatic thoughts which prevent engagement in therapy and result in slow progress are often similar to those which prevent recovery in a more general sense. They should be identified and questioned just like any other negative automatic thoughts. (For a fuller discussion, see Beck *et al.* 1979, Chapters 14 and 15.)

Negative automatic thoughts are a product of errors in processing, through which perceptions and interpretations of experience are distorted. These include:

- *Overgeneralization*, making sweeping judgements on the basis of single instances. Thus a depressed person who made one mistake might conclude: 'Everything I do goes wrong'.

- *Selective abstraction*, attending only to negative aspects of experiences. Thus a person might state 'I didn't have a moment's pleasure today', not because this was true, but because pleasures had failed to enter conscious awareness.

- *Dichotomous reasoning*, thinking in extremes. Thus a patient might discount a less than perfect performance because: 'If I can't get it 100 per cent right, there's no point in doing it at all'.

- *Personalization*, taking responsibility for things that have little or nothing to do with oneself. Thus a depressed person who failed to catch the eye of a friend in the street might think: 'I must have done something to offend him'.

- *Arbitrary inference*, jumping to conclusions on the basis of inadequate evidence. Thus someone who had problems with a first homework assignment might conclude: 'This therapy will never work for me'.

Negative automatic thoughts relate to the full range of depressive symptomatology. Behavioural and motivational symptoms are associated with an expectation of negative outcomes (e.g. 'I can't do it'). Affective symptoms relate to cognitions which differ in content according to the nature of the perceived impact on the personal domain. Sadness, for example, is associated with thoughts of loss (e.g. 'Everything I ever valued has gone'), anxiety with thoughts of risk or threat (see Chapter 3). Cognitive symptoms may be precipitated or intensified by negative automatic thoughts. Thus ruminations about current problems may hamper concentration and memory, leading on to further distressing thoughts (e.g. 'My mind is going'). Similarly, somatic symptoms may be intensified by negative interpretations of their significance (e.g. 'If I don't sleep, I'll go mad').

Identifying negative automatic thoughts

Patients usually first practise identifying negative automatic thoughts with the therapist, and then develop their skills through self-monitoring homework assignments. The Dysfunctional Thoughts Record, illustrated in Fig. 6.4, can routinely be used for this purpose. The column heads on the record sheet act as a guide to the sequence of steps involved. The patient is taught:

DATE	EMOTION(S) *What do you feel?* *How bad was it (0–100)?*	SITUATION *What were you doing or thinking about?*	AUTOMATIC THOUGHTS *What exactly were your thoughts? How far did you believe each of them (0–100%)?*	RATIONAL RESPONSE *What are your rational answers to the automatic thoughts? How far do you believe each of them (0–100%)?*	OUTCOME *1. How far do you now believe the thoughts (0–100%)?* *2. How do you feel (0–100)?* *3. What can you do now?*
Sat.	Sad 80 Empty 80 Guilty 90	Evening out with ex-husband	We're never going home together again, because of the stupid way I've handled my life. Things are never going to be as good again. I don't deserve any happiness because of the hurt I've caused him. 90%	There's nothing I can do to alter what has happened in the past. 100% There is no point dwelling on what might have been. 70% I don't know that things will never be as good again because I can't see into the future. 90% I'm still young and there are lots of people in my situation who end up having a happy life and do lots of things they never would have done if things hadn't changed. 75% In fact, the future could be better for me than the past—if I'm honest with myself, the marriage just wasn't working out for either of us. 70%	1. 60% 2. Sad 50 　 Empty 50 　 Guilty 70 3. Don't dwell on the past. Put your energy into planning future pleasures.

Fig. 6.4 Dysfunctional thoughts record: Mrs R

(1) to identify unpleasant emotions;

(2) to identify the situation in which these occur; and

(3) to identify associated negative automatic thoughts.

These steps will now be described in greater detail:

Identifying unpleasant emotions

Mood-change in a negative direction is a signal that automatic thoughts are present (it is usually easier for patients to notice changes in how they feel than to monitor thoughts directly). Patients record what the emotions are (e.g. sad, angry, guilty) and rate them for intensity on a 0–100 scale. A rating of 100 means that the emotion is as strong as it could possibly be, 50 that it is moderately strong, and so on. Intensity of emotion and belief in negative automatic thoughts (see below) are rated because challenging thoughts rarely undermines belief in them or removes the distress with which they are associated immediately and completely. Rating scales make small changes obvious. However, some people do not like them, usually because they become over-conscientious about accuracy ('Now, was it 73 or 74?') or because they feel that numbers render the process of therapy mechanical. If so, it may be necessary to devise another way of measuring change, for example assessing whether the patient feels better, worse, or the same after challenging particular thoughts.

Identifying the problem situation

Patients briefly describe the situation in which the emotions occurred, indicating what they were doing (e.g. 'talking to my husband' or 'watching TV') or the general topic they were thinking about (e.g. 'thinking about my mother-in-law coming for the weekend' or 'worrying about the way I feel').

Identifying associated negative automatic thoughts

Patients record what went through their minds when they began to feel bad, and rate how far they believe each thought on a 0–100 scale. A rating of 100 means that they are totally convinced, 50 that they only half believe the thought, and so on. Negative automatic thoughts include not only thoughts in words, but also images (see Chapter 3). They must be recorded accurately, word for word. If it is not possible to write them down when they occur, patients may find it helpful briefly to jot down or make a mental note of what happened and to return to it later for fuller analysis.

Common problems in identifying negative automatic thoughts

Patient avoids recording thoughts

Depressed mood makes it difficult for people to distance themselves from their negative thoughts. Indeed, enhancing awareness of depressing thoughts before the skills to deal with them are available can be painful and aversive. Patients who are prepared for this, and have accepted the treatment rationale, are less likely to take refuge in avoidance. It may also initially be helpful to agree to limit the time spent focusing on distressing thoughts, and to provide other means of controlling them (e.g. a programme of absorbing activities).

No negative automatic thoughts

If no negative thoughts can be identified in a particular upsetting situation, it may be helpful to ask: 'What was the meaning of that situation for you? What did it say about you/your situation/your future?' Questions such as these reveal the implicit personal significance of events. For instance, a patient who had just begun therapy became depressed and agitated before each treatment session. She could not find any thoughts that might account for how she felt. When asked for the meaning of coming for treatment, however, she stated, 'It shows how far I've gone downhill. I shouldn't need this kind of help. I should be able to manage alone.'

Missing core depressing thoughts

It is important to look for thoughts, images, or meanings powerful enough to account for the emotions experienced. One patient described how a cake she made got a little burnt in the baking. The emotion she reported was hopelessness, rated at 90 per cent. The thought originally identified was, 'I made a mess of that.' This thought did not appear to the therapist to 'fit' the degree of emotion experienced. Further questioning revealed another much more depressing thought: 'I'm completely useless.' To ensure that core depressing thoughts of this kind are correctly identified, the therapist may find it useful to ask, 'If I thought this, would I feel as bad as that?' If the answer is 'no', the search should continue.

Asking for explanations rather than thoughts

Therapists sometimes fail to obtain accurate reports of cognitions because their exploratory questions do not clearly show patients what is wanted. 'Why?' questions fall into this category. For example, 'Why were you upset?' could be answered in a number of ways, none of which would provide concrete information about the person's thinking processes, e.g. 'I have a complex from when I was little' (historical explanation), 'I was just coming up to my period' (biological explanation), 'That's the sort of person I am' (personality explanation), 'Anybody would get upset about something like that' (human nature explanation). None of these answers are much use to the cognitive therapist. The exploration of upsetting incidents should be directed towards the point where the therapist can ask the question, 'What exactly went through your mind at that moment?' This question shows the patient exactly what the therapist wants to know. As a general rule, 'why' questions are to be avoided. It is better to substitute questions beginning with 'what' or 'how'.

Testing negative automatic thoughts

There are two main methods of searching for more realistic and helpful alternatives to negative automatic thoughts: verbal challenges to their validity, and behavioural experiments designed to test them in action.

Verbal challenging

The goal of verbal challenging, in the interests of generalization and prevention, is to teach patients how to re-evaluate their thinking for themselves. This goal will not be attained if the therapist is doing all the work. So the main change strategy involves *eliciting* alternatives from the patient through systematic but sensitive questioning, rather than *supplying* alternatives through debate, lecturing, or interpretation. Useful questions patients can ask themselves include:

1. What is the evidence?'
2. What alternative views are there?
3. What are the advantages and disadvantages of this way of thinking?
4. What logical errors am I making?

Each of these will now be discussed in more detail.

What is the evidence? The evidence used to support a negative automatic thought is likely to be distorted in two major ways. First, positive information (contrary evidence) is less easily recalled than negative information (supporting evidence) (Clark and Teasdale 1982). This means that the patient, without realizing it, forms conclusions on the basis of a biased sample. Secondly, neutral or positive information that *does* become available is interpreted as negative and, by the same token, genuine negative information as even more negative than the facts would warrant. It follows that:

(1) efforts should be made to uncover disconfirmatory evidence of which the patient is not initially aware; and

(2)   the validity of apparently negative evidence should be carefully questioned.

The dialogue below illustrates this point.

Patient   'My husband doesn't love me any more.'
Therapist 'That must be a very distressing thought. What makes you think that he doesn't love you?'
Pt   'Well, when he comes in in the evening, he never wants to talk to me. He just wants to sit and watch TV. Then he goes straight off to bed.'
Th.   'OK. Now, is there any evidence, anything he does, that goes against the idea that he doesn't love you?'
Pt   'I can't think of any. Well, no, wait a minute. Actually it was my birthday a couple of weeks ago, and he gave me a watch which is really lovely. I'd seen them advertised and mentioned I liked it, and he took notice and went and got me one.'
Th.   'Right. Now how does that fit with the idea that he doesn't love you?'
Pt   'Well, I suppose it doesn't really, does it? But then why is he like that in the evening?'
Th.   'I suppose him not loving you any more is one possible reason. Are there any other possible reasons?'
Pt   'Well, he has been working very hard lately. I mean, he's late home most nights, and he had to go in to the office at the weekend. So I suppose it could be that.'
Th.   'It could, couldn't it? How could you find out if that's it?'
Pt   'Well, I could say I've noticed how tired he looks and ask him how he's feeling and how the work's going. I haven't done that, I've just been getting annoyed because he doesn't pay any attention to me.'
Th.   'That sounds like an excellent idea. How would you like to make that a homework task for this week?'

This illustrates how homework can be used to gather information to clarify issues on which existing evidence is inadequate. It should be noted, incidentally, that the patient's negative perspective may in fact be correct. In this particular case, tiredness was indeed the explanation for the husband's behaviour. But the patient could have been right.

What alternative views are there?   In the example given above, a possible alternative explanation for the husband's behaviour was relatively easily available. This is not always the case. Supplementary questions include:

1.   What would you have thought about this before you got depressed? (Provided that the depression has not lasted for a long time, people can normally recall that before its onset they thought about things differently. Current fluctuations in mood can be used in the same way, e.g. 'On a day when you are feeling relatively OK, what would you think about this?')

2. What might someone else whose views you trusted think about this?

3. What would you say to another person who came to you with this problem? (People are often much better at solving others' problems than their own. One can use this facility to generate alternative views.)

It is important that alternatives generated are related to the facts. Otherwise, patients may see them merely as empty reassurances.

What are the advantages and disadvantages of this way of thinking? This question is particularly useful when questioning self-critical thoughts. Many people see self-criticism as necessary and constructive, and do not notice it undermining attempts to overcome their difficulties:

Therapist 'It sounds as if you are very hard on yourself when you try something and it doesn't work out.'

Patient 'I don't think so. I mean, if I didn't have high standards for myself, I'd never do anything.'

Th. 'So in order to keep yourself going at all, you have to be hard on yourself?'

Pt 'That's right.'

Th. 'Now, you have a little girl, don't you? When she was learning to talk, how did you help her? Did you pick on all the mistakes she made, and get angry with her when she used the wrong word?'

Pt 'No, I didn't.'

Th. 'What do you think would have happened if you had done so?'

Pt 'Well, I suppose she might have got discouraged and stopped trying.'

Th. 'Now how does that fit with the way you are with yourself?'

Pt 'Well, yes, I do get fed up and want to give up.'

Th. 'So what might happen in fact if you stopped being so hard on mistakes and encouraged yourself more?'

Pt 'You mean be towards myself as I might to someone else who was trying to learn something new?'

Th. 'Exactly. What might be the advantages of experimenting with that approach over the next week?'

Pt 'Well, I suppose it might make it easier to keep trying.'

What logical errors am I making? This is particularly helpful where a patient regularly makes the same mistake. Useful questions include the following (more examples will be found in the handout on pp. 255–31):

(1) Am I condemning myself as a person on the basis of one event? (overgeneralization);

(2) Am I concentrating on my weaknesses and forgetting my strengths? (selective abstraction);

(3)   Am I thinking in all-or-nothing terms? (dichotomous reasoning);

(4)   Am I taking responsibility for something which is not my fault? (personalization);

(5)   Am I jumping to conclusions? (arbitrary inference).

On the Dysfunctional Thoughts Record, answers to these and similar questions are recorded in the column headed 'Rational response'. Each is rated for belief on a 0–100 scale, in the same way as the original negative automatic thoughts. Then the effectiveness of the answers is assessed in the final column of the record sheet. First, belief in the original negative thoughts is re-rated, the goal being a reduction in belief. Secondly, the intensity of the distressing emotions that accompanied the original thoughts is re-rated, the goal being a reduction in intensity. Finally, the patient sets up a behavioural experiment which will test the validity of the answers in action.

Behavioural experiments

Verbal challenging of automatic thoughts is routinely followed by behavioural assignments through which new ideas are put to the test. These may involve taking action to improve an unsatisfactory external situation, or finding more effective ways of reacting to an external situation that cannot be improved. Questioning negative thoughts encourages patients to evaluate realistically the costs and advantages of acting differently, and to prepare for a range of possible outcomes. So it opens the way to changes in behaviour. These in turn produce consequences that contradict the original thoughts and thus further erode their credibility. Thus, within cognitive behaviour therapy, behaviour change is a means of testing the validity of negative automatic thoughts, and not an end in itself. Sometimes new behaviours already exist within the person's repertoire, but have been blocked by negative thoughts. So, for example, a person might know *how to* express disagreement, but be inhibited from doing so by thoughts such as 'If I disagree, they won't like me.' In other cases, the patient may not simply be blocked by negative thoughts, but may not know *how to* act more effectively. In this case, new behaviours such as assertiveness, social skills, problem-solving, or study skills may need to be learned in therapy.

The steps involved in setting up a behavioural experiment are similar to the steps involved in carrying out scientific research, that is:

1.   *Make a prediction.*   Specify the thought which the experiment will test, e.g. 'If I tell my wife how bad I feel, she will be angry with me.'

2.   *Review existing evidence for and against the prediction.*   This in

itself may undermine evidence supporting negative predictions and bring contradictory evidence which had been unperceived or discounted to light.

3. *Devise a specific experiment to test the validity of the prediction.* It must be clear to both therapist and patient exactly what the patient will do. In addition, the experiment should be set up in such a way as to maximize the chances of a positive outcome. In the example above, for instance, the way in which the husband expresses his feelings could be discussed, and role-played if necessary.

4. *Note the results.* Like all homework assignments, behavioural experiments should be set up as 'no lose situations' (p. 183) which will be of value whether they turn out as the patient wishes or not. If the experiment 'works' (the wife does *not* get angry), so much the better. The patient has acquired experiential evidence that negative thoughts can be incorrect. In this case, the next step is to build on what has been learned so that the specific lesson can be generalized to other situations. If, on the other hand, the experiment does not 'work' (the wife *does* get angry) this too is valuable information. What went wrong? Was it something the patient did? Were his good intentions undermined by further negative thoughts? Once the problem is identified, plans can be made to handle the situation more effectively next time round. Thus even apparently negative results can be used constructively.

5. *Draw conclusions.* As a final step, it is often helpful to formulate a rule encapsulating what has been learned. In the example given above, the conclusion was: 'Don't make assumptions about how other people will react to you: find out for yourself.'

Common problems in challenging negative automatic thoughts

Rational responses make no difference

Rational responses change the intensity of distressing emotions and belief in negative automatic thoughts only if the patient believes them. This is one reason why they should be elicited from patients, rather than supplied by the therapist. An answer which makes sense to the therapist will not necessarily make sense to the patient. Similarly, attempts to reassure without any call on factual evidence (e.g. 'You'll be OK') and injunctions (e.g. 'Don't be silly') are not helpful. That said, it is not necessary for patients to believe all their answers 100 per cent from the outset. Challenging negative thoughts successfully is a skill; it requires practice. When apparently valid answers do not lead to any reduction in distress or in belief in the original thoughts, this usually means that the patient has reservations about their validity. These 'yes, but . . .'s can be answered in their turn.

Being contaminated by the patient's thinking

Therapists sometimes fall into the trap of thinking that patients are justified in being depressed, especially where their life circumstances are difficult. Provided there is good evidence that the 'cognitive triad' is present, the therapist should assume that a change in perspective is possible. Not all people in genuinely difficult situations are depressed: some maintain a positive, problem-solving stance and guard their self-esteem despite their difficulties. What is it about *this* person's thinking that prevents him or her from doing so?

Challenging the impossible

Facts cannot be challenged. Sometimes what the therapist interprets as a depressive distortion turns out to be objectively true. This is one reason why it is important to establish what evidence supports the patient's views. Similarly, it is not possible to challenge questions. Negative automatic thoughts associated with anxiety, for example, often take the form of queries about the future, e.g. 'What if I can't cope?' Such questions usually disguise negative predictions. It is the therapist's task to find the prediction, i.e. to turn the question into a statement which can then be rated according to how far the patient believes it, and challenged. In the above example this might be, 'I won't be able to cope. Belief: 80 per cent.'

Step 4.   Preventative strategies

A major advantage of psychological treatments for depression over anti-depressant medication is that they can reduce the risk of relapse. Cognitive behaviour therapy is particularly rich in this respect. In addition to teaching the wide range of depression management skills described above, it decreases vulnerability to future episodes by undermining the fundamental assumptions on which depressive thinking is based.

Identifying and challenging dysfunctional assumptions

Identifying dysfunctional assumptions

Once the patient can skilfully identify and challenge negative automatic thoughts, the focus of treatment shifts to dealing with the dysfunctional assumptions which underlie them. These have certain recognizable characteristics:

   1.   *They do not reflect the reality of human experience.* So, for example,

the belief 'I should always be strong' ignores human vulnerability. In this sense assumptions are 'unreasonable'.

2. *They are rigid, overgeneralized, and extreme*, taking no account of variations in circumstances.

3. *They prevent rather than facilitate goal-attainment*, as when perfectionist standards produce anxiety that inhibits performance.

4. *Their violation is associated with extreme and excessive emotions*, e.g. depression and despair rather than sadness or regret. When their terms are met, the positive emotions experienced are equally strong, e.g. elation rather than pleasure or contentment.

5. *They are relatively impervious to ordinary experience*. This is partly because, although the individual acts *as if* they were true, they are often unformulated and hence largely unconscious. In addition, abandoning them may be attended by apparently unacceptable risks, e.g. 'If I stop putting everyone else first all the time, no one will like me any more.'

Beck, Hollon, Young, Bedrosian, and Budenz (1985) have grouped dysfunctional assumptions in terms of three central areas of concern: *achievement* (high standards of performance, the need to succeed, etc.), *acceptance* (the need to be liked, loved, etc.), and *control* (the need to control events, the need to be strong, etc.). In a given situation, any of these may be operative. So people might avoid close relationships because they feared being unable to meet the other's standards (achievement), because they feared rejection (acceptance), or because they feared their life might be taken over (control). Beck, Epstein, and Harrison (1983) have further grouped assumptions in terms of superordinate dimensions which they suggest may influence the kind of events that precipitate depression, the pattern of symptomatology, and the way people respond to treatment. They identify two dimensions: '*sociotropy*' (which emphasizes the importance of interpersonal relations), and '*autonomy*' (which emphasizes the importance of independence and freedom of choice). These dimensions, which are not mutually exclusive, are much broader in scope than specific dysfunctional assumptions. In this sense they are more akin to 'personality variables', influencing what people feel, think, and do throughout their lives and across a wide range of different situations. Groupings such as these may be used clinically to extend understanding of particular patients, and to guide the way in which treatment is carried out. For example, a highly autonomous person might find it difficult to accept suggestions emanating from the therapist, and be tempted to terminate therapy prematurely because they 'should' be able to manage alone. In contrast, a highly sociotropic person might be over-eager to please the therapist, and have difficulty in operating independently between sessions. Both these habitual response patterns can be used to advantage, in the first case by capitalizing on self-help aspects of treatment, in the second by using the patient's desire to please to mobilize him or her before encouraging greater independence.

Identifying dysfunctional assumptions can be more difficult than catching negative automatic thoughts because, rather than discrete events occurring in consciousness, they are generalized rules which may never have been formulated in so many words. They may need to be inferred rather than observed, using clues such as these:

1. *Themes* which emerge during treatment, e.g. preoccupation with doing things well, or with rejection.

2. *Logical errors* in automatic thoughts which may reflect similar errors in underlying dysfunctional assumptions, e.g. dichotomous reasoning: 'If we have another argument, I'm leaving' (thought); 'If you can't agree with someone, there's no point in having a relationship at all' (assumption).

3. *Global self-evaluations,* e.g. 'stupid', 'childish', 'weak', may reflect standards of behaviour which are not otherwise explicit. Global evaluations of others often serve the same function.

4. *Memories, family sayings.* People sometimes have vivid memories of childhood experiences which seem, at least intuitively, to 'match' current beliefs. One woman believed it was absolutely necessary to defer to others' wishes at all times. She vividly remembered her mother leaving the house with the threat that she would not love her any more unless she did as she was told. Although she was now in her forties, any sign of disapproval still produced in her the same feeling of despair. Useful questions for identifying memories of this kind include: 'Can you recall feeling this way before?', 'When did you first have this feeling?', and 'Does this remind you of anything in your past?'

5. *High mood* often indicates that the terms of an assumption have been met, just as low mood signals its violation. So, for example, a person who believes it is necessary to be liked all the time will be delighted (rather than simply pleased) when someone likes them.

6. *Downward arrow.* This technique (Burns 1980, pp. 235–41) involves identifying in the usual way a problem situation and the unpleasant emotions and negative thoughts experienced within that situation. Rather than challenging the thoughts themselves, the therapist asks: 'Supposing that was true, what would that mean to you?' This and similar questions (e.g. 'What would that say about you?', 'What would happen then?', 'If so, what would be so bad about that?') are repeated until it is possible to formulate a statement general enough to encompass

Situation: Session with patient who reported feeling no better at the end
Emotions: Guilty, anxious, depressed
Thoughts: That was a terrible session—we didn't get anywhere

Supposing that was true, what would it mean to you?

The patient won't get better

Supposing they didn't, what would that mean to you?

That I had done a bad job

And supposing you had, what would that mean to you?

That I was a lousy therapist

Supposing you were a lousy therapist, what then?

Sooner or later I'd be found out

And what does that mean, 'found out'?

That every one would know I was no good and despise me
It would prove that my success up to now is a con, pure luck

**i.e. To think well of myself, and to have others think well of me, I
have to succeed at every single thing I do**

Fig. 6.5 Downward arrow technique: physician heal thyself

not only the original problem-situation, but also other situations where
the same rule is operating. An example is given in Fig. 6.5.

Challenging dysfunctional assumptions
Once a dysfunctional assumption has been identified, questioning and
behavioural experimentation are used to find a new, more moderate and
realistic rule. Helpful questions include:

In what way is the assumption unreasonable? This question, like 'What is the evidence?', calls for an assessment of the facts as far as they can be ascertained. Does the assumption fit the way the world works? In what way does it fail to reflect the reality of human experience? For example, it is unreasonable to demand that life should always be fair, because the fact of the matter is that it is not.

In what way is the assumption unhelpful? Does it help the patient to get what they want out of life, or does it hinder them? A valuable strategy here is to list the advantages and disadvantages of holding the belief. It often becomes clear that the belief has more drawbacks than pay-offs, and that many pay-offs are more apparent than real. For example, perfectionist assumptions may genuinely produce high-quality performance on occasion. However, they often arouse a degree of anxiety which is incompatible with quality performance, and may lead to avoidance of challenges and opportunities.

Where did the assumption come from? Adopting a historical perspective is unusual in cognitive behaviour therapy. In some cases, however, understanding how dysfunctional assumptions were formed promotes distance from them. What was relevant to the child may clearly be less so to the adult. In the example given above under 'Memories and family sayings', the patient as a child had believed that *survival* depended on averting her mother's displeasure. As an adult, required for the first time systematically to re-evaluate the consequences of displeasing others, she realized that her current need was determined by circumstances that no longer held true. Pleasing others, in other words, was rarely a matter of life or death. At the same time, understanding the original significance of rejection made sense of the strength of her adult emotions.

What would be a more moderate alternative which would confer the advantages of the dysfunctional assumption without its disadvantages? Dysfunctional assumptions are usually extreme in their demands. This is reflected in the language in which they are expressed (shoulds, oughts, musts; absolutes like always, never, everyone). Formulating an alternative, which takes account of shades of grey, prepares the person to deal effectively with occasions which, in the terms of the original assumption, would count as failures and lead to depression. One patient, for example, believed that asking for help was a sign of personal inadequacy. His assumption was, 'You should always be able to deal with everything yourself, no matter how bad you feel.' Over the course of therapy, a more helpful and realistic alternative was formulated, 'It's good to be able to deal with problems independently. But it's not fair on myself to expect to be able to do it all the time. I'm only human, and I need help sometimes, just like anyone else. So: deal with it if you can, but if you can't, take all the help you can get.' Alternatives to dysfunctional assumptions can be written on flash-cards for patients to read repeatedly until acting in accordance with them becomes second nature (see Chapter 3, p. 88).

As with negative automatic thoughts, verbal challenges to dysfunctional assumptions should always be tested and reinforced by changes in behaviour. Given the likelihood that assumptions are long-standing, change is unlikely to occur overnight. Behavioural experiments may well need to be repeated over a more lengthy period than experiments relating to specific thoughts, and in a wider variety of situations. Experiments may take a number of forms, including: gathering information about other people's standards (rather than assuming one's own are universal); observing what other people do (an indication of their differing standards); acting against assumptions and observing the consequences (which may well provoke considerable anxiety); and testing out the new rule in action. The man in the example above made a point of asking for help at work, at home, and with his friends, even when he did not really need it. He discovered that this did not lead to any catastrophic consequences; in fact, his relationships improved because people began to realize that he was not invulnerable and liked him the more for it.

Use of set-backs

Throughout treatment, patients regularly practise cognitive, behavioural, and cognitive–behavioural depression-management skills. Thus their ability to deal with increasingly difficult situations grows. Provided patients are taught to expect them as a normal part of recovery, set-backs which occur while treatment is still under way provide an invaluable opportunity to practise. They demonstrate in action that what has been learned can be used to control recurrences of depression.

Preparation for the future

As the end of treatment approaches, many patients worry that they will be unable to cope alone. These worries are dealt with in the same way as other upsetting cognitions. It is important to encourage the patient to express them, and to evaluate the evidence for their validity. The patient might, for example, be given a homework assignment to find answers to questions such as these: 'What evidence is there that this therapy can work for you?', 'What have you learned from the sessions?', 'How can you build on what you have learned so as to make yourself as independent and confident as possible by the end of treatment?', 'Accepting that you may experience problems again at some time, what kind of things are likely to set you back? How could you deal with them?', 'Who is there at home who could help you if necessary?', 'What arrangements have you made to contact your therapist, if your best efforts do not work?'

It may be possible to identify specific events in the future which could lead to depression, e.g. retirement, the death of a parent, or children leaving home. Therapist and patient can work together to draw up contingency plans for how to deal with these situations. On a more general level, it may be valuable to summarize whatever techniques the patient has found helpful in the form of a 'first-aid kit' containing, on the one hand, the difficulties experienced by that particular individual when they become depressed (e.g. spending a lot of time in bed ruminating, being self-critical) and, on the other hand, specific techniques which have been used successfully to overcome these (e.g. planning the day so that pleasure and mastery are maximized, being tolerant with oneself, and using praise and encouragement rather than putting oneself down). The summary is kept readily available, in a place known to the patient and perhaps to their spouse or to a close friend, so that it can be put to immediate use if depression recurs.

What if cognitive behaviour therapy fails?

A small proportion of depressed patients fail to respond to cognitive behaviour therapy (Blackburn and Bishop 1983; Fennell and Teasdale 1987a). Unfortunately, these are not easy to identify before starting treatment, though the difficulty of working with them often becomes only too evident after a small number of sessions. To avoid arousing false hopes of quick recovery in therapist and patient, it may be worthwhile initially always to contract for only five or six sessions. Where it becomes clear that a person is unlikely to respond without a lengthy intervention (for example, because they have major difficulties in establishing a collaborative therapeutic relationship), or that cognitive behaviour therapy is not the treatment of choice (for example, because serious marital difficulties emerge), treatment can then be extended or terminated relatively gracefully.

The decision to terminate treatment, and what alternatives to recommend, depend in essence on the therapist's assessment of the factors maintaining the depression. Where these are judged to be primarily cognitive, but chronic, generalized, and accompanied by extensive behavioural deficits, long-term therapy may be needed. There is no reason why cognitive behaviour therapy should not be extended in this way. Where maintaining factors appear to be interpersonal, marital or family therapy may be more appropriate. Again, this could be carried out within a cognitive–behavioural framework. Where maintaining factors appear to be biochemical, physical treatment might be advocated, alone or in combination with cognitive-behavioural techniques. (For a fuller discussion of difficult patients and treatment failures, see Beck *et al.* 1979, Chapters 14 and 15; Rush and Shaw 1983.)

Research findings

Early studies with subclinical populations (e.g. Shaw 1977; Taylor and Marshall 1977) and single-case series (e.g. Rush, Khatami, and Beck 1975) have now been followed by a growing body of full-scale controlled trials of cognitive behaviour therapy for depression. The main findings of these studies are summarized below. More detailed reviews of the literature are provided by: Blaney (1977); Weissman (1979); Kovacs (1980); Miller and Berman (1983); Latimer and Sweet (1984); Vallis (1984); Williams (1984*a, b*); Teasdale (1985).

Immediate effects of specific cognitive–behavioural interventions

Preliminary evidence shows that interventions designed to reduce the frequency or intensity of depressing thoughts can have an immediate beneficial effect on mood. These include distraction (e.g. Teasdale and Rezin 1978; Davies 1982 [cited in Williams 1984*a*]; Fennell and Teasdale 1984; Fennell and Teasdale 1987*b*) and challenging, as opposed to simply focusing on or exploring, depressing thoughts (e.g. Blackburn and Bonham 1980; Teasdale and Fennell 1982).

Post-treatment effects of cognitive behaviour therapy

Studies assessing post-treatment outcome reliably show cognitive behaviour therapy to be at least as effective in reducing depression as tricyclic antidepressants, and suggest that on average little is gained by combining the two (Rush, Beck, Kovacs, and Hollon 1977; Blackburn *et al.* 1981; Hollon, Evans, and DeRubeis 1983; Murphy, Simons, Wetzel, and Lustman 1984; Teasdale, Fennell, Hibbert, and Amies 1984; Beck *et al.* 1985).

Long-term effects of cognitive behaviour therapy

Encouraging findings from five studies suggest that cognitive–behavioural therapy may be more effective in preventing relapse than antidepressant drugs (Kovacs *et al.* 1981; Hollon *et al.* 1983; Simons, Murphy, Levine and Wetzel, 1986; Zimmer, Axmann, Koch, Giedke, Pflug, and Hiemann, 1985; Blackburn, Eunson, and Bishop 1986).

Recommended reading

Beck, A. T. (1967). *Depression: clinical, experimental and theoretical aspects.* Harper and Row, New York.

Beck, A. T. (1976). *Cognitive therapy and the emotional disorders.* International Universities Press, New York.

Beck, A. T. and Greenberg, R. L. (1974). *Coping with depression.* Available from: The Center for Cognitive Therapy, Room 602, 133 South 36th Street, Philadelphia, PA 19104, USA.

Beck, A. T., Rush, A. J., Shaw, B. F., and Emery, G. (1979). *Cognitive therapy of depression*. Guilford, New York. (Paperback edition: 1987.)

Blackburn, I. M. (1987). *Coping with depression*. Chambers, Edinburgh.

Burns, D. D. (1980). *Feeling good*. New American Library, New York.

Emery, G. (1981). *A new beginning: How to change your life through cognitive therapy*. Simon and Schuster, New York.

Hollon, S. D. and Kriss, M. R. (1984). Cognitive factors in clinical research and practice. *Clinical Psychology Review* 4, 35–76.

Rush, A. J. and Shaw, B. F. (1983). Failures in treating depression by cognitive–behavioural therapy. In *Failures in behaviour therapy*, (ed. E. B. Foa and P. M. G. Emmelkamp), pp. 217–28. Wiley, New York.

Williams, J. M. G. (1984). *The psychological treatment of depression: A guide to the theory and practice of cognitive–behaviour therapy*. Croom Helm, London.

APPENDIX: HANDOUTS FOR PATIENTS

Please note these should *not* be used without the help of a qualified therapist.

How to activate yourself

The problem

Depression is a vicious circle. It slows you down, mentally and physically. Everything becomes an effort, and you tire easily. You do less, and then blame yourself for doing less. You come to believe that you *can* do nothing, and that you will never get over your depression. Then you feel even more depressed. It becomes even more difficult to do anything. And so it goes on.

Overcoming the problem: activity scheduling

Becoming more active is one way of breaking the vicious circle. It has a number of advantages:

Activity makes you feel better At the very least, it takes your mind off your painful feelings. It can give you the sense that you are taking control of your life again, and achieving something worthwhile. You may even find that there are things you enjoy, once you try them.

Activity makes you feel less tired Normally, when you are tired, you need rest. When you are depressed, the opposite is true. You need to do *more*. Doing nothing will only make you feel more lethargic and exhausted. And doing nothing leaves your mind unoccupied, so you are more likely to brood on your difficulties, and to feel even more depressed.

Activity motivates you to do more In depression, motivation works backwards. The more you do, the more you feel like doing.

Activity improves your ability to think Once you get started, problems which you thought you could do nothing about come into perspective.

In spite of these advantages, getting going again is not easy. This is because the gloomy, pessimistic thoughts which are typical of depression stand in your way. When you are depressed, you may think that you are doing nothing, achieving nothing, and enjoying nothing. It may be difficult to organize your time productively, or to involve yourself in things you normally enjoy. When you are faced with something you want to do, you may find yourself thinking: 'I won't enjoy it', 'I'll only make a mess of it', or 'It's too difficult.' Thoughts like these stop you from taking action and help to keep you in the vicious circle.

Later on in therapy, you will learn how to work directly on depressing thoughts which stop you from getting down to what you want to do. Your goal will be to notice and challenge the thoughts, so that they no longer stand in your way. First of all, though, you need to get a detailed idea of exactly what you *are* doing, and how much pleasure and satisfaction you get from what you do. What you discover will help you to plan your time so as to get the most out of each day's activities. This is called 'activity scheduling', and you will find details on how to do it below. There are two steps involved: self-monitoring, and planning ahead.

Step I: Self-monitoring

'Self-monitoring' simply means observing your pattern of activities. It involves keeping a detailed record of what you do, hour by hour. You can do this in a notebook or diary, or your therapist will give you a special record-sheet.

Your record will show you in black and white how you are spending your time, and will make you aware of how much satisfaction you get from what you do. This will allow you to test thoughts like 'I'm not doing anything', or 'I don't enjoy anything I do', and to see if they hold water when compared with the facts. You may well find that you are more active and competent than you assumed, and that you are enjoying yourself more than you thought. Even if this is not the case, you will have a factual record to help you find out more about what is getting in your way, and to form a basis for changing how you spend your time.

How to do it

For the next few days, in your diary or on your record-sheet, write down:

1. *Your activities*   Record exactly what you do, hour by hour.
2. *Pleasure and mastery*   Give each activity a rating between 0 and 10 for pleasure (P) and for mastery (M). 'P' refers to how much you enjoyed what you did. So 'P10' would mean that you had enjoyed something very much. 'P0' would mean that you had not enjoyed it at all. You could use any number between 0 and 10 to show how much you had enjoyed a particular activity. 'M' refers to how much mastery you experienced in what you did. How much of an achievement was it, given how you felt? 'M10' would mean that what you did was a real achievement. 'M0' would mean that it was not an achievement at all. Again, you could use any number between 0 and 10 to show how much mastery was involved in a particular activity.

Common problems in self-monitoring

Thinking you are doing nothing   Sitting in a chair in front of the television is an activity. So are going to bed, and staring out of the window brooding. You are never doing 'nothing'. But some activities may be less helpful to you than others. It will help you to identify these if you specify on your record-sheet what they are, rather than simply writing 'nothing'.

Underestimating your achievements   'M' should be rated for how difficult an activity is for you *now*, not how difficult it was for you before you got depressed, or how difficult another person might find it. When you are depressed, things which would normally be very easy become difficult. Even getting out of bed, or making a slice of toast, can be a major achievement, given how you feel. Beware of thoughts like 'But I should be able to do this better', or 'So what? Any fool could do this.' This will only keep you trapped in depression's vicious circle. Take a stand against them by making sure that you give yourself credit for what you do.

Delaying your ratings   It is important to rate your activities for P and for M *at the time*. If you wait until later, your depression will colour how you see your day, and may well cause you to ignore or devalue good things you have done. When people are depressed, bad things that happen are easily noticed and remembered. In contrast, good things are often blotted out or discounted. If you make your ratings *at the time*, this bias in how you see things is less likely. Immediate ratings will also help you to become sensitive to even small degrees of pleasure and mastery, which might otherwise go unnoticed.

Step II: Planning ahead

Now that you can see how you are spending your time, the next step is to plan each day in advance, making sure that you include activities which will give you a sense of pleasure and mastery.

Planning ahead will allow you to feel that you are taking control of your life, and will give you a sense of purpose. The framework you give yourself will prevent you from sinking into a swamp of minor decisions ('What shall I do next?'), and will help you to keep going even when you feel bad. Once the day's activites are laid out in writing, they will seem less overwhelming. You will have broken the day down into a series of manageable chunks, rather than a long shapeless stretch of time which you must somehow fill.

How to do it

1. *Plan your activities*   Every evening, or first thing in the morning, set aside time to plan the day ahead. Find out which time suits you best to do this, remembering that you are likely to be able to plan most realistically and constructively when you are feeling relatively well and clear-headed. If you find it difficult to remember to make time to plan ahead, give yourself reminder cues. Put up signs around the house, for example, or ask someone to remind you that 7.30 is your time for planning tomorrow. As far as possible, try to ensure that your planning time is not interrupted, and that

there are no other pressing demands to distract you. Turn off the television, and take the phone off the hook.

Aim for a balance between pleasure and mastery in your day. If you fill your time with duties and chores, and allow no time for enjoyment or relaxation, you may find yourself feeling tired, resentful, and depressed at the end of the day. On the other hand, if you completely ignore things you have to do, you may find your pleasure soured by a sense that nothing has been achieved, and your list of necessary tasks will mount up. You may find it helpful to aim for the pattern of activities you found most rewarding in the past. There is a fair chance that, once you get going, you will find this pattern works for you again.

Encourage yourself by starting the day with an activity which will give you a sense of mastery or pleasure, and which you have a good chance of completing successfully. This is particularly important if you have trouble getting going in the morning. And plan to reward yourself with a pleasurable or relaxing activity when you tackle something difficult. You might, for example, set aside time to have a cup of coffee and listen to your favourite radio programme when you have spent an hour doing housework. Avoid bed. Beds are for sleeping in, not for retreating to during the day. If you need rest or relaxation, plan to achieve it in some other way.

To begin with, you may find that trying to plan a whole day at a time is too much for you. If so, break the day down into smaller chunks, and deal with them one at a time.

2. *Record what you actually do*   Put your plan into practice. Write down how you in fact spend your time on your record sheet, just as you did at the self-monitoring stage. Rate each activity out of 10 for mastery and pleasure.

3. *Review what you have done*   At the end of each day, review what you have done. Take the time to sit down and examine how you spent your day, how much pleasure and mastery you got from what you did, and how far you managed to carry out the activities you had planned. This will help you to see clearly how you are spending your time, what room there is for improvement, and what changes you might like to make in the pattern of your day.

If you have managed overall to stick to your plan, and have found what you did reasonably satisfying, this gives you something positive to build on. If on the other hand you did not stick to your plan, or you got little satisfaction from what you did, this will give you valuable information about the kind of things that are preventing you from making the most of your time. What exactly was the problem? Did you over-estimate what you could do in the time available? Did you feel too tired to carry out everything you had planned? Did you aim too high, forgetting to take into account how you feel at the moment? Did you spend your day doing things that you felt you *ought* to do, rather than things that would give you pleasure and help you to relax? Were your best efforts blocked by pessimistic thoughts? If you can find out what went wrong, you can learn from these experiences. Use what you have found out to help you plan in future.

Coping with practical tasks

Depression often leads people to put off practical tasks they need to carry out. The pile mounts, and in the end they feel completely overwhelmed. You can help yourself to get started on things you need to do by following these steps:

1. *Make a list of all the things you have been putting off*, in whatever order they occur to you.

2. *Number the tasks in order of priority*   Which needs to be done first? If you cannot decide, or it genuinely does not matter, number them in alphabetical order. The important thing at this stage is to do *something*.

3. *Take the first task and break it down into small steps*   What exactly do you have to do in order to complete it?

4. *Rehearse the task mentally, step by step*   Write down any practical difficulties you may encounter, and work out what to do about them.

5. *Write down any negative thoughts* that come to you about doing the task, and answer them if you can (see below). If you cannot find answers, simply note the thoughts down (recognizing them for what they are), put them to one side for later discussion with your therapist, and concentrate on what you are doing.

6. *Take the task step by step*, dealing with difficulties and negative thoughts as they occur, just as you did in your mental rehearsal.

7. *Write down what you have done* on your activity schedule, and rate it out of 10 for P and M, as soon as you have completed the task.

8. *Focus on what you have achieved*, not on all the other things you still have to do. Watch out for negative thoughts that will make you devalue or discount what you have done. Write these thoughts down, and answer them if you can. If not, note them and put them to one side for later discussion with your therapist.

9. *Take the next task* and tackle it the same way.

Common problems with planning head

Not being able to get going   If you have difficulty getting down to a particular activity, tell your body in detail what to do. 'Get on with it' is too vague. 'Legs, walk. Hand, pick up pen. Now write', will give you the impetus to begin. As soon as you have told yourself what to do, do it. Do not allow any pause for doubts to creep in.

Being too rigid   Your plan is a guide, not a god. It is not carved on stone tablets. It is there to help you, not to rule your life. So, for example, something unexpected may happen to throw you off schedule. A friend drops in unexpectedly, or the washing-machine breaks down. At this point, you may feel that your efforts to plan your day have been wasted: unless you can stick to what you have planned, you might just as well not bother.

There are a number of things you can do to cope with the unexpected:

- *Accept the disruption* Accept that things have not worked out the way you thought they would, and continue with your original plan when you can. Your friend leaves at 4 o'clock. What did you have scheduled for that time?

- *Think of alternatives* Some of the activities you have planned may depend on factors beyond your control, such as the weather or other people's health. Supposing, for example, you plan a picnic, have something up your sleeve in case it rains. Or supposing you had planned to spend the weekend with an old friend and at the last minute she comes down with flu, look for an alternative that you will enjoy, rather than giving up and doing nothing in particular.

- *Do not try to make up things you have missed* If for some reason you cannot do what you had planned at a particular time (you wanted to clean the bedroom and ended up talking to your son about his holiday plans), do not go back and try to do it later. Move on to the next activity on your plan, and re-schedule what you missed for next day. Similarly, if you find that you finish an activity sooner than planned, leave your next activity until the time you had scheduled. Fill the gap with something you enjoy. You may find it useful to have a list of pleasurable activities handy so that you have something to choose from.

Being too specific or too general You need not write down what you intend to do in nit-picking detail. Listing every piece of furniture and ornament you have to dust is too specific. Equally, do not be too general. 'Housework', for example, is too general for you to feel clear about what it is that you are aiming to do. So you will not know when you have achieved your goal. Schedule your activities roughly by the hour or half-hour. Experience will tell you how long each activity is likely to take.

Planning for quality, not quantity Write down the amount of time you are going to spend on a particular activity, not how much you are going to do in that time. When the time is up, stop. How much you do in a given period may depend on factors outside your control (e.g. interruptions, machines breaking down), or on other problems (e.g. concentration difficulties, fatigue). If you tell yourself you *must* weed the whole garden this afternoon and you do not do it, you will probably think of yourself as a failure and give yourself no credit for what you *have* done. If on the other hand, you set yourself to weed for an hour, then how much you do is neither here nor there. Reward the effort, not the outcome.

Expecting miracles Your immediate goal is to carry out what you have planned as best you can, not to get over your depression. You will probably feel less depressed when you are doing some things than when you are doing others. And if you work steadily at becoming more active, you will eventually feel better. But no single thing you do is likely to produce a miracle cure. Don't expect to be over your depression after an hour's television, or cleaning out the cupboard under the stairs. If you do, you will only disappoint yourself.

Stopping when the going gets tough   Quit an activity when you are winning, not when you have exhausted yourself, or when things are going badly. This will leave you feeling good about what you have achieved, and ready to carry on.

Thoughts that stop you activating yourself

We have already discussed how pessimistic, gloomy thinking can get in the way of your attempts to activate yourself, and trap you in the vicious circle of depression. The most powerful way to overcome your depression is to identify your depressing thoughts when they occur, and to challenge them. You will learn how to do this later in therapy. In the meantime, monitoring what you do and planning ahead will give you a good opportunity to start becoming more aware of depressing thoughts that block progress and get in your way.

In the last section of this handout, you will find some examples of the kind of thoughts that may be preventing you from becoming more active, together with some possible answers to them. These are not the *right* answers, nor the *only* answers. They are just some suggestions. The answers which work for you personally may be quite different. With practice you will learn to find effective answers, which change how you feel and help you to tackle your difficulties constructively, for yourself.

Automatic thoughts	Possible answers
I can't do anything—there are too many practical difficulties.	There are always practical difficulties involved in doing anything—it's part of life. What would I do about them if I wasn't depressed? Is there anyone who could give me advice with things I don't know how to handle?
I can't keep a schedule—I've never been a record-keeper.	Keeping written records is a skill that I can learn. I may not have done this before, but that doesn't mean to say I can't do it. After all, I've used lists before, for shopping and to remember what to take on holiday. I could start by listing all the things I have to do.
There's too much to do—I won't be able to cope.	Believing that is all part of depression. It may not be true. If I write down what I need to do, it won't seem so overwhelming. I don't have to do it all at once. I can take things one at a time.
It's too difficult.	It only seems difficult because I'm depressed. I've done more difficult things than this in the past.
I won't know how to go about it.	The idea is to have a go, not to produce a perfect performance. It's better to try and find out how I do than not to do anything at all.

I don't want to.

That's true. But whether I want to or not, what is in my best interests? Which will make me feel better and more in control of things? Doing it? Or not doing it?

I'm not up to it just now, I'll wait till I'm feeling better.

I won't know if I'm up to it until I try. If I wait till I'm feeling better, I'll never do it. Doing it will make me feel better.

It's too late, I should have done it before.

Maybe it would have been better if I'd done it before. But the fact is I didn't. Feeling guilty is not going to help me. Better late than never—do it now instead of wasting time in regrets.

I can't decide what to do first.

It really doesn't matter. The important thing at this stage is to do *something*. Take the thing that comes first in the alphabet. Once you get going, it will probably be clearer what to do next. If not, just go on down the alphabet.

There's no point in trying. I'll only make a mess of it and feel worse.

I don't know that till I try. Nobody's asking for a five-star performance. Even if I do make a mess of it, it's not the end of the world—I can learn from my mistakes if I don't take them too seriously.

I won't enjoy it.

How do I know? I'm not a fortune-teller. I might enjoy it more than I think, once I get involved in what I'm doing. That has happened before.

I won't be able to do everything I've planned.

No one does everything they've planned all the time, so there's no need to feel badly about it. Before I got depressed, if I didn't get everything done, I just put it forward to next day. Do what you can, and forget what you can't. The world won't end because I don't clean out the attic today.

I'm not doing anything.

Am I sure of that? Or is it that I'm not giving myself credit for what I do? Why not keep a record for a few days, and see. Maybe I just *think* I'm not doing anything.

I don't do anything worthwhile.

I didn't see it that way before I got depressed. I was doing much the same

	then as I am now, but I could see that it was worthwhile, even though none of it was very dramatic or exciting. If I discount everything I do, I will only get discouraged.
I don't deserve to enjoy myself. I should get on with all the things I've got to do.	Doing things I enjoy will help me to feel better. That's what I want. Also, if I'm more relaxed and feeling better, I'm likely to do what I've got to do more efficiently, instead of getting in a muddle and dashing from one thing to another. I know that from experience; I get more done when I give myself breaks that when I plough on non-stop.
So I cleaned the car. So what?	Normally, cleaning the car would be nothing very special. But given the way I feel, it is in fact very difficult. So doing it is an achievement. I deserve to give myself credit for that. M10.

How to deal with negative thoughts

The problem

People who are depressed typically think in a biased, negative way. They have negative views of themselves (e.g. 'I'm no good'), the world (e.g. 'Life has no meaning'), and the future (e.g. 'I will always feel this way').

Negative thoughts like these have several characteristics. They are:

- *automatic*—they just pop into your head without any effort on your part;

- *distorted*—they do not fit all of the facts;

- *unhelpful*—they keep you depressed, make it difficult to change, and stop you from getting what you want out of life;

- *plausible*—you accept them as facts, and it does not occur to you to question them;

- *involuntary*—you do not choose to have them, and they can be very difficult to switch off.

Thoughts like these can trap you in a vicious circle. The more depressed you become, the more negative thoughts you have, and the more you believe them. The more negative thoughts you have, and the more you believe them, the more depressed you become. The main goal of cognitive therapy is to help you to break out of this vicious circle.

Overcoming the problem

You have probably already discussed examples of your own negative thoughts with your therapist, and looked at the effect they have on how you feel and what you do. The time has now come to make negative thinking your main focus. This is the heart of cognitive therapy: learning to recognize when you are thinking negatively, to look for more positive and realistic ways of viewing your experiences, and to test these out in action.

At first, you may not find it easy to catch and answer your thoughts. Answering negative thoughts is like any other skill—it takes time and regular practice to be able to do it with ease. So do not feel discouraged if you have difficulties to start with. In sessions, you and your therapist will work together on identifying and answering thoughts, and your homework assignments will give you plenty of opportunity to practise on your own. The more you practise, the sooner answering thoughts will come naturally to you. The steps involved are described in turn below.

Step I: Becoming aware of negative thoughts

The first step in overcoming negative thinking is to become aware of your thoughts, and of their effects on you.

Negative thoughts make you feel bad—anxious, sad, depressed, hopeless, guilty, angry. Instead of being overwhelmed by these feelings, you can learn to use them as a cue for action. Notice when your mood changes for the worse, and look back at what was running through your mind at that moment. Over the course of a few days, you will become more sensitive to changes in your feelings, and to the thoughts that spark them off. You may well find that the same thoughts occur again and again.

How to do it

The best way to become aware of negative thoughts is to write them down as soon as they occur. You can do this on a *Dysfunctional Thoughts Record* (you will find an example of a completed record below). Write down:

1. *The date*
2. *The emotion(s)* you felt. Give each one a rating out of 100 for how bad it was. A rating of 0, for example, would mean no emotion, 50 a moderate degree of emotion, and 100 an emotion as strong as it could be. You could score anywhere between 0 and 100.
3. *The situation* What were you doing when you started to feel bad? This includes, in general terms, what you were thinking about at the time. Only put down the general topic here (e.g. 'Thinking about how difficult life is'). What precisely was going through your mind should go in the next column.
4. *The automatic thought(s)* What thoughts were running through your mind at the time you started to feel bad? Try to record them as accurately as possible, word for word. Some of your thoughts may take the form of images

in your mind's eye, rather than words. You might, for example, imagine yourself being unable to cope with a situation in the future. Write down exactly what the image was, just as you saw it.

There may be times when you cannot identify any thoughts or images as such. If so, ask yourself what the meaning of the situation is. What does it tell you about yourself, your situation, your future? This may give you a clue as to why the situation is so depressing, or what is making you so anxious, or angry, or whatever. An argument, for instance, might mean to you that a relationship is at an end, or even that you will never be able to have a proper relationship with anybody. Once you can identify the meaning, you will be able to challenge it just as you would challenge any other thought. (Details on how to do this are in 'Step II: Answering negative thoughts' below.)

When you have written down your negative thoughts, images, or meanings, give each one a rating out of 100 according to how far you believe it. A rating of 100 would mean you believed a thought completely, 0 that you did not believe it at all, 50 that you half believed it, and so on. You could score anywhere between 0 and 100.

Common problems in recording negative thoughts

Timing   Ideally, it is best to record your thoughts and feelings immediately they occur. But of course this is not always possible. It would look odd, for example, if you got your record sheets out in the middle of a party or a meeting! In this case, make a mental note of what has distressed you, or jot down a reminder on any handy piece of paper. Then set aside time in the evening (say, 20 minutes) to make a proper written record. Run through an 'action replay', trying to recall in as much detail as possible what happened, how you felt, and what your thoughts were.

Avoiding writing down your negative thoughts   Beware of excuses that keep you from focusing on your thoughts and emotions. You may say to yourself, for instance, 'I'll do it later', or 'It would be better to forget all about it'. You may find that you are very unwilling to look your thoughts in the face. Perhaps you are afraid they will overwhelm you, or think that they are stupid. It is quite natural to want to avoid thinking through unpleasant experiences, but doing so is the best way to combat your depression. If you find yourself making excuses, this is probably because you have hit upon something important, so make yourself write it down. You can then divert yourself by engaging in a distraction exercise if you want to. But ignoring the thoughts will not make them go away.

Step II: Answering negative thoughts

Once you have learned to become aware of negative thinking, the next step is to evaluate the thoughts you identify, and to look for more helpful and realistic alternatives.

How to do it

There are four main questions you can use to help you find answers to your negative thoughts:

DATE	EMOTION(S) What do you feel? How bad is it (0–100)?	SITUATION What were you doing or thinking about?	AUTOMATIC THOUGHTS What exactly were your thoughts? How far do you believe each of them (0–100%)?
8th December	Tense 90 Angry 90 Despair 75	Dog next door barked for half an hour	I can't stand this. 80% Why can't they shut up? We've saddled ourselves with a house that will always be spoiled by that dog barking and we'll never get away from it
9th December	Panic 80 Anxiety 80	Car engine overheating; icy road, getting dark	I don't know what to do 100% It's too dangerous to go on—I'll do something to the car 80% But I can't stop here or I'll cause an accident 80%
14th December	Lonely 70 Helpless 60 Unhappy 90	At work people grumbling, not wanting or trying to make things work	I don't want to be here 100% I can't leave because I need the money 100% They don't care, so I have to do everything 90% I have nothing in common with anyone here 90%

Dysfunctional Thoughts Record I

1. *What is the evidence?*   Do the facts of the situation back up what you think, or do they contradict it?

2. *What alternative views are there?*   There are many different ways to look at any experience. How else could you interpret what has happened? Get as many alternatives as you can, and review the evidence for and against them. When you consider it objectively, which alternative is most likely to be correct?

3. *What is the effect of thinking the way you do?*   How does it influence how you feel and what you do? What are the advantages and disadvantages of thinking this way? Can you find an alternative which will be more helpful to you?

4. *What thinking errors are you making?*   Depressed people typically distort how they see their experiences in systematic ways. They jump to conclusions, overgeneralize from specific things that happen, take responsibility for things that are not their fault, and so on. Which of these errors can you find in your own thinking?

Further on in this handout you will find 20 more specific questions, grouped together with examples under these four main headings. You can use these to help you find alternatives to your negative thoughts. Remember that the examples are only possibilities. The answers which work for you personally may be quite different. You will need to find these for yourself.

It is extremely important to record and answer as many thoughts as possible every day. Writing them down will allow you to distance yourself from them. In the end, you will probably be able to answer them in your head as they occur. But if you try to do this at first, the thoughts will often be too strong for the answers and will wipe them out. Writing the answers down gives them power; there they are, in black and white. You may need to work out answers to 50 or 100 thoughts on paper before you can do it in your head with ease—if then. All the same, finding effective answers will become easier and easier the more you practise.

Record-keeping

Use the *Dysfunctional Thoughts Record* to record your answers as follows (you will find an example of a completed record sheet below):

1. *Rational response*   Write down all the answers you can think of to each thought. Give each answer a rating out of 100 according to how far you believe it. A rating of 100 means you believe it completely, 0 that you do not believe it at all, 50 that you half believe it, and so on. You could score anywhere between 0 and 100.

2. *Outcome*
    (a) Go back to the original *negative automatic thoughts*. Now that you have answered them, how far do you believe them? Give each one a new rating out of 100.

    If your answers have been effective, you should find that your belief has decreased to some extent. If it has not, it may be that you are disqualifying the answer in some way—telling yourself it is just a rationalization, or that it may apply to other people but not to you. Write these 'yes, but ... 's down in the negative automatic thoughts column and answer them in the same way that you answered the original thoughts.

Do not expect your belief in the negative thoughts to disappear completely in one go. They have probably been around for a long time, whereas the answers may be quite new to you. It will take time and practice to build up belief in them, and you will probably need to test them out in action.

(b) Look back at the *emotion* column and check how you felt before you answered the negative thoughts. What are your emotions now, in the light of the answers you have found? Rate each one out of 100.

Again, if your answers have been effective, you should find that your painful emotions have decreased to some extent. Do not be discouraged if they have not disappeared completely. This will take time and practice.

(c) Work out an *action plan*. What can you do, either to change the situation for the better, or to test out the answers to your negative thoughts? How would you like to handle the situation differently next time it occurs? What will you do if you find yourself thinking and feeling this way again? Try to work out a strategy you can use in future, whenever you find yourself facing a similar difficulty. (You will find more details about how to test your thoughts in action under 'Step III' below.)

Common problems in answering negative thoughts

The need for practice Standing back, questioning, evaluating, and answering our thoughts is not something we normally do. You may well find it difficult at first to be objective and to find answers which affect your feelings to any great extent. You will have the opportunity to practise in sessions with your therapist, and also by yourself, so give yourself a chance to get the hang of it, and do not be discouraged if at first you cannot always find effective answers. Would you expect to win Wimbledon after six tennis lessons?

Dealing with extreme distress You will probably find it particularly difficult to find rational alternatives to your negative thoughts when you are feeling very badly upset. In this case you may find it helpful simply to write down what is distressing you, to distract yourself until you are feeling calmer, and then to return to what you have recorded and look for answers. You will be in a better position to do so once you are feeling better. Beware of making the situation worse by telling yourself that you are a failure, or that the therapy will not work for you.

Setting perfectionist standards Your record does not have to be a literary masterpiece. Nor do you have to find the one right answer, or the answer which you think your therapist would approve of. A good answer is one which changes

DATE	EMOTION(S) What do you feel? How bad is it (0–100)?	SITUATION What were you doing or thinking about?	AUTOMATIC THOUGHTS What exactly were your thoughts? How far did you believe each of them (0–100%)?	RATIONAL RESPONSE What are your rational answers to the automatic thoughts? How far do you believe each of them (0–100%)?	OUTCOME 1. How far do you now believe the thoughts (0–100%)? 2. How do you feel (0–100)? 3. What can you do now?
7 Jan	Disappointed 75	Finished making curtains & found hems were not straight	I spent all day on that and now look at it. It's worse than before I started. 100% What a waste 90% I should have done it better. 90% I'll never get it right 80%	I did get the linings right and that's the biggest job 100% I can redo the hems another time 70% I did the best I could – you can't do better than that 90%	1. 30% 2. 25 3. It's not the end of the world. Leave it for a few days and then treat it as a separate job – have another go.
15 Jan	Anxious 65 guilty 50	Spoke to sister's husband on phone when she was out	I've said something wrong 60%	All you did was talk about the weather! You'd have felt worse if you hadn't had a conversation at all. You did manage to talk to him, and for you that's an achievement. 70% You've got flu just now – that always makes conversation difficult 70% Don't worry about it – he was quite friendly so there's no evidence you did wrong 65%	1. 0% 2. 0. 0. 3. Forget the whole thing – except remembering that you've done something you usually avoid, and that's an achievement.

Dysfunctional Thoughts Record II

the way you feel and reduces your belief in your negative thoughts, and which opens up avenues for action. No one answer will do for everybody. You have to find the ones which work for you.

Putting yourself down Watch out for self-criticism when you are recording your thoughts. You may find yourself thinking, for example, 'I must be really stupid to think this way'. Remember that negative thinking is a sign of depression, which you can overcome, not of lack of intelligence.

The need for repetition Do not get discouraged if you find the same thoughts occurring again and again. If you have been depressed for some time, thinking negatively will have become a well-established habit. It will take time to break it. The more often a particular thought occurs, the more opportunity you will have to answer and change it.

Twenty questions to help you challenge negative thinking

What is the evidence?

1. *Am I confusing a thought with a fact?* The fact that you believe something to be true, does not necessarily mean that it is. Does what you think fit the facts? Would it be accepted as correct by other people? Would it stand up in court, or be dismissed as circumstantial? What objective evidence do you have to back up your thoughts, and to contradict them?

Automatic thoughts	*Possible answer*
When I met Peter in the street today, he didn't smile at me. I must have done something to offend him.	It is true that he didn't smile at me, but I have no reason to think that he is offended with me. It was probably nothing at all to do with me. Maybe he just had a lot on his mind.

2. *Am I jumping to conclusions?* This is the result of basing what you think on poor evidence. For instance, depressed people often believe that others are thinking critically about them. But none of us are mind-readers. How can you *know* what someone else is thinking? You may be right, but do not jump to conclusions. Stick to what you can be sure of. If you do not have enough evidence to make a sound judgement, see if you can find out more of the facts before you make up your mind.

Automatic thoughts	*Possible answer*
My husband didn't eat that chocolate cake I baked for him. He thinks I'm a terrible cook.	All I know for sure is that he didn't eat it. I don't actually know whether he thinks I'm a terrible cook or not. Maybe he just wasn't hungry. I can ask him.

What alternatives are there?

3. *Am I assuming my view of things is the only one possible?* There is more than one way of seeing any situation. How would you have reacted before you

got depressed? How would you react even now, on a day when you were feeling relatively well? How might another person see things? What would your reaction be if a friend told you about the situation that is distressing you? Would your thinking be so black if another person was in that situation instead of you?

Automatic thoughts	*Possible answer*
That was a terrible mistake. I will never learn to do this properly.	If I wasn't depressed, I would probably shrug my shoulders and put it down to experience. I would do what I could to set things right, and learn from my mistake. Tom made just the same mistake last week, and he made a joke of it.

What is the effect of thinking the way I do?

4. *Do negative thoughts help or hinder me?* What do you want? What are your goals? Do you want to overcome your depression, to be happy, and to make the most of your life? Is the way you are thinking now helping you to achieve this? Or is it standing in your way?

Automatic thoughts	*Possible answers*
This is hopeless. I should be able to do better than this by now. I'm never going to get the hang of answering my thoughts.	What I want is to get over my depression. Thinking this way is not going to help me to do that. It just makes me feel worse. It's no good telling myself I should be doing better by now. What I need is practice, and if I keep putting myself down I will give up instead of practising.

5. *What are the advantages and disadvantages of thinking this way?* Many distorted thought patterns do have some pay-off. That is what keeps them going. For example, they may allow you to avoid situations you find difficult. But do the disadvantages outweigh the advantages? If so, it may be worth your while to work out a new way of looking at things which will give you the advantages, but avoid the disadvantages, of the old way.

Automatic thoughts	*Possible answers*
I must make a good impression at this party.	*Advantage* I'll go out of my way to talk to people. If they do like me, I'll feel marvellous. *Disadvantage* If somebody doesn't seem to like me, I'll feel terrible and think badly of myself. So in fact telling myself I *must* make a good impression just puts pressure on me, and makes it hard to relax and enjoy myself. It is impossible for everyone to like me all the time. If they do, that's very nice. But if they don't, it's not the end of the world.

6. *Am I asking questions that have no answers?* This means questions like 'How can I undo the past?', 'Why aren't I different?', 'What is the meaning of life?', 'Why does this always happen to me?', 'Why is life so unfair?', and so on. Brooding over unanswerable questions is a guaranteed way to depress yourself. If you can turn them into answerable questions, so much the better. If not, do not waste time on them. Turn your thoughts towards something more constructive instead.

Automatic thoughts	*Possible answers*
When will I be better again?	I can't answer that. Going over and over it just makes me worried and up-set. I would do better to spend the time working out what I *can* do to help myself get over this depression as quickly as possible.

What thinking errors am I making?

7. *Am I thinking in all-or-nothing terms?* Nearly everything is relative. People, for instance, are not usually all good or all bad. They are a mixture of the two. Are you applying this kind of black-and-white thinking to yourself? Look for the shades of grey.

Automatic thoughts	*Possible answers*
I did that really badly. I might as well not bother at all.	The fact is, I didn't do it as well as I wanted to. That does not mean that it was no good at all. I can't expect to get everything 100 per cent right. If I do, I'll never be satisfied.

8. *Am I using ultimatum words in my thinking?* Watch out for words like 'always', 'never', 'everyone', 'no one', 'everything', and 'nothing'. The chances are that the situation is in fact less clear-cut than that. Mostly it is a case of sometimes, some people, and some things.

Automatic thoughts	*Possible answers*
Everything always goes badly for me.	What, 'everything'? That is an exag-geration. Some things do go badly for me, just as they do for everyone else, but some things go well.

9. *Am I condemning myself as a total person on the basis of a single event?* Depressed people often take difficulties to mean that they have no value at all as a person. Are you making this kind of blanket judgement? You are made up of thousands of thoughts, feelings, and actions. It is not fair to judge yourself as a person on the basis of any single one. This is especially true when you are depressed, because you will be biased to notice your weaknesses and faults, and to ignore your strengths and assets.

Automatic thoughts	*Possible answers*
I was so irritable with the children this morning. I'm a terrible mother and a wicked person.	The fact that on a particular day, at a particular time, in particular circumst-ances, I was irritable, does not make

me a terrible mother or a wicked person. I can't reasonably expect never to
be irritable, and asking myself depressed by writing myself off completely is
not going to help me to be nicer to the
children when they get in from school.

10. *Am I concentrating on my weaknesses and forgetting my strengths?* When people become depressed, they often overlook problems they handled successfully in the past, and forget resources and assets which would help them to overcome current difficulties. Instead they focus on failures and weaknesses. It may become difficult to think of a single good quality or talent. It is important to try to keep a balanced view of yourself. Of course there are things you are not very good at, things you have done that you regret, and things about yourself you would prefer to change. But what about the other side of the equation? What are the things you *are* good at? What do you like about yourself when you are not depressed? What do other people value in you? How have you coped with past difficulties in your life? What are your assets and resources?

Automatic thoughts

I've made a complete mess of my life. I hate myself. Why go on trying?

Possible answers

That's not true. There are many things I have done well. I just can't see them clearly because the depression is getting in the way. If I was such a hopeless mess, I would have no friends. But I do have friends, and a husband and children who love me. That must mean something. And the fact that I'm trying to fight my depression is a sign of strength.

11. *Am I blaming myself for something which is not really my fault?* For example, depressed people often blame themselves for being depressed. They may put it down to lack of willpower, weakness, or inadequacy. They think they should pull themselves together and stop being so pathetic. When they find this is impossible, they can become harshly self-critical. In fact, depression is a very common problem; at any one time, more than one in ten people are experiencing symptoms of depression. Scientists have been studying depression for many years, and are still not certain what causes it. Depression is genuinely a difficult problem to solve, and blaming yourself for it will only make you more depressed.

Automatic thoughts

I must be really stupid to have these distorted thoughts.

Possible answers

Stupidity is one possible reason. But when I look at myself as a whole, there's not much evidence that I'm stupid. I have these thoughts because I'm depressed. That's not my fault, and I am doing what I can to sort it out. Once I'm feeling better, I'll think quite differently.

12. *Am I taking things personally which have little or nothing to do with me?* When things go wrong, depressed people often believe that in some way this is directed at them personally, or that it has been caused by them. In fact, it may have had nothing to do with them.

Automatic thoughts
Mary doesn't like me at all. She would never have shouted at me like that if she did.

Possible answers
I am not the only person Mary shouts at. She is always on edge when things are not going well for her, and she shouts at whoever is around. I've seen her do it. She will get over it, and will probably apologize.

13. *Am I expecting myself to be perfect?* Depressed people often set very high standards for themselves. For example, they may think that they should be able to deal with everything just as well when they are badly depressed as they would if they were feeling fine. This is simply not realistic, and merely opens the way to self-criticism and more depression. It is just not possible to get everything 100 per cent right all the time. If you expect to do so, you are setting yourself up to fail. Accepting that you cannot be perfect does not mean that you have to give up trying to do things well. But it means that you can be realistic, and take how you feel into account when you set targets for yourself. That makes you more likely to succeed. Success makes you feel better, and the next step is then that much easier. Also, it means that you can learn from your difficulties and mistakes, instead of being upset and paralysed by them. Remember: If a thing is worth doing, it is worth doing badly.

Automatic thoughts
This is not good enough. I should have finished everything I planned to do.

Possible answers
I can't always expect to carry out everything I plan. I'm not God—I'm fallible, like any other human being. It would have been nice if I had finished, but the fact that I haven't is not a disaster. Better to focus on what I have done, not on what I have failed to do. This way I will be encouraged to try again.

14. *Am I using a double standard?* You may be expecting more of yourself than you would of another person. How would you react to someone else in your situation? Would you be so hard on them? Or would you use praise and encouragement to help them tackle their difficulties? You can afford to be as kind to yourself as you would to someone else. It will not lead to collapse.

Automatic thoughts
I'm pathetic. I shouldn't be so upset by trivial things.

Possible answers
If someone else was upset by this situation, I would not think it was trivial. I would be sympathetic, and try to help them find a solution to the problem. I certainly wouldn't call them pathetic—

I could see that it wouldn't help. I can
do the same for myself. It will give me
the courage to carry on.

15. *Am I only paying attention to the black side of things?* Are you, for
instance, focusing on everything that has gone wrong during the day, and forgetting or discounting things you have enjoyed or achieved?

Automatic thoughts	*Possible answers*
That was a really terrible day.	Hang on a moment, I was late for a meeting, and I had a disagreement with my daughter, but on the whole my work went well, and I enjoyed the cinema this evening. So, all in all, it was not a bad day. Only remembering the bad things is part of depression. Watch out for it.

16. *Am I over-estimating the chances of disaster?* Depressed people often
believe that if things go at all wrong, disaster is sure to follow. If the day starts
badly, for example, it can only get worse. These ideas can act as self-fulfilling
prophecies. But how likely is it in fact that what you expect will happen? What
can you do to change the course of events?

Automatic thoughts	*Possible answers*
I didn't get all my work done today. I'll get the sack.	When was the last time they sacked someone in this firm for not having time to finish a job? It's perfectly nor-mal not to finish on time, when we all have to work under such pressure. If my boss comments, I can explain the situation to him.

17. *Am I exaggerating the importance of events?* What difference does a
particular event make in your life? What will you think about it in a week, a
month, a year, 10 years? Will anyone else remember what happened? Will you?
Even if you do, will you feel the same about it? Probably not.

Automatic thoughts	*Possible answers*
I made a real fool of myself yesterday. I'll never be able to face them again.	Don't make a mountain out of a mole-hill. Most people didn't even notice. I don't suppose anyone who did thought much of it—they were probably too busy thinking of themselves. If it had happened when I wasn't depressed, I would have laughed about it. It cer-tainly makes a good story.

18. *Am I fretting about the way things ought to be, instead of accepting and
dealing with them as they are?* Are you allowing events in the world at large to
feed your depression? Telling yourself life is not fair and people are brutes? It is

sad that there is so much suffering in the world, and you may decide to do what you can to change things. But getting depressed about it does nothing to help.

Automatic thoughts	*Possible answers*
That TV programme about old people was terribly upsetting. Life is so cruel. It shouldn't be like this.	Things are as they are, and to want them different is unrealistic, like wishing I was 6 feet tall. The fact is that I am not. Getting depressed about it is not going to help the situation. Why not see if I can visit someone in the Old People's Home down the road? That at least is something I *can* do.

19. *Am I assuming I can do nothing to change my situation?* Pessimism about the chances of changing things is central to depression. It makes you want to give up before you even start. But you cannot know that there is no solution to your problems until you try. Is the way you are thinking helping you to problem-solve? Or is it making you turn down possible solutions without even giving them a go?

Automatic thoughts	*Possible answers*
It's no good. I will never sort this out.	If I tell myself that, I certainly won't. I will sit down and work out what I need to do, step by step. Even if some of my solutions didn't work before, that doesn't mean to say they won't work now. I can work out what went wrong, and how to get round it.

20. *Am I predicting the future instead of experimenting with it?* The fact that you have acted a certain way in the past does not mean that you have to act the same way in the future. If you predict the future, instead of trying something different and finding out what happens, you are cutting off the possibility of change. Change may be difficult, but it is not usually impossible.

Automatic thoughts	*Possible answers*
I'll never manage to stand up for myself. I never have.	The fact that I never have stood up for myself does not mean that I never can. If I do stand up for myself, I will feel uncomfortable at first. But if I stick with it, it will become easier. Also other people will respect me more. And I will respect myself. No one respects a doormat—they just walk on it.

Step III: Taking action to test negative thoughts

Arguing against your negative automatic thoughts may not be enough in itself to convince you that they are incorrect. You will need to build up a body of experience which contradicts them. The best way to do this is to act on your rational answers and find out for yourself whether they are in line with the facts and helpful to you, or whether they need to be changed. Taking action allows you to test your answers in the real world. It helps you to break old habits of thinking and to strengthen new ones.

Testing predictions

People are like scientists. We make predictions (e.g. 'If I press the switch, the light will come on', 'He will not like it if I contradict him', 'If I stand in the rain, I will get a cold'), and we act on them. We use information from what happens to us, and from what we do, to confirm our predictions or to change them.

Depression makes it difficult for us to make realistic predictions, or to test them with an open mind. When depressed people make predictions (e.g. 'I won't be able to cope', 'Everyone will think I'm an idiot', 'If I say what I think, I will be rejected'), they tend to see them as facts, not as hunches which may or may not be correct. So it is difficult to stand back and look at the evidence objectively, or to test out the prediction in action and see if it *does* fit the facts. After all, what is the point? The result is a foregone conclusion.

The final step in overcoming negative thinking is to test what you think in action. In order to do this, you need to find out what you are predicting, to review existing evidence (e.g. past experience), and to work out what you need to do in order to discover whether your negative thinking fits the facts.

These are the steps involved in taking action to test negative thoughts:

1. *State your prediction* clearly (the negative automatic thought).

2. *Review the existing evidence* for and against it. What does past experience tell you, when you look at it objectively? What would you predict for another person in this situation?

3. *Work out an action plan* which will help you to find out if your prediction is correct or not.

4. *Make a note of the results* There are two main possibilities:

    (a) *Your prediction is not borne out* That is, your negative thoughts are shown by experience to be incorrect. This demonstrates through action (rather than just argument) how distorted depressed thinking can be. So much the better.

    (b) *Your prediction is borne out* That is, your negative thought is shown by experience to be correct. Do not despair. This is valuable information. Find out what you were doing to bring about this result. Can you work out ways of handling the situation differently in future so that things turn out better? This may involve behaving differently so as to change the situation. But, of course, some situations cannot be changed. Even so, you may still be able to change how you think about an unchangeable situation, so that you feel differently about it. When you have decided what needs to be done, work out *a new action plan*.

5. *Draw conclusions on the basis of your results* What do they tell you about yourself, or about the way depression affects you? What general rules can you draw up which will help you to deal better with similar situations in future?

Below you will find two examples showing how to test negative thoughts in action. If there is anything which does not make sense to you, ask your therapist to explain.

Example 1

Colin has been invited to a party. The thought of it fills him with panic. He is convinced that he will have nothing to say to anyone, and that he will not enjoy himself. This depresses him, because he believes that unless he can get on at parties, he will lose contact with all his friends.

1. *Prediction* If I go, I will not be able to talk to anyone, and I will have a terrible time.

2. *Review of existing evidence* Before I got depressed, I used to enjoy parties. It's true that since I got depressed I haven't got much pleasure out of them. Still, there have been one or two I enjoyed. This will be all old friends. They know how I have been, and won't expect a lot of me. If I don't go, I will miss an opportunity for pleasure, which will make me feel better if it does work out.

3. *Action plan* Go, and see what happens. Use distraction beforehand to stop anxiety building up. Talk to people I know first. Relax, and listen to what they have to say.

4. *Results* Did not enjoy it. Left early. What went wrong? Spent the whole evening thinking how happy everyone else looked, and telling myself how different things were for me. So busy thinking about myself, I couldn't concentrate on anything that was going on.
   New action plan Next time, work harder at answering negative thoughts beforehand, and distracting myself while I'm there. In the meantime, practise distraction exercises every day, and see if I can arrange to see friends in other situations, where it will be easier. Start by phoning Pete and suggesting a game of squash.

5. *Conclusions* My original prediction was correct, but mainly because I was so preoccupied with negative thoughts. Even so, two friends have been in touch since, so one bad evening does not necessarily mean that I'll lose contact with everyone completely.

Example 2

Linda has been depressed for some time. She has tried several antidepressant drugs, without much success. Recently she was referred for cognitive therapy. She has had eight sessions, and has learned how to identify her depressing thoughts and to find more realistic and helpful alternatives to them. Things seemed to be going well, but in the last few days she has been feeling more and more depressed. She is beginning to doubt if the treatment will work, and feels like giving up. Hopelessness is making her think that suicide may be the only solution. The action plan below was worked out in session with her therapist.

1. *Prediction* I'm back to square one. There's no point in doing anything—nothing will work. I'm always going to be like this. The only answer is to kill myself.

2.	*Review of evidence*	It is true that I feel much worse than I did last week. But it is not true that I am back to square one. Even now, I'm not as bad as when I went into hospital last. I am doing the housework, looking after the children, doing my job. To be truthful, I am getting a little satisfaction out of it, so it's not a complete failure. I *have* been feeling very bad, but set-backs are to be expected. Disappointment at the contrast to feeling so much better is making it worse. Dealing with my thoughts and feelings is a new skill, and it will take time before I can do it easily all the time. After all, I've been depressed for three years, but I've only been getting this treatment for a few weeks. In fact, when I think about it, I can already deal with about 75 per cent of my depression, as opposed to 25 per cent before I started these sessions. Suicide is not the answer. Evidence that things have changed since I started therapy shows it can work.

3.	*Action plan*	Don't over-react—this is probably a set-back, no more and no less. Go back to basics. Plan your time carefully so that you do things that you can enjoy and which give you a sense of achievement. Keep busy. If you can find alternatives to your negative thoughts, do it. But if you can't, don't worry about it—you will be able to do so once you are better. In the meantime, distract yourself. And talk to Paul [husband]—you know it helps when you do, instead of keeping it all bottled up.

4.	*Results*	It worked! Not at once, but within a couple of days I was much better, back to answering my thoughts properly, and feeling a lot less depressed.

5.	*Conclusions*	Accept set-backs as part of the process of recovery, not the end of the world. Keep using what I have learned to deal with my depression. Watch out for the tendency to be hard on myself when things go wrong—it doesn't help. Remember hopelessness is part of being depressed—it doesn't necessarily reflect the way things really are.

7

Somatic problems

Paul M. Salkovskis

The treatment of somatic problems is one of the oldest applications of psychological approaches (Lipowski 1986*a*). Particularly influential was the writing of Galen, in second-century Rome. Galen's view that the 'passions' such as anger, fear, and lust were important causes of illness continued to be influential until the eighteenth century. More recently, two approaches have been important; firstly, *psychosomatic medicine* attempted to establish a psychological causation for physical disorders such as asthma, eczema, and ulcers (e.g. Alexander 1950). This field, which was strongly influenced by psychoanalysis, has now declined leaving behind little of practical application (Schwartz and Weiss 1978), although an unfortunate effect is that psychological treatment of somatic conditions is sometimes thought to imply that the problems being treated are 'all in the mind'.

The other more recent approach was *psychophysiological*; this view emphasizes the importance of considering psychological processes rather than diagnostic categories. The foundation of this approach is experimental work in which physiological responses are measured during experimental tasks which probe particular psychological processes (e.g. listening to stimuli, reacting by pressing a button when stimuli occur). Such experiments aim to examine whether particular types of stimuli or psychological reactions consistently produce characteristic physiological reactions (stimulus–response specificity); and whether different individuals react in characteristic ways to stimuli (individual–response specificity). Thus, particular stressors might be responsible for the development of specific disorders in vulnerable individuals. These concepts can help explain why some people develop headaches in response to stress when other people do not, and why some stresses precipitate headaches and others do not.

It is important to note that much of the early work on somatic disorders was based on patients who were seen after several previous medical referrals, ineffective attempts at treatment, and a variety of potentially conflicting explanations of the problem. There is now greater emphasis on liaison work, with those involved in psychological treatment working in primary or secondary medical settings. This type of work results in a change both in the characteristics of the patients themselves (e.g. their problems tend to be less chronic and they have had fewer physical interventions) and in the way in which psychological treatment is viewed (i.e. not as a last resort).

Approaches to somatic problems

The understanding of psychological approaches to somatic problems has been influenced by the tendency to refer for psychological treatment as a 'last resort' and the resulting high rates of complicating psychological conditions in clinic populations. That is, as patients' problems become more chronic and they become more distressed with the failure of medical treatment, they perceive themselves as having a psychological problem arising out of their chronic physical condition. Although this perception leads to acceptance of psychiatric referral, it is often for problems the patient regards as subsidiary. Sometimes, the patient is told after many months or even years of medical investigation that there is no further medical treatment and that the only avenue for further help is through the acceptance of psychological help. The way in which patients are referred can have important implications for their willingness to accept psychological treatment. This will be dealt with below when the crucial issue of engagement in treatment is discussed. A further effect of this referral pattern is that some clinicians and researchers in psychiatry regard phenomena such as hypochondriasis, headache, or sleep disturbance as secondary to other clinical syndromes, most commonly depression (e.g. Kenyon 1964).

Two major areas of work in behaviour therapy have been influential in the increasing application of cognitive–behavioural approaches to somatic problems. The first area adopted was Lang's (1970) view that psychological responses could best be described in terms of the interaction between loosely coupled response systems: *subjective*, *behavioural*, and *physiological*. This view brought with it the notion that behavioural or cognitive interventions could have effects on physiology, and thus provided the foundation for a great deal of subsequent work in behavioural medicine (e.g. Latimer 1981). The second important area in which psychological approaches were applied to somatic problems was learned voluntary control of physiological responses, known as *biofeedback* (Birk 1973). Measurements of physiological activity are displayed to the patient, who is set the task of changing the display. However, the therapeutic promise of biofeedback has not been realized. Even when control is learned, it does not generalize well beyond the laboratory and seldom exceeds the clinical improvement obtained by other procedures such as relaxation. Biofeedback assumes a link between specific physiological responses and particular disorders; the validity of this assumption has been questioned in some instances (e.g. Philips 1976).

The nature of the problems

Somatic presentations of psychological problems fall into three broad categories;

(1) problems where there are observable and identifiable disturbances of bodily functioning;

(2) problems where the disturbances are primarily of perceived symptoms, sensitivity to or excessive reaction to normal bodily sensations; and

(3) a mixed group.

The major conditions included in these categories are shown in Table 7.1. In fact, there is considerable overlap between these categories (e.g. hypochondriacal patients are often reacting to minor symptoms such as headaches or skin blemishes). Nevertheless, the extent of physical pathology can have an effect on the interventions used and on the targets of treatment.

Amongst the most common somatic problems seen in general practice and psychiatric settings are insomnia, headache, irritable bowel syndrome, and hypochondriasis. As a variety of different factors can be important in the causation and maintenance of these and other conditions, this chapter focuses on the general principles of treatment for somatic conditions and considers aspects of these four specific problems as a way of illustrating the application of the general principles. Throughout the chapter, particular attention will be paid to factors which contribute to anxiety about health (called hypochondriasis when very severe), while specific sections are devoted to insomnia, headache, and irritable bowel. Health anxiety is dealt with most extensively because it is an important source of distress in most somatic conditions, whether or not anxiety is directly involved in their maintainance.

An important principle in the cognitive–behavioural approach to somatic conditions is that patients' problems should be positively formulated in psychological terms even when complicated by the presence of an actual physical condition. This means that those conducting psychological treatment do not have to rely on the unsatisfactory practice of diagnosing psychological problems by exclusion. The more sophisticated and directly psychological approach is particularly necessary when physiological factors play a major role in the problem. In such instances, it is not sensible to rule out any physical conditions before proceeding with psychological treatment because 'if it is not physical, it must be psychological'.

However, it is necessary to obtain a realistic description of the patient's physical state, the likely course of any physical condition, and any physical limitations which might affect psychological treatment. This provides

Table 7.1 Major somatic presentations with a significant psychological component, or where there is evidence of responsiveness to cognitive–behavioural intervention

1. *Problems where there is an observable and identifiable disturbance of bodily functioning*
   Irritable bowel syndrome Abdominal pain and change in bowel habit including both constipation and/or diarrhoea
   Hypertension High blood pressure
   Tics and spasms Involuntary muscular movements or contractions
   Asthma
   Insomnia Perceived and actual difficulty with sleep, associated with the complaint of daytime fatigue; divided into difficulty in falling asleep (onset insomnia), disturbed sleep with frequent waking, early morning wakening, and unsatisfying sleep
   Sleep disorders Nightmares, sleepwalking, enuresis, movement problems (bruxism, nocturnal head rocking), sleep apnoea, snoring
   Psychogenic vomiting
   Difficulties with swallowing and eating
   Skin conditions Lesions, irritations, or irruptions of the skin, often exacerbated by scratching (eczema, psorasis)

2. *Problems where the disturbance is primarily one of perceived symptoms, sensitivity to or excessive reaction to normal bodily sensations*
   Hypochondriasis Preoccupation with the fear of having or belief that one has a serious disease, not (fully) accounted for by physical condition; resistant to 'medical reassurance'; includes illness phobia
   Somatization disorder Many minor physical complaints, characterized by the patients' belief that they are 'sickly'
   Idiopathic pain disorder preoccupation with pain
   Hysterical conversion Loss of or alteration in physical functioning suggesting a physical disorder
   Dysmorphophobia Preoccupation with an imagined defect of physical appearance.

3. *Problems in which the basis of symptoms varies or is uncertain*
   Headache Pain in the region of head (including facial pain); divided into migraine and tension headache, *maybe* due to functional disturbances of muscular contraction and cerebrovascular functioning respectively
   Disproportionate breathlessness Perceived obstruction of the upper airways in the absence of sufficient objective impairment of physiological functioning
   Functional chest pain/cardiac neurosis Pain in the cardiac region, usually mimicking disturbed cardiac functioning
   Vestibular symptoms Dizziness, tinnitus
   Chronic pain Pain which endures beyond the normal course of healing, or which arises from a degenerative condition—includes low back pain

Eating disorders (anorexia nervosa, bulimia nervosa), panic attacks, and sexual problems are covered in Chapters 8, 3, and 11.

a context for a working cognitive–behavioural hypothesis which is formulated by identifying factors currently maintaining the patient's problem and the distress experienced. Treatment is then designed to test this hypothesis, which is modified as necessary on the basis of progress. This approach can also be successfully applied when somatic symptoms coexist with other psychological problems (for instance, insomnia, headache, and irritable bowel are commonly associated with anxiety disorders) and for patients presenting with somatic complaints arising from another psychiatric condition (e.g. depression and loss of appetite; panic attacks and cardiac symptoms [Katon 1984; Chapter 3]). In each instance, the psychological conceptualization is crucial.

General conceptualization of somatic problems with a psychological component

Within medical psychology and behavioural medicine, several theoretical models are now being applied to account for the effectiveness of a range of psychological treatments. There are two principal approaches;

(1) adopting the medical diagnostic framework, then applying psychological principles within this framework, with the assumption that different psychological factors operate in different diagnoses;

(2) adopting a primarily psychological conceptualization, applying psychological principles to patients with specific diagnoses (Marteau and Johnston 1987), with attention to specific medical diagnostic groups as a secondary consideration.

The second option is most consistent with the cognitive–behavioural approach, and is adopted here. Although no single conceptualization can fully account for the problems experienced by all patients, there are some common concepts relevant to the psychological treatment of most somatic problems, and these are summarized below.

1. Patients commonly believe that their problems have a physical cause or manifestation; this perception may be accurate, exaggerated, or completely inaccurate. However, when patients have a distorted or unrealistic belief that their bodily functioning is, or is going to be, impaired in harmful ways, this belief is a source of difficulty and anxiety.

2. Patients base exaggerated beliefs on observations which convince them that their belief may be true. There may be symptoms and signs which are falsely interpreted as evidence of bodily impairment, or the evidence may arise from the patient's understanding (or misunderstanding) of communications from medical practitioners or others. Sometimes, signs, symptoms, and communications indicating that some aspect of the patient's bodily functioning is slightly different from the norm or ideal are interpreted as evidence of serious impairment.

3.   The patients' somatic problems are threatening in two ways, both of which impair their ability to live life to the full:

(a)   the degree of handicap or disability arising from the problem; and

(b)   the emotional reaction to the problem, particularly anxiety about its potential causes and consequences, anger, and depression.

Either or both of these factors can lead patients to seek help.

4.   The reaction to perceived impairment can include changes in mood, cognitions, behaviour, and physiological functioning. These changes can maintain the problem itself (in disorders where there is little or no continuing physical basis for the condition), increase the degree of handicap arising from a condition with an identifiable physical basis, and increase the emotional reaction to the perceived impairment of functioning. Psychological treatment is directed at changing the factors which maintain both distress and handicap.

5.   Problems which *originally* had a physical causation may later be maintained by psychological factors.

Conceptualizing hypochondriasis and anxiety about health

Hypochondriasis is when the *predominant* disturbance is anxiety about health, either as the fear of having, or the belief that one has, a serious physical illness. Many patients with specific somatic disorders have lesser degrees of anxiety about their health. One of the first tasks in psychological treatment of any somatic condition is to assess the extent to which health anxiety is contributing directly or indirectly to the patient's distress and the presenting problem itself. This is not to say that health anxiety is always involved in the maintainance of all types of somatic problems, only that it is commonly involved and is particularly open to psychological intervention. Assessment of the specific somatic problem may reveal other maintaining factors co-existing with anxiety about health, and it is often helpful to intervene in both areas. Obtaining some reduction of anxiety about health early in treatment of somatic problems is often a goal which can be achieved rapidly and will enhance the effectiveness of other interventions, particularly when health anxiety is initially intense. An important illustration of this is the effect of health beliefs on compliance with medical regimes (Becker, Maiman, Kirscht, Haefner, Drachman, and Taylor 1979).

Factors maintaining preoccupation with worries about health

Figure 7.1 illustrates the main ways in which psychological factors operate to maintain anxiety and preoccupation with health. It is important to remember that, in many patients, these physical and psychological factors interact with other mechanisms involved in the maintainance of somatic

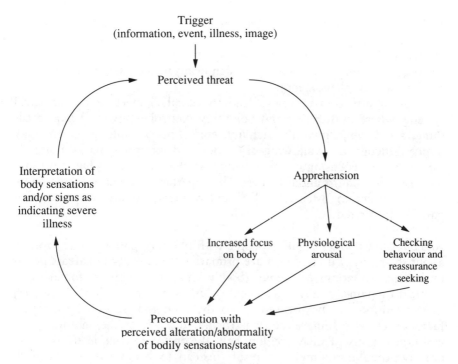

Fig. 7.1. Hypothesized maintaining mechanisms in hypochondriasis

changes, interacting with the factors described here rather than overriding them.

Increased physiological arousal This stems from the perception of threat and leads to an increase in autonomically mediated sensations; these sensations are often interpreted by the patient as further evidence of illness. For example, a patient noticed an increase in sweating and had the thought that this was a sign of a serious hormonal imbalance; sweating increased when this thought occurred, which provided further evidence of 'disturbance'. A patient with irritable bowel problems noticed abdominal discomfort and became anxious about losing control of her bowels, which made her stomach churn. Discomfort and pain then increased, resulting in frightening thoughts about incontinence and so on.

Focus of attention Normal variations in bodily function (including those which give rise to bodily sensations) or previously unnoticed aspects of appearance or bodily function may come to patients' attention and be perceived as novel. Patients may conclude that these perceived changes represent pathological departures from 'normal'. For example, a patient noticed that the roots of his fingernails looked pale and that he had white spots on his nails, and interpreted this as a sign of a 'hormone problem'. He found this observation extremely upsetting, and could not believe that he could have missed something so significant in the past, which meant it must be a new phenomenon.

Focus of attention may also lead to actual changes in physiological systems where both reflex and voluntary control is involved (e.g. breathing, swallowing, muscular activity, etc.). For example, a patient may notice difficulty in swallowing dry foods and interpret this as a sign of throat cancer. Focusing on swallowing can then lead to undue effort and increased discomfort and difficulty. The experience of pain is increased by focus of attention (Melzack 1979) independently of the way in which pain is interpreted.

Avoidant behaviours   Unlike people with phobias, patients with worries about their physical condition are primarily anxious about threats posed by internal situations or stimuli (bodily sensations such as stomach discomfort or pains, bodily signs such as lumps under the skin). However, their attention can be focused on to these internal stimuli by external factors such as reading about a particular disease, or the enquiries of a concerned spouse. Patients seldom have the option of completely avoiding anxiety-provoking stimuli, so resort instead to behaviours designed to minimize bodily discomfort and to behaviours which they believe may prevent feared disasters. The belief that danger has been averted sustains the patients' beliefs; e.g. 'If I hadn't used my inhaler, I would have suffocated and died', 'I never exercise because it might kill me.'

In some patients prone to anxiety about their health, behaviours such as bodily checking and reassurance seeking are reinforced by a temporary reduction of anxiety; as with obsessional patients, this is at the expense of a longer-term increase in anxiety and preoccupation (see Chapter 5). In reassurance seeking, the patient's intention is to draw the attention of others to his or her physical state so that any physical abnormality would be detected (and hence decrease long-term risk). In fact, checking and reassurance seeking focus patients' attention on their fears and prevent habituation to the anxiety-provoking stimuli. In some instances, persistent distress, impairment of normal behaviour, and frequent requests for medical consultation, investigations, and reassurance persuade sympathetic physicians to opt for more drastic medical interventions. These can sometimes include surgery or powerful medication, which patients may take as confirmation of their fears, thereby worsening their symptoms and complaints, and sometimes adding new iatrogenic symptoms to those already present (e.g. side-effects from the medication).

Some behaviours have a more direct physical effect on the patient's symptoms. For example, a patient who noticed persistent weakness reduced his activities, stopped playing sport, and reduced the amount he walked. After some months, he noticed that the weakness was getting worse (actually due to unfitness), which confirmed his initial fears that he was suffering from multiple sclerosis. Pain patients frequently reduce the amount of exercise they take and adopt exaggerated postures in attempts to moderate their pain. As a result of this behaviour, the pain (which may originally have been muscular) worsens, and the patient begins to experience pain from other muscles persistently held in awkward positions. A patient with pains in his testicles frequently pressed them to check whether the pain was still there; he did this for periods of up to 15 minutes, sometimes with only two or three minutes between. Not surprisingly, the pain increased, and his disability with it. Other common behaviours include excessive use of things such as inappropriate medication (prescribed or not), corsets, sticks, crutches, etc.

Beliefs and misinterpretation of symptoms, signs, and medical communications The most important aspect of health anxiety and a crucial component in the complaints of many patients with somatic problems is the misinterpretation of innocuous bodily changes, or of information provided by doctors, friends, or the media. Patients take these changes and communications as evidence that they are suffering from a more serious problem than is really so. This is especially likely when exaggerated beliefs that patients have about the nature of symptoms or illness result in a *confirmatory bias* with respect to illness-related information. As a result, such patients selectively notice and remember information which is consistent with their negative beliefs about their problems. For instance, a patient saw a neurologist about headaches and dizziness; the neurologist told him that if he had a brain tumour it would have worsened and then killed him. The patient, who believed that any sensations in the head were a sign of something internally wrong, later told his therapist that the neurologist had said that he had a fatal brain tumour, because he was noticing his symptoms more which he thought meant that his tumour was getting worse. He believed that the neurologist telling that he had nothing seriously wrong with him was an example of 'breaking it gently'.

In the majority of somatic conditions, aspects of these factors may contribute directly to the maintainance of the problem as well as to anxiety about health. The relative importance of these factors and mood disturbance (particularly depression) in the maintainance of common somatic problems is summarized in Table 7.2.

The scope of the problem

Reports of the prevalence of somatic problems vary, but it is clear that they are extremely common. Headaches and sleep disturbance alone can

Table 7.2 Involvement of cognitive, physiological, and behavioural components in the maintainance of common somatic problems

	Physiological arousal	Avoidance of activities	Checking, reassurance	Symptom misinterpretation	Disturbed mood
Irritable bowel	+/−	+	+	+/−	−
Hypertension	+	−	−	−	−
Insomnia	+/−	−	−	+/−	+/−
Hypochondriasis	−	+	+ +	+ +	+/−
Chronic pain	+/−	+ +	+ +	+	+/−
Headache	+	+	+/−	+/−	−
Vestibular problems	+/−	+	+	+ +	−

+ An important factor; + + a very important factor; − a factor which is seldom important; +/− this factor can be important, but can also be absent.

be found, at some time, in over 90 per cent of the population. Few of these problems reach the point where patients consult their general practitioners. Nevertheless, it has been estimated that 30−80 per cent of patients who consult primary-care physicians present with symptoms for which the physical basis does not fully justify the degree of distress experienced (Barsky and Klerman 1983). Only the most intractable and complicated problems are seen in the psychiatric clinic.

Assessment

Introducing and facilitating the assessment

Introducing the assessment and its purpose is important in patients who believe that they have been wrongly referred for psychological treatment because their problems are entirely physical (and therefore require physical treatment). These beliefs can make the initial interview particularly difficult, especially when the patients have only agreed to attend with the intention of convincing the therapist that they are physically unwell and that assessment and treatment should be medical rather than psychological. One of the therapist's initial tasks is to discover the patient's attitude to the referral, concentrating particularly on any thoughts the patient may have about its implications. For instance, the patient might be asked, 'When your doctor told you that he was referring you for a psychological opinion, what was your reaction?', then, 'How do you feel about it now?' Quite frequently the response will be something like, 'The doctor thinks the problem is imaginary', or, 'He thinks I'm crazy.' If the patient has worries of this type, it is important to allay these fears before proceeding to further assessment. A helpful way of eliciting the patient's co-operation is to explain:

'My job includes treatment of a variety of problems which are not obviously psychological, but which may involve psychological factors. For instance, I am often asked to help people who have very severe migraine headaches, people who have stomach ulcers, people who have high blood pressure, people who are worried about their health, and so on. In each of these problems, there is often a real physical problem involved, but psychological treatment can be helpful by reducing stress which contributes to the problem, helping with extra stress arising from the problem itself, or helping people adjust to having the problem. Actually, it is very unusual to find someone who isn't at least a little worried about their problem, whatever caused it in the first place.'

A further useful tactic is to tell the patient:

'I only know a small amount about your problems at this stage. The purpose of this interview is for me to find out more about your problems and the way they have been affecting you. It may be that psychological help is or is not right for you—you don't have to decide that at this stage. What I would like to do is for us to discuss your problem, then see if there might be anything which we could work on. Then we could discuss whether my kind of treatment would be helpful.'

Sometimes it may be necessary to devote 15–20 minutes to a discussion of this type. The therapist's target is to engage the patient sufficiently to be able to assess the problem collaboratively; engaging the patient in treatment is a later goal (see below), but this is neither necessary or desirable at this stage. No treatment should be offered until the therapist has reached a positive psychological formulation of the patient's problems. A small proportion of patients resist discussing anything other than physical symptoms, despite the techniques described above. With these patients, engagement in assessment has to be carried out along the lines used to begin treatment (p. 253).

For example, the therapist might say, 'I understand your doubts about whether or not discussing psychological aspects of your problem is appropriate, because you feel convinced your problem is entirely physical. However, over the last six months, has there ever been even a moment when you had even a fraction of one per cent of doubt?', then, 'Just for the moment, could we consider that doubt as an exercise in making sure you have covered every possibility for dealing with your problem. So bearing in mind that we are talking about only a minimum of doubt ... '

General assessment

The assessment interview proceeds along the lines discussed in Chapter 2, with emphasis on the physiological concomitants of the problem and the patients' beliefs about their physical state (see Table 7.3 for a summary of the main points of the assessment). Attention is paid to any events, thoughts, images, feelings, or behaviours which precede or accompany the problem. For instance, headache patients are asked whether they have

Table 7.3 Summary of principal areas of assessment

Interview
  Patient's attitude to referral and to the problem
  Details of the problem: cognitive, physiological, behavioural, affective; history
    of previous treatments
  What makes it worse and what makes it better
  Degree of handicap: social/occupational/leisure
  Beliefs about origin, cause, and course of the illness
  General beliefs about the nature and meaning of symptoms

Self-monitoring
  Diaries of target problem, associated thoughts, mood, behaviours, medication
    use, consequences of the problem

Questionnaires
  Anxiety, depression, specific questionnaires

Physiological measurements
  Specific criterion measures where appropriate
  Defining any perceived variation in bodily function involved

noticed anything which makes the problem worse or better. Have they ever noticed any patterns according to the day of the week, time of the month, or time of the year? When the headaches occur, what goes through their mind at the time? When the symptoms are at their worst, what does the patient think is *the worst things that could happen*? Patients who are very anxious are often preoccupied with thoughts about what will eventually happen to them, although such thoughts can be very difficult to elicit. This difficulty is especially marked when patients are actively trying not to dwell on their fears. In this type of cognitive avoidance the attempts to suppress thoughts of disaster (sometimes through frantic reassurance seeking about the symptoms experienced) can result in frequent and unpleasant breakthroughs of terrifying thoughts or images. The effects of this cognitive avoidance is therefore a paradoxical increase in preoccupation with vague fears of 'the worst'. An example of this was a patient who noticed that she became very tense when worried; her doctor told her not to worry, and that it was possible to become tense to the point of rigidity and yet still be able to breathe. She interpreted this as meaning that this was what was going to happen to her, and sought a medical solution to her stiffness, believing it to be the sign of a serious wasting disease. An alternative, more helpful line of enquiry is to ask, 'What do you think is the cause of your problems?', 'How do you think that would work to produce the symptoms you get?' The therapist should enquire about *visual images* related to the problem. For example, a patient who complained of pain in her legs was able to identify a visual image of her legs being amputated every time she noticed a twinge in her knees; this image was associated with an increase in both anxiety and perceived pain.

Exaggerated dysfunctional beliefs about health and illness which may convince patients that they are suffering from a serious illness should be assessed. Examples are, 'Physical symptoms are always a sign that there is something wrong with your body', 'It is possible to know, with absolute certainty, that you are *not* ill.' Another frequent problem occurs in patients who believe health professionals are likely to make errors of diagnosis with potentially serious consequences. Such beliefs may occur as a result of personal experience or because of examples publicized in the media. Assessing these beliefs is an important part of the initial assessment; later in treatment, they can be challenged as described in Chapters 3 and 6. A related issue is the overinclusive cognitive style adopted by some patients with respect to health matters.

For example, a patient repeatedly told the therapist that he *must* discover the cause of his rash, and that the doctors *should* give him a reason for his problems. The therapist asked, 'Why *must* you discover the cause; does everything have to have a cause that could be identified?' The patient replied, 'I have always been the type of person who had to know the cause of a problem; for example, I would *completely* take my car apart to find why there was a rattle; a rattle means that there is something wrong which is going to get worse.' Thus, being told that, 'We have ruled out, beyond reasonable doubt, the possibility that your symptoms indicate a serious condition' would be unlikely to be helpful unless these beliefs were modified.

Behaviours which are consequences of patient's symptoms or anxiety are assessed in detail. This includes what patients' actually do (e.g. go home, lie down, take tablets), but also other less obvious voluntary actions (focusing on their body, distraction, asking for reassurance from others, reading medical textbooks). Anything patients *make themselves do or think* is inquired about. The patient is asked, 'When the problem starts to bother you, is there anything you tend to do because of the problem?', 'Are there any things you try to do when the problem is there?', 'How would your behaviour be different if the problem were to clear up tomorrow?' Reassurance seeking from medical or non-medical sources should be specifically assessed.

Assessment should also include enquiry about avoidance which *anticipates* symptoms and anxiety, and any associated thoughts. For example, patients often report that they habitually avoid a particular activity, although they cannot identify an associated thought. The therapist could ask, 'If you had *not* been able to avoid that activity . . . what was the worst thing that could have happened then?' Patients with pain, hypo-

chondriasis, irritable bowel, and headache often have anticipatory behaviours of this type, and therefore report few immediately identifiable
negative thoughts. Avoidance functions in a similar way to that observed
in phobic anxiety (see Chapter 4, p. 100), and is assessed in similar ways.
For instance, 'Are there things that your problem prevents you from
doing?'

Once a general account of the problem has been gained, a more
detailed description of recent episodes is elicited. This is best done as a
narrative progression through a recent occasion which the patient vividly
recalls: 'The last time your pain was so severe that it stopped you from
walking was on Tuesday. What was the first sign that it was getting
bad?', as the description progresses, useful questions are, 'What went
through your mind when you noticed that the pain was worse?', 'What
happened next?', 'At that time, what did you think was the worst thing
that could happen?', 'Did you try to do anything to stop that happening?', 'What did you want to do then?'

Self-monitoring

A full formulation is seldom possible immediately after the first assessment session; further assessment should include a period of self-
monitoring (which is also useful as a baseline against which to measure
the effectiveness of treatment) and completion of self-report questionnaires. When self-monitoring is begun, the patient is asked to keep records about the relevant variables, (e.g. the target problem, thoughts
associated with episodes, general mood, and behaviours), in the way
described in Chapter 2. The therapist should stress that at this stage
patients should describe the thoughts and behaviours associated with the
problem, rather than attempt to establish any links between them.

At least one further assessment session is helpful, usually after the
therapist has examined medical and psychiatric notes where these are
available. The intervening period also allows time for self-monitoring
data to be gathered and discussed. Aspects of the patient's history which
may intensify the degree of distress the patient experiences should be
considered. For example, an outstanding competitive runner developed
chronic pain and obesity following a fall in which he damaged his legs so
badly that he was never able to walk properly again. Whenever he noticed
pain, he had the thought, 'Life isn't worth living if I can't run again;
nothing else is worthwhile.'

Physicians and other professionals currently involved in the patient's
care should be contacted for their opinion, and to indicate the therapist's
involvement. It is important to establish and agree the medical limits
which may be imposed on treatment. Treatment often includes medication reduction, exercise programmes, and so on; these should be conducted in co-operation with the physicians involved. In the second

session, the results of self-monitoring are examined and the process of engaging the patient in treatment starts.

Self-monitoring can be either individualized or standardized. An example of the use of a standardized self-monitoring sheet for a headache patient is shown in Fig. 7.2. Self-monitoring is usually on the basis of a daily diary. This would include the variables which the initial assessment suggested may be important. Although criterion measures (e.g. headache intensity) are kept constant, other details recorded in the diary (e.g. thoughts of brain tumours, stressful events, coping behaviours) may vary as treatment progresses and the formulation is refined. Later in treatment, the application and effectiveness of coping techniques learned in therapy may also be recorded.

For example, in a patient with chronic pain the assessment suggested that he was restricting his physical activities, spending most of his mornings in bed. An activity diary revealed that his afternoon and evenings were usually spent lying on a couch in one position. Extension of the diary to include his thoughts and mood every time his clock struck the hour (so that he had an identifiable signal for his self-recording) revealed gloomy thoughts centred on the hopelessness of the future. This led into a discussion of the role of *mental* as well as physical inactivity, and ways in which he could try to improve his situation *regardless of his medical condition*. He was asked, 'Alright, supposing for the moment that the pain were never to improve. How would you want to set about coping with that?'

Medication use should be included in self-monitoring, and can be regarded as an illness behaviour which fosters preoccupation, sometimes because of side-effects.

For example, a patient with mild asthma was experiencing several attacks of anxiety each day, and was constantly in a state of some agitation. She was asked to monitor her breathlessness, general anxiety, anxiety attacks, and use of inhalers. It emerged from these records that episodes of anxiety in the afternoon were five times more likely after she had used her inhaler more than three times. Restricting her use of the inhaler resulted in a dramatic reduction in anxiety, as a preliminary to a fuller programme of treatment (see p. 256).

Questionnaires

Although many questionnaires for somatic problems have been produced, few have proven useful in routine clinical practice (Bradley and Prokop 1982). The McGill Pain Questionnaire can be useful with pain patients as it measures the sensory, affective, and evaluative components of pain as well as its intensity (Melzack and Torgerson 1971). In headache patients, the Headache Questionnaire (Blanchard and Andrasik 1985, p. 8) is useful. None of the questionnaires which measure somatization and illness behaviour have demonstrated clinical usefulness. Measurement of anxiety and depression in patients with a somatic presentation are a

Fig. 7.2 An example of a completed headache diary, showing (a) the ratings as given on the front of the booklet; (b) the section for recording the location of head pain and activities avoided (heads are the key for location); (c) the headache chart itself, with the upper section being for the recording of medication (The author is grateful to Clare Philips who originally supplied the prototype for this form)

a)

RATING SCALE (0–5)

0 No headache
1 Very low level—aware of it only at times
2 Pain level can be ignored at times
3 Painful, but can continue work
4 Severe, makes concentration difficult
5 Intense, incapacitating

Time woke .... *7.30 a.m.*
Time went to sleep..... *11.15 p.m.*

b)

Time of day	Activity avoided, etc.	Location
a.m.	Not invited neighbour round Sat down for half hour at 12.00	16 , 17, 14 , 6
p.m.	Went to bed 4–5 pm Wouldn't take kids to park Avoided talking, noise	16 , 17, 14, 6,15, 13, 4

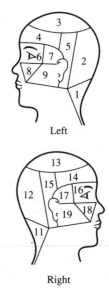

Left

Right

Figure 7.2 *(Cont'd)*

c) Medication

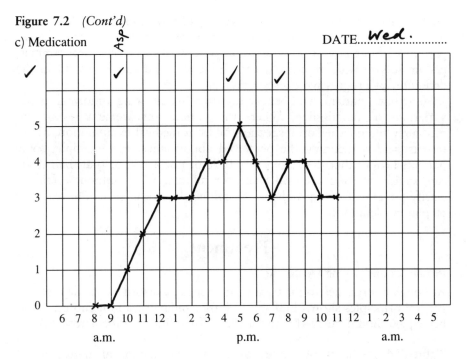

special problem, because questionnaires relevant to these states rely commonly on a large proportion of physical symptoms. The Hospital Anxiety and Depression scale (Zigmond and Snaith 1983) was devised to overcome this problem, and has the advantages of being short, easy to score, and relatively sensitive to change.

Physiological measurements

For patients with an identifiable physiological correlate of their problem, direct measurement of this is sometimes useful as a way of evaluating progress and providing both patient and therapist with feedback about the efficacy of treatment (e.g. periodic measurement of blood pressure; measurement of the size of inflamed areas in patients with skin conditions). Measurements can be included as self-monitoring during assessment; thus, the patient with intermittent episodes of high blood pressure can be taught to measure blood pressure at different times of day, before and after particular activities, and so on. In patients where respiratory factors such as hyperventilation may play a role in the problem, measurement of $_pCO_2$ is sometimes helpful (Salkovskis, Clark, and Jones 1986), although this is not always easy to arrange, and any evidence of hyperventilation must be considered in the context of the psychological assessment of what symptoms experienced mean to the patient (Salkovskis 1988c). There are simple devices which measure amount of activity and which are of great value with a variety of problems, particularly pain. For example, pedometers allow comparisons of activity at different periods within a day or on different days; as part of exercise programmes, pedometers provide rapid and easy feedback, and can be useful in the definition of progressive exercise targets.

Sometimes, patients will believe that they are showing abnormal bodily variations or functioning. Where the somatic involvement is not immediately plain either on inspection or from medical examination, attention is paid to defining the perceived abnormality. For example, some patients believe that they sleep very little or not at all, or that their heart rate should never exceed 60 beats per minute. When interview fails to clarify the extent of a problem, physiological assessment can have a role to play in definition.

Treatment

Principles underlying treatment

Although approaches to the treatment of specific disorders are diverse, the general principles shown in Table 7.4 are similar for all diagnoses. These principles should guide the application of specific treatment techniques.

Table 7.4 General principles of cognitive–behavioural treatment of somatic problems

---

1. Aim is to help the patient identify what the problem *is*, not what the problem is not
2. Acknowledge that the symptoms really exist—and that the treatment aims to provide a satisfactory explanation for the symptoms
3. Distinguish between giving relevant information as opposed to reassuring with irrelevant or repetitive information
4. Treatment sessions should never become combative; questioning and collaboration with the patient is the preferred style, as in cognitive therapy in general
5. Patient's beliefs are invariably based on evidence which they find convincing; rather than discounting a belief, discover the observations which the patient believes to be evidence of illness and then work collaboratively with the patient on that basis
6. Set a limited period contract which fulfils the therapist's requirements while respecting the patient's worries
7. The selective attention and suggestibility typical of many patients should be used to demonstrate the way in which anxiety can arise from innocuous circumstances, symptoms, and information
8. What the patients have understood about what has been said during the treatment sessions must *always* be checked by asking them to summarize what has been said and its implications for them.

Treatment techniques

Specific treatment techniques for somatic problems are outlined in this section. In some patients, assessment may suggest the application of some of the treatment techniques outlined in Chapters 3, 4, 5, 10, and 12. However, where reluctance to engage in treatment is present, it must be dealt with before treatment commences.

Engagement in treatment

Patients who initially believe their problem is primarily physical are difficult to engage in treatment, since they do not believe that psychological treatment is appropriate. This belief will lead to non-compliance with interventions (Rosenstock and Kirscht 1979). Establishing engagement usually follows from assessment. On the basis of a preliminary conceptualization of the problem, the therapist summarizes what the patient has said, emphasizing the role of the patient's *symptoms, thoughts, beliefs*, and *behaviours*, presenting the conceptualization in these terms. The acceptability of this conceptualization is discussed with the patient. Before treatment can proceed beyond this stage, the therapist and patient must agree on treatment goals. Many patients are willing to attend for a psychological assessment, but have a different set of goals from the therapist, who is attempting to arrive at a psychological formulation for treatment of the patient's problem. Patients, on the other hand, may regard the therapist as a potential ally in their attempts to rule out physical illnesses or to have their beliefs about the medical basis of their problems accepted as true. For instance, they may intend to prove to the therapist that they are not 'mad', or regard the therapist as a new source of expert reassurance. Unless these different expectations of treatment and how it should proceed can be reconciled, therapy is unlikely to be effective. However, the therapist should not expect patients to 'admit' that their problems are 'just anxiety', when they are seeking treatment for what they believe is an undiagnosed physical illness, or one which is more severe or handicapping than has been recognized.

This impasse can be resolved by careful discussion which neither rejects the patient's beliefs nor adds weight to them. The therapist first indicates full acceptance that the patient *experiences* physical symptoms and that the patient believes that these symptoms are due to a serious physical illness. The therapist can explain that people generally base such beliefs on particular observations which seem to be convincing evidence that they are ill. However, it is also possible that there may be alternative explanations of the observations which they have made (see also p. 257). Further assessment and treatment then involve the examination of the evidence and possible alternative explanations, and includes the use of specific tasks designed to test out alternative explanations. The patient is explicitly informed that, in this new way of dealing with the problem, physical tests and checks would not be a part of treatment, nor would reassurance and lengthy discussions of symptoms be useful.

Before patients decide about the acceptability of this new approach to the problem, the usefulness of the two alternative ways (new and old) of tackling the problem should be considered. How long had the patients been trying to solve their problem and rid themselves of symptoms by exclusively medical means? How effective had this been? Had they ever properly tested the alternative psychological approach suggested by the therapist. It is then proposed that patients commit themselves to work with the therapist in this new way for four months, and dates are specified. If they were able to do all the things agreed with their therapist and the problem has not improved at all at the end of that time, then it would be reasonable to come back to their original way of tackling the problem, and the therapist would then be happy to reconsider the problem from a more physical perspective. In this way, the patients are not asked to give up their view of their problems, but to consider and test an alternative for a limited period. In patients who believe that they may have a physical illness which is being neglected this is an attractive proposition. The transcript below illustrates this approach in the second session with a 57-year-old woman.

Therapist 'So you believe that you have a serious physical problem that the doctors haven't picked up. Is that right?'

Patient   'Yes, that's right.'

Th.   'So that thought is very upsetting, and makes you unhappy in a variety of ways. The main ways it affects what you do is it interferes with you being on your own, and it stops you doing things you enjoy, such as tennis. It also has stopped you from eating very much, which might be making eating still more difficult. Is that right?'

Pt   'Yes. Sometimes I will be on my own, but I won't if I can help it.'

Th.   'Right. In general, when people have fears, they usually have reasons for those fears. In your instance, the reasons for your fear about your health are the pains you get, your loss of weight, difficulty eating and swallowing, and bowel problems. These all suggest to you that you are ill, especially as they come every day. Is there any other evidence that makes you think you are ill?'

Pt   'Yes, it's not a lump, it's a horrible feeling in the throat, tight, when it gets to here it's sore. My doctor checked me, but this has only got worse since I had the X-rays, not before; then it didn't stop me from eating. My waterworks are a problem too. It's very frightening, I can't deal with it. Those are the main things, they make me think I have the same as my mother.'

Th.   'Right; so these all make you think the worst; you think you have cancer, like your mother.'

Pt   'Yes.'

Th.	'There are also some things which make you think you have anxiety as well; for instance, towards the end of our last meeting, you said that the sleep problem was anxiety about dying in your sleep, that you fight sleep. So your sleeping problem is explained by being worried?'
Pt	'Yes, I think so.'
Th.	'Now, you also have problems with pain, eating, waterworks, and bowels. These make you think you are ill. One worry about these is that the doctors would not take these seriously because you've had similar problems in the past.'
Pt	'How would they know if I had something seriously wrong with me organically? This is different from the past. I can't work through it now.'
Th.	'The doctor has listened to the symptoms, but you are worried that he pays too much attention to your previous problems.' [Briefly discusses the way diagnoses are made.] 'He thinks you have a kind of phobia about your health, and the symptoms come from anxiety.' [Discusses symptoms of anxiety, asks patient to identify whether she experiences any of these, describes effects of anxiety on pain and appetite . . .] 'What's your reaction to this kind of idea?'
Pt	'I can say to you that when my symptoms are starting to lift, then I'll believe I'm alright.'
Th.	'OK. I have a proposition for you. Your worry is that there is something physically wrong with you, and I understand why the things we have discussed make you think that. We've also gone over things which make me think you have a type of phobia of being ill. So, there are two possibilities, and we need to consider both of them. The two possibilities are the one you believe and I doubt, which is that there is something physically wrong with you. The other possibility I believe and you doubt; this is that you are getting very anxious and having upsetting thoughts. These thoughts make you do things which focus you more on your worries, and can produce symptoms in your body, change your eating. Is that a good summary?'
Pt	'Yes, that's just it.'
Th.	'Recently, how much have you tried to act as if you were ill and deal with the problem in that way?'
Pt	'Like going to my GP? Yes, he's checked up on me a lot.'
Th.	'Has that been a help in making the symptoms less?'
Pt	'No, because . . . he gave me medicals, nothing was found. I'm saying, what am I to do?'
Th.	'It sounds like you have tried to put the problem right by dealing with it as if it were a physical problem. I've been suggesting that anxiety might be a big part of your problem. How much have you tried to deal with it in that kind of way, as if the problem were anxiety? Have you given that a try?'
Pt	'Em . . . [long pause] I can't say I have.'
Th.	'You haven't tried to deal with it like anxiety?'
Pt	'No.'
Th.	'You've tried dealing with it as a physical problem. How about making

	a bargain for just three months; in those three months, to deal with it as an anxiety problem. You try to deal with it as anxiety; if you are able to do all the things we work out together to deal with your anxiety, and at the end of three months the problem is not improving, then we will look at it again from a physical angle.'
Pt	'I understand.'
Th.	'It seems like a sensible way of doing it; if you do this and it works then the problem's gone. If it doesn't help, then that's also good, because you can turn round and say "Ah ha, I got my anxiety down, and the problem is still there; you need to look at it again." Does that seem alright?'
Pt	'I see. Where do we start?'

A summary and consolidation would then follow. The sessions should be audio-taped; the patient can then listen afterwards and summarize the important points.

Changes in medication and physical aids, diet, and lifestyle
Considerable changes in somatic disorders can be made by simple interventions.

Medication and physical aids Many patients take medication which was intended to help their problems but has become counterproductive. For example, there is evidence that a *reduction* in pain may occur in as many as 40 per cent of pain patients when (prescribed or non-prescribed) medication is withdrawn. Palliative medication of this type should be discontinued as soon as is possible, in co-operation with the prescribing physician. On occasions, reduction of medication has to be very gradual; rarely, supervised withdrawal as an inpatient is necessary. Other medication which commonly has a paradoxical beneficial effect when withdrawn includes laxatives, which can increase pain and impair bowel functioning in irritable bowel patients; hypnotics, which may impair quality of sleep (and can produce early wakening) in insomnia; and inhalers for non-asthmatic breathlessness (over-use can produce anxiety as a side-effect). Medication which is being prescribed for a disorder which is *not* present usually increases anxiety, because the act of taking it focuses the patient's attention and bolsters the belief in the supposed illness. For example, this was understandable in a chest-pain patient who believed that he had a heart condition, was told that he was healthy by a cardiologist, but was also given, 'little white tablets to put under his tongue when the pain gets bad'. Similar effects can occur with physical aids, particularly corsets, crutches, and wheelchairs, which can also increase weakness and muscle pain.

Taking medication or using physical aids over a long period as a means of symptom relief may have paradoxical effects in three ways:

(1)   direct effects, e.g. hypnotics adversely affecting sleep pattern, laxatives leading to bowel pain and sluggishness;

(2)   effects on judgements of abnormality and impairment, e.g. the belief that six hours' sleep each night must be a problem if tablets are prescribed for it, that occasional constipation must be abnormal if it merits laxatives;

(3)   effects on the belief that there is a serious underlying condition, e.g. the breathless patient given an inhaler.

Dietary and lifestyle factors   The role of allergic dietary factors in physical presentations is contentious (Rippere 1983). If there is evidence from the assessment that symptoms may be related to particular substances, then patients could be asked to monitor the effects of excluding these factors. This is followed by gradually re-introducing them, the patient being kept unaware of precisely when this happens (Mackarness 1980). It is sometimes worth considering whether a patient's disorder might be related to occupational exposure to particular substances. In one patient, for example, exposure to styrene at work was associated with breathlessness, and simply identifying this fact dealt with the patient's anxiety. Often, the reaction to dietary factors is an obvious direct link, sleeplessness and caffeine intake being one of the best known. Also frequently encountered are problems resulting from excessive alcohol intake, e.g. hangover (headache), sleep impairment, or more general physical problems. Patients can be unaware that their consumption is excessive, or may be ashamed to admit it. Eliminating alcohol consumption can then be illuminating. Cigarette-smoking can produce problems such as poor circulation and breathlessness. Poor physical fitness is implicated in some problems: patients who take little exercise may experience muscle pain when they do and may have problems sleeping. Exercise often has beneficial effects on bowel function in irritable bowel syndrome. Furthermore, changing from a diet of french fries and hamburgers, for example, to one with more roughage is almost invariably beneficial.

Changing beliefs about the nature and consequences of the problem

Anxiety about health involves the interpretation of bodily sensations, physical changes, or medical communications as more dangerous than they really are. In particular, the *future development* of a medical condition (real or imagined) may be perceived as more threatening than is truly the case. In problems with a substantial basis in anxiety, treatment involves changing the way in which patients evaluate the meaning of symptoms. Changing beliefs initially involves identifying negative thoughts and the evidence upon which they are based.

For example, a patient who had recently developed tinnitus, and who believed that the tinnitus would become so intense as to drive him to despair and possibly suicide, rated his belief in this thought as 85/100. Questioning revealed that, when the tinnitus began, the patient had noticed a progression from no noise to a level equivalent to a whisper in the space of two days. He had also become intensely depressed and anxious over the subsequent week. Following that, the condition had been stable; however, the patient believed that tinnitus progressed in a stepwise fashion, and that each step would magnify his anxiety and depression to a comparable degree to the time when his tinnitus began. He was extrapolating from the early experience of tinnitus to what he believed the likely progression would be. When this basis for his worries was made explicit, it was written down and the patient considered it carefully in the light of his general experience. He noted that when anxiety and depression result from a series of significant events, they do not develop cumulatively (as in having a bad week where everything goes wrong). He also recognized that when a friend developed diabetes, his subsequent response was less than his initial reaction.

Through questioning, he was able to generate an alternative description of his tinnitus, namely that it had gradually built up over a period of months or even years, and that he had only noticed it after seeing a TV programme about hearing defects; the shock of noticing tinnitus, and worries about having a brain tumour had increased the extent to which he focused on the noise, leading to further increases in perception. He then rated his belief in this alternative as being 80/100, and re-rated his original thought as only 30/100. A behavioural experiment was devised to test his thoughts. He recorded his anxiety and the perceived intensity of tinnitus during a game of football, compared to a period spent sitting at home thinking about all the possible things which might happen to him as a result of tinnitus. He found the results of this experiment so convincing that he re-rated his initial thoughts about how the tinnitus might drive him to suicide at only 5/100.

This combination of discussing the basis of negative beliefs, self-monitoring, and behavioural experiments is applicable to a wide range of reactions involving anxiety or depression as a response to physical symptoms or fears. Ratings indicate to the therapist and patient how successful belief change has been. Dual ratings of belief are often helpful; for example: 'I would like you to rate the thought "the tinnitus will become so intense as to drive me to suicide" on a 0–100 scale, where 0 is "I don't believe this at all" and 100 is "I am completely convinced that this is true." Right now, how much do you believe this?' Then: 'When it is very quiet and you particularly notice the tinnitus, what would the rating be then?' Often, the presence of the symptom produces substantial differences in belief ratings; the negative thoughts should be identified and challenged for situations where beliefs would be at their strongest, because this disconfirmation has the biggest impact on the patient's behaviour. Behavioural experiments are a very powerful way of changing patients' beliefs about the origin and nature of symptoms. In a behavioural experiment, the aim is to demonstrate to patients that their symptoms can be influenced by factors other than the ones they believe are responsible.

For example, a patient who believed that difficulty swallowing was a sign of throat cancer was asked to swallow repeatedly then describe the effects of this. She was surprised to discover that she found it increasingly difficult to swallow, and that the therapist experienced the same thing when he swallowed repeatedly. The importance of this observation was that she would frequently check her throat by swallowing a number of times.

Another patient noticed numbness in her head, which she believed to be a sign of a brain tumour. When she focused on this and thought of brain tumours, the numbness worsened; when describing aloud a picture in the therapist's office, she no longer noticed the numbness. While discussing this experiment, she recalled that thinking of brain tumours usually provoked symptoms; the therapist asked her what she made of that observation. She replied that it seemed very unlikely that thinking about a tumour would make it worse, and it made it seem very likely that the problem was her response to anxiety about a tumour.

(Several other examples are described in this chapter and Chapter 3.)

Changing behaviour

The majority of behaviours involved in somatic problems are perceived by the patient as serving a preventative function, and are therefore relatively difficult to modify without attention to the underlying beliefs.

Behaviours directly related to the problem   When illness behaviour is prominent, treatment strategies aim to elicit and demonstrate the role of behaviours in maintaining anxiety, preoccupation, and physiological disturbance. The use of questioning as part of guided discovery can be helpful. Direct demonstration is particularly convincing when changing behaviour can be shown to have an effect on symptoms. The patient and therapist design experiments to

(1)   test the patient's belief that the behaviour is 'keeping them safe' from serious harm; and

(2)   to see if behaviours which the patient believes relieve symptoms really do so.

For example, a patient was frightened that she had AIDS because she had a number of symptoms which had been reported in the media as characteristic of AIDS. Questioning revealed that she had been particularly frightened by lumps and pain in her neck and armpits. As a result of this fear, she frequently prodded and manipulated these areas, resulting in worsening of the pain, some superficial inflammation and swelling. She and the therapist carried out an experiment in which both prodded their necks in the same way for three periods of five minutes during a session. The increase in pain and inflammation was sufficient to convince her that her behaviour was implicated in the production of the symptom.

Another example was a patient with irritable bowel, in whom self-monitoring indicated that she felt anxious if she had any sensations of fullness in her lower bowel. She frequently used laxatives and suppositories in order to get rid of these feelings. It was hypothesized that these disturbed her bowel function and increased her sensitivity to sensations from the lower bowel; she agreed to desist from the use of suppositories and laxatives for a period of three weeks, monitoring bowel function during this time. She found that she experienced less sensations of fullness, and learned to discriminate urges to defecate better. Both bowel habit and anxiety improved as a result of this intervention.

In many instances, avoidance behaviours maintain the patients' pre-occupation with disease by preventing the patient accessing information which contradicts negative interpretations of symptoms.

For example, a pain patient believed that the reason she was not confined to a wheelchair was because she had restricted her physical activity, stayed in bed when the pain was severe, and so on. When she started an exercise programme she was astonished that this did not result in deterioration of her condition.

A patient believed that he had prevented himself from having a stroke by focusing his attention on trying to, 'make the blood flow more freely', by the exertion of will-power, and that should he stop this he would then have a stroke (belief rated 95/100). He was obviously reluctant to stop doing this so the therapist suggested that he try to *bring on* a stroke in the session by effort of will. Surprised by this suggestion, he said after some discussion that it was not possible; he was able to generalize this to his efforts to prevent a stroke (belief rating dropped to 10/100). He was able to prevent his efforts at control outside the session, his belief dropped to 0/100, and he ceased to worry about having a stroke.

Further examples of the specific application of techniques to change pain behaviours and beliefs are described in detail by Philips (1988).

Reassurance   In patients anxious about their health, a variety of behaviours can occur which have the same effect as obsessional checking (p. 130). These reassurance-seeking behaviours focus attention on patients' worries, reducing their anxiety in the short term, but increasing pre-occupation and other aspects of the problem in the longer term (Salkovskis and Warwick 1986; Warwick and Salkovskis 1985). Such behaviours can include requests for physical tests, physical examination, or detailed discussion of symptoms in an attempt to *rule out* possible disease. Although most non-anxious patients seeking medical help respond to properly delivered reassurance in which illness is 'ruled out', patients anxious about their health respond differently; repeated and 'stronger' reassurance quickly becomes counterproductive as the patients selectively attend to and misinterpret the reassurance itself. For example, a patient was told, 'These headaches are certainly caused by tension; if they persist, then I'll send you for a skull X-ray to put your mind at rest'; he interpreted this as a sign that the doctor believed that he might have a brain tumour. Repeated attempts to 'prove' to patients that they are *not* ill, either through medical tests or verbal persuasion, are more likely to increase anxiety.

The ways in which patients seek reassurance vary tremendously, including subtle ways, such as 'casual' conversations in which symptoms are mentioned. Several doctors may be consulted simultaneously and friends and families questioned repeatedly, in ways which do not seem to be connected to health worries. For example, one patient would dress up but not make up before going out, then ask her husband how she looked, and whether she was unduly pale and ill-looking. As noted earlier, bodily checking is often a prominent feature, and can produce problems of its own (e.g. inflammation, pain, tenderness). The role of reassurance-seeking in maintaining patients' problems must be explained to them in a way which they clearly understand. For example, a patient who wanted to repeatedly discuss his symptoms in case he had developed cancer asked why the therapist would not discuss symptoms. The therapist was aware that the interview was developing into an unproductive argument:

Therapist 'Do you think that you really need this?'
Patient 'Well, it would make me feel better.'
Th. 'OK. I guess that if that's what will help I ought to go over the symptoms with you. And I think I really ought to do it properly. I have a lot of time now, which I'm happy to spend with you, so long as it deals with the problem properly. How many times would I have to reassure you to last until the end of the year?'
Pt 'Until the end of the year?'
Th. 'Yes; there seems little point in doing something like this, which you have done lots before, unless it's really going to work this time. Is three hours enough for the rest of the year?'
Pt 'But . . . it won't last for the rest of the year.'
Th. 'I see. How long will it last?'
Pt 'Probably for the rest of the day. Then I'll probably get worried again.'
Th. 'So, however much reassurance you get it never lasts?'
Pt 'No. Sometimes the more I get the more I want.'
Th. 'You are saying that however much reassurance I give you, it isn't going to last very long before you are going to get worried again, and it might even make you more worried. As we have already identified anxiety about your health as one of your major problems, do you think that reassurance is an effective treatment, or should we look for alternatives?'

Where reassurance-seeking is a major feature of a patient's difficulties, it is helpful to devise a behavioural experiment demonstrating the effects of reassurance (Salkovskis and Warwick 1986). This experiment can also function as an engagement strategy in patients who are reluctant to start treatment without a 'final test'. For example, a last physical investigation before psychological treatment starts is discussed and arranged on the strict understanding that it is regarded as unnecessary for the patient's physical health, but may be helpful in the psychological assessment. Self-monitoring of anxiety about health, belief in specific illness-related thoughts, and need for reassurance are all regularly rated on a 0–100 scale over the period prior to and after the test. If anxiety is reduced in an enduring way, then this is helpful in any case. If, as is much more common, anxiety is reduced only briefly, this is used as the basis for discussion about the way in which reassurance keeps anxiety going. The demonstration also engages the patient in treatment and establishes a collaborative relationship. It provides a clear rationale for controlling reassurance-seeking and thereby helps the patient to tolerate the initial anxiety caused by behaviour change. A similar strategy is to ask patients to specify exactly what procedures would *fully* convince them that they are *not* suffering from the feared illness. The therapist then adopts the role of the interested sceptic, asking things like, 'Yes, but would that *really* be convincing? How could you be really sure that the doctor was properly aware of how to use the test?', and so on; this is to illustrate that it is *never* possible to be certain that illness is not present, in the same way as it is never possible to be sure that a satellite will not fall on their heads as they walk down the street. This discussion is related to the importance of reassurance in maintaining anxiety, preoccupation, and illness beliefs.

Families and others involved with the patient must be included in such discussions and shown how to deal with requests for reassurance. A role-play may be used, in which the patient asks the relative for reassurance and the relative answers (without non-verbal criticism) in previously agreed terms. For example, a relative might reply, 'As we agreed at the clinic, it does not help you if I give you reassurance. I'm not going to respond at all after this.' The relative then either leaves or talks about unrelated things. Except as a stopgap at times when the patient is *especially* stressed, this type of strategy is of little use without the patient's agreement (see also Chapter 5, p. 153).

Other coping strategies
A range of specific techniques has been used with somatic patients, particularly those for general management of stress and anxiety. Many patients experience stress which is unrelated to their somatic presentation but which makes the somatic problem more difficult to cope with. The techniques described elsewhere in this book (particularly in Chapters 3, 4, 10, and 12) should be applied when assessment indicates that general stress is contributing to the patient's problems. Applied relaxation (see

Chapter 3, p. 92) is helpful for these patients, and for problems in which the main bodily symptoms which frighten the patient are the result of muscle tension or autonomic nervous-system arousal.

The techniques developed by Borkovec (Borkovec, Robinson, Pruzinsky, and DePree 1983) are helpful in patients in whom anxious ruminations and worry play a major part; particularly sleep problems, pain, and somatization. The nature of the patient's worries is assessed and summarized thus:

'So what happens is that when you worry you go over your problems time and time again in your head. Doing this never solves them, but you find it hard not to worry. Is that right?' Having agreed this, the therapist proceeds, 'OK, it would not be sensible to tell you to stop worrying; you obviously would do that if you could. Instead, I'm going to ask you to postpone your worrying. How this works is that, when you notice that you are worrying, you write down the topic of your worries in a notebook, and carry on. Then you set aside about half an hour or an hour each evening as worry time, and go over your worries at that time.'

This is given as homework; when discussed at the next session, the patient often reports that it was very difficult to worry at the worry time; the problems did not seem to matter. The therapist asks what can be made of this, leading to the conclusion that, 'When worries come up, they seem very upsetting because they get out of proportion, and because anxiety makes it difficult to think about them properly. Later on, they can be considered properly and don't seem to be such a problem. You can learn from this that the things you worry about are not as upsetting as they seem at the time. On the other hand, it also helps sort out the "real worries"; things which continue to be a problem later often need problem-solving. This procedure helps you tell the difference.'

Specific disorders: the application of general and specific techniques

In this section, the most important specific treatment techniques for particular problems are outlined and used to illustrate the general principles of treatment described above. Some of the specific interventions described below and elsewhere in this book apply to several problems; for instance the techniques described in Chapters 3, 6, and 12 for the management of stress and anxiety, such as relaxation (as adapted in the headache section) can be useful for most somatic problems.

Headache

Headache has traditionally been divided into a number of diagnostic groupings; clinically, those most commonly encountered are migraine and tension headache (sometimes called muscle contraction headache). The relative utility of these diagnoses with respect to psychological treatment has been the subject of some debate (Bakal 1982; Blanchard and Andrasik 1985). Treatment studies suggest that headaches principally vary in pain intensity rather than other dimensions. Research shows that the most effective psychological treatment is a combination of cognitive, relaxation, and behaviour-change strategies (Philips 1988).

In addition to a general assessment, a neurological opinion is strongly suggested if the headaches are associated with sensory or motor deficits (including twitching, effects on speech), if the patient has a previous history of cancer, if the onset or serious exacerbation of headaches has been recent or was associated with any type of head injury. Other physical disorders which can cause headaches include eye problems and dental factors, particularly malocclusion, in which the patient's 'bite' is misaligned. Reduction of excessive medication is important for headache sufferers; as many as 40 per cent of patients experience a long-term improvement in headache when they reduce or stop analgesic medication. The contraceptive pill has been implicated in headache; counselling with respect to alternative forms of contraception may therefore be important (Philips 1988). Dietary factors are reviewed during self-monitoring and before starting treatment. Most commonly implicated are cheese, caffeine, and alchohol (particularly red wine); smoking may also contribute.

The rationale for the psychological treatment of headache should be related to the information derived during the assessment (p. 244). It might be outlined as:

'The cause of headaches of the kind you have is stress and anxiety. By this I mean that headaches are the way that your body is responding to your present worries. This is not a simple response; it is not simply that when you get worried, you immediately get a headache, but instead that worries build up, and eventually get to the point where a headache happens. Sometimes, worries build up, but only when you relax does the headache happen, probably because you have difficulty winding down. For instance, the records you kept show that you are most likely to get headaches on Tuesdays, after your busy Mondays.'

'Once it starts, the headache itself is an important source of stress, particularly when headaches persist over a longer time. For example, supposing you had drunk too much the night before, you would not enjoy the headache, but would think "Oh well, what do I expect? At least it will go away, and next time I'll know to drink less." However, with headaches, you have identified a different set of thoughts, which are "Here's the headache again—these are ruining my life, I can't do anything about them." When they are particularly bad, you have thoughts like 'Maybe I have a brain tumour." When you compare these different types of thoughts, how stressful do headaches seem to you?'

In this way, the material gathered during the assessment is woven into the rationale, and used to illustrate points the therapist wishes to make. In the last section of the above example the therapist has prepared the way for a description of the rationale for cognitive treatment. A common question raised here is, 'Why do I get headaches? I know other people who are more stressed, and who don't.' This is dealt with by discussing the way different people react to the same stress in different ways; 'For example, some people sweat a lot under stress, others blush, and so on. In your case, you get headaches.' The specific rationale for the treatment itself might be explained as follows:

'Stress tends to be something we accept as part of daily life. Many people enjoy a certain amount of stress in their life. However, it can get out of control and then become unpleasant. The aim of treatment is to allow you to have more control over stress and, in particular, over its physical effects on you. There are a number of ways in which you can learn this control; the main ones we will be covering in treatment are to do with the effect your thoughts have on how you react to stressful situations; finding ways of changing your lifestyle, which can increase the efficiency with which you use time; and learning how to relax.'

Further questioning is encouraged and then the therapist proceeds to discuss specific techniques. The relaxation method used is *applied relaxation* (fully described in Chapter 3, p. 92), with additional emphasis on self-monitoring of the first signs of headache. Often, patients are able to identify the pre-headache state up to two hours before a headache develops, and can use applied relaxation, time management, and problem-solving strategies to abort the headache (see Chapter 3 for details of time management and Chapter 12 on problem-solving).

Relaxation is taught by the therapist within a session; tapes of the relaxation procedures recorded during the therapy session are given to the patient at the end of each session as an adjunct to home practice. Cognitive treatment is based on an analysis of stressful situations and the thoughts associated with them, along the lines outlined in Chapters 3, 4, and 6. As in most of the treatments described in this book, it is emphasized that practice and application between sessions is an important determinant of success.

Insomnia

There are a wide variety of presentations and patterns of insomnia; however, approaches to psychological treatment mostly depend on the modification of the common factor of worry (Borkovec 1982; Borkovec *et al.* 1983). This is a key variable in the treatment of insomnia in two complementary ways. First, when people worry (that is, go over unsolved or unsolvable problems in their mind in a way which is unlikely to lead to their solution), they experience increased arousal; increased arousal prevents sleep since, by definition, sleep involves a state of diminished arousal. Secondly, sleep is considered by most people to be essential to healthy functioning so difficulty in sleeping can be a source of considerable worry. Thus, worry can be both a cause and an effect of perceived sleep disturbance; patients with sleep problems are usually in a vicious circle of worry leading to perceived sleep disturbance leading to worry about sleep disturbance leading to further perceived sleep disturbance, and so on. Successful treatments for insomnia are usually based on this hypothesis, so that treatment is carried out on the basis of

(1) optimizing conditions for sleep to occur;

(2) reducing worry about events *other* than sleep problems; and

(3) reducing worry about sleep problems.

Assessment determines where emphasis should lie.

In the above description, *perceived* sleep disturbance is emphasized: while the report of difficulty sleeping is usually the presenting complaint, the basis of the complaint is not always clear. There is a poor relationship between complaint of disturbed sleep and actual disturbance; for instance, some patients who complain of disturbed sleep show a normal pattern when measured using EEG, while many non-patients showing patterns which deviate considerably from the 'norm' are perfectly happy with their sleep (Coates and Thoresen 1981). The 'norm' is of dubious usefulness with respect to sleep; many patients believe that they should have 'a good eight hours', and that anything short of this has to be 'made up'. This belief is inaccurate; often it is helpful to describe sleep as being, 'a bit like appetite; some people need lots of food, others never seem to eat at all. Both ways are normal, depending on the individual.' Two important factors contribute to the desynchrony between reports of sleep problems and physiological recordings. Some patients complain of onset insomnia but show a normal sleep latency; when wakened in the early stages of sleep they report that they have not yet fallen asleep (Borkovec, Grayson, O'Brien, and Weerts 1979). A further factor is that time perception is affected as sleep nears, so that the period prior to sleep onset often appears longer than is really the case. Taken together, these factors mean that, in cases of this kind, a sufficient goal of treatment is that patients become happy with their sleep. In other cases, treatment efforts can be directed at the target physiological response itself (i.e. sleep), at antecedent conditions (i.e. stress, worry), as well as at the appraisal of the condition.

Assessment

This normally begins with a detailed description of the patient's current sleep pattern, including variations related to shift work, young children, and so on. The emphasis is on assessing the extent to which the patient has a regular sleep pattern. Intake of stimulant drugs (especially caffeine), sleeping tablets, and alcohol are assessed, together with exercise habits. In some patients, the interview assessment may reveal a clear reason for anxiety about sleep; for example, a patient reported that, 'It might seem strange to you, but I think that I'm not going to wake up, so I try not to go to sleep.' These patients often complain of tiredness, and seldom mention their fears unless specifically asked. The assessment also considers the patient's beliefs about 'normal' sleep, thoughts and behaviours surrounding going to bed, the sleeping environment, and coping used when unable to sleep. The therapist should elicit the patient's thoughts on recent occasions on which sleep was difficult, focusing on any current concerns which may be intruding as worry. Patients are asked, 'Supposing this problem were to worsen over the next month, so that it was four or five times as bad, what is the worst thing that could possibly happen?' The reply to this question should indicate the extent to which the difficulty sleeping is itself a worry. This usually provides the basis for education about sleep, which is the first stage of treatment. Sleep diaries supplement information gained from the interview. Interview assessment is followed by a period of self-monitoring of those variables which the formulation suggests are important.

Education

This is planned around the beliefs the patient has about sleep. The therapist provides basic information about sleep, and patients are encouraged to construe sleep in these terms. The belief that sleeplessness can harm or significantly impair performance is discussed, sometimes by using accessible literature (e.g. Oswald 1966). Behaviours which are not conducive to sleep are described and alternatives planned; examples include stopping caffeinated drinks after six in the evening, banning the taking of naps during the day, and reinstating a regular sleep pattern by setting regular times for going to bed and for getting up.

Cognitive strategies

Cognitive interventions focus on modifying the negative thoughts related to sleep, especially those which occur when the patient is having difficulty with getting to sleep. This involves identifying and challenging the negative thoughts, as described earlier in this chapter and in Chapters 2, 3, and 4. Beliefs concerning the negative effects of not sleeping are particularly common, and contribute to a vicious circle of worry about not sleeping—not sleeping—worry about not sleeping . . .

For example, a patient believed that, if deprived of sleep he would die of fatigue. He read the description of experiments described in Oswald (1966) in which subjects were kept awake using loud noises, flashing lights, and electric shocks. After initial surprise that the experiments were allowed, he realized that this indicated they were not harmful. He laughed when he read that subjects eventually went to sleep; his belief rating that lack of sleep could kill changed from 90 to 0 per cent. A flash-card was constructed, on which the thought, 'Not sleeping will kill me' was written; on the other side, he wrote the results of the above discussion (including the words, 'Not sleeping will make me go to sleep!'), so that he could go over the card before going to bed.

Many patients have less drastic beliefs related to performance. For example, a bank clerk believed that lack of sleep impaired her arithmetic ability, possibly leading to major problems at work. She agreed to test this out by doing pre-arranged mental arithmetic tasks (in a set time) on days when she had slept well the night before and on days when she had not. She was surprised that there was no difference. This was followed up by keeping a diary of her mood, errors in her work, and trying to relate that to tiredness; she found that lack of sleep could affect her mood but not her performance.

Assessment should have revealed the extent to which sleep problems are related to worry about general life situation, specific events, and so on. If there is evidence that the patient has some deficits in general problem-solving abilities, then problem-solving techniques as outlined in Chapter 12 should be used, particularly directed at those problems which the patient tends to worry about when trying to go to sleep. Other techniques for dealing with more ephemeral worries have been described above (p. 263).

Relaxation

Once education and dealing with worry about sleep itself is complete, a more comprehensive treatment programme is commenced if necessary. This includes relaxation as described in Chapter 3; the major modification is that the relaxation techniques should proceed up to 'release only' with the addition of cue-controlled relaxation, practised in bed. As regular, rhythmic stimuli are conducive to sleep, relaxation is done in a very rhythmic way, finishing with pleasant and rhythmic mental images; for example, patients can be asked, 'Imagine, vividly, like you can see and hear it right now, lying on a warm beach, feeling very sleepy. Watch the waves rolling in and hear them swishing down, again and again.'

Stimulus control

Once relaxation has been started, stimulus control procedures are added. This can be explained to the patient as follows:

'Sleeping is something we do so often that it tends to become a bit of a habit, and lots of habits accumulate around it. Some of these habits are deliberate, but many are automatic. For instance, going into the kitchen can make you feel hungry, because you usually eat in the kitchen. In the same way, one of the things which can make people more sleepy is being in bed or even being in the bedroom. One of the things which can make sleeping a problem is getting into *bad* habits. For instance, if you used your bedroom as an office, then this would make it harder to sleep. Another thing which can happen if you have problems sleeping is that you associate the bed with lying awake worrying. The idea of the treatment is to find ways you can get into better sleeping habits.'

After dealing with any questions, stimulus control is described, so that everything around going to bed and the bedroom is associated with sleep and nothing else. Activities which do not go well with sleep are identified; these usually include reading, eating, watching TV, worrying, and so on. Often, a diary of bedtime activities helps pin-point problem activities. All activities (other than sleep and sex) are excluded from the bedroom. The therapist might say:

'Go to bed at your regular time. If, when you go to bed, you find that you are worrying, get up after 10 minutes and go into another room. Stay up as long as you want, and return to bed when you start to feel sleepy. Repeat this as many times as you have to; it is important that you remember that bed is for sleeping, not worrying; do your worrying in another room. For the first few nights you might find that you sleep very little or even not at all; don't worry about that, it's just a sign that you are breaking out of the old, bad habits before establishing new ones.'

(See also Lacks 1987.)

Finally, the strategies to be used around bedtime are outlined; usually these include some evening exercise and a light snack an hour before going to bed.

Paradoxical techniques

These can be helpful in cases which are resistant to other treatment. The patient is told, 'It would be useful to discover the thoughts which occur *just before* you fall asleep. When you go to bed, try to notice the thoughts you are having. Try your hardest *not* to fall asleep, just notice your thoughts. Although you may get almost no sleep at all tonight, it will be a great help in the future.' This reduces concern about not sleeping, and facilitates sleep in those in whom this is a major factor. Demonstrating this can be a useful assessment device, and helps illustrate the role of worry. It is most effective in patients who believe that sleep disturbance is a sign not of worry but of illness.

Irritable bowel

Irritable bowel syndrome is defined as persistent abdominal discomfort and/or alteration of bowel habit. It is a major problem in medical and non-medical settings; some sources have suggested that it accounts for 60 per cent of patients with digestive complaints, and may be present in 14 per cent of the general population (Latimer 1981; Ford 1986). The striking relationship between irritable bowel problems and anxiety suggests that cognitive, behavioural, and physiological factors all need to be considered. In individuals who believe that they have a bowel problem (regardless of actual gastrointestinal changes), stress or anxiety can increase this perception and may be accompanied by actual changes in the bowel. This perception of gastrointestinal disturbance further increases the patients' anxiety and the patients may develop behaviours to cope with the perceived problem, including avoidance behaviours, changes in toilet use, and use of medication such as laxatives. Assessment usually reveals a pattern of interaction between preoccupation, behavioural changes, and the perception of altered gastrointestinal function. (An example of the way in which behavioural change can bolster dysfunctional beliefs is described on p. 260.) Dietary factors should always be considered in gastrointestinal problems; increasing the proportion of dietary fibre may bring about a substantial reduction in symptoms.

Many patients who complain of irritable bowel problems are severely restricted in their activities. It is not uncommon for this restriction to assume similar proportions to that seen in agoraphobia. It is based on the fear of unexpected incontinence, particularly when this would be socially embarrassing, and sometimes on the prior occurrence of mild incontinence (or 'near' incontinence; see below). More commonly, patients notice abdominal sensations and infer that incontinence would have been inevitable had they not escaped from the situation. Patients are usually aware of the way in which anxiety worsens their symptoms, so anticipatory anxiety often becomes a major obstacle to their activity. The avoidance resulting from patients interpreting symptoms as a sign of feared catastrophes is very similar to the avoidance associated with panic attacks (Chapter 3); panic and irritable bowel often co-exist.

For example, a 48-year-old married female patient was referred for irritable bowel problems. She was unable to attend social functions for longer than half an hour; when she left the house, she always wore incontinence pads. She frequently had abdominal pain, urge to defecate, and diarrhoea, particularly when under stress of any kind, including anticipatory anxiety related to social occasions. The principal thoughts she experienced when she noticed abdominal discomfort and urge were, 'I am going to lose control of my bowels'; this was sometimes accompanied by an image of leaving a room, smelling terribly and leaking copiously through her clothes. She said that she had been incontinent once before, it had been humiliating, and she was not prepared to risk it again. The other evidence that she would be incontinent in social situations was the experience of symptoms under stress, and the way in which she would hold on for as long as possible then, 'only just make it...the force would be terrible...' when she finally got to the toilet. Her fear was that, 'It might happen like that when I'm talking to someone.' During the early stages of treatment, it became clear that the reported incontinence had been a very slight leak, which she acknowledged had been completely unnoticed by everyone present. This discrepancy between the incident and her description of it reflected the way she thought about it; simply identifying this was helpful. Therapy proceeded along the following lines:

Therapist 'On the occasion when you did lose control, was it like when you finally go to the toilet?'

Patient   'No. It was just a little bit, nobody apart from me would have noticed; I had had gastroenteritis as well at that time.'

Th.   'So you think that because it happened a little bit, it could happen with all the force you get when you go after holding back?'

Pt   'Yes. There have been many times when I have only just managed to get there in time; one of these times I won't make it; just 10 seconds longer and that would be it.'

Th.   'You have the thought that one of these times you won't make it. Apart from that once, you have always made it, however far it is to the toilet, however long you had to wait?'

Pt   'I suppose so, yes.'

Th.   'Could we just go over the last time you "just made it". You rushed to the toilet, then sat down, and even although you were still trying to hold back you couldn't?'

Pt   'No, I was not trying to hold back then; I just let go.'

Th.   'I see; when you go to the toilet, you let go. If we compare that to the one time you were very slightly caught short, does that suggest anything to you?'

Pt   'I see what you mean. I've been thinking that what happens when I go to the toilet is what will happen in public, but that might not be true.'

Th.   'Maybe. The only time it has happened it wasn't like that.'

The patient was thus shown that the many instances she regarded as 'near misses', (and therefore evidence that she was constantly at risk of a very embarrassing incident) may not have been 'near misses' at all. A behavioural experiment was set up, in which she held back for an extra 10 seconds before emptying her bowels. In this way, the chances of an accident were more realistically assessed. Treatment progressed as usual in graded exposure to feared situations, emphasizing the point that the patient was testing her thoughts by reducing avoidance (going to more social functions, staying longer, leaving off the incontinence pads, and so on). She also learned applied relaxation and more general cognitive–behavioural stress-management procedures, including problem-solving and time management.

An additional technique which is frequently helpful is the downward arrow technique (p. 204), in which the full consequences of losing bowel control are explored. In the following dialogue, this technique was used with a patient who had been unable to change his behaviour. Each step, however unlikely, was written down for later consideration (e.g. the evidence for each step was reviewed and rated).

Therapist   'You say that it would be awful if you did have an accident. Alright, just supposing you did. What would be so bad about that?'

Patient   'Everyone would notice.'

Th.   'Supposing everyone did notice; what would be bad about that?'

Pt   'They'd be disgusted.'

Th.   'If they really were disgusted, why would that be a problem.'

Pt   'Well . . . they'd never speak to me again.'
Th.   'What would be bad about that?'
Pt   'I'd lose all my friends, be all alone.'

This can be taken yet further; however, this was sufficient for this patient, who was able to see that his friends would not desert him if he had an 'accident'; rather, they would be sympathetic and helpful, as he would if the roles were reversed. His rating of the likelihood of being ostracized fell to 0 per cent, and he was prepared to go into situations he had previously avoided in order to test out whether his fears of incontinence were justified or not.

Special considerations in other conditions

Some of the more important considerations affecting the treatment of specific medical conditions, together with relevant references in the area, are summarized in Table 7.5. Several general texts also have good sections on the problems listed below, especially Williams and Gentry (1976) and Gentry (1984).

Difficulties in treatment

The areas where problems are most likely to emerge are the attitude of the patient towards the likely effects and effectiveness of treatment, and the attitude of other professionals.

Expected effects of treatment
It is important that the therapist helps patients define clear and appropriate treatment goals; these seldom involve a 'cure', and often acknowledge that changes will occur in the longer term. Simply making the targets (and their limitations) explicit early in therapy is helpful, often combined with regularly scheduled reviews of progress in which the aims are restated and reformulated. If patients come to treatment with the view that with psychological help they will be able to exert 'mind over matter', the therapist should help the patient to adopt a more realistic view. By the same token, when patients are completely hopeless about the prospects of any change it can be useful to review with them what small changes would be helpful in their day-to-day life and then to discuss the extent to which anything would be lost if the patient carried out a small 'experiment' to see if it might be possible to move towards this limited goal. Sometimes it is helpful to make the initial targets overtly psychological (e.g. 'Not to get depressed when I notice I feel dizzy').

Attitudes of other professionals
The attitudes of other professionals can be problematic because they may act as a powerful counter to the therapist's efforts. Careful co-ordination

Table 7.5 Special considerations in the treatment of some specific somatic problems, including key treatment references where available

---

Hypertension:
Blood pressure should be periodically monitored. Patel has had considerable success using relaxation combined with meditative and biofeedback procedures. (Patel, Marmot, and Terry 1981; Johnston 1984; Leenan and Haynes 1986).

Tics and spasms
Positive practice has been widely used, in which the patient is required to repeatedly mimic the muscular contraction for concentrated periods (Bird, Cataldo, and Parker 1981).

Asthma
Panic-like symptoms are common in some patients when there is no airway obstruction; panic attacks sometimes culminate in asthma attacks and vice versa, making panic treatment important (see Chapter 3). Detailed self-monitoring and behavioural experiments (sometimes using peak-flow meters) are used to help the patient discriminate between an attack of anxiety and asthma proper. Panic/anxiety management and exposure strategies can be helpful when used to abort attacks and build up tolerance to stress. (Creer 1982; Johnston 1984).

Sleep disorders
Sleep problems associated with deep or deepening sleep (bruxism [teeth grinding], jactatio capitis nocturna [head rocking], nocturnal enuresis, and snoring) may benefit from an alarm system, in which the occurrence of the undesired behaviour is conditioned to (associated with) wakening to a loud noise. Some indication that strategies used for insomnia can be helpful, as can be stress management. (Lindsay, Salkovskis, and Stoll 1982; Delprato and McGlynn 1986).

Psychogenic vomiting
Careful assessment must discriminate from bulimia (Chapter 8). Procedures used usually include detailed analysis of eating pattern. Slowing of eating rate and increasing exposure to avoided foods *in small, regular amounts* are helpful. Explanation should include some reference to the effects of trying to eat a large meal when very little has been eaten for some time. Relaxation is often helpful.

Skin conditions
The principal intervention used in eczema is the reduction of scratching, some of which goes on with minimal awareness. The rationale is that scratching provides instant relief but worsens the problem over the longer term. Self-monitoring increases awareness; an alternative behaviour is then substituted for scratching the affected area. This includes gently patting the affected area or scratching an area which is not affected. (Risch and Ferguson 1981; Melin, Fredericksen, Noren, and Swebelius 1986).

Table 7.5 *(Cont'd)*

Somatization disorder
 Similar to the treatment of hypochondriasis, with the predominant belief which
 needs to be modified being that the patient is vulnerable to illness (Lipowski
 1986*b*).

Dysmorphophobia
 Cognitive interventions directed at changing beliefs about the area of concern,
 and reducing checking of all kinds are suggested. Care is required in eliciting
 the evidence the patient has for their beliefs; often this may be things said in
 the past or misinterpretation of present behaviour of others in the social
 environment.

Disproportionate breathlessness
 Changes in breathing pattern can be involved in many instances. These include
 hyperventilation and paradoxical breathlessness, and normal respiration at full
 tidal volume (i.e. breathing with the chest full). Demonstration of the effects of
 these manoeuvres as part of a behavioural experiment are followed up by
 homework which includes cued self-monitoring and change. For example, a
 yellow dot is pasted to the patient's watch, then he attends to and changes (if
 necessary) his breathing pattern at that time.
 Sometimes includes 'hyperventilation syndrome', which is better viewed as
 panic/hypochondriasis (Chapter 3; Salkovskis 1988*c*).

Vestibular problems
 In chronic dizziness, exercises involving graded exposure to abrupt head movements and other manoeuvres which induce dizzy sensations may be especially
 helpful. In tinnitus, both relaxation and cognitive interventions designed to
 help patients make more realistic interpretations of their symptoms have been
 used with considerable success. (Hallam and Stephens 1985; Beyts 1987).

Chronic pain (see also the section on headache above)
 A wide range of avoidance behaviours dominate the picture in many chronic
 pain patients, and can make the assessment of cognitions difficult (see also p.
 247). Reducing avoidance is an important component of treatment. Enhancing
 perceived control is a crucial variable. Agreeing a rationale for a treatment
 which involves increasing physical exercise is important. The *explicit* objectives
 of treatment are to bring about gradual change in the quality of the patient's
 life by limiting or reducing the degree of behavioural handicap and anxiety
 experienced; if pain reduction also results, then this is an additional bonus.
 Increased exercise levels can also increase tolerance for pain. Cognitive procedures stress that 'hurt does not necessarily equal harm'. (Weisenberg, 1987;
 Philips 1988).

with all other professionals involved is the key to this problem. If colleagues are either very over- *or* underenthusiastic about treatment, problems can arise. With overenthusiasm, the patient's expectations can readily be modified. Difficulties are greater when another professional is communicating opinions or advice which conflict with those of the psychologically oriented therapist, such as, 'Don't let anyone tell you that your problem is psychological—it's purely physical.' The problem is tackled in the first instance by examining the remarks in context, and by liaison with the other professional. It is not helpful to counter-attack by criticizing the other professionals or their judgement; patients are usually unable to discriminate between these opinions, and hence have their confidence eroded in both, rightly thinking that a degree of incompetence is implied by the very existence of such overt squabbling. Disagreements between professionals and inconsistent management can increase patients' doubts about the validity of the diagnoses or formulations offered, and hence adversely affect compliance.

Conclusions

The psychological management of somatic problems is a challenging undertaking because the majority of patients have chronic and previously intractable conditions, and because an unwillingness to engage in psychologically based treatment is a frequent complicating difficulty. Nevertheless, considerable change or total relief is possible in many patients. For others, even relatively small improvements can make a tremendous difference to the quality of life. In some of the more intractable conditions described here, the aims of therapy should be more limited. Reasonable targets might be:

(1) gradual improvement over longer periods;

(2) bringing about small changes which are helpful to the patient;

(3) arresting deterioration;

(4) helping patients lead a fuller life within the constraints of their problem; and

(5) reducing distress associated with the problem (anxiety, depression, and demoralization).

Recommended reading

Blanchard, E. B. and Andrasik, F. (1985). *Management of chronic headaches: a pyschological approach*. Pergamon, New York.

Clark, D. M. and Salkovskis, P. M. (in press). *Cognitive therapy for panic and hypochondriasis*. Pergamon, New York.

Gentry, W. D. (1984). *Handbook of behavioral medicine*. Guilford, New York.

Kellner, R. (1986). *Somatization and hypochondriasis.* Praeger, New York.

Lacks, P. (1987). *Behavioural treatment for persistent insomnia.* Pergamon, New York.

Leenan, F. H. H. and Haynes, R. B. (1986). *How to control your blood pressure and get more out of life.* Grosvenor House Press, Montreal.

Philips, H. C. (1988). *The psychological management of chronic pain: a manual.* Springer, New York.

Warwick, H. M. C. and Salkovskis, P. M. (1989). Hypochondriasis. In *Cognitive therapy: a clinical casebook,* (ed. J. Scott, J. M. G. Williams, and A. T. Beck), pp. 78–102. Routledge, London.

Weisenberg, M. (1987). Psychological intervention for the control of pain. *Behaviour Research and Therapy* **25**, 301–12.

Williams, R. B. and Gentry, W. D. (1976). *Behavioural approaches to medical treatment.* Ballinger, Cambridge, Mass.

8

Eating disorders

Christopher G. Fairburn and Peter J. Cooper

Introduction

This chapter is concerned with the treatment of the two major 'eating disorders', anorexia nervosa and bulimia nervosa. Although their exact prevalence is unknown, it is clear that these disorders constitute a significant source of psychiatric morbidity. The chapter does not address the treatment of obesity, although cognitive behavioural procedures are widely used in the management of this major medical problem. The omission may be justified on three grounds: first, there are limitations on space; second, several first-rate treatment manuals are available; and third, obesity is not a 'psychiatric' disorder *per se* and its treatment is rarely part of psychiatric practice. For further information on obesity, the reader is referred to the excellent book by Garrow (1988); and for information on cognitive–behavioural approaches to its treatment, the book by Mahoney and Mahoney (1976) may be recommended.

Uniting anorexia nervosa and bulimia nervosa are certain highly characteristic extreme concerns about shape and weight. These concerns, or overvalued ideas, are peculiar to anorexia nervosa and bulimia nervosa and are therefore of great diagnostic significance (Fairburn and Garner 1988). They have been described in various terms: for example, as a 'morbid fear of fatness' (Russell 1970), a 'pursuit of thinness' (Bruch 1973), and as a 'weight phobia' (Crisp 1967). The essence of this 'core psychopathology', as it has been termed, is that these patients judge their self-worth or value almost exclusively in terms of their shape and weight. As a result, they are preoccupied with thoughts about their shape and weight, they assiduously avoid weight gain or 'fatness', and many strive to be thin.

Various behaviours designed to control body weight are also a feature of anorexia nervosa and bulimia nervosa. These include extreme dieting, self-induced vomiting, the misuse of purgatives or diuretics, and vigorous exercising. In anorexia nervosa the result is that the patients are underweight. In bulimia nervosa this is not necessarily the case since these patients' attempts to diet are punctuated by episodes of overeating. In both disorders there is an associated 'general psychopathology' which

Table 8.1 DSM III R diagnostic criteria for anorexia nervosa and bulimia nervosa (American Psychiatric Association 1987)

Anorexia nervosa
A. Refusal to maintain body weight over a minimum normal weight for age and height, e.g. weight loss leading to maintenance of body weight 15 per cent below that expected; or failure to make expected weight gain during period of growth, leading to body weight 15 per cent below that expected
B. Intense fear of gaining weight or becoming fat, even though underweight
C. Disturbance in the way in which one's body weight, size, or shape is experienced, e.g. the person claims to 'feel fat' even when emaciated, believes that one area of the body is 'too fat' even when obviously underweight
D. In females, absence of at least three consecutive menstrual cycles when otherwise expected to occur (primary or secondary amenorrhoea—a woman is considered to have amenorrhoea if her periods occur only following hormone (e.g. oestrogen) administration)

Bulimia nervosa
A. Recurrent episodes of binge eating (rapid consumption of a large amount of food in a discrete period of time)
B. A feeling of lack of control over eating behaviour during the eating binges
C. The person regularly engages in either self-induced vomiting, use of laxatives or diuretics, strict dieting or fasting, or vigorous exercise in order to prevent weight gain
D. A minimum average of two binge-eating episodes a week for at least three months
E. Persistent overconcern with body shape and weight

---

consists of a wide range of neurotic symptoms with depressive features being particularly prominent.

A recently published set of diagnostic criteria for anorexia nervosa and bulimia nervosa is shown in Table 8.1. According to these criteria, the two diagnoses are not mutually exclusive. However, the usual clinical convention is that the diagnosis of anorexia nervosa 'trumps' that of bulimia nervosa. This has the effect of restricting the diagnosis of bulimia nervosa to individuals of average or above average weight.

The clinical features of anorexia nervosa and bulimia nervosa

The principal clinical features of anorexia nervosa and bulimia nervosa are listed in Table 8.2. See Garfinkel and Garner (1982) and Fairburn, Cooper, and Cooper (1986a) for more complete descriptions of anorexia nervosa and bulimia nervosa respectively. Three points are worth noting about the psychopathology of the two disorders, each of which has major implications for treatment.

Table 8.2 The main psychopathlogical features of anorexia nervosa (AN) and bulimia nervosa (BN)

Specific psychopathololgy
1. Characteristic extreme concerns about shape and weight. Assessment of self-worth almost exclusively in terms of shape and weight
2. Behaviour designed to control shape and weight
   extreme dieting
   self-induced vomiting
   misuse of purgatives and diuretics
   rigorous exercising (especially AN)
3. Episodes of bulimia (especially BN)
General psychopathology
1. Range of depressive and anxiety symptoms
2. Obsessional features (especially AN)
3. Poor concentration
4. Impaired social functioning

1. *Most features of anorexia nervosa and bulimia nervosa appear to be secondary to these patients' overvalued ideas concerning their shape and weight.* These secondary features include the extreme dieting (and resultant low weight in anorexia nervosa), self-induced vomiting, misuse of purgatives and diuretics, excessive exercising, and preoccupation with shape and weight. Even the episodes of overeating seen in all patients with bulimia nervosa, and in about 50 per cent of those with anorexia nervosa, are probably a secondary feature in that it is widely thought that they are in part a consequence of the extreme attempts to diet (Polivy and Herman 1985). The overvalued ideas concerning shape and weight and certain associated errors of reasoning (see Table 8.5) lead the patients to adopt strict and inflexible dietary rules, minor transgressions of which are viewed as evidence of poor self-control and are followed by a temporary abandonment of control over eating. Physiological factors may also encourage episodes of overeating in those patients who are significantly underweight and in those who are eating very little. In many patients both cognitive and physiological mechanisms probably operate.

The fact that most features of anorexia nervosa and bulimia nervosa appear to be secondary to the patients' extreme concerns about shape and weight has clear implications for management. In particular, it suggests that these overvalued ideas must be modified if there is to be full and lasting recovery. This prediction has yet to be tested (see Fairburn 1988). Nevertheless, the modification of these overvalued ideas is one of the major goals of cognitive–behavioural treatments for anorexia nervosa and bulimia nervosa.

2. *Some features of anorexia nervosa are due to 'starvation'.* Certain features of anorexia nervosa are probably a direct result of starvation (Garner, Rockert, Olmsted, Johnson, and Coscina 1985). These include preoccupation with food and eating, episodes of overeating, depressed mood and irritability, obsessional symptoms, impaired concentration, reduced outside interests, loss of sexual appetite, and social withdrawal. In support of this suggestion is the finding that in the majority of patients many of these features disappear with simple weight restoration. It is partly for this reason that restoration of weight to a healthy level is an essential aspect of the treatment of anorexia nervosa. Two features, however, do not consistently improve with weight restoration, the episodes of overeating and the depressive features. Many of the subgroup of patients in whom depressive features persist despite weight restoration seem to have a co-existing depressive disorder.

3. *Many features of bulimia nervosa are a secondary psychological response to loss of control over eating.* (The same is true of those patients with anorexia nervosa who have episodes of bulimia.) Research into the nature of the general psychopathology of bulimia nervosa (Cooper and Fairburn 1986) and its response to treatment (Fairburn, Cooper, Kirk, and O'Connor 1985) suggests that many features may be regarded as a secondary psychological reaction to loss of control over eating in people who place great store on their shape and weight. These features most notably include the depressive and anxiety symptoms, social withdrawal, and impaired concentration. In the majority of cases these symptoms do not require direct therapeutic attention in their own right. Instead, they are reversed by simply enhancing the patient's control over eating.

The treatment of bulimia nervosa

The treatment of bulimia nervosa will be considered before that of anorexia nervosa for two reasons. First, although bulimia nervosa was described more recently than anorexia nervosa, its treatment has been the subject of more research. Secondly, there is wide agreement that the treatment of choice for bulimia nervosa is some form of cognitive behaviour therapy (Agras 1987; Wilson 1987). However, the current enthusiasm for cognitive–behavioural treatments for bulimia nervosa is perhaps somewhat excessive since the evidence that they are significantly more effective than other approaches is weak (Fairburn, in press). The findings of three recent controlled studies indicate that patients with bulimia nervosa can benefit to a similar degree from treatments which cannot be regarded, at least in terms of most conventional definitions, as forms of cognitive behaviour therapy (Kirkley, Schneider, Agras, and Bachman 1985; Fairburn, Kirk, O'Connor, and Cooper 1986b; Fairburn, in press). Nevertheless, it is the case that cognitive–behavioural treatments have been the most extensively evaluated of the psychological treatments for the disorder and that the research findings indicate that patients benefit in the short term. Little is known about the maintenance of change following cognitive behaviour therapy. The findings of a recent five-year follow-up study suggest that the improvements are maintained (Fairburn, O'Connor, and Anastasiades, in preparation).

It is well established that the great majority of patients with bulimia nervosa may be managed on an out-patient basis. There are three indications for hospitalization: if the patient is too depressed to be managed as an out-patient or there is a risk of suicide; if the patient's physical health is a cause for concern, severe electrolyte disturbance being the most common problem; and if the eating disorder proves refractory to out-patient care. In our experience working with NHS catchment area populations of patients, these indications apply in less than 5 per cent of cases.

The cognitive–behavioural approaches to the treatment of bulimia nervosa have three properties in common. First, they are based upon the cognitive view of the maintenance of bulimia nervosa. This view is presented explicitly to patients and provides the rationale for most treatment procedures. Secondly, these treatments aim not only to change these patients' behaviour, but also to change their attitudes to shape and weight and, where relevant, more fundamental cognitive 'distortions'. Thirdly, they use a combination of cognitive and behavioural treatment procedures. These treatments are generally outpatient-based, last between three and six months, and involve 10–20 treatment sessions. Most make use of the following procedures: cognitive restructuring using techniques similar to those developed by Beck and colleagues for the treatment of depression (Beck Rush, Shaw, and Emery 1979; Chapter 6 of this volume); self-monitoring of relevant thoughts and behaviour; education; the use of self-control measures to establish a pattern of regular eating; and various other measures designed to eliminate dieting. Some programmes employ additional elements, including relapse prevention techniques, training in problem-solving, and exposure with response prevention. One particular cognitive–behavioural treatment will be described in this chapter. It is probably the most intensively studied of the cognitive–behavioural treatments for bulimia nervosa. A detailed manual was published in 1985 (Fairburn 1985). This is an updated version of that manual.

With this approach, treatment is conducted on an individual basis and lasts about five months. The treatment is semi-structured, problem-oriented, and primarily concerned with the present and future rather than the past. It is an active process with responsibility for change residing with the patient. The therapist provides information, advice, support, and encouragement. Three stages in the treatment may be distinguished, with each containing several different elements designed to deal with relatively specific areas of difficulty. In the first, the cognitive view of bulimia nervosa is outlined, and behavioural techniques are used to help patients regain control over eating. The emphasis of the second stage is on the examination and modification of problematic thoughts and attitudes. In addition, behavioural procedures are used both to erode any tendency to diet and to modify concerns about shape and weight. In the final stage, the focus is on the maintenance of change.

A cognitive–behavioural treatment manual

This treatment suits most patients with bulimia nervosa. Although a definite treatment 'package' is described, in clinical practice treatment should be adapted to suit the needs of the individual patient. For certain subgroups of patients, most notably those who are either significantly overweight or underweight, major modifications to the treatment programme are required. An outline of these modifications is given on p. 302.

Table 8.3   Major topics to cover when assessing the current state of patients with bulimia nervosa (Fairburn and Hope 1988)

---

1. *The exact nature of the problem as seen by the patient*
2. *Specific psychopathology*
(a) Attitudes to shape and weight
      degree of importance attached to shape and weight
      reaction to changes in weight
      reaction to comments on appearance
      desired weight
(b) Eating habits
      attempts to diet
      episodes of 'overeating'
      sense of control over eating
(c) Methods of weight control
      dieting (see above)
      self-induced vomiting
      use of purgatives or diuretics
      exercising
3. *General psychopathology*
(a) Neurotic symptomatology especially depressive symptoms and suicide risk
(b) Interpersonal functioning
(c) Self-esteem, assertiveness, perfectionism
4. *Social circumstances*
5. *Physical health*
      Weight and weight history
      (NB Check electrolytes of patients who are vomiting or taking purgatives or diuretics)

In describing the treatment it is assumed that the patient is female since the great majority of people with bulimia nervosa are women.

Stage 1

Stage 1 lasts four weeks and appointments are twice weekly. Patients who do not have frequent bulimic episodes need a less intensive initial intervention. On the other hand, if the patient's eating habits are extremely disturbed—for example, when overeating is almost continuous—it is advisable, if at all possible, to see the patient three or more times a week.

Interview 1

In this interview the patient's history should be taken and the structure, style, and goals of treatment should be described. The major points to cover when assessing the patient's current state are listed in Table 8.3.

The cognitive view of the nature of bulimia nervosa (See Fairburn *et al.* 1986*a*.) This should be discussed in detail with reference to Fig. 8.1. There are four major points to emphasize:

1. Although dieting is undoubtedly a response to binge-eating, it also maintains binge-eating through both the psychological and physiological mechanisms mentioned earlier.

2. Self-induced vomiting and, to a lesser extent, purgative and diuretic misuse, also encourage binge-eating since belief in their effectiveness

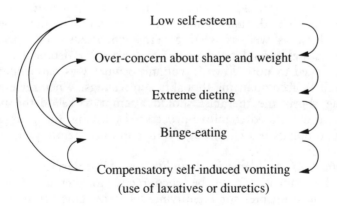

Fig. 8.1 The cognitive view of the maintenance of bulimia nervosa

as means of reducing calorie absorption removes normal constraints against overeating.

3. Overconcern about shape and weight, particularly the tendency to judge self-worth in terms of shape and weight, promotes extreme dieting and thereby maintains the eating problem.

4. Overconcern about shape and weight is often associated with long-standing feelings of ineffectiveness and worthlessness.

In describing the cognitive view of bulimia nervosa it is the therapist's goal to persuade the patient that there is a need for both behaviour and cognitive change. Some patients find this view difficult to comprehend. The therapist should return to it throughout treatment and, whenever possible, reinforce it using specific clinical illustrations.

Monitoring The patient should be shown how to monitor her eating. She should be given written instructions on monitoring (see Table 8.4) together with an example of a typical completed monitoring sheet (see Fig. 8.2). The rationale for monitoring should be explained: it helps both the therapist and patient examine her eating habits and the circumstances under which problems arise; and helps the patient modify both her eating habits and problematic thoughts and feelings. It is not uncommon for patients to be reluctant to monitor especially if they are ashamed of their eating habits. This potential difficulty should be openly discussed.

Interview 2

Review of monitoring sheets This interview and all subsequent interviews should centre on a detailed review of the patient's monitoring sheets. Each sheet should be discussed in great depth with the patient taking the lead. The therapist's aim is to understand why the patient eats what she does, as well as what governs when she eats. Episodes of 'excessive eating' should be discussed in particular detail. The patient should be asked to note down in column 6 what was happening at the time as well as accompanying thoughts and feelings. When reviewing the monitoring sheets the therapist should attempt to relate the patient's behaviour to associated cognitive processes by asking, for example, 'Exactly what thoughts passed through your mind just before you ate this?'

Identification of problematic thoughts In this interview and henceforward the patient should be encouraged to identify problematic thoughts. The principles for identifying such thoughts are described in Chapters 3 and 6. It is our experience that certain of the procedures used in conventional cognitive therapy (for example, the completion of dysfunctional thought records) are not of value when treating patients with

Table 8.4 Instructions for monitoring

The purpose of monitoring is to provide a detailed picture of your eating habits. It is central to treatment. At first, writing down everything you eat may seem inconvenient and irritating, but soon it becomes second nature and of obvious value.

A sample monitoring sheet is shown overleaf. A separate sheet (or sheets) should be used each day with the date and day of the week noted at the top.

Column 2 is for recording *all* the food and liquid you consume during the day. Each item should be written down as soon as possible after it has been eaten. Recalling what you ate some hours earlier is not sufficient. Obviously, if you are to record your food intake in this way, you will have to carry your monitoring sheets around with you. Calories should not be recorded. Instead, provide a simple description of what you ate. Meals should be distinguished using a bracket. A meal may be defined as a 'discrete episode of eating which was controlled, organized, and eaten in a normal fashion'.

Column 1 is for noting when food or liquid is consumed.

Column 3 should give the place the food is eaten. If this is your home, the room should be specified.

Column 4   Asterisks should be placed in this column adjacent to eating which you felt was excessive. It is essential to record all the food eaten during 'binges'.

Column 5 is for recording episodes of vomiting and the taking of laxatives or diuretics.

Column 6 is used as a diary to record those thoughts and feelings which you think influenced your eating. For example, you may feel that an argument precipitated a 'binge': in that case the argument should be noted down on the sheet together with the feelings you experienced and the actual thoughts which passed through your mind. You may wish to record other events even if they had no effect on your eating. In Column 6 you should also record your weight each time you weigh yourself.

Every treatment interview will include a careful review of your monitoring sheets. You must therefore remember to bring them with you.

eating disorders. What is essential is that the patient's problematic thoughts are identified and that she successfully modifies them. It is also our experience that the emphasis during the first stage of treatment should be merely on helping patients to become adept at identifying problematic thoughts and feelings, and not usually on helping them to question their thoughts and feelings. Of course, the thoughts should be used whenever possible to reinforce the cognitive view of the disorder.

DAY: Wednesday   DATE: 7th November

TIME	FOOD AND LIQUID CONSUMED	PLACE	B	V/L	CIRCUMSTANCES
7.45	1 apple 1 grapefruit 1 black coffee	Kitchen			Depressed. Feel fat.
3.10	1 egg sandwich 1 bread roll 1 doughnut	Work " "	* * *		Bought more food from canteen. Shouldn't have eaten the egg sandwich — too much. Bound to be a terrible day now.
3.45	1 doughnut 1 cup tea 1 danish pastry 2 cups of tea	" " " "	* * *	V	Can't stop eating. Help. Weighed myself — 9st 4lb. Cried. MUST NOT EAT AGAIN TODAY
8.20	1 slice of toast 1 slice toast	Kitchen "	* *		
8.35	1 slice toast 1 diet coke	" "	*		
8.40	Whole packet of shortbread biscuits	"	*		Give up. I can't go on like this. Hate myself.
8.52	1 bowl of cereal 2 glasses of water		*		Feel completely bloated.
9.05	1 bowl of cereal		*	V L	Weighed 9st. 5lb. Wish I was dead. -16 Nylax

Fig. 8.2 A monitoring sheet illustrating the eating habits of a patient with bulimia nervosa. It is typical of a patient in the early stages of treatment. (B = bulimic episodes; V/L = vomiting or laxative use; * = episodes of eating viewed by the patient as 'excessive')

Weekly weighing   In this interview or the next one, the patient should be asked to weigh herself once a week and to record her weight on the monitoring sheet each time she does so. Many patients find this task difficult and, if necessary, graded tasks should therefore be set. For example, if the patient is weighing herself six times a day, the therapist should begin by asking her to weigh herself once a day or once every other day. The therapist should explain that there are two reasons for asking her to weigh herself once a week. First, it is reasonable that she monitors her weight since her eating habits will change during treatment. Weighing once a week is an appropriate way of doing this, whereas weighing more frequently often leads to undue concern with inconsequential fluctuations in weight. It should be explained that body weight naturally fluctuates by a few pounds from day to day and that these fluctuations represent, in the main, changes in fluid balance. Day-to-day fluctuations in weight cannot therefore be used to infer long-term weight change in either direction. It is only legitimate for the patient to conclude that her weight has changed if there is evidence of a consistent trend over several weeks.

The second reason for asking the patient to weigh herself weekly is because it provides an excellent means for identifying certain common problematic thoughts concerning shape and weight. Immediately after weighing herself, the patient should write down her weight on the reverse of the monitoring sheet as well as exactly what went through her mind as she saw the number appear on the scales. Later on in treatment the patient may be asked to write down in advance of weighing her anticipated thoughts should she find she has gained two pounds, lost two pounds, or remained the same weight. Then, she should weigh herself and record her actual thoughts. The patient should decide on which day of the week she will weigh herself. A week-day morning is usually best.

Interviews 3–8

Each of these treatment sessions centres on a review of the patient's monitoring sheets. At the end of each interview the patient should be set a limited number of clearly specified tasks. At the subsequent interview the therapist and patient should review her attempts to fulfil these tasks, and further ones should be set. Since patients with bulimia nervosa tend to be excessively self-critical, any successes, however modest, should be highlighted. In addition, the sessions should include the following components.

Clarification of the cognitive view of bulimia nervosa   The therapist should repeatedly return to the cognitive view of the disorder. When information emerges which reinforces some aspect of this view, it should be emphasized. For example, if an episode of overeating is precipitated by the breaking of a dietary rule, for instance eating chocolate, this may be used to illustrate the important point that the presence of rigid dietary rules promotes intermittent overeating. The aim is to help the patient gain an understanding of the mechanisms which perpetuate the eating problem and to appreciate the need for both behaviour and cognitive change.

Education   The patient should be provided with information on a number of topics.

1.   *Body weight and its regulation.* Patients should be told what their weight represents as a percentage of the average weight for their age and height (i.e. standard weight). They should be advised against having a precise desired weight. Instead, they should accept a *weight range* of approximately six pounds in magnitude. This weight range should not extend below 85 per cent of their standard weight since at such a weight they will be liable to experience the physiological and psychological sequelae of starvation. The patient should also be advised against choosing a weight range which necessitates anything more than moderate dietary restriction, since restraint of this type is prone to encourage these patients to overeat. In practice, it is best that patients postpone deciding upon a specific weight range until they have regained control over eating and entered the second stage of treatment.

2.   *The physical consequences of binge-eating, self-induced vomiting, and purgative misuse.* All patients should be informed about the physical complications of bulimia nervosa. These include electrolyte disturbance in those who vomit or take purgatives; salivary gland enlargement, which may give the patient's face a chubby appearance; erosion of the dental enamel of the inner surface of the front teeth; intermittant oedema, particularly in those who take large quantities of purgatives or diuretics; and menstrual irregularities. Only the electrolyte disturbances are medically serious and, even so, they rarely need treatment in their own right. Usually it is sufficient to focus on the treatment of the eating problem itself, since normalization of eating habits will result in their reversal. The same is true of all the other physical abnormalities other than the dental damage which is permanent. In the case of menstruation there may be a significant delay before the onset of regular monthly periods.

3.   *The relative ineffectiveness of vomiting and purgative use as means of weight control.* The main point to emphasize is that 'binges' usually involve the consumption of a large amount of energy (calories) and that self-induced vomiting does not retrieve everything that has been eaten. Patients should be informed that purgatives have a minimal effect on energy absorption and that, like diuretics, their effect on body weight is short term and the result of changes in fluid balance.

4. *The adverse effects of dieting.* There are three forms of dieting: avoiding eating for periods of time, avoiding eating certain types of food, and restricting the total amount of food eaten. Most patients with bulimia nervosa practise all three forms of dieting, often to an extreme degree. Typically they have rigid dietary rules which are impossible to obey, particularly at times of stress. The patients tend to view the resulting deviations from these rules as evidence of their poor self-control rather than seeing that the rules themselves are at fault. The usual consequence is the temporary abandonment of self-control. Patients think that they have 'broken' their diet and that they might as well 'give up', perhaps resolving to re-start dieting the next day. Once control has been relinquished, other factors actively encourage overeating. These include the pleasure which results from eating 'banned' foods; distraction from current problems; and a temporary alleviation of feelings of depression and anxiety. The point the therapist needs to stress to patients is that dieting encourages overeating. The aim is to help the patients arrive at the conclusion that she must learn not to diet. This point needs to be made repeatedly throughout treatment.

Advice regarding eating, vomiting, and purgative use

1. *The prescription of a pattern of regular eating.* The patient should be asked to restrict her eating to three or four planned meals each day, plus one or two planned snacks. There should rarely be more than a three-hour interval between eating times and the patient should always know when she is next due to eat. This eating pattern should take precedence over other activities. Between these times the patient should do her utmost to refrain from eating. Thus her day should be divided into segments by meals and snacks. The benefits of adopting this pattern of eating should already be clear to the patient. By eating regularly, unrealistic attempts to delay eating are avoided, thereby eliminating one type of dietary restraint. The therapist should explain that this pattern of regular eating has the effect of displacing the alternating overeating and dietary restriction which characterizes most of these patients' eating habits. Obviously, the pattern must be tailored to suit the patient's daily commitments and usually it needs to be modified to accommodate weekends. Patients whose eating habits are severely disturbed should be advised to introduce the meals and snacks in a gradual manner: first, they should concentrate on the part of the day when their eating is least disturbed (usually mornings); then, they should gradually extend the pattern of eating until it encompasses the entire day.

Some patients are reluctant to eat meals or snacks since they think that this will result in weight gain. They may be reassured that the converse usually occurs, since the introduction of this eating pattern will decrease their frequency of binge-eating and thereby significantly reduce their overall calorie intake. Despite such reassurances, however, it is common for patients to select meals and snacks which are low in calories. No objection need be raised to this tendency since, at this stage in treatment, the emphasis is primarily on establishing a regular pattern of eating. The introduction of this eating pattern may be set up by the therapist as an 'experiment' designed to demonstrate whether or not the patient can eat meals and snacks without gaining weight.

2. *Stimulus control and allied measures.* The well-established stimulus control techniques used in the treatment of obesity should be used to help patients adhere to the prescribed eating pattern (see Mahoney and Mahoney 1976 for details). These techniques may be applied individually or in combination and their use must be tailored to the individual patient's needs and circumstances. They include the following:

- Not engaging in any other activity while eating. Eating should be a 'pure experience'. Patients should not eat while engaged in other activities (for example, watching television, reading, talking on the telephone, etc.). They should be told that if they eat in the way suggested they will avoid 'automatic eating' and as a result will eat less. They will come to enjoy their food more. They should be encouraged to savour their food.

- Confining eating to one room in the house and within that room having a specific place for eating. If feasible, this place should be exclusively used for eating and for no other purpose. When eating, the patient should formalize the act as much as possible by setting her place, etc. She should never eat in the same place as she works (for example, at her desk or at her seat at work).

- Limiting the supply of food available while eating. For example, if bread is going to be eaten, the patient should obtain the desired number of slices from the loaf and return the remainder to where it is stored. If she wants another slice, she should only get this after she has finished what she had intended to eat, and has thought carefully whether she really wants to continue eating. (Unsliced loaves are easier to resist overeating.) The same principle applies to the eating of cereals, etc. Supplies of food should not be left on the table where the patient is eating. The patient should have to get up and leave her place if she wishes to extend her meal or snack. She should never eat directly from containers since it is difficult to keep track on the quantity of food consumed. When eating by herself, the patient should prepare one portion at a time.

- Practising leaving food on the plate. Frequently patients feel guilty if they leave food uneaten. They should practise leaving food which is in excess of their requirements. Usually they feel that this is wasteful, but they should be reminded that the waste is minimal in comparison with the food that they eat but do not want.

- Throwing away left-over food. Left-overs should be discarded and, if necessary, made inedible.

- Limiting exposure to 'danger' foods. The patient should keep as little 'problem-food' as possible in the house. Any such food that has to be stored should be kept out of sight and in one room (usually the kitchen).

- Planning shopping and sticking to a shopping list. This list should be composed after the patient has eaten rather than when she is hungry. The patient should never decide what to buy when she is in a shop. When shopping, the patient should take only sufficient money to purchase the goods on the shopping list. At times when her control is poor, she should carry as little money as possible. She should also have a bias towards selecting foods which need preparation rather than those which can be eaten immediately.

- Avoiding, if possible, being the food dispenser for others. If children need food packed for them, they may be able to do so for themselves, or perhaps another member of the family could help.

3. *Alternative behaviour.* These have several important uses. First, they help patients resist urges to eat or vomit (for example, when feeling full). Secondly, they may be used preventively to decrease the frequency of occurrence of situations liable to result in binge-eating. To this end the patient should be asked to prepare a list of pleasurable activities which might serve as a substitute for binge-eating. Such activities may include visiting or telephoning friends, taking exercise, playing music, or having a bath. Having drawn up such a list, the patient should be asked to engage in each possible activity whenever she feels the urge to overeat. Another use of alternative behaviour is to enhance patients' self-esteem. Many patients give a history of having abandoned pursuits which they previously enjoyed and found rewarding. The therapist should encourage patients to resume such activities.

4. *Advice regarding vomiting.* Some patients ask for advice regarding vomiting. In general, the therapist should emphasize that effort should be focused on changing eating habits rather than on stopping vomiting. With reference to the cognitive view, the therapist should explain that if the patient stops overeating she is unlikely to continue vomiting. However, it should be added that if the patient is capable of reducing her frequency of vomiting, she should do so. Furthermore, she must never decide what to eat with the foregone assumption that she will subsequently vomit.

5. *Advice regarding purgatives and diuretics.* Having explained the ineffectiveness of these measures at preventing food absorption, the therapist should ask patients to cease taking these drugs and to throw away their supplies. It is surprising how many patients can do so. However, a minority cannot. Such patients should be given a withdrawal schedule during which the drugs are gradually phased out. In some cases this will result in a temporary period of weight gain due to rebound water retention.

6. *Interviewing the patient's friends or relatives.* In most cases at some point in the latter half of Stage 1 the therapist should arrange for a joint interview with the patient and the people with whom she lives. The aims of the joint interview are to bring the patient's problem into the open and to elicit appropriate social support. By getting the patient to explain to her relatives and friends the principles of treatment, the latter may be helped to understand how they can be of assistance. It is often tempting for them to take over and impose control over the patient's eating. It should be explained that external control by others is ineffective in the long term since the patient must learn to tackle the problem herself.

Progress during Stage 1

In the great majority of cases, Stage 1 results in a marked reduction in the frequency of binge-eating and an improvement in mood. In those cases in which significant mood disturbance persists, the possibility that there may be a co-existing depressive disorder must be considered.

Patients whose eating habits have not shown some improvement rarely benefit from Stage 2 of treatment. The therapist should therefore review other treatment options. For example, it may be appropriate to offer the patient a period of in-patient care during which she will be subject to external controls. Alternatively, Stage 1 may be extended for a week or so. This is justified when the patient has made significant gains but is still binge-eating at least once a day. However, it must be stressed that protracted intensive contact is inadvisable. If by the end of eight weeks the patient's eating habits have not significantly improved, this treatment approach should be abandoned.

Stage 2

Stage 2 of treatment lasts eight weeks and appointments are held at weekly intervals. In comparison with Stage 1, treatment is much more cognitively oriented. Some patients react adversely to the decrease in appointment frequency. In such cases interview 9 should be devoted to the consolidation of progress, and the homework assignments should be similar to those used earlier.

The elimination of dieting

This is one of the major goals of treatment. The therapist should remind the patient that dieting encourages binge-eating and it is therefore essential that she ceases to diet. Abandoning dieting does not mean that she will necessarily gain weight since much of her calorie intake will have been from 'binges'. The patient may be informed that in most cases there is minimal weight change as a result of treatment (see Fairburn *et al.* 1986*b*).

The patient's avoidance of specific types of food, the second of the three types of dieting, may be assessed by asking her to visit a local supermarket and note down all foods that she would be reluctant to eat because of their possible effect on her shape or weight. The avoided foods should be ranked in order of the degree of reluctance that she would have eating them and then categorized into four groups of increasing difficulty. Each week the therapist should ask the patient to eat the foods from one of the four groups, starting with the easiest and moving on to the most difficult. The foods should be eaten as part of a planned meal or snack and only at times when the patient senses that she has a reasonable degree of control over eating. At first the amount of the food eaten is not important, although the eventual goal is that the patient is capable of eating normal quantities with impunity.

The elimination of the third form of dieting, restriction over the total amount of food eaten, is achieved in a manner equivalent to the introduction of avoided foods. By direct questioning and detailed scrutiny of the monitoring sheets, it should be possible to determine whether the patient is eating too little. If this is the case, the patient should be asked to eat more until she is consuming at least 1500 calories each day.

A small number of patients find it impossible to obey these behavioural instructions. They may prove incapable of introducing 'banned foods' or they may go on to overeat and perhaps also vomit. Such patients may benefit from a form of 'therapist-assisted exposure' (Rosen and Leitenberg 1985; Wilson 1988). This involves arranging for the patient to eat the avoided foods in the treatment session and then helping her combat the urge to overeat or vomit. Such sessions need careful planning, with the patient being made fully aware of what is being proposed and the rationale for it. The food to be eaten should be consumed early in the session, the remainder of which should be devoted both to helping the patient cope with the resulting feelings and to identifying and questioning associated thoughts (see p. 294). Usually a series of such sessions is needed, with different types of food being dealt with in turn. Between sessions the patient should practise eating these foods without subsequent overeating or vomiting, and without disrupting her regular eating pattern.

Patients should be encouraged to relax certain other controls over eating. For example, some patients who are highly calorie-conscious dislike eating foods whose calorie content is uncertain. They may even insist on preparing their own food so that they know its composition. Such patients should be encouraged to eat foods whose calorie content is difficult to determine. All patients should practise eating in a variety of different circumstances (e.g. restaurants, dinner parties, picnics, etc.) and they should try to eat as varied a diet as possible.

Cognitive restructuring

By the beginning of Stage 2 the patient should be ready to learn how to question *problematic thoughts*. The principles used are similar to those described in Chapters 3 and 6. The 'cognitive distortions' of patients with anorexia nervosa and bulimia nervosa are relatively stereotyped and have been described in detail elsewhere (Fairburn *et al.* 1986a; Garner and Bemis 1982, 1985). Typical examples of these distortions are given in Table 8.5. Three procedures may be used to elicit problematic thoughts.

1. *The patient may be given homework assignments which will be likely to provoke problematic thoughts.* Such assignments include weekly weighing, eating a 'banned food' or one whose calorie content is not known, inspecting herself in a full-length mirror, comparing her figure with that of other women, wearing clothes which reveal her shape (e.g. a leotard or swimming costume), engaging in activities which invite comparison with others' shape (e.g. exercise classes), or trying on clothes in shops. The patient should be asked to record on her monitoring sheets the actual thoughts which pass through her mind when performing such assignments.

2. *The patient may be asked to record her thoughts under certain naturally occurring circumstances.* Situations most often associated with problematic thoughts include 'overeating' (signified by an asterisk on the monitoring sheets), seeing her reflection, and receiving comments about her appearance.

3. *Thoughts may be provoked in the treatment session.* For example, the patient may be asked to imagine being told that she looks more 'healthy' than she used to, or that her appetite has 'improved'. Alternatively, she might imagine putting on clothes which feel tight or discovering that her weight has increased.

Having identified a problematic thought, this should be examined. There are four steps in this process:

1. *The thought should be reduced to its essence.* For example, the thought 'I feel fat' may have several different meanings, including 'I am overweight', 'I look overweight to myself', 'I look overweight to others',

Table 8.5 Typical cognitive distortions of patients with anorexia nervosa or bulimia nervosa (reprinted from Garner and Bemis 1982)

Selective abstraction, or basing a conclusion on isolated details while ignoring contradictory and more salient evidence.
Examples:
'I just can't control myself. Last night when I had dinner in a restaurant, I ate everything I was served, although I had decided ahead of time that I was going to be very careful. I am so weak.'
'The only way that I can be in control is through eating'
'I am special if I am thin.'

Overgeneralization, or extracting a rule on the basis of one event and applying it to other dissimilar situations.
Examples:
'When I used to eat carbohydrates, I was fat; therefore, I must avoid them now so I won't become obese.'
'I used to be of normal weight, and I wasn't happy. So I know gaining weight isn't going to make me feel better.'

Magnification, or over-estimation of the significance of undesirable consequent events. Stimuli are embellished with surplus meaning not supported by an objective analysis.
Examples:
'Gaining five pounds would push me over the brink.'
'If others comment on my weight gain, I won't be able to stand it.'
'I've gained two pounds, so I can't wear shorts any more.'

Dichotomous or all-or-none reasoning, or thinking in extreme and absolute terms. Events can be only black or white, right or wrong, good or bad.
Examples:
'If I'm not in complete control, I lose all control. If I can't master this area of my life, I'll lose everything.'
'If I gain one pound, I'll go on and gain a hundred pounds.'
'If I don't establish a daily routine, everything will be chaotic and I won't accomplish anything.'

Personalization and self-reference, or egocentric interpretations of impersonal events or overinterpretation of events relating to the self.
Examples:
'Two people laughed and whispered something to each other when I walked by. They were probably saying that I looked unattractive. I have gained three pounds . . . '
'I am embarrassed when other people see me eat.'
'When I see someone who is overweight, I worry that I will be like her.'

Superstitious thinking, or believing in the cause–effect relationship of non-contingent events.
Examples:
'I can't enjoy anything because it will be taken away.'
'If I eat a sweet, it will be converted instantly into stomach fat.'

---

or it may refer to unpleasant affective states which make the patient feel unattractive.

2.　*Arguments and evidence to support the thought should be marshalled.* For example, if the patient has gained weight, this fact could be said to support the thought 'I am getting fat', especially if weight gain in the past has resulted in obesity.

3.　*Arguments and evidence which cast doubt on the thought should be identified.* Using the example above, if the patient has only gained a few pounds in weight, this cannot be equated with imminent obesity. The notion of 'getting fat' should be examined and operationalized. Using Socratic questioning the patient should be encouraged to consider such issues as 'At what stage does one become "fat"?', 'Can "fatness" be reduced to a specific shape or weight (for example, clothes size)?', and 'If so, am I actually approaching this shape or weight?' In generating counter-arguments, the patient should consider what other people would think given the particular situation. Would others conclude they were getting fat if they had gained a few pounds in weight? The patient should ask herself whether she is applying one set of standards to herself while applying another, less rigorous, set to others. She should check that she is not confusing subjective impression (for example, feeling fat) with objective reality (for example, being statistically overweight). She should look out for errors of attribution: for example, could the weight gain be due to premenstrual fluid retention rather than overeating? In addition, she should check for 'errors of reasoning': for example, there may be dichotomous thinking, selective abstraction, or overgeneralization (see Table 8.5).

4.　*The patient should aim to reach a reasoned conclusion which should then be used to govern her behaviour.* This conclusion should provide a response to the specific problematic thought. Some patients may choose to recite this response each time that the thought occurs.

Occasionally, behavioural experiments may be used as a means of obtaining supplementary information relevant to the thought in question. For example, many patients are convinced that they are fat or that parts of their bodies are fat. Often they have never discussed this thought before. In such cases it may be appropriate to suggest that the patient ask a trusted female friend for her uncensored view on the patient's figure. It is also quite common for patients to insist that on some days they are 'fat' and that on others they are 'thin' or 'less fat'. This proposition can be tested by suggesting that, for a period of a week or two, the patient decide each morning whether or not she is 'fat', and then see whether this impression matches up with her actual weight. Almost invariably, the two are found not to be closely related.

Once the patient has acquired the knack of examining problematic thoughts in sessions, she should practise the technique on her own, writing down the steps on the back of the day's monitoring sheet. She should be encouraged to practise this technique as often as possible and her attempts to do so should be examined in each treatment session.

The techniques for identifying and questioning *problematic attitudes* also resemble those used in other disorders (see Chapters 3 and 6). In patients with anorexia nervosa and bulimia nervosa typical examples include the following:

- I must be thin because to be thin is to be successful, attractive, and happy.
- I must avoid being fat because to be fat is to be a failure, unattractive, and unhappy.
- Self-indulgence is bad since it is a sign of weakness.
- Self-control is good because it is a sign of strength and discipline.
- Anything less than total success is utter failure.

Clearly such beliefs and values are extreme forms of widely held views. It is their strength, personal significance, and inflexibility which makes them problematic. When examining and questioning such attitudes, it is important that the therapist helps the patient consider what she gains by adhering to them. For example, by judging her self-worth in terms of her shape or weight, the patient is provided with an objective and simple measure of her strengths and weaknesses. By showing that she can influence her shape and weight, and overcome her need to eat, she is demonstrating that she is capable of exerting control over her life. By concluding that she is 'fat', she is providing herself with a convenient excuse for a host of interpersonal problems. Usually it is clear that most of the benefits are short term. In contrast, the long-term consequences are usually disadvantageous. The therapist should try to help the patient articulate these disadvantages. For example, most patients will admit that they are unlikely ever to be satisfied with their shape or weight. Thus, if they are to retain a belief and value system in which shape and weight are given high priority, they are likely to remain perpetually dissatisfied with themselves. In addition, by being preoccupied with shape and weight, patients may fail to recognize and tackle more fundamental problems, for example, unassertiveness, low self-esteem, and difficulties with relationships.

In most cases the origin of the patient's beliefs and values may also usefully be explored. This helps the patient gain an understanding of the development and maintenance of the problem, thereby giving her a sense of mastery over the past as well as some guidance as to how to ensure that the problem does not recur in the future. The patient should therefore be asked to reflect on the evolution of the eating problem. She should consider its earliest roots, the influence of her family and peers, and the role of social pressures to be slim. She should distinguish between factors that are likely to have contributed to the development of the problem, and factors that have served to maintain it. Some patients become particularly interested in the influence of socio-cultural factors. They may be recommended books such as *Fat is a feminist issue* (Orbach 1978), *Womansize* (Chernin 1983), *Hunger strike* (Orbach 1986), and *Never satisfied* (Schwartz 1986). However, they should be advised against following advice contained in these books without first discussing the matter with the therapist.

When examining problematic thoughts and attitudes it is always essential that conclusions be drawn. In general, the therapist should encourage the patient to adopt less extreme and more flexible beliefs and values. For example, with regard to the issue of self-control, the patient may decide that some degree of self-control is desirable, but it is counterproductive to demand of oneself total self-control in all spheres at all times. Having reached a conclusion, the patient should repeatedly remind herself of it and use it to govern her behaviour. Occasionally this may mean behaving in a manner that seems alien. For example, if the patient discovers that she has gained some weight, she may choose to wear clothes that highlight her figure rather than clothes that disguise it. Such behaviour would be compatible with the conclusion that 'I should not evaluate myself in terms of my shape and weight'.

Some patients are resistant to cognitive restructuring. Usually this resistance stems from a fear of the unknown, a feeling that therapy is becoming unacceptably intrusive, and a realization that certain fundamental and private aspects of themselves are going to be brought out into the open. This reluctance to embark on cognitive restructuring is understandable. Nevertheless, patients should be reminded of the rationale for exploring their thoughts and attitudes and they should be encouraged to embark upon the enterprise. Usually their reticence diminishes after one or two sessions, especially if the potential benefits of such self-exploration are becoming evident.

A minority of patients seem incapable of engaging in cognitively oriented tasks. While they appear to understand their rationale and are willing to do the necessary homework, they seem unable to identify their thoughts. This inability to examine cognitive processes effectively precludes cognitive restructuring. With such patients this part of treatment is best abandoned: instead, the therapist should concentrate on those behavioural interventions which seem most likely to promote cognitive change.

Addressing other cognitive distortions

In some cases, but not all, it is important to address cognitive distortions unrelated to the specific psychopathology of the eating problem. The most common is negative self-evaluation. Others frequently encountered include unassertiveness and extreme perfectionism (see Garner and Bemis 1985 for details of a cognitive–behavioural approach to their treatment).

Training in problem-solving

Once the patient is overeating on an intermittent rather than regular basis the circumstances under which these episodes occur should become clear. Training the patient in problem-solving is intended to help her cope with such circumstances by giving her a technique for dealing with difficulties which might otherwise have resulted in binge-eating. The procedure used resembles that described in Chapter 12.

From the monitoring sheets the therapist should identify an episode of poor control over eating and its precipitants. Then, using this example, the therapist should teach the patient the principles of problem-solving. The therapist should explain that while many problems seem overwhelming at first, if they are approached systematically they are often manageable. Training in problem-solving is intended to help the patient tackle day-to-day difficulties.

Problem-solving is a logical process which follows certain common-sense steps. These are as follows:

Step 1. The problem should be identified and specified as precisely as possible. It may emerge that there are two or more co-existing problems, in which case each should be considered in turn. Re-phrasing the problem may be helpful.

Step 2. Alternative ways of coping with the problem should be identified. The patient should generate as many solutions as possible. Some solutions may immediately seem nonsensical or impracticable. Nevertheless, they should be included in the list of possible alternatives. The more solutions that are generated, the more likely a good one will emerge.

Step 3. The likely effectiveness and practicality of each potential solution should be considered.

Step 4. One alternative should be chosen. This is often an intuitative process. Sometimes a combination of solutions is best.

Step 5. The steps required to carry out the chosen solution should be defined.

Step 6. The solution should be acted upon.

Step 7. The entire problem-solving process should be evaluated the following day in the light of subsequent events. The patient should be encouraged to review each of the steps of problem-solving and decide how the process might have been improved.

The patient should be encouraged to practise problem-solving whenever the opportunity arises. If any difficulty occurs or is foreseen, the patient should write 'problem' in column 6 of her monitoring sheet, and then on the back write out each of the problem-solving steps. She should be told that her problem-solving skills will improve with practice, and that the technique may be applied to any day-to-day difficulty. If she uses the technique effectively, it will improve her ability to cope with situations which would previously have led to episodes of binge-eating. In addition, by encouraging her to look out for forseeable difficulties, it should lead to a reduction in the frequency with which potential problems arise.

Addressing body image misperception and disparagement

Some patients with bulimia nervosa exhibit unequivocal body image misperception in which they overestimate the size of part or all of their body. Clinical experience with patients with anorexia nervosa suggests that this disturbance fails to respond to direct modification (Garfinkel and Garner 1982) and it is our impression that the same is true of patients with bulimia nervosa. However, preliminary evidence suggests that, in patients who respond to psychological treatments, body image misperception resolves without the need for specific interventions (Cooper and Steere, in preparation). If the phenomenon is particularly prominent, the therapist should help the patient acknowledge the misperception and function in spite of it. The patient should be provided with all the evidence indicating that she misperceives her shape, and she should be encouraged to re-attribute the misperception to her eating disorder. As suggested by Garner and Bemis (1982), she should be told that it is as if she were colour blind with respect to her shape. Whenever she sees herself as fat, she should remind herself that she misperceives her shape and that she should judge her size both according to the opinions of trusted others and on the basis of the information provided by weekly weighing.

The term 'body image disparagement' refers to feelings of extreme revulsion toward one's body. It is not often found in anorexia nervosa, but it is present in some patients with bulimia nervosa. Usually patients with body image disparagement do their utmost to avoid seeing their bodies. For example, they may dress and undress in the dark; they may avoid mirrors; they may wear shapeless clothes; and, in more extreme cases, they may bathe or shower wearing a chemise. Treatment involves 'exposure'. Rather than avoiding seeing herself, the patient should seek out opportunities to see and reveal her body, for example by looking in mirrors, going to swimming baths or saunas, or attending aerobics classes.

Progress during Stage 2

In the great majority of cases, Stage 2 results in a consolidation of the gains made during the first phase of treatment. Binge-eating becomes infrequent or ceases altogether, while problematic thoughts and attitudes toward body shape and weight become less prominent. Occasionally progress is sufficiently rapid to justify shortening the course of treatment. However, the therapist should beware of judging progress simply in behavioural terms. It is quite possible for the patient to improve behaviourally while retaining the problematic attitudes which, according to the cognitive view, maintain the disorder. In such cases, progress is likely to be spurious and short-lived. On the other hand, if some cognitive and behavioural problems remain despite the completion of Stage 2, this is not necessarily an indication for extending treatment. Experience suggests that little is gained from protracted courses of treatment.

Stage 3

Stage 3, the final stage in treatment, consists of three interviews at two-week intervals. The aim of this stage is to ensure that progress is maintained following termination. With patients who are still symptomatic (the majority) and concerned at the prospect of finishing treatment, reassurance should be given that it is usual for there to be continuing improvement following the end of treatment (see Fairburn *et al.* 1986*b*).

Preparation for difficulties in the future ('relapse prevention')

It is most important to ensure that the patient's expectations are realistic. Many patients hope that they will never overeat, vomit, or take purgatives again. This expectation should be challenged since it makes them vulnerable to react catastrophically to any lapse, in that they will regard a return of their symptoms as evidence of complete relapse. The distinction between a 'lapse' and 'relapse' should be discussed (see Marlatt and Gordon 1985; Brownell, Marlatt, Lichtenstein, and Wilson 1986). Underlying the former term is the view that there are degrees of deterioration, whereas the latter has the connotation that one is either 'sick' or 'well'. The two terms also have different implications with regard to the patient's ability to influence the situation: a 'lapse' or 'slip' can be corrected, whereas 'relapse' implies that one requires outside help.

The patient should be reminded that most people 'overeat' at times and that this is neither abnormal nor a sign that control over eating is deteriorating. Patients are liable to be oversensitive to any sign that they are 'overeating' and they are prone to label normal overeating as 'binge-eating'. This is not appropriate. Patients should be able to allow themselves to overeat at times and not view this negatively.

During this final stage of treatment patients should be asked to consider what therapeutic ingredients they found most helpful. They should prepare a written plan for dealing with future times when they sense their eating is becoming a problem. In the penultimate session this plan should be discussed in detail and on the basis of this discussion the patient and the therapist should prepare a 'maintenance sheet' in which the plan is formally outlined.

When discussing the future the patient should be told to expect occasional setbacks. The eating problem will constitute an Achilles' heel since eating and/or vomiting are likely to remain her response to stress. She should be reminded that she has developed skills for dealing with the eating problem during treatment and she should be able to use these again. In addition, she should be encouraged to review why any setbacks have occurred and how she might prevent them from recurring in the future.

As a matter of routine the risks of dieting must be re-emphasized. It should be explained that the patient may well be tempted to diet at some time in the future (for example, after childbirth), but must have serious reservations about doing so. Reasonable indications for dieting should be discussed: these are if one is clearly overweight compared to one's norm, or if there are medical reasons to diet.

Difficult subgroups of patients with bulimia nervosa

Certain well-recognized subgroups of patients with bulimia nervosa have special needs and their treatment must be modified accordingly. Their treatment usually takes considerably longer than that of 'uncomplicated' cases.

Underweight patients (below 80 per cent standard weight)

These patients used to be regarded as belonging to the so-called 'bulimic group' of patients with anorexia nervosa. With them, the initial emphasis is on weight restoration (see p. 307), although this can be done in combination with the elements of Stage 1.

Overweight patients (over 120 per cent standard weight)

These patients are particularly difficult to treat. Settling on a reasonable target weight range is often problematic since a high one frequently seems appropriate; and encouraging them not to diet is invariably met with resistance. If some degree of dietary restriction does seem appropriate, then a diet which is not likely to encourage binge-eating should be chosen. In general it is best to recommend that they cut down on the size of portions rather than avoiding any particular foodstuffs or skipping meals or snacks. At the same time they should be helped to increase their daily level of energy expenditure.

'Multi-impulsive' patients

A small minority of patients with bulimia nervosa are also dependent upon alcohol or drugs, and some describe difficulty controlling 'impulses' in general (Lacey and Evans 1986). Usually the drug or alcohol problem needs to be tackled before the problems with eating are addressed. A period of in-patient care may be indicated.

Diabetic patients

When bulimia nervosa and diabetes co-exist, there is often a negative interaction between the two disorders. As Szmukler (1984) remarks, 'Rarely, if ever, can one find one illness being used so clearly in the service of another.' Some diabetic patients, for example, capitalize on the weight-losing properties of their disease in their attempts to lose weight: their desire for thinness overrides their desire for good physical health. The treatment of such patients is complicated. Close collaboration is needed between the therapist and physician, with the latter having to accept during the course of treatment that there will almost inevitably be periods of poor glycaemic control.

Patients with long-standing negative self-evaluation

Some patients with bulimia nervosa have a tendency to judge themselves particularly harshly. They evaluate all aspects of themselves negatively and often have done so for many years. These patients respond least well to short-term psychological treatments (Fairburn, Kirk, O'Connor, Anastasiades, and Cooper 1987). Some benefit from longer-term cognitively oriented psychotherapy of the type described by Garner and Bemis (1985).

Group therapy, in-patient treatment and the use of drugs in the treatment of bulimia nervosa

There are several reasons why group therapy for patients with bulimia nervosa is an attractive proposition. Apart from its cost-effectiveness, group therapy might help reduce these patients' sense of shame and isolation and, given that certain of the treatment procedures are used in a standard way (for example, education, procedures for establishing a pattern of regular eating, and those designed to tackle dieting), it seems reasonable to expect that it might be as effective as individual treatment. The data suggest that this is not the case (Garner, Fairburn, and Davis 1987). The major problem is that there is a high attrition rate with group treatment. It seems that group theapy is not well tolerated by these patients. As yet, there has been no comparison of a group and individual version of the same treatment programme.

The limited indications for in-patient treatment have already been discussed. In general, it should be brief and regarded as a preliminary to out-patient care. The external controls provided by the hospital environment, while often bringing relief to patients, can mislead them and the staff into believing that problems are being solved. Often this is not the case. The hospital structure does allow the patient to be introduced both to a pattern of regular eating and to the consumption of a balanced diet, and in this environment some cognitive change can also be achieved, but rarely is hospital a suitable environment for patients to learn how to control their eating. For this reason the risk of relapse on discharge is high. A transitional period of day-patient care can be beneficial since it allows the gradual transfer of control over eating from the hospital to patients while, at the same time, exposing them to some of the difficulties of everyday life.

With regard to pharmacological treatments, the only drugs shown to have promise in the treatment of bulimia nervosa are antidepressants (Agras and McCann 1987). It has been claimed that they are a specific treatment for the disorder. Research to date indicates that they are superior to placebo, even in those patients who do not have significant depressive symptoms. Few patients, however, make a complete recovery and the disturbed attitudes to shape and weight tend to persist. There has been no systematic research into the maintenance of change with drug treatment, nor have the effects of drug discontinuation been investigated. The clinical impression is that the benefits that are obtained with drug treatment tend to be lost once the drugs are discontinued. For this reason we suggest that antidepressant drugs are only indicated for those patients who are thought to have a co-existing depressive disorder. Such patients often do benefit from treatment with antidepressants, but almost always they also require treatment for the eating problem itself along the lines already described.

The treatment of anorexia nervosa

There has been little systematic research into the treatment of anorexia nervosa. Therefore firm recommendations about management must be based mainly on clinical experience. The major reason for the relative lack of research is that the treatment of anorexia nervosa takes, at the minimum, many months and running a treatment study over such a long period presents considerable practical difficulties. The studies which have been conducted have usually focused on the treatment of only one feature of the disorder, for example the weight loss, and the findings have correspondingly elucidated only a small aspect of general management. There is, therefore, no comprehensive approach to treatment grounded in sound empirical research. Instead, therapeutic recommendations derive largely from the experience of clinicians who specialize in the treatment of these patients. While these recommendations are of considerable assistance to the practising non-specialist clinician, they must be viewed with some caution since experts tend to see a disproportionate number of severe and difficult cases. This may explain the emphasis in the literature on hospital treatment, while outcome studies from non-specialist centres indicate that the majority of patients may be managed on an out-patient basis (e.g. Morgan, Purgold, and Welbourne 1983).

Although there are widely divergent views on the nature of anorexia nervosa, there is consensus on the areas of disturbance which need to be addressed in treatment. First, there is the problem that the disorder is 'ego-syntonic' with patients not recognizing that they are in need of help. Once this difficulty has been overcome, a central task is to tackle the state of starvation and to treat those physical complications that require attention. Since these patients have markedly disturbed eating habits and engage in a variety of extreme methods of weight control, these behaviours need to be addressed, as do the associated problematic attitudes to shape and weight. General psychological symptoms, usually of an affective or obsessional nature, also sometimes require attention. Finally, relationships within the patients' families are frequently disturbed, as may be their overall interpersonal functioning. The remainder of this chapter provides general guidelines for dealing with each of these areas.

Treatment setting
Treatment may be on an in-patient, day-patient, or out-patient basis. The appropriate setting depends on the clinical state of the patient and, of course, on the facilities available. There are six main indications for admission to hospital. First, patients need to be admitted if weight loss is severe. As a general guideline, a body weight of under 60 per cent of average for age, sex, and height is an indicant for admission. Secondly, if weight is being lost at a rapid rate, admission should be considered. Thirdly, patients with life-threatening physical complications, for example severe hypokalaemia, need medical treatment in hospital. Fourthly, patients who are at risk of suicide usually require admission. Fifthly, some patients may need to be admitted because, for a variety of reasons, their social circumstances are not conducive to out-patient management. Lastly, some patients who have failed to respond to out-patient treatment benefit from a period in hospital. Even if hospitalization is needed, however, it must be remembered that in-patient treatment is a preliminary to outpatient care, which is always the mainstay of treatment.

Little has been written on the day-patient treatment of patients with anorexia nervosa and no empirical work has been conducted. It is likely that admission to hospital could, in many cases, be avoided if specialist day-hospital facilities were available. The potential advantages of day-patient treatment have yet to be fully exploited.

Treatment modality

A wide range of treatments have been advocated for anorexia nervosa. The cornerstone of in-patient management is nursing care. Generally such care will be sufficient to ensure a satisfactory rate of weight gain and adequate progress in changing patients' eating habits. When nursing care proves insufficient, operant behavioural strategies are indicated (Bemis 1987). With many patients it is appropriate to involve their family in treatment. Russell and colleagues (Russell, Szmukler, Dare, and Eisler 1987) have shown that with patients whose disorder began at an early age (before the age of 19 years) and in whom it has not become chronic (less than three years in duration), out-patient family therapy is markedly superior to supportive psychotherapy following in-patient weight restoration.

In recent years there has also been interest in the use of cognitive–behavioural strategies in the management of these patients (Garner and Bemis 1982, 1985). Like cognitive–behavioural therapy for bulimia nervosa, the central aim is to alter the patient's thinking about shape and weight on the assumption that such change is a prerequisite for full and lasting recovery. No cognitive–behavioural treatment for anorexia nervosa has been specified in any detail, although the major areas to be addressed have been identified and a range of therapeutic strategies described. The approach has yet to be evaluated and it cannot, therefore, be recommended with the same confidence as cognitive–behavioural treatments for bulimia nervosa. Nevertheless, since the two disorders share a common psychopathology, there are reasonable prima-facie grounds for assuming that the cognitive approach is of value.

Drugs have not been found to confer significant clinical benefit in the general management of the disorder (Russell, Checkley, and Robinson 1986). Three classes of drugs have a limited role in a minority of cases. First, extreme anxiety sometimes makes it difficult for patients to re-start eating while in hospital. Such patients may benefit from the short-term prescription of minor tranquillizers. Major tranquillizers are not indicated. Secondly, some patients have a co-existing depressive disorder which requires independent treatment. In practice, it is often difficult to determine at presentation whether a patient's depressive symptoms reflect an independent psychiatric disorder, whether they are due to starvation, or whether they are a secondary psychological reaction to some distressing feature of the disorder. It is usually best to postpone any decision about the use of antidepressant drugs until the state of starvation has been reversed. If significant depressive symptoms persist following weight restoration, treatment with antidepressants is indicated. Drugs may also be useful in the management of postprandial fullness. Some patients experience profound gastric discomfort following eating and report that this persists for many hours. This is due to the delay in gastric emptying that occurs in anorexia nervosa. In such patients, a brief course of the peripheral dopamine antagonist domperidone may be helpful (Russell, Freedman, Feiglin, Jeejeebhoy, Swinson, and Garfinkel 1983).

Weight restoration

It is in the nature of anorexia nervosa that these patients are reluctant to gain weight or, at best, find weight gain difficult to achieve. One of the first steps in treatment is therefore to persuade patients of the necessity of restoring their weight to a healthy level. This is frequently a difficult task because many patients will not have come for treatment of their own volition and see no need for weight gain. In such circumstances it is often helpful to focus discussions on aspects of patients' lives which they find distressing and which are likely to be secondary to starvation and therefore reversible with weight gain (see p. 280). This approach should be set in the broader context of educating patients about the nature of anorexia nervosa and the importance of cognitive factors (see Garner *et al.* 1985). The aim is to help patients realize that they have a well-recognized clinical condition. Referring them to a lay text on anorexia nervosa (e.g. Abraham and Llewellyn-Jones 1987) can be useful in this regard. The wider social costs of having anorexia nervosa should be pointed out and patients should be encouraged to consider what activities they would be engaging in and what interests they would be following had they not developed the disorder. They should be helped to ask fundamental questions about what has motivated them in their endeavours to be thin. If such matters are discussed in a sensitive and non-judgemental way, it is uncommon for patients not to come to recognize and admit that they do have problems for which they need help. Nevertheless, it must be acknowledged that some patients continue steadfastly to maintain that they are perfectly well and in no need of treatment. In such cases it may be necessary to accept that the patient is not at present amenable to treatment. These patients should be referred back to their family doctor for general monitoring of their physical and psychological health. If, however, their physical or psychological state is seriously disturbed, it is occasionally necessary to use the Mental Health Act to permit treatment.

Patients sometimes argue that it is inappropriate to expect them to begin eating normally and gain weight until the 'underlying cause' of their behaviour is understood and resolved. While this view should be received sympathetically, patients must also be reminded of the impact of starvation on their thinking and emotional responses (see p. 280). It should be explained that weight restoration, although only a small part of treatment, is needed not only to restore their physical health, but also to enable them to engage effectively in psychological treatments designed to address these more central problems.

In-patient weight restoration

When weight restoration is to be accomplished in hospital, the main therapists are the nurses (Russell 1977). Patients should, within a few days of admission, be introduced to the consumption of regular meals and snacks; and, if possible, by the end of two weeks these should be of a normal quantity and composition, consisting of about 2000 kcal a day. A goal should be set with the patient of a weight increase of about 1.5 kg a week, with the patient being weighed each morning. Average-sized meals and snacks will not be sufficient to achieve this rate of weight gain since between 3000 and 5000 kcal a day are likely to be required. Rather than requiring patients to eat abnormally large or frequent meals, it is our view that the additional calories are best provided in the form of energy-rich drinks which the patient may be encouraged to view as 'medicine'. It is useful to explain in advance to patients that they may well have strong urges to vomit, exercise, or take purgatives and that this is understandable given their fears about weight gain. They should use the nursing staff to help them resist these urges. Clearly, however, total reliance cannot be placed on the patients' ability to approach nursing staff. Therefore patients should be closely supervised after eating. It is, of course, also important that patients' concerns about weight restoration are recognized and openly discussed. In individual therapy sessions the thoughts responsible for distress and resistance to weight gain should be identified and questioned.

The decision about what constitutes a satisfactory target weight is problematic. Sometimes it is possible to use patients' premorbid weight as a guide if there was a period when they were eating normally and were approximately the same height as at present. Often no such 'natural' weight can be identified. Generally, the target weight should be at least 90 per cent of average for the age, height, and sex of the patient. The choice of target weight should be presented in the context of the cognitive view of the disorder: not only should it be a weight at which the physical and psychological effects of starvation are no longer present and at which normal hormonal functioning is restored, but it should also represent a weight at which eating without dieting is possible. It is important that the target is a weight range of about (2.5 kg) since it is normal for weight to fluctuate from day to day. Once patients enter the target weight range, the high calorie supplements should be phased out, leaving them consuming a normal diet sufficient to maintain their weight.

If the nursing care required for this type of management programme is not available, or if this regime fails to produce a satisfactory rate of weight gain, an operant programme is indicated (Bemis 1987). The strict and complex operant programmes which have at times been recommended are probably no more effective than simpler more 'lenient' approaches, and the latter are therefore to be preferred (Touyz, Beumont, Glaun, Phillips, and Cowie 1984). For example, a minimum rate of weight gain of 0.75 kg every four days may be set with patients being given responsibility for achieving this target. They should have full 'privileges' and should participate in ward activities. It should be agreed, however, that if the target is not met, they will spend the next four days on 'bed rest' so that eating and exercise levels may be more closely supervised. (There should be no other restrictions.) If the four days of bed rest result in at least 0.75 kg weight gain, then the patient may resume normal ward activities. Simple regimes of this type have several advantages. They are easily understood by staff and patients alike and are straightforward to administer; they are economical in staff time; they enhance autonomy and are less degrading than some 'traditional' programmes; and they are probably as effective. Most patients require few, if any, periods of bed rest.

With in-patient weight restoration regimes of the type described, body weight is usually restored to a healthy range within 2–3 months and the patient discharged home 2–4 weeks later. It is important that the transition from in-patient to out-patient care is carefully orchestrated and, if possible, there should be continuity in ongoing psychotherapy. Detailed and comprehensive descriptions of in-patient treatment programmes are provided by Vandereycken and Meermann (1984), Andersen (1985), and Agras (1987).

Out-patient weight restoration

For most patients, weight restoration is conducted on an out-patient basis. Sometimes it is worthwhile scheduling frequent appointments at first to get weight gain started; for example, twice weekly sessions for two or three weeks. Patients should monitor their food intake (as described on p. 284) and be instructed to eat regular meals and snacks. The expected rate of weight gain should be lower than that for in-patient treatment, 0.5 kg per week being an adequate minimum. Weight gain should be monitored by the therapist, with patients being weighed at the beginning of each treatment session. Again, energy-rich supplements may be needed. In the initial phase of treatment an empirical approach should be adopted to determine precisely what calorie intake is necessary to achieve the desired rate of weight gain. Like in-patient weight restoration, the process should be set within the framework of a cognitive approach to treatment (see below).

The management of physical complications

Most of the physical complications of anorexia nervosa are reversed by the restoration of a healthy body weight and normal eating habits. One exception is amenorrhoea: frequently there is some delay in the return of regular menstrual periods. Although this does not represent a medical problem, some patients see absence of menstruation as evidence of an ongoing physical disturbance and may therefore be distressed by amenorrhoea. In such cases it may be appropriate to induce menstruation by the use of clomiphene or luteinizing-hormone releasing hormone.

Normalizing eating habits

Patients who are admitted to hospital for weight restoration should immediately be prescribed regular meals and snacks. As noted, the goal should be that, over the course of the first few weeks in hospital, these should be increased until they amount to approximately 2000 kcal daily. Patients frequently exclude a wide range of foods from their diet because they are perceived as 'fattening'. Regular behavioural tasks should therefore be set involving patients' starting to eat these avoided foods, thereby widening their diet. In individual therapy sessions the thoughts provoked by eating such foods should be identified and questioned using the procedures described earlier (p. 294). It is useful if the introduction of new foods is supervised by a dietician, since patients frequently hold rigid and erroneous views about diet and health, and respond well to these views being challenged by a dietary expert. Patients must also be encouraged to eat in normal social circumstances. Initially, they should simply be required to eat with other patients on the ward. Later, they should practise eating with friends and relatives and at restaurants. When patients are approaching their target weight range, external controls over their eating should be gradually withdrawn. Patients should be allowed to make their own decisions about the composition and quantity of the food that they eat, and they should eat with friends or family at weekends. Unless considerable attention is paid to the maintenance phase of treatment, the risk of relapse after discharge is considerable.

For patients managed on an out-patient basis, similar strategies should be used. Clearly, under these circumstances it is much more difficult for the therapist to influence the rate of progress. It is essential that patients monitor their food intake and that the monitoring sheets be closely scrutinized by the patient and therapist during treatment sessions. Each session should end with specific tasks being set and these should be reviewed at the subsequent appointment. Although close monitoring of eating habits and the prescription of highly structured meal plans are essential in the early stages of treatment, once a healthy body weight is being maintained, these strictures may be gradually relaxed.

In the process of normalizing eating habits it is often useful to involve family members in a more active way than would be appropriate with patients with bulimia nervosa. Family members may be informed by patients of the particular goals they are trying to achieve, since this declaration can serve to strengthen motivation. Family members may also act as consultants to patients on matters such as the quantity or variety of food that it is appropriate to eat. Often the patient's eating will have become an area of considerable conflict within the family. With young patients, family sessions should be held in which responsibility for over-seeing the patient's eating is entrusted to the parents (Russell *et al.* 1987). With older patients, it is essential that the responsibility for change resides with the patients and that the amount of help received from others is for them and their therapists to decide.

It is important that patients be repeatedly reminded that they must learn not to diet (see p. 289). While this should be done with all patients, it is particularly apposite for those who have experienced episodes of overeating. The management of such patients' eating should closely follow the programme outlined for bulimia nervosa with appropriate modification to accommodate weight restoration.

Modifying weight control measures

In addition to severely restricting their food intake, patients with anorexia nervosa frequently engage in other extreme methods of weight control. The adverse effects of vomiting and of purgative and diuretic misuse (p. 288) should be emphasized in the course of educating the patient about the nature of the disorder. Using graded tasks, patients should learn to eat without vomiting afterwards. With regard to purgatives and diuretics, once a collaborative therapeutic relationship has been established, patients should be asked not to take these drugs. The majority are immediately able to cease doing so. The remainder should be given a graded withdrawal schedule.

Many patients find it difficult establishing a normal level of exercising. Patients admitted to hospital for weight restoration should not be allowed to take vigorous exercise in the early stages of treatment. It is important that they recognize that exercise is a potential means of weight control and that they must therefore ration the amount and type of exercise that they take. They should check their motives for exercising and only exercise for pleasure and not with the aim of altering shape or weight. A similar approach should be used with out-patients.

Modifying problematic attitudes

In our opinion, the procedures described above for educating the patient, inducing weight gain, and normalizing eating habits are best conducted within the framework of a cognitive approach to the nature and treatment of the disorder. This is equivalent to the cognitive view of the nature of bulimia nervosa (see p. 283). In practice this means that patients should be helped to articulate and examine the thoughts and attitudes which motivate their disturbed behaviour and make change difficult. In the early stages of treatment, patients should simply articulate thoughts concerned with shape and weight and record them on monitoring sheets. Later, when they have gained a significant amount of weight and the psychological effects of starvation have begun to dissipate, formal cognitive restructuring is possible along the lines described for bulimia nervosa (see p. 294).

Garner and Bemis (1982, 1985) have provided an analysis of the 'cognitive distortions' of patients with anorexia nervosa in terms of the 'errors of reasoning' delineated by Beck and colleagues. As can be seen from Table 8.5, these are mainly concerned with ideas about the significance of shape and weight and the importance of adhering to particular dietary rules. Using cognitive restructuring procedures, such thoughts and attitudes and the associated errors of reasoning may be identified and questioned. Providing training in problem-solving (see p. 299) is sometimes of value since it not only provides patients with a means of dealing with the multitude of choices and decisions they are faced with in day-to-day life but it also enhances their general sense of self-control.

Addressing other cognitive distortions

Patients with anorexia nervosa usually have a low opinion of themselves compared to others. The consequence is that shape and weight tend to become the sole way in which they gauge their self-worth. The cognitive techniques discussed earlier may be employed to question this mode of assessing self-worth. They should also be used to address their tendency to view themselves as ineffectual and inadequate (Garner and Bemis 1982, 1985).

Body image misperception

Body image misperception is common in anorexia nervosa. As noted earlier, there is no evidence that it responds to direct intervention. The approach to its management should be the same as that described for patients with bulimia nervosa (p. 300).

General psychopathology

Patients with anorexia nervosa present with a range of psychological symptoms, notably depressive, anxiety, and obsessional features. Most of these symptoms disappear, or are markedly attenuated, once weight has been restored to a healthy level. Symptoms which remain should be treated in the usual way.

Family and social functioning

With young patients it is essential that their parents be actively involved in treatment. With many older patients it is also appropriate to involve the family to some degree. This is particularly important when the patients' relationships with their parents have become one of constant conflict surrounding food and eating. A wide range of techniques may be used (see Sargent, Liebman, and Silver 1985; Russell *et al.* 1987): for example, it is useful for parents to be kept informed of the patient's endeavours to change and, when appropriate, for the patient to solicit their help, for example in normalizing eating habits. With patients who have had unremitting anorexia nervosa for many years, the parents may have learnt to accomodate to the patient's behaviour and perhaps contribute to its perpetuation. In such circumstances, rather than attempting to alter the entire family's attitude to the patient and her disorder, it may be more appropriate to help the patient leave home and function autonomously.

For many patients with anorexia nervosa crucial developmental years have been devoted to the pursuit of thinness and self-control. Recovery from the disorder precipitates such patients into social circumstances and personal feelings with which they may be ill-equipped to cope. Therapists should therefore be prepared to provide long-term support, advice, and encouragement to help them deal with a broad range of difficulties, particularly those of an interpersonal nature.

Progress of treatment

The intensity of treatment, in terms of the frequency of appointments and its duration, varies greatly. Some patients can be treated exclusively as out-patients, seen weekly initially and then fortnightly, and discharged within a few months. This is not, however, the norm. For the great majority of patients a lengthy period of out-patient treatment is necessary. Treatment often takes between 12 and 18 months, although in the later stages appointments need not be frequent.

The management of the chronic patient

Some patients present with a long history of anorexia nervosa which includes a series of unsuccessful attempts at treatment. Many of these patients have had multiple hospital admissions for weight restoration which, in terms of the limited goal of weight gain, may have been successful, but which appear to have had no beneficial effect on the long-term course of the disorder. With such patients it is necessary to adjust one's therapeutic goals, since anorexia nervosa has become for them a mode of existence (Casper 1987). However, it is never appropriate to abandon all hope of change since recovery, even after a 12-year history, does sometimes occur (Theander 1985).

In general, the admission to hospital of such chronic patients is only indicated if life is threatened. Often it is not the patient's absolute weight which dictates whether hospitalization is indicated, since this may have been low for many years, but rather a fall in weight. The purpose of admission should not be to restore weight to a statistically or even medically desirable level, but merely to reach the point at which the patient in question appears to function optimally. Out-patient treatment should be supportive and essentially aimed at helping her lead as fulfilling a life as is possible given the disorder. Vigorous efforts to alter such patients' eating habits and to cajole them into gaining weight are wholly inappropriate. Such tactics are demoralizing for the patient. They tend to distance these patients from the very support that they need, and may also increase the already significant risk of suicide. The appropriate therapeutic stance is a non-threatening one which aims to maximize the patient's dignity and self-respect.

Acknowledgements

C. G. F. is grateful to the Wellcome Trust for their support.

Recommended reading

Fairburn, C. G. (1985). Cognitive behavioral treatment for bulimia. In *Handbook of psychotherapy for anorexia nervosa and bulimia*, (ed. D. M. Garner and P. E. Garfinkel), pp. 160–92. Guilford Press, New York.

Fairburn, C. G. and Hope, R. A. (1988). Disorders of eating and weight. In *Companion to psychiatric studies*, (4th edn), (ed. R. E. Kendell and A. K. Zealley), pp. 588–604. Churchill-Livingstone, Edinburgh.

Garner, D. M. and Bemis, K. M. (1985). Cognitive therapy for anorexia nervosa. In *Handbook of psychotherapy for anorexia nervosa and bulimia*, (ed. D. M. Garner and P. E. Garfinkel), pp. 107–146. Guilford Press, New York.

Garner D. M. and Garfinkel, P. E. (ed.) (1985). *Handbook of psychotherapy for anorexia nervosa and bulimia*. Guilford Press, New York.

Garner, D. M., Rockert, W., Olmsted, M. P., Johnson, C., and Coscina, D. V. (1985). Psychoeducational principles in the treatment of bulimia and anorexia nervosa. In *Handbook of psychotherapy for anorexia nervosa and bulimia*, (ed. D. M. Garner and P. E. Garfinkel), pp. 513–72. Guilford Press, New York.

9

Chronic psychiatric handicaps

John Hall

Introduction

Behavioural treatment approaches to the handicaps of chronic psychiatric patients have developed within the past 20 years. The classic text of Ayllon and Azrin (1968) described the development of ward-wide treatment regimes using tokens as a way of immediately rewarding adaptive behaviour, and led to many therapeutic and research token-economy programmes being introduced (Matson 1980). Ward-wide token programmes have now been superseded by individual and group behavioural programmes within wards or hostels, and among the most promising developments are those involving treatment in family settings.

Until 10 or 15 years ago virtually all treatment of chronic disabling psychiatric conditions took place in institutional settings, so other treatments available for these patients have been primarily large-group ward-based programmes and therapeutic-community regimes, such as those described by Clark (1964). Since the introduction of phenothiazine drugs in the mid-1950s, maintenance medication has been widely used with chronically disabled patients, and the more recent introduction of depot neuroleptic medication has reduced the problem of non-compliance with orally administered medication. Currently, the most appropriate use of behavioural procedures is in the setting of a stable and facilitating social and physical environment, with sensitive use of maintenance medication for many patients, and involving those relatives still in contact with the patient.

The problems

Many psychiatric and psychological problems, such as eating disorders and phobic problems, may be long standing and chronic, but most of them can either improve substantially with treatment, or permit a reasonable and continuing level of social, domestic, and occupational adjustment. By contrast, the patients considered in this chapter are those with disabling chronic conditions who are unable to sustain a full range of independent social and functional skills.

The severely chronically disabled patient has been recognized from the earliest days of asylum treatment. Throughout the build-up of the asylum system, to the peak number of 150 000 in-patients in England in 1955, chronically disabled patients formed the majority of the residents. Many psychiatric hospitals still have some very old 'old long-stay' patients who may have been continuously resident in hospital for 60 years or more, some of whom are still surprisingly active, and may be seen as potential candidates for behavioural programmes.

At the other end of the age spectrum come the young adults who may have never been in hospital continuously for more than three months, yet who are clearly deteriorating socially, and who may be actively deluded and periodically violent. In between these two extremes lie a heterogeneous range of patients, resident in a range of hospital, hostel, group-home, lodging, and domestic settings, with a range of social contact varying from normal to extreme social isolation.

Changes in policy regarding the discharge of long-stay patients, and the retention in acute wards and general adult services of new 'high contact' patients, young but possibly already seriously disabled, mean that in most localities professional staff concerned with chronically disabled psychiatric patients will be asked to deal with a wide range of symptomatology and levels of handicap. Diagnostically, schizophrenia is the most frequent condition encountered, among both old long-stay and more recently admitted patients. Other patients display chronic anxiety-related conditions, long-standing personality or conduct disorders (often with histories of offending), moderate levels of mental handicap in people with behavioural disturbance, and neurological or degenerative conditions, such as head injury sustained after a road traffic accident.

Most attention has been paid to chronic schizophrenic patients, whose symptoms are often classified as 'positive'—such as auditory hallucinations—or 'negative'—such as poverty of affect and apathy. Apart from specifically symptomatic problems, an inability to maintain normal social interaction is often seen, in the most extreme cases sometimes leading to elective mutism. From a behavioural viewpoint, these symptoms and difficulties can be categorized as *deficits* of behaviour, such as loss of self-care skills like washing or shaving, or as behavioural *excesses*, such as a high rate of shouting. In general, there is little correlation between the level of behavioural deficits and of behavioural excesses in individual patients (Wing 1961).

Many chronic schizophrenic patients are slow, in speech and motor movements as well as in their rate of carrying out tasks. Some have impaired concentration, so they are easily distracted and influenced by peripheral stimulation. Many lack everyday skills of self-care, and the most handicapped may have very low levels of motivation.

Causes of the problems, and maintaining factors
The three-fold classification of causes of schizophrenic disability of Wing (1975) is widely accepted in Britain, using categories of primary, premor-

bid, and secondary handicaps. In this scheme, *primary handicaps* are those that arise from the nature of the psychiatric disorder, and it is typically the emergence of these handicaps that leads to diagnosis. *Premorbid handicaps* are those that existed before the psychiatric condition ever arose; it is well established that patients with a chronic course to their schizophrenic illness tend to have lower levels of educational attainment, occupational stability, and social stability before any symptoms are apparent. These factors are often important in indicating the probable final level of outcome of behavioural treatment. *Secondary handicaps* are those which arise from the experience of illness by the patient, or by those in contact with the patient; these adverse personal reactions may persist in some patients even when primary symptoms have disappeared. For example, a patient may have previously seriously damaged items of household equipment, such as a car, washing machine, or television, so that opportunities to use those items are now effectively lost in the family setting.

Three other causes of chronic psychiatric disability need to be considered. Until 20 years ago, chronic patients were only studied in hospitals, and it was then impossible to untangle secondary handicaps from the specific effects of institutional living. Only by studying chronically disabled patients living at home, with no history of admissions (Creer and Wing 1974), has it been possible to identify *handicaps specifically attributable to institutionalization*. Secondly, *iatrogenic handicaps*, or handicaps secondary to physical treatment, may need to be recognized: there are now very few leucotomized long-stay patients, but long-term administration of major tranquillizers carries the risk of side-effects, such as tardive dyskinesia, which may be irreversible. Lastly, chronic patients may show a *raised pain threshold* or may simply *not present a range of physical ailments for treatment*, and they have three times the expected level of morbidity from chronic medical illnesses (Amdur 1981).

An important factor in treating chronic psychiatric disability is the general level of activity and stimulation to which the patient is exposed. Under-stimulating environments tend to produce higher levels of apathy and social withdrawal. It is equally important to avoid over-stimulating environments (Wing and Brown 1970), and for that reason it is usually desirable, whenever possible, to transfer chronic patients as soon as possible from busy and sometimes hectic admission wards. Another more specific maintaining factor is the nature and quantity of the verbal interaction between patients and direct carers, be they family members or staff. A fascinating study (Gelfand, Gelfand, and Dobson 1967) suggested that patients, rather than ward staff, may in a natural ward setting be the better modifiers of other patients' deviant behaviour. Hall, Baker, and Hutchinson (1977) suggest that there may be a number of 'therapeutic ingredients' which can affect the behaviour of chronically disabled patients, apart from the specific effects of behavioural procedures. These ingredients include change of any kind (including change of ward); the degree of structure of the overall social environment; provision of personally relevant activities and possessions; and social expectations.

A special feature of work with chronic psychiatric patients is the limited extent to which many patients can be expected to take responsibility for their own treatment. However, it is important not to remove from patients social responsibilities or opportunities which they can continue to assume or enjoy, and only the 'minimum therapeutic dose' of help or assistance should be given in those areas of the patient's life where it is necessary.

Whatever the level of motivation, it is important to involve patients as fully as possible in determining therapeutic objectives and eliciting their own perception of their needs, difficult though this may be (MacCarthy, Benson, and Brewin 1986). This can be achieved by asking patients in what areas of their life *they* would like some improvement, and by asking them to rank, or arrange in order of importance to them, some pre-prepared cards listing possible therapeutic goals or areas of unmet need. However, the loss of motivation already noted, and the possible loss of insight by patients into the consequences of their actions, may mean that another person may have to take some responsibility for day-to-day functioning of the patient. This 'other person' may be an individual, such as a parent or a community psychiatric nurse, or may be a group of people, such as a team of ward nurses. The psychologist or psychiatrist working behaviourally with these patients then has the added task of training and teaching these direct carers the concepts and practices described in this chapter.

Assessment

The assessment of chronically psychiatrically handicapped people is similar in many respects to the assessment of mentally handicapped and elderly people. When assessing chronic psychiatric patients it may thus be helpful to consider using those assessment instruments developed mainly for the mentally handicapped (e.g. the Handicaps, Behaviour and Skills (HBS) schedule of Wing and Gould 1978), for the elderly (e.g. the CAPE system of Pattie and Gilleard 1979), or for the physically handicapped.

The assessment of chronic patients should emphasize current behaviour, looking especially at the remaining *assets*, or residual skills of the patient, at the *deficits*, or behavioural losses of the patient, and at the *deviations*, or oddities or excesses of behaviour. The potential target problems—those which are likely to be treated—should be the focus of a functional analysis, to see if there is any relationship between the antecedents, the associated events, and the consequent events surrounding the target events which could then be exploited for treatment. The general methods used include rating methods, and the direct observation of behaviour, usually in association with time-sampling procedures and coding of observed behaviour, as described in any of the standard texts on behavioural assessment (see, for example, Haynes 1978).

The assessment of chronic psychiatric patients has traditionally relied on the use of rating scales (Hall 1979), either completed on the basis of a one-to-one interview by (usually) a psychiatrist, or completed by ward staff on the basis of relatively unstructured direct observation of general behaviour on the ward. Rating scales continue to have a use for general screening purposes, for assessing general improvement, and for initially identifying areas of functioning which will then require more detailed assessment.

Examples of well-designed and useful rating scales are the Krawiecka, Goldberg, and Vaughn (1977) interview-based scale, and the Baker and Hall (1983) ward-behaviour-based REHAB scale. The Krawiecka scale is completed by a psychiatrist on the basis of a semi-structured interview, yielding a set of five-point ratings of the degree of severity of eight symptomatic items. Four of the items rate the level of specific psycho-pathology (such as coherently expressed delusions), and four rate specific areas of unusual behaviour (such as psychomotor retardation). The RE-HAB scale is completed by ward staff at the end of a one-week observation period, and leads to a deviant-behaviour score (based on seven items) and a general-behaviour score (based on 16 items). For example, two of the deviant-behaviour items cover incontinence and physical aggression, and two of the general-behaviour items describe relating to other people on the ward, and the quality of speech.

Time-sampling involves the observation of the patient at predetermined intervals, chosen to cover the greatest possible part of the patient's waking day. Coding of behaviour involves the identification of a number of categories (such as the mutually incompatible behaviours of sitting, standing, walking, running, lying down; and other behaviour such as talking to self, talking to other patients, talking to care staff, shouting) which are relevant to the target behaviour, and which can be rapidly and reliably entered by an observer on a record sheet.

An important factor in determining time-sampling schedules, and in establishing appropriate coding categories, is the common finding with chronic patients that rates of behaviour in general will be low, and most behaviour will be relatively simple. This permits the use of schedules and coding categories allowing observation of groups of up to five or six patients quite satisfactorily.

Apart from the assessment of *current behaviour*, it will be important to have some knowledge of the *past behaviour* of the patient, as recorded in hospital records, and as reported by the patient and by those who know him or her well. For example, it may become apparent that particularly disturbed episodes have in the past been preceded by particular events, such as meeting a given person, or going to a given place. Hospital records should be interpreted cautiously, especially with long-stay patients, as they may be unreliable, and very rarely give a precise description of a patient's behaviour in the past.

More important will be an assessment of the *current environment* of the patient, as this may place a limit on the range of adaptive behaviour the person can display. A number of standard checklists now exist to assess the physical environment in which a patient lives, as well as the social aspects of that environment, as illustrated by the 'restrictive-practices' checklist used by Wykes (1982). This checklist covers, for example, the extent to which external doors are locked, the level of restriction on possession of knives, matches, and money, and the tolerance of the use of alcohol.

The reality of many settings in which chronic patients live is that the only available assessor for most areas of a patient's life may be an untrained and harassed assistant, or relative, with no special assessment skills. This means that most assessment and monitoring procedures should use a simple vocabulary level and writing style, clearly laid out to minimize omissions and clerical errors, and have basic instructions on *every* chart or response sheet—separate manuals always get lost! Despite the reservations which have been expressed about the level of involvement of patients in their treatment, self-assessment by the patient should be encouraged whenever possible. An example would be a simple self-recording chart placed by a patient's bed-space, requiring the patient to enter a tick every time he or she has been to the local shop or post office. Self-assessment can help the patient to remain clear about the goals of any intervention, even if the results of the self-assessment are psychometrically unreliable.

Table 9.1 illustrates the sequence of assessments and information-gathering which might be involved in introducing a ward-wide behavioural programme, or programme in a day-hospital.

Whenever possible the patient should be interviewed. However, particular skills are required in interviewing chronically disabled patients. Since they may have a poor tolerance of over-intrusive questions, it is important with many patients to ask relatively few questions in an interview and to limit the length of the session. Since they may be slow in answering questions, it is important to give them ample opportunity to reply before prompting them. Because of the possibility of some disturbance in their thinking, questions should be as direct as possible, without any qualifying clauses or phrases. It can be easier to obtain answers from some patients by asking them to write them down, or by asking them to point to the right answer on a pre-prepared card, than by expecting a

Table 9.1 Sequence of assessments and information-gathering prior to treatment

---

1. Assess all patients with standard measures (including a standard general-behaviour rating scale, and a standard psychiatric rating)
2. Gather other basic information (interviewing patient, staff, or relatives where necessary and possible), including: age of patients, sex, physical and medical status, current daily activity, social network with other patients
3. Consider whether any grouping of patients would be helpful, and whether any patients are too frail, too disturbed, etc. to fit into the proposed group
4. Identify on a group or individual basis any common problems or frequently occurring deficits which are likely to be amenable to treatment, and gather any other relevant information (e.g. any remaining interests or assets of patients)
5. Develop a change-sensitive measure for each identified problem—for example, a time-sampling measure of positive use of leisure time, or a checklist of specific steps in self-care—and collect baseline observations
6. Select (initially) either one or two problems common to several patients
             or a few patients with unique problems, where improvement in each problem would be of great significance to the patient, or to care staff or family

---

spoken answer. Outright refusal to be interviewed, including having the patient walk away, is not uncommon, but a significant proportion of non-responders usually respond if approached again a day or two later. Many relatives of chronically disabled patients know surprisingly little about the nature of the patient's condition, and they are likely to be better informants if *their* questions are answered first.

An initial assessment would involve a standard general-behaviour rating with at least an indication of major areas of behavioural disturbance. This would help to ensure that the therapeutic goals are set at a realistic level, and that major areas of disturbance are taken into account in detailed therapeutic planning. This would be accompanied by a general clinical assessment of physical state (including significant physical illness and necessity for any maintenance medication). Subsequent assessment on a group or individual basis would concentrate on relatively limited target areas (such as meal-time behaviour, or frequency of disturbed shouting), assessed mainly by direct observation (with use of time-sampling procedures) and by use of specific checklists, which may have to be specially designed. Since interventions with these patients may take at least several months, all assessment measures should be selected so they can be used regularly over considerable periods of time. There are several useful detailed reviews on assessment practice with chronic patients (Hall 1981; Shepherd 1984; Wallace 1986).

Factors regarding suitability for treatment

Treatment aimed at improving behavioural deficits is usually more effective than treatment aimed at reducing the rate of deviant or inappropriate behaviour. Given that the most common deficits are social, positive factors indicating suitability for treatment include evidence that the patient still retains some degree of social skill; maintains some interaction with other patients, relatives, and staff; and can still converse appropriately with other people. Any evidence that some new skill has been acquired recently, or some old interest re-awakened, is also a positive factor.

Given the inability of some patients to voice their own wishes, there are ethical issues relevant to the way in which chronic patients should be treated. If hospital in-patients cannot clearly express their own wishes, it is unacceptable that by default they are not treated at all, yet equally there are limits beyond which some treatments cannot be imposed. This dilemma is particularly acute for the small but significant number of chronic patients in a health district who may be continually detained under a Section of the 1983 Mental Health Act, and whose treatment should be carefully considered by local staff in the light of the Zangwill report (1979) (see also Gostin 1986). The Zangwill report lays down guidelines for the use of behavioural programmes with patients, in particular suggesting how agreements on the objectives and procedures of programmes should be reached, and how minimum standards of accommodation, etc. must be ensured.

The presence of active psychotic symptoms is not by itself a barrier to successful treatment, and indeed the behavioural treatment of such symptoms is described later in the chapter. In general, continued levels of disruptive or violent behaviour make it difficult for treatment to be offered. A history of heavy drinking is also a poor predictor of successful treatment in a community setting.

If it is likely that the patient will remain in a sheltered residential setting, then useful selection factors for treatment are the continued presence of some specific interests, a reasonable level of verbal comprehension, and evidence of continuing social responsiveness. If it is likely that the patient may move to a more independent way of life, ability to take any medication regularly may be important. If the family of the patient are still in contact, then their relationship to and mode of interaction with the patient should be assessed. The implications of recent research on patterns of patient–family interaction suggests that where interaction is characterized by high levels of face-to-face contact, hostility, over-involvement, and critical comments, returning the patient to family care without trying to change the behaviour of the family carries a high risk of relapse (see section on treatment of new long-term patients, p. 333).

Treating chronic psychiatric handicap

Some patients with relatively mild chronic disabilities may be seen as out-patients while living in their own home and continuing to work. However, the majority of patients presenting for treatment will be living somewhere along the dimension of hospital ward/hostel/group home/ sheltered lodging/parental home, or will be attending during the day somewhere along the dimension hospital occupational therapy department/mental health day-centre/multi-use centre, or both. Many of the patients will be treated for at least part of the time on a group basis, often for no better reason than insufficient therapist time to treat patients individually. Treatment will be described under four headings, which together will cover the main practical points in treating chronic patients:

- designing a cognitive–behavioural milieu for groups;
- designing individual programmes for patients;
- the long-stay: treating large groups of patients in hospital and hostels;
- the new long-term: treating individuals in families.

Designing a cognitive–behavioural milieu for groups

All wards and day-centres necessarily have some sort of 'milieu' or atmosphere, but it may not be specifically recognized as a major treatment tool. When treating chronic patients, as much of their waking time as possible should be spent in a stable milieu which can exploit the gains of any specific individual- or group-treatment programmes. Any therapist working with these patients in non-domestic settings is likely to spend at least as much time maintaining this general milieu, as in the detail of individual programmes.

An important first task is to agree with the direct-care staff some overall therapeutic goals: there is a risk with some behavioural approaches that treatment is seen as a number of independent programmes following each other with no overall cohesion, and with little ability to attract the commitment of staff. However, there are a number of superordinate therapeutic goals currently in vogue, including the encouragement of high levels of 'personalization' or of 'engagement', or the promotion of the 'least restrictive environment' (see, for example, MIND 1983). *Personalization* refers to the encouragement and creation of events, possessions, and daily routines which are personal and unique to each patient; *engagement* refers to actual use of recreational and occupational material and equipment, and actual conversation or collaboration with neighbouring patients, rather than passively sitting by or next to materials or people.

A particularly influential concept is that of 'normalization', developed by Wolfensberger and Glenn (1975). This approach presupposes that society has refused to accept disabled and handicapped people as equal members, and has devalued them by consigning them to segregated environments or by refusing access to 'normal' facilities. The argument assumes that if mentally disabled people have access to 'normal' facilities, they will become and feel 'equal', and hence acquire new repertoires of behaviour. There is the risk that these philosophies will be trotted out as mere jargon or slogans: others see these views as offering cohesion to otherwise unconnected staff practices.

It is usually helpful to have a period of several weeks when these general ideas can be explained to, and explored by, all the staff involved in a programme. This may be done by regular meetings with key staff members. Photocopies of useful articles or chapters should be freely available. Paying a visit to another hospital which is trying the same sort of treatment approach is often highly effective, quite apart from the 'day out' atmosphere which usually ensues! Which overall conceptual system to choose will depend on local need and circumstances: however, failure to adopt an overall conceptual framework means that inadequate and implicitly passive goals such as 'return to the community', or 'provision of a homely environment' will often guide staff thinking.

An important attribute of the general milieu of the ward or unit should be its stability. Chronic patients typically take a long time to respond to programmes, and if they remain on an acute admitting ward they can be affected by the sudden disruptive episodes which occur there. One component of stability is consistency in staffing, with as low a level of staff turnover as can be achieved. Equally, movements of patients should be minimized: impromptu discharge decisions because of pressure to admit someone else, and patient movements made for purely administrative reasons should be avoided.

Another component of this stability is consistency in staff practices, and consistency of the overall framework, so that even relatively infrequent episodes of disturbed behaviour by a patient will be dealt with in a similar way. For example, observing a number of physical attacks by a patient may reveal several types of staff response, such as: scolding, separating the assailant and victim, avoiding the situation by leaving the room, or forcing an apology. An appropriate response to attacks should be agreed with the staff. Consistency is also important in general ward 'rules', such as the times residents have to go to bed, or whether they are allowed alcohol in their rooms (see Lavender 1985, for a useful discussion of staff practices).

This level of consistency usually requires some formal staff training, covering *all* direct-care staff and emphasizing practical skills. Milne (1986) gives a detailed account of how to design a ward-oriented training programme for nurses. The aim of these programmes is to produce skill change that will generalize to the ward setting after the programme has been completed. Such training courses typically cover topics such as: causes of chronic psychiatric impairment; monitoring and recording what patients do; general principles of learning; and promoting new and adaptive skills. The teaching methods used in such courses should include not only written and spoken information, but 'iconic' (in Milne's notation) learning from viewing videos or live demonstrations, and 'enactive' learning from practical involvement in projects, rehearsal, and role-play. Barker (1982) and Butler and Rosenthal (1985) indicate the detailed content required for such courses.

Designing individual programmes for patients

There is a considerable body of research showing that behavioural methods can be used with individual chronic patients, and can modify a wide range of symptomatic behaviour, including the experience and behavioural concomitants of auditory hallucinations. A number of review articles, such as those by Baker (1975), Gomes-Schwartz (1979), and Matson (1980) indicate the range of problems treated and range of techniques used. The problems treated include delusions (usually those which are consistent and long-standing), and other forms of thought disorder (such as disturbed associations) which in treatment terms may be formulated as speech disorders, disorders of emotional expression, and perceptual disorders. A number of the techniques used are described later in this section, but others used include satiation (the repeated or constant presentation of a stimulus until the inappropriate response is exhausted), time-out (withdrawal from the setting for a short period of time when disturbed behaviour is occurring), and playing back to patients videotapes of their own behaviour.

The degree of modification of behaviour which can be achieved with individual patients is highly variable. While in general the individual rate of change may be relatively slow, there are certainly cases reported where all the major symptoms demonstrated by an individual have been suppressed (see, for example, Nydegger 1972). The relationship between change in symptomatic, or disturbed, behaviour, and adaptive or social functioning is often low, so it is important to determine in advance the main general area of behaviour which is chosen for both intervention and regular monitoring. The target behaviour initially selected should be chosen with care: ward staff or families may be sceptical of the value of behavioural techniques, so the initial targets should be those where change is most likely, and where change will be seen as most relevant.

The whole range of behavioural techniques can be used with chronic patients. With elective mutism, for example, it may be necessary to start with shaping techniques, so that the most rudimentary approximations to speech are immediately reinforced with some material reinforcement, such as a soft drink or a biscuit. Imitation procedures (which involve the patient following move-by-move the actions of the therapist, if necessary with manual prompting) may also be useful where the initial rate of behaviour is very low, although this technique carries with it a slight risk of an over-developed tendency to imitate the therapist in irrelevant ways.

A classic individual case study by Ayllon and Michael (1959) demonstrated the way in which selective attention by nurses could shape the behaviour of an individual patient, in that case holding a broom. Meichenbaum and Cameron (1973) developed a 'self-instruction' procedure with new chronic patients, encouraging patients to think aloud and to give themselves instructions, such as 'I must be coherent', then going on to internalize this thinking strategy. Meichenbaum's work is of interest in this early use of cognitive techniques, and in the way he developed chains of previously unrelated behavioural elements to produce complex behaviour change.

A dressing programme

A detailed example of how to modify deficits in dressing illustrates a number of key points. Many chronic patients look odd: this may be for a variety of reasons, including odd gait as a result of maintenance medication, and poorly fitting clothes because of lack of individualized clothing facilities. This indicates the need for a proper assessment of *why* particular patients appear unusual, before trying to improve their ability to dress themselves.

The assessment could include the construction of an individual checklist, checking every day for a week exactly what aspects of appearance *look* unusual—such as 'hair not brushed' or 'shirt incorrectly buttoned'. It could also include direct observation of the patient washing and dressing in the morning, noting what the patient does—this might well reveal that the patient sleeps in most of his or her day clothes, and hence does not practise dressing every day anyway.

However, many chronic patients may have difficulties both in dressing themselves at the beginning of the day—thereby placing a considerable burden on ward staff or families—and in maintaining a neat appearance during the day. A pre-condition for a satisfactory dressing programme is a supply of appropriate clothing of the right size, a space easily accessible to the patient where the clothing can be kept, and a suitably private space, with a mirror, where the clothing can be laid out prior to being put on. Very often no immediate feedback is given to such patients after dressing, so any subsequent statements such as 'You look smart today' will not be perceived by the patients as related to their own earlier behaviour. Any praise or encouragement of the patient should be given within a few seconds of the satisfactory completion of a stage of dressing.

With very disabled patients, backward chaining techniques may be helpful, so that when a patient is first learning how a shirt should be put on, the shirt is first put on by a member of staff or family, and the patient only has to do up the last button or two. At the next stage the patient has to do up more buttons, and *last of all* learns how to put on the shirt. This technique, used widely with severely mentally handicapped people, is applicable to any cognitively impaired person showing deficits in such everyday skills.

Chronic patients may be able to dress themselves but their appearance may then deteriorate during the day. This can be tackled by checking the appearance of the patient at regular intervals during the day, if necessary for particular items of clothing (checking that the tie is fastened, fly zip done up, shoes laced) and giving the patient appropriate informational feedback, praise, and material reinforcement (such as a cigarette). A common reason why clothing can deteriorate with such patients is that holes may be burnt through clothing by tobacco ash or stubs dropping on the clothing: this may suggest a specific programme in how to use ashtrays appropriately. The pattern of tobacco use in a long-stay ward can be significant in its own right, since it may be the focus of a high proportion of patient–patient interaction.

Individual treatment programmes must be monitored, to ensure that change is occurring and that targets are regularly reviewed. This is best achieved by direct observation of the programme being carried out, and implies that someone with an adequate knowledge of both behavioural methods in general and the specific programmes in particular, is available to observe a sample of the programme. Ideally an unqualified member of staff can carry out this task, but otherwise the professional staff member supervising the programme will need to do it. This procedure also assumes that direct-care staff know they will be observed, and that the observer is able to provide feedback to staff both accurately and non-offensively.

Another important practical point is to build variability into individual programmes from their inception—for example, in who runs them, where they take place, and at what time of day they occur—otherwise the improvement will be unlikely to spread (or generalize) to other settings or to other relationships (Shepherd 1980). When a patient is being prepared for discharge, or for transfer from one setting to another, it is essential that individual programmes are carried out on at least a proportion of occasions in the post-transfer setting before final transfer takes place.

The 'long-stay'—treating large groups of patients in hospitals and hostels

Despite the reduction in the total numbers of long-stay patients in psychiatric hospitals, most hospitals have a number of wards which are home to 20, 30, or more chronic patients. Staffing levels on these wards may be very low, with only two or three staff on duty at any one time: staff availability is the crucial determinant of the complexity of any group programme that can be tried. Group programmes will be more relevant if members of the group are relatively similar in their level of functioning for the target behaviour in question. A preliminary group survey, using the assessment techniques already described, may be helpful in initially identifying broad groupings of patients, and then levels of specific skills within a group. A survey of this sort may sometimes lead to some inter-ward transfers to increase the homogeneity of groupings within a ward, but such transfers should not interfere with existing friendships unless absolutely essential, and should be as infrequent as possible.

An important skill in designing group behavioural programmes in this type of setting is to identify therapeutic targets that are applicable to the widest number of patients, and which present several opportunities a day for intervention to occur. Improvement of meal-time behaviour is an example of such a target: a reasonably acceptable standard of eating and drinking, like the standard of dress and appearance, is important in the acceptability by the wider community of the chronically psychiatrically disabled. In addition, meal-times take place three times a day and consti-tute a major part of the work-load of care staff. Apart from the improve-ment of purely functional eating skills, such as a reduction in dribbling, or an increase in the appropriate use of forks and spoons (as opposed to eating inappropriately with fingers), meal-times are also significant oppor-tunities for the improvement of social communication and co-operation.

In detail, such a programme might focus on appropriate posture while sitting; use of appropriate implements; self-help in serving food on to plates, pouring out drinks, clearing dishes away; and encouraging com-munication with the patient sitting next to the target patient. A clear, simple statement of the required standard of behaviour would be written down—perhaps in large writing on a card—to be used as a prompt by staff members when necessary. When the programme first begins, care staff would observe whether or not the required standard of behaviour had occurred, and as soon as possible reinforce appropriately. This might involve positive feedback about goals attained (e.g. 'Well done, you sat up close to the table'); feedback about goals not yet attained, but expected (e.g. 'Try to hold your fork right'—said while demonstrating the correct grip); social praise and encouragement; and material—or token—reinforcement, where that is part of the programme. It should not be forgotten that each such reinforcement also constitutes an individual social interaction, which can otherwise be very rare in such settings.

Another example of a group target which might be appropriate in this type of setting is carrying out a ward task or job. The overall level of patient activity during a day can be quite low, and there is a risk that nothing may happen between highly structured activities such as mealtimes. It is possible to examine all the tasks available on a ward—such as hoovering the ward, setting the tables, doing the washing-up, sorting out ward clothing—and to grade or classify them so that tasks can be assigned to those capable—or nearly capable—of carrying them out. Each task leads to a 'job card' (Fig. 9.1), available to both staff and patients, which gives the steps involved in each job, and the criterion for satisfactory performance. It is very important to ensure that jobs are changed every 2–4 weeks, to encourage some flexibility of performance, and so avoid that phenomenon of traditional wards, the patient who makes the tea so well because he has been doing the same job for 17 years.

Rewards and reinforcements

Many ward programmes use some form of material reward, or, by using tokens to give later access to material goods, become examples of 'token economies' (p. 7). It is a paradox that controlled trials suggest that token economies are the group treatment of choice for long-stay patients, yet their effectiveness is not due to the operant conditioning rationale that led to their development. Recent reviews of token economies (Hall and Baker 1986) suggest that the complex social interaction systems inherent in their application are the key therapeutic ingredients in their effectiveness. This has important practical implications, since it suggests that appropriate delivery of the tokens with associated feedback and specific guidance is the main process to get right, and that the actual exchange of tokens for material goods is redundant.

The use of tokens can have another benefit: while in theory the physical nature of the token is unimportant, the use of plastic educational money as tokens helps to re-introduce relative cash values into the day-to-day lives of chronic patients. Many patients make a once-a-day purchase of

---

GRADE 3 JOBS
JOB No. 1
BREAKFAST

1. Wash hands
2. Set trolley: Top—cornflakes, wheatflakes, dishes, milk
   Bottom—trays
3. After cereals, remove trolley and clean
4. Set trolley with containers, servers, plates
5. Remove trolley, put containers on small trolley
6. Hand in card

Fig. 9.1 Example of a job card for monitoring the attainment of specific tasks

sweets or tobacco, and then never have to make another cash-relevant decision during the day. The use of tokens, viewed in this way, helps them to make more choices and decisions during the day.

If any sort of material reward or reinforcement is used, it is essential to check that the reinforcement used in one setting with a patient is compatible with that available in any other settings. For example, it may be possible for a patient to have some hospital earnings from attendance at a workshop, some money or goods available from a visiting relative, and some goods available, via tokens, from the ward regime. In these circumstances the money and goods available from all other sources should be monitored, so that the goods available from the ward regime constitute a high enough proportion of total income to be significant to the patient, from the point of view of his internal 'economy'.

For the relatively disabled patient, return to the world of work may be highly unlikely, so therapeutic targets should include recreational and social activity. These could include engagement in individual hobbies or interests, such as model-making or stamp collecting, games such as draughts or bingo, and some physical activity. Since a considerable proportion of long-stay patients may be relatively old, techniques designed for use with the elderly may be incorporated into the ward regime.

'*Reminiscence*' *techniques* are one of the main psychological interventions which have been used with the elderly. In reminiscence therapy, groups of older people are encouraged to share memories of common interest, elicited by use of old newspapers and other 'prompt' materials. As individual and group memories emerge, members of the group are encouraged to see what challenges they overcame in the past, and so to adopt a more positive approach to the present. (See Wisocki 1984, for further details of behavioural methods with the elderly.) It may also be appropriate to withdraw positively or 'retire' older patients from day activities, such as attending an industrial therapy workshop, which are no longer age-appropriate. When older patients continue to attend such workshops by force of habit, their work rate is often extremely low, and their workshop attendance may prevent them from joining in more appropriate activities.

Monitoring and programme review

If a number of targets are used in a ward programme, the progress of individual patients should be monitored so that levels of target performance can be modified periodically. When there has been an improvement in a patient's behaviour, there should be some evidence of stable change before moving to a more demanding level of behaviour. There is little point in reviewing programmes more often than once a month, since the rate of behaviour change is usually relatively slow. Reviewing behaviour too frequently may lead staff to attach significance to changes of behaviour that are minor fluctuations, and not true indications of improvement.

There is some evidence (Hall *et al.* 1977) that when too many aspects of a patient's behaviour are identified as targets, any improvement in those target areas may be matched by deterioration in some non-target behaviours. This indicates the limited ability of some patients to attend to more than a few targets at once, and suggests initially limiting the number of target areas for individual patients to three or four at most. Stable improvements in those areas may then justify increasing the number of targets.

Since there is bound to be some turnover in direct-care staff, any staff training course needs to be continually repeated, with basic manuals or guides to the ward programme available to new staff members as soon as they join the ward. As well as turnover in the staff, hopefully there will be some turnover in patients, as improved patients move to a more independent environment. New patients admitted to the ward may be less competent than the original patients were, so that slowly the level of disability of the patients increases. It will then be necessary periodically to review the whole programme—say every two years or so—to ensure that the ward regime fits the needs of the current patients.

Recent approaches to hostel care

The previous section concentrated on the treatment of relatively large groups of more disabled patients. Attention is now being paid to the treatment of smaller groups of ostensibly less disabled patients—usually termed 'new long-stay'—in hostel settings. In practice, the residents in some hostels may be more disabled than the patients in some wards of the nearby hospital: this section is therefore relevant to the care of relatively competent patients, whatever the setting in which they live.

The term 'new long-stay' is used imprecisely in the research literature, but it usually describes those people who have been in a psychiatric hospital continuously for more than 9 or 12 months, without any longer periods spent in hospital. Despite their relatively short psychiatric histories, such people may have had periods in prison, in Salvation Army or Church Army hostels, and may have had very little experience of work or of a normal independent social existence. They may thus have difficulties in looking after their own money, and may be relatively unskilled socially so they cannot live independently.

Although they may still have psychiatric symptoms, such people do not require the relatively high levels of supervision offered in a hospital setting, and may be able to co-operate reasonably well with others. They may be best cared for by living in a hostel situated in an ordinary street, which enables them to retain existing skills, interests, and social contacts, while being offered positive therapeutic help and a degree of protection from exploitation.

Under these circumstances a different organizational approach to the use of cognitive–behavioural intervention strategies has to be developed. A frequently used system is to have a psychologist or psychiatrist act as advisor to both hostel and an associated day-centre, and to offer courses of, for example, social skills training in the day-centre. Since hostel residents may be able to take more collective responsibility for their lives together than is possible in a ward, residents and staff may be able to agree on common roles and procedures.

Wykes (1982) and Garety and Morris (1984) have both described one example of such a hostel, illustrating how behavioural techniques can be used in such situations. This particular hostel is home to 14 residents, and has been converted from a large detached Victorian house. Most of the residents have needed a great deal of individual attention, with their own routine worked out by a psychologist. A major problem has been to maintain resident responsibility for those tasks which they *can* undertake, even though they may do them slowly and inefficiently. The individual care routines are then carefully reviewed each week.

Both descriptions of this unit have focused upon management practices that maintain an appropriate therapeutic milieu for this group of clients. These include the promotion of optimistic attitudes towards residents; the lowest possible level of restictiveness consistent with offering a safe environment; and individualized intervention programmes, as opposed to 'block' programmes.

There is at present little research-based guidance on how best to bring about these changes. It has been traditional to describe the set of objectives given in the previous paragraph as resident-oriented, as opposed to institutionally-oriented, and to consider these two types of orientation as dimensionally opposite. Conning (1986) has, however, suggested that these two orientations are better considered as two dimensions which may vary independently, so suggesting that there is no one simple set of rules for organizing a care environment.

The sort of hospital-hostel just described will, by definition, form only part of the total range of provision for the chronically mentally disabled in a particular locality. Häfner (1985) has noted the erosion of the role of the traditional mental hospital implied by these changes, so that the five main functions which need to be carried out—treatment, accommodation, occupation, social provision, and leisure activities—may now be carried out by five separate organizations. Under these circumstances it is important to co-ordinate the policies of each organization in order that together the needs of residents are met fully—without overprovision or duplication—and in order that different units interface closely, so that residents can move from one to another with as little stress as possible on them.

From a behavioural point of view, it is then helpful for one organization to take the responsibility for co-ordinating all the treatment programmes for any one individual resident. As already discussed, it would be very confusing if behavioural programmes were being carried out by, say, three organizations without any consistency in management practices, targets, or contingencies. Again, it is important to establish that a simple programme works at all and is acceptable to both residents and staff, before trying anything too complex.

The new long-term—treating individuals in families

Until 15 years ago, very little was known about the treatment of chronic psychiatric disability in family settings. Recently both research workers (Vaughn and Leff 1976) and voluntary organizations (Creer and Wing 1974) have become interested in how families cope with a schizophrenic member. Initial interest focused on measures of Expressed Emotion (EE)—a measure both of the level of critical comments directed at, and emotional involvement with, the identified relative—as a predictor of relapse in the family setting. More recently, a number of structured programmes have been developed, directed at changing attitudes and behaviour of the family carers.

The distinguishing features of this approach are the emphasis on a clearly structured educational programme about the nature of schizophrenia, and the direct approach to modifying of interactions within the family. Different programmes emphasize different components of this approach. Some stress support for the families, others stress problem-solving skills, while others stress the educational component. Research studies have noted the interaction of drug effects with behavioural treatment effects in the programmes, indicating the need for careful use and monitoring of phenothiazine medication.

In general, the educational programmes aim to give a clear account of the main presenting problems of schizophrenia, and describe simply how family members can understand and respond to those problems. The programmes may make use of lectures, videos, or booklets, or a combination of educational methods. Since family members may not be highly literate, it may be worth checking, by use of one of the standard 'readability' formulae (e.g. Gunning's 'FOG' index, Gunning 1952) that written information can be understood by people of less than average ability. The content of the programmes typically includes: an explanation of the nature of schizophrenia, including the role of environmental stress; a description of the manifestations of schizophrenia, as experienced by family members; an explanation of the purpose of medication; and advice

Table 9.2 Examples of information sections from a family education programme (from Smith and Birchwood 1987)

Section 1
Brief outline on the development of the concept of schizophrenia, and epidemiological information about who could develop schizophrenia. Simple explanations of possible causal factors, e.g. the role of genetic and biochemical abnormalities, though the lack of conclusive evidence is stressed. The role of possible environmental stress, including family factors, in the development and course of the illness. Families are reassured that they are not reponsible for causing the illness, though their important role in the recovery process is stressed. A guarded but hopeful prognosis for the majority of patients is given.

Section 4
How to help relatives to identify support services in terms of available hospital and community resources. Addresses of local and national branches of various organizations are given, including self-help and family support groups, and a short reference list to encourage further reading is provided. General advice is given to encourage relatives to look after their own needs:
  (1) Look after your own needs by carrying on with or taking up activities that you used to do. (Relatives carry out a homework exercise to articulate their past and ideal lifestyles.)
  (2) Do not centre your life round the patient too much.
  (3) Do not worry about giving the individual responsibilities around the house—e.g. household tasks—but do not overburden him immediately after discharge.
  (4) Try to plan and do things with the patient which the whole family enjoy—e.g. trips out.
  (5) Map out your social support network and talk about your problems and difficulties with friends.
  (6) Expect bad times when things fail and expect stress, frustration, and some unhappiness.

---

on how families can plan their lives to accommodate their schizophrenic relative. Table 9.2 gives an example of the information included in one particular programme (Smith and Birchwood 1987).

Milne's (1986) book on the training of behaviour therapists has two useful chapters on the training of parents, relating primarily to the parents of handicapped children, which would be helpful in the detailed design of educational programmes for the parents of schizophrenic sufferers.

Other programmes have particularly emphasized relative support groups, and family meetings. Earlier observations of families had shown that some families (usually those with low levels of EE in the relatives) had developed effective coping mechanisms without benefit of theory, so it has been hoped that these coping strategies will be picked up by other families. Family meetings in the home are widely used to involve the patient in discussions on how best to cope with specific problems in family life. In a family meeting the therapist may help the family to pin-point problems, and then work with them to generate a range of possible solutions, choose and implement the solution which looks most promising, and then review progress. This approach is described in detail in Chapter 12. The therapist may also focus on general communication within the family, encouraging families to be specific and clear in their views, and to express both positive and negative feelings clearly. Leff and Vaughn (1985) summarize recent work emphasizing the family work aspect of this approach. The results of this approach seem promising. Strachan (1986) has systematically reviewed four studies, all conducted with a randomized design and with at least one comparison condition. Typically, the results show less social withdrawal and lower rates of relapse for the patients, and more positive attitudes displayed by relatives.

This form of structured family behavioural therapy is of considerable interest, for at least two reasons. Some direct-care staff can also be hostile or rejecting in their interactions with chronic patients, and might benefit from the treatment approaches usually given to family members. Secondly, it gives greater prominence than any of the other approaches considered in this chapter to the information given to both patient and carers about the nature of the psychiatric disability. It suggests the desirability of giving to patient and carers, as quickly as possible after it becomes probable that the patient will be chronically disabled, direct and specific information about the nature of the condition, rather than waiting until chronicity is already well advanced.

However, it has already been pointed out that the 'active ingredients' of these psychosocial treatment regimes are not yet clear (Barrowclough and Tarrier 1984). Also, of course, a substantial proportion of new long-term or high-contact patients may have exhausted the tolerance of their families, or may have chosen a more solitary lifestyle, and are no longer in contact with their family of origin. Nonetheless, this form of intervention has wide potential applications, and increases the range of treatment methods available for chronic patients.

Conclusions

Chronic psychiatric handicaps can be very severe, and thus both the *rate* of improvement, and the probable *degree* of improvement, of an individual patient may be limited. Because of this, and because of the historically limited use of positive rehabilitative methods with many chronic patients, many direct-care staff do not believe that chronic patients can improve. A critical first step in any treatment programme should thus be to demonstrate that change is possible. This implies that the first patient treated, or the first target area chosen, should be one where positive treatment response is possible. The evidence of real-life improvement, validly demonstrated by a recording or monitoring method which the staff trust, is a more effective motivator to direct-care staff than the most statistically elegant research report.

Treatment programmes for this client group are often prophylactic, not curative. The long-term maintenance of a structured ward regime, or of an altered pattern of family communication, is necessary to maintain changes in patient behaviour. These programmes are thus particularly sensitive to staff changes, or major organizational changes in a ward.

Historically, large psychiatric hospitals have offered 'block' treatment regimes, based on the expectation that scores of patients could conveniently be treated in an identical way. This chapter has pointed out the extremely heterogeneous nature of the problems and needs presented by the several hundred chronic patients who will live in a typical Health District of a quarter of a million people. Community care programmes, and the range of hostel and day-care facilities they have created, have only further emphasized the varied careers of individual patients, and the individualized treatment facilities that should be available to them. Chronic psychiatric problems are highly individual, as the following three case vignettes illustrate:

David was a 39-year-old computing graduate, a heavy drinker and previously a marijuana smoker, repetitively loping about the ward, expressing suicidal ideas but hoping to share his life with Eva, previously wife to his best friend.

Mervyn was aged 31, with a 14-year psychiatric history and seven previous admissions, who coped adequately with an isolated job at a water works but who was bored and frustrated at home with his highly critical father and physically ill mother.

Jane was 52, with six previous admissions going back 30 years, and had been found wandering in the local cemetery in a thin dress in autumn, with no food in her squalid flat, and was exhausting the tolerance of the local church which she irregularly attended.

In order to help these three individuals, behavioural and cognitive methods could be used to: provide a relevant day activity programme for David, and modify his beliefs about the possibility of a close relationship with Eva; provide a relevant evening and weekend recreational programme for Mervyn, and modify the pattern of interaction with his father; provide suitable hostel accommodation, with appropriate management practices, for Jane, and teach her basic skills in the areas of choice of clothing and purchase of food.

Each of these individuals require a different mix of interventions (see Shepherd 1984 for an extended description of an individual treatment programme). In order for those interventions to be delivered over a period

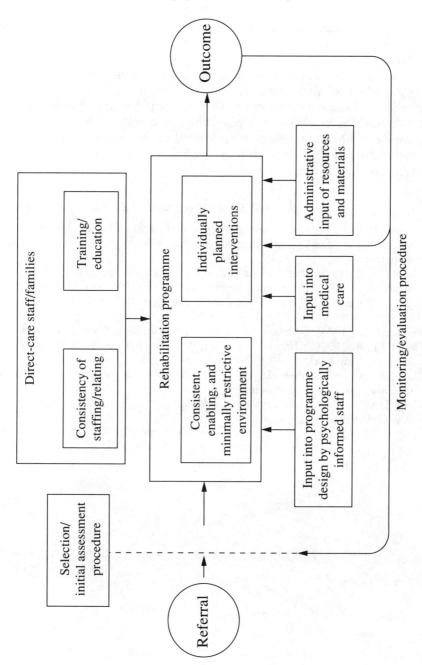

Fig. 9.2 Elements of a comprehensive therapeutic system for chronically disabled patients

of time, a considerable amount of organizational skill is required to bring together the clinical and administrative resources required for a treatment programme.

Figure 9.2 illustrates how these resources combine together to form a comprehensive therapeutic system. It is paradoxical that only as the number of chronic patients in British psychiatric hospitals has dropped by a half have psychiatrists and psychologists developed behavioural and cognitive treatment methods with some demonstrated efficacy, so these patients can now be helped both in hospital and community settings more effectively than before.

Recommended reading

Falloon, I. R. H. (1985). *Family management of schizophrenia: a study of the clinical, social, family, and economic benefits.* John Hopkins University Press, Baltimore.

Matson, J. L. (1980). Behavior modification procedures for training chronically institutionalised schizophrenics. In *Progress in behaviour modification*, Vol. 9, (ed. M. Herson, R. M. Eisler, and P. M. Miller), pp. 167–202. Academic Press, London.

Shepherd, G. (1984). *Institutional care and rehabilitation.* Longman, London.

Talbott, J. A. (1984). *The chronic mental patient: five years later.* Grune and Stratton, New York.

Watts, F. N. and Bennett, D. H. (1983). *Theory and practice of psychiatric rehabilitation.* Wiley, Chichester.

Wing, J. K. and Morris, B. (1981). *Handbook of psychiatric rehabilitation practice.* Oxford University Press.

10

Marital problems

Karen B. Schmaling, Alan E. Fruzzetti, and Neil S. Jacobson

Introduction

Cognitive–behavioural marital therapy in historical context

Behavioural treatment approaches to marital distress have evolved extensively since their introduction (Stuart 1969; Patterson and Hops 1972) less than two decades ago. These early behavioural interventions emphasized simple social exchange theory and contracting. Recently, a more broad-based view of interventions has been designed to increase positive, pleasing behaviours, improve communication, develop problem-solving skills, alleviate sexual problems, restructure harmful or distorted thinking patterns spouses might have, find ways to circumvent destructive conflict escalation, and attempt to change larger patterns of behaviours that result in marital discord.

Because early approaches defined marital satisfaction as the preponderance of positive interactions between spouses, initial behavioural interventions sought to replace negative interactions with positive ones by identifying and increasing pleasing behaviours. Largely based on learning theories developed in the laboratory and inspired by the work of B. F. Skinner, the behavioural view considered interactions between distressed spouses to be under *aversive control*: controlled by punishment or the threat of negative consequences. Thus, those first behavioural interventions aimed to shift the focus from aversive control to *positive control*, where spouses would behave positively not to avoid punishment but to please the other spouse (and consequently be pleased in return). These concepts continue to provide the theoretical underpinnings of much of present-day behavioural marital therapy, but both theory and practice have expanded to include a number of important innovations.

Social learning theory (Bandura 1977) particularly has contributed to our understanding of the cognitive–perceptual processes that are important in working with distressed couples. An important implication of this view is that the clinician must assess the *attributions* that spouses make for their own and their partner's behaviour. Attributions are the beliefs spouses have about the causes of, or reasons for, each other's behaviours. In addition to assessing the *perceived causes* of behaviours, a marital therapist must assess the way in which each spouse interprets the *impact* of their own and their partner's behaviour (*cognitive style*). With careful assessment the skilled therapist can learn where to focus interventions to help change or restructure problematic attributional or cognitive styles.

This chapter presents a view of cognitive–behavioural marital therapy as it might be applied to the short-term treatment of marital problems in any out-patient service.

Presenting problems

Couples or individuals seek marital therapy to address a variety of problems. Couples may seek therapy because of increased frequency or severity of arguments, a specific problem or set of problems they are unable to solve, unhappiness about their sexual relationship, or simply report vague and non-specific dissatisfaction with their relationship. It is also common for couples to report feeling 'trapped' in their 'stale' relationship, and seek therapy as a final attempt at resolution before seeking separation or divorce. Sometimes an extramarital affair or major life change precipitates the decision to enter marital therapy.

Marital problems may also be the reason for a husband or wife seeking individual therapy. In such cases it is likely that either the other spouse has refused to accompany the presenting spouse or that the presenting spouse does not identify marital problems *per se* as the cause of his or her current difficulties. Thus, marital problems may often be implicated when an individual seeks individual therapy for depression, anxiety, etc., or seeks medical attention for associated somatic complaints. A full assessment of the marriage in these cases will ascertain whether marital therapy is indicated or possible.

Causes of marital distress: a cognitive–behavioural theory

Distressed couples generally have few pleasant and rewarding interactions but many angry, blaming, or punishing ones. Interactions of distressed couples are often characterized by *reciprocated negative behaviour*: if one spouse behaves negatively, the partner is likely to respond in kind, and thus starts a chain of escalating negative interaction (Gottman 1979).

Such a chain of negative behaviours in a couple having marital problems might start with one spouse *expecting* to be criticized for not completing some household task that he or she normally performs. When the other spouse begins to ask about the task, even if the question is neutral both in tone and wording, the first spouse (expecting criticism) responds with a criticism of something the other did or did not do. The questioning spouse senses the critical tone and feels attacked, so attacks back, and so forth. Thus the components of this argument are a negative expectation of one spouse from the other, and reciprocated negative behaviours (*escalating criticism*).

Distressed couples are *reactive*: positive or negative events have a powerful influence on how spouses feel about or evaluate the relationship at any given time (Jacobson, Follette, and McDonald 1982). Non-distressed couples are less affected by moment-to-moment variation. In the example above, a spouse in a non-distressed couple would probably not have had the expectation of criticism, so the aggressive and hostile exchange might not have taken place at all. Rather, the simple question would probably have been answered directly and in a non-hostile manner, precluding a reciprocal negative response. High reactivity in distressed couples may increase the likelihood of misunderstanding and poor communication. Since spouses are so used to feeling attacked, they may cease listening carefully to one another and instead be preparing a counter-attack to the initial (perceived or expected) criticism.

Distressed relationships are further characterized by an inability to resolve conflict. Lack of conflict resolution skills leave couples with a backlog of unresolved fights and conflicts that have built up over the history of their relationship. A history of such unresolved conflicts may also contribute to negative expectations about future conflicts and make engagement in constructive problem-solving even less likely to occur in their relationship.

Reinforcement erosion occurs when partners lose the satisfaction that was once present in the relationship. This might be attributed to habituation: behaviours that were pleasing at one time are not as important any more. They may fail to appreciate each other's efforts, take each other for granted, or have new and different needs that their partners have not yet learned to meet. One or both spouses may have stopped doing some of the nice things that formerly helped to provide many warm feelings between them.

Moreover, all of the above factors may be integrated into *destructive patterns* of neglect, criticism, arguments, and negative expectations and beliefs concerning the other spouse and the relationship.

Assessment

Assessment of target problems

Therapy usually begins with two or three sessions of assessment, unless there is an acute crisis. The purposes of the assessment sessions are to determine a couple's suitability for marital therapy and to gain an understanding of their situation. The focus is on gathering information: couples are told that no changes are to be expected during the assessment phase because the treatment will proceed only after the therapist learns enough about the couple and their problems to make an informed decision about the course of therapy, and indeed whether marital therapy is indicated at all.

Approaching the first few sessions in this manner has important benefits besides those already stated. First, it helps to reduce unrealistic expectations about the power of therapy to bring immediate and large-scale changes. On the other hand, if some improvements are made early in therapy the couple may work quite hard for further positive results.

The first session: initial conjoint meeting

The first conjoint session should focus on relationship strengths as well as problem areas, helping the therapist to begin to understand both spouses and their relationship. In order to set the tone for therapy and gather as much pertinent information as possible, there are two important general areas in which to focus attention in the first session.

1. *Problem areas*　After briefly answering any immediate questions that the couple might have, the therapist should focus directly upon the couple's presenting problems. This is accomplished by asking them 'What caused you to seek an appointment just now?', or 'So, just what do the two of you think are the problems?', while alternating between spouses, being sure to give each a full opportunity to be heard without inter-ruptions. If one spouse repeatedly interrupts the other, this is a significant pattern to note, but also to stop quickly. Gently ask the impatient spouse to wait until the other has finished, and point out that the other spouse will then have a chance to explain fully his or her position. Gentle enforcement of respectful conversation is not only vital for a successful session, but also begins to give couples some objective limits for their behaviour outside therapy.

　Also important is information about how long the couple has perceived the problem(s), what steps (including previous therapy) they have taken to help alleviate their difficulties, what has worked, and what has not been successful. If the couple has had previous therapy that was not helpful, the therapist must be sure not to attempt the same interventions a second time. Not only are they likely to be ineffective, but the therapist's credibility would be harmed in the process. Each partner's complaints about the marriage need to be behaviourally specified. Couples are unlike-ly to do this naturally or easily, so the therapist must help them clarify their formulation. For example, 'He never pays attention to me' is vague, and the therapist might ask, 'What does "being attentive" mean to you? What are examples of what you wish him to do that would mean he was being attentive to you?' By contrast, 'He touches me in an affectionate way during sex, but not at other times' is more specific.

　In the context of the couple's presenting problems, it is important to ask who initiated therapy, how each spouse currently feels about being in therapy, and what goals each person has for therapy. If both spouses are quite willing participants, it bodes well for therapy and the therapist may begin therapy expecting active participation from the couple. If one or

both spouses is reluctant, their expectations about therapy and willingness to participate fully must be assessed, and later addressed at the
roundtable (third session) at which time a decision will be made about the
appropriateness of therapy.

2. *Relationship history* This part of the session should be introduced
by a statement like:

'I realise that the problems we've been talking about are quite difficult ones,
and I am beginning to get a sense of what things have been like for you lately.
What I would like to do now is turn our attention back to the beginning of your
relationship and talk about things like how you met, what attracted you to each
other, a little about your wedding, things like that. We'll have lots more opportunities to talk about problem areas, so I'd like this time to be focused on those
more positive aspects of your relationship. So, don't bring up problem areas,
because I'll just have to interrupt you to postpone those things until another
time.'

After setting the parameters for discussion, the therapist should help the
partners trace the history of their relationship, including how they met,
the courtship phase, what attracted each spouse to the other, fun things
they have done together, and how they made the decision to marry.

By the time couples come in for therapy they frequently are focused
largely on negative aspects of each other and their marriage. There is
often relief, hopefulness, and even a cheery response as the therapist
redirects the couple's attention to more positive aspects of each partner
and more positive phases in the history of the relationship.

The first session is also the place to answer any questions the couple
may have about marital therapy and to outline any other expectations the
therapist has for them. For example, in order to maximize the value of
therapy the therapist should require that the couple be living together
during the programme and that neither spouse be involved in an extramarital sexual relationship. The rationale for this is that it is only by
devoting themselves completely to the therapy and their marital relationship that they can know how satisfying their relationship could be, and
only in this way will therapy be maximally helpful for them.

Questionnaires are often useful as adjuncts to the assessment process.
Several common 'paper-and-pencil' tests quickly identify areas of conflict
and give the therapist normative information about the presenting couple
vis-à-vis other couples seeking marital therapy. Spouses may even complete questionnaires and return them by mail before the first session,
helping the therapist to direct questioning efficiently early in therapy.

Any of the following questionnaires may be useful:

(1) Dyadic Adjustment Scale (Spanier 1976) provides a global measure
    of marital satisfaction, is widely used, and norms are available;

(2) Areas of Change Questionnaire (Weiss, Hops, and Patterson 1973) is a measure of the degree of dissatisfaction with a number of common presenting problems;

(3) Marital Satisfaction Inventory (Snyder 1981) yields a comprehensive MMPI-like profile of distress in nine content areas for each spouse, plus Global Distress and validity scale scores; and

(4) Marital Status Inventory (Weiss and Cerreto 1980) provides what the authors of this chapter fondly refer to as the 'number of toes out the door', i.e. how many specific steps the spouse has taken toward divorce or separation.

In the UK the Maudsley Marital Questionnaire (Crowe 1978) and the Golombok Rust Inventory of Marital Satisfaction (Rust, Bennun, Crowe, and Golombok 1986) are also used.

Session 2: Interviews with individual spouses
Brief individual sessions usually follow the initial conjoint session (usually 30–45 minutes with each spouse). The primary purpose of these interviews is to understand the spouses better as individuals and hence develop a fuller picture of the relationship while building rapport. It may be informative to ask questions of each individual that may be too threatening to be addressed in a conjoint setting. Examples of these include asking 'Do you love your spouse', 'Do you like your spouse', or 'If you could have a magic wand and make things in your marriage absolutely ideal, what would you change? How would things be?' Individual sessions are also used to explore any suspicions or concerns that the therapist has about contraindications to therapy (e.g. extramarital sexual affairs or imminent divorce).

Beware the person who has already decided to divorce but attends therapy to prove to his or her partner that they have tried everything; or the spouse who wants to enter treatment so that he or she will have a 'safe' place in which to make a significant self-disclosure (e.g. that she or he is having an affair). In such cases, the willingness of the spouses to participate fully in the spirit of marital therapy must be carefully determined.

The individual interviews can be used to explore a number of other areas including:

(1) individual psychopathology;
(2) sexual difficulties;
(3) sexual and physical abuse as a child;
(4) history and characteristics of past significant relationships; and
(5) relevant information about the family of origin (e.g. the person's

relationship to family members, parents' marital relationship, patterns of conflict, and emotional expression in the family of origin).

Finally, it is important to ask each person at the end of the individual interviews if anything which has been discussed should be kept secret from the other spouse. For reasons both practical and ethical, wishes of non-disclosure should be respected, although the therapist should encourage spouses to be as open as possible with each other.

Assessment of suitability for marital therapy

Marital therapy is usually not indicated when a spouse refuses to give up an extramarital affair, or when one spouse has decided to seek a divorce. Another contraindication for marital therapy is a history of unstable relationships attributable to severe character disturbance or personality disorder; it may be best to work with the personality difficulties in individual therapy before conjoint therapy. Physical abuse may be a contraindication for marital therapy, especially if the batterer has problems with alcohol or substance abuse or dependence. Marital therapy can involve discussion of volatile topics and a spouse who has difficulty with anger control may be at higher risk for abusing his or her spouse during therapy. Anger-management training may be a prerequisite for conjoint work with such couples. Similarly, control over, or abstinence from, alcohol and substance abuse need to be gained before marital therapy. Ambiguous issues may need to be addressed openly in the roundtable session (below) before agreeing to proceed with treatment (e.g. an agreement or contract may be made to limit alcohol use).

These and other relative contraindications for marital therapy are discussed in the later section on client characteristics that are related to therapeutic failure ('Limitations of treatment', p. 367).

Session 3: The roundtable session

A roundtable discussion follows these initial interviews. The therapist presents a formulation of the couple's strengths and weaknesses, problems, the proposed treatment plan, and any concerns about the couple's ability to work on their relationship in therapy. The therapist must engage the couple in a conversation about their relationship and about the proposed course of marital therapy, setting the tone of mutual responsibility which will follow throughout.

The proposed treatment plan might include the order in which the skills or problem areas will be addressed, and an estimate of the number of sessions spent working on each area. If the couple and therapist agree to work together, the therapist may outline the couple's role and responsibility in the treatment and change process: the couple must commit themselves to putting effort into improving their relationship both during the sessions (by attending, arriving on time, etc.) and outside therapy (by doing assignments between sessions). A crucial topic in the roundtable is the induction of the *collaborative set*. To contradict the blaming stance so frequently seen in distressed couples, successful therapy involves both partners beginning to accept mutual responsibility, compromise, and working together.

Treatment structure

Structure of each session

It is preferable to hold 90-minute therapy sessions, initially on a weekly basis. Each session generally consists of the following components (in approximate order):

(1) setting an agenda for the current session (5 minutes);

(2) evaluation of progress in therapy to date (10 minutes);

(3) debriefing assignments (15 minutes);

(4) new 'business', i.e. introduction of new topics and/or skills (45 minutes); and

(5) assigning tasks to be completed before the next session (15 minutes).

Setting the agenda is usually a brief process, but crucial to the success of the session. The therapist might say something like this:

'What I had planned for our session for today was to first check how you've been feeling about what we've been doing in therapy, then find out how your home assignment went. Then I thought we could practise your problem-solving skills by working on one of your major problems, with me as the back-seat driver. Finally, of course, we'll talk about some things you can do over the next week, considering what you feel you need to work on at this point in therapy.

Is there anything really significant that happened during the last week that would keep us from using this agenda? How does this sound to you?'

Evaluating progress might utilize any of several techniques, and should be included in some form each session. The couple might be asked to rate daily their happiness or satisfaction with their partner or relationship in 12 areas (see Table 10.1). These ratings are averaged for the week and may be graphed over the course of therapy. Couples should be asked in the session how well the graphs reflect how the previous week went and how accurately their ratings reflect their overall impressions. Any discrepancies between their overall impressions and their graphs should be explored. For example, daily ratings may be used to help pin-point factors that contribute to positive vs. negative feelings from day to day.

Another use of the graphs is to note what areas of the relationship are increasingly satisfying. If the areas worked on in therapy are not showing improvement, the therapist and couple need to explore why (e.g. while working on communication, ratings in this area should show improvement; if not, the reason must be found and addressed).

An important way to monitor progress involves taking spouses' 'affective temperature' (Jacobson, Berley, Melman, Elwood, and Phelps 1985), and this should be employed from time to time during the course of therapy. This is an opportunity for the therapist to be less structured and simply explore with the couple how they feel about the therapy and about their partner as a result of the therapy. This topic is best broached with open-ended questions from the therapist such as, 'How have you been feeling about what we've been doing in therapy?', and 'How have your feelings about being married to (your partner) changed as a result of the therapy?'

Another method to evaluate therapeutic progress is to review the events of therapy. The therapist may do this, but it is preferable if the couple are prompted to recall what has been happening and why the therapy has focused on these areas. The therapist may ask a broad question such as: 'What have we been working on these past few weeks, and how does it fit in to your goals for therapy?' In this way the therapist helps the couple to conceptualize the therapy and their relationship as a process that evolves and changes over time. This approach contrasts with the notion, typical of distressed couples, that their relationship is static and that there is nothing that can be done about it. Providing a sense of therapeutic history, as well as a sense of purposeful and logical progress toward

Table 10.1 Areas of marital satisfaction

How does each spouse feel today about his or her partner in the following areas of their marriage?

Rate 1–10, completely unhappy–completely happy

1. Consideration
2. Affection
3. Household responsibilities
4. Rearing of children
5. Social activities (as a couple or with other people)
6. Money
7. Communication
8. Sex
9. Occupational (or academic) activities
10. Own independence
11. Partner's independence
12. Overall:
    A. Your marriage
    B. Yourself

---

agreed-upon goals, sets the stage for the couple to be receptive to and excited about beginning work in new areas.

The next phase of the session is devoted to a *review of the tasks assigned* for the previous week. It is essential that the therapist conveys to the couple the central importance of between-session assignments: improving their relationship should not be confined merely to the 90 minutes spent in marital therapy each week, and each session's agenda is predicated upon completion of whatever tasks were assigned the previous session.

The focus of this review should be on what went well. Success should of course be rewarded, and particular attention addressed to what the couple found useful in the assignment. If the assignment went poorly, it is important to find out why: did they fail to allocate sufficient time, had they had an argument, was the assignment inappropriate (too difficult or too many tasks), did they not understand the task, or what? If the reasons for difficulty are not readily apparent, one way to investigate is to have the couple actually try their tasks again, in the session. This may give the therapist additional information to help adjust future assignments so the couple are more likely to succeed.

If the couple have not done their assignment it may be preferable to cancel or postpone the session, rather than try to forge ahead and present new skills. When the couple have not practised, let alone mastered, old skills, the acquisition of newer skills is doomed to fail. Of course, sufficient time must be spent with couples who do not attempt their between-session tasks to emphasize the importance of these assignments, to explore the reasons for non-compliance, and to help them find ways to complete future assignments.

The *introduction of new 'business' or new topics* comprises the bulk of each session. New business should be introduced within the framework of a review of new skills attained so far in therapy, with an emphasis on the logical progression of skills and topics (e.g. good communication skills must be attained before embarking on problem-solving tasks). The specific techniques or skills that may be introduced are discussed in the next section of this chapter.

Finally, each session closes with an *assignment of relevant tasks* to be completed before the next session, with careful checking to be sure both the tasks themselves and their rationale are understood. The therapist may ask, 'I want to make sure we're all clear on what you're going to be doing for homework this week. Could one of you just say again what your understanding is of what we've agreed upon?' In the early stages of therapy the therapist should assign quite specific tasks, but in the latter stages the couple should be given increasing responsibility for planning the assignments. The couple may be asked, 'What do you feel you need to work on over the next week—what tasks do you think you should try?'

One way to facilitate successful completion of assignments is to anticipate difficulties couples might have and include in the assignment ways to avoid pitfalls. For example, the therapist could ask, 'What might prevent you from completing this homework?' Any problems they anticipate (e.g. they will be too tired, they will not have time alone, etc.) should be addressed in a problem-solving discussion. It may be necessary to help the couple schedule a day, and a specific block of time during that day, when they will do their tasks, and assign some responsibility to each spouse for actually getting the assignment done (e.g. while both agree not to schedule anything else on Monday evening when they are fresh, the wife might be responsible for finding a babysitter so that they can have peace and quiet when they do their assignment, and the husband will provide pencils and paper).

Therapist characteristics and approach

Structuring

The therapist should structure time within sessions in order to accomplish the agenda, and structure material over the course of therapy to maintain steady and efficient progress.

Session time should be actively structured by the therapist. The therapist must not only consider in advance time and material to be covered when setting the agenda, but also control the flow of the session and interrupt destructive behaviour. For example, often one spouse is especially verbal, and particularly skilled at delivering a verbal litany of complaints about his or her partner. In many such cases the other spouse increasingly withdraws when these verbal tirades begin.

In order to promote the idea of collaboration (as noted in the round-table section), to facilitate engagement of the quiet spouse into the therapeutic enterprise, and to interrupt this negative interaction pattern, the therapist must quickly intervene. This might be accomplished by modelling a more appropriate expression of anger, asking the relentless partner to focus on his or her own behaviours (self-focus), or simply by interrupting the pattern and initiating a discussion of ways to alter this destructive cycle.

In all cases the therapist should be supportive but quite firm in his or her expectations and reasons for cutting off one spouse's speaking. After the first interruption, the therapist should share responsibility for monitoring the pattern with the husband or wife by interrupting in this manner: 'Hold on, I'm going to interrupt you right there. OK, why am I stopping you?'

Additionally, the therapist should continually bear in mind the overall structure of the therapy so that the important issues are addressed. Either spouse or the couple together may use side-tracking or denial to avoid confronting difficult and important issues. Only with vigilant attention to progress *vis-à-vis* each problem area can the therapist promote changes in an efficient and effective manner.

Instigating

Through a careful blend of direction, support, timing, firmness, and cajoling, the therapist must foster couples' abilities to change problem behaviours in their lives outside therapy. This includes inducing compliance with between-session assignments, helping couples to behave more collaboratively (see roundtable) both in and between sessions, and carefully titrating the amount of responsibility assigned to couples to help them learn and practise skills on their own. By the end of therapy couples should feel empowered to be their 'own therapists'.

Teaching

Cognitive–behavioural marital therapy techniques are often educational, so one major task of the therapist is to teach, and sometimes to model, new skills. When a technique is to be practised in a session or outside therapy, the therapist should go over the rules, principles, guidelines, and rationale, increasingly requesting the spouses themselves to provide the rule or rationale. Each partner should be given feedback about his or her performance, beginning with successful aspects and then moving on to provide suggestions for improvement in other areas. Feedback should be connected to a rule or principle. For example:

Sue   'Stan, when you fix yourself a sandwich for a midnight snack and leave the jars unscrewed and the bread bin open on the counter, I feel annoyed that I have to clean up after you.'

Therapist 'Sue, I really liked how specific you were about the problem—I felt like I knew exactly what you saw when you came into the kitchen after Stan fixed his snack. I think it's important to start out by telling Stan, though, what you appreciate. What's your understanding of why it is important to tell him what you appreciate before you tell him what you don't appreciate?'

Sue   'Because he'll be more receptive to my problem and he'll know I'm not just paying attention to the annoying stuff he does. I could start with, "Stan, I really like the way you make snacks on your own and don't ask me to get things for you."'

Creating positive expectancies

It is important for the therapist to be positive and enthusiastic about the couple's progress and prognosis, yet also to be realistic. A healthy dose of realism often involves the sober appraisal that the couple must work diligently and collaboratively both in and out of the sessions in order to establish and maintain improvements.

If the couple show significant improvement it is very important for the therapist to *predict setbacks*, both to prevent disillusionment for the couple and to enhance the therapist's credibility. Any prediction that the couple may back-pedal should be balanced with the hopeful and more positive expectation that momentum is likely to be regained, and further progress realized.

Providing emotional nurturance

It is essential that the therapist encourages expressions of the couple's emotional responses to each other and to the process of therapy. Careful attention to emotions, with considerable support, comfort, and understanding regarding the sensitive nature of marital therapy, helps to ease this difficult and sometimes discouraging endeavour as well as to humanize its potentially mechanistic flavour.

There are a number of ways to explore spouses' feelings within the structure of therapy. First, there should be routine discussion of feelings early in each session when progress is evaluated. Also, whenever a spouse responds in an incongruous or ambivalent manner the therapist needs to explore the underlying feelings (e.g. if a spouse says, 'it was okay . . . I guess', in response to the therapist's query about the preceding week). Finally, support and understanding are always indicated during emotionally sensitive or hurtful times.

Alliance balancing

Work with couples often involves shifting the alliance between the spouses. Not every comment or question to one spouse needs to be balanced immediately with attention to the other spouse. However, the overall quality of interaction should be relatively even-handed across therapy. This may be problematic if one spouse is, for example, aggressive or manipulative. Like a therapeutic relationship with any difficult client, marital therapists need to find those vulnerable aspects of each spouse with which they can be empathic. Sometimes this may entail reappraising the overtly hostile behaviour that the spouse displays, with therapeutic focus on more positive behaviours.

Achieving a balance does *not* mean that the therapist has to find arbitrary changes for one spouse to make in order to balance real changes of the other. For example, if both spouses are employed yet the wife is also responsible for child-care and household responsibilities, and both agree this is not equitable, the majority of changes must be made by the husband. The wife's role in this case may be simply to acknowledge and/or reward him for his efforts, not to make changes herself in other areas as compensation.

Treatment interventions: Techniques

Overview

The interventions that follow are described separately as if they were discrete 'intervention modules' to be employed in a prescriptive manner. While the techniques are delineated in a logical order, each new intervention is somewhat predicated upon successful mastery of earlier ones, and the therapist should integrate the various interventions over the course of therapy to maximize their usefulness.

Therapy may begin by trying to renew some warm feelings by having spouses do some nice things for each other in an attempt to provide some immediate relief from current difficulties and to provide a basis for later interventions. A focus on improving communication typically follows, because this is a basic requisite for learning to solve problems in a systematic manner that is not overly emotionally charged. A problem-solving approach may then be employed through the remaining sessions to resolve a variety of presenting problems. This may be followed with attention to the sexual or affectional aspects of the marriage. Specific sessions toward the end of therapy may be reserved for work on preventing relapses and generalizing improvements across a wide array of areas in a couple's lives. Woven throughout therapy are cognitive interventions and conflict-management strategies, depending upon events that occur over the course of therapy.

Couples may bring skills in some areas to therapy, so that the therapist will need to spend only enough time in those areas to assess their skills. Other couples may seek therapy to address a very specific problem area (e.g. child-rearing). Specific, limited interventions may be chosen in such cases. Integrating and weaving these differing techniques into a coherent whole, unique to the couple, is the challenge which faces the marital therapist.

Behaviour exchange

Behaviour exchange engages both spouses in activities designed to increase each other's marital satisfaction. The term 'behaviour exchange' indicates the essence of this technique: an exchange of behaviours which are pleasing to each partner. Typically these activities are thoughtful, fairly simple, low-effort behaviours that can be readily incorporated into spouses' daily repertoires. Behaviour exchange is designed to induce short-term positive changes in the pattern of interaction early in therapy, and to have immediate effects in the couple's life outside of therapy, and thereby lay the groundwork needed for work on other major issues.

Behaviour exchange is commonly used in the early stages of therapy because the warm feelings it may foster often encourage a new sense of collaboration between spouses. Moreover, these initial improvements enhance the therapist's credibility. Behaviour exchange is also designed to counteract the spouses' selective focus on each other's negative behaviours, alleviate their feelings of helplessness about their distress, and begin to reverse their adversarial stance of blaming each other for their problems. Although much of the work of behaviour exchange is completed outside the therapy session, success rests upon full comprehension by the couple of the integral place of these exercises in therapy and on complete understanding of the tasks themselves.

The rationale for behaviour exchange, just as in all interventions in cognitive behaviour therapy, is carefully discussed with the couple. The rationale includes:

(1) establishing control over marital happiness rather than leaving things to chance or waiting for the partner to change;

(2) learning to pin-point specific behaviours that make the difference between a good day and a bad one, and that lead to positive feelings about the relationship versus negative feelings; and

(3) finding out that maintaining a good marriage requires daily effort.

The therapist should introduce behavioural exchange with a reminder to the couple to be collaborative and focus on themselves, as they had agreed during the roundtable discussion. Each spouse is asked, 'What could you do to improve your spouse's satisfaction with your relationship?' Each spouse is helped to pin-point specific behaviours that could have a positive effect on the other spouse's marital happiness. Initially, each spouse should do this without input from the partner. The therapist should encourage each of them to focus on small steps and easy, low-effort things which could increase the other's satisfaction.

If either spouse gets stuck, there are several prompts the therapist can give:

1. Remind the spouse of a problem area that was defined during the roundtable and ask, 'We discussed how being affectionate is a problem in your relationship. Focus on yourself and think about what small things you could do to make that part of your relationship a little better.'

2. Prompt them to think of activities from their courtship or other more satisfying times that could be initiated now.

3. Ask them to fantasize: If their only goal in life were to please the partner, what would they do?

If an individual or couple has particular difficulty creating a list of positive behaviours, the therapist might provide a questionnaire or supplement to help with ideas (e.g. the Spouse Observation Checklist, Patterson 1976).

Each spouse should generate as long a list as possible with specific ideas for what each could do to please the partner, including specific details of the situation and timing of each pleasing behaviour.

One couple began therapy with the wife complaining that her husband worked too much, leaving too little time to help her with chores or to pay attention to her. While the husband had complaints of his own, the following was a partial list of behaviours he could engage in to improve his wife's satisfaction:

1. Take a cup of coffee to Sally in bed before I go to work.
2. Bring home a rose.
3. Offer to take her to the movie of her choice.
4. Do a load of laundry.
5. Pick up all the old newspapers and take them out.
6. Wash and vacuum her car.
7. Offer to rub her back before she goes to sleep.
8. Ask her how her day went.
9. Apologize if I catch myself being preoccupied with work.

Once adequate lists had been developed (and reviewed with the therapist), the couple's assignment was to begin to do some of the things on the list, with the goal of each pleasing the other spouse. Additionally, spouses should be instructed to begin to pay attention to *all* efforts their partners make and to acknowledge or reward these efforts. The couple should be reminded not to assume that just because something is on the list it will be performed, nor should they think that just because the partner does something nice it is present on the list. In this way, the therapist helps their *attributions* about each other's behaviours to be positive (see 'Cognitive interventions', below).

Because behaviour exchange is sometimes viewed as mechanical, it is helpful to point out to couples that the assignment emphasizes the spouses' *choice* of what behaviours are to be employed. Furthermore, spouses should be encouraged to do only those things that feel comfortable. Hopefully, however, each spouse will feel inspired during the week and try to do a number of things to please the partner.

Some spouses come into therapy feeling that they have done all they can and have given a great deal to the other. It may be that one spouse has done things that are not as pleasing or as important to the partner as that spouse believes (e.g. spouses are sometimes ignorant about what pleases their partner so their efforts are genuine but misguided). While acknowledging the feelings of injustice such spouses might have, the therapist must remind the couple that both partners have agreed to collaborate in a new effort to make their relationship work and that the current task is to do some nice things. In that way, the focus will turn to recognizing each other's efforts and providing feedback.

Behaviour-exchange homework is generally one of the first opportunities for the therapist to assess how willing and/or able the couple is to
work collaboratively in therapy. A review of the assignment might start
with a question such as, 'What did you choose to do to try to please your
partner over the last week?' Steer the focus of the discussion to the
positive aspects of what went well; reward spouses for trying new behaviours even if they did not work out well; ask the receiver, 'What was
important about that [new behaviour] for you?', so that the spouse learns
what the behaviour means to the receiving spouse; ask the receiver how
he or she gave credit for or acknowledged the effort being made by the
giver; and ask the receiver if the behaviour is something she or he would
like to continue (to begin providing the giver with feedback).

Discuss what did not go well and why. If the couple did not do the
homework the therapist must explore the reasons (see above: 'Instigat-
ing', p. 350) and address the problem. If they did the assignment but did
not give their partners adequate credit, it might be that positive behaviours were ignored (intentionally or not), diminished, or even refused.
Perhaps the attributions one spouse made about the other's efforts need
to be explored and/or reformulated (see 'Cognitive interventions', below).
It is essential for the therapist to help the partners find ways to reward
each other for their efforts.

Cognitive interventions

In distressed relationships, spouses' emotional responses to their partners
are dependent upon their *thoughts* about their partners' behaviour and
the *meaning* they ascribe to it, rather than just the behaviour itself.
Relabelling or reinterpreting partner behaviour is a powerful intervention
that may be employed during any phase of therapy. Because the therapist
should be constantly on the lookout for distorted and/or dysfunctonal
thinking, and should intervene regardless of the content or phase in the
therapy, cognitive interventions are an integral part of cognitive–
behavioural marital therapy.

As with other therapy procedures, it is helpful to give the patients a
rationale for focusing on their thoughts. The rationale varies depending
on the circumstances and the particular problematic thinking pattern.
One rationale is simply that even if the negative assumptions about a
spouse's behaviours are *partially* true, there are likely to be other more
positive things contributing to the partner's behaviour as well, and that
the angry or hurt spouse might feel better if he or she thought about the
partner's behaviour differently.

For example, one spouse may *attribute* the cause of some behaviour of
the partner in a negative manner that affects the tenor of their conversation and interactions. In one couple, the wife (Kara) interpreted her
husband Paul playing quietly with their children on the floor after coming

home from work as evidence of his laziness and lack of commitment to the family. It seemed that these attributions about Paul permeated many of their interactions. Being careful not to engage in a truth-seeking enterprise (and not allowing Kara to ridicule or degrade Paul), the therapist simply asked, 'How might you think of Paul's behaviour in a different way, a way that would not result in your being so angry?' After exploring some alternatives with the therapist, Kara said that one alternative might be that 'despite having worked really hard all day, Paul still is making the effort to play with the children rather than just relaxing by himself.' Kara noted that this explanation was just as reasonable, or valid, as the previous one, and that she felt much warmer toward Paul when thinking about his behaviour this way.

It is common for both spouses to have unreasonable negative thoughts or hurtful attributions about their partners. In such cases, the therapist may involve both partners in this explorative process, perhaps linking negative thoughts with hurtful responses, which in turn contribute toward negative thoughts in the partner, and so on.

To continue the above example, after exploring both spouses' thoughts Paul noted that he believed that no matter what he did Kara would not stop thinking of him as lazy, so he had given up trying to be more ambitious. The therapist pointed out how each person's assumptions affected their feelings about the other's behaviour, and hence about each other. Both partners agreed to challenge their own negative assumptions and to try to find positive explanations for each other's behaviour.

Of course, it is not always certain that the negative attributions a spouse makes about the partner's behaviour are inaccurate. In such cases the therapist must clarify the *intent* of the first partner and also clarify the *impact* it has on the other partner.

Intent is explored by the therapist, who models good communication skills (see below) in trying to gain one spouse's perspective on his or her behaviour. With the other spouse the therapist must explore the impact of the behaviour on two levels:

(1) identifying the thoughts that the spouse has when faced with ambiguous behaviour by the partner (e.g. when a husband comes home from work and does not kiss his partner, she might think he did not kiss her 'because he did not want to'); and

(2) identifying the underlying assumptions that gave rise to the dysfunctional thoughts: what do the thoughts *mean* (e.g. she might think 'he doesn't care about me').

After exploring both the thoughts and their meaning, the therapist should help the couple to gather evidence to test if the negative attribution or thought (or *pattern* of thinking) is indeed distorted or if it is truly based in reality (see Chapter 6 for a fuller discussion of testing negative automatic thoughts). If the thoughts appear distorted, possible alternative assumptions and thoughts are explored. The therapist may assign the spouse to monitor (in writing) his or her negative automatic thoughts about the partner, providing a rational response to each one (see Fig. 6.4 for an example of this format). If the thoughts are reality-based, this indicates that behaviour change or compromise is needed on the part of the partner, requiring *problem-solving* or *trouble-shooting* interventions (see below).

Communication training

Not only are communication skill deficits a common presenting problem of couples, but difficulties with expressive and receptive communication skills are linked to a host of other typical complaints: lack of understanding, insufficient attention to each other, poor listening, conflict escalation, and difficulty solving problems.

Expressive skills include the speaker identifying his or her own thoughts, feelings, wishes, etc., then expressing them in the first person, in a specific and clear manner (e.g. 'When you don't help get the children ready for bed I feel frustrated', or 'It really makes me happy when you come home and ask me how my day went'). Receptive skills include non-verbal listening and attending (making eye-contact, head-nodding, etc.), empathizing, paraphrasing, and other expressions of good listening and understanding. These communication skills are the building blocks for the problem-solving techniques in the following section.

One way to introduce communication training is to say:

'When you came in for therapy you said that you felt poor communication was a big problem in your marriage. I have some specific ideas for ways that you can improve your communication. Better communication will help you feel closer and more intimate with one another, and it will help you to understand each other's feelings, likes and dislikes, and desires. These skills will probably help regardless of what is being discussed, even if it is unpleasant.'

Start the discussion with defining the two distinct roles in communication, those of *speaker* and *listener*. The therapist will first be an active participant in these exercises and will model and/or role-play each skill, but then should move to more of a 'coaching' role with the couple. There are a number of exercises delineated below that are designed to teach and practise each communication skill. The therapist should approach these exercises in the order provided, beginning with the more elementary receptive skills and then moving on to more difficult expressive skills as quickly as the couple master each level. The therapist should always be the one to model the *negative* behaviours in these exercises. In fact, he or she can even exaggerate the roles to help lighten the process with a touch of humour.

Exercises:

1. The therapist models *negative non-verbal listening* (e.g. looking away, shifting in the chair, doodling) while each spouse in turn talks about a neutral topic (such as how he or she spent the day). Ask each spouse how they *felt* (angry, sad, frustrated, ridiculed, hurt) during the exercise and what *thoughts* they had while they were talking and not being attended to (perhaps one spouse thought 'What I say isn't important', or 'I never get any respect'). This exercise often uncovers many dysfunctional automatic thoughts that may be amenable to cognitive exploration and intervention (see above). Ask each spouse to be collaborative and give examples of things he or she does at times that qualify as negative non-verbal listening.

2. The therapist, then each spouse, practise *positive non-verbal listening* behaviours (sitting forward, making eye-contact, nodding) while listening to the other spouse talking about a neutral topic. Ask each spouse how attended to or listened to she or he felt.

3. The therapist models *negative verbal receptive skills* (interrupting, finishing sentences, cross-complaining, etc.) in an exaggerated and humorous way. Ask each to focus on him/herself and give an example of what he or she does that is a negative listening skill.

4. Teach them to *paraphrase*: listen to the intent of what their partner is saying, rephrase the partner's statement in a *tentative* and questioning manner (e.g. 'I think . . . ?', or 'It sounds like you're saying that . . . ?'), and check out the accuracy either verbally ('Is that right?', or 'Is that what you meant?', or 'Did I capture your meaning?') or non-verbally (raising eyebrows, or giving a questioning look). The therapist may need to model paraphrasing, but usually this exercise can start by having each spouse in turn paraphrase the therapist (who might describe his or her feelings about some event or interaction—perhaps even modelling something related to a presenting problem). Spouses also need to learn to stop the speaker when he or she has said more than they can paraphrase back (e.g. 'wait a second, I want to see if I've got that so far . . . ').

5. Next the couple will be ready to paraphrase each other. Each spouse in turn should choose a positive topic: a behaviour exchange exercise that he or she liked, a pleasant memory of something the couple did together, or something positive involving the spouse.

6. The next exercise involves *recognizing and expressing emotions*, building on Exercise 5. It is often helpful to provide a list of 'feeling' words (Table 10.2) so the couple can test how a number of different emotive words fit, and begin to express themselves using more precise language. Have the couple paraphrase each other, with the speaker again talking about anything associated with positive feelings about the partner,

and the listener concentrating on understanding the emotional impact the event had on the speaker (e.g. 'When you pick me up from work and we go to dinner or a show I feel really cared for', or 'I am delighted when you call me at work to see how my day is going; it makes me feel warm and close to you').

Often, spouses will express their thoughts about an event as if they were stating feelings ('I feel that was the right thing to do' vs. 'I felt satisfied or pleased because I agreed with what you did'). In such cases the therapist needs to point out the difference between thoughts and feelings about events, perhaps model a 'feeling statement', and/or prompt the partner for his or her feelings.

Assignments to be done at home during communication training generally involve each spouse switching roles between speaker and listener and

Table 10.2 Examples of 'feeling' words to help partners link their spouse's behaviour with their emotions

Positive	Negative
calm	disappointed
warm	frustrated
happy	alone
delighted	trapped
close (to partner)	ashamed
content	bored
secure	restless
strong	nervous
elated	tired
turned on	lonely
excited	depressed
trustful	rebellious
responsive	guilty
satisfied	tense
relaxed	embarrassed
sexy	distant
loving	powerless
proud	unhappy
energetic	empty
special	angry
affectionate	vulnerable
paid attention to	insecure
loved	hurt
pleased	afraid
important (to partner)	confused

practising specific skills (appropriate to their progress) for 10–20 minutes, several nights a week. This way each spouse has an opportunity to practise both expressive and listening skills at each skill level several times during the week. It can also be quite useful to have the couple make an audio-recording of these exercises for the spouses themselves and/or the therapist to review.

Problem-solving

Problem-solving is an important component of most cognitive behaviour therapies, and especially when working with couples (see Chapter 12 for a full description of problem-solving across a wide array of settings and situations). Along with the communication skills described above, problem-solving skills provide the couple with a framework to be their own 'therapists' with many subsequent problems.

Problem-solving training has two discrete phases: *problem definition* and *problem solution*. This two-phase process helps couples to avoid proposing changes before the problem has been defined, and helps them to continue to redefine the problem when a solution to the originally defined problem has not been found.

In the problem-definition phase, one spouse starts by commenting positively about something the partner does that is related to the problem. This is followed by a specific description of the problem, then by his or her emotional response to the problem.

In the spirit of collaboration, the first spouse states how she or he contributes to the problem and what his or her own role is in the problem. Inducing the complainant to make this statement is crucial because

(1) it reduces the accusing nature of problem definition, helps the other spouse to feel less attacked, and encourages that spouse to listen and engage in the problem-solving endeavour; and

(2) it is consistent with the collaborative approach, which never allows one partner to be responsible for 100 per cent of any problem or 100 per cent of any solution.

Explaining this rationale to the couple usually facilitates their compliance with this format.

The partner is encouraged to summarize the other person's statements and to show willingness to work with the spouse to solve the problem which has been identified. The first spouse then paraphrases this statement as well. A problem definition might go like this:

Sally 'I really appreciate the effort you make to come home on time, and feel as though you really care about me when you ask me how my day was, but when you come home from work, throw your stuff down on the couch, and start complaining about how awful your day has been and don't ask me how I am, I feel hurt and ignored.'

James 'I think you're saying that you like it and feel I'm paying attention to you when I do ask you how your day was, but when I don't do that, and instead come home all fired up from all the junk that's gone on at the office and maybe can't seem to focus on anything else, especially you, you feel hurt and ignored, is that right?'

Sally 'Yes, that's how I feel. I guess that I do think I contribute to this problem because I've never told you how important it is to me to have a bit of your attention when you come home. I've never asked you, and you probably didn't know. I guess I sometimes might snap at you, too, because you don't give me the attention I want.'

James 'So it seems you think your part in this is that you haven't told me before how you felt about this, about how important it is to you, did I get that?' [Sally nods.] 'And that sometimes you could be more cheery when I get home?' [Sally agrees.] 'I can see how this is a problem for you and our relationship and I really want to work with you on this and find a way to resolve it.'

Sally 'You're saying you are willing to work with me on this problem?'

James 'Right.'

The first step in the problem-solution phase is to *brainstorm* and generate a list of potential solutions. Any solution is acceptable, and spouses should not censor their own solutions or start to evaluate their own or their partner's solutions. Solutions should continue to be suggested until the couple cannot think of any more, and each one should be written down. The therapist may add suggestions to the discussion, perhaps including a few humorous ones to ease the tension of the situation. A list for Sally's and James' problem might include:

1. James will run around the neighbourhood for 15 minutes to work off any tension from work before he sets foot in the door.
2. When James comes home he'll find Sally and give her a hug, then they'll ask each other about how their days were. Each gets five minutes to talk about their day.
3. If James needs more time to complain about work, he will ask Sally is she's willing to listen and she'll set a time limit for how long she wants to listen. If she does not, James will call a friend.
4. James will contact a job counsellor to talk about career options.
5. Sally will put her hand across James' mouth and start talking about herself if James forgets and starts to complain about work without asking.
6. James will never talk about work with Sally.
7. Sally will make a 'selfish' demand for equal time if she listens to James' complaints about work, such as ask for a back rub, or to sit on his lap while watching TV.
8. Sally will use her best listening skills when James talks about work, and he will also listen with interest when she talks about her day.
9. James will quit his awful job.

10. James will talk with his boss about how his job could be made more tolerable.

After the couple has brainstormed a list of potential solutions, each solution is evaluated by four criteria:

1. Is it absurd?
2. Would this solution help solve the problem?
3. What are the pros for this solution? and
4. What are the cons for this solution?

The ultimate agreement is likely to be a combination of the most helpful solutions on the list that have the fewest negative consequences. The change agreement should include who will do what when, where, and how, in specific terms. The ultimate agreement to Sally and James' problem might be:

James will talk with his boss about his concerns within the next week and explore changes that could be made to make his job more tolerable. If his boss or his position is not flexible, James will call the therapist for names of job counsellors and will explore other job options.

When James comes home from work, he will find Sally and be affectionate (e.g. give her a hug and kiss) and each will tell the other how it feels to see the partner. Both partners will then talk for five minutes each about how their days went. If James or Sally want more time to talk about something bad that happened during their day that does not involve a complaint about the partner, she or he can ask for the spouse's time. The spouses will be free to refuse or set a limit to the time each thinks he or she would be able to be a good listener. The spouse who needed to talk can call a friend if there is a need to talk further about the day's problems.

The solution needs to be checked to ensure that each spouse can do the things he or she has agreed to do. The therapist needs to play devil's advocate and question anything that seems implausible, unlikely to be carried out, or likely to be a block to its success. In the solution above, for example, what will James and Sally do if the job is inflexible and the job counsellor is unhelpful? What will they do if James forgets to be affectionate and just launches into a barrage of complaints about his day? In order to explore potential pitfalls, the therapist should ask the questions, 'What might prevent you from carrying out this agreement? What would get in the way?'

An effective progression in problem-solving is to start with more minor problems involving practical issues (e.g. who makes dinner, when), and then move onto more global, thematic, and emotional issues.

Affection and sexual enrichment

It is not uncommon for couples who present for marital therapy to also have some specific sexual dysfunction. For these couples, therapy time is

devoted to ameliorate the dysfunction(s). The treatment of sexual dysfunctions is discussed in Chapter 11.

With couples who have no specific sexual dysfunction it is often important at an appropriate point in therapy to emphasize affection and the
enhancement of the sexual relationship. Timing will depend upon how
important these areas are relative to other presenting issues.

Couples can benefit from applying behaviour exchange, communication
training and problem-solving skills to issues regarding intimacy, sexuality,
and affection. Because discussing these issues may be difficult and/or
emotionally-charged, the therapist must be sensitive to whatever fears
couples may have and the possible tendency to avoid these topics. The
rationale for work in the areas of affection, intimacy, and sexual enrich-
ment is that work in these areas helps foster closeness, not just the
reduction of conflict as in most of the therapy.

There are a number of exercises the couple may try, depending on an
assessment of their needs, strengths, and weaknesses. The reader is
directed to Chapter 11 in this volume and, in addition, Kaplan (1974,
1979), Zilbergeld (1978), and Barbach (1983) for a more complete discussion of these and other exercises. Useful exercises might include:

(1) sharing a memory of a positive affectional experience;

(2) guided fantasy exercises about ideal affection and sexual situations;

(3) communication exercises for giving feedback when receiving affection and during sex;

(4) non-genital and genital sensate focus;

(5) problem-solving regarding initiation and refusal of sexual activity;
and

(6) brainstorming other ways to enhance sexuality, perhaps including
new sexual behaviours.

Reducing conflict: trouble-shooting

Sometimes couples will come to sessions angry and frustrated, seemingly
unable to focus on new business and proceed with the session. This
generally occurs when they have had an unsolved argument during the
week. *Trouble-shooting* is a technique designed to teach couples *conflict
de-escalation* (keeping conflict from getting increasingly more hostile and
damaging), which facilitates conflict resolution. The goals of trouble-
shooting are both cognitive and behavioural: to help the couple understand their thoughts and feelings during the argument, and to make them
aware of behavioural options to stop the escalation of the argument so
they can turn their attention to a resolution of the conflict. Two steps are
involved in trouble-shooting:

1.   *Reconstruction* of the argument (in session) involves an exploration

of the intent and impact of each step in the argument, and clarification of the feelings, thoughts, and assumptions of each spouse at each step. The therapist must be careful to give both spouses an opportunity to present their perspectives on the argument, their thoughts and feelings at the time of the conflict, and their thoughts and feelings during the reconstruction.

2. *Exploration* of the cognitive and behavioural options of each spouse at each step that might have reduced the negative feelings or de-escalated the conflict. This may be accomplished by simply asking each spouse 'What was a different way of thinking about your partner's actions at that time', or 'What else could it have meant?' At each step, the therapist should ask (and sometimes have each spouse write down) 'What might you have *done* differently at that point to keep things from getting worse?' By keeping track of the options for behavioural change at each step, the couple compiles numerous possible ways to modify their own actions in future conflict situations. The therapist should, of course, point out how one spouse can influence the other's behaviour by also doing something differently. This approach helps each spouse to take responsibility for his or her own actions, decreases blaming of the other, and shows both spouses ways for reducing conflict situations.

Identifying and altering negative patterns of interaction

In the course of trouble-shooting, it may be possible to identify particular *themes* of conflict and the couple's typical *pattern* of conflict escalation. It may be useful to think of these characteristic dysfunctional interactional patterns as 'dances', where both partners know the 'steps' and work together in the escalation of conflict. Sullaway and Christensen (1983) have identified several common themes about which couples often have difficulty:

1. In the *demand/withdraw* pattern, one spouse typically demands more and more attention or affection from his or her partner, who initially was somewhat withdrawn. The increasing demands result in this partner withdrawing still further.

2. In the *relationship vs. work-oriented* pattern (or, affiliation vs. independence; Jacobson and Margolin 1979) one spouse puts a higher priority on the relationship, while the other spouse is more focused on career or vocational interests.

3. With the *emotional/rational* pattern, there is one emotionally escalating partner (stereotypically the wife) who is matched with an increasingly rational, non-emotional, and logical partner (stereotypically the husband).

Simply identifying the conflict pattern may be helpful for some couples. In such cases just examining the conflict process is sufficient for both spouses to eliminate the destructive pattern. Alternatively, patterns of arguments about the above themes or others may be addressed in the problem-solving format described earlier. However, during an argument spouses are not as likely to engage in a collaborative problem-solving effort, and conflict often escalates too rapidly for couples to be able to attempt rational problem-solving. The most practical intervention may be to help the couple to identify their pattern of conflict escalation and some early warning signs of their 'dance'.

Early signs of impending conflict escalation might include emotional arousal, a pattern of verbal accusations, or the invocation of sensitive topics. The therapist should help each spouse identify as many warning signs as possible early in the conflict. For example, a spouse might identify these early warning signs: 'I'm starting to sweat and feel tense, and these are signs that things might explode.' Then, when either or both spouses identify these indicators they can cut off or redirect their discussion, thereby thwarting the established destructive conflict pattern: 'In this situation, things have got out of hand in the past. We need to take time out and I need to go for a walk before we can talk about this constructively.'

These interactional patterns can have widespread impact on the relationship because many minor problems may be manifestations of the same theme. For example, 'He doesn't ask me about my day', 'He doesn't tell me how he feels', and 'He never wants to go anywhere together' are all complaints involving the theme of the wife's desire for more closeness and the husband's desire for more independence (and foretell his subsequent withdrawal). Rather than having arguments about each of these specific instances of the general theme, and rather than having a whole series of problem-solving sessions, the couple could resolve this set of issues together if the theme were properly identified.

Helping to generalize treatment gains throughout therapy

The success of therapy depends on how well the skills learned in the therapy sessions are carried out in the home environment. Diligent completion of assignments between sessions is crucial to the success of marital therapy because these exercises are the bridge between successful therapy and the couple's ability to maintain or even advance their gains after therapy is over.

In addition to assigning increasing responsibility to couples for their exercises while fading out therapist involvement, the therapist should tie each exercise, rule, or role-play to a principle, thus helping the couple to generalize from the specific to the general in order to apply the principle to future situations. After working on one problem area the therapist should regularly ask 'In what other areas could you apply this solution?', and/or 'At what times wouldn't this agreement work?', and help the couple to generalize from their specific agreements. This discussion might be backed up by a homework assignment in which the couple agree to use the technique in a novel situation.

It is also important that the couple understand the rationale for employing each skill so that, for example, if one spouse begins problem-solving it is understood by the partner to be 'because my partner will be more receptive to working on this problem with me', rather than 'because the therapist told us to'.

There are a number of other techniques the therapist might employ to enhance generalization; for example by lengthening the time between sessions as the couple nears termination. With two weeks between sessions couples have more time for practice on their own and there is a greater opportunity for pitfalls to be identified. Rather than viewing new difficulties in a negative manner, couples should try to identify situations or problems that might result in new difficulties so that they can be addressed before termination (see 'Preventing relapse', below).

Another option is to dispense with formal termination of therapy and instead lengthen the time between sessions to six months or one year at a time. The knowledge that the couple will have a regular 'booster session' may provide motivation for them to practise and employ the skills learned, and the booster sessions themselves allow an opportunity to address new problems that might emerge over time.

The therapist should urge the couple to become their 'own therapists' by holding regularly scheduled meetings in a manner similar to attending therapy sessions. The couple should begin early in therapy to hold these 'state of the relationship' meetings every week and should continue to meet weekly, two-weekly, or monthly after therapy ends. The partners should use the time to discuss how well their relationship is working, engage in problem-solving, and/or just to have a specific time to tell each other how they are feeling about their marriage. They should do this even when their relationship has few or no apparent problems (perhaps especially at those times).

Preventing relapse

Regardless of the extent of progress or skill level a couple achieve, some lapses into old negative patterns or the rekindling of old problems inevitably occur. One way to reduce relapses (Marlatt and Gordon 1985) includes two basic components:

(1) anticipate and intervene to prevent the situations or behaviours that would increase the likelihood of a relapse; and

(2) establish strategies to help the patients recover from small setbacks to avert a complete relapse.

Much of the termination phase of therapy is devoted to work regarding the anticipation and correction of slips and lapses.

Toward the end of therapy it is important to direct the couple's attention to future events, dates, activities, etc. that might be stressful or have precipitated difficulties in the past. Some examples might include whether to have children (or additional children) or not; how they will deal with common parenting issues; if they are a two-career couple, what they will do if one of them receives an attractive job offer in another city; how they will spend their leisure time or 'disposable' income if they become more affluent, or, conversely, what will they do if a financial crisis occurs; or how they will deal with an ageing parent. Having anticipated a difficult situation, they may be able to problem-solve in advance, and hence build into their lives important coping or resolution strategies.

As was noted previously, distressed couples are reactive: greatly affected by the immediate situation, and hence liable to over-react to minor difficulties. The second aspect of the relapse-prevention model is to minimize the impact of slips on the relationship, perhaps by identifying and minimizing spouses' reactivity. This might include additional cognitive work (see 'Cognitive interventions', p. 355), imagining lapses and planning adaptive, non-destructive responses.

The therapist should work with the couple to identify signs that they are slipping back into old, negative patterns. Signs of an impending relapse might include skipping or avoiding formal problem-solving sessions or 'state of the relationship' meetings, or decreases in pleasurable activities, including sexual and social activities together. Recognition of these signs of a likely lapse could prompt the couple to

(1) use their relationship skills to define and solve the problems; and/or

(2) consider re-entering marital therapy.

Outcome

Limitations of treatment

Five characteristics of couples seem to be related to poor outcome with cognitive–behavioural marital therapy (Jacobson *et al.* 1985).

1. Individuals with *severe emotional or behavioural problems* (e.g. depression, schizophrenia, intellectual deficiencies) are likely to be more difficult to treat for marital distress. Marital therapy can be successful, if difficult, with couples in which there is the complication of individual psychopathology. A successful outcome is more likely if these individual problems are recognized early and treated, rather than left unrecognized or denied, and untreated. For couples in which a spouse has severe

individual psychopathology, marital therapy can be a useful adjunct to the primary treatment (e.g. medication, individual psychotherapy) for the individual with problems. Where there is evidence that some problems are the *result* of marital distress, marital therapy would be the primary treatment of choice. For example, depression is especially common among married women and marital distress is the most common complaint to precede a depressive episode (Paykel, Myers, Dienelt, Klerman, Lindenthal, and Pepper 1969).

If one or both partners have *unrecognized or denied* problems (e.g. alcohol or substance abuse or dependence, and/or physical violence in the marriage) marital therapy is not likely to be effective until these problems have been dealt with directly. For example, it is usually preferable for a husband who is physically abusive to his wife to be referred for individual or group therapy to increase anger-management skills; the wife needs to be protected and may benefit from involvement in a group for battered women.

2.   Therapy is based on the assumption that spouses can be rewarding to each other. Therefore, it is a poor prognostic sign if in the initial interview a couple have difficulty addressing questions such as 'What first attracted you to each other?', and 'What have you done together that was fun?' It is extremely difficult to induce attraction or passion, especially when it was never there to begin with. A couple may have decided to marry without knowing one another well, or for reasons not entirely rooted in their attraction to, and happiness with, one another (e.g. unplanned pregnancy).

3.   A couple may present with *differing expectations of therapy*. The therapy framework is based on the assumption that the couple are committed to remaining together; the emphasis on skills training in therapy is not appropriate for helping couples who have already decided to split up. Therapy is unlikely to be effective when one spouse has already decided to leave the relationship.

4.   The spouses may be generally compatible, attracted to one another, and able to please each other, yet have developed *an apparently insurmountable problem* in their relationship. A common example is whether or not to have children. If one spouse strongly wishes to have children and the other does not, there is no easy compromise, since a choice in either direction would sacrifice one spouse's position. Since problem-solving is based on finding solutions that are acceptable to both spouses any major problem with only two possible outcomes is seemingly insoluble.

5.   Some couples are *unwilling to accept the assumptions and premises on which cognitive-behavioural marital therapy is based*. Such spouses may be unwilling to be collaborative, accept responsibility for problems,

or accept compromise solutions, despite the therapist's best efforts. Some spouses will balk at what they perceive to be the mechanistic nature of the skills-training exercises and will not accept the rationales presented for why assignments between sessions and practice are necessary. Some couples feel that a focus on the present is not in their best interests and insist that they need psychodynamically oriented therapy or other work that involves more attention to spouses' family of origin and attaining insight into their problems.

Results of controlled research trials

Many studies have examined the effectiveness of earlier versions of behavioural marital therapy, which usually were limited to behaviour exchange and communication/problem-solving interventions. While the efficacy of newer cognitive–behavioural marital therapy formats, such as those described in this chapter, needs to be investigated, a review of outcome studies of earlier approaches of this kind (Baucom and Hoffman 1986) showed this approach to be fairly effective in alleviating marital discord. This type of marital therapy seems to be quite effective in reducing communication problems, decreasing reported problem areas, and increasing overall marital satisfaction.

A more stringent re-analysis of the data from four outcome studies using these earlier cognitive–behavioural marital therapy approaches found more modest results than had been previously suggested (Jacobson, Follette, Revenstorf, Baucom, Hahlweg, and Margolin 1984). This re-analysis found that by the end of therapy about half of treated couples showed significant improvement, and approximately one-third of couples appeared to be non-distressed. However, clinically significant statistical improvements were often limited to just one spouse in the couple.

Despite the need to be cautious about treatment gains using any approach, it is important to note that over the past 15 years cognitive–behavioural marital therapy has consistently been found to be as or more effective than any other type of marital therapy.

Recommended reading

Gottman, J., Markman, H., Notarius, C., and Gonso, J. (1976). *A couple's guide to communication*. Research Press, Champaign, Illinois.

Guerney, B. (1977). *Relationship enhancement*. Jossey-Bass, San Francisco.

Jacobson, N. S. and Gurman, A. S. (ed.) (1986). *Clinical handbook of marital therapy*. Guilford Press, New York.

Jacobson, N. S. and Margolin, G. (1979). *Marital therapy: Strategies based on social learning and behavior exchange principles*. Brunner/Mazel, New York.

Stuart, R. B. (1980). *Helping couples change: A social learning approach to marital therapy*. Guilford Press, New York.

11

Sexual dysfunctions

Keith Hawton

Sexual dysfunctions were formerly thought to arise almost entirely from early childhood experiences, especially abnormalities in childhood sexuality and child–parent relationships. Individual psychoanalytic therapy aimed at providing insight into unconscious conflicts was regarded as the treatment of choice. During the late 1950s and 1960s, behavioural therapy approaches, especially systematic desensitization, were introduced for some sexual difficulties. These were derived from a very different rationale, namely that most sexual problems are acquired (at whatever stage in life) in ways explained by learning theory and can therefore be changed using treatment methods based on learning principles.

The treatment available for people with sexual dysfunctions altered substantially following the publication in 1970 of the Masters and Johnson book *Human sexual inadequacy*. This described a novel and systematic approach, which subsequently became known as 'sex therapy', and which formed the initial basis of therapy as described in this chapter. It represented a considerable extension of the original behavioural concepts, with its particular emphasis on communication skills, education, and the involvement of both partners.

There was considerable enthusiasm for the Masters and Johnson approach during the 1970s, both because of the outstanding results they reported, and because the approach seemed to have common-sense validity and was relatively easy to learn and apply. Although this initial surge of enthusiasm was somewhat tempered when therapists found that they could not usually achieve the results they had been led to expect, it still represents the most effective psychological treatment available for the considerable number of couples who seek help for sexual disorders. However, it has also developed substantially since its introduction, particularly in terms of greater flexibility and variety of approaches, and lately with more emphasis on cognitive aspects of treatment.

While sex therapy is the most complex of current psychological approaches to sexual dysfunctions, other simpler approaches are also available for helping people with relatively mild problems. Often these are components of sex therapy—for example, education and practical advice. Sex therapy was originally introduced for the treatment of couples, which meant that there was little to offer the individual without a partner who presented for help. A significant recent development has been the adaptation of sex therapy to help individuals without partners. A further development has been the use of sex therapy to help people with physical handicaps (e.g. neurological disorders).

It is important to be aware that sexual dysfunctions can be due to physical as well as psychological factors. Indeed, recent findings suggest that many cases, especially of erectile dysfunction, may in the past have been misdiagnosed as psychogenic. However, it is probable that in almost every case where there is a physical basis for a sexual difficulty, psychological factors will have developed secondarily to complicate the situation. Thus while this chapter is directed primarily at patients without physical disorders, psychological treatments of the kind described here also have a significant place in the management of many people with sexual difficulties related to physical disorders.

The nature of sexual dysfunctions

A reasonable working definition of sexual dysfunction is *the persistent impairment of the normal patterns of sexual interest or response*. Thus sexual dysfunctions are distinguished from sexual deviations or variations, which are sexual behaviours that are regarded as qualitatively abnormal and may be harmful to other people. However, this definition is not entirely satisfactory because, first, it is virtually impossible to define the range of 'normal patterns' of sexuality; and, secondly, whether or not a person's sexual function is dysfunctional will depend on whether the person or his or her partner thinks there is a problem, and this may be influenced by expectations generated by other factors, including, for example, friends, the media, and medical opinion.

There is no universally accepted method of classifying sexual dysfunctions. The classification used here groups sexual dysfunctions in four categories—*sexual interest, arousal, orgasm,* and *other problems* which cannot be included in any of the first three groups (Table 11.1). Two important dimensions in describing sexual problems are the time of onset and the extent of the problem. The terms *primary* and *secondary* dysfunctions are used respectively to describe problems that have been present from the onset of sexual activity and those which developed after a period of satisfactory sexual functioning. The terms *total* and *situational* are used respectively to describe problems that are present in all sexual situations and those that only occur in some situations (e.g. sex with regular partner) but not others (e.g. sex with casual partner, during masturbation).

Within each category of sexual dysfunction there may be considerable variation. For example, the category of erectile dysfunction includes men

Cognitive behaviour therapy

Table 11.1 Classification of sexual dysfunctions

Category	Sexual dysfunctions	
	Women	Men
Interest	Impaired sexual interest	Impaired sexual interest
Arousal	Impaired sexual arousal	Erectile dysfunction
Orgasm	Orgasmic dysfunction	Premature ejaculation
		Retarded/absent ejaculation
Other	Vaginismus	Painful ejaculation
	Dyspareunia	Dyspareunia

who can obtain an erection when with a partner but who lose it during sexual intercourse, men who can only obtain partial erections, men who experience erections only when on their own, and men who never have erections under any circumstances. There are notes on each of the sexual dysfunctions of women and men in Tables 11.2 and 11.3 in order to assist the reader when trying to categorize a person's sexual dysfunction and to convey a fuller picture of the more common sexual difficulties.

A further sexual difficulty, *lack of sexual satisfaction*, is not appropriately grouped with the sexual dysfunctions, but is important among people who seek help. Most couples who seek help from sexual dysfunction clinics are dissatisfied with their sexual relationships (Frank, Anderson, and Kupfer, 1976); some of these do not have clear dysfunctions but specifically complain of 'lack of enjoyment'. Many factors may contribute to such complaints, including general relationship difficulties, partners no longer finding each other attractive, and boredom with unvaried sexual activity. Sometimes, however, this problem may be secondary to impaired sexual interest (Bancroft 1983).

Apart from lack of sexual satisfaction and specific complaints of sexual dysfunction, people with sexual difficulties may come to professional attention with a variety of other presentations, including depression, insomnia, gynaecological complaints, and infertility. Detection of their sexual problems may then depend on the skill of the professional worker, willingness to enquire about sexual adjustment, and awareness that such presentations may indicate sexual difficulties.

Causes of sexual dysfunction

Sexual dysfunctions can be caused by many factors. While the emphasis in this chapter is on those problems which have a psychological basis, it is imperative that the reader is aware of the importance of physical factors, including illness, surgery, and medication, as causes of sexual problems

Table 11.2 Notes on the sexual dysfunction of women

Impaired sexual interest (Other terms—'low libido'; 'inhibited sexual desire'). The most frequent dysfunction in women. Levels of 'normal' interest vary greatly between women. Sexual interest reflected in frequency of sexual acts with partner, sexual thoughts, and masturbation. Best guide to secondary dysfunction is comparison with previous level of interest. Distinguishing total primary dysfunction from lower end of normal range can be difficult. NB Often associated with general relationship difficulties (Hawton and Catalan 1986) and with depression (Weissman and Paykel 1974).

Impaired sexual arousal Failure of normal physiological responses (e.g. vaginal engorgement and lubrication) to sexual stimulation and lack of sensations usually associated with sexual excitement. Uncommon in women with unimpaired sexual interest, except following menopause and shortly after childbirth. Can occur in women with major inhibitions about sexuality.

Orgasmic dysfunction Usually includes absent or very infrequent orgasm. Important for therapeutic purposes to distinguish women who cannot experience orgasm with a partner but can through masturbation on own, from those who cannot or have never masturbated. Secondary orgasmic dysfunction often associated with general relationship difficulties (McGovern, Stewart, and LoPicollo 1975).

Vaginismus Sexual intercourse impossible or extremely painful because of spasm of vaginal muscles when penetration attempted (often a history of failure to insert tampons). Usually a primary problem, although may occur as a secondary problem following vaginal trauma or infection. Women with vaginismus often have distorted ideas about capacity and other characteristics of vagina. Most women with vaginsmus are otherwise normally sexually responsive (Duddle 1977).

Dyspareunia Pain during sexual intercourse. May be localized at entrance to vagina ('superficial', e.g. mild vaginismus, lack of arousal, vaginal infections, Bartholin's cyst) or 'deep' in vagina (physical cause likely—e.g. pelvic infection, endometriosis—although can be due to lack of arousal). Gynaecological assessment indicated.

(reviewed in, for example, Bancroft 1983; Hawton 1985, 1987). However, as noted above, even in cases associated with physical disorders physiological reactions to the disorder may have exacerbated the problem and can be amenable to sex therapy. For example, men with early peripheral nerve damage because of diabetes often become anxious when they find it more difficult to obtain and maintain an erection. As a result of this anxiety the erectile response may be considerably more impaired. In such cases a cognitive–behavioural approach to treatment may be highly appropriate.

It is useful to group causal influences into *predisposing factors* (those

Table 11.3   Notes on the sexual dysfunctions of men

Impaired sexual interest   (See Table 11.2.) Uncommon presenting problem (in UK but not USA), but is underlying cause in some cases of erectile dysfunction. Secondary impaired sexual interest often associated with general difficulties in relationship with partner, or with depression. In both primary and secondary cases organic causes (e.g. hypogonadism) should be excluded.

Erectile dysfunction   Most common problem among men who seek help—men often older than those with other dysfunctions. Range considerable (see p. 371). Erectile mechanism and response vulnerable to a variety of factors, both psychological (e.g. anxiety, distraction, performance demands) and physical (e.g. diabetes, circulatory problems, spinal cord lesions, antihypertensive medication).

Premature ejaculation   Difficult to define—probably best to use couple/individual's assessment of whether man's control is satisfactory (NB some people have unreasonable expectations). Usually a primary problem. Rapid masturbation might be a predisposing factor. Rapid ejaculation common in young men having first sexual encounters, at times of stress, and when sexual outlets have been temporarily unavailable—only persistent unwanted rapid ejaculation should be regarded as dysfunctional.

Retarded/absent ejaculation   Relatively uncommon dysfunction which affects both ejaculation and experience of orgasm. Should be distinguished from retrograde ejaculation when, due to physical disease, surgery (e.g. prostatectomy), or medication (e.g. thioridazine) orgasm experienced but ejaculate passes into the bladder. Ejaculation may occur with masturbation but not with a partner, or only in sleep, or never (suggests a physical cause). Retarded ejaculation—sexual stimulation needs to be continued for excessively long time before ejaculation occurs.

Painful ejaculation and dyspareunia   Painful ejaculation (or a burning sensation in the urethra after ejaculation) usually the result of infection (e.g. urethritis, prostatitis, cystitis). Extreme sensitivity of glans penis after ejaculation is normal. Dyspareunia (pain during sexual intercourse) also usually due to physical cause (e.g. tight foreskin, torn frenulum, infection).

---

which make a person vulnerable to developing a sexual problem), *precipitants* (the factors which lead to the appearance of a sexual problem), and *maintaining factors* (psychological responses to a sexual problem, attitudes, and other stresses which cause the problem to persist or worsen). In any one patient there is usually an interaction between these factors. For example, a 35-year-old man had never been confident about his ability as a lover ever since early adolescence when he was frequently teased by other boys because of his delayed puberty (*predisposing factor*). After a party at which he had been drinking heavily he failed to get an erection when attempting to make love to his wife (*precipitant*). Subsequently he became anxious whenever they began sexual activity because

Table 11.4 Psychological factors which may contribute to sexual dysfunction

---

Predisposing factors
Restrictive upbringing, including inhibited/distorted parental attitudes to sex
Disturbed family relationships, including poor parental relationship, lack of affection
Traumatic early sexual experiences, including child sexual abuse and incest
Poor sex education

Precipitants

Discord in general relationship	Random failure
Childbirth (although this may also cause sexual difficulties because of depression or physical factors)	Depression/anxiety
	Traumatic sexual experience
	Ageing
Infidelity	Psychological reaction to
Dysfunction in partner	organic factor

Maintaining factors

Performance anxiety (e.g. a man's need always to be an expert lover, or a woman's to have an orgasm whenever sex occurs in order to please her partner)	Loss of attraction
	Discord in general relationship
	Fear of emotional intimacy
	Inadequate sexual information (e.g. about how to stimulate the partner effectively)
Fear of failure (e.g. of loss of erection)	
Partner demands	
Poor communication (especially about each partner's sexual needs or anxieties)	Restricted foreplay (e.g. such that the female partner is not adequately aroused)
Guilt (e.g. about an affair)	Depression/anxiety

---

he thought he was losing his ability to get an erection (*maintaining factor*), and as a consequence he experienced persistent erectile failure. While maintaining factors are usually the most relevant from the therapeutic standpoint, the therapist often needs to attempt to understand (and help the patients do likewise) the predisposing factors and precipitants of a particular dysfunction.

The common predisposing factors, precipitants and maintaining factors which contribute to sexual dysfunctions are listed in Table 11.4. Some of the factors are speculative. Thus, while clinical experience and common sense suggest their relevance to sexual dysfunction, they may not have been investigated in a way which conclusively demonstrates a causal association. Child sexual abuse provides a good example. While women reporting abuse experiences are fairly common among clients of sexual dysfunction clinics, and samples of women who have been sexually abused in childhood report high rates of sexual dysfunction, the exact extent to which sexual abuse results in subsequent sexual dysfunction is unclear.

Barlow and colleagues have recently put forward some interesting ideas concerning the way anxiety and particular patterns of thinking combine to maintain sexual dysfunction (Beck and Barlow 1984; Barlow 1986). In summary, the findings of several research studies suggest that men with psychogenic erectile dysfunction experience negative affect, especially anxiety, in sexual situations, and tend to report that they are less aroused than indicated by objective physiological measures. Furthermore, when faced by stimuli related to sexual performance (e.g. partner's sexual arousal) they become concerned about performance and therefore distracted from the erotic stimuli, with a consequent reduction in arousal. These findings have implications for sex therapy because they emphasize the need to help patients to focus their attention on erotic thoughts and stimuli instead of on thoughts about performance (e.g. 'I shall never be able to keep this erection'). This is likely to be more effective than simply encouraging relaxation in sexual situations.

Assessment

Most of the rest of this chapter will be concerned with the treatment of couples, although some of the principles of sex therapy can be utilized in helping individuals without partners.

Aims of assessment

The aims can broadly be summarized as follows:

1. To define the nature of the sexual problem and what changes are desired.
2. To obtain information which allows the therapist to formulate a tentative explanation of the causes of the problem in terms of predisposing factors, precipitants, and maintaining factors.
3. To assess what type of therapeutic intervention is indicated on the basis of this formulation.
4. To initiate the therapeutic process, both by opening up discussion of sexual matters and by encouraging the partners to think about causal factors and possible solutions.

General aspects of assessment interviews

The therapist should explain the aims of the interview to both partners before the assessment begins. Initially the partners should be interviewed separately. This will allow each partner to be more forthright, and provides them with equal opportunity to express views on the problem. In this chapter it will be assumed that the therapist is working alone. However, co-therapists might adopt the policy of each therapist taking a detailed history from the same-sex partner, and then, during an interview with the other partner, briefly assessing his or her attitudes to the sexual problem.

Usually three-quarters of an hour with each partner is sufficient. Many patients become embarrassed during the initial interview. The therapist must be alert to this, and acknowledge it, perhaps by explaining how understandable it is that discussion of intimate personal matters is embarrassing, but, at the same time, emphasizing the need to obtain a clear understanding of the problem. One reason for embarrassment can be the patient feeling that he or she lacks the appropriate vocabulary to discuss sexual matters with a professional. It is important therefore to establish an agreed vocabulary, whether it be based on clinical or colloquial terminology. For example, the therapist might begin a question concerning ejaculation as follows: 'When you ejaculate . . . , do you call this . . . "coming"? . . . OK, when you come do you find . . . ?'

Therapists inexperienced in interviewing patients with sexual problems are also likely to feel embarrassed. In part this can be overcome through practice role-play interviews with colleagues. However, practice with patients is the best way of gaining confidence.

After the partners have been interviewed separately they should then be seen together. This allows the therapist a chance to explore any discrepancies between their individual accounts. However, at the end of the individual interviews the therapist should check if any information has been given which the person does not wish to be revealed to the partner. Obviously the therapist must explicitly respect confidentiality if the person requests it, but should discuss possible difficulties if the partner has revealed something which might be vital to resolving the sexual problem (e.g. an affair, sexual variation, or sexual trauma, of which the partner is unaware). The conjoint interview also allows the therapist to assess how the partners relate to each other, especially whether they are supportive of each other and share responsibility for the problem. Finally, the therapist should describe his or her understanding of the problem and discuss the possible therapeutic plans.

Assessment schedule

The areas that should be covered during the individual assessment interviews are listed in Table 11.5. A few points are made below about aspects of some of these areas.

The therapist should first establish whether there is actual sexual dysfunction, or whether a couple's complaint is due to misinformation (e.g. expectation that the female partner must always experience orgasm whenever they have sexual intercourse). In trying to define a couple's sexual

Table 11.5 Areas to cover during the assessment interviews with each partner

---

1. *The sexual problem*—its precise nature and development; desired changes in the sexual relationship (i.e. goals)
2. *Family background and early childhood*—including relationships with parents, parental relationship, family attitudes to sexuality
3. *Sexual development and experiences*—including attitudes to puberty, onset of sexual interest, previous sexual experiences and problems, masturbation, traumatic sexual experiences (e.g. sexual abuse), homosexuality
4. *Sexual information*—source, extent, whether the person thinks he or she lacks information, and therapist's assessment of level of sexual knowledge
5. *Relationship with partner*—including its development, previous sexual adjustment, general relationship, children and contraception, infidelity, commitment to the relationship, feelings and attraction towards the partner
6. *School, occupation, interests, religious beliefs*
7. *Medical history*—including any current medication
8. *Psychiatric history*
9. *Use of alcohol and drugs*
10. *Appearance and mood* (mental state)
11. *Physical examination* (if appropriate)

---

problem the therapist should be aware that what is initially presented as a difficulty may not be the fundamental problem. For example, sometimes a couple complain that the man has premature ejaculation, when in fact he is able to sustain intercourse for a reasonable length of time, but his partner has difficulty reaching orgasm. Of course the reverse situation may also occur (e.g. a woman's apparent difficulty in experiencing orgasm may reflect her partner's poor ejaculatory control).

The therapist should obtain specific information, especially when assessing the presenting sexual problem. One of the most effective means of doing this is to enquire in detail about a recent occasion of sexual activity when the problem occurred. This should cover:

(1) the specific behaviour which occurred;

(2) what the person was thinking before, during and after it;

(3) how he or she felt about it.

People often find it difficult at this stage to say what they were thinking. If this is the case, the therapist might suggest some possibilities (e.g. for a man with erectile dysfunction—'Did you find yourself thinking, "Will I be able to keep my erection"?'; for a woman with orgasmic dysfunction—'Were you thinking that he might get bored with stimulating you for so long?'). This type of questioning will help to introduce the notion that the cognitive aspects of the problem may be at least as important as the behavioural aspects.

Having clearly established the pattern of sexual difficulty the therapist should enquire what changes the patient would like to achieve. The therapist needs to establish whether the partners share common goals, or whether there is any major discrepancy between their aims. Clearly, if there is a discrepancy, this needs to be resolved *before* therapy begins.

In the assessment of background factors, the parental relationship is important because not only will this have provided an initial model for the individual, but (and this is extremely common) the person may, unwittingly, be using this as a standard against which his or her current relationship is judged. Attempts to establish a different sort of relationship are sometimes thwarted because the patient has an underlying assumption that the parental relationship is 'how things ought to be'.

The pattern of previous sexual relationships can provide important clues to factors relevant to the current difficulty. For example, people who have problems concerning emotional intimacy (i.e. the ability to sustain a close relationship in which there is mutual caring, trust, and open communication) may describe several previous relationships in which sex was initially satisfactory but subsequently deteriorated, usually because of loss of interest and, or failure to become aroused.

It is vital to enquire about masturbation, for several reasons. First, it has important diagnostic implications when, for example, trying to establish whether erectile dysfuncton is a situational or total problem, or whether an individual's loss of interest in sex, or orgasmic dysfunction, is total or confined to sex with the partner. Also, a pattern of rapid masturbation to ejaculation may be a predisposing or maintaining factor in premature ejaculation. Secondly, attitudes to masturbation may provide clues to the origin of the current sexual difficulty. For example, guilt about masturbation may indicate general inhibitions about sex. Thirdly, masturbation may be a necessary element in therapy, especially when treating total primary orgasmic dysfunction or premature ejaculation, and when treatment is conducted with an individual without a partner (Hawton 1985). A useful way of broaching what can be an embarrassing topic is to ask, 'When did you find out about masturbation?'

Increasingly often a history of sexual abuse is found in people with sexual difficulties. This should always be asked about directly (e.g. 'Have you ever had an upsetting sexual experience, perhaps involving an older person or someone in your family?'), although the therapist should be aware that some people may be unwilling to reveal such experiences at the initial assessment. Enquiry about homosexuality (e.g. 'Have you felt sexually attracted to people of your own sex?') is also important, not only because current homosexual interest may be relevant in understanding the sexual problem, but because patients of both sexes often incorrectly think their difficulty may be the result of hidden homosexual tendencies, relying on an isolated homosexual experience in adolescence as evidence for this.

The therapist should question the patient directly about how well informed he or she feels about sexuality (e.g. 'Do you know as much about sex as you think you ought to?'). However, it is important also to make an independent assessment of this on the basis of the person's answers throughout the interview. Patients who say they 'know all about it' are often remarkably ignorant.

A clear picture should be established of the development of the relationship with the partner, both sexually and in general. In particular, the therapist should determine whether the sexual relationship has ever been satisfying. It is important to assess the couple's general relationship because sexual and general relationship problems often co-exist. Aspects that should be focused on include how the partners feel towards each other, their commitment to the relationsip, how easily they can communicate with each other (both generally and about sex), and whether any affairs have occurred during this relationship. A useful and often revealing initial question is, 'How would you compare your relationship with that of other couples you know—worse than average, average, better than average?' Another key question concerns what will happen to the couple if the sexual problem is not resolved. Sometimes the dysfunctional partner assumes incorrectly that the other partner will leave if things do not improve.

Sexual difficulties, especially impaired sexual interest, are common in people with psychiatric disorders, particularly depression. Therefore it is important to assess whether there is any evidence of current psychiatric disorder. Also, the therapist should enquire about any previous psychiatric problems. Not only may this have prognostic implications (p. 403), but some sexual dysfunctions, especially impaired sexual interest and erectile dysfunction, begin during an episode of psychiatric disorder (Schreiner-Engel and Schiavi 1986). The effects of depression on self-esteem and other important cognitive factors may be very relevant to the persistence of the sexual problem.

Details of the physical examination to exclude physical disorder will not be provided here (see Hawton 1985). Obviously, the therapist should be alert to any possible organic aspects of the problem. Non-medical therapists working in this field ought to have access to a medical practitioner who can advise when medical referral is indicated. Physical examination can also have important therapeutic functions, especially reassurance. In the treatment of vaginismus a vaginal examination is occasionally an important factor in achieving progress (p. 392). Such strategies should only be used by medically qualified therapists.

Choice of treatment

Psychological approaches to sexual problems can broadly be grouped into *brief counselling* and *sex therapy*. Brief counselling, including education and advice, will be appropriate for many people with sexual difficulties, especially those seen in general practice. The usual indications will be:

(1) the sexual problem is of recent onset and appears to be uncomplicated;

(2) the main need is for education;

(3) the couple have gone some way to resolving the problem themselves; and

(4) it is unclear whether sex therapy is necessary, and therefore brief counselling seems a sensible initial approach.

Individuals without partners may also largely be treated using brief approaches (Hawton 1985).

Indications for sex therapy

There are no absolute guidelines for when to offer sex therapy. Reasonable indications include:

(1) sexual problems of long duraton (at least a few months);

(2) efforts by the couple themselves to solve the problem have proved unsuccessful;

(3) the problem is likely to be caused or maintained by psychological factors (e.g. aversive previous sexual experience, performance anxiety, poor self-esteem);

(4) the problem is threatening the overall relationship between the partners.

Further factors which should be taken into account in deciding whether sex therapy is appropriate include:

General relationship Sex therapy should not be offered, at least initially, if the sexual difficulty is largely symptomatic of problems in the couple's general relationship. In such a situation marital therapy may be more appropriate. Furthermore, even if the sexual difficulty is not of this kind, a poor general relationship usually rules out sex therapy until the couple's overall relationship has improved. When a therapist is in doubt, a few sessions, say three, of sex therapy might be offered to test whether this approach is likely to help. However, it is preferable to prolong the assessment over two or three sessions, spaced over a few weeks. Having the couple attempt some non-sexual homework assignments (see Chapter 10) can often clarify the situation.

Psychiatric disorder   Major psychiatric disturbance usually precludes sex therapy until the disorder has been adequately treated. However, minor psychiatric symptoms, such as mild to moderate depression or anxiety, are not necessarily contraindications to sex therapy, especially if the symptoms appear, in part at least, to be caused by the sexual difficulty.

Alcoholism   Sex therapy should not be offered if either partner has a major current problem of alcohol abuse, because poor compliance and general relationship difficulties are likely to interfere with treatment.

Pregnancy   Clinical experience indicates that it is unwise to begin sex therapy if the female partner is pregnant, because the natural loss of sexual interest which often occurs in late pregnancy limits the chances of success. It is best to reassess the couple some 3–6 months after the birth to see if there is still a problem.

Motivation   It is not easy to assess accurately the enthusiasm of partners to engage in the sex-therapy programme. Sometimes apparently highly motivated partners never engage, while a partner who appears poorly motivated at the outset may become more enthusiastic once the potential benefits of the programme become clearer. It is important to recognize that apparently poor motivation may reflect lack of understanding of either the rationale or aims of treatment. However, it is pointless offering sex therapy when it is clearly unacceptable to one or both partners.

Overview of sex therapy

The stages and components of sex therapy are summarized in Fig. 11.1. *Assessment* has already been described. The *formulation*, which is usually presented at the beginning of the second therapy session, provides a basis from which to initiate therapy (although the assessment interviews and the formulation can themselves also have important therapeutic benefits). The three principle ingredients of the treatment programme are:

(1) *graded homework assignments*, which are presented throughout therapy;

(2) *counselling* (including the cognitive aspects of therapy) which will be necessary whenever blocks are encountered in the programme of homework assignments; and

(3) *education*, which occurs throughout therapy, and is also the focus of a specific treatment session.

While all three components are integrated in treatment, it will be clearer to the reader if they are described separately. *Termination* of therapy is also important, especially in terms of prevention of further difficulties. A *follow-up session* a few months after treatment ends can be therapeutic as well as allowing the therapist to check whether a couple's progress has been maintained.

General relationship therapy will be necessary for some couples, either at the onset of treatment or subsequently. However, the author does not think it advisable to try to carry out *full* sex therapy and marital therapy programmes in parallel. A useful principle in sex therapy is to adhere to addressing issues in the sexual relationship unless difficulties in the general relationship impede this to the extent that the latter must be dealt with. Approaches for helping with general relationship problems were described in the previous chapter.

Couples should be told at the outset of treatment that there will be specific review sessions and that treatment will be terminated if the partners or the therapist feel it is not proving effective. The third session (not counting the assessment) is a useful time for the first review because it can encourage early involvement in the homework assignments. It also provides an early 'escape route' for either the partners or the therapist. The last point is important because progress (in terms of carrying out the homework assignments) by this stage is a very good indication of the likely eventual outcome (Hawton and Catalan 1986).

At the start of treatment the couple should also be told that while treatment sessions will usually be conducted with both partners, the therapist may wish to see the partners individually at some stage in order to obtain their views about progress. This can also allow the partners to discuss factors that they did not feel able to mention during the assessment but which may be very relevant to the progress of treatment (Haw-

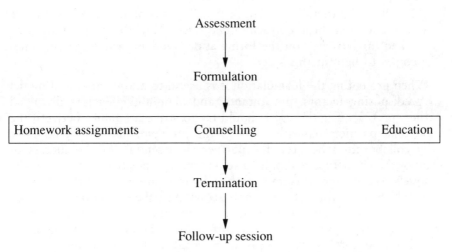

Fig. 11.1 Stages and components of sex therapy

ton, Catalan, Martin, and Fagg 1986). Weekly treatment sessions, lasting 30 minutes to an hour, are the most practical for therapists and couples. Sometimes, when progress is slow, it is worth switching to twice-weekly sessions for a couple of weeks. During the later stages of the programme the sessions might be more widely spaced (e.g. fortnightly), and a longer gap, of say three or four weeks, is usually arranged between the penultimate and final sessions of treatment. This allows for consolidation of progress, helps ensure that the couple take full responsibility for their relationship, but also provides a chance for discussion of any remaining difficulties. The follow-up session is in part an extension of this process. The length of treatment can vary greatly, but between 8 and 20 sessions are sufficient to complete treatment with virtually all couples.

Formulation

At the beginning of sex therapy the couple should be presented with a brief and simple account of the nature of their problems and possible contributory factors. It is best to present the formulation at the start of the treatment session when the homework assignments are going to be described. The aims of the formulation are:

1. To help the couple understand their difficulties—this can be a source of encouragement, especially if the therapist also explains how common such problems are.

2. To point out likely contributory factors, particularly the maintaining factors which will be the focus of therapy, and thus establish a rationale for the treatment approach.

3. To allow the therapist to check that the information obtained in the assessment has been correctly interpreted. Thus the couple should be asked for feedback on the formulation. New information sometimes comes to light at this stage.

When presenting the formulation it is useful to adopt the causal model of predisposing factors, precipitants, and maintaining factors discussed earlier (p. 373). The therapist should try to strike a balance between the individual partners' contributions to the problem, and thus emphasize why collaboration between the partners is essential for the success of therapy. The therapist should also emphasize positive aspects of the couple's relationship. It is important to indicate any parts of the formulation which are hypothetical, emphasizing that these can be tested out during treatment, and to explain that new information is likely to become apparent as therapy proceeds. The formulation should be recorded in the couple's case notes so that it can be referred to during therapy.

Table 11.6 Summary of a formulation

Jane, aged 28, and Peter, aged 36, had presented because Jane lacked interest in sex and disliked sexual intercourse

At the end of his assessment the therapist explained that *the problem* appeared to be Jane's lack of interest in sex, and also the pain she experienced during sexual intercourse, which occurred because she was not fully aroused.

Predisposing factors
Several factors had contributed to Jane originally feeling uncertain about sexuality, especially:
(1) her inhibited upbringing in which she was encouraged to regard sex as 'dirty';
(2) her lack of sex education and consequent poor sexual information; and
(3) her guilt about her only previous sexual relationship, which had been with an older, married man
When their relationship began, Peter had lacked confidence in his sexual ability, largely because his first wife had left him for another man

Precipitants
Understandably, both partners were very hesitant and uncertain when their sexual relationship began. As a result, Jane did not become very aroused and therefore sexual intercourse was painful. Subsequently whenever they attempted to make love Jane immediately started to feel anxious, worrying whether sexual intercourse would again be painful. Therefore she hardly got aroused at all, intercourse was just as uncomfortable as she had feared it would be, and she gradually lost interest in sex altogether.

Maintaining factors
The problem appeared to have persisted because both partners thought each sexual episode would be a failure and anticipatory anxiety prevented Jane feeling any interest in sex. Furthermore, Jane and Peter found it difficult to discuss the problem and hence work out possible solutions.

The positive features in this case included the fact that Jane and Peter's general relationship was happy and affectionate, the relatively short duration of the problem (15 months), and the clear enthusiasm of both partners to overcome the difficulty

---

A summary of a formulation, illustrating the points above, is given in Table 11.6.

The presentation and discussion of the formulation need not take long, say 15–20 minutes. Once this stage has been completed, the therapist should explain that it is important for both partners to be involved actively in treatment because both contribute in some way to the problem and a collaborative approach is the only one likely to succeed. After this the initial homework assignments can be discussed.

Homework assignments

Before describing what the therapist wants the couple to do during the first week, the overall homework assignments should be explained. These are:

1. To provide a structured approach which allows the couple to rebuild their sexual relationship gradually.
2. To aid identification of the specific factors which are maintaining the sexual dysfunction. These include cognitions and attitudes, especially those not apparent at the outset.
3. To provide the couple with specific techniques to deal with particular problems.

Most therapists use a basic programme of homework assignments which they apply in the treatment of the majority of couples, although there has to be flexibility about the emphasis on each stage, depending on the nature of a couple's problem and their rate of progress. The stages of this programme, which are labelled using the terminology introduced by Masters and Johnson (1970), are:

(1) *Non-genital sensate focus*, which is intended particularly to help a couple establish physical intimacy in a comfortable and relaxed fashion, and to allow open communication about feelings and desires;
(2) *Genital sensate focus*, which aims to facilitate sexually arousing caressing, without undue anxiety;
(3) *Vaginal containment*, which is an intermediate stage before full sexual intercourse begins.

These three stages will be described first, before examining specific strategies which may be grafted onto this programme in order to deal with particular problems. However, it must be emphasized that the homework assignments are only one element in treatment and if used alone will rarely bring success. Blocks to progress with the homework assignments occur in the treatment of most couples, and are to be expected. The therapist must use counselling skills (described later) to help a couple understand the reasons for the difficulties and assist them to overcome them.

There are some important general principles concerning the instructions for the homework assignments.

1. The instructions must be detailed and precise.
2. The therapist should always check that the couple have fully regis-

tered and understood the instructions before the treatment session ends.

3. When giving new instructions the therapist should ask the couple how they feel about them and whether they anticipate any difficulties. If problems are anticipated, the therapist should endeavour to resolve their fears before they attempt the assignment. For example, a woman was very apprehensive about moving from non-genital to genital sensate focus. When asked what she thought might happen she said she feared that stimulation of her husband's genitals would arouse him so much that he would demand sexual intercourse. When the husband was asked for his views he reassured her that this would not be the case and that indeed he would welcome her providing him with more sexual stimulation.

4. A couple should not be asked to move on to the next stage of the programme until they have mastered the current assignments.

5. A couple should never be left with the option of moving from one stage to the next between treatment sessions depending on how they progress, because the uncertainty can be detrimental to progress.

6. The couple should be informed that the therapist will be asking for detailed feedback on progress at the next treatment session.

Non-genital sensate focus

This stage, which is beneficial for most couples with sexual dysfunction, is especially helpful for couples whose whole sexual relationship is impaired (e.g. by anxiety or pessimistic attitudes resulting from repeated failures) and those who find it difficult to discuss their physical relationship.

Before describing the initial assignments, the therapist should explain the aims of this stage, namely to help the partners develop a sense of trust and closeness, to become more aware of what each likes, and to encourage communication.

The couple are first requested to refrain from sexual intercourse and touching of each other's genitals and the woman's breasts. It should be explained that this is to ensure that they are not continually confronted by those aspects of sexuality most likely to cause anxiety, and to enable them to concentrate on rebuilding their physical relationship by first learning to enjoy general physical contact.

They are then instructed that during the following week one partner, when he or she feels like it, should invite the other partner for a homework session. This invitation should be explicit (e.g. 'I would like to try the caressing that the therapist suggested. Would you?'), and the other partner should accept the invitation if he or she is feeling either positive or neutral about it. If feeling negative, it is important that the partner says so but tries to explain why. These instructions are intended to open up communication and avoid partners feeling pressurized by each other. After the first session of caressing the pattern of inviting then alternates, so that the onus is on the other partner to invite next time.

The caressing sessions can occur wherever the couple wish, as long as they feel comfortable, warm, and there is no risk of them being disturbed. The eventual aim might be for the partners to be naked during sessions, with some low lighting in the room. Initially, however, they should begin at a stage which they will not find too threatening.

Non-genital sensate focus should begin with one partner (the one who gave the invitation) exploring and caressing the other partner's body all over, except the 'no-go' areas. The partners should do this in a way that gives pleasure to both of them. The other partner should try to concentrate on the sensations elicited by the caressing and provide feedback on what he or she likes and dislikes and how things could be improved (e.g. by being firmer, lighter, slower, or faster). Guiding the partner's hands can be a good way of doing this. During the early sessions this exercise may often be like a massage. The partners should swap round when they wish to, so that the 'passive' partner now takes over caressing. The session can go on as long as the partners want it to (usually between 10 minutes and half an hour) but they should avoid becoming bored.

Sexual arousal is not the objective at this stage, but if either or both partners does become aroused they are encouraged to enjoy this but not go beyond the agreed limits of caressing. Some couples find that a lotion (e.g. K-Y jelly or baby lotion) enhances the pleasure of sensate focus. There is no restriction on masturbation, should either partner wish to relieve sexual tension, but for the present this should be restricted to self-masturbation, not in the partner's presence.

While not wanting to impose too rigid a schedule it is important that the therapist makes it clear that the couple are expected to apply themselves during treatment and that three sessions of homework per week would be a reasonable frequency to aim for. Couples should be forewarned that they may find these sessions lacking in spontaneity at this stage, but that this is understandable when working at solving a problem. Most couples find their sessions become more spontaneous as therapy progresses.

Reactions to non-genital sensate focus

Initial reactions to this stage vary according to the nature of a couple's difficulties. Some couples immediately find non-genital sensate focus enjoyable. Others initially react negatively, and report, for example, not having had enough time for homework sessions, breaking the ban on sexual intercourse, negative feelings (e.g. tension, boredom), or one partner being unable to offer an invitation. The ways in which therapists can help couples overcome such problems are discussed later (p. 397). Only when this stage is well established should the couple progress to genital sensate focus.

Genital sensate focus

The aims of this stage should be explained to the couple, namely to make their caressing more sexual and arousing, but also to encourage them to continue discussing their feeling and desires.

To begin with the couple are asked to continue their pattern of alternate inviting and taking turns at caressing, but to extend this to include both partners' genitals and the woman's breasts. This should initially be gentle and exploratory, without sexual arousal being the objective. Instead, the partners should concentrate on the relaxed giving and receiving of erotic pleasure. If arousal occurs, then it should be enjoyed. The therapist must explain in some detail the types of caressing that couples like (see, for example, Kaplan 1987), emphasizing the need for this stage to be added to the previous one, not to replace it. Guiding the partner's hand can again be a useful means of helping the partner learn what is enjoyable. Lotion can also be used at this stage if the couple wish. When this stage is progressing well the couple are instructed to include mutual caressing as well as taking turns at being active and passive. Should either or both partners wish to experience orgasm they should feel free to do so, but this should not become the goal of the sessions.

Some of the specific techniques for dealing with particular dysfunctions are introduced at this stage (see below).

Reactions to genital sensate focus

As with non-genital sensate focus, some couples immediately find genital sensate focus pleasurable while others react adversely. This stage is particularly likely to generate anxiety, especially about sexual arousal or intimacy. The reader is reminded of Barlow's work discussed earlier which indicates that sexual arousal in dysfunctional individuals often results in attention to non-erotic cognitions and stimuli (p. 376). It is important, therefore, that the therapist specifically encourages partners to focus on pleasurable sensations. However, such encouragement may not be sufficient to deal with this particular problem; instead, the thoughts and attitudes which cause distraction may need to be explored (see p. 398).

Vaginal containment

This stage is an intermediate one in the introduction of sexual intercourse to the therapy programme. It is a relatively minor stage for couples whose

difficulties have by now largely resolved. For others it is extremely important, especially when vaginal penetration is a key step (e.g. vaginismus,
premature ejaculation, erectile dysfunction).

The couple are instructed that when they are both feeling relaxed and
sexually aroused the woman should introduce her partner's penis into
her vagina and the partners should then lie still, concentrating on any
pleasant genital sensations. The best positions for vaginal containment
are often the female-superior position or a side-by-side position. This is
important in the treatment of vaginismus because it helps the woman
retain a sense of control. Also, many men find that their ejaculatory
control is better in this position than in the male superior position
(although the reason for this is unclear). The therapist must describe the
position to be used in some detail, especially if the presenting problem
was the female partner's vaginismus and she has never had sexual intercourse. Drawings (e.g. Kaplan 1987) can be helpful.

The couple are asked to maintain containment as long as they wish,
and then to return to genital and non-genital pleasuring. They might
repeat containment up to three times in any one session.

Once this stage is well established the couple should introduce movement during containment. Sometimes it is best to suggest that the woman
starts moving first. This is again important if she presented with vaginismus as it allows her to maintain control over the situation and hence
allays fears of her being hurt. If all previous stages have progressed well
this final stage does not usually pose any major difficulties, except for
some men with premature ejaculation (see below). Subsequently the couple might, if they wish, experiment with different sexual positions.

This completes the general programme of homework assignments used
in sex therapy with most couples. Now the procedures which can be
superimposed on this programme for the treatment of specific sexual
dysfunctions will be described.

Procedures for specific sexual dysfunctions of women

Orgasmic dysfunction

If a woman has never experienced orgasm, masturbation training might
be considered, because most women find it easier initially to experience
orgasm on their own. This is summarized in Table 11.7. However, while
this approach is the treatment of choice for a woman who does not have
a partner, many couples will prefer to try to resolve the problem in the
context of their conjoint sexual activity.

A woman who can experience orgasm on her own should be encouraged to show her partner how she likes being stimulated, hand-on-hand
guidance being a good means of doing this. The therapist should emphasize the importance of clitoral stimulation for female orgasm. If the

Table 11.7 Summary of a masturbation training programme that may be used for women

---

The following steps should be recommended. The pace at which the woman proceeds should be dictated by how comfortable she is with the programme, not by a rigid schedule. At each stage the woman's attitudes to what she is being asked to do and what she has just done must be explored. Further cognitive work may be needed if highly negative attitudes are identified.

1. *General self-examination* This self-awareness exercise may be especially helpful if the woman has any negative attitudes to her body. She should examine herself generally while naked, and identify three aspects of her body she likes and three which she likes less. The attitudes to her body should be explored at the next treatment session. The aim is to get the woman 'in touch' with her body, and to help her develop a rational appreciation of it.

2. *Genital self-examination* Visual examination of genitals, using a mirror, identifying various areas that have previously been pointed out on a diagram by the therapist, followed by exploration of the genitals with the fingers, both outside and inside.

3. *Pelvic muscle exercises* (see p. 392).

4. *Masturbation* Genital stimulation to produce sexual arousal, with attention focused on erotic experiences or sensations.

5. *Adjuncts to masturbation* The following might be suggested in order to enhance sexual arousal:
   Erotic literature
   Sexual fantasies (Friday [1975] can help women who do not find it easy to have fantasies).
   Vibrator, if orgasm has not occurred after several weeks of regular masturbation. Anxieties about using one, especially of becoming dependent on it, must be discussed. Most women who become orgasmic with a vibrator are soon able to reach orgasm without it.

---

woman is unable to reach orgasm in spite of apparently adequate stimulation a vigrator might be suggested (Yaffe and Fenwick 1986). It is important to reassure the couple that this need only be a temporary measure. The therapist should also discuss the range of female orgasmic responsivity, emphasizing that many perfectly normal women experience orgasm on only some occasions of sexual activity but that sex for them is nevertheless extremely enjoyable and rewarding.

Once orgasm is possible with manual stimulation a 'bridge manoeuvre' (Kaplan 1987) can be used to help the woman become orgasmic during sexual intercourse. The partner (or the woman herself) should provide clitoral stimulation manually during vaginal containment, combined with slow pelvic thrusting by the woman. When she feels herself approaching orgasm she should begin vigorous pelvic thrusting, and continue to obtain clitoral stimulation, if possible, by pressing her clitoris against her partner's pelvis. Some women will eventually be able to experience orgasm during sexual intercourse without manual stimulation, but many will continue to need clitoral stimulation. Whatever the outcome the couple should be reassured that either is perfectly normal.

Vaginismus

There are several stages in the treatment of vaginismus:

1. *Helping the woman develop more positive attitudes towards her genitals* After the therapist has fully described female sexual anatomy, preferably using a photograph or diagram, the woman should be encouraged to examine herself with a hand mirror on several occasions. Extremely negative attitudes (especially concerning the appearance of the genitals, or the desirability of examining them) may become apparent during this stage, possibly leading to failure to carry out the homework. Some women find it easier to examine themselves in the presence of the partner; others may only get started if the therapist helps them do this first in the clinic. If this is necessary a medically qualified female therapist should be involved.

2. *Pelvic muscle exercises* These are intended to help the woman gain some control over the muscles surrounding the entrance to the vagina. If she is unsure whether or not she can contract her vaginal muscles she should be asked to try to stop the flow of urine when she next goes to the toilet; the pelvic muscles are used to do this. The woman can later check that she is using the correct muscles by placing her finger at the entrance to her vagina where she should be able to feel the muscle contractions. Subsequently she should practise firmly contracting these muscles an agreed number of times (e.g. 10) several times a day.

3. *Vaginal penetration* Once the woman has become comfortable with her external genital anatomy she should begin to explore the inside of her vagina with her fingers. This is partly to encourage familiarity and partly to initiate vaginal penetration. Negative attitudes may also become apparent at this stage (e.g. concerning the texture of the vagina, its cleanliness, fear of causing damage, and whether it is 'right' to do this sort of thing). The rationale for any of these objections must be explored. At a later stage the woman might try using two fingers and moving them around. Once she is comfortable inserting a finger herself her partner should begin to do this under her guidance during their homework sessions. A lotion (e.g. K-Y or baby lotion) can make this easier. Graded vaginal dilators were used in Masters and Johnson's original programme and are still used

today in many clinics. However, clinical experience has shown that the use of fingers is just as effective.

4. *Vaginal containment* When vaginal containment is attempted the pelvic muscle exercises and the lotion should also be employed to assist in relaxing the vaginal muscles and making penetration easier. This is often a difficult stage and the therapist therefore needs to encourage the woman to gain confidence from all the progress made so far. Persisting concerns about possible pain may need to be explored, including how the woman might ensure that she retains control during this stage.

Dyspareunia

If dyspareunia is caused by psychological factors, especially failure of arousal, therapy should largely be concerned with helping the woman become aroused through the sensate focus programme. However, even in such cases, and also in those where pain is due to a physical cause (e.g. endometriosis), advice on positions for vaginal containment and sexual intercourse in which there is less deep vaginal penetration (e.g. both partners lying on their sides, face-to-face) can be helpful.

Impaired sexual interest

No particular procedures are used in the treatment of this problem, the main emphasis being on setting the right circumstances for sexual activity, reducing anxiety, establishing satisfactory foreplay, focusing attention on erotic stimuli and cognitions, and resolving general relationship issues. Inhibitions about sexual behaviour or arousal often become obvious during treatment and will need to be explored (p. 398). Crowe and Ridley (1986) have found that negotiating a weekly timetable for sexual activity which represents a compromise between each partner's ideal frequency can be helpful.

Impaired sexual arousal

The general programme of homework assignments is also the main strategy for helping with this problem. The use of sexual fantasies can sometimes aid arousal (e.g. Friday 1975). However, since this is unacceptable to some couples, the therapist must broach the topic with sensitivity and caution. An oestrogen cream, or depot hormone replacement in women who have undergone hysterectomy, can greatly help women troubled by vaginal dryness (Bancroft 1983).

Procedures for specific sexual dysfunctions of men

Erectile dysfunction

Men with psychogenic erectile dysfunction will usually start experiencing erections during either non-genital or genital sensate focus. If the therapist suggests that during the initial phase the man tries *not* to have an erection this can have the opposite effect. As noted earlier, men with erectile dysfunction often have difficulty attending to erotic stimuli, especially when an erection develops, tending instead to think about the quality of their erection or whether they will be able maintain it. The therapist should specifically encourage the man to focus his attention on the pleasurable sensations he experiences during his partner's genital caressing (the use of a lotion can often heighten these sensations), areas of his partner's body that he finds arousing, and the pleasure of witnessing his partner's sexual arousal.

Once erections are occurring regularly the therapist should suggest that the couple stop their caressing during a session and allow the erection to subside. They should then resume their caressing—usually the man's erection will return, especially if his partner stimulates his genitals in a teasing and/or slow fashion. This waxing-and-waning exercise, which should be repeated two or three times each session, can help to dispel a man's fear that any loss of erection means that the erection will be lost completely and will not return.

When containment is introduced to the programme this should initially be kept brief, with the woman providing extra genital stimulation if there is any loss of erection.

Premature ejaculation

During genital sensate focus the couple should be taught either the stop-start (Semans 1956) or squeeze techniques (Masters and Johnson 1970).

The *stop-start technique* consists of the man lying on his back and focusing his attention fully on the sensation provided by the partner's stimulation of his penis. When he feels himself becoming highly aroused he should indicate this to her in a pre-arranged manner at which point she should stop caressing and allow his arousal to subside. After a short delay this procedure is repeated twice more, following which the woman stimulates her partner to ejaculation. At first the man may find himself ejaculating too early, but usually control gradually develops. Later a lotion can be applied to the man's penis during this procedure which will increase his arousal and make genital stimulation more like vaginal containment.

The *squeeze technique* is an elaboration of the stop-start technique, and probably only needs to be used if the latter proves ineffective. The couple proceed as with the stop-start procedue. When the man indicates he is becoming highly aroused his partner should apply a firm squeeze to his penis for about 15–20 seconds with her fingers in the position shown in Fig. 11.2. This inhibits the ejaculatory reflex. As with the stop-start technique this is repeated three times in a session and on the fourth occasion the man should ejaculate. Both procedures appear to help a man develop more control over ejaculation, perhaps because he gradually

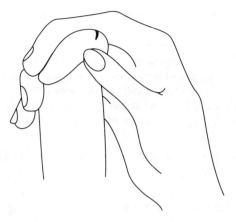

Fig. 11.2 Squeeze technique

acquires the cognitive techniques associated with ejaculatory control, or perhaps because he gradually becomes accustomed to experiencing sexual arousal without getting anxious.

Once either technique is successfully established the couple should proceed to vaginal containment, using the female superior position (p. 390). If the man becomes highly aroused he must indicate this to his partner who then lifts off him and either allows his arousal to subside or assists this with the squeeze technique. Most couples eventually become able to have full sexual intercourse with reasonable ejaculatory control, usually without the aid of either specific technique.

Retarded/absent ejaculation

When a man has never ejaculated, except in his sleep, an individaul masturbation training programme is usually recommended initially. Such a programme is outlined in Table 11.8. When ejaculation is possible on masturbation but not with the partner, or only with difficulty, the emphasis of the genital sensate focus programme is on the woman stimulating her partner's penis, at first gently and later more vigorously, using a lotion to enhance arousal and reduce friction. Some men find that self-stimulation helps at this stage. The man is encouraged to focus his attention on the sensations he is experiencing. If ejaculation occurs, in later sessions he should try to ejaculate close to his partner's vaginal entrance. Subsequently he should penetrate his partner when near to ejaculation and continue vigorous thrusting. The male superior position is recommended for this problem because this usually facilitates ejaculation. Increased stimulation of the glans penis can be provided during sexual intercourse by the woman (or man) gently pulling the skin at the basis of the penis downwards.

Table 11.8 Summary of a masturbation training programme that may be used for men

---

A masturbation training programme can be useful in the treatment of retarded/ absent ejaculation, premature ejaculation, or erectile dysfunction, although the type of programme will differ according to the presenting sexual dysfunction. In each case, the man's attitudes to what has been suggested must be explored first.

The following steps might be suggested in the treatment of *retarded/absent ejaculation:*

1. *Exploration of genitals and surrounding areas*—with the hands and fingers to identify areas of sensitivity.

2. *Masturbation*—varying the intensity of stimulation. Use of a lotion to heighten arousal and prevent soreness. When arousal is high, vigorous masturbation may result in ejaculation.

3. *Adjuncts to masturbation*:
   Sexual fantasies (Friday [1980] may help men who have difficulty generating sexual fantasies.
   Erotic literature
   Vibrator

In the treatment of *premature ejaculation*, the man should be encouraged to prolong masturbation for a fixed period (e.g. 15 minutes) before ejaculating. Later he should use a lotion in order that he can become used to more intense stimulation and higher arousal.

In the treatment of *erectile dysfunction*, during masturbation the man should allow his erection to subside for a while before continuing self-stimulation, and repeat this two or three times. This can help the man develop confidence in his erectile capability.

Impaired sexual interest

Again, as for women (p. 393), there are no psychological procedures used specifically for this problem, the main emphasis being on establishing a rewarding pattern of sexual behaviour and resolving any contributory interpersonal issues. The negotiated weekly timetable approach for discrepancies between partners' levels of sexual desire (p. 393) does not appear to be very effective when it is the male partner whose sexual interest is impaired.

Counselling

There are several non-specific aspects of sex therapy which may be important in the therapeutic process. These include the extent to which the therapist adopts an understanding and caring approach, the confidence the therapist shows in the programme, and the extent to which the couple are encouraged, especially when gains are made, even if these are relatively small. However, the emphasis in this section is on how to help couples when they encounter blocks during treatment.

Blocks during treatment
Difficulties may occur at any stage in the therapy programme but broadly can be divided into those which occur early on and those which occur later.

Early difficulties
These may present in a variety of ways, for example:

(1) failure to get started on the homework assignments;
(2) breaking the ban on sexual intercourse;
(3) complaints that the homework sessions lack spontaneity, or seem artificial or contrived;
(4) the sessions evoke negative feelings, such as tension or boredom.

Early difficulties may be of no great significance, or they may indicate major problems (e.g. general relationship difficulties, especially resentment).

Later difficulties
These can also present in various ways, for example:

(1) the couple stop having homework sessions;
(2) the sessions cease being pleasurable;
(3) the ban on sexual intercourse is broken.

Later difficulties are especially common in the treatment of erectile dysfunction and vaginismus.

The management of difficulties
The first step is to ensure that the couple understood the treatment instructions. If they did, then the therapist should obtain a detailed and precise account of what happened. One can broadly divide difficulties in sex therapy into those that are minor and those that are major.

Minor difficulties
These include problems such as a couple finding the initial homework sessions lacking in spontaneity, or having trouble getting started on the programme because of embarrassment. In some cases it will be appropriate simply to acknowledge the problem and reassure and encourage the couple. This might be so, for example, when a couple report that their

initial sessions seemed rather contrived. The therapist should explain that this is understandable and to be expected, but that in order to overcome a sexual problem like theirs it is necessary to approach it in a systematic fashion; the couple will find that as they begin to get pleasure out of their sessions these will feel more spontaneous. When a couple have difficulty getting started on sensate focus because of embarrassment the therapist should help them agree on an acceptable starting point. They might, for example, begin with cuddling and caressing fully clothed.

Major difficulties

More serious difficulties are usually indicated by problems such as very negative responses to homework assignments, persistent breaking of the ban on sexual intercourse, or cessation of homework sessions. Management of such difficulties is the crux of effective sex therapy.

A cognitive model that can be useful when trying to understand and explain negative responses to homework assignments is shown in Fig. 11.3. This demonstrates how failure to carry out the agreed homework assignments, or to enjoy them, results from cognitive processes (thoughts or images). However, because the underlying cognitions are often automatic (i.e. fleeting, over-learned habits of thinking) a person may not be

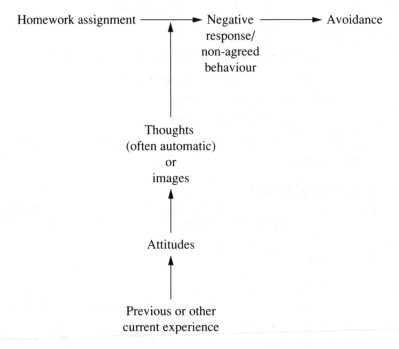

Fig. 11.3　A cognitive model useful in explaining major difficulties during homework assignments

very aware of them. The cognitions evoked by a homework assignment will usually reflect more general attitudes to sexuality, and these will often have resulted from previous, or other current, experiences. The following case provides an example:

A woman who presented with lack of interest in sex became very tense when the homework assignments progressed to the stage of genital sensate focus. She experienced revulsion when her partner began caressing her genitals, thinking, 'He cannot be liking this, he is only doing it because he feels he has to.' Underlying this was a general disgust with her genitals. This was the result of her father having sexually abused her repeatedly during her late childhood and early adolescence. He had fondled her genitals during these episodes, leaving her feeling dirty and guilty.

The thoughts and attitudes underlying difficulties in sex therapy are often idiosyncratic. The therapist's first task is to help the couple develop understanding. This can begin by explaining that feelings or behaviours do not arise out of the blue but that they are based on thoughts or images. The couple can then be encouraged to identify the cognitions which occur when they encounter problems. Some couples are able to do this fairly easily, while others require considerable help. A useful approach is to assist the couple to think of as many explanations (however unlikely they seem) as they can, and then to help them evaluate each in turn until a likely explanation for the difficulty can be found. Often the therapist will have to put forward at least some of the possibilities. The following example illustrates this procedure:

A couple entered sex therapy because the woman had orgasmic dysfunction. They had no homework sessions during the first two weeks, the man refusing all his partner's invitations and not feeling able to offer an invitation himself. However, neither partner could explain this. The following list of possible explanations was arrived at:

(1) the man feared that if they began caressing he would get sexually aroused and not be able to control himself;

(2) he was unsure how to caress his partner in a way she would find pleasurable;

(3) he did not want to initiate a process which might result in his wife becoming more sexually responsive and possibly seeking another partner;

(4) he felt unable to give his wife pleasure because of continuing resentment about an affair his wife had three years previously.

Eventually the man recognized that the last explanation was the most likely. He was then asked to discuss further his feelings and thoughts about this episode, following which it became apparent that while he had forgiven his wife for the affair, he thought she might compare his sexual technique with that of the other man. His wife experienced considerable surprise about this, and was able to reassure him that this had never happened.

Some thoughts underlying difficulties during sex therapy concern the nature of a homework assignment (e.g. it is wrong, unpleasant), while others concern the possible consequences of the behaviour (e.g. failure, humiliation, loss of control). A helpful approach to understanding the reasons for difficulties is to pose the questions 'What if you did do . . . ?; How would you feel?; What might the consequences be?'

In trying to understand the reasons for a difficulty it may not be possible to identify early experiences that have shaped current attitudes. Fortunately, this does not usually matter. The important thing is to identify automatic thoughts or images, and also the underlying attitudes from which these stem. Having done so, the therapist's task is to encourage the partners to review the evidence for these thoughts or beliefs, and then to examine other ways of interpreting the situation. Because dysfunctional beliefs associated with sexual problems often arise out of misunderstandings or myths about the opposite sex, the presence of the partner can greatly facilitate this aspect of therapy. The following example illustrates this:

When a young couple in which the man had premature ejaculation started sensate focus, he was able to caress his wife, but when it was her turn to caress him he persuaded her to have sexual intercourse. This happened twice in the first week of treatment. Exploration by means of the approach described above revealed that the image of his passively accepting his wife's caressing made him anxious. This was because of his underlying beliefs that 'real men' are the leaders in sexual activity and that being passive in this way was effeminate.

The therapist asked the man what evidence he had to support his beliefs. The patient said: 'My friends think the same way' and 'Women always expect men to take the lead . . . it's natural that way.' The therapist encouraged the man to ask his wife what she thought about this. She responded: 'You and probably most men think that, but that is because you never ask the woman. Sometimes I would like to be able to have a say in when sex happens. I also often wish you would let me caress you . . . at the moment I daren't because if I start you take this to mean that I want to have sex *now*. I am sure you would enjoy sex more if I could spend more time giving you pleasure . . . and I would feel less pressured by you.' The man was very surprised by this, and subsequently agreed to find out what it would be like if his wife caressed him as part of the sensate focus exercise.

In some cases, extensive therapeutic work will be necessary before progress is possible. Indeed, the focus of therapy might have to change temporarily. This was the case in the example noted above of the man who felt resentful about his wife's affair. Two sessions of treatment had to be devoted to helping the man express his feelings and anxieties about the affair before further specific work on their sexual problem was possible.

Occasionally, no progress can be made in developing understanding of why a couple have encountered a major difficulty. Under these circumstances it is worth considering seeing the partners separately to find out whether important information is being withheld by one of them, although before doing this the therapist should stress the need for any new information to be shared in subsequent conjoint sessions.

Education

Education about sexuality should occur both informally throughout treatment, and more formally in the shape of recommended reading and an educational session.

Reading material

Many couples find it helpful if they read a suitable book about sexuality during the early part of the programme. Delvin (1974) is a good example. Books aimed specifically at women (e.g. Phillips and Rakusen 1978) or men (e.g. Zilbergeld 1980) are also useful, but should be read by both partners.

Educational session

Because ignorance or misinformation are often important contributory factors in sexual dysfunction, it is worth devoting most of one treatment session (somewhere between the third and sixth sessions) to provision of sexual information. With the aid of drawings or photographs the therapist should describe, in simple terms, sexual anatomy and the stages of sexual arousal. Thus, for example, the genitalia of both sexes are described, including the changes that occur with sexual arousal and orgasm. Myths about sexuality (Zilbergeld 1978; Hawton 1985) should be addressed (e.g. 'a man automatically knows how to caress a woman'; 'sex is only really successful when the partners reach orgasm simultaneously'). This session should be tailored to the couple's educational level and needs. For example, with an older couple it is useful to describe in a reassuring fashion the normal effects of ageing on sexuality.

Clinical experience has shown that the educational session can be an extremely important part of the treatment programme, and it is particularly appreciated by couples (Hawton *et al.* 1986). It should therefore be included in the treatment of all couples. Fuller details of how the educational session can be conducted have been provided elsewhere by the author (Hawton 1985, p. 172).

Termination

The final phase of sex therapy begins once a couple have largely overcome their sexual difficulty, usually when vaginal containment has been completed. The end of treatment must be planned just as carefully as the rest of the programme. The following strategies are suggested:

1. *Prepare the couple for termination from the start of treatment.* Thus when a couple enter treatment they should be told the likely duration of the programme. Setting a time-frame can help encourage a couple to work on the homework assignments.

2. *Towards the end of treatment extend the intervals between sessions.* Once a couple are getting towards the end of the programme and are more confident about their ability to overcome any further problems, the intervals between the last two or three sessions might be extended to two or three weeks.

3. *Prepare the couple for further problems.* The therapist should explain that some couples encounter further difficulties after treatment has ended, and ask them to discuss how they would deal with them should this happen. Couples often find that good communication, an accepting attitude, and reintroduction of some of the stages of the treatment programme, allow them to overcome such problems (Hawton *et al.* 1986).

4. *Follow-up assessment.* Couples often welcome the opportunity to report on subsequent progress a few months after the end of sex therapy. A follow-up assessment also allows the therapist to evaluate the short-term effectiveness of treatment. A final appointment roughly three months after treatment ends should therefore be part of the agreed programme.

Outcome of sex therapy

Methods of assessing progress

There are several standardized self-rating questionnaires which may be used to evaluate the effects of sex therapy. The Golombok Rusk Inventory of Sexual Satisfaction (GRISS) is one recently introduced in the UK (Rust and Golombok 1986). A far more lengthy American questionnaire is the Sexual Interaction Inventory (LoPiccolo and Steger 1974). Some questionnaires, such as the Maudsley Marital Questionnaire (Crowe 1978), can be used to evaluate both general and sexual aspects of a relationship.

Many therapists will prefer to use brief rating-scales, which can be completed by both themselves and the partners, in order to record progress and to monitor their own effectiveness. Three scales might be used, one to assess changes in the presenting problem, one which records a couple's current satisfaction with their sexual relationship, and a third concerning the couple's satisfaction with their general relationship. Changes in the presenting problem might be rated on a scale such as:

(1) presenting problem resolved;

(2) presenting problem largely resolved, although difficulty still experienced;

(3) some improvement, but presenting problem largely unresolved;

(4) no change;

(5) problem worse.

A couple's satisfaction with their sexual, or general, relationship might be recorded on a scale such as:

(1) completely satisfied with the sexual (general) relationship;

(2) largely satisfied with the sexual (general) relationship, but some dissatisfaction;

(3) some satisfaction with the sexual (general) relationship, but largely dissatisfied;

(4) complete dissatisfaction with the sexual (general) relationship.

Results of treatment

There have been several reports of uncontrolled studies of outcome following sex therapy. Approximately two-thirds of patients appear to gain substantial benefits from treatment (Duddle 1975; Bancroft and Coles 1976; Milne 1976; Hawton and Catalan 1986).

Controlled studies comparing sex therapy with other approaches (e.g. systematic desensitization, self-help, postal treatment, and brief therapist contact) have also been reported (for reviews see Sotile and Kilmann 1977; Wright, Perreault, and Mathieu 1977; Kilmann and Auerbach 1979; Hawton 1985). However, the design of nearly all these studies has been far from satisfactory, particularly with regard to matching of groups of subjects for important prognostic variables. In the main, they indicate the superiority of sex therapy over other approaches, but often the differences have not been vast (e.g. Mathews *et al.* 1976).

Important pre-treatment factors which have been shown to predict outcome are the quality of a couple's general relationship, the overall quality of their sexual relationship, the extent to which they find each other attractive, their apparent motivation, and serious psychiatric disorder (O'Connor 1976; Whitehead and Mathews 1977; Hawton *et al.* 1986; Whitehead and Mathews 1986). Active engagement in the homework assignments by the third treatment session is also an important indicator of likely outcome (Hawton *et al.* 1986).

Long-term follow-up studies have shown that while the immediate benefits of sex therapy are often not fully sustained, many couples remain reasonably satisfied with both their sexual and general relationship (De Amicis, Goldberg, LoPiccolo, Friedman, and Davies 1985; Hawton *et al.* 1986). There are, however, marked differences in outcome for different sexual dysfunctions. Of the male dysfunctions, erectile problems and premature ejaculation do best. Of the female dysfunctions, vaginismus usually has an excellent outcome which is sustained. However, many women with impaired sexual interest, while often showing some initial improvement, have considerable problems when followed up.

Reasons for failure, and alternative approaches

The main reason why couples might not benefit from sex therapy include major general relationship difficulties, a desire on the part of one or both partners to maintain the status quo (perhaps because of fear of the possible consequences of changes in the sexual relationship), and psychiatric disorder or major psychological difficulties of one or other partner. Fear of emotional intimacy is one example in the last category; in such cases individual psychotherapy, possibly on a cognitive–behavioural basis, might be a preferable initial approach.

Other alternative approaches include marital therapy for couples with difficulties in their general relationship, individual therapy (Hawton 1985) where one partner refuses to be involved, and physical treatments, such as hormone replacement, where there is a clear indication that this is appropriate.

Conclusions

Sex therapy is a well-established approach for helping couples with sexual dysfunctions. It consists of an attractive blend of behavioural, counselling, and educational treatment strategies. All three components are important, with counselling usually being essential when couples encounter difficulties in carrying out homework assignments. Cognitively based counselling can be an effective approach to helping with major difficulties. It is important for therapists to be flexible in this approach, being prepared to adjust the treatment programme according to each couple's progress and the difficulties they encounter. Therapists must be prepared, if necessary, to help couples with general relationship issues, either as a prelude to sex therapy or if such problems begin to interfere with progress. Sex therapy can be very effective and rewarding, with approximately two-thirds of couples deriving significant benefits by the end of treatment.

Recommended reading

Background and therapy

Bancroft, J. (1983). *Human sexuality and its problems*. Churchill Livingstone, Edinburgh.

Hawton, K. (1985). *Sex therapy: a practical guide*. Oxford University Press, Oxford.

Kaplan, H. S. (1987). *The illustrated manual of sex therapy*, (2nd edn). Brunner/ Mazel, New York.

Self-help

Barbach, L. G. (1976). *For yourself: the fulfilment of female sexuality*. Signet, New York.

Brown, P. and Faulder, C. (1979). *Treat yourself to sex: a guide for good loving*. Penguin, London.

Delvin, D. (1974). *The book of love*. New English Library, London.

Heiman, J., LoPiccolo, L., and LoPicollo, J. (1976). *Becoming orgasmic: a sexual growth program for women*. Prentice Hall, New Jersey.

Phillips, A. and Rakusen, J. (1978). *Our bodies ourselves*. Penguin, London.

Yaffe, M. and Fenwick, E. (1986). *Sexual happiness: a practical approach*. Dorling Kindersley, London.

Zilbergeld, B. (1980). *Men and sex*. Fontana, London.

12

Problem-solving

Keith Hawton and Joan Kirk

Introduction

This chapter provides practical guidance on a general approach to helping people manage personal issues. In keeping with the cognitive–behavioural methods of treatment for specific disorders which have been described in this book, it demands a collaborative approach in which therapist and patient work together actively. The aims of problem-solving are to:

(1) assist patients to identify problems as causes of dysphoria;
(2) help them recognize the resources they possess for approaching their difficulties;
(3) teach them a systematic method of overcoming their current problems;
(4) enhance their sense of control over problems;
(5) equip them with a method for tackling future problems.

The first stage of problem-solving involves helping patients define the problems they are facing. Then they are helped to generate potential solutions to the problems, following which the most attractive solutions are tested out. Problem-solving also involves identifying difficulties (both practical and cognitive) that patients may have with these initial stages, and ways of overcoming them. Where testing and evaluation of possible solutions indicates that they are inappropriate, then either modified or new solutions are sought and tested out.

The problem-solving approach is attractive for both professionals and patients in that it is easily learned and can be applied in a wide range of situations commonly encountered in psychiatric practice. It is appropriate that problem-solving is described in the final chapter of this book because it is frequently a component in the therapeutic approaches to many of the specific disorders which have already been described.

Problem-solving is often a brief method of intervention. The extent to which cognitive strategies are employed in this approach varies from being minimal, particularly in the treatment of people who are not amenable to psychological approaches, to being the main techniques for facilitating progress.

Historical aspects

In view of its wide applicability, it is surprising that little attention has been paid to problem-solving in the psychiatric literature. It is mainly psychologists who have described the approach and attempted to assess the importance of its various components (D'Zurilla and Goldfried 1971; D'Zurilla and Nezu 1980). Somewhat more attention has been paid to problem-solving recently as a result of the interest in crisis intervention, although even in the literature on crisis intervention descriptions of this approach are sparse. In the social-work field the approach called task-centred casework (Reid and Epstein 1972) is quite closely allied to problem-solving.

When is problem-solving applicable?

The potential uses of problem-solving in psychiatry, social work, general practice, and counselling are wide-ranging. It is very relevant, for example, in the management of crisis. The nature of crises has been discussed in detail elsewhere (Caplan 1961; Brandon 1970; Bartolucci and Drayer 1973). Caplan's (1961) definition is that a crisis is 'when a person faces an obstacle to important life-goals that is, for a time, insurmountable through the utilization of customary methods of problem-solving. A period of disorganisation ensues, a period of upset, during which many abortive attempts at solutions are made.' Clearly, problem-solving may also be relevant before this state has developed. Furthermore, it can be incorporated into many other treatments in order to help patients develop efficient strategies for dealing with stress (e.g. pp. 179 and 299).

The range of problems for which a problem-solving approach is likely to be relevant and effective includes: threatened loss (e.g. of an important relationship or of personal status), actual loss, conflicts in which a person is faced by a major choice (e.g. whether or not to leave a situation, take on a new role), marital and other relationship problems, work difficulties (e.g. how to alter current working relationships), study problems, coping with boredom, difficulties concerning child care, and dealing with handicaps resulting from either physical or psychiatric illness. Often individuals come to attention initially not because of their problems, but because of their symptoms (e.g. insomnia, depression, anxiety) or behaviour (e.g. suicide attempts). Only after careful assessment might the problems associated with these become apparent.

Broadly speaking, one can divide people who can be helped by problem-solving into

(1) those who generally cope well but are not doing so at present, perhaps because of illness or the nature of the dilemma they face; and

(2) those with poor coping resources.

For this second group, problem-solving may involve longer-term intervention than with the first group.

As noted above, problem-solving is often an important component in the treatment of any of the specific psychiatric and psychological problems described in other chapters in this book. It can also be a central approach for helping patients with schizophrenia and their families solve difficulties which may be maintaining or exacerbating the psychotic disorder (Falloon, Boyd, and McGill 1984).

Assessment

The principles of assessment for problem-solving are precisely those of cognitive–behavioural assessment in general that were described in Chapter 2. The fundamental decision which determines if problem-solving is currently applicable for a patient concerns whether the person is so severely disabled by psychiatric symptoms or disorder that he or she cannot at present be expected to take responsibility, even with the support of the therapist, for managing the problems that require attention. For example, a patient with marked retarded or agitated depression is very unlikely to be able to engage in the steps necessary for problem-solving until there has been some reduction in the severity of the affective disturbance. Similarly, when a person is in a severe state of crisis, especially if suicidal, problem-solving will usually be inappropriate until the level of disorganization and helplessness which often characterizes such a state has been reduced. Attention to exacerbating factors (e.g. sleep disturbance, lack of supports) can often bring this about, following which problem-solving may then be very appropriate.

Procedure

The key steps in assessment relevant to problem-solving are listed in Table 12.1. The thoroughness and accuracy of the assessment of prob-

Table 12.1 Steps in assessment for problem-solving

1. Identify the patient's problems
2. Identify the patient's resources—assets and supports
3. Obtain information from other sources
4. Decide whether problem-solving is appropriate
5. Decide on practical arrangements—who will be involved, likely number of sessions, duration, timing, etc.
6. Establish a therapeutic contract—including the patient's and therapist's responsibilities in problem-solving

lems will determine whether the problem-solving process is initiated in a potentially successful fashion. While errors made at this stage do not preclude a successful outcome, they may undermine the approach and cause therapy to be prolonged, especially if at a later stage it becomes apparent that problems were either incorrectly identified or that other important problems were overlooked. This does not necessarily mean that a single interview allows assessment of all of a patient's problems—the assessment phase often needs to be extended over two or three therapy sessions, partly to allow the patient to carry out homework (e.g. diary-keeping or other self-monitoring) which can assist in the identification of problems. Indeed, assessment should continue throughout therapy, with the original formulation being revised if necessary in the light of any new information which might emerge.

Identifying the patient's problems

This initial step is of central importance, and must be a collaborative exercise. The aim should be to draw up a written problem-list, with each problem clearly specified. Sometimes people present for help complaining of problems which are not clearly described (e.g. 'difficulty getting on at work', 'study problems'). The therapist's task is then to help the patient be more specific (e.g. 'What is it about work which is difficult?', 'Could you go into more detail about the problem you are having with studying?'). Only then can possible goals and strategies relevant to overcoming the problem be identified. However, people may present with dysphoric or other symptoms, either aware that these relate to difficulties but unclear about their precise nature, or apparently unaware that their symptoms relate to life problems. This can apply to a wide range of symptoms and behaviour (e.g. anxiety, depression, alcohol abuse, eating disorders). Careful self-monitoring of fluctuations in the presenting symptoms, the circumstances in which such changes occur, and the patients' thoughts at the time, may be necessary to identify the contributory problems and hence establish the relevance of problem-solving.

For example, a middle-aged man presented with unexplained anxiety, which he described as occurring throughout the day. After keeping a daily diary, rating his anxiety hourly on a 0–10 scale, it became apparent that this symptom fluctuated a great deal. His most severe ratings were when he was at home unoccupied. His notes concerning what he was thinking at the time revealed that he was worrying about the poor state of the roof of his house and his inability to get enough money to have it repaired. His financial problems then became the focus of problem-solving.

The following tactics are helpful in identifying problems, especially when patients initially present with a largely undifferentiated array of difficulties.

1. Listen carefully to the patient's description of the problems. If the patient is having difficulty identifying problems, then a question such as, 'What is upsetting you most?' may help.

2. Make an initial attempt to list the patient's problems, paraphrasing where necessary what the patient has said, and write down these problems once the patient has verified that they are correct.

For example:
Therapist   'You seem to be saying that you have three different problems; first, the fact you and your husband rarely seem to be able to discuss matters which are upsetting you both; secondly, the very different ideas the two of you have about disciplining your children; and, thirdly, the daily arguments which occur as a result of the first two difficulties. Does that sound like a reasonable summary of what you have told me so far?'

3. Explore whether there are any other problems which may not have been presented. Going through a checklist, such as that shown in Table 12.2, can often be a useful way of ensuring that nothing important is missed.

For example:
Therapist   'Before we look at these problems in more detail I wonder if there is anything else troubling you. For example, do you and your husband have any financial problems . . . is your house OK . . . ?'

4. Obtain a detailed description of all the apparent problems. When a problem is episodic (e.g. arguments with spouse, difficulties with colleagues at work) it is useful to have the patient describe the most recent occasion on which it occurred. The therapist should also ask in what ways the patient would like things to be different. Asking the patient what he or she would like to happen if there was a magic wand to wave

Table 12.2 A checklist of potential problem areas

---

   1. Relationship with partner or spouse
   2. Relationship with other family members, particularly young children
   3. Employment or studies
   4. Finances
   5. Housing
   6. Legal
   7. Social isolation and relationships with friends
   8. Use of alcohol and drugs
   9. Psychiatric health
  10. Physical health
  11. Sexual adjustment
  12. Bereavement and impending loss

---

can help initiate exploration of desired changes. The interrelationships between problems may also become clearer at this stage.

Now the therapist and patient should draw up and write out a detailed problem list. As noted above, this stage may need to be extended over two or more sessions, partly because it can take quite a long time to get an accurate detailed assessment of the patient's problems, and partly because the patient may need to spend time collecting further information (e.g. by daily record-keeping—see p. 18) and thinking about the problems. To reiterate the point made earlier, this stage should not be rushed or else the effectiveness of problem-solving may be reduced and treatment may eventually take longer than necessary.

The following case illustrates how a problem-list emerged following an assessment:

Mary was a 32-year-old married woman with two children. She was referred because she had been depressed for the past five months, since shortly after she had, through redundancy, lost her job as a supervisor in a carpet store. She particularly missed the friends she had made at work and had gradually abandoned previously rewarding activities, such as gardening. She did not think her husband understood how she felt, and her problem was made worse by her mother's intrusiveness, including her insistence that Mary telephone her daily. The problem-list agreed between Mary and her therapist was as shown in Table 12.3.

Identifying the patient's resources

As far as possible, problem-solving utilizes skills possessed by the patient. The patient's resources include both general personal assets and strengths, and available supports. These (especially assets and strengths) can be difficult to assess at times of stress and difficulty. Essentially one is aiming to find out how capable the person might be of overcoming the current problems and how quickly.

Table 12.3 Mary's problem list

1. Unemployment: lost job through redundancy six months ago
2. Low self-esteem—secondary to problem 1
3. Lack of social contacts—secondary to problem 1
4. Depression: worse during week days—secondary to problems 1, 2, 3, and 7
5. Loss of interest in usual hobbies, especially gardening—secondary to problem 4
6. Mother's intrusiveness: daily telephone calls, twice-weekly visits, many critical comments on Mary's lifestyle
7. Difficulty communicating with husband: he refuses to discuss any of Mary's problems

Personal assets and strengths   There are several factors which are potentially important here:

(1) how the person has coped in the past with problems, especially any which were similar to the current difficulties—it may be helpful for the therapist to identify an example with the patient (e.g. previous loss or failure) and then ask for a detailed description of how such a problem was approached and resolved;

(2) the degree to which escape methods (especially alcohol) or avoidance have been used to cope in the past;

(3) the extent of current dysphoria—thus, while a person may have shown excellent coping ability in the past, marked current psychological symptoms (especially depression, anxiety, and sleep disturbance) can severely interfere with current ability;

(4) the extent to which the person can formulate potential solutions to any of the problems which have been identified (e.g. Therapist: 'What thoughts have you had about what you might do in order to overcome this problem?').

Supports   Three factors in particular should be investigated in assessing an individual's actual or potential supports:

(1) whether the person has a confident (e.g. Therapist: 'Is there anyone with whom you can discuss personal problems? . . . Have you found it helpful in the past if you shared things that were worrying you? . . . Do you think he/she would mind if you talked about this problem?');

(2) whether there are any other professionals who are available to help in tackling the current difficulties (e.g. general practitioner, social worker, clergyman); and

(3) 'environmental factors' which may have a bearing on both the current problems and the person's general quality of life. These include housing and finance, but also interests and employment, and especially whether these are a source of self-esteem.

Information from other sources

If there are significant other people, including professionals, relatives, and friends, who can provide further information about the patient's difficulties these should be consulted. It is important that the patient is fully informed and has willingly consented to this (e.g. Therapist: 'Now you have told me about the problems you and your husband are having. In order to get a full picture of things and to see what we can do about them I would like to talk to your husband. Are you happy for me to do that? . . . If so, could you ask him? . . . what do you think?')

Suitability for problem-solving

Several factors should be taken into account when assessing whether problem-solving is an appropriate therapeutic approach for a patient's difficulties:

1. *The patient's problems can be specified.* As emphasized already, the crux of effective problem-solving is the clear initial definition of problems. However, a patient's problems may not be easily disentangled at first, and prolonged assessment and considerable help from the therapist may be necessary before the precise nature of the problems becomes clear (furthermore, as therapy proceeds, problems identified at the outset often need to be redefined or subdivided). If after thorough assessment the therapist and patient are unable to agree on the nature of the patient's problems, then there is little point in proceeding with problem-solving.

2. *The patient's goals seem realistic.* During the initial assessment of problems, as already noted, the therapist should ask the patient what changes in the problems are desired. Sometimes, a patient's goals will clearly be inappropriate or over-ambitious. For example, a man who had recently separated from his wife, she having formed a new relationship, insisted that his main goal was to get her back. The wife had made it absolutely clear to both patient and therapist that she would never consider a reunion. Failure to negotiate a goal which is likely to be attainable will preclude problem-solving, at least with regard to the specific problem.

3. *Absence of severe acute psychiatric illness.* Because the patient's active collaboration is essential, problem-solving may not be feasible when a patient is in the acute phase of a major psychiatric illness, although it may become highly appropriate once the illness has become less severe. Thus, problem-solving should not be attempted with a severely retarded or agitated depressed patient, nor with a very deluded patient with schizophrenia. However, problem-solving is often possible and appropriate with other depressed patients and less disturbed patients with schizophrenia. It can be a very useful approach with suicidal patients (Hawton and Catalan 1987), except when the current risk of a suicidal act is so high that the main initial focus of treatment has to be on protecting the patient from himself or herself (usually by becoming a hospital in-patient). Even in very distressed patients, however, problem-solving can often begin as soon as there has been even slight amelioration of their distress. Current alcoholism may preclude problem-solving, but this approach can be helpful when control over drinking has developed.

4. *Agreement on initial contract.* As noted below, it is necessary to establish a clear contract concerning the nature, aims, and extent of problem-solving. Both therapist and patient must be reasonably satisfied

with this contract before problem-solving proceeds. The therapist should also emphasize that the aim is not just to deal with present problems, but also to teach the patient an approach which might be used to manage future difficulties.

It should be noted that 'psychological-mindedness' on the part of the patient is *not* a prerequisite for problem-solving. This is essentially a practical approach, although, as will be seen later, cognitive aspects of therapy are very important in some cases.

Practical arrangements

The practical arrangements should be clarified from the outset, and include who is to be involved, the likely number of treatment sessions, and their duration and timing, etc. A decision may have to be made about whether or not anybody other than the therapist and patient will be included in the treatment sessions, and when this should occur.

This approach often involves relatively brief therapeutic contact—say 4–6 treatment sessions—although the duration will depend on the extent of the patient's problems, the patient's resources, the number of problems to be tackled, and the goals. Therapy sessions might last between 30 and 60 minutes, although later sessions can often be relatively brief. Problem-solving may be most effective, especially when the patient is facing a crisis, if the initial therapy sessions (say Sessions 1 to 3) are quite close together, perhaps three sessions in a fortnight, although practical constraints may preclude this. Relatively frequent initial sessions can help engage the patient. Less frequent sessions later can encourage the patient's autonomy. It is worthwhile building into the initial contract a review session (Session 3 or 4 is usually the best) when the overall progress will be assessed by both therapist and patient, and a decision made whether to proceed. This can help sustain the patient's efforts and provide reinforcement when progress has occurred, while also allowing therapy to be terminated less abruptly if it is not effecting any changes.

Sometimes, especially when a patient is very distressed or depressed, an offer of emergency telephone access to either the therapist or other professionals might be considered. This may serve as a comfort for the patient, even if it is unlikely to be used, or as an important means of preventing a crisis developing. However, the decision whether or not to offer such emergency access requires careful deliberation. Sometimes therapists take on too much responsibility for their patient's problems, and this can undermine the patient's sense of autonomy and therefore inhibit problem-solving.

Therapeutic contract

The points made in the previous section should be discussed and agreed with the patient. There should also be rough agreement at this stage about which problems are to be the focus of treatment and what are the likely goals. Finally, the responsibilities of both patient and therapist must be made clear, especially for patients whose compliance is in doubt.

For example, the therapist might say: 'I think it would be helpful for us to be clear about what we are each going to put into treatment, because it is obviously going to take quite a commitment on both sides. I will keep the appointments and help you all I can, especially if you run into difficulties. Similarly, you will need to attend the agreed sessions, work actively on your problems, and be open and frank about what sort of progress you make. At this stage can you see any problems with that kind of commitment?'

Stages and strategies in problem-solving

The steps to follow in problem-solving are summarized in Table 12.4. This brief outline indicates the overall therapeutic approach. Most of the rest of this chapter is devoted to detailed description of the various stages, including how to help patients anticipate and overcome difficulties, and specific strategies to assist progress.

Procedure

An agenda of items to be dealt with should be agreed at the beginning of each treatment session, usually following a general enquiry about how the patient has been getting on since the previous session. The agenda might be introduced by the therapist as follows:

'Let's set the agenda for today. I think we should begin by looking at how you have got on with the homework assignments we agreed last time, and whether you had any difficulties with them. If there have been any difficulties we need to look at ways of overcoming them. We also need to decide on what you should try and do before we next meet. Is there anything else you would like to discuss today?'

Table 12.4 Steps in problem-solving

---

1. Decide which problem(s) to be tackled first
2. Agree goal(s)
3. Work out steps necessary to achieve goal(s)
4. Decide tasks necessary to tackle first step
5. Review progress at next therapy session, including difficulties that have been encountered
6. Decide next step, depending on progress, and agree subsequent tasks
7. Proceed, as above, to agreed goal(s), or redefine problems and goals
8. Work on further problems (if necessary)

Choice of problem(s) to be tackled first

It is often best initially to focus on one problem. This might be the central and most important problem for the patient. However, sometimes it is preferable to choose a problem which appears relatively easy to solve. This is especially the case when dysphoric symptoms are marked, partly because these may impair the person's ability to deal with a more complex problem and partly because successful resolution of one problem can engender hope, a belief that more substantial problems can be solved, and an improvement in the patient's self-esteem, usually resulting in reduction in symptoms.

For example, Mary, whose problem-list is shown in Table 12.3, had gradually given up her social contacts and interests. It seemed appropriate to focus problem-solving initially on her beginning to renew these activities because this was likely to make her feel better and more able to face the task of seeking work.

The patient must ultimately decide which problem wll be pursued first. However, the therapist's role is to ensure that the patient chooses a problem likely to be manageable at this stage.

It is not always necessary to confine the early sessions rigidly to one problem, but the therapist should beware of encouraging a patient to take on too much. At the beginning it is more important to get problem-solving started than to try to effect major changes.

Agree goal(s) and target(s)

During the initial assessment the patient and therapist should have identified general goals. Now the therapist must help the patient establish more precise targets for each of the general goals. These should be realistic, and, whenever possible, they should be described in behavioural terms, as outlined in Chapter 2. The therapist's role is to help the patient with both these aspects of goal-setting. Once agreed, the problem, goals, and targets should be recorded in writing.

For example, Mary (p. 411) agreed that the general goals in relation to problem 3 in her list in Table 12.3 fell into two groups: (1) establishing contact with previous friends; and (2) initiating new informal relationships. The specific targets were:

- one face-to-face contact per week with any of her friends;
- one phone call per week with any of her friends;
- one regular 'social' commitment per week, e.g. yoga, painting class;
- to help in children's school one afternoon per week.

Sometimes patients are very unclear about their goals. If this is the case, the therapist can often help using one of the cognitive strategies (e.g. brainstorming, two-column technique) described later (p. 420).

Work out steps necessary to achieve goal(s)

The therapist now needs to help the patient decide on the steps necessary to tackle the problem. Sometimes only one step will be required. In other cases several steps may be necessary, the later steps often not being clear at this stage, especially if the problem is complex, or is one involving a choice situation (e.g. whether the patient should or should not change job, leave a partner, etc.). The therapist should dissuade the patient from opting immediately for what appears to be the most obvious solution. Instead, the patient should be encouraged to generate a list of possible solutions (see p. 420), however unlikely some of them may seem.

Decide initial tasks

Having established the overall direction of problem-solving, the next important stage is to decide in detail on the tasks necessary to complete the first step. The tasks must be realistic and practical, and planned in detail, including factors such as what, when, with whom, how often, etc. Thus in the case of Mary, the first step she planned towards her target of 'one regular social commitment per week' was to go to the Citizens' Advice Bureau to find out what recreational classes were available locally.

The therapist must ask the patient to anticipate the likely consequences of the task, and especially any foreseeable difficulties. Cognitive rehearsal (p. 421)— that is, encouraging patients to go through in their imagination exactly what needs to be done and what might happen—can aid identification of the initial tasks and any possible difficulties. If difficulties are foreseen, the therapist can encourage the patient to work out what might be done to circumvent or minimize them. Once the initial tasks have been agreed, they should be written down, ideally by the patient, and both patient and therapist should keep a copy. Furthermore, patients often find it helpful if they keep a diary in which they can record the tasks, what they actually manage to do, and the outcome, including any changes in symptoms and satisfaction which occurred. The form of the diary should be set out in detail (p. 18), so that attention is focused on the specific tasks rather than general topics.

Finally, the therapist should explain what will happen in the next therapy session.

For example, 'When we next meet I'd like to go over in detail with you how you have been getting on. We can talk about any difficulties you have had and, if necessary, work out other ways of trying to sort out this problem. At the end of each meeting, just like today, we'll agree on what you are going to try and do before the next session.'

Review progress

At the next treatment session, having reviewed with the patient what had been agreed, the patient is asked for a detailed account of progress in terms of the agreed tasks. If the patient has kept a diary, the therapist and patient should go over this together. Any positive efforts by the patient to carry out the agreed tasks should be praised, even if the result has been disappointing—difficulties can provide further understanding of the patient's problems which can then be used to formulate tasks more likely to succeed. For example, 'You are clearly upset that after all your effort things didn't work out as planned. But let us look at what we have learned from this.'

At this point, progress may be roughly grouped into three categories—success, partial success, and no progress.

Success in carrying out the initial task   If the patient has successfully negotiated the initial step, the therapist should ask what benefits have resulted (e.g. improved self-confidence, mood, understanding). Then the next step should be addressed using the same approach as described in 'Decide initial tasks', above.

Partial success   If the patient has been partly successful in tackling the first step, the therapist and patient must decide whether more time is required to complete the task, or whether difficulties have come to light which are impeding progress. These might include both practical difficulties and attitudes or beliefs, especially concerning possible consequences of attempting the full task. Solutions to practical difficulties can often easily be identified, although the therapist should encourage the patient to generate these. The brainstorming technique for identifying possible solutions (see p. 420) and the method of examining the potential outcomes for alternative strategies (see p. 421) can be helpful. It is also useful to examine fears about the possible consequences of solving the problem, or patients' doubts about their ability to manage tasks. This can be achieved by looking at alternative strategies, especially action versus no action, and by asking the patient to rehearse in imagination what needs to be done. Where a significant belief is identified it may be necessary to outline briefly the cognitive model (p. 171), and to get the patient to question the validity of the belief, perhaps by examining the evidence for and against the belief. Eventually it is usually possible to decide whether the patient should now attempt the original task, or whether another approach to the problem is necessary.

Thus, for example, Mary made one attempt to telephone a friend. Getting no reply she was unable to repeat the telephone call. However, with the therapist's help she was able to identify the reason for this, namely her fear that her friend would be uninterested in seeing her. After examining the evidence for this belief she agreed that it would be helpful to telephone the friend in order to find out whether her fears were justified.

No progress A similar approach should be used if the patient has made no progress, including when the patient has failed to attempt the agreed tasks(s). It may become apparent either that the initially agreed task was too difficult, and that a smaller step needs to be tried, or that a new approach to the problem is necessary.

Thus in Mary's case, she had agreed to discuss with one of her children's teachers the possibility of helping in school one afternoon per week. However, because she felt embarrassed about not having been to the school for several weeks she had not been able to do this. Therefore the initial task was changed to her spending a week going to school with her children and talking informally with their teachers.

Further possibilities include the therapist having failed to detect the seriousness of psychiatric disorder, which should then become the focus of therapy; or a patient's unwillingness to take responsibility for the resolution of his or her problems. If the latter is suspected, the therapist must openly discuss this possibility with the patient.

For example, the therapist might say, 'I am concerned that we spent quite a lot of time working out ways you might tackle some of your problems, but so far you have not managed to try any of these. As your problems are part of your everyday life we are not going to make any progress unless you do try things out. I think it would be helpful therefore to stand back and question whether the goals you have set are really that important for you at this stage.'

However, the therapist must be wary of being too ready to assume that a patient is unwilling to take responsibility until every effort has been made to initiate problem-solving. Unwillingness to get started may reflect a patient's low self-esteem or fears about the consequences of trying to change.

Subsequent stages of therapy

While problem-solving is in progress it is imperative that the patient always has tasks to attempt between sessions. Thus the treatment sessions can largely be viewed as means of facilitating the patient's efforts to effect changes in his or her everyday life. The tasks agreed at the end of the second and subsequent sessions will depend on progress so far, and the results of examining any difficulties the patient may have had.

If problem-solving proceeds step-by-step until a problem is solved, a decision whether to move to a further problem should be made. If the initial problem has been a relatively major one, patients not uncommonly say that they feel confident that they can now deal with their remaining problems. If further problems are tackled in therapy, the approach should be as described. However, the therapist must encourage the patient to take increasing responsibility for identifying solutions to problems. When the problem-solving approach has not been successful for a particular problem, the problem should be re-examined in terms of possible alternative goals. In the case of Mary, after she had spent several weeks trying to improve communication with her husband (problem 7 in Table 12.3) she realized that he was unlikely to change. At this point she started to consider the possibility of leaving him.

Cognitive and other strategies in problem-solving

There are several therapeutic strategies which can be of value in problem-solving. Some of these have been described in other chapters, and therefore will receive only brief mention here.

Generating possible solutions to problems   Following careful and thorough assessment of a patient's problems, the appropriate solutions and necessary steps to achieve these often becoming glaringly obvious. On the other hand, the solutions may be unclear, or the therapist may be able to work out a reasonable solution, but wants to encourage the patient to come up with ideas in order to encourage self-sufficiency. *Brainstorming* is one approach to helping a patient generate ideas. The patient is asked to suggest as many potential solutions as possible, however unlikely they seem. At this stage the patient is asked not to evaluate the potential usefulness of any of the possibilities because otherwise each proffered solution may be dismissed as useless in some way, and the generation of new alternatives impaired. For example, the therapist might say,

'The next step for us is to try and think of as many possible solutions to the problem as we can. But an important condition at this stage is that we do not consider *at all* whether or not a solution is practical, impossible, or whatever. You'll be very good at seeing the drawbacks to any solution you come up with, and would probably very quickly get dragged down into thoughts about how difficult the situation is. To avoid that, we need to try and keep more open-minded, so that you get the opportunity to think round the problem. We're aiming for as many solutions as we can, say between six and ten, including some extreme ones.'

If the patient finds it difficult to generate solutions, the therapist can put forward possibilities. Suggestion of solutions which are clearly inappropriate and therefore easily rejected can facilitate the involvement of the patient in this process. Suggestion of *extreme solutions* can often lead the patient into unexplored avenues and hence produce other novel solutions. All possible solutions are written down. Once a substantial list has been produced the patient can then be helped to examine the advantages and disadvantages of each solution. Sometimes a solution which at first seems highly unlikely may, on closer examination and modification, become a potentially valuable one.

For example, Mary was helped to brainstorm possible solutions to the problem of her intrusive mother (problem 6 in Table 12.3). She generated the following list, including some extreme solutions:
(1) ask her not to visit or telephone any more;
(2) ask her to reduce her visits and telephone calls;
(3) leave the country;
(4) change telephone number and go ex-directory;
(5) discuss the problem with her mother;
(6) do nothing and accept the status quo.
After examining in detail the advantages and disadvantages of each solution, Mary decided that the fifth one, which she had previously regarded as impossible, was the more appropriate in the first instance.

Examining alternatives   The problems faced by a patient often consist of making a choice between two very different courses of action, or two potential solutions to a problem. A useful strategy in these circumstances is the *two-column* or *pros and cons technique*. This is very simple, and consists of writing down the advantages and disadvantages, including likely outcomes, of each possibility. Each of the pros and cons may be given relative weightings if appropriate. The therapist may first have to demonstrate this to the patient. When the decision is a very difficult or important one the patient might be given this as a homework task. This technique often results in the most appropriate course of action becoming clearer, or it indicates that further information must be obtained by the patient in order to give further weight to one or other alternative. As the list is generated the patient and therapist work collaboratively on assessing the probable accuracy of each statement.

The pros and cons approach was used when Mary was considering the possibility of leaving her husband. The therapist explained it by saying, 'It's often useful at this stage to use what is called the "two-column" technique, which is basically listing the "pros" and "cons" for a particular line of action. It seems that you are now endlessly worrying about the problem, going over and over the situation, but hardly being able to see the wood for the trees. It is very common to concentrate on the negative aspects of the situation—in this case, the negative aspects of staying and the negative aspects of leaving. It can be more helpful to focus on what the advantages of a particular course of action would be, and to write down a list of the pros and cons so that you are not simply going round in circles.' At the end of this exercise she had produced the list of pros and cons shown in Table 12.5.

Cognitive rehearsal   This strategy has already been introduced in this chapter (p. 417). It refers to the detailed rehearsal in imagination of a particular task, including the details of the steps taken and the consequences. It is useful for helping a patient develop confidence in attempting a task, in identifying possible pitfalls that were not immediately obvious,

Table 12.5 Mary's list of pros and cons for leaving her husband

Pros	Cons
Reduce her day-to-day distress	Possible loneliness
Improved relationship with children if less tense	Difficulty coping financially
	Children will miss their father
Greater freedom to develop new career	Loss of contact with in-laws
Increased contact with friends	Greater dependence on mother
Allow her to develop new confiding relationships	Loss of sexual relationship
	Shame of broken marriage
	Splitting up of family home

and in establishing more clearly the likely consequences, including advantages and disadvantages, of a course of action.

Role-play and role-reversal   When a patient's problem concerns an inter-personal issue, role-playing a homework assignment can have similar effects to cognitive rehearsal. It has the advantage that patient and therap-ist can evaluate the patient's performance and then, if necessary, try other approaches. Occasionally, role-reversal, in which the therapist plays the patient and the patient plays the significant other person, can be very useful. This is especially relevant when there is a difficulty in behaving assertively, because the patient can get a feel of the likely impact of different sorts of interaction on the significant other. This procedure was used to help Mary prepare herself to discuss intrusiveness with her mother. Role-reversal was particularly useful in this case because it helped Mary to realize that giving her mother specific examples of intrusiveness might be less upsetting than to discuss intrusiveness in more general terms.

Activity scheduling   This technique, which was fully described in Chap-ter 6, is useful in problem-solving, especially when dealing with problems concerning organization of time (see also p. 72). *Study problems* provide an excellent example. Students with study problems often report that their tasks seem overwhelming and they do not know where to begin; therefore, they either work excessively long hours but in a disorganized or overinclusive fashion, or give up trying altogether. The therapist should first help the student draw up a list of priorities for the topics or subjects to be addressed in a study programme. In doing this, the time available will be a major factor, especially if there is an examination close at hand. Next the student should identify some relatively simple tasks relevant to the first priority subject and decide what the objectives are to be. An activity schedule can be used to plan how the student will allocate time to these tasks. A useful general principle is that while completion of a task should be the main objective, the student should decide how long he or she can effectively work in a single stretch (with a maximum of three hours), and keep to that time, even if a task is not completed. The therapist can also help the student work out a schedule which involves regular breaks. Subsequent treatment sessions will involve examining to what extent the student kept to the schedule, problems that were encountered, and then planning a new schedule. Gradually the student can be encouraged to take over the planning.

Challenging erroneous beliefs Difficulties in carrying out problem-solving tasks may be due to beliefs people have about either their ability to manage a task effectively or fear of the consequences of trying. The ways in which erroneous beliefs (erroneous in the sense that they are either incorrect or distorted) can be examined and modified have already been discussed in relation to depression (p. 192) and anxiety states (p. 73), and similar principles can be applied in problem-solving. Erroneous beliefs are often ill-formed in the patient's mind, and the therapist must help the patient identify their precise nature.

For example, a man regarded as too difficult the task of telling his boss the ways in which his job was unsatisfactory and how it might be improved. On closer examination it became apparent that the patient believed that his boss would respond by becoming angry and that as a result his job would be made even worse. The therapist then encouraged him to recall other situations in which he had asserted himself with his boss, and the consequences of doing so; to list the advantages and disadvantages of speaking to his boss; and to predict how he might respond if he were in his boss's position.

Contingency management Occasionally patients can be encouraged to pursue problem-solving by agreeing to reward themselves on completion of a task. For example, a patient might agree that if a task is completed within a certain time he or she will buy a treat, such as an article of clothing.

Providing information and advice The emphasis in problem-solving is on encouraging patients to take responsibility for their problems and to develop their coping skills. Nevertheless, provision of information and advice can be helpful when a person is lacking information, misinformed, or seeking specific advice. For example, a patient might be reassured when told that a decline in sexual interest is common during depression, or when the reasons for physical symptoms in anxiety-provoking situations (p. 57) are explained. Similarly, a therapist might give specific advice concerning, for example, how to make contact with a helping agency (e.g. Citizens' Advice Bureau, Cruse, Shelter, Family Planning Clinic, a sexual minorities group). Whenever possible, patients should be encouraged to obtain further information for themselves.

Termination

The patient should be prepared from the outset for the end of therapy. There should be an early agreement about the likely duration of therapy and number of treatment sessions. As termination comes closer the therapist should plan how this can be accomplished most effectively. It is often helpful if there is a gap of two or three weeks between the penultimate and final treatment sessions. This can allow the patient more time to apply the approach and develop confidence in his or her ability to cope unsupported by the therapist. It also allows time for more difficulties to occur, and these can then be examined in terms of how the patient dealt with them. During the final treatment phase the patient should be encouraged to plan strategies for tackling problems likely to occur in future and be reminded of the steps in problem-solving. Some patients find it helpful if the steps are written down.

Therapists must plan carefully when to end therapy. There may be a temptation to go on too long, perhaps in the belief that patients can be helped with all their problems. Once a patient has made reasonable progress and indicates increased confidence in dealing with remaining problems, the therapist should avoid prolonging treatment, especially if the patient can formulate plans for approaching the more important remaining problems. Failure to progress can be another reason for ending therapy, and this is discussed below.

Monitoring progress and evaluating outcome

Both therapist and patient will find it helpful if the patient's progress in problem-solving is monitored in some way. A diary (p. 46) can provide a detailed record of the patient's progress.

Simple measures of goal achievement can be used if clear goals have been defined at the outset. An assessment for each goal can be made at the end of treatment—e.g. 'goal achieved', 'some progress', 'no change'. An alternative approach is to rate changes in the original problems—e.g. 'problem resolved', 'some improvement', 'no change', 'worse', 'problem no longer relevant'. If patient and therapist make such an assessment together, it can provide helpful feedback to the patient on changes that have been made.

Self-ratings of self-esteem or ability to cope in particular situations may also provide useful information about progress. Changes in symptoms can be assessed through self-report questionnaires, such as the Beck Depression Inventory (Beck, Ward, Mendelsohn, Mock, and Erbaugh 1961; see

p. 175) or the Spielberger Anxiety scale (State) (Spielberger, Gorsuch, and Lushene 1970), or even simpler self-report measures such as visual analogue mood scales (p. 46).

Reasons for failure
Problem-solving may fail for a number of reasons.

Psychiatric disorder
As noted earlier, severe psychiatric disorder usually precludes problem-solving, at least for the present. Sometimes problem-solving will fail because the severity of the psychiatric disorder was not apparent at the outset, was poorly assessed, or has become more severe. The therapist will need to ensure that the psychiatric condition is properly treated before proceeding with problem-solving. However, therapists must be careful not to attribute to psychiatric disorder poor progress due to lack of confidence or low self-esteem.

Low self-esteem and lack of confidence
Poor progress in problem-solving may be the result of a person's self-esteem or confidence being so low that any tasks appear daunting. If this is so, the therapeutic approach may have to be altered to focus on these issues, using the approach described for the treatment of depressed patients (p. 202). Where lack of confidence prevents a patient applying problem-solving strategies without considerable help from the therapist, treatment may have to be prolonged and termination more gradual.

The patient's problems reflect long-standing personality difficulties
If the key problems are the result of long-standing personality difficulties, the patients may need to understand the latter before he or she can attempt to change. Some patients, for example, appear to destroy promising personal relationships because they cannot tolerate emotional intimacy. The origins of such difficulties may be insecure childhood or early adolescent relationships with one or both parents. While a cognitive–behavioural approach can be useful for such problems, dynamic psychotherapy would be another option.

Conclusions
Problem-solving represents a logical, systematic, and reasonably easily learned approach which can be used to help patients in many psychiatric and non-psychiatric settings. It has the advantage of being based on common-sense principles, and is therefore attractive to patients as well as to therapists. Problem-solving is sometimes the only treatment approach that needs to be used. However, it can be an adjunct to other psychological and physical treatments.

Recommended reading

Bancroft, J. (1986). Crisis intervention. In *An introduction to the psychotherapies*, (2nd edn), (ed. S. Bloch), pp. 113–32. Oxford University Press, Oxford.

Brandon, S. (1970). Crisis theory and possibilities of therapeutic intervention. *British Journal of Psychiatry* 117, 627–33.

D'Zurilla, T. J. and Goldfried, M. R. (1971). Problem solving and behaviour modification. *Journal of Abnormal Psychology* 78, 107–26.

Falloon, I. R., Boyd, J. L., and McGill, C. (1984). Problem-solving training. In *Family care of schizophrenia*, pp. 261–84. Guilford Press, New York.

Haaga, D. A. and Davison, G. C. (1986). Cognitive change methods. In *Helping people change: a textbook of methods*, (3rd edn), (ed. F. H. Kanfer and A. P. Goldstein), pp. 236–82. Pergamon Press, New York.

Hawton, K. and Catalan, J. (1987). *Attempted suicide: a practical guide to its nature and management*, (2nd edn). Oxford University Press, Oxford.

References

Abraham, S. and Llewellyn-Jones, D. (1987). *Eating disorders: the facts.* Oxford University Press, Oxford.

Abramson, L. Y., Seligman, M. E. P., and Teasdale, J. D. (1978). Learned helplessness in humans: critique and reformulation. *Journal of Abnormal Psychology* **87**, 49–74.

Agras, W. S. (1987). *Eating disorders: management of obesity, bulimia and anorexia nervosa.* Pergamon, New York.

Agras, W. S. and McCann, U. (1987). The efficacy and role of antidepressants in the treatment of bulimia nervosa. *Annals of Behavioral Medicine* **9**, 18–22.

Agras, S., Sylvester, D., and Oliveau, D. (1969). The epidemiology of common fears and phobias. *Comprehensive Psychiatry* **10**, 151–6.

Alexander, F. (1950). *Psychosomatic medicine, its principles and application.* Norton, New York.

Amdur, M. A. (1981). Death in aftercare. *Comprehensive Psychiatry* **22**, 619–26.

American Psychiatric Association (1980). *Diagnostic and statistical manual of mental disorders,* (3rd edn). American Psychiatric Association, Washington DC.

American Psychiatric Association (1987). *Diagnostic and statistical manual of mental disorders,* (3rd edn, revised). American Psychiatric Association, Washington DC.

Amies, P. L., Gelder, M. G., and Shaw, P. M. (1983). Social phobia: a comparative clinical study. *British Journal of Psychiatry* **142**, 147–79.

Andersen, A. E. (1985). *Practical comprehensive treatment of anorexia nervosa and bulimia.* Johns Hopkins University Press, Baltimore.

Ayllon, T. and Azrin, N. (1968). *The token economy.* Appleton Century Crofts, New York.

Ayllon, T. and Michael, J. (1959). The psychiatric nurse as a behavioral engineer. *Journal of the Experimental Analysis of Behavior* **2**, 323–34.

Bakal, D. A. (1982). *The psychology of chronic headache.* Springer, New York.

Baker, R. D. (1975). Behavioural techniques in the treatment of schizophrenia. In *Handbook of schizophrenia,* (ed. A. Forrest, and J. Affleck), pp. 215–41. Churchill Livingstone, Edinburgh.

Baker, R. D. and Hall, J. N. (1983). *REHAB*: a multipurpose assessment instrument for long-stay psychiatric patients. Vine Publishing, Aberdeen.

Bancroft, J. (1983). *Human sexuality and its problems.* Churchill Livingstone, Edinburgh.

Bancroft, J. and Coles, L. (1976). Three years' experience in a sexual problems clinic. *British Medical Journal* i, 1575–77.

Bandura, A. (1977). Self-efficacy: toward a unifying theory of behavioral change. *Psychological Review* **84**, 191–215.

Barbach, L. (1983). *For each other.* New American Library, New York.

Barker, P. (1982). *Behaviour therapy nursing.* Croom Helm, London.

Barlow, D. H. (1986). Causes of sexual dysfunction: the role of anxiety and cognitive interference. *Journal of Consulting and Clinical Psychology* **54**, 140–8.

Barlow, D. H. and Craske, M. G. (1988). The phenomenology of panic. In *Panic: psychological perspectives*, (ed. S. Rachman, and J. D. Maser), pp. 11–36. Lawrence Erlbaum, Hillsdale NJ.

Barlow, D. H. and Wolfe, B. E. (1981). Behavioral approaches to anxiety disorders: a report on the NIMH-SUNY, Albany, research conference. *Journal of Consulting and Clinical Psychology* **49**, 448–54.

Barlow, D. H., Hayes, S. C. and Nelson, R. O. (1984). *The scientist practitioner*. Pergamon, Oxford.

Barlow, D. H., Blanchard, E. B., Vermilyea, J. A., Vermilyea, B. B., and Di Nardo, P. A. (1986). Generalized anxiety and generalized anxiety disorder: description and reconceptualisation. *American Journal of Psychiatry* **143**, 40–4.

Barlow, D. H., Cohen, A. S., Waddell, M. T., Vermilyea, B. B., Klosko, T. S., Blanchard, E. B., and Di Nardo, P. A. (1984). Panic and generalised anxiety disorders: native and treatment. *Behavior Therapy* **15**, 431–49.

Barrowclough, C. and Tarrier, N. (1984). 'Psychosocial' interventions with families and their effects on the course of schizophrenia: a review. *Psychological Medicine* **14**, 629–42.

Barsky, A. J. and Klerman G. L. (1983). Overview: hypochondriasis, bodily complaints and somatic styles. *American Journal of Psychiatry* **140**, 273–81.

Bartolucci, G. and Drayer, C. S. (1973). An overview of crisis intervention in the emergency rooms of general hospitals. *American Journal of Psychiatry* **130**, 953–60.

Baucom, D. H. and Hoffman, J. A. (1986). The effectiveness of marital therapy: current status and application to the clinical setting. In *Clinical handbook of marital therapy*, (ed. N. S. Jacobson, and A. S. Gurman), pp. 597–620. Guilford Press, New York.

Beck, A. T. (1967). *Depression: clinical, experimental and theoretical aspects*. Harper and Row, New York.

Beck, A. T. (1970). Cognitive therapy: nature and relation to behavior therapy. *Behavior Therapy* **1**, 184–200.

Beck, A. T. (1976). *Cognitive therapy and the emotional disorders*. International Universities Press, New York.

Beck, A. T. (1988). Cognitive approaches to panic disorder. In *Panic: psychological perspectives*, (ed. S. Rachman, and J. D. Maser), pp. 91–110. Lawrence Erlbaum, Hillsdale NJ.

Beck, A. T. and Greenberg, R. L. (1974). *Coping with depression*. Available from: The Center for Cognitive Therapy, Room 602, 133 South 36th Street, Philadelphia, PA 19104, USA.

Beck, A. T., Emery, G., and Greenberg, R. (1985). *Anxiety disorders and phobias: a cognitive perspective*. Basic Books, New York.

Beck, A. T., Epstein, N., and Harrison, R. P. (1983). Cognitions, attitudes and personality dimensions in depression. *British Journal of Cognitive Psychotherapy* **1**, 1–16.

Beck, A. T., Laude, R., and Bohnert, M. (1974). Ideational components of anxiety neurosis. *Archives of General Psychiatry* **31**, 319–25.

Beck, A. T., Epstein, N., Brown, G., and Steer, R. A. (in press). An inventory for measuring clinical anxiety: psychometric properties. *Journal of Consulting and Clinical Psychology*

Beck, A. T., Rush, A. J., Shaw, B. F., and Emery, G. (1979). *Cognitive therapy of depression*. Guilford Press, New York.

Beck, A. T., Hollon, S. D., Young, J. E., Bedrosian, R. C., and Budenz, D. (1985). Treatment of depression with cognitive therapy and amitriptyline. *Archives of General Psychiatry* **42**, 142–8.

Beck, A. T., Ward, C. H., Mendelson, M., Mock, J., and Erbaugh, J. (1961). An inventory for measuring depression. *Archives of General Psychiatry* **4**, 561–71.

Beck, J. G. and Barlow, D. H. (1984). Current conceptualizations of sexual dysfunction: a review and an alternative perspective. *Clinical Psychology Review* **4**, 363–78.

Becker, M. H., Maiman, L. A., Kirscht, J. P., Haefner, D. P., Drachman, R. H., and Taylor, D. W. (1979). Patient perceptions and compliance; recent studies of the health belief model. In *Compliance in health care*, (ed. R. B. Haynes, D. W. Taylor, and D. L. Sackett), pp. 78–109 Johns Hopkins University Press, Baltimore.

Bellack, A. S. and Hersen, M. (1988). *Behavioral assessment: a practical handbook*, (3rd edn). Pergamon, New York.

Bellack, A. S. and Schwartz, J. S. (1976). Assessment for self-control programs. In *Behavioral assessment: a practical handbook*, (ed. M. Hersen and A. S. Bellack), pp. 111–42. Pergamon, Oxford.

Bemis, K. M. (1987). The present status of operant conditioning for the treatment of anorexia nervosa. *Behavior Modification* **11**, 432–64.

Bernstein, D. A. and Borkovec, T. D. (1973). *Progressive relaxation training: a manual for the helping professions*. Research Press, Champaign Ill.

Beyts. J. P. (1987). Vestibular rehabilitation. In *Scott Brown's diseases of the ear, nose and throat, Vol 2*, (ed. B. Dix and S. D. G. Stephens), pp. 532–57. Butterworths, London.

Bibb, J. L. and Chambless, D. L. (1986). Alcohol use and abuse among diagnosed agoraphobics. *Behaviour Research and Therapy* **24**, 49–58.

Bird, B. L., Cataldo, M. F., and Parker, L. (1981). Behavioral medicine for muscular disorders. In *Handbook of clinical behavior therapy*, (ed. S. M. Turner, K. S. Calhoun, and H. E. Adams), pp. 406–46. Wiley, New York.

Birk, L. (1973). *Biofeedback: behavioral medicine*. Grune and Stratton, New York.

Blackburn, I. M. and Bishop, S. (1983). Changes in cognition with pharmacotherapy and cognitive therapy. *British Journal of Psychiatry* **143**, 609–17.

Blackburn, I. M. and Bonham, K. G. (1980). Experimental effects of a cognitive therapy technique in depressed patients. *British Journal of Social and Clinical Psychology* **19**, 353–63.

Blackburn, I. M., Eunson, K. M., and Bishop, S. (1986). A two-year naturalistic follow-up of depressed patients treated with cognitive therapy, pharmacotherapy and a combination of both. *Journal of Affective Disorders* **10**, 67–75.

Blackburn, I. M., Bishop, S., Glen, A. I. M., Whalley, L. J., and Christie, J. E. (1981). The efficacy of cognitive therapy in depression: a treatment trial using cognitive therapy and pharmacotherapy, each alone and in combination. *British Journal of Psychiatry* **139**, 181–9.

Blanchard, E. B. and Andrasik, F. (1985). *Management of chronic headaches: a psychological approach*. Pergamon, New York.

Blaney, P. H. (1977). Contemporary theories of depression: critique and comparison. *Journal of Abnormal Psychology* **86**, 203–23.

✗ Borkovec, T. D. (1982). Insomnia. *Journal of Consulting and Clinical Psychology* **50**, 880–95.

Borkovec, T. D. and Sides, J. K. (1979a). The contribution of relaxation and expectancy to fear reduction via graded, imaginal exposure to feared stimuli. *Behaviour Research and Therapy* **17**, 529–40.

Borkovec, T. D. and Sides, J. K. (1979b). Critical procedural variables related to the physiological effects of progressive relaxation: a review. *Behaviour Research and Therapy* **17**, 119–25.

✓ Borkovec, T. D., Grayson, J. B., O'Brien, G. T., and Weerts, T. C. (1979). Relaxation treatment of pseudoinsomnia and idiopathic insomnia: and electroencephalographic evaluation. *Journal of Applied Behavior Analysis* **12**, 37–54.

✗ Borkovec, T. D., Robinson, E., Pruzinsky, T., and DePree, J. A. (1983). Preliminary exploration of worry: some characteristics and processes. *Behaviour Research and Therapy* **21**, 9–16.

Bornstein, P. H., Bach, P. J., Heider, J. F., and Ernst, J. (1981). Clinical treatment of marital dysfunction: a multiple baseline analysis. *Behavioral Assessment* **3**, 335–43.

Boyd, J. H. (1986). Use of mental health services for the treatment of panic disorder. *American Journal of Psychiatry* **143**, 1569–74.

Boyd, J. H. and Weissman, M. M. (1982). Epidemiology. In *Handbook of affective disorders*, (ed. E. S. Paykel), pp. 109–25. Churchill Livingstone, Edinburgh.

Bradley, L. A. and Prokop, C. K. (1982). Research methods in contemporary medical psychology. In *Handbook of research methods in clinical psychology*, (ed. P. C. Kendall, and J. N. Butcher), pp. 591–650. Wiley, New York.

Brandon, S. (1970). Crisis theory and possibilities of therapeutic intervention. *British Journal of Psychiatry* **117**, 627–33.

Brown, G. W. and Harris, T. O. (1978). *Social origins of depression: a study of psychiatric disorder in women*. Tavistock Publications, London.

Brownell, K. D., Marlatt, G. A., Lichtenstein, E. and Wilson, G. T. (1986). Understanding and preventing relapse. *American Psychologist* **41**, 765–82.

Bruch, H. (1973). *Eating disorders: obesity, anorexia nervosa and the person within*. Basic Books, New York.

Burns, D. (1980). *Feeling good*. New American Library, New York.

Butler, G. (1985). Exposure as a treatment for social phobia: some instructive difficulties. *Behaviour Research and Therapy* **23**, 651–7.

Butler, G. (1989). Issues in the application of cognitive and behavioral strategies to the treatment of social phobia. *Clinical Psychology Review*, in press.

Butler, G. and Mathews, A. (1983). Cognitive processes in anxiety. *Advances in Behaviour Research and Therapy* **5**, 51–62.

Butler, G., Cullington, A., Hibbert, G., Klimes, I., and Gelder, M. (1987b).

Anxiety management for persistent generalised anxiety. *British Journal of Psychiatry* **151**, 535–42.

Butler, G., Cullington, A., Munby, M., Amies, P., and Gelder, M. (1984). Exposure and anxiety management in the treatment of social phobia. *Journal of Consulting and Clinical Psychology* **52**, 642–50.

Butler, G., Gelder, M., Hibbert, G., Cullington, A., and Klimes, I. (1987a). Anxiety management: developing effective strategies. *Behaviour Research and Therapy* **25**, 517–22.

Butler, R. J. and Rosenthal, G. (1985). *Behaviour and rehabilitation.* John Wright, Bristol.

Caplan, G. (1961). *An approach to community mental health.* Tavistock, London.

Casper, R. C. (1987). Psychotherapy in anorexia nervosa. In *Handbook of eating disorders. Part 1: anorexia and bulimia nervosa,* (ed. P. J. V. Beumont, G. D. Burrows, and R. C. Casper), pp. 255–69. Elsevier, Amsterdam.

Catalan, J., Gath, D., Edmonds, G., and Ennis, J. (1984). The effects of non-prescribing in general practice: I controlled evaluation of psychiatric and social outcome. *British Journal of Psychiatry* **144**, 593–603.

Cautela, J. R. (1967). Covert sensitization. *Psychological Reports* **20**, 459–68.

Cautela, J. R. and Upper, D. (1976). The Behavioral Inventory Battery: the use of self-report measures in behavioral analysis and therapy. In *Behavioral assessment: a practical handbook,* (ed. M. Hersen, and A. S. Bellack), pp. 77–109, Pergamon, New York.

Cawley, R. (1974). Psychotherapy and obsessional disorders. In *Obsessional states,* (ed. H. R. Beech), pp. 259–90. Methuen, London.

Chambless, D. L. and Goldstein, A. J. (1982). *Agoraphobia: multiple perspectives on theory and treatment.* John Wiley, New York.

Chambless, D. L., Caputo, G. C., Bright, P., and Gallagher, R. (1984). Measurement of fear of fear in agoraphobics: the body sensations questionnaire and the agoraphobic cognitions questionnaire. *Journal of Consulting and Clinical Psychology* **52**, 1090–7.

Chambless, D. L., Caputo, G. C., Jasin, S., Gracely, E., and Williams, C. (1985). The mobility questionnaire for agoraphobia. *Behaviour Research and Therapy* **23**, 35–44.

Chernin, K. (1983). *Womansize: the tyranny of slenderness.* The Women's Press, Wellingborough.

Christensen, H., Hadzi-Pavlovic, D., Andrews, G., and Mattick, R. (1987). Behavior therapy and tricyclic medication in the treatment of obsessive-compulsive disorder: a quantitive review. *Journal of Consulting and Clinical Psychology* **55**, 701–11.

Clark, D. H. (1964). *Administrative therapy.* Tavistock, London.

Clark, D. M. (1983). On the induction of depressed mood in the laboratory: evaluation and comparison of the Velten and musical procedures. *Advances in Behaviour Research and Therapy* **5**, 27–50.

Clark, D. M. (1986a). A cognitive approach to panic. *Behaviour Research and Therapy* **24**, 461–70.

Clark, D. M. (1986b). Cognitive therapy of anxiety. *Behavioural Psychotherapy* **14**, 283–94.

Clark, D. M. (1988). A cognitive model of panic attacks. In *Panic: psychological perspectives*, (ed. S. Rachman, and J. D. Maser), pp. 71–90. Lawrence Erlbaum, Hillsdale NJ.

Clark, D. M. and Beck, A. T. (1988). Cognitive approaches. In *Handbook of anxiety disorders*, (ed. C. Last, and M. Hersen), pp. 362–85. Pergamon, New York.

Clark, D. M. and Salkovskis, P. M. (in press). *Cognitive therapy for panic and hypochondriasis*. Pergamon, New York.

Clark, D. M. and Teasdale, J. D. (1982). Diurnal variation in clinical depression and accessibility of memories of positive and negative experiences. *Journal of Abnormal Psychology* 91, 87–95.

Clark, D. M., Salkovskis, P. M., and Chalkley, A. J. (1985). Respiratory control as a treatment for panic attacks. *Journal of Behavior Therapy and Experimental Psychiatry* 16, 23–30.

Clark, D. M., Salkovskis, P. M., Gelder, M., Koehler, K., Martin, M., Anastasiades, P., Hackmann, A., Middleton, H., and Jeavons, A. (1988). Tests of a cognitive theory of panic. In *Panic and phobias II*, (ed. I. Hand, and H. U. Wittchen), pp. 149–58. Springer-Verlag, Heidelberg.

× Coates, T. J. and Thoresen, C. E. (1981). Treating sleep disorders: few answers, some suggestions and many questions. In *Handbook of clinical behavior therapy*, (ed. S. M. Turner, K. S. Calhoun, and H. E. Adams), pp. 240–89. Wiley, New York.

Conning, A. (1986). *Individual differences in designing treatments for chronic psychiatric patients*. Unpublished M. Phil. dissertation. University of London.

Cooper, P. J. and Fairburn, C. G. (1986). The depressive symptoms of bulimia nervosa. *British Journal of Psychiatry* 148, 268–74.

Cooper, P. J. and Steere, J. A. (in preparation). Body image disurbance in bulimia nervosa: changes following treatment.

Coryell, W. and Winokur, G. (1982). Course and outcome. In *Handbook of affective disorders*, (ed. E. S. Paykel), pp. 93–106. Churchill-Livingstone, London.

Costello, C. G. (1972). Depression: loss of reinforcement or loss of reinforcer effectiveness? *Behavior Therapy* 3, 240–7.

Creer, C. and Wing, J. K. (1974). *Schizophrenia at home*. National Schizophrenia Fellowship, Surbiton.

Creer, T. L. (1982). Asthma. *Journal of Consulting and Clinical Psychology* 50, 912–21.

Crisp, A. H. (1967). The possible significance of some behavioural correlates of weight and carbohydrate intake. *Journal of Psychosomatic Research* 11, 117–31.

Crowe, M. J. (1978). Conjoint marital therapy: a controlled outcome study. *Psychological Medicine* 8, 623–36.

Crowe, M. and Ridley, J. (1986). The negotiated timetable: a new approach to marital conflicts involving male demands and female reluctance for sex. *Sexual and Marital Therapy* 1, 157–77.

Davison, G. C. (1968). Systematic desensitisation as a counterconditioning technique *Journal of Abnormal Psychology* 73, 91–9.

De Amicis, L. A., Goldberg, D. C., LoPiccolo, J., Friedman, J., and Davies, L. (1985). Clinical follow-up of couples treated for sexual dysfunction. *Archives of Sexual Behavior* **14**, 467–89.

De Jong, R., Treibe, R., and Henrich, G. (1986). Effectiveness of two psychological treatments for inpatients with severe and chronic depressions. *Cognitive Therapy and Research* **10**, 645–63.

Delprato, D. J. and McGlynn, F. D. (1986). Innovations in behavioral medicine. In *Progress in Behavior Modification*, Vol. 10, (ed. M. Hersen, and R. M. Eiser), pp. 67–122.

Delvin, D. (1974). *The book of love*. New English Library, London.

Dollard, J. and Miller, N. E. (1950). *Personality and psychotherapy: an analysis in terms of learning, thinking, and culture*. McGraw-Hill, New York.

Duddle, C. M. (1975). The treatment of marital psycho-sexual problems. *British Journal of Psychiatry* **127**, 169–70.

Duddle, C. M. (1977). Etiological factors in the unconsummated marriage. *Journal of Psychosomatic Research* **21**, 157–60.

DuPont, R. L. (1982). *Phobia: a comprehensive summary of modern treatments*. Brunner/Mazel, New York.

Durham, R. C. and Turvey, A. A. (1987). Cognitive therapy vs. behaviour therapy in the treatment of chronic general anxiety. *Behaviour Research and Therapy* **25**, 229–34.

D'Zurilla, T. J. and Goldfried, M. R. (1971). Problem solving and behavior modification. *Journal of Abnormal Psychology* **78**, 107–26.

D'Zurilla, T. J. and Nezu, A. (1980). A study of the generation of alternatives process in social problem solving. *Cognitive Therapy and Research* **4**, 73–81.

Ellis, A. (1962). *Reason and emotion in psychotherapy*. Lyle Stuart, New York.

Emmelkamp, P. M. G. (1982). *Phobic and obsessive-compulsive disorders: theory, research and practice*. Plenum, New York.

Emmelkamp, P. M. G. and Geisselbach, P. (1981). Treatment of obsessions: relevant vs. irrelevant exposure. *Behavioural Psychotherapy* **9**, 322–9.

Emmelkamp, P. M. G., Visser, S., and Hoekstra, R. J. (1988). Cognitive therapy vs. exposure *in vivo* in the treatment of obsessive-compulsives. *Cognitive Therapy and Research* **12**, 103–14.

Emmelkamp, P. M. G., van der Helm, M., Van Zanten, B., and Plochg, I. (1980). Treatment of obsessive-compulsive patients: the contribution of self-instructional training to the effectiveness of exposure. *Behaviour Research and Therapy* **18**, 61–6.

Emmelkamp, P. M. G., Mersch, P. P., Vissia, E., and van der Helm, M. (1985). Social phobia: a comparative evaluation of cognitive and behavioural interventions. *Behaviour Research and Therapy* **22**, 365–9.

Eysenck, H. J. (1952). The effects of psychotherapy: an evaluation. *Journal of Consulting Psychology* **16**, 319–24.

Fairburn, C. G. (1985). Cognitive–behavioral treatment for bulimia. In *Handbook of psychotherapy for anorexia nervosa and bulimia*, (ed. D. M. Garner, and P. E. Garfinkel), pp. 160–92. Guilford Press, New York.

Fairburn, C. G. (1988). The uncertain status of the cognitive approach to bulimia nervosa. In *Psychobiology of bulimia nervosa*, (ed. K. Pirke, D. Ploog, and W. Vandereycken). pp. 129–36. Springer-Verlag, Heidelberg.

Fairburn, C. G. (1988). The current status of psychological treatments for bulimia nervosa. *Journal of Psychosomatic Research* **32**, 635–45.

Fairburn, C. G. and Garner, D. M. (1988). Diagnostic criteria for anorexia nervosa and bulimia nervosa: the importance of attitudes to shape and weight. In *Diagnostic issues in anorexia nervosa and bulimia nervosa*, (ed. D. M. Garner, and P. E. Garfinkel), pp. 36–55. Brunner/Mazel, New York.

Fairburn, C. G. and Hope, R. A. (1988). Disorders of eating and weight. In *Companion to psychiatric studies*, (4th edn), (ed. R. E. Kendell, and A. K. Zealley), pp. 588–604. Churchill Livingstone, Edinburgh.

Fairburn, C. G., Cooper, Z., and Cooper, P. J. (1986a). The clinical features and maintenance of bulimia nervosa. In *Handbook of eating disorders: physiology, psychology and treatment of obesity, anorexia and bulimia*, (ed. K. D. Brownell, and J. P. Foreyt), pp. 389–404. Basic Books, New York.

Fairburn, C. G., O'Conner, M., and Anastasiades, P. (in preparation). The outcome of bulimia nervosa: a five year follow-up study.

Fairburn, C. G., Cooper, P. J., Kirk, J., and O'Connor, M. (1985). The significance of the neurotic symptoms of bulimia nervosa. *Journal of Psychiatric Research* **19**, 135–40.

Fairburn, C. G., Kirk, J., O'Connor, M., and Cooper, P. J. (1986b). A comparison of two psychological treatments for bulimia nervosa. *Behavioural Research and Therapy* **24**, 629–43.

Fairburn, C. G., Kirk, J., O'Connor, M., Anastasiades, P., and Cooper, P. J. (1987). Prognostic factors in bulimia nervosa. *British Journal of Clinical Psychology* **26**, 223–4.

Falloon, I. R. H., Boyd, J. L., and McGill, C. W. (1984). *Family care of schizophrenia*. Guilford, New York.

Fennell, M. J. V. and Teasdale, J. D. (1982). Cognitive therapy with chronic, drug-refractory depressed outpatients: a note of caution. *Cognitive Therapy and Research* **6**, 455–9.

Fennell, M. J. V. and Teasdale, J. D. (1984). Effects of distraction on thinking and affect in depressed patients. *British Journal of Clinical Psychology* **23**, 65–6.

Fennell, M. J. V. and Teasdale, J. D. (1987a). Cognitive therapy for depression: individual differences and the process of change. *Cognitive Therapy and Research* **11**, 253–71.

Fennell, M. J. V. and Teasdale, J. D. (1987b). Distraction in neurotic and endogenous depression: an investigation of negative thinking in major depressive disorder. *Psychological Medicine* **17**, 441–52.

Ferster, C. B. (1973). A functional analysis of depression. *American Psychologist* **28**, 857–70.

Finlay-Jones, R. and Brown, G. W. (1981). Types of stressful life events and the onset of anxiety and depressive disorders. *Psychological Medicine* **11**, 803–15.

Foa, E. B. (1979). Failures in treating obsessive-compulsives. *Behavior Research and Therapy* **17**, 169–76.

Foa, E. B. and Emmelkamp, P. M. G. (1983). *Failures in behavior therapy*. Wiley, New York.

Foa, E. B. and Goldstein, A. (1978). Continuous exposure and strict response prevention in the treatment of obsessive-compulsive neurosis. *Behavior Therapy* 9, 821–9.

Ford, M. J. (1986). The irritable bowel syndrome. *Journal of Psychosomatic Medicine* 30, 399–410.

Frank, E., Anderson, L., and Kupfer, D. J. (1976). Profiles of couples seeking sex therapy and maritial therapy. *American Journal of Psychiatry* 133, 559–62.

Freund, B., Steketee, G. S. and Foa, E. B. (1987). Compulsive activity checklist (CAC): pychometric analysis with obsessive-compulsive disorder. *Behavioral Assessment* 9, 67–79.

Friday, N. (1975). *My Secret Garden*. Virago, London.

Friday, N. (1980). *Men in Love*. Arrow, London.

Gambrill, E. D. (1977). *Behavior modification; handbook of assessment, intervention and evaluation*. Jossey-Bass, San Francisco.

Garakani, H., Zitrin, C. M., and Klein, D. F. (1984). Treatment of panic disorder with imipramine alone. *American Journal of Psychiatry* 141, 446–8.

Garety, P. A. and Morris, I. (1984). A new unit for long-stay psychiatric patients: organisation, attitudes and quality of care. *Psychological Medicine* 14, 183–92.

Garfinkel, P. E. and Garner, D. M. (1982). *Anorexia nervosa: a multidimensional perspective*. Brunner/Mazel, New York.

Garner, A. (1980). *Conversationally speaking*. McGraw-Hill, New York.

Garner, D. M. and Bemis, K. M. (1982). A cognitive-behavioral approach to anorexia nervosa. *Cognitive Therapy and Research* 6, 123–50.

Garner, D. M. and Bemis, K. M. (1985). Cognitive therapy for anorexia nervosa. In *Handbook of psychotherapy for anorexia nervosa and bulimia*, (ed. D. M. Garner, and P. E. Garfinkel), pp. 107–46. Guilford Press, New York.

Garner, D. M., Fairburn, C. G., and Davis, R. (1987). Cognitive–behavioral treatment of bulimia nervosa: a critical appraisal. *Behavior Modification* 11, 398–431.

Garner, D. M., Rockert, W., Olmsted, M. P., Johnson, C., and Coscina, D. V. (1985). Psychoeducational principles in the treatment of bulimia and anorexia nervosa. In *Handbook of psychotherapy for anorexia nervosa and bulimia*, (ed. D. M. Garner, and P. E. Garfinkel), pp. 513–72. Guilford Press, New York.

Garrow, J. S. (1988). *Obesity and related diseases*. Churchill Livingstone, Edinburgh.

Gelder, M. G., Bancroft, J. H. J., Gath, D. H., Johnston, D. W., Mathews, A. M., and Shaw, P. M. (1973). Specific and non-specific factors in behaviour therapy. *British Journal of Psychiatry* 123, 445–62.

Gelfand, D. M., Gelfand, S., and Dobson, W. R. (1967). Unprogrammed reinforcement of patients' behaviour in a mental hospital. *Behaviour Research and Therapy* 5, 201–7.

Gentry, W. D. (1984). *Handbook of behavioral medicine*. Guilford Press, New York.

Gitlin, B., Martin, J., Shear, M. K., Frances, A. J., Ball, G., and Josephson, S. (1986). Behavioral therapy for panic disorder. *Journal of Nervous and Mental Disease* 173, 742–3.

Gittleson, N. (1966). The fate of obsessions in depressive psychosis. *British Journal of Psychiatry* 112, 67–79.

Goldfried, M. R. and Davison, G. C. (1976). *Clinical behavior therapy*. Holt Rinehart and Winston, New York.

Goldfried, M. R. and Robins, C. (1983). Self-schema, cognitive bias, and the processing of therapeutic experiences. In *Advances in cognitive–behavioral research and therapy*, Vol. 2, (ed. P. C. Kendall), pp. 33–80. Academic Press, New York.

Gomes-Schwartz, B. (1979). The modification of schizophrenic behavior. *Behavior Modification* 3, 439–68.

Gostin, L. (1986). *Institutions observed*. King Edwards Hospital Fund for London, London.

Gottman, J. M. (1979). *Marital interaction: experimental investigations*. Academic press, New York.

Griez, E. and van den Hout, M. A. (1986). CO_2 inhalation in the treatment of panic attacks. *Behaviour Research and Therapy* 24, 145–50.

Gunning, R. (1952). *The technique of clear writing*. McGraw-Hill, New York.

Häfner, H. (1985). Changing patterns of mental health care. *Acta Psychiatrica Scandinavica*, Supplement No. 319, 71, 151–64.

Häfner, J. and Milton, F. (1977). The influences of propranolol on the exposure *in vivo* of agoraphobics. *Psychological Bulletin* 7, 419–25.

Hall, J. N. (1979). Assessment procedures used in studies on long-stay patients: a survey of papers published in the British Journal of Psychiatry. *British Journal of Psychiatry* 135, 330–5.

Hall, J. N. (1981). Psychological assessment. In *Handbook of psychiatric rehabilitation practice*, (ed. J. K. Wing, and B. Morris), pp. 17–28. Oxford University Press, Oxford.

Hall, J. N. and Baker, R. D. (1986). Token economies and schizophrenia: a review. In *Contemporary issues in schizophrenia*, (ed. A. Kerr, and R. P. Snaith), pp. 410–19. Gaskell, London.

Hall, J. N. Baker, R. D., and Hutchinson, K. (1977). A controlled evaluation of token economy procedures with chronic schizophrenic patients. *Behaviour Research and Therapy* 15, 261–83.

Hallam, R. S. and Stephens, S. D. G. (1985). Vestibular disorders and emotional distress. *Journal of Psychosomatic Research* 29, 408–13.

Hammen, C. L. and Glass, D. R. (1975). Depression, activity, and evaluation of reinforcement. *Journal of Abnormal Psychology* 84, 718–21.

Hardy, A. B. (1982). Phobic thinking: the cognitive influences on the behavior and effective treatment of the agoraphobic. In *Phobia: a comprehensive summary of modern treatments*, (ed. R. L. Dupont), pp. 93–8. Brunner/Mazel, New York.

Hawton, K. (1985). *Sex therapy: a practical guide*. Oxford University Press, Oxford.

Hawton, K. (1987). Sexual problems associated with physical illness. In *Oxford textbook of medicine*, (ed. D. J. Weatherall, J. G. G. Ledingham, and D. A. Warrell), pp. 245.40–245.43. Oxford University Press, Oxford.

Hawton, K. and Catalan, J. (1986). Prognostic factors in sex therapy. *Behaviour Research and Therapy* 24, 377–85.

Hawton, K. and Catalan, J. (1987). *Attempted suicide: a practical guide to its nature and management*, (2nd edn). Oxford University Press, Oxford.

Hawton, K., Catalan, J., Martin, P., and Fagg, J. (1986). Long-term outcome of sex therapy. *Behaviour Research and Therapy* 24, 665–75.

Haynes, S. N. (1978). *Principles of behavioral assessment*. Gardner Press, New York.

Heide, F. J. and Borkovec, T. D. (1984). Relaxation-induced anxiety: mechanisms and theoretical implications. *Behaviour Research and Therapy* 22, 1–12.

Heimberg, R. G., Dodge, C. S., and Becker, R. E. (1987). Social phobia. In *Anxiety and stress disorders*, (ed. L. Michelson, and L. M. Ascher), pp. 281–309. Guilford Press, New York.

Hibbert, G. A. (1984). Ideational components of anxiety: their origin and content. *British Journal of Psychiatry* 144, 618–24.

Himadi, W. G., Cerny, J. A., Barlow, D. H., Cohen, S., and O'Brien, G. T. (1986). The relationship of marital adjustment to agoraphobia treatment and outcome. *Behaviour Research and Therapy* 24, 107–15.

Hodgson, R. and Rachman, S. J. (1977). Obsessional-compulsive complaints. *Behaviour Research and Therapy* 15, 389–95.

Hollon, S. D. (1980). Cognitive–behavioral treatment of drug-induced pan-situational anxiety states. In *New directions in cognitive therapy: a casebook*, (ed. G. Emergy, S. D. Hollon, and R. C. Bedrosian), pp. 120–38. Raven Press, New York.

Hollon, S. D. and Kriss, M. R. (1984). Cognitive factors in clinical research and practice. *Clinical Psychology Review* 4, 35–76.

Hollon, S. D., Evans, M., and DeRubeis, R. J. (1983). Final report of the cognitive-pharmacotherapy trial. Paper presented at the World Congress on Behavior Therapy, Washington, DC, December.

Jacobson, E. (1938). *Progressive relaxation*. University of Chicago Press, Chicago.

Jacobson, N. S. and Margolin, G. (1979). *Marital therapy: strategies based on social learning and behavior exchange principles*. Brunner/Mazel, New York.

Jacobson, N. S., Follette, W. C., and McDonald, D. W. (1982). Reactivity to positive and negative behavior in distressed and non-distressed married couples. *Journal of Consulting and Clinical Psychology* 50, 706–14.

Jacobson, N. S., Berley, R. A., Melman, K. N., Elwood, R., and Phelps, C. (1985). Failure in behavioral marital therapy. In *Failures in family therapy*, (ed. S. Coleman), pp. 91–134. Guilford Press, New York.

Jacobson, N. S., Follette, W. C., Revenstorf, D., Baucom, D. H., Hahlweg, K., and Margolin, G. (1984). Variability in outcome and clinical significance of behavioral marital therapy: a re-analysis of outcome data. *Journal of Consulting and Clinical Psychology* 52, 497–504.

Johnston, D. W. (1984). Biofeedback, relaxation and related procedures in the treatment of psychophysiological disorders. In *Health care and human behaviour*, (ed. A. Steptoe, and A. Mathews), pp. 267–300. Academic Press, London.

Jones, M. C. (1924). The elimination of children's fears. *Journal of Experimental Psychology* 7, 382–90.

Katon, W. (1984). Panic disorder and somatization. *The American Journal of Medicine* 77, 101–6.

Kaplan, H. S. (1974). *The new sex therapy.* Brunner/Mazel, New York.

Kaplan, H. S. (1979). *Disorders of sexual desire and other new concepts and techniques in sex therapy.* Brunner/Mazel, New York.

Kaplan, H. S. (1987). *The illustrated manual of sex therapy*, (2nd edn). Brunner/Mazel, New York.

Kendall, P. C. (1984). Cognitive processes and procedures in behavior therapy. In *Annual review of behavior therapy; theory and practice*, Vol. 10, (ed. C. M. Franks, G. T. Wilson, P. C. Kendall, and K. D. Brownell), pp. 123–63. Guilford Press, New York.

Kenyon, F. E. (1964). Hypochondriasis: a clinical study. *British Journal of Psychiatry* 110, 478–88.

Kilmann, P. R. and Auerbach, R. (1979). Treatments of premature ejaculation and psychogenic impotence: a critical review of the literature. *Archives of Sexual Behavior* 8, 81–100.

Kirk, J. W. (1983). Behavioural treatment of obsessive-compulsive patients in routine clinical practice. *Behaviour Research and Therapy* 21, 57–62.

Kirkley, B. G., Schneider, J. A., Agras, W. S., and Bachman, J. A. (1985). A comparison of two group treatments for bulimia. *Journal of Consulting and Clinical Psychology* 53, 43–8.

Klerman, G. L. (1986). Current trends in clinical research on panic attacks, agoraphobia and related anxiety disorders. *Journal of Clinical Psychiatry* 47, 37–9.

Kovacs, M. (1980). The efficacy of cognitive–behavioral therapy for depression. *American Journal of Psychiatry* 137, 1495–501.

Kovacs, M., Rush, A. J., Beck, A. T., and Hollon, S. D. (1981). Depressed outpatients treated with cognitive therapy or pharmacotherapy: a one-year follow-up. *Archives of General Psychiatry* 135, 525–33.

Krawiecka, M., Goldberg, D., and Vaughn, M. (1977). A standardised psychiatric assessment scale for rating chronic psychotic patients. *Acta Psychiatrica Scandinavica* 55, 299–308.

Lacey, J. H. and Evans, C. D. H. (1986). The Impulsivist: a multi-impulsive personality disorder. *British Journal of Addiction* 81, 641–9.

Lacks, P. (1987). *Behavioral treatment for persistent insomnia.* Pergamon, New York.

Lader, M. and Marks, I. M. (1971). *Clinical anxiety.* Heineman, London.

Lang, P. J. (1968). Fear reduction and fear behavior: problems in treating a construct. In *Research in psychotherapy*, Vol. III, (ed. J. M. Schlien), pp. 90–103. American Psychological Association, Washington DC.

Lang, P. J. (1970). Stimulus control, response control and the desensitization of fear. In *Learning approaches to therapeutic behavior*, (ed. D. J. Levis), pp. 148–73. Aldine Press, Chicago.

Last, C. G. (1987). Simple phobias. In *Anxiety and stress disorders: cognitive–behavioral assessment and treatment*, (ed. L. Michelson, and L. M. Ascher), pp. 177–90. Guilford Press, New York.

Latimer, P. R. (1981). Irritable bowel syndrome: a behavioral model. *Behaviour Research and Therapy* 19, 475–83.

Latimer, P. R. and Sweet, A. A. (1984). Cognitive versus behavioral procedures in cognitive behavior therapy: a critical review of the evidence. *Journal of Behavior Therapy and Experimental Psychiatry* **15**, 9–22.

Lavender, A. (1985). Quality of care and staff practices in long-stay settings. In *New developments in clinical psychology*, (ed. F. N. Watts), pp. 70–83. Wiley, Chichester.

Lazarus, A. A. (1968). Learning theory and the treatment of depression. *Behaviour Research and Therapy* **6**, 83–9.

Lazarus, A. A. (1971). *Behavior therapy and beyond*. McGraw Hill, New York.

Leenan, F. H. H. and Haynes, R. B. (1986). *How to control your blood pressure and get more out of life*. Grosvenor House Press, Montreal.

Leff, J. P. and Vaughn, C. (1985). *Expressed emotion in families*. Guilford Press, New York.

Lewinsohn, P. M. (1974a). A behavioral approach to depression. In *The psychology of depression: contemporary theory and research*, (ed. R. J. Friedman, and M. M. Katz). Winston, Washington, DC.

Lewinsohn, P. M. (1974b). Clinical and theoretical aspects of depression. In *Innovative methods in psychopathology*, (ed. K. S. Calhoun, H. E. Adams, and K. M. Mitchell), pp. 63–120, Wiley, New York.

Lewinsohn, P. M., Sullivan, M. J., and Grosscup, S. J. (1982). Behavioral therapy: clinical applications. In *Short-term psychotherapies for depression*, (ed. A. J. Rush), pp. 50–87. Wiley, New York.

Lewinsohn, P. M., Munoz, R. F., Youngren, M. A., and Zeiss, A. M. (1978). *Control your depression*. Prentice-Hill, New Jersey.

Ley, P. (1979). Memory for medical information. *British Journal of Social and Clinical Psychology* **18**, 245–55.

Liberman, R. P., King, L. W., De Risi, W. J., and McCann, M. (1975). *Personal effectiveness*. Research Press, Champaign, Ill.

Lindsay, S. J., Salkovskis, P. M., and Stoll, K. (1982). Rhythmical body movements in sleep: a brief review and treatment study. *Behaviour Research and Therapy* **20**, 523–7.

Lipinski, D. P. and Nelson, R. O. (1974). The reactivity and unreliability of self-recording. *Journal of Consulting and Clinical Psychology* **42**, 118–23.

Lipowski, Z. J. (1986a). Psychosomatic concepts in historical perspective. In *Proceedings of the 15th European conference on psychosomatic research*, (ed. J. H. Lacey, and D. A. Sturgeon), pp. 1–5. John Libbey, London.

Lipowski, Z. J. (1986b). Somatization: a borderland between medicine and psychiatry. *Canadian Medical Association Journal* **135**, 609–14.

LoPiccolo, J. and Steger, J. C. (1974). The sexual interaction inventory: a new instrument for the assessment of sexual dysfunction. *Archives of Sexual Behavior* **3**, 585–95.

MacCarthy, B., Benson, J., and Brewin, C. R. (1986). Task motivation and problem appraisal in long-term psychiatric patients. *Psychological Medicine* **16**, 431–8.

McGovern, K. B., Stewart, R. C., and LoPiccolo, J. (1975). Secondary orgasmic dysfunction, I: analysis and strategies for treatment. *Archives of Sexual Behavior* **4**, 265–75.

Mackarness, R. (1980). *Chemical victims*. Pan Books, London.

McNally, R. J. (1987). Preparedness and phobias: a review. *Psychological Bulletin* **101**, 283–303.

Mahoney, M. H. and Mahoney, K. (1976). *Permanent weight control*. Norton, New York.

Marks, I. M. (1969). *Fears and phobias*. Academic Press, New York.

Marks, I. M. (1975). Behavioral treatment of phobic and obsessive-compulsive disorders: a critical appraisal. In *Progress in behavior modification*, Vol. 1, (ed. M. Hersen, R. M. Eisler, and P. M. Miller), pp. 66–158. Academic Press, New York.

Marks, I. M. (1981). *Cure and care of neurosis*. Wiley, New York.

Marks, I. M. (1987). *Fears, phobias and rituals*. Oxford University Press, Oxford.

Marks, I. M. and Gelder, M. G. (1966). Different ages of onset in varieties of phobia. *American Journal of Psychiatry* **123**, 218–21.

Marks, I. M. and Mathews, A. M. (1979). Standard self-rating for phobic patients. *Behaviour Research and Therapy* **17**, 263–7.

Marks, I. M., Stern, R. S., Mawson, D., Cobb, J., and McDonald, R. (1980). Clomipramine and exposure for obsessive-compulsive rituals: I. *British Journal of Psychiatry* **136**, 1–25.

Marlatt, G. A. and Gordon, J. R. (1985). *Relapse prevention: maintenance strategies in the treatment of addictive behaviors*. Guilford Press, New York.

Marteau, T. M. and Johnston, M. (1987). Health psychology: the danger of neglecting psychological models. *Bulletin of the British Psychological Society* **40**, 82–5.

Masserman, J. H. (1943). *Behavior and neurosis: an experimental psychoanalytic approach to psychobiologic principles*. University of Chicago Press, Chicago.

Masters, W. H. and Johnson, V. E. (1970). *Human sexual inadequacy*. Churchill, London.

Mathews, A. M. (1985). Anxiety states: a cognitive–behavioural approach. In *Psychological applications in psychiatry*, (ed. B. P. Bradley, and C. Thompson), pp. 41–59. Wiley, Chichester.

Mathews, A. M., Gelder, M. G., and Johnston, D. W. (1981). *Agoraphobia: nature and treatment*. Guilford Press, New York.

Mathews, A. M., Bancroft, J., Whitehead, A., Hackmann, A., Julier, D., Bancroft, J., Gath, D., and Shaw, P. (1976). The behavioural treatment of sexual inadequacy: a comparative study. *Behaviour Research and Therapy* **14**, 427–36.

Matson, J. L. (1980). Behavior modification procedures for training chronically institutionalized schizophrenics. In *Progress in Behavior Modification*, Vol. 9, (ed. M. Hersen, R. M. Eisler, and P. M. Miller), pp. 167–202. Academic Press, London.

Mattick, R. P. and Peters, L. (1988). Treatment of severe social phobia: effects of guided exposure with and without cognitive restructuring. *Journal of Consulting and Clinical Psychology* **56**, 251–60.

Mavissakalian, M. and Barlow, D. H. (1981). *Phobia: psychological and pharmacological treatment*. Guilford Press, New York.

Meichenbaum, D. H. (1975). Self-instructional methods. In *Helping people change: a textbook of methods*, (ed. F. H. Kanfer, and A. P. Goldstein), pp. 357–91. Pergamon, New York.

Meichenbaum, D. H. and Cameron, R. (1973). Training schizophrenics to talk to themselves: a means of developing attentional controls. *Behavior Therapy* **4**, 515–34.

Melin, I., Fredericksen, T., Noren, P., and Swebelius, B. G. (1986). Behavioural treatment of scratching in patients with atopic dermatitis. *British Journal of Dermatology* **115**, 467–74.

Melzack, R. (1979). Current concepts of pain. In *Research in psychology and medicine*, Vol. 1, (ed. D. J. Oborne, M. M. Gruneberg, and J. R. Eiser), pp. 13–19. Academic Press, London.

Melzack, R. and Torgerson, W. S. (1971). On the language of pain. *Anesthesiology* **34**, 50–9.

Metzner, R. (1963). Some experimental analogues of obsession. *Behaviour Research and Therapy* **1**, 231–6.

Meyer, V. (1966). Modification of expectations in cases with obsessional rituals. *Behaviour Research and Therapy* **4**, 273–80.

Michelson, L. (1986). Treatment consonance and response profiles in agoraphobia: the role of individual differences in cognitive, behavioural and physiological treatments. *Behaviour Research and Therapy* **24**, 263–75.

Miller, R. C. and Berman, J. S. (1983). The efficacy of cognitive behavior therapies: a quantitative review of the research evidence. *Psychological Bulletin* **94**, 39–53.

Milne, D. (1986). *Training behaviour therapists*. Croom Helm, London.

Milne, H. B. (1976). The role of the psychiatrist. In *Psychosexual problems*, (ed. H. Milne and S. J. Hardy), pp. 65–87. Bradford University Press, Bradford.

MIND (1983). *Common concern*. MIND, London.

Morgan, H. G. Purgold, J., and Welbourne, J. (1983). Management and outcome in anorexia nervosa: a standardized prognostic study. *British Journal of Psychiatry* **143**, 282–7.

Mowrer, O. H. (1947). On the dual nature of learning—a reinterpretation of 'conditioning' and 'problem solving'. *Harvard Educational Review* **17**, 102–48.

Mowrer, O. H. (1960). *Learning theory and behavior*. Wiley, New York.

Mowrer, O. H. and Mowrer, W. M. (1938). Enuresis—a method for its study and treatment. *American Journal of Orthopsychiatry* **8**, 436–59.

Munby, M. and Johnston, D. W. (1980). Agoraphobia: the long-term follow-up of behavioural treatment. *British Journal of Psychiatry* **137**, 418–27.

Murphy, G. E., Simons, A. D., Wetzel, R. D., and Lustman, P. J. (1984). Cognitive therapy and pharmacotherapy: singly and together in the treatment of depression. *Archives of General Psychiatry* **41**, 33–41.

Nisbett, R. E. and Ross, L. (1980). *Human inference: strategies and shortcomings of social judgement*. Prentice-Hall, Englewood Cliffs NJ.

Noyes, R., Anderson, D. J., Clancy, M., Crowe, R. R., Slymen, D. J., Ghoneim, M. M., and Hinrichs, J. V. (1984). Diazepam and propranolol in panic disorder and agoraphobia. *Archives of General Psychiatry* **41**, 287–92.

Nydegger, R. V. (1972). The elimination of hallucinatory and delusional material by verbal conditioning and assertive training: a case study. *Journal of Behavior Therapy and Experimental Psychiatry* **3**, 225–7.

O'Connor, J. F. (1976). Sexual problems, therapy, and prognostic factors. In

Clinical management of sexual disorders, (ed. J. K. Meyer), pp. 74–98. Williams and Wilkins, Baltimore.

O'Leary, K. D. and Wilson, G. T. (1975). *Behavior therapy: application and outcome*. Prentice Hall, Englewood Cliffs NJ.

Orbach, S. (1978). *Fat is a feminist issue*. Paddington Press, London.

Orbach, S. (1986). *Hunger strike*. Faber and Faber, London.

Ost, L. G. (1987). Applied relaxation: description of a coping technique and review of controlled studies. *Behaviour Research and Therapy* 25, 397–410.

Ost, L. G. (1988). Applied relaxation v. progressive relaxation in the treatment of panic disorder. *Behaviour Research and Therapy* 26, 13–22.

Ost, L. G. and Hugdahl, K. (1981). Acquisition of phobias and anxiety response patterns in clinical patients. *Behaviour Research and Therapy* 19, 439–47.

Ost, L. G. and Sterner, U. (1987). Applied tension: a specific behavioural method for treatment of blood phobia. *Behaviour Researcha and Therapy* 25, 25–30.

Ost. L. G., Jerremalm, A., and Johansson, J. (1981). Individual response patterns and the effects of different behavioural methods in the treatment of social phobia. *Behaviour Research and Therapy* 19, 1–16.

Ost, L. G., Johansson, J., and Jerremalm, A. (1982). Individual response patterns and the effects of different behavioural methods in the treatment of claustrophobia. *Behaviour Research and Therapy* 20, 445–60.

Ost, L. G., Lindahl, I. L., Sterner, U., and Jerremalm, A. (1984). Exposure *in vivo* versus applied relaxation in the treatment of blood phobia. *Behaviour Research and Therapy* 22, 205–17.

X Osward, I. M. (1966). *Sleep*. Penguin, London.

Patel, C., Marmot, M. G., and Terry, D. J. (1981). Controlled trial of biofeedback aided behavioural methods in reducing mild hypertension. *British Medical Journal* 282, 2005–8.

Patterson, G. R. (1976). Some procedures for assessing changes in marital interaction patterns. *Oregon Research Institute Bulletin* 16(7), 1–29.

Patterson, G. R. and Hops, H. (1972). Coercion, a game for two: intervention techniques for marital conflict. In *The experimental analysis of social behavior*, (ed. R. E. Ulrich, and P. Mountjoy), pp. 424–40. Appleton-Century-Crofts, New York.

Pattie, A. H. and Gilleard, C. J. (1979). *The Clifton Assessment Procedure for the Elderly (CAPE)*. Hodder and Stoughton, Sevenoaks.

Paul, G. L. (1966). *Insight vs desensitisation in psychotherapy*. Stanford University Press, California.

Paykel, E. S., Myers, J. K., Dienelt, M. N., Klerman, G. L., Lindenthal, J. J., and Pepper, M. P. (1969). Life events and depression: a controlled study. *Archives of General Psychiatry* 21, 753–60.

Peveler, R. and Johnston, D. W. (1986). Subjective and cognitive effects of relaxation. *Behaviour Research and Therapy* 24, 413–20.

Phillips, A. and Rakusen, J. (1978). *Our bodies ourselves*. Penguin, London.

Philips, H. C. (1976). A psychological analysis of tension headache. In *Contributions to medical psychology*, Vol. 1, (ed. S. Rachman), pp. 91–114. Pergamon, Oxford.

Philips, H. C. (1988). *The psychological management of chronic pain: a manual*. Springer, New York.

Polivy, J. and Herman, C. P. (1985). Dieting and binging: a causal analysis. *American Psychologist* **40**, 193–201.

Rachman, S. J. (1977). The conditioning theory of fear-acquisition: a critical examination. *Behaviour Research and Therapy* **15**, 375–87.

Rachman, S. J. (1978*a*). An anatomy of obsessions. *Behaviour Analysis and Modification* **2**, 253–78.

Rachman, S. J. (1978*b*). *Fear and courage*. Freeman, San Francisco.

Rachman, S. J. (1979). Psychosurgical treatment of obsessional compulsive disorders. In *The psychosurgery debate*, (ed. E. Valenstein), pp. 113–28. Freeman, San Francisco.

Rachman, S. J. and De Silva, P. (1978). Abnormal and normal obsessions. *Behaviour Research and Therapy* **16**, 233–8.

Rachman, S. J. and Hodgson, R. (1974). Synchrony and desynchrony in fear and avoidance. *Behaviour Research and Therapy* **12**, 311–18.

Rachman, S. J. and Hodgson, R. (1980). *Obsessions and compulsions*. Prentice Hall, Englewood Cliffs NJ.

Rachman, S. J. and Seligman, M. E. P. (1976). Unprepared phobias: "be prepared". *Behaviour Research and Therapy* **14**, 333–8.

Rachman, S. and Teasdale, J. (1969). *Aversion therapy and behavior disorders: an analysis*. University of Miami Press, Coral Gables.

Rachman, S. J. and Wilson, G. T. (1980). *The effects of psychological therapy*. Pergamon, Oxford.

Rachman, S. J., Hodgson, R., and Marks, I. M. (1971). The treatment of chronic obsessional neurosis. *Behaviour Research and Therapy* **9**, 237–47.

Rachman, S. J., Cobb, J., Grey, S., McDonald, R., Mawson, D., Sartory, G., and Stern, R. (1979). The behavioural treatment of obsessive-compulsive disorders with and without chlomipramine. *Behaviour Research and Therapy* **17**, 462–78.

Rapee, R. (1985). Distinctions between panic disorder and generalised anxiety disorder. *Australian and New Zealand Journal of Psychiatry* **19**, 227–32.

Rehm, L. P. (1982). Self-management in depression. In *Self-management and behavior change: from theory to practice*, (ed. P. Karoly and F. H. Kanfer). pp. 552–70. Pergamon, New York.

Reid, W. and Epstein, L. (1972). *Task-centered casework*. Columbia University Press, New York.

Rimm, D. C. and Masters, J. C. (1979). *Behavior therapy*, (2nd edn). Academic Press, New York.

Rippere, V. (1983). Behavioural diagnosis of food addictions. *Newsletter of the Society for Environmental Therapy* **3**, 21–4.

Risch, C. and Ferguson, J. (1981). Behavioural treatment of skin disorders. In *The comprehensive handbook of behavioural medicine*, Vol. 2 (ed. J. M. Ferguson, and C. B. Taylor). MTP, Lancaster.

Robins, L. N., Helzer, J. E., Weissman, M. M., Orvaschel, H., Gruenberg, E., Burke, J. D., and Regier, D. A. (1984). Lifetime prevalence of specific psychiatric disorders in three sites. *Archives of General Psychiatry* **41**, 949–58.

Rosen, J. C. and Leitenberg, H. (1985). Exposure plus response prevention treatment of bulimia. In *Handbook of psychotherapy for anorexia nervosa and bulimia*, (ed. D. M. Garner, and P. E. Garfinkel), pp. 193–209. Guilford Press, New York.

Rosenberg, M. (1965). *Society and the adolescent self image.* Princeton University Press, Princeton.

Rosenstock, I. M. and Kirscht, J. P. (1979). Why people seek health care. In *Health psychology,* (ed. G. C. Stone, F. Cohen, and N. Adler), pp. 161–88. Jossey Bass, San Francisco.

Rush, A. J. (1982). *Short-term psychotherapies for depression.* Guilford Press, New York.

Rush, A. J. and Shaw, B. F. (1983). Failures in treating depression by cognitive-behavioral therapy. In *Failures in behavior therapy,* (ed. E. B. Foa, and P. M. G. Emmelkamp), pp. 217–28. Wiley, New York.

Rush, A. J., Khatami, M., and Beck, A. T. (1975). Cognitive and behavior therapy in chronic depression. *Behavior Therapy* 6, 398–404.

Rush, A. J., Beck, A. T., Kovacs, M., and Hollon, S. D. (1977). Comparative efficacy of cognitive therapy and pharmacotherapy in the treatment of depressed outpatients. *Cognitive Therapy and Research* 1, 17–37.

Russell, D. McR., Freedman, M. L., Feiglin, D. H. I., Jeejeebhoy, K. N., Swinson, R. P., and Garfinkel, P. E. (1983). Delayed gastric emptying and improvement with domperidone in a patient with anorexia nervosa. *American Journal of Psychiatry* 140, 1235–6.

Russell, G. F. M. (1970). Anorexia nervosa: its identity as an illness and its treatment. In *Modern trends in psychological medicine,* Vol. 2, (ed. O. W. Hill), pp. 131–64. Butterworths, London.

Russell, G. F. M. (1977). General management of anorexia nervosa and difficulties in assessing the efficacy of treatment. In *Anorexia nervosa,* (ed. R. A. Vigerskyi), pp. 277–89. Raven Press, New York.

Russell, G. F. M., Checkley, S. A., and Robinson, P. H. (1986). The limited role of drugs in the treatment of anorexia and bulimia. In *Pharmacology of eating disorders: theoretical and clinical developments,* (ed. M. O. Carruba and J. E. Blundell), pp. 151–67. Raven Press, New York.

Russell, G. F. M., Szmukler, G. I., Dare, C., and Eisler, I. (1987). An evaluation of family therapy in anorexia nervosa and bulimia nervosa. *Archives of General Psychiatry* 44, 1047–56.

Rust, J. and Golombok, S. (1986). The GRISS: a psychometric instrument for the assessment of sexual dysfunction. *Archives of Sexual Behaviour* 15, 153–61.

Rust, J., Bennun, I., Crowe, M., and Golombok, S. (1986). The Golombok-Rust Inventory of Marital State (GRIMS). *Sexual and Marital Therapy* 1, 55–60.

Salkovskis, P. M. (1985). Obsessional-compulsive problems: a cognitive–behavioural analysis. *Behaviour Research and Therapy* 25, 571–83.

Salkovskis, P. M. (1988a). Intrusive thoughts and obsessional disorders. In *current issues in clinical psychology,* Vol. 4, (ed. D. Glasgow and N. Eisenberg), pp. 96–110. Gower, London.

Salkovskis, P. M. (1988b). Phenomenology, assessment and the cognitive model of panic. In *Panic: psychological perspectives,* (ed. S. Rachman, and J. D. Maser), pp. 111–36. Lawrence Erlbaum, Hillsdale NJ.

Salkovskis, P. M. (1988c). Hyperventilation and anxiety. *Current Opinion in Psychiatry* 1, 76–82.

Salkovskis, P. M. (1989). Obsessions and compulsions. In *Cognitive therapy:*

a clinical casebook, (ed. J. Scott, J. M. G. Williams, and A. T. Beck) Routledge, London.

Salkovskis, P. M. and Warwick, H. M. C. (1985). Cognitive therapy of obsessive-compulsive disorder—treating treatment failures. *Behavioural Psychotherapy* 13, 243–55.

Salkovskis, P. M. and Warwick, H. M. C. (1986). Morbid preoccupations, health anxiety and reassurance: a cognitive behavioural approach to hypochondriasis. *Behaviour Research and Therapy* 24, 597–602.

Salkovskis, P. M. and Warwick, H. M. C. (1988). Cognitive therapy of obsessive-compulsive disorder. In *The theory and practice of cognitive therapy*, (ed. C. Perris, I. M. Blackburn, and H. Perris), pp. 376–95. Springer–Verlag, Heidelberg.

Salkovskis, P. M. and Westbrook, D. (1987). Obsessive-compulsive disorder: clinical strategies for improving behavioural treatments. In *Clinical psychology: research and development*, (ed. H. R. Dent), pp. 200–13. Croom Helm, London.

Salkovskis, P. M., Clark, D. M., and Jones, D. R. O. (1986*b*). A psychosomatic mechanism in anxiety attacks; the role of hyperventilation in social anxiety and cardiac neurosis. In *Proceedings of the 15th European conference on psychosomatic research*, (ed. J. H. Lacey, and D. A. Sturgeon), pp. 239–45. John Libbey, London.

Salkovskis, P. M., Jones, D. R. O., and Clark, D. M. (1986*a*). Respiratory control in the treatment of panic attacks: replication and extension with concurrent measurement of behaviour and pCO_2. *British Journal of Psychiatry* 148, 526–32.

Sargent, J., Liebman, R., and Silver, M. (1985). Family therapy for anorexia nervosa. In *Handbook of psychotherapy for anorexia nervosa and bulima*, (ed. D. M. Garner, and P. E. Garfinkel), pp. 257–79. Guilford Press, New York.

Schreiner-Engel, P. and Schiavi, R. C. (1986). Lifetime psychopathology in individuals with low sexual desire. *Journal of Nervous and Mental Disease* 174, 646–51.

Schwartz, G. E. and Weiss, S. M. (1977). What is behavioral medicine? *Psychosomatic Medicine* 39, 377–81.

Schwartz, H. (1986). *Never satisfied: a cultural history of diets, fantasies and fat.* The Free Press, New York.

Seligman, M. E. P. (1971). Phobias and preparedness. *Behavior Therapy* 2, 307–20.

Seligman, M. E. P. (1975). *Helplessness.* Freeman, San Francisco.

Semans, J. H. (1956). Premature ejaculation: a new approach. *Southern Medical Journal* 49, 353–7.

Shaw, B. F. (1977). Comparison of cognitive therapy and behavior therapy in the treatment of depression. *Journal of Consulting and Clinical Psychology* 45, 534–51.

Shapiro, M. B. (1961*a*). A method of measuring psychological changes specific to the individual psychiatric patient. *British Journal of Medical Psychology* 34, 151–5.

Shapiro, M. B. (1961*b*). The single case in fundamental psychological research. *British Journal of Medical Psychology* 34, 255–62.

Shepherd, G. (1980). The treatment of social difficulties in special environments. In *The social psychology of psychological problems*, (ed. P. Feldman, and J. Orford), pp. 249–78. Wiley, Chichester.

Shepherd, G. (1984). *Institutional care and rehabilitation*. Longman, London.

Simons, A. D., Lustman, P. J., Wetzel, R. D., and Murphy, G. E. (1985). Predicting response to cognitive therapy for depression: the role of learned resourcefulness. *Cognitive Therapy and Research* 9, 79–89.

Simons, A. D., Murphy, G. E., Levine, J. L., and Wetzel, R. D. (1986). Cognitive therapy and pharmacotherapy for depression: sustained improvement over one year. *Archives of General Psychiatry* 43, 43–9.

Smith, J. V. and Birchwood, M. J. (1987). Specific and non-specific effects of educational interventional with families living with a schizophrenic relative. *British Journal of Psychiatry* 150, 645–52.

Snyder, D. K. (1981). *Marital Satisfaction Inventory (MSI): manual*. Western Psychological Services, Los Angeles.

Solomon, R. L. and Wynne, L. C. (1954). Traumatic avoidance learning: the principles of anxiety conservation and partial irreversibility. *Psychological Review* 61, 353–85.

Sotile, W. M. and Kilmann, P. R. (1977). Treatment of psychogenic female sexual dysfunction. *Psychological Bulletin* 84, 619–33.

Spanier, G. B. (1976). Measuring dyadic adjustment: new scales for assessing the quality of marriage and similar dyads. *Journal of Marriage and the Family* 38, 15–28.

Speilberger, C., Gorsuch, R., and Lushene, R. (1970). *State-trait anxiety inventory manual*. Consulting Psychologist Press, Palo Alto, California.

Spitzer, R. L., Endicott, J., and Robins, E. (1978). *Research diagnostic criteria (RDC) for a select group of functional disorders*, (3rd edn). New York Psychiatric Institute, New York.

Stern, R. and Marks, I. (1973). Brief and prolonged flooding. *Archives of General Psychiatry* 28, 270–6.

Sternberg, M. (1974). Physical treatments in obsessional disorders. In *Obsessional states*, (ed. H. R. Beech), pp. 291–306. Methuen, London.

Storr, A. (1979). *The art of psychotherapy*. Secker Warburg, London.

Strachan, A. M. (1986). Family intervention for the rehabilitation of schizophrenia: toward protection and coping. *Schizophrenia Bulletin* 12, 678–98.

Stuart, R. B. (1969). Operant-interpersonal treatment of marital discord. *Journal of Consulting and Clinical Psychology* 33, 675–82.

Sullaway, M. and Christensen, A. (1983). Assessment of dysfunctional interaction patterns in couples. *Journal of Marriage and the Family* 45, 653–60.

Szmukler, G. I. (1984). Anorexia nervosa and bulimia in diabetics. *Journal of Psychiatric Research* 28, 365–9.

Taylor, F. G. and Marshall, W. L. (1977). Experimental analysis of a cognitive–behavioral therapy for depression. *Cognitive Therapy and Research* 1, 59–72.

Teasdale, J. D. (1985). Psychological treatments for depression: how do they work? *Behaviour Research and Therapy* 23, 157–65.

Teasdale, J. D. and Fennell, M. J. V. (1982). Immediate effects on depression of cognitive therapy intervention. *Cognitive Therapy and Research* 6, 343–51.

Teasdale J. D. and Rezin, V. (1978). The effects of reducing frequency of negative thoughts on the mood of depressed patients—tests of a cognitive model of depression. *British Journal of Social and Clinical Psychology* 17, 65–74.

Teasdale, J. D., Fennell, M. J. V., Hibbert, G. A., and Amies, P. L. (1984). Cognitive therapy for major depressive disorder in primary care. *British Journal of Psychiatry* 144, 400–6.

Telch, M. J., Agras, W. S., Taylor, C. B., Roth, W. T., and Gallen, C. C. (1985). Combined pharmacological and behavioural treatment for agoraphobia. *Behaviour Research and Therapy* 23, 325–36.

Theander, S. (1985). Outcome and prognosis in anorexia nervosa and bulimia: some results of previous investigations, compared with those of a Swedish long-term study. *Journal of Psychiatric Research* 19, 493–508.

Touyz, S. W., Beumont, P. J. V., Glaun, D., Phillips, T., and Cowie, I. (1984). A comparison of lenient and strict operant conditioning programmes in refeeding patients with anorexia nervosa. *British Journal of Psychiatry* 144, 517–20.

Trower, P., Bryant, B., and Argyle, M. (1978). *Social skills and mental health*. Methuen, London.

Tyrer, P. and Owen R. (1984). Anxiety in primary care: is short-term drug treatment appropriate? *Journal of Psychiatric Research* 18, 73–9.

Vallis, T. M. (1984). Second generation studies of cognitive therapy for depression: recommendations for future research. Paper presented at the Meeting for the Society for Psychotherapy Research, Alberta, Canada, June.

Vandereycken, W. and Meermann, R. (1984). *Anorexia nervosa: a clinician's guide to treatment*. de Gruyter, Berlin.

Vaughn, C. E. and Leff, J. P. (1976). The influence of family and social factors on the course of psychiatric illness. *British Journal of Psychiatry* 129, 125–37.

Waddell, M. T., Barlow, D. H., and O'Brien, G. T. (1984). A preliminary investigation of cognitive and relaxation treatment of panic disorder: effects on intense anxiety v. 'background' anxiety. *Behaviour Research and Therapy* 22, 393–402.

Wallace, C. J. (1986). Functional assessment in rehabilitation. *Schizophrenia Bulletin* 12, 604–30.

Watson, J. B. and Rayner, R. (1920). Conditioned emotional reactions. *Journal of Experimental Psychology* 3, 1–14.

Warwick, H. M. C. and Salkovskis, P. M. (1985). Reassurance. *British Medical Journal* 290, 1028.

Watson, D. and Friend, R. (1969). Measurement of social-evaluative anxiety. *Journal of Consulting and Clinical Psychology* 33, 448–57.

Weisenberg, M. (1987). Psychological intervention for the control of pain. *Behaviour Research and Therapy* 25, 301–12.

Weiss, R. L. and Cerreto, M. C. (1980). The Marital Status Inventory: development of a measure of dissolution potential. *American Journal of Family Therapy* 8, 80–95.

Weiss, R. L., Hops, H., and Patterson, G. R. (1973). A framework for conceptualising marital conflict, technology for altering it, some data for evaluating it. In *Behavior change: methodology, concepts, and practice*, (ed. L. A. Hammerlynck, L. C. Handy, and E. M. Mash), pp. 309–42. Research Press, Champaign Ill.

Weissman, M. M. (1979). The psychological treatment of depression: evidence for the efficacy of psychotherapy alone, in comparison with, and in combination with pharmacotherapy. *Archives of General Psychiatry* **36**, 1261–8.

Weissman, M. M. and Merikangas, K. R. (1986). The epidemiology of anxiety and panic disorders. *Journal of Clinical Psychiatry* (suppl.) **46**, 11–17.

Weissman, M. M. and Paykel, E. S. (1974). *The depressed woman: a study of social relationships.* University of Chicago Press, Chicago.

Whitehead, A. and Mathews, A. (1977). Attitude change during behavioural treatment of sexual inadequacy. *British Journal of Social and Clinical Psychology* **16**, 275–81.

Whitehead, A. and Mathews, A. (1986). Factors related to successful outcome in the treatment of sexually unresponsive women. *Psychological Medicine* **16**, 373–8.

Williams, J. M. G. (1984a). Cognitive behaviour therapy for depression: problems and perspectives. *British Journal of Psychiatry* **145**, 254–62.

Williams, J. M. G. (1984b). *The psychological treatment of depression: a guide to the theory and practice of cognitive behaviour therapy.* Croom Helm, London.

Williams, R. B. and Gentry, W. D. (1976). *Behavioral approaches to medical treatment.* Ballinger, Cambridge Mass.

Wilson, G. T. (1987). Cognitive–behavioral treatment for bulimia nervosa. *Annals of Behavioral Medicine* **9**, 12–17.

Wilson, G. T. (1988). Cognitive–behavioral treatments of bulimia nervosa: the role of exposure. In *Psychobiology of bulimia nervosa*, (ed. K. Pirke, D. Ploog, and W. Vandereycken), pp. 135–45. Springer-Verlag, Heidelberg.

Wing, J. K. (1961). A simple and reliable subclassification of chronic schizophrenia. *Journal of Mental Science* **107**, 862–75.

Wing, J. K. (1975). Impairments in schizophrenia: a rational basis for social treatment. In *Life history research in psychopathology*, Vol. 4, (ed. R. D. Wirt, G. Winokur, and M. Roff), pp. 237–68. University of Minnesota Press, Minneapolis.

Wing, J. K. and Brown, G. W. (1970). *Institutionalisation and schizophrenia.* Cambridge University Press, Cambridge.

Wing, L. and Gould, J. (1978). Systematic recording of behaviour and skills of retarded and psychotic children. *Journal of Autism and Childhood Schizophrenia* **8**, 79–97.

Wisocki, P. A. (1984). Behavioral approaches to gerontology. In *Progress in behavior modification*, Vol. 16, (ed. M. Eisler, R. M. Eisler, and P. M. Miller), pp. 121–58. Academic Press, New York.

Wolfensberger, G. and Glenn, L. (1975). *Program analysis of service systems: a method for the quantitative evaluation of human sciences.* National Institute of Mental Retardation, Toronto.

Wolpe, J. (1958). *Psychotherapy by reciprocal inhibition.* Stanford University Press, California.

Wolpe, J. (1961). The systematic desensitization treatment of neurosis. *Journal of Nervous and Mental Diseases* **132**, 189–203.

Wolpe, J. (1982). *The practice of behavior therapy*, (3rd edn). Pergamon, New York.

Wolpe, J. and Lang, P. J. (1964). A fear survey schedule for use in behaviour therapy. *Behaviour Research and Therapy* **2**, 27–30.

Wright, J., Perreault, R., and Mathieu, M. (1977). The treatment of sexual dysfunction. *Archives of General Psychiatry* **34**, 881–90.

Wykes, T. (1982). A hostel-ward for 'new' long-stay patients: an evaluative study of 'a ward in a house'. In *Long-term community care: experience in a London borough. Psychological Medicine Monograph Supplement* **2**, 59–97.

Yaffe, M. and Fenwick, E. (1986). *Sexual happiness: a practical approach.* Dorling Kindersley, London.

Young, J. E. and Beck, A. T. (1982). Cognitive therapy: clinical applications. In *Short-term psychotherapies for depression*, (ed. A. J. Rush), pp. 182–214. Guilford Press, New York.

Zangwill Report (1979). *Report of the joint working party to formulate ethical guidelines for the conduct of programmes of behaviour modification.* HMSO, London.

Zigmond, A. S. and Snaith, R. P. (1983). The hospital anxiety and depression scale. *Acta Psychiatrica Scandinavica* **67**, 361–70.

Zilbergeld, B. (1978). *Male sexuality: a guide to sexual fulfillment.* Bantam, New York.

Zilbergeld, B. (1980). *Men and sex.* Fontana, London.

Zimmer, F. T., Axmann, D., Koch, H., Giedke, H., Pflug, B., and Heimann, H. (1985). One-year follow-up of cognitive behavioural therapy alone. Paper presented at the 15th Annual Meeting of the European Association for Behaviour Therapy. Munich, September.

Index